Pleasure Of Ruins

kansas city public library
KC
kansas city, missouri
Books will be issued only
on presentation of library card.
Please report lost cards and
change of residence promptly.
Card holders are responsible for
all books, records, films, pictures
or other library materials
checked out on their cards.

DATE DUE

3-4-67			

PLEASURE OF RUINS

Rose Macaulay

WALKER AND COMPANY
NEW YORK

First published in 1953.
This reprinted edition first published in the United States of America in 1966 by Walker & Company, a division of Publications Development Corporation

Library of Congress Catalog Card Number: 66-24080

Manufactured in Great Britain

ELEGY ON A PILE OF RUINS

Aspice murorum moles, praeruptaque saxa! (Janus Vitalis)
Omnia tempus edax depascitur, omnia carpit. (Seneca)

In the full prospect yonder hill commands,
O'er barren heath and cultivated plains,
The vestige of an ancient abbey stands,
Close by a ruin'd castle's rude remains.

Half buried there lie many a broken bust,
And obelisk, and urn, o'erthrown by Time;
And many a cherub there descends in dust
From the rent roof, and portico sublime.

Where rev'rend shrines in gothic grandeur stood,
The nettle, or the noxious night-shade spreads;
And ashlings, wafted from the neighb'ring wood,
Through the worn turrets wave their trembling heads.

I left the mantling shade in moral mood . . .
Sigh'd, as the mould'ring monuments I viewed.

Inexorably calm, with silent pace,
Here Time has pass'd—What ruin marks his way!
This pile, now crumbling o'er its hallow'd base,
Turn'd not his step, nor could his course delay.

How solemn is the cell o'ergrown with moss
That terminates the view, yon cloister'd way!
In the crush'd wall, a time-corroded cross
Religion-like, stands mould'ring in decay!

Near the brown arch, redoubling yonder gloom,
The bones of an illustrious chieftain lie,
As trac'd among the fragments of his tomb,
The trophies of a broken Fame imply.

Though to the clouds his castle seem'd to climb,
  And frown'd defiance to the desp'rate foe;
Though deem'd invincible, the conqueror, Time,
  Levell'd the fabric, as the founder, low.

The lizard, and the lazy lurking bat,
  Inhabit now, perhaps, the painted room
Where the sage matron and her maidens sat,
  Sweet-singing at the silver-working loom.

Though his rich hours in revelry were spent,
  With Comus, and the laughter-loving crew,
And the sweet brow of Beauty, still unbent,
  Brighten'd his fleecy moments as they flew:

Vain then are pyramids, and motto'd stones,
  And monumental trophies rais'd on high!
For Time confounds them with the crumbling bones,
  That mix'd in hasty graves unnotic'd lie.

Hither let Luxury lead her loose-robed train;
  Here flutter Pride, on purple-painted wings:
And from the moral prospect learn—how vain
  The wish that sighs for sublunary things!

JOHN CUNNINGHAM. *Poems chiefly Pastoral* (1766)

* * * * *

Has not that ruin, says he, a good effect? . . . Those pines which hang nodding over those broken Arches, that murmuring cascade, and those Fauns and Satyrs dancing to its sound, I assure you begin to raise very wild ideas in my head. Whence is it, my friend, that the imagination even of a good-natured man is more enraptured with these rude appearances of Nature, these prospects of the ruinous kind, than with the most smiling views of plenty and prosperity?

A Dialogue on Stowe (1746)

CONTENTS

LIST OF ILLUSTRATIONS

ILLUSTRATIONS IN TEXT

ACKNOWLEDGMENTS

DURING the three years of writing this probably over-lengthy book, I have received from a great number of kind, generous and clever friends more valuable help, in the way of information, suggestions, transport and assistance of all kinds, than can be easily acknowledged. Inevitably, since memory is capricious, any such list must have omissions, which will vex the omitter but not, one imagines, the omitted. Here, anyhow, is a list of some to whom I owe thanks:

Dr Gilbert Murray, Mr Cecil Gould, Mr Christopher Hussey, Mr Victor Cunard, Lord Kinross, Sir Kenneth Clark, Mr John Summerson, Sir Ronald Storrs, Mr Robin McDouall, Mr Iain Colquhoun, Dr Charles Mitchell and the staff of the Warburg Institute, Mr John Hayward, the Reverend Gervase Mathew, Mr Theophilus Magabgab, Dr Batista i Roca, Mr Patrick Leigh Fermor, Mr Daniel George, the Reverend Gerard Irvine, Mr Soames Jenyng, Mr C. D. Ley, Mr Alan Pryce-Jones, Mr Cyril Connolly, Mr Roger Hinks, Mr Clough Williams-Ellis, Mr Stewart Perowne, Mr Alan Morton, Miss Jean Smith, Mr Julian Huxley, those members of the Irak Petroleum Company who so kindly gave me hospitality and transport in Syria, Mr G. L. Harding, Mr T. Canaan and Miss Kirkpatrick, who showed me the fabulous desert city of Jerash where they were digging and reconstructing. Mrs Kurz, for her valuable help with the illustrations, and Miss Susan Lister, who so patiently and expertly read the proofs. Finally, my long-suffering publishers, and, as usual, the indefatigable staff of the London Library.

My thanks are also due to the following for permission to reproduce the paintings, drawings and photographs in their possession: the Metropolitan Museum, New York, for illustration No. 1; *Country Life* for No. 3; Wayland Dobson, Esq., for No. 4; the Soane Museum for Nos. 8, 25, 30; the Staedel, Frankfort, for No. 21; the British Museum for Nos. 23, 33, 34, 43, 44, 49, 57; Messrs Wildenstein & Co. Ltd. for No. 27; the Staatliche Museen, Berlin, for No. 46, the Victoria & Albert Museum for Nos. 48 and 65; the Tate Gallery for No. 54; the Musée Condé, Chantilly, for No. 59; Editions Tel for No. 60; Mr John Piper and the Walker Art Gallery, Liverpool, for No. 70; Mr John Piper and the Leicester Galleries for No. 71.

INTRODUCTION

THE approach to ruins in this highly selective book will be seen to be that of a pleasurist. It is not architectural or archaeological, nor in any other way expert. Its aim, however incoherently kept in view and inadequately achieved, is to explore the various kinds of pleasure given to various people at various epochs by the spectacle of ruined buildings. Here and there, and particularly in the first section, and in the pages on Rome, I have made some attempt to trace the growth and development of this strange human reaction to decay. Elsewhere the emphasis is on the ruins themselves, and the impression they individually make, by their beauty, or their strangeness, or their shattered intimidations that strike so responsive a nerve in our destruction-seeking souls. Or, more usually, by their mere picturesqueness. "I am living in the Capuchin Convent," Byron wrote from Athens, "Hymettus before me, the Acropolis behind, the Temple of Jove to my right, the Stadium in front, the town to my left; eh, Sir, there's a situation, there's your picturesque!" Or, as Marie Lloyd used to sing, "I am very fond of ruins, ruins I love to scan". That is the common human sentiment; when did it consciously begin, this delight in decayed or wrecked buildings? Very early, it seems. Since down the ages men have meditated before ruins, rhapsodized before them, mourned pleasurably over their ruination, it is interesting to speculate on the various strands in this complex enjoyment, on how much of it is admiration for the ruin as it was in its prime—*quanta Roma fuit, ipsa ruina docet*—how much aesthetic pleasure in its present appearance—*plus belle que la beauté est la ruine de la beauté*—how much is association, historical or literary, what part is played by morbid pleasure in decay, by righteous pleasure in retribution (for so often it is the proud and the bad who have fallen), by mystical pleasure in the destruction of all things mortal and the eternity of God (a common reaction in the Middle Ages), by egotistic satisfaction in surviving—(where now art thou? here still am I)—by masochistic joy in a common destruction—*L'homme va méditer sur les ruines des empires, il oublie qu'il est lui-même une ruine encore plus chancelante, et qu'il sera tombé avant ces débris*—and by a dozen other entwined threads of pleasurable and melancholy emotion, of which the main strand is, one imagines, the romantic and conscious swimming down the hurrying river of time, whose mysterious reaches, stretching limitlessly behind, glimmer suddenly into view with these wracks washed on to the silted shores. More intellectual than any of these emotions are those two learned, noble and inquisitive pleasures, archaeology and antiquarianism, which have inspired so much eager research, such stalwart, patient and prolonged investigation, such ingenious and erroneous deductions and reconstructions, and have been rewarded by those exquisite thrills of triumph and discovery which must be as exciting as finding a new land. These are, no doubt, the highest and purest of ruin-pleasures, but are reserved for the few.

Then there is the host of minor pleasures—looting, carrying away fragments (a treat enjoyed by great looters and small, from Lord Elgin and the Renaissance nobles and popes to the tourist pocketing stone eggs from fallen Corinthian capitals). There is the pleasure of constructing among the ruins a dwelling or a hermitage (for the enterprising and eccentric company of the Stylites, this is apt to be on the tops of pillars), of being portrayed against a ruinous background (very large, the ruins very small, as William Lithgow before Troy, and Goethe seated on a fallen column in the Campagna), of writing or cutting one's name, as all good tourists have done in all times, of self-projection into the past, of composing poetry and prose, of observing the screech owl, the bat, and the melancholy ghost, and the vegetation that pushes among the crevices and will one day engulf.

Whatever its complex elements, the pleasure felt by most of us in good ruins is great. "A monument of antiquity," wrote Thomas Whately in 1770, "is never seen with indifference . . . No circumstance so forcibly marks the desolation of a spot once inhabited, as the prevalence of Nature over it. *Jam seges est ubi Troja fuit* is a sentence which conveys a stronger idea of a city totally overthrown than a description of its remains." We might be still more delighted to see Troy or Athens, Corinth, Paestum or Rome, as they stood two thousand odd years ago; but that cannot be; this broken beauty is all we have of that ancient magnificence; we cherish it like the extant fragments of some lost and noble poem.

Unthinking ἰδιῶται, unversed in their own emotions, not knowing that they love ruins, reveal it not in words, but by continually making more of them; more and more and more This book is a random excursion into the fantastic world that the ἰδιῶται (including Time, their chief) have made and left, a shattered heritage, for us to deplore and to admire Many of the ruins here mentioned I have seen, many not. Some I have not seen for many years, and since I saw them they have suffered change. Ruins change so fast that one cannot keep pace: they disintegrate, they go to earth, they are tidied up, excavated, cleared of vegetation, built over, restored, prostrate columns set on end and fitted with their own or other capitals; fresh areas of ancient cities are exposed, scattered ruins assembled together in railed enclosures, ruin-squatting populations expelled from castles and abbeys, walls repaired. Even between typing and printing, printing and publication, drastic changes in ruins everywhere occur; one cannot keep pace. One must select for contemplation some phase in a ruin's devious career, it matters little which, and consider the human reaction to this; or merely enjoy one's own.

"A heartless pastime", Henry James called his own ruin-questing (and this was a title I considered for my book), "and the pleasure, I confess, shows a note of perversity". Indeed, I fear this may seem to many a perverse book. For, out of this extremely ruinous world (in which there are, above and under the earth, far more ruined than unruined buildings), I have only had space to select a few ruinous objects, a ruin here and a ruin there, to illustrate the human attitude towards them, and the odds are against any one's finding here more than a few of their own favourite ruins. I have not attempted to deal with all types of ruin; I have, for instance, no separate sections for theatres, forums, aqueducts, arches, baths or bridges, each of which could have filled long chapters; but they have had to come in, all too cursorily, with the rest; and a chapter to be called "Mouldering Mansions" never got past a rough draft. Still, it may be held that this book, whatever it lacks, does not suffer from brevity, so perhaps it is for the best.

I

ART, FANTASY AND AFFECTATION

SINCE to be fascinated by ruins has always, it would seem, been a human tendency, it is of some interest to try and trace the development of its expression in literature and art. It is pretty safe to suppose that the earliest ruin pleasure was inextricably mixed with triumph over enemies, with moral judgment and vengeance, and with the violent excitements of war, and the earliest extant literature in all languages deals largely with all these haunts of the catastrophic imagination of man; to say that man found pleasure in celebrating such disasters by word and picture is not quite the same as to say that he found emotional joy in the contemplation of the ruinous results. Or is it? One cannot distinguish too nicely, or too sharply define the separation of aesthetic pleasure from vindictive. In what proportions, for instance, were the elements mixed in the magnificent poetic ruin pictures painted in windy words by the Hebrew poets, in those impassioned invectives described meiotically by commentators as "discourses directed against foreign nations"? The vengeance of the Lord, the fall of the proud, the desolation of the rich and powerful: but, beyond all these, surely a profound, passionate, poetic pleasure in ruin as such. Out come the screech-owls, the dragons, the satyrs, the bitterns, the serpents, the jackals, the bats, even the moles, all the familiar creatures of ruin that haunt demolished cities and glooming fancy, the vineyards are trodden down and laid waste, the briars and thorns spring up, houses, now great and fair, shall stand desolate, the Lord shall hiss for flies from Egypt and bees from Assyria, and they shall come and stay. As for Babylon (said Isaiah, writing nearly two centuries before that city fell in 538 B.C., as it might be Piranesi or Hubert Robert or Monsú Desiderio or Pannini or James Pryde or Joseph Gandy drawing and painting fantastic pictures of the imaginary ruin of well-known buildings)—as for Babylon,

"wild beasts of the desert shall lie there, and their houses shall be full of doleful creatures, and owls shall dwell there, and satyrs shall dance there, and the wild beasts of the islands shall cry in their desolate houses, and dragons in their pleasant palaces: and her time is near to come. . . . Thy pomp is brought down to the graves, and the noise of thy viols· the worm is spread under thee and the worms cover thee. How art thou fallen from heaven, O Lucifer, son of the morning! how art thou cut down to the ground. . . . I will also make it a possession for the bittern, and pools of water: and I will sweep it with the besom of destruction, saith the Lord of hosts."

Similarly, Edom, of whom Isaiah (or, more probably, another poet) wrote:

"the cormorant and the bittern shall possess it; the owl also and the raven shall dwell in it: and he shall stretch out upon it the lines of confusion, and the stones of emptiness . . . and thorns shall come up in her palaces, nettles and brambles in the fortresses thereof. and it shall be a habitation of dragons and a court for owls. The wild beasts of the desert shall meet with the wild beasts of the island, and the satyr shall cry to his fellow; the screech owl also shall rest there. . . There shall the great owl make her nest and lay and hatch . . . there shall the vultures also be gathered, every one with her mate."

Jeremiah (school of) filled the ruined Babylon with sea monsters, which had presumably swum up the Euphrates, and the city had, not unnaturally, become " an astonishment and a hissing, without an inhabitant "—but the confused excitement of the composite ruin-picture which follows is too great for any but Hebrew scholars to disentangle. Ezekiel's account of Nebuchadrezzar's siege and destruction of Tyre is more admirable.

"And they shall make a spoil of thy riches and make a prey of thy merchandise: and they shall break down thy walls and destroy thy pleasant houses: and they shall lay thy stones and thy timber and thy dust in the midst of the water. . . . And I will make thee like the top of a rock: thou shalt be a place to spread nets upon; thou shalt be built no more. . . "

1 The Adoration of the Kings, by Hieronymus Bosch (c. 1460-1516)

2 Woodcut from *Hypnerotomachia Poliphili*, 1499

3 Scotney Castle *Country Life* photograph

There is the dwelling on past glories which puts an edge on the forlornness of ruin; the rich ships, the fine linen broidered sails, the blue and purple from the isles, the luxurious wares, the wealthy merchants who traded in the fairs, the jewellery, the spices and the wine. "Thy builders have perfected thy beauty . . .", but it shall all "fall into the midst of the seas in the day of thy ruin", and "the merchants shall hiss at thee; thou shalt be a terror, and never shalt be any more".

It is all there, ruin-triumph with its several ingredients; and again in Zephaniah's lament for Nineveh, pleasantly mournful with cormorants and bitterns in the lintels, and all the beasts of the nations, it is obvious that round the walls of every desert city, however mighty and extensive, the animals prowled, waiting their chance; and they had only to wait.

It seems obvious, too, that the ruin excitement of Hebrew prophets was greater, more ecstatic, than that of most of their contemporaries, or even their successors. The Chinese, for example, seem on the whole to have always taken a view of ruins both more tranquil and more sad They have always, it appears, liked to produce a pleasing and terrible effect in their gardens by decorating them with decaying buildings, ruined castles, palaces, temples or half-buried triumphal arches and "whatever else may serve to indicate the debility, the disappointments and the dissolution of humanity, which . . . fill the mind with melancholy and incline it to serious reflection."[1] So wrote Sir William Chambers of them in the eighteenth century, but possibly he did not know. Chinese comments on the ruins they saw have been, on the whole, tearful.

"The wind howls in the pines, the rats fly at my approach and hide under the old tiles. What monarch once had this palace built, of which there only remain ruins on a mountain side? . . The owner of this palace had beautiful dancers, who are to-day one with the cold dust. He had chariots, and warriors. Of all this pomp, of all this glory, what remains? A marble horse lying in the grass I should like to express my great sadness in an enduring poem, but I weep, and my pencil trembles."[2]

[1] Sir William Chambers, *Dissertations on Oriental Building* (1772)
[2] From 170 *Chinese Poems*, trans Arthur Waley (Constable, 1923).

So wrote an early anonymous poet before the ruins of a palace. Another, in the first century B.C., returning to his home after a long lifetime as a soldier, met a villager who said to him:

That over there is your house,
All covered over with trees and bushes.
Rabbits had run in at the dog-hole,
Pheasants flew down from the beam of the roof.
In the courtyard was growing some wild grain,
And by the well some wild mallows.
I'll boil the grain and make porridge,
I'll pluck the mallows and make soup
Soup and porridge are both cooked,
But there is no one to eat them with.
I went out and looked towards the east,
While tears fell and wetted my clothes.[1]

Then, two centuries or so later, Ts'ao Chih looked down from a mountain on the war-ruined city of Lo-Yang, and he too was sick at heart.

In Lo-Yang how still it is!
Palaces and houses all burnt to ashes.
Walls and fences all broken and gaping,
Thorns and brambles shooting up to the sky. . . .
I turn aside, for the straight road is lost:
The fields are overgrown, and will never be ploughed again.
I have been away such a long time
That I do not know which street is which.
How sad and ugly the empty moors are!
A thousand miles without the smoke of a chimney.
I think of the house I lived in all those years:
I am heart-tied and cannot speak[1]

But the great ruin centuries in China were not yet. During the T'ang Dynasty (618–905) "innumerable poems record Reflections on visiting a Ruin", or on "the site of an old city. The details are ingeniously varied, but the sentiments are in each case identical."[1] That stormy period all over the world produced ruin everywhere; but few poets to record it. In the great days of Greek literature, there were the poets, and often the ruins, and certainly the climate

[1]From 170 *Chinese Poems*, trans. Arthur Waley (Constable, 1923).

of ruin, but little sentimental dwelling on actual ruins. Homer, for all his tremendous siege, war, victories, defeats and catastrophes, for all his noise and clash of battle, murder and sudden death, dwells little on the pathos and pity of ruined buildings. Nor do the historians of the ruins made by the Persians in the fifth century dwell much on them; the destroyed Acropolis is described neither by historian, philosopher nor poet; there was no notion of sentimentalizing ruin. So little notion that, when Phrynichus put on his tragedy about the Persian destruction of Miletus, the Athenian audience burst into tears, and the dramatist was heavily fined and his play forbidden. The ruin of Miletus was sheer tragedy, no one (except Phrynichus) wanted tragedies written about it, or romantic poems made.

But by the second century B.C. ruin poetry garlanded Corinth and the wreckage made by the Roman soldiery in Greece.

"Where is thy far-famed beauty, Doric Corinth?" [wrote Antipater of Sidon soon after the destruction] "Where thy crown of towers and thy ancient possessions? Where the temples of the blessed, the homes and the matrons? . . . Not a trace is left of thee, ill-fated city, but war has seized and devoured all. We alone, the Nereids, Ocean's daughters, remain, lamenting like halcyons thy griefs."

The poetic exaggeration of the ruin-elegizer is there; sacked Corinth, though a sorry sight, was not as annihilated as all that. But its noble ruins, and the other ruined Grecian cities, lying unrestored for a century, sank into men's imaginations and consciousness, sank into the dark chasms of the mind and soul where catastrophic desires gape, uneasily and greedily, for fulfilment. Inverted, such desires disguise themselves as lamentation. Cicero, passing by Corinth just before it was rebuilt as a Roman town, was deeply moved.

"At Corinth the sudden sight of the ruins had more effect on me than on the actual inhabitants, for long contemplation had had the hardening effect of length of time upon their souls."[1]

Nor did moralizing lack Cicero's friend Servius Sulpicius Rufus, passing that way in 45 B.C., was moved to the kind of

[1] Cicero, *Disputations*.

sermon in stones which ruins have frequently evoked. Having had from Cicero melancholy letters about Tullia's death, he felt that such paternal weakness should be better controlled. Observing about him all these once so flourishing towns, of which Corinth had been the greatest, now lying prostrate and dismembered before his eyes, he thus admonished himself:

"Hem! We little human beings resent it if one of us, whose lives are naturally shorter, has died in his bed or been slain in battle, when in this one region there lie flung down before us the corpses of so many towns. Pray, Servius, control yourself, and remember that you were born a human being Believe me, I was not a little fortified by these reflections. . . ."

Such reflections, one may hazard, might prove less fortifying to the bereaved parent than to the bereaved parent's friend.

The ancient ruins of Mycenae, too, became a romantic symbol of fallen greatness and antiquity. "More waste than any goat-fold ", poets were writing in the second century A.D., six centuries after Mycenae's destruction, gazing with reverent awe at those mighty stones, little higher than the ground. "The goat-herds," they said, "pointed thee out, and an old man said, 'Here stood the city rich in gold, the city that the Cyclops built' " Thus the poet Alpheius, and Pompeius, overcome by the same emotion, makes the Cyclopean ruin give tongue:

"Though I, Mycenae, am but dust here in the desert, though I am poorer to behold than any stone, he who looks on the glorious city of Ilion whose walls I trampled and emptied the house of Priam, shall know how mighty I was of old. . . ."

But we are, and long before the time of these two admirers, arrived at an age of ruin-sentiment, which was never wholly to fade. One can see it in many of the Hellenistic and later wall paintings in the villas of rich Romans at Pompeii and Herculaneum—landscapes and buildings conveying an atmosphere of romantic desolation, pastoral scenes set with houses or temples partly fallen, with bare, twisted boughs of trees thrusting out of broken columns, shafts of pillars standing among distorted rocks, tottering arches and blasted trees. Against such desolate backgrounds temples and country altars stand, satyrs and nymphs embrace, Europa rides her bull, Polyphemus sits among his flocks watching Galatea swim by on her dolphin, Pan flutes outside a broken-pillared house. In one pretty country scene (of the fourth Pompeiian style) there stands by a little lake a group of three columns which looks like the Temple of Saturn as it is to-day. It would seem that, among poetic rural landscapes, sometimes almost Watteau-like in their gay suggestion of *fêtes champêtres*, their elegant shrines, railed bridges arching over smooth water, pretty houses and temples, al fresco tables that may be altars but have the air of being all set for a picnic—it would seem that into the idyllic poetry and peace of such scenes the painters would from time to time intrude a more melancholy poetry, the romance of ruin-sentiment, an almost macabre desolation of fantasy (as in the Pompeiian fresco of the wooden horse being taken into Troy among broken pillars and blasted trees). Many of the artists were Greek, many of the Pompeiian and Herculanean paintings were copies of Greek originals, the Greeks were used to seeing about their country the ruins the Romans had made of their cities and buildings. Also, they loved catastrophic tales; how should they not paint ruin decoratively round the rooms of the Roman rich? Of what they painted round their own walls in Greece we have few relics remaining, but there is no reason to think it different, or that, among the gods and men, shepherds and nymphs, fauns and little loves, processions, battles and garlands, landscapes and temples and cities, which doubtless bloomed thereon like nosegays, the poetry of ruin did not also make its gesture.

Ruin-sentiment, then, was already distinguishable in literature and art. The evidence for it in architecture at that time is more doubtful. Were ruins built as well as painted? It is, in the nature of things, a difficult question to solve; how be certain whether a building we see in a ruinous state to-day was so built, or has suffered destruction and decay? The evidence for the artificial ruins of the eighteenth and early nineteenth centuries is external; they were continually written and talked about. We have no such evidence in classical literature: we do not find Cicero or Verres writing to order ruined temples for their villas, nor Pliny describing the prospects in his Tuscan garden as terminated by broken triumphal arches, nor Horace rejoicing in ruins on his Sabine farm. Though it seems unlikely, on the face of it, that the ingenious, antiquity-loving, pleasure-tasting emperors, greedy consuls and governors, voluptuaries and men of letters, who decorated the Campagna, the bays of Naples and Baiae, and Roman Greece, with their extravagant palaces, villas and gardens, should not have thought of throwing up here and there some elegant ruin, we have no indication that they did so. The landscape gardens characteristic of a later age always existed among civilized peoples; even Eden, according to Milton, was most carefully and skilfully tended and laid out, with vistas, rivulets, bridges, aromatic trees and shrubs. Persians and Greeks and Romans of substance planned and enjoyed their country estates with discerning eyes for the picturesque. Not Shenstone himself described the Leasowes with more detail and delight than Pliny his property in Tuscany, that *regionis forma pulcherrima*, with natural amphitheatre, woods, hills, vineyards, flower-jewelled meadows nourished by clear rills, gardens with terraces and banks, box-trees cut into animals, marble basins full of splashing water: "You would think it not a real but a painted landscape, drawn with exquisite beauty." Like the eighteenth-century gentlemen, Pliny saw his landscape like a picture. He admired the picturesque; but his pictorial landscape was, so far as we know (and the garrulous Pliny would have told us), exquisitely sufficient without a ruined tower embosomed mid his tufted trees. They had learned by the eighteenth century that no landscape was properly pictorial without this delightful adjunct. Apart from this difference, so pertinent to our thesis, the descriptions we have of Roman and English estates, across the gulf of seventeen centuries and of a shattered world rebuilt by barbarians and wistfully looking for classical form, could serve for either age. The Romans too, said, in effect, enthusiastically describing their carefully laid out *fermes ornées*:

Would the curious stranger know
Whence delights so various flow?
They're the most refined part
Both of nature and of art;
Rising from the chrystal floods,
Rivers, meadows, hills and woods;
Feather'd songsters on the trees,
Flowers cluster'd round with bees;

Spacious oxen, prancing steeds,
Nibbling flocks on fatt'ning meads;
Tinkling brooks and pearly rills,
Groves on pleasurable hills,
Vistas planted, clumps of firs,
Octagons and cylinders.[1]

One would like to believe that the Roman gentlemen added to all this the Ruined Object so dear to later gardeners. Hadrian, in particular, who had seen and lost his heart to the antique buildings, ruined and whole, of much of Europe, Asia and Egypt; and who had the agreeable notion of reproducing many of them in his immense Tibur Villa—did he not set up some noble ruins among the rest? But no description of the Villa mentions any, and we conclude that his preference, like that of other rich Roman collectors of Greek antiquities, was for the antique but whole.

But the Roman world was to become a world of ruins. The barbarian tide swept in like a ravening sea, breaking down the walls, leaving wreckage in its wake; the cities, plundered of their stones and marble by citizens and foes, crumbled away like wave-stormed cliffs. In the minds of Romans and barbarians the gigantic ruins brooded, formidable unlaid ghosts; whether they liked it or not, men became ruin-haunted, ruin-minded. Gregory the Great preached ruin from St. Peter's: "*Destructae urbes, eversa sunt castra . . . desolatione civium . . . frequentia ruinarum. . . .*" Two centuries later the English monk Alcuin contrasted ruined Rome with her past greatness:

Roma, caput mundi, mundi decus, aurea Roma,
Nunc remanet tantum saeva ruina tibi.

The contrast impressed the simplest and the most learned minds, leaving in them that blend of pleasure and romantic gloom which has always been the basic element in ruin-sensibility, and which was never to fade from the European consciousness. Like an undulant fever, it rose and fell, reaching its peak in the seventeenth, eighteenth and nineteenth centuries, but never wholly absent. Christianity, with its storm-ridden conscience, the northern Goths and Celts with their nostalgia for violent catastrophe, combined to develop the darkly ruinous mind of torn

[1]Anon., 1744.

Europe, that loved the desolation it bewailed. The Anglo-Saxons sang dirges of woe over ruins, that throb with pleasurable pity; as the seventh-century elegy traditionally supposed to be for Roman Bath, sacked and destroyed by the West Saxons in 577, of which I give a version by a modern poet.

Wonder holds these walls. Under destiny destruction
Castles has split apart; gigantic battlements are crumbling,
Roofs sunk in ruin, riven towers fallen,
Gates and turrets lost, hoar-frost for mortar,
Rain-bastions beaten, cleft, pierced, perished,
Eaten away by time. Earth's fist and grasp
Holds mason and man, all decayed, departed;
The soil grips hard; there a hundred generations
Of the people have dwindled and gone . . .
Magnificent rose the fortresses, the lavish swimming-halls,
The profuse and lofty glory of spires, the clangour of armies,
The drinking-halls crammed with every man's delight,
Till that was overturned by steadfast fate.
The broad walls were sundered: the plague-days came:
The brave men were rapt away by the bereaver,
Their war-ramparts razed to desolate foundations,
Their cities crumbled down. . . .
. . . And so these halls are wastes,
The once purple gates, and the bricks and wood are lying
Scattered with the smashed roofs. Death crushed that place,
Struck it flat to the hill, where once many a man
Brilliant with gold and adazzle with costliest war-trappings,
Happy, proud and wine-flushed, glittered there in his battle-armour,
Gazed over his treasures, on the silver and the curious stones,
On the rich goods and possessions, on the preciously-cut jewels,
And on this splendid city of the far-spread kingdom.
The stone courts stood then; the hot stream broke
Welling strongly through the stone, all was close and sweet
In the bright bosom of the walls; and where the baths lay
Hot at the heart of the place, that was the best of all. . .[1]

And so on. The poet would seem to have had somewhat confused ideas of what Roman Bath had been like, and of the reason for its downfall; but the ruined city obsessed his imagination. The same melancholy inspired his West Saxon contemporary who wrote

[1] *The Ruin*. Translated from Anglo-Saxon by Edward Morgan (*Horizon*, 1949).

The Wanderer, a poem of more general application and more philosophic musing

". . . A wise man will perceive how mysterious will be the time when the wealth of all this age will lie waste, just as now in diverse places throughout the earth walls are standing beaten by the wind and covered with rime. The bulwarks are dismantled, the banqueting halls are ruinous. . . . He then who in a spirit of meditation has pondered over this ruin, and who with an understanding heart probes the mystery of our life down to its depth, will call to mind many slaughters of long ago, and give voice to such words as these: What has become of the steed, of the squire? . . . What has become of the banqueting houses? Where are the joys of the hall? O shining goblet! O mailed warrior! O glory of the prince! How has that time passed away, grown shadowy under the canopy of night as though it had never been! There remains now of the beloved knights no trace save the wall wondrously high, decorated with serpent forms . . ."[1]

The poet ends with mourning over fate and tribulation. "Desolation will hold sway throughout the wide world." Here was the northern imagination, brooding over the waste places, here, indeed, was English spleen, which was to play its part in creating a great literature. Unhaunted by the sense of ruin, English literature must have developed on other lines.

The acceptance of ruin as a natural doom was heightened by the sense of God's judgments and of the transient values of this world. With *l'an mil* and the end of the world just ahead, what were a few ruins less or more? The apprehensively-waiting human race spent much time in composing hymns and prayers anticipatory of the universal catastrophe, when all the world should in ruins lie. It really did not seem of much importance if all cities and buildings should collapse, pending the dire event. The crisis passed: but the sense of the ephemeral nature of cities and buildings remained. In illuminated manuscripts walls and castles fell, towers, arches and churches crashed, and men fell head downwards among them; a reckless abandonment to *bouleversement* obtained. Christians triumphed over the fallen pagan world whose ruined monuments stood about among the dazzling sanctuaries of the New Jerusalem which sprang from their loins. Yet there

[1] *The Wanderer*, trans. N. Kershaw.

were signs, as time passed, of a new spirit of wistful admiration. The grim denunciatory triumph of Jerome and the early Popes became in the scholarly and classically-minded monk Hildebert of Lavardin, who visited Rome in 1116, a passionate and romantic enthusiasm, tempered with a note of religious apology.

"*Pars tibi, Roma, nihil*" [he exclaimed]. "There is nothing thy equal, Rome, almost wholly ruined as thou art. How great thou wert when whole, thou teachest broken. Long ages have destroyed thy splendour; the arches of the Caesars and the ancient temples lie fallen. . . . This can be said: Rome was! But neither years nor flames nor the sword can wholly wreck her beauty. The care of men so built Rome that no efforts of the gods can undo her."

It was a new tone, and one increasingly to be heard. But, in a second stanza, Hildebert made Rome reply to his apostrophizing that she used in the old days to have vain gods, great armies, many citizens, mighty walls, but now that the images and the superstitious altars and the palaces and triumphal arches were fallen, she served the one true God and placed all her hopes in the Cross. Hildebert had remembered that he was a clergyman.

He also makes it clear—and this is an interesting note to be heard so early—that he wants no Roman ruin restored or reconstructed; all are irreparable, matchless, and [he adds] examples, as they stand, of divine chastisement. It is apparent that he was fascinated by the mighty ruins as they were now, as well as by their past greatness; he was well on the road to the Renaissance view of the beauty of ruin as such, and would, with his emotions if not with his mind, have rejected the dictum of St. Thomas Aquinas that "*quae enim diminutae sunt, hoc ipso turpia sunt*". He took the more Gothic view, which spread over the world with its bitter-sweet gloom, gloom at once so bitter and so sweet that it is not easy to disentangle its melancholy strands. It was, of course, by no means only Gothic; it was a tenth-century Persian poet who mourned the great ruined city of Tus near the Turkestan border, desolated by invading hordes.

Last night by ruined Tus I chanced to go;
An owl sat perched where once the cock did crow.
Quoth I, "What message from this waste bring'st thou?"
Quoth he, "The message is woe, woe, all's woe."[1]

[1]Shahid of Balkh, *Early Persian Poetry* (trans. A V. W. Jackson, 1920).

Another Persian, in the next century, dwelt lovingly on ruin, if his English translator renders him rightly. There is the true morbid note in

> They say the Lion and the Lizard keep
> The courts where Jamshyd gloried and drank deep:
> And Bahrám, that great Hunter—the Wild Ass
> Stamps o'er his head, and he lies fast asleep.

Arab poets were seized by the same emotion at the sight of ruin. Even the Bedouins, writes a tenth-century Spanish-Arab poet, wept over the ruins of the desert camps abandoned by the tribes; he himself addresses a compassionate poem to the ruined and deserted stones. Fallen greatness, desertion, vanished glory, the whole ruinous climate, were dear both to Arabs and Spaniards. Modern Arabs have lost this sense: to them an ancient ruin is either a sheltering place or a quarry for stones.

As to those tough Goths, the crusaders, who made it their business and their sport to over-run the infidel lands and hold them down, throwing up castles on the foundations of ancient or Byzantine fortresses all over Syria and Greece, they seem to have felt little interest in their dimly realized predecessors who had erected those mighty buildings in ages of which, in their barbarian ignorance, they knew next to nothing. But they saw Athens, Thebes (where they lived in feudal state), Byzantine Mistrà and the cities of the Morea; they stormed down the incomparable coast of Syria, finding and making ruins all the way; and however little they knew or cared about the ancient ruins, they must have entered into their consciousness. They were accompanied too by chroniclers, such as William of Tyre, who did know something, and who reported on Tyre's incomparable situation in the sea, her fortifications and walls, her causeway and islands. The Frankish knights and princes built all down the coast and islands and all over the Levant their massive castles: if past ruins said little to their practical minds, present defences meant much. No ruin-poetry, in verse or prose, came out of those picturesque incursions into lands where every step would, in a later age, have invited it; the crusaders have left no such sentiments on record; interesting ruins provided no such solace for the troops as was afforded to scholarly warriors in latter-day campaigns in ancient lands, or as was attributed by the rather simple-minded Elizabethan authors of *Titus Andronicus* to the Gothic troops fighting Rome in the third century, one of whom reports that

> from our troops I strayed
> To gaze upon a ruinous Monastery,
> And as I earnestly did fix mine eye
> Upon the wasted building . . .

This passage can scarcely be taken as evidence that ruin-gazing was a normal pastime for Gothic troops of the late third century, or, indeed, that there existed at that time any "ruinous monasteries" in the country round Rome for them to gaze at; the conception is Elizabethan; it seemed to the writer natural, even for troops, to turn aside and gaze at these wasted buildings that stood in decayed or shattered beauty about their own countryside. Between themselves and the Gothic soldiery, a whole new world of ideas and emotions had surged and stormed, the Renaissance had dawned and opened windows on to a past whose ruins lay strewn like jewels about the earth. Rome was the centre; from the fourteenth century on archaeological studies were enthusiastically pursued there. Cola di Rienzo hunted among the broken sculptures for inscriptions and went nobly and patriotically mad; Petrarch, arriving in the ruinous capital from his North Italian home, was overcome and inspired to poetry and prose which stirred the world to realization of its great heritage and to indignation against those who did not cease to plunder and spoil it. Eager scholars flocked to Rome to marvel at her mighty wrecks, while the magnificent new Rome of palaces and churches rose out of the quarried ancient splendour. The mournful note of other-worldly resignation ("all passes but God") was sounded less often; pagan humanists such as Poggio Bracciolini, a century after Petrarch, wrote with passion of the buildings founded for eternity that lay prostrate and broken, and of the stupendous remains that survived. His list of these was only one guide among many; ruin-worship and ruin-knowledge yearly increased. This zestful curiosity was embodied in the antiquarian humanist Aeneas Silvius, later Pope Pius II, who roved the world to admire its sights, travelling in a litter to Tusculum, Tibur and Ostia, full of inquisitiveness, romantic excitement, and gout. Roman ruin-tending became a science; imitation of antique structures had for some time been a fashion among connoisseurs; we find late medieval and early Renaissance buildings with imitation antique columns and actual fragments of antique friezes incorporated. From this it would seem a short step to the erecting of imitation ruins. In painting, ruins were fashionable in religious pictures from the quattrocento on; annunciations and nativities occurred in tottering and blasted palaces or stables, against a background of broken Roman arches and shattered columns (possibly symbolic).[1] Leonardo enumerated as good subjects for painting 'mountains, ruins, rocks, woods, great plains, hills and valleys . . ." and almost every artist threw in fragments of antique towers, temples and broken pillars to adorn his landscape.

In 1467 came the first full-length literary ruin rhapsody; Francesco Colonna's *Hypnerotomachia* (the Strife of Love in a Dream), illustrated with woodcuts of the two lovers walking and rhapsodizing through a paradise of fallen columns, broken sculptures, capitals lying overgrown with shrubs, abandoned and dilapidated temples. Polifilio and Polia, walking out, saw a very ancient building surrounded by a sacred wood on a river bank. A great part of the white marble walls still stood, and a mole of a neighbouring port; it was a ruin well enough preserved. From the cracks in mole and wall grew samphire and many herbs and flowers, covering also the temple steps. This ravaged building lay partly demolished on the earth; huge columns of pink-grained stone lay broken, without base or capital; all was mouldering with age. Concerning it, Polia addressed to Polifilio a ruin-discourse. "Admire", said she, "my dearest Polifilio, this monument all in ruins and upset, an immense heap of broken stones. Once it was a magnificent temple, where great solemn rites were performed before a multitude of spectators. But now it is annihilated and ruined and totally abandoned. Its name was Polyandrion. It contains a number of small vaults in which are buried those who died of a tragic love. The interior is dedicated to Pluto. . . ."

Polifilio examined the temple, deciphering the inscriptions, and searched it for passages, then descended steps into the darkness of

[1] I have to thank Sir Kenneth Clark for calling my attention to what may be the earliest Renaissance ruin picture, Maso's "St. Silvester and the Dragon", in Santa Croce (1340). The fashion did not rage until the next century.

a large subterranean vault. There he found several ruined chapels, one whole one, and some paintings. With the keenest pleasure he went from one fragment to another, delighted at the sight of so many antique objects. Then he wandered through an ancient court, bordered by broken and vegetation-grown pillars, old trees, wild olives and brambles; perhaps, he thought, it had been a ride for horses. So in his dream he wandered on, in an ecstasy of ruinous antiquity.

Intoxicated by this ecstasy the sixteenth century thundered in; architecture, painting, literature, spoke of ruin with one voice. And very early in the century we come on a mention of a sham ruin, of the kind that was to become two centuries later a raging fashion. So casually, so without surprise, is it referred to by Vasari, that one cannot but suppose it one of many such. "A house which, representing a ruin, is a very beautiful thing to see," writes Vasari, was built about 1510 by Girolamo Genga in the park of the Duke of Urbino at Pesaro; it had a staircase copied from that of the Belvedere in Rome. A present-day writer about the Urbino palace and grounds mentions a villa that was "never finished"; but Vasari should know, and he tells us it was built for a ruin. How many more of these were there? They were not written about, gossipped about, written up, as the later follies were; they took their places quietly, decorating gardens and landscapes with broken arches and columns, believed, no doubt, by later generations to have fallen into ruin. How can one tell? Increasingly, ruin assumed its place as the romantic background, the foil to the practical bustle of living, the broken arch through which a distant vista showed, stretching into infinity, stretching back to the long dim reaches of the past. One read du Bellay's lament for the antiquities of Rome:

Ces vieux palais, ces vieux arcs que tu vois,
Et ces vieux murs. . . .

One saw paintings of them; if one could afford to travel, one saw Rome itself, and returned with Rome in one's soul. One heard tales from travellers to Greece and Syria, from Aleppo merchants, from the deserts where Babylon's monstrous ruins sprawled and the supposed tower of Babel rose, so full of serpents, scorpions and probably dragons that no one dared approach it. Ruin loomed all about the mysterious margins of the known world. And in Britain abbeys and monasteries fell like broken trees beneath the brutal axe, and stood in shattered, decaying magnificence to haunt men's souls. The Dissolution did much to add the dimension of ruin to British life; a half-superstitious reverence and awe surrounded and englamoured those fallen, tree-grown shrines that silently (unless they were appropriated for mansions) went more to earth as the seasons passed over their roofless frames and sprouting aisles where the encircling woods pressed in and foxes made their lairs. The melancholy beauty of ruins as such sank deeply into the human mind Webster's Delio and Antonio in the *Duchess of Malfi* expressed a common feeling.

DELIO. This fortification.
Grew from the ruins of an ancient Abbey:
And to yond side o' the river lies a wall
(Piece of a cloister) which in my opinion
Gives the best echo that you ever heard;
So hollow and so dismal, and withal
So plain in the distinction of our words
That many have supposed it is a spirit
That answers.
ANTONIO. I do love these ancient ruins:
We never tread upon them, but we set
Our foot upon some reverend history. . . .
. . . But all things have their end:
Churches and Cities (which have diseases like to men)
Must have like death that we have.
ECHO. *Like death that we have.*
DELIO. Now the Echo hath caught you.
ANTONIO. It groan'd (me thought) and gave
A very deadly accent?
ECHO. *Deadly accent*
DELIO. I told you 'twas a pretty one: You may make it
A huntsman, or a falconer, a musician,
Or a thing of sorrow.
ECHO. *A thing of sorrow.*
ANTONIO. Aye sure, that suits it best.

Indeed, the catastrophic ruinousness of much Elizabethan and Jacobean drama voice the growing sensibility, even as did the enthusiastic descriptions of the antiquaries. Leland, Stow,

Camden, Speed fed, with their careful historical researches and reports, the imaginations of the generations that followed them, seventeenth-century enthusiasts like Aubrey, Wood, Dugdale and Hearne. The antiquary became a familiar type, guyed by such popular satirists as John Earle.

"He is a man strangely thrifty of time past. . . . He is one that hath that unnatural disease to be enamoured of old age and wrinkles, and loves all things (as Dutchman do cheese) the better for being mouldy and worm-eaten . . . a broken statue would almost make him an idolater. A great admirer he is of the rust of old monuments, and reads only those characters where time hath eaten out the letters. He will go you forty miles to see a saint's well or a ruined abbey. . . . Printed books he condemns, as a novelty of this latter age, but a manuscript he pores on everlastingly, especially if the cover be all moth-eaten. . . . His grave does not fright him, for he has been used to sepulchres, and he likes death the better because it gathers him to his fathers."[1]

That was in 1628. The type persisted, becoming more common as the century went on. It would go anywhere to see a ruined abbey, and would, "with a melancholy delight", as Anthony Wood put it, spend time in "taking a prospect" of it. Interest grew not only in the medieval but in the classical past. Fed by history, poetry and translations, the romantically-minded looked back indiscriminately to Gothic castles and abbeys, Virgilian pastoral landscapes, Grecian gods, nymphs and dryads, Roman monuments and temples. Two centuries of ruin painting began Artists had always painted ruins, either for decoration, or historically, or for some symbolic religious purpose, but never before with such fervour. The seventeenth and eighteenth century explosion of ruin-feeling into paint and architecture was a climax, the coming to a head of an age-old emotion never inarticulate, but never fully finding its voice until, for various reasons, the climate and circumstances of the seventeenth century touched it off. The subject became an artistic obsession, reaching its most extreme violence in Salvator Rosa and the Neapolitan ruin fantasia painter Monsú Desiderio. The fierce, ruin-minded, banditti-haunted Salvator

"was, in a minor degree, a kind of Byron. He opened a new vein

[1] John Earle, *Microcosmographie* (1628).

4 Neapolitan Fantasy. Oil painting by Francesco Desiderio (fl 1623-31)

5 Section of tower in the Désert de Retz, Forest of Marly, nr. Paris. Etching by G. L. Le Rouge, *Jardins Anglo-Chinois*, 1785

of sentiment, and discovered the rhetorical form in which it could be conveyed. . . The artist who invents stage properties which can be borrowed with effect is sure of success, and the minor painters of the eighteenth century came to rely on Salvator's banditti and shaggy fir trees" (and still more on his ruins) "as their successors of the 1930s relied on Picasso's harlequins and guitars. Neither would have obtained currency had they not also fulfilled some half realized dream of the period. As Dr. Johnson said of Sterne, His nonsense suits their nonsense."[1]

Whatever the components and complex causes of that dream—and dreams come and go on the capricious winds of fashion—painters

"began to cherish ruin in itself and for its own sake; and, just as Caravaggio and the Neapolitan figure painters were absorbed in the divergence of human beings from an ideal type, so the painters of landscape in the decay of buildings . . . The imagination thus set loose did not merely copy ruins. It built them in a kind of philosophic sport. It was a lunar spirit which led to the construction of dead cities and disquieting arcades of fancy. In this strange form of creation it seemed as if ruin fed upon ruin and propagated after its own nature, filling a world of dream with spongy products of unreason. Such are the paintings of a mysterious Monsú Desiderio. . . ."[2]

whose wild and irrationally decadent towers, spires, palaces and statues tumble so startlingly yet exquisitely on to strange quays, in an elegant nightmare of decay. Desiderio was the most fantastic of the seventeenth-century ruin artists, Salvator Rosa the most intense. It was Rosa who brought the savage world of rocks, ruins and brigandage into the general artistic consciousness. "Precipices, mountains, torrents, wolves, rumblings, Salvator Rosa," as Horace Walpole exclaimed from the grandeur of the Savoy mountains. Here was the awful wildness of Gothic ruin, of frowning towers, baronial halls, shattered cowsheds, castles of Otranto, the true rust of the barons' wars.

Meanwhile, greater artists, Claude, the two Poussins, were painting tranquil classical landscapes, where broken arches and columns stand above luminous water under luminous skies. Everywhere was ruin, horrid or lovely, infernal or divine; it

[1] Sir Kenneth Clark, *Landscape into Art* (Murray, 1950).
[2] William Gaunt, *Bandits in a Landscape* (Studio Ltd, 1937).

decorated the visible landscape, it moulded men's dreams. Troops of lesser artists imitated the masters in this; ruin became more than an artistic fashion; it was a mystique; almost a religion; it gave its devotees the most ecstatic satisfaction. Ghisolfi, Pannini, Piranesi, Guardi, followed in the next century; later Hubert Robert made ruin his chief concern. Ruins were accepted as part of the scenery, like trees and water, young ladies produced pseudo-Rosas, all broken walls and ivied crags; ruinous landscapes were limned with hot pokers. Every traveller to Italy brought home prints, drawings and water-colour sketches in the *genere panniniano*, while the rich connoisseur (and most rich tourists were connoisseurs) beautified his private art collection with original paintings. Such enthusiasm for the art of another country had not been seen since rich Romans looted Greek sculptures during the prodigal centuries after the conquest of Greece. "The love for fine paintings", said Defoe, "so universally spread itself among the nobility and persons of figure all over the kingdom, that it is incredible what collections have been made by English gentlemen since that time; and how all Europe has been rummag'd, as we say, for pictures to bring over hither." And with the pictures came the ruins.[1]

It is tempting to over-estimate the contribution made by ruin paintings to popular sensibility. They were, after all, only one side of the great tide of romanticism that swept Europe about the turn of the century; a tide not new, but increased in force and apparency. If people painted and admired ruin pictures, it was (apart from mere fashion) because they got from them a satisfaction they needed. The human race is, and has always been, ruin-minded. The literature of all ages has found beauty in the dark and violent forces, physical and spiritual, of which ruin is one symbol. The symbols change; the need does not. Oedipus, Clytemnestra, Atreus, Medea, children slain and served up in pies to their parents, all the atrocious horrors of Greek drama, of Seneca, of Dante's hell, of Tasso, of the Elizabethans and Jacobeans—these have a profoundly ruinous and welcome gloom, far greater than that of the romantic ruined towers, the bats, toads and ghosts that were so fashionable in eighteenth-century

[1]See E. M Manwaring, *Italian Landscape in eighteenth-century England* (1925), for an admirable account of the influence of Italian painters on English sentiment.

poetry. Shakespeare, Marlowe, Webster, Ford, have all the properties—mass murder, torture, rape, loathsome dungeons and caves, haunted castles, minatory ghosts, witches, blasted heaths, blindings, madness, owls and flitting bats, adders and speckled toads, monstrous passions, suicide, revenge; it is indeed a ruined and ruinous world they inhabit and portray, and no eighteenth-century ruin poet can hold a candle to them. The ghastly owl shrieks his baleful note in both; the horrid worms twine about the cold corpse in the mouldering grave; there was not much that the later century could add.

What it did add was a kind of cheerful enjoyment of the dismal scene, a brisk, approving gaiety, expressed in firm octosyllabic or decasyllabic lines, with satisfied enumerations of the gloomy objects perceived; and a good moral at the end, as in Dyer's *Grongar Hill*.

> 'Tis now the raven's bleak abode;
> 'Tis now th' apartment of the toad;
> And there the fox securely feeds;
> And there the poisonous adder breeds,
> Conceal'd in ruins, moss and weeds;
> While ever and anon there falls
> Huge heaps of hoary, moulder'd walls. . . .
> A little rule, a little sway,
> A sun-beam in a winter's day
> Is all the proud and mighty have
> Between the cradle and the grave.[1]

He went on to *The Ruins of Rome*, drawing a similar moral:

> The city gleam'd
> With precious spoils: alas, prosperity! . . .
> Sudden the Goth and Vandal, dreaded names,
> Rush as the breach of waters, whelming all
> Their domes, their villas; down the festive piles,
> Down fall their Parian porches, gilded baths,
> And roll before the storm in clouds of dust.
> Vain end of human strength, of human skill,
> Conquest and triumph, and domain and pomp,
> And ease, and luxury! O luxury. . . .
> What dreary change, what ruin is not thine?[2]

[1] John Dyer, *Grongar Hill* (1727).
[2] John Dyer, *The Ruins of Rome* (1720).

Other poets envisaged horrific earthquakes:

> Still greater horrors strike my eyes.
> Behold convulsive earthquakes there,
> And shatter'd lands in pieces tear,
> And ancient cities sink, and sudden mountains rise.
> Thro' opening mines th' astonished wretches go
> Hurry'd to unknown depths below.
> The bury'd ruin sleeps; and naught remains
> But dust above and desart plains.[1]

As the century proceeded, fashionable gloom increased. By 1745 it was a mode which young poets adopted with fervour. Young Thomas Warton, at seventeen, produced his devoutly imitative *Pleasures of Melancholy*; in his hands the well-kept church and studious cloister where Milton had aspired to walk with Melancholy, became a "ruin'd abbey's moss-grown piles", where the moon looks through the window, and instead of the pealing organ,

> sullen sacred silence reigns around,
> Save the lone screech-owl's note, who builds his bow'r
> Amid the mould'ring caverns dark and damp, . . .

Come midnight, he desired to be in some hollow charnel, with a taper, and a few ghosts to conduct him through the vaults. He imagines himself a hermit looking down from his cavern on "the piles of fall'n Persepolis", vaulted halls horrid with thorn and thieves,

> Whence flits the twilight-loving bat at eve,
> And the deaf adder wreathes her spotted train,
> The dwellings once of elegance and art.
> Here temples rise, amid whose hallow'd bounds
> Spires the black pine, while thro' the naked street
> Once haunt of tradeful merchants, springs the grass:
> Here columns heap'd on prostrate columns, torn
> From their firm base, increase the mould'ring mass.
> Far as the sight can pierce, appear the spoils
> Of sunk magnificence! a blended scene
> Of moles, fanes, arches, domes and palaces,
> Where, with his brother Horror, Ruin sits![2]

[1] John Hughes, *The Ecstasy* (1735).
[2] Thomas Warton, *Pleasures of Melancholy* (1745).

So the mood swelled and grew: ruin, horror, gloom, adders, toads, bats, screech-owls, ivy, wasted towers, Gothic romance, multiplied cheerfully, in poetry, prose and paint. The vast ruined vaults of Piranesi soared before nostalgic eyes; the dark roads stretched back to a formidably romantic past that haunted the mind, an escape from the utilitarian present; before the century's end there was to be Goethe, innumerable writers of Gothic romances, and Hubert Robert of the Ruins, who saw little else worth his painting, and even put the Louvre into picturesque wreckage, as Joseph Gandy later put the Bank of England. Painters, poets, novelists and the general public had come to express articulately what they had from the earliest times unconsciously felt—that

> there's a fascination frantic
> in a ruin that's romantic.

Should they desire to know why, Diderot could tell them. He exhorted Robert (one would think unnecessarily) to realize that ruins have a poetry of their own. "You don't know," he said, "why ruins give so much pleasure. I will tell you. . . . Everything dissolves, everything perishes, everything passes, only time goes on. . . . How old the world is. I walk between two eternities. . . . What is my existence in comparison with this crumbling stone?"[1]

Be that as it may, the realization of mortality does seem to have been the dominant emotion to which ruins then led; or possibly it was only the emotion best understood. To-day we are perhaps more objective: we consider the ruined building itself, its age and its history—"the visible effects of history in terms of decay".[2] More simply, ruin is part of the general Weltschmerz, Sehnsucht, malaise, nostalgia, Angst, frustration, sickness, passion of the human soul; it is the eternal symbol. Literature and art have always carried it; it has had, as a fashion, its ups and downs, but the constant mood and appetite is there.

The symptoms do, however, vary at different stages of history and culture; and early in the eighteenth century one charming new symptom emerged. The wind of fashion blew (who can predict when or why it blows?), and it was natural that the active

[1]Quoted by W Gaunt, *Bandits in a Landscape* (Studio Ltd, 1937).
[2]John Piper, *Pleasing Decay* (*Architectural Review*, Sept. 1947).

and outdoor British should be blown by it from their contemplation of ruin in pictures and literature and ancient abbeys into their gardens and parks, where they could throw up new ruins of their own. "Take thy plastic spade, it is thy pencil," advised William Mason in his poem *The English Garden*; and

> If Nature lend
> Materials fit for torrent, rock or arch,
> Produce new Tivolis.

Producing new Tivolis, ruined temples and all, proved an immensely charming occupation for estate-owners, and ruins came into their own as objects in a landscape, picturesque and exciting in themselves and artistic in their relation to the design of the whole.

So began the fashion of building artificial ruins, which raged over Europe through the eighteenth century and well into the nineteenth. Few phases of social and cultural life have been more instructively, entertainingly and extensively written about since its inception.[1] It has been so well dealt with that there is little left to say of it; we all know how ruins, classical Gothic, and even Chinese, sprang up in every fashionable gentleman's grounds, in Great Britain, France, Germany, Austria and the Netherlands; how garden vistas terminated in ruined Objects, classical temples adorned lakes; Baalbek, Palmyra and Paestum lifted their towers on wooded slopes, Gothic castles, bearing "the true rust of the Barons' Wars" were commissioned as lodges in parks; cowsheds and dairies, built Roman-ruin-fashion, stood in the cattle yards of *fermes ornées*, landscapes were laid out with ruined temples or abbeys at advantageous points, and ruinated hermitages, complete with hermit, hidden in thickets. It was a delicious game; everyone in the fashionable world played it, and many of slender means did, in a simpler manner, what they could, even though they could not afford, for the most part, to have the temples of Ionia reproduced from the plates in *Ionian Antiquities*, and erected under the inspection of Mr Nicholas Revett, as Lord Le Dispenser did with the portico of the ruined Temple of

[1] Among recent excellent books may be instanced *The Picturesque* (Christopher Hussey, 1937), *The Gothic Revival* (Sir Kenneth Clark, 1927), *Italian Landscape in eighteenth-century England* (E. M. Manwaring, 1925). Earlier treatments of aspects of the subject are too many to mention.

Bacchus at Teos, which rose very exactly and beautifully in his grounds near High Wycombe.

As students of its vast literature will know, the game had its rules, and these differed between one expert and another. Lord Kames, for instance, in his *Elements of Criticism* (1762), laid down that ruins should be rather Gothic than Grecian, for the former

"exhibits the triumph of time over strength; a melancholy, but not unpleasant thought; a Grecian ruin suggests rather the triumph of barbarity over taste; a gloomy and discouraging thought."

Then,

"a ruin affording a kind of melancholy pleasure ought not to be seen from a flower-parterre, which is gay and cheerful. But to pass from an exhilarating object to a ruin has a fine effect, for each of the emotions is the more sensibly felt by being contrasted with the other."

He instanced the Chinese, who introduced into their gardens rough rocks, dark caverns, trees decayed or rent by tempests and lightning, buildings in ruins or half-consumed by fire. (One would like to know for how long the Chinese had been doing this.) "But," he added, "to relieve the mind from the harshness of such objects, the sweetest and most beautiful scenes always succeed." Lord Kames had another theory, unshared by many of his fellow ruin-fans: he thought that buildings, even ruinous buildings, should look firm and stable, for "what appears tottering and in hazard of tumbling produces in the spectator the painful emotion of fear, instead of the pleasant emotion of beauty". The conceit of putting up buildings that looked about to fall he called "a kind of false wit in architecture": it is unlikely that he cared for the pictorial ruin effects of Monsú Desiderio.

Since early in the century theorists had expounded their principles on the lay-out of garden ruins. One of the first was Batty Langley, in his *New Principles of Gardening* (1728). Ruins in the old Roman manner, he said, should be used to terminate walks; they may be either painted on canvas, or actually built of brick and covered with plaster. Built ruins had not by then come in extensively; which was actually the first in this country we are not likely to discover; there seem no allusions to any earlier than those in Stowe Park, but these are mentioned without surprise in

1728, and it is usually safe to assume examples of any style earlier than those that come into general notice. If the Italians were building artificial ruins in 1510, they may well have existed in other countries a little later. But the records are uncommunicative. In any case, now that the thing had become a craze, many orderly minds felt that it needed direction. So out the instructions and maxims poured

"In wild and romantic scenes" [wrote Thomas Whately in 1770] "may be introduced a ruined stone bridge, of which some arches may be still standing, and the loss of those which are fallen may be supplied by a few planks, with a rail, thrown over the vacancy. It is a picturesque object· it suits the situation, and the antiquity of the passage, the care taken to keep it still open, tho' the original building is decayed . . . give it an imposing air of reality."

Ruins may also, he says, be on the model of Tintern Abbey, roofless, twined with ivy, and the floor turf-grown. A few trees and a cottager's shed will look well amid the remains of a temple, and convey a strong notion of antiquity. "A material circumstance to the truth of the imitation is that the ruin appear to be very old", and a semblance of antiquity may be given by judiciously arranged ivy and cracks. There should be a certain congruity: in a British scene the semblance of an ancient British monument, "an object to be seen at a distance, rude and large, and in character agreeable to a wild view", looks better than a classical temple.

Richard Jago, in his long didactic poem *Edge-Hill* (1767), is particular about appropriate sites: "To every structure give its proper site", placing the mimic fane and mouldering abbey in the vale, preferably among pines, while the castle, the broken arch or mouldering wall, should "crown with graceful pomp the shaggy hill".

The proportions, shapes and designs of Gothic barns, cowsheds and hermitages, of ruined classical and oriental temples, arches and colonnades, filled many useful and beautiful volumes. There was no excuse for any one's not knowing how ruins should be built in his grounds: the difficulty was only in getting it skilfully done, by the right architect. As the Reverend William Gilpin observed, "It is not every man who can build a house who can execute a ruin." But, early in the century, the architects rose to this new opportunity for their skill, and the ruins went up. First the fortified Gothic castles and farms, unruined, like Vanbrugh's fortified buildings at Castle Howard; then Lord Bathurst's Alfred's Hall, a sham ruined castle set in woods in his grounds; there followed sham façades innumerable, rising, blandly and naively sly, charmingly and tranquilly hypocritical shells, on what their constructors called eminences, all over the gentlemen's grounds of Britain. In the landscape gardens ruins were to be surprised in hidden nooks, wood-screened; like Mr. Hamilton's Roman mausoleum (or triumphal arch?) at Pain's Hill, and his large Gothic ruin by the lake, standing among that delicious wilderness of follies; and Mr Shenstone's Gothic ruins at the Leasowes. The most celebrated ruin-builder, Sanderson Miller, leaped to fame with his Folly at Edgehill, in 1743, and, two years later, with his castle in Hagley Park. Edgehill, though not the first sham Gothic ruin, became perhaps the best known; with its two round towers joined by a high wooden bridge, and its ruined cottages across the road, it is instantly charming to the eye, and was an immediate success. Still charming to-day, and still a success, it is now an inn. Even more famous was Miller's castle in Hagley Park

"Mr Lyttelton [Shenstone wrote to Lady Luxborough] has near finish'd one side of his castle. It consists of one entire Tow'r, and three stumps of Tow'rs, with a ruin'd Wall betwixt them [here he drew a sketch of it, not very like]. There is no great Art or Variety in the Ruin, but the Situation gives it a charming effect, the chief Tow'r is allowedly about ten feet too low."

Horace Walpole lost his heart to this castle, which served as lodge for the park keeper. To quote once again his best-known remark: "There is a ruined castle, built by Miller, that would get him his freedom even of Strawberry: it has the true rust of the Barons' Wars."

So thought almost everyone.

"While with cheerful step you climb the hill [wrote an admirer] your eye will, delighted, repose . . . on the remains of an old dusky building, solemn and venerable, rearing its gothic turret among the bushy trees, called

THE RUIN

"Upon the first glimpse of this becoming object, which adds so much dignity to the scene, one cannot resist an involuntary pause—struck with its character, the mind naturally falls into reflections . . . and I make no doubt that an antiquarian . . . would sigh to know in what era it was founded, and by whom:—what sieges it had sustained—what blood had been spilt upon its walls: and would lament that hostile discord or the iron hand of all-mouldering time, should so rapaciously destroy it. . . . In reality it is nothing but a deception, designed and raised here by the late noble possessor . . . it is a modern structure, intended not merely as an object only, to give a livelier consequence to the landscape, but for use. . . . the massy stones which have tumbled from the ruinous walls are suffered to lie about . . . in the most neglected confusion: this agreeably preserves its intention as a ruin, and the climbing ivy which already begins to embrace the walls with its gloomy arms will soon throw a deeper solemnity over the whole, and make it carry the strongest face of antiquity."[1]

Such was the reaction of our ancestors to these becoming objects. Not that applause was universal. Lady Luxborough, an enthusiast for Shenstone's laid-out landscape at the Leasowes, wrote firmly: "I like even a root seat at the Leasowes better than I do this modern ruin of an ancient castle." The stones for the castle were brought from a neighbouring quarry, the framework of the windows from the ruined thirteenth-century abbey at Halesowen.

Meanwhile, a few miles away, Shenstone was happily laying out his *ferme ornée*, that celebrated triumph of landscape gardening, described in prose and verse by so many admirers, from Dodsley and Goldsmith to the cobbler poet, James Woodhouse. It was one of the earlier and most charming of its kind, complete with groves, vistas, walks, hill, meandering rills, lake, urns, artless cascades, a serpentine river and, of course, ruins; "the rudest, the most simple, and the most captivating scene". There was "a simple cottage, dressed up in the form of a small ruin . . . the bold church-like Gothic windows give it a solemn air, and add a graceful lustre to the groves and fields that surround it". This "ruinated priory" was fitted up with reliquaries and ornaments from Halesowen Abbey and elsewhere; to-day there is only a fragment left. In its day it was, though ruinated, habitable;

[1] Joseph Heeley, *The Beauties of Hagley and the Leasowes* (1777).

Shenstone put in it a tenant, who paid "tolerable poundage". He wrote of it to his friend Richard Graves; one room was to have "Gothic shields round the cornice"; an army of workmen were employed on making a piece of water below it. Graves enjoyed the Leasowes very much; some years later he put both it and its owner into two satirical novels.

No one could say that this fashionable hobby did not give much pleasure all round. The sources of this pleasure were explored by many writers at the time. Their effect on the imagination, Whately suggested, was profound.

"All remains excite an enquiry into the former state of the edifice, and fix the mind in a contemplation of the use it was applied to . . . they suggest ideas which would not arise from the buildings if entire. . . . Whatever building we see in decay, we naturally contrast its present to its former state, and delight to ruminate on the comparison. It is true that such effects properly belong to real ruins; they are, however, produced in a certain degree by those which are fictitious; the impressions are not so strong, but they are exactly similar. . . . At the sight of a ruin, reflections on the change, the decay, and the desolation before us, naturally occur, and they introduce a long succession of others, all tinctured with that melancholy which these have inspired. . . ."[1]

Sometimes the reflections induced were moral, as those inspired by the ruinous Temple of Modern Virtue in Stowe Park, contrasting so significantly with the orderly grandeur of the noble Temple of Ancient Virtue, where in a circle

a sacred band
Of Princes, Patriots, Bards and Sages stand. . . .
Acknowledged Benefactors of Mankind.

Though the ruined temple looked well, it bore a sad moral, as was noticed by two visiting gentlemen in the 1740s, whose comments are recorded in *A Dialogue on Stowe*. Callophilus, introducing his friend Polypthon to the famous ornamental park, so rich in statues, temples, grottos, bridges, cascades, and the other outcomes of "Cobham's pleasing toils", indicates a Ruin.

"Has not that ruin," says he, "a good effect? How romantick is yon Hermitage! Those pines which hang nodding over those

[1]Thomas Whately, *Observations on Modern Gardening* (1770).

broken Arches, that murmuring cascade, and those Fauns and Satyrs dancing to its sound, I assure you begin to raise very wild ideas in my head. Whence is it, my friend, that the imagination, even of a good-natured man, is more enraptured with these rude appearances of Nature, these prospects of the ruinous kind, than with the most smiling views of plenty and prosperity?"

After discussing this, Polypthon begs to be informed what the ruin means. A contrast, he supposes, in the landscape. Something more, says Callophilus:

"You have just seen the flourishing condition of Ancient Virtue; see the ruinous state of modern. That heap of stones . . . appear, you see, in the utmost disorder. Most of them have broke loose from all ties of society."

Polypthon returned that he was "glad to find his walk grown a little more moral." He thought the ruin "a very elegant piece of satyr, upon my word!" and was "most prodigiously taken with it".[1]

Some visitors, however, concentrated entirely on the temple's artistic aspect, and admired its wanton frescos.

> See where the *Ruin* lifts its mould'ring head!
> Within, close-sheltered from the peering day,
> Satyrs and Fauns their wanton Frolicks play. . . .[2]

Stowe was the first of the celebrated landscape parks with ruins; it was also considered by most people the finest; though Bishop Herring of Bangor, returning from Wales mountain-intoxicated, remarked that had he seen Stowe on his way home, he would have "thrown out some very unmannerly reflections upon it; I should have smiled at the little niceties of art, and beheld with contempt an artificial ruin, after I had been agreeably terrified with something like the rubbish of a creation." But most people fully agreed with Mr. George Bickham—

> O how charming the walks to my fancy appear,
> What a number of temples and grottos are here![3]

[1] *A Dialogue on Stowe* (1751 edition)
[2] George West, *Stowe, The Gardens of the Right Honourable Richard Lord Viscount Cobham* (1732).
[3] George Bickham, *Stowe* (1756).

Stourhead too. Indeed, Stourhead, with its wooded slopes stretching round its large and beautiful lake, and its classical temples and grottos set along the shores, and the Baalbek Temple of the Sun hidden in the high woods above, is actually a finer affair.

As the century advanced, ruins became more Gothic; the pastoral Augustan landscape grew ever craggier and shaggier; ruined abbeys and barns ousted classical temples. The mixture of styles and periods, condemned by purists, continued. The Italian influence of that great gardener, William Kent, which created so many landscapes where

> Fair temples, opening to the sight,
> Surprise each turn with new delight,

yielded increasingly to the taste for British antiquity in a state of dilapidation. Sanderson Miller, the designer of Edgehill and the Hagley ruin, had his hands full of commissions. Some of his effects were stagey, lacking solidity, like the castle façade ordered by Lord Chancellor Hardwicke for his park at Wimpole. Admiring Hagley Castle, he had, wrote George Lyttelton to Miller, "a mind to build one at Wimple himself", but Lyttelton had, not unnaturally, advised him to have his rather different, so now "he wants no house, nor even room in it, but merely the walls and semblance of an old castle, to make an object from the house". As the back and one side would be closed by a wood, only the front and the right side need be built. The materials would be a mixture of flint pebbles and other stone; there were also bricks in the neighbourhood.

So there the stage castle stands on its hill to this day, with an air as if it might be made of canvas and plaster; as, indeed, many sham ruins were. Ralph Allen's Sham Castle, erected on Bathwick Hill above Bath, so that Mr Allen could see it from his own house, is also a façade. But most of the Follies, of whatever material built, stood four-square, like "the pompous piles of Hagley", or Lord Bathurst's "lowly pile", whose

> crusted, mould'ring wall
> Threats the beholders with a sudden fall. . . .
> This pile the marks of rolling centuries wears,
> Sunk to decay—and built but twenty years.[1]

[1]Edward Stephens (1769)

Sometimes, like Sir Edward Turner's affair, they fell down. "Come and deplore the ruin of my ruin," he wrote to Sanderson Miller.

By the last quarter of the century British Gothic had gained a temporary victory over foreign classical, and the moss-grown ruinated medieval sham stirred more hearts than a

poor Baalbec dwindled to the eye,
And Paestum's fanes with columns six feet high,

or than the Roman arch that mingles with the Chinese elegance at Kew. For the perfect ruin, there had to be ivy, an owl (preferably screech), a raven and a few bats in the tower, a broken arch, with moss, trees thrusting through Gothic windows, a toad, an adder, and perhaps a fox. There might, too, be a hermit; but in that case the roof must not be so ruinated as to let in the rain; a ghost was less trouble.

Such a fashion could not be permanent: it defeated itself, as time went on, by its excesses. Even Walpole wearied of it, observing that "Taste, when not under the guidance of good sense, will degenerate into whimsical conceits and absurdities which instantly detect themselves." It is noticeable that no ruins figure among the Gothic gimcrackeries of Strawberry. When it was damaged by an explosion near by, its owner wrote ruefully, "Never did it look so Gothic in its born days." But he had no "cow-house in baronial style", nor did he

Build of old disjointed moss-grown stone
A time-struck abbey.

Perhaps, with his wit and his acute social sense, he foresaw in the near future the literary joke that ruin-mania, together with the landscape gardening craze, was to become.

"The Doric portico, the Palladian bridge, the Gothic ruin, the Chinese pagoda, that surprise the stranger, soon lose their charms to their surfeited master. . . . But the ornament whose merit soonest fades is the hermitage, or scene adapted to contemplation. It is almost comic to set aside a quarter of one's garden to be melancholy in."

Of course it partly depended on how skilfully the illusion was produced. Joseph Heeley, the enthusiast for the Leasowes, condemned such deceptions as adorning the gable end of a barn with a large Gothic window to give it the appearance of a chapel: "this betrays a very childish taste" as do cascades made of tin. But the priory at the Leasowes, the ruined castle at Hagley, and many others, were not in the least objectionable—they were "real, and what the nearest inspection justifies".[1]

There is a defensive note here. By the late 1770s, though the fashion was still unabated, it was also the fashion to guy it, as Richard Graves did. He forestalled by a generation Peacock and *Headlong Hall*, where the guests are conducted over the estate by their enthusiastic host, who shows them with pride every feature of his landscape garden. One of the guests particularly admires a ruined tower on a point of rock overgrown with ivy, but thinks it would be a great deal improved by polishing the walls, and by a plantation of spruce firs, by blowing up part of the rock, and changing the building into a more elegant shape. *Nightmare Abbey*, too, with its tower "ruinous and full of owls", has moved a long way from the early naïve enthusiasm.

> "I remember the good time [wrote someone], when the price of a haunch of venison with a country friend was only half an hour's walk upon a hot terrace, a descent to the two square fish-ponds overgrown with frog-spawn, a peep into the hog-stye, or a visit to the pigeon house. How reasonable was this, when compared with the attention now expected from you to the number of temples, pagodas, pyramids, grottos, bridges, hermitages, caves, towers, etc."[2]

The fashion was a gift to the satirists; but it could not be killed by guying, and was going strong all through the Regency. Beckford, in 1796, thought of building Fonthill Abbey as "a sort of habitable ruin", a convent of which only part had survived; but in the end he wanted something more grandiose. But most of his contemporaries were still agreed that "the mouldering ruins of ancient temples, theatres, and aqueducts . . . are in the highest degree picturesque", and were eager for "a little taste of everything at Tusculum".

Though the fashion flourished also on the continent, some

[1] Joseph Heeley, *The Beauties of Hagley and the Leasowes, etc.* (1777)
[2] R. Cambridge, *The World*, no. 76 (quoted by E. F. Carritt in *A Calendar of British Taste*, 1949).

French critics thought that the English, with their well-known lack of balance, went a good deal too far. The Prince de Ligne, for instance, though his own gardens at Beloeil were tastefully decorated with these elegant whimsies, condemned the English *templomanie* and sham Gothic. He himself liked to have temples within reason—a Chinese temple for a pigeon-house, an Indian temple to eat cream in, and even "*une tour qui a l'air d'être ancienne comme le monde, et que j'ai fait faire dans un genre ridicule, gothique, et singulier*". But as to English ruins,

> *J'aime les ruines lorsqu'elles offrent une idée des choses respectables qui s'y sont passées, et des gens célèbres qui les habitaient; mais quand on voit la Grécie de plusieurs Anglais et la Gothie de Mr Walpole, on est tenté de croire que c'est le délire d'un mauvais rêve qui a conduit leur ouvrage. J'aime autant son château d'Otrant, celui de la Tamise est tout aussi fou, et n'est pas plus gai.*[1]

All these columns, he thought, half-standing, half-buried, resembled a game of skittles; the pieces of wall, the remains of buildings, were still more ridiculous. One was tempted to ask, why has no one cleared away all these fragments? It was with difficulty that he could admire anything English, Stau, Twiknam, Chisswig, Wimmelton, most of the famous gardens of "mylords atrabilaires" were as little agreeable in his eyes as their owners. Nor did Italian gardens please him. French were the best; he admired very much M. de Monville's Désert de Retz, near Marly, which was then in building, and particularly its main feature, the broken column, forty-four feet round, fitted with rooms—an idea all his own. He had advised M. de Monville to build round it a ruined colonnade, and to erect a pyramid. The whole group of buildings seemed to him most picturesque.

As, indeed, it is. There are few more engaging conceits, in that age of engaging conceits, than this Anglo-Chinese French garden, created on the sloping ground running down from the forest of Marly near St. Germain-en-Laye It was partly designed for its owner by Hubert Robert the ruin-painter, and it has some of the eerie fascination of his pictures. To study it thoroughly, even when one has seen it, one should look at the plan and engravings in Le Rouge's *Jardins Anglo-Chinois*, which shows it as it was.

[1]The Prince de Ligne, *Coup d'Œil sur Belœil* (1778)

6 Design for a ruined object Batty Langley, 1728

7 'Roman' ruin at Kew Etching from G L Le Rouge, *Jardins Anglo-Chinois*, 1785

8 The Bank of England in Ruins, a Fantasy
Water-colour by J M Gandy (1771-1845)

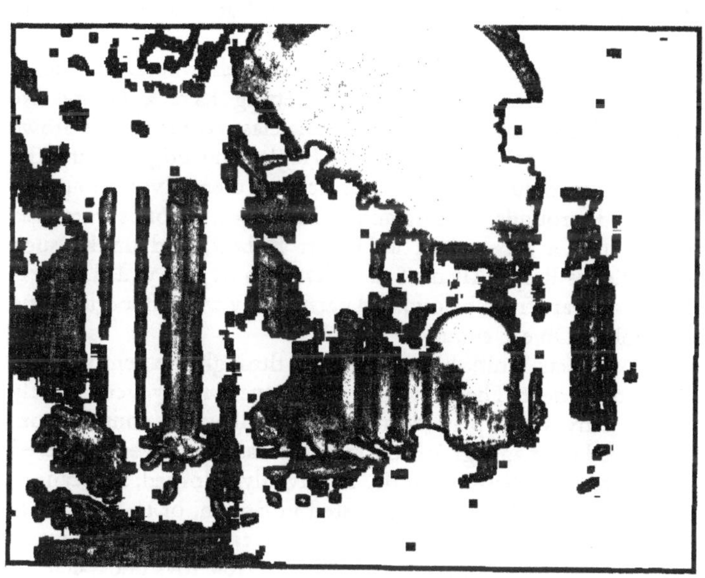

9 The Grande Galerie of the Louvre in Ruins, a Fantasy
Oil painting by Hubert Robert (1733-1808)

To-day it is more ruinous than it was built to be, and more overgrown; the excellent photographs illustrating an article on it by Mr Osvald Sirén in a recent number of the *Architectural Review* show it as it has lately been. It lies in a woody park, untended and in parts impassable; the chief building is a house in the shape of a broken column, with rooms fitted neatly, on four stories, round a spiral stairway running up inside. Now uninhabited and disused, it is decaying and creeper-grown, and trees have encroached upon it till it is half hidden. It used to be topped by a jagged parapet, shrub-grown, standing high against the sky. The interior, with its circular walls and oval rooms, is delightful. A little way from it are a creeper-covered ice-house, pyramid-shaped, and fragments of walls and arches of the artificial ruin of a small Gothic church. This, and the ruined urn, and the circular Temple of Pan, are all now more ruinous than when they were built, and drowned in the woods that creep on about them. Even the Maison Chinoise, which was not built as a ruin, is now heartrending in decay; it is the prettiest of French-Chinese houses, with its jutting belled eaves, its lantern top, its charmingly-furnished, but now tattered, torn and dilapidated five rooms.

There is nothing quite like this Désert elsewhere. Its ruined fantasies in their romantic woody setting have a gnome-like charm and grace far removed from the classical dignity of Stowe or Stourhead, or the Gothic rust of Hagley and Edgehill, and the hundreds of their kind that had seeded themselves about the parks and grounds of England. The Désert inspires romantic dreams, like a Piranesi or a Hubert Robert; and unlike such banal piles as Ralph Allen's Sham Castle on its hill, which, nevertheless, appears from below, and particularly when floodlit, a fine and foolish Object enough.

Such Objects multiplied themselves through the century, and well into the next. They have not all survived; many were flimsily built of canvas and plaster; a kind of Hollywood construction, they served their age, gratified a transient taste, and were gathered to the earth they had so lightly, so trivially, adorned. We cannot know how many bogus ruins existed in Britain, or in Europe, at the peak of the craze Nor, I fancy, can we easily know how many are left to-day; still one comes on these amiable toys unexpectedly in unadvertized spots; exploring the laurel-shaded garden of some charming little house tucked away in the purlieus of Kensington and Holland Park, one finds, concealed by potting-shed or garage, delightful fragments of Gothic ruin embedded in ivied walls, the heads of monks or gargoyles peering down from the corbels of arches at the little Austin in the shed.

Of the well-known ruin follies, there must still be many hundreds. Among the most remarkable are the arches, columns and ruined temple put up in the early nineteenth century by the side of Virginia Water. There is nothing flimsy or transient about these, for their stones are genuine Roman antiques from Leptis Magna in North Africa. The British Consul in Tripoli persuaded, it seems, the Bey of that city in 1816 to present the ruins of Leptis to the Prince Regent; the stones were shipped to London and lay in the British Museum courtyard till 1826, when George IV had them erected at Virginia Water, in the noble form we see. They were then surrounded by statues, but these were ill-used by the public and soon removed. This transported Leptis has given immense pleasure ever since to those with a taste for the grandiose and superb.

Politics, passion, and religion have played their parts in ruin-building. The Duke of Norfolk of 1780 gratified his pro-American Whig bias by running up on his estate at Greystoke two anti-British ruins, calling them after two victories of our late colonists, Bunker's Hill and Fort Putnam. As to religion, besides all the ruined churches put up by triumphing atheist or wistful agnostic to symbolize the decay of superstition, one may see at the top of a steep and rugged hill in Somerset a very ruinous Gothic ruin which marks "the birthplace of Primitive Methodism": it is called Mow Cop Castle, and why it was built in ruin form is anyone's guess; perhaps it was put up by an episcopalian.

As to passion, ruins have been flung up in jealous rage, like that erected by Lord Belvedere in West Meath in 1740. When Lady Belvedere ran off with her brother-in-law, whose house, a few miles away, was in full view of the earl's windows, the earl saw nothing for it but to build a ruined abbey (the ruin was, presumably, symbolic of his shattered domestic life) about fifty yards from his house, blocking from view his brother's offensive mansion. Rather more ivy-clad than in 1740, it is otherwise said to be as good as new. No doubt there are other such, conceived in passion and put up in rage. And more, perhaps, whose ragged and crumbling walls symbolize the frustration and exasperation of some ruined and tormented architect or landed gentleman or lady. It is held by some thinkers that sex frustration has not infrequently been the inspiration of such ruins: there are, it seems, some elegant follies flung up by a frustrated Countess near Warsaw in 1820; what, or who, caused the frustration we do not now recall, though it may be known in Warsaw, but its fruits are agreeable enough.

Sometimes real ruins seem to have induced, by force of suggestion, bogus ones. As on Chapel Island, near Conishead (so christened by Mrs Radcliffe in her *Tour of the Lakes*), where, at the end of the eighteenth century, the ruined shell of a chapel stood; in 1823, when Colonel Bradyll's new mansion at Conishead Priory was building, shams sprouted about it like mushrooms; they included a high-gabled wall of slate, pierced by lancet windows. This suggestive effect of actual ruins is not uncommon; it would seem to be the working in reverse of the principle by which hens produce actual eggs when confronted by sham ones in their nest. The same principle may be responsible for the sham-ruin entrance of Croxton Rectory, Lancashire, which seems built of pieces of a genuine ruin; and for the fascinating jumble of Gothic ecclesiastical ruins erected by the enterprising early Victorian owner of the now public gardens behind Abingdon Abbey; they are a particularly imposing folly, constructed out of stones taken from St. Helen's church during its restoration; there are arches, a tower, great fragments of broken wall, part of a cloister, and a fine perpendicular window apparently taken from the church; the whole affair lying picturesquely in tree-shaded gloom. The Borough Council is said, perhaps unjustly, to have it in mind to demolish this charming sham in which it sees no sense; it has put up a cold notice at the entrance to the gardens, "These are not the ruins of the Abbey", vouchsafing no further information.

Sometimes ruins have been intentionally manufactured by destruction, not in anger or in arson, but in aesthetic enthusiasm. In 1836 Mr Hussey, the grandfather of the present owner of Scotney Castle in Kent, moved by this enthusiasm and desirous of building himself a new and more commodious house to live in, abandoned his ancient fortified manor house by the lilied moat, the tower surviving from the fourteenth-century castle, the Elizabethan brick mansion with its great hall and oak staircase and priest's hiding-hole, and the three-storey house in the style of Inigo Jones that had been built on to it in the mid-seventeenth century, the three buildings forming an exquisite composite single mansion. Mr Hussey had a fine new house quarried out of the hillside high above the old castle; and, in order to see from his windows a picturesque object, had the seventeenth-century part of the old house partially and fashionably ruined. The attic storey, all but one window, was destroyed, the roof removed, the walls shattered into jagged roughness at the top. He achieved his picturesque object; from the first it must have been beautiful; to-day, creeper-grown and the colour of lichen, standing with the grey and rust-coloured barbicaned castle tower against a steep wilderness of quarry flowers behind, and at its foot the lily moat reflecting sky, trees, tower and ruined mansion, to-day it makes an exquisite picture. If ever ruin-making has justified itself, this has; the scene has a harmonious grace, the grace achieved in greater or less measure by many time-struck or fate-struck ruins, and by few shams. These are apt to balance between the melancholy banal and the gay absurd; some are philistine, like the group of follies in Brussels, presented to the eccentric nineteenth-century painter, Antoine Wiertz. All have the interest of commemorating a period taste, of having once gratified that eternal ruin-appetite which consumes the febrile and fantastic human mind. Sometimes the appetite is appeased by the imaginary demolition of famous buildings, as Hubert Robert ruined the Louvre and Joseph Gandy the Bank of England, and as an artist in the *Strand Magazine* of the 1890's presented exciting and romantic ruins of St Paul's, Westminster Abbey, the Houses of Parliament, and Buckingham Palace. Some have thought this fanciful ruination silly: "*Pourquoi détruire, dis-le moi . . . A le détruire mieux que toi Tant de gens si bien réussissent*," a critic of the 1796 Salon apostrophized Robert.

Some follies commemorate the activities of a group; of these is the ruined castle of Türkensturz, built in 1826, near the ancient Lower Austrian castle of Seebenstein, where a group of noblemen, among them the emperor's brother Johann, used to meet to indulge their mood of romantic feudal medievalism, which had down the centuries furnished Austria and Germany with so many magnificent examples of the real thing.

The hobby has persisted sporadically into our own day, though our present surfeit of real ruins has now probably halted it. But the talented architect, Mr Clough Williams-Ellis, who built the Italianate town of Portmeirion on a hill above the Merioneth coast, has erected two fine ruins in his grounds: a tall castle in the hills near his house (the house is now disastrously burnt down), and a ruined fort down on the sea, which is used to bathe from. Standing on a rock above a small cove, backed by a wooded hill-side, it has an imposing and singular air, with its arches, little towers and solid brick walls, and the Atlantic running in waves against its rocky base.

How many more have been built during this century, matching in brick and stone the canvases of Mr John Piper, where ruin, lightning and storm make lurid drama of elegant mansions and towered halls? But it is probable that, though a few genuine ruins about the place are apt to breed emulating shams, such a surfeit as we have now sustained causes a strong reaction of distaste, a Thomist yearning for the whole and strong—("*primo quidem integritas sive perfectio: quae enim diminutae sunt, hoc ipso turpia sunt*")—and in that case we shall not see the revival of this eccentric and ingenious pastime for some time to come. With all the ruins any one could desire at hand, to build new ones would seem redundant.

Not that the ruin-craving has past; indeed, its unconscious urge may be working, with inverted zest, to create more of them in all lands. Literature and art are still ruin-grounded; still the bat flits.

> Whilst in the air a ghastly bat, bereft
> Of sense, has flitted with a mad surprise
> Out of the cave this hideous light had cleft,
> And he comes hastening like a moth that hies
> After a taper; and the midnight sky
> Flares, a light more dread than obscurity.
> 'Tis the tempestuous loveliness of terror. . . .[1]

But it may be hard, in the future, to treat ruins as toys

[1]Shelley, *Medusa*.

II

THE STUPENDOUS PAST

I

THE ascendancy over men's minds of the ruins of the stupendous past, the past of history, legend and myth, at once factual and fantastic, stretching back and back into ages that can but be surmised, is half-mystical in basis. The intoxication, at once so heady and so devout, is not the romantic melancholy engendered by broken towers and mouldered stones; it is the soaring of the imagination into the high empyrean where huge episodes are tangled with myths and dreams; it is the stunning impact of world history on its amazed heirs. Such ascendancy has been swayed down the ages by the ruins of Troy, of Crete, Mycenae, Tyre, Nineveh, Babylon, Thebes, Rome, Byzantium, Carthage, and every temple, theatre and broken column of classical Greece; it is less ruin-worship than the worship of a tremendous past.

Such worship would stir and overset the Roman emperors when they paid their pious visits to Troy. One of the pleasanter relations concerning the emperor Caracalla is the strange histrionic ecstasy which overtook him on such an occasion. A head never very well balanced had been turned (says the learned Dr Richard Chandler) by the writings of Philostratus, and Caracalla had become Troy-minded to excess. What he saw before him was, of course, the Graeco-Roman Ilium; but he believed it Homer's Troy, and was overcome with a passion to imitate Achilles, as he had previously, when in Macedonia, fancied himself Alexander. After adorning what passed for his hero's tomb with floral garlands and crowns, he felt the need of a Patroclus to mourn and obsequize with funerary rites. To require was, with Caracalla, to obtain, and the timely decease of his favourite freedman occurred forthwith. The emperor, in his Achillean role, caused to be erected a large pyre, had the corpse and a miscellaneous variety of slain animals placed on it, poured on it a libation, and (causing some mirth among the spectators) cut off one of his few remaining locks of hair to throw on the flames. He then emulated Alexander by running naked with his retinue round the hero's tomb, and concluded the celebrations by distributing money among his troops to reward them for having taken Troy. Subsequently he had a bronze statue of Achilles erected on a column near Cape Sigeum.

This ecstasy, this orgiastic conjuring of the past, this upsurging of furious fancies, seems very admirable in Caracalla, and indeed, in others, for it has descended in varying degrees and in a variety of forms on many millions of ruin-tipplers, and visits to Troy, in particular, have usually produced some strong Trojan intoxication. Xerxes, for instance, sacrificed there a thousand oxen and much costly wine; Alexander did his course round the Achilles tomb, sacrificed to Priam on the altar of Jupiter Hircius, donned some of the arms preserved in the Temple of Athene as those of Trojan warriors, and made grandiose plans for the enlargement and embellishment of Ilium. Julius Caesar, hunting Pompey over land and sea, across the Bosphorus and into Asia Minor, arrived on the Rhoetian promontory and wandered about the ruins of burnt Troy (for Ilium had been destroyed and slaughtered by Fimbria forty years before) among the mighty shades, seeking the vestiges of Apollo's walls. All he found (says Lucan, who surely exaggerated) was the enveloping forest, rotting oak thickets growing over the palaces of kings and the temples of gods; all Pergama lay buried, *etiam periere ruinae.* "*De leur pompeux débris le temps a fait sa proie.*" Unknowing, he crossed the dusty banks of the little winding stream that had been Xanthus, stepped on a grassy mound, and was warned by a Phrygian local that there lay the ashes of Hector. "Do you not see," this native patriot also asked him, "the altars of Jupiter Hirceas?" Caesar, though at the time Pompey-minded, was far from indifferent to the ancient shrine of his forbears; he built an altar of turf, burned incense on it, and prayed to the gods who guarded these sacred ashes, asking for himself a prosperous future, vowing that Rome should restore Troy, that a Roman Pergamon should arise. Then, having his business with Pompey, he hurried back to his waiting fleet and was away to Egypt's shores.

Rome did rebuild Ilium, which fell at last again to ruin; ruin on ruin Troy lies, and for centuries lay, among the other ruins on Troy plain, and travellers for a thousand years or so were happily confused as to what they saw, taking for Priam's Troy the glorious sea-washed columns and palaces of Alexandria Troas, founded after Alexander's death on the shore miles away. "How was it possible," Gibbon demanded severely, "to confound Ilium and Alexandria Troas?" But it was, until the great nineteenth-century Trojan excavations, only too possible, and to go into Trojan raptures among the broken pillars and magnificent vaulted arches standing by the sea's edge has always been among the more stirring ruin-pleasures. There was, for instance, that zealous traveller Mr Thomas Coryat, who, in the year 1612, arrived on the Trojan shore opposite Tenedos with a ship's company of fourteen Englishmen and a Jew, all well-weaponed against hostile Turks. Near the shore they saw extensive ruins, the remains of a goodly fortress, parts of a strong wall, many grey marble pillars standing upright among wheat, marble sepulchres, two of which, Coryat was sure, contained King Ilus and King Priam. "I affirme nothing certainly, only I gesse, as another industrious traveller would do . . . that one of these goodly monuments might be the Sepulcher of King Priamus." Such guesses are among the ruin-tasters' imaginative enjoyments. Coryat spent his afternoon guessing. Ascending from the shore among pillars, ancient stones, and growing corn, he guessed that the fragments of the great buttressed wall on his left were first built by Ilum, Troy's fourth king, when he enlarged the city, and rebuilt by Priam. Then he guessed that he saw Priam's palace, fair and stately, built of square white stones and adorned with arches and gates and pieces of white marble exquisitely carved: Coryat helped himself to some of these to carry home, "to reserve them in my safe custodie for memorable antiquities while I live. At the top of the middle arch there are two prittie holes in which Bees do breed honey." He got more pleasure than buried Ilium on the mount of Hissarlik could have given him; the pleasure swelled into drama when one of the company, observing his antiquarian eagerness, in merry humour drew his sword and knighted him, dubbing him the first English Knight of Troy. Coryat, above himself with Trojan fervour, replied,

> Lo heere with prostrate knee I doe embrace
> The gallant title of a Trojane Knight.
> In Priams Court which time shall ne'er deface;
> A grace unknowne to any British Wight. . . .

Volleys of shot were discharged by the musketeers, and the Trojan knight delivered an extemporary oration of some length on their happiness at being in ancient Troy, visited by so many heroes of antiquity but by so few of the British. As he spoke he grew more wholly convinced that they stood in the court of the ancient Trojan kings, even identifying sites of castles and forts which had served for granaries during "the decanal siege of the city". Pointing to the green corn that thrust among the stones, he quoted, inevitably, "*Jam seges est ubi Troja fuit*", and moralized on the inconstancy of fortune, remembering other noble cities buried in their ruins—Nineveh, Babylon, Tyre, Carthage, Numantia, Athens, Thebes, Lacedaemon, Corinth, "none of which I believe do yield these stately ruins that you now behold." Finally, as ruin-seers will (and this must be listed high among ruin-pleasures) he pointed a moral. "You may observe . . . one of the most pregnant examples of Luxurie that ever was in the World in these confused heaps of stones . . . For Adulterie was the principall cause of the ruines of this Citie," and London, our new Troy, was in a bad way too, "being as much poluted with extravagant lusts as ever was the old Troy".

On the way back to the sea, lying among broken arches and stones, they saw a plough, which they held in turn, "that if we live to be old men we may say in our old age, we had once holden the Plough in the Trojan Territorie". They ascended a little mount by the sea which Coryat conjectured had been made by the Trojans so that they look over their walls, and by darts, slings and arrows annoy the Greeks riding at anchor off-shore. Not for five hundred pounds, said Coryat, would he have missed all these notable sights: he advised all his travelling countrymen to visit "this famous place, as being farre the most worthiest of all the ruined places in the world".[1]

[1]Thomas Coryat, *Coryats Crudities* (1611).

But there was one pleasure that he missed, which had been enjoyed by Mr William Lithgow three years before. Mr Lithgow, an equally enthusiastic Trojan, and perhaps more of an egoist, first took the measurements of such walls as he saw (what walls they were, neither he nor we are very clear), and then indulged in another familiar pleasure, that of portraying himself, or being portrayed before the ruins. Here is his portrait, clad *en Turque* standing "by the eastern gate of that sometimes noble city, with a piece of a high wall, as yet undecayed". Some bunches of grapes denote vineyards, over the fragments of Priam's pretended palace an eagle hovers, and the Simois snakes round the picture. The ruins are small and dumpy, Mr Lithgow much larger. "Beneath my feet lie the two tombs of Priam and Hecuba his queen" (two small oblong boxes). "Under them the encircling hills of Ida, at my left delicious fields of olives and figs." He captions the picture with verse.

> "Loe, here's mine effigie, and Turkish suit . . .
> Plac'd in old Ilium. . . ."

and so on. A gratifying picture to draw: here he stood, in old Ilium, dominating the legendary city; if he did not, like Caracalla, imagine himself a Greek or Trojan hero, he towered over the heroic scene with the sapience of later ages and advantages of survival. "*Jam Lithgow est ubi Troja fuit*," he seems to say.

Quoting the classics at Troy has been since the age of Homer an inevitable pastime. Or is our unclassical century now sending to Ilium ships and coaches fraught with happy, unlettered hordes whose only pleasures in ancient ruins are the time-honoured joys of inscribing on them their names, and of being photographed on broken columns and mouldered walls? Be this as it may, most visitors to Troy have gone Homer or Virgil in hand, to re-read local history on the spot; they "read the Iliad deliciously on the tomb of Achilles and of Priam," and inscribe Greek texts on broken stones. Sometimes, pursuing the matter further, they read about famous visitors of antiquity. After reading Homer (wrote M. Guys, secretary to Louis XVI, to his son on his travels) one should read again Lucan's *Pharsalia*, which relates Caesar's visit to Troy, and translate it into French verse. Remember, M. Guys reminded his son, how we translated Horace together at Tivoli, before the Temple of Sibyl. Young M. Guys derived much pleasure from comparing his lot favourably with that of La Fontaine, who had never been to Troy, but had written, with wistful longing:

Ilion, ton nom seul a des charmes pour moi . . .
Qui pût me retracer l'image de ces lieux.

"But I," wrote young M. Guys, "have seen the place where they claim that Troy was built . . . and, without being inspired like our Fabulist, I taste all the pleasure that he coveted."

Indeed, one tastes great pleasure on Troy's site; and the labours of archaeologists have made it more apparent than it was to M. Guys, Mr Coryat, Mr Lithgow, or indeed Julius Caesar, where this site was. Layer below layer, theory after theory, have been during the last eighty years exposed; and now we see the ruins of the great Mycenaean walls and towers of Homer's Troy unearthed, standing among the later Hellenic walls, and those of the great Roman city built on these. All are marked with their successive periods; in imagination city after city rises over that wide and stony plain, looking across the Scamander to Sigeum and the sea. It is a tremendous sight. Not picturesque; not even beautiful; but magnificent in its domination, and in its evocation of the greatest legend of history. Such a pleasure, as Lady Mary Wortley Montagu observed, to see the site of what had been the greatest city of the world. But Lady Mary was too early. The Hissarlik mound was in her day yet undug, and she, shrewder and less confused than most of her contemporaries, wrote, "All that is left of Troy is the ground on which it stood, for, I am firmly persuaded, whatever pieces of antiquity may be found round it are much more modern, and I think Strabo says the same thing." However, she derived pleasure from seeing "the point of land where poor old Hecuba was buried," and the burial place of Achilles, "where Alexander ran naked round his tomb, which no doubt was a great comfort to his ghost". She found large stones, on which "Mr W. plainly distinguished" inscriptions, and had them conveyed to her ship, but the captain discouraged this pleasure, and she had to be content, for the most part, with copying the inscriptions, and, Homer in hand, admiring his "exact geography". She enjoyed too Alexandria Troas, which she conjectured to be the remains of the city begun by Constantine for his projected capital; she "took the pains of rising at two in the morning to view coolly those ruins which are commonly shewed to strangers . . . where 'tis vulgarly reported Troy stood". Hiring an ass, she made a tour of the ancient walls, which were of vast extent, and was delighted with all she saw and surmised.

So, indeed, must all have been who, looking on Alexandria Troas and less well informed than Lady Mary, took these romantically beautiful ruins for old Troy. On the whole our ancestors, intoxicated with this agreeable delusion, probably enjoyed themselves more than we, who are faced with the formidable pile of excavated and stratified ruins on Hissarlik. But even to those travellers who were not deceived, Alexandria Troas has always seemed delightful. How happy, for instance, was Dr Robert Wood, that learned traveller, who, landing on the Sigean promontory in 1750, proceeded down the coast with horses, guides, camp equipage and a tent, till he came to the ruins opposite Tenedos, lying in a beautiful shelving landscape crowned with woods, and knew them for the Macedonian Troas. How happy, too, a few years later Dr Richard Chandler, in love with that Asiatic beach, where "the waves broke with an amusing murmur" and the soft wind wafted fragrance. At the ancient port of Troas a solemn silence prevailed; nothing lived but some partridges and a fox; among long dry grass and thickets of low oak stood granite pillars half-buried in sand and corroded with sea, bearing still the scars of ropes that had once tied ships to them. The great wall, broken and towered, stretched many miles round what had been a magnificent city of buildings, theatres and temples, and now was deserted forest. In vaulted substructures, beneath swarms of hanging and flitting bats, banditti and their horses had made their homes. the great broken aqueduct marched against the sky. Dr Chandler spent his days making plans and views of the principal ruins, picnicking under a spreading tree before the arcade; in the evening he and his party returned to their headquarters in a vineyard, dined on delicious roast kid, and slept; "the starry sky was our canopy," and they woke to breakfast on grapes, figs, honeycomb and coffee. The romantic archaeologist passed his days in the deepest content: as another visitor to Alexandria Troas wrote a little later, "time glides away most rapidly on a tide of pleasure."

Even those who have visited these enchanting ruins while pursuing the apostle of the Gentiles on his breathless and busy expeditions about Asia Minor, Syria, Macedonia and the Isles, and have called at this port where the young man Eutychus was preached to sleep and almost to death, had he not been revived by the magnanimous preacher, are apt to forget both St Paul and Eutychus and, gazing on the beauty of Troas, launch into lyrical descriptions of the sea-washed, oak-grown ruin, its columns bristling among the waves. Alexandria Troas, rich colony of Macedon and Rome, founded in memory of Alexander, cherished as heir of the sacred Ilium, plundered and destroyed by Turks down the ages, lives on in its own right.

As to Ilium itself, it is a city of the ancestral mind; its cycle of tales rings down the centuries, the holy mythos of Hellenes and Romans, the great romantic legend of the Middle Ages, the ancestor of all the later Troys. It is not the mighty excavated walls on Hissarlik that dominate the Troad plain; it is the memory of the battling and the siege, the Trojans behind their walls, the Greeks encamped without, the slain heroes, the crafty horse, the victory and the flaming fall, the greatness and the ruin of sacked Troy. The pleasures of association are here at their least earth-bound, with however diligent enquiry we explore Troy's site, examining stones and pots and shards, weighing Schliemann against Dörpfeld, distinguishing Mycenaean from pre- and post-Mycenaean, from Hellenic, from Roman.

As to the enterprising and learned, if not always reliable, Schliemann, the twelve years he spent in pioneer excavation, enthusiastically burrowing, turning up city below city, settlement below settlement, finding nine layers of culture, each with its pots and pans, its jewellery, idols and stones, jumbling them together, confusing the strata, forming magnificent theories and every few years writing a book about them—these years must have been ruin-pleasure in its purest, most enthusiastic, inquisitive, adventurous and rewarding form. The noble, heady pleasure of digging up great legendary cities lost for two thousand and more years: there is, it is said, nothing like it.

As in all great ruins, a hundred minor and less noble pleasures have flourished in Troy and its ruined neighbours of the plain. Professional guides were early there; in the fourth century the Emperor Julian found in the Graeco-Roman Ilium

> "a population of guides making what they could out of the tourist, with the aid of the remains of Priam's town, and anything the tourist asked for that happened to be missing they did not hesitate to supply. There was a hero-shrine . . . where sacrifices were still burnt before a statue of Hector, and to balance Hector a statue of Achilles had been recently added. . . . It seems a pity that the guides stopped short of showing an authentic wooden horse"[1]

Though, as to that, we have no evidence that they did.

There has been, too, much relic-looting; one may doubt if any visitor to the Troad has come empty-handed away. Some, like Lady Mary Montagu, took large inscribed stones; many have, like Coryat, broken off and pocketed carved marbles; Mark Anthony took the statue of Ajax from the Rhoetian shore and carried it to Egypt to gratify the Egyptian woman. Later the Venetians, who always coveted statues, filled their galleys with deities from the broken temples; while the Turks took cargoes of columns to build and decorate Stamboul. Early in the fifth century a vessel was so weighted with large columns from Alexandria Troas that it could not be launched until a bishop was found to exorcise obstructive demons. For these reasons the Troad cities are as we see them to-day. All intelligent tourists have acquired some Trojan treasure, the higher-minded among them remarking that the Turks would take what they did not. For all intelligent tourists, and most less intelligent, have always been, in some degree or other, antiquarians; antiquarianism is the main basis of *Ruinenempfindsamkeit*, and however far one looks back into history one finds it working hotly in the human breast. Travellers, from Homer onward, have gazed on Troy and on Troy's ruins because Troy was great, but more because Troy was ancient, ruined and fallen. They would have preferred, we should prefer now, to see the great city as she was; but, gazing on her ruins, we build her in our minds.

[1]Dorothy Brooke, *Pilgrims were They All* (Faber, 1934).

2

As also we build Tyre. Since the vindictive passion of Ezekiel against Tyre some twenty-six centuries back produced one of the major Hebrew poems of invective, the reports of Tyre's death have always been exaggerated. Ruined she has been, again and again; desolate and diminished she is; but always she has risen again, Phoenician, Roman, medieval, modern, standing on her successive ruins in the sea. The prophet's wishful "thou shalt be built no more" has never come to pass, though generations of visitors to Tyre have mournfully repeated the words as they gazed on the fallen fishing city; to do so is one of the Tyrian pleasures.

It all began when Tyre said of Jerusalem, "Aha, she is broken. I shall be replenished, now she is laid waste." This turned Ezekiel and the Lord against Tyre, the rich fair in which all the world traded, the joyous city whose antiquity was of ancient days, the garden of God, adorned with precious stones, the crowning city whose merchants were princes, the rich jewel in the midst of the seas. The Lord, taking sides with the xenophobe Ezekiel, said to Tyre:

"Behold, I am against thee, and will cause many nations to come up against thee like the waves of the sea, and they shall destroy the walls of Tyrus and break down her towers. It shall be a place for the spreading of nets in the midst of the sea . . . thou shalt be built no more. The princes of the sea shall say, How wast thou destroyed that wast inhabited by seafaring men, the crowned city that was strong in the sea. Thou shalt be no more; though thou be sought for, yet shalt thou never be found again."

And so on. So travellers, gazing on the one-time mistress of the sea, mourn, "What city is like Tyre, the destroyed in the midst of the sea?" No doubt they said this of the ancient Palaeotyrus on the mainland, when the Tyrians abandoned it after its siege by Nebuchadnezzar and built the magnificent new Tyre on the island. No doubt Alexander said it when, after his seven months' siege, he entered the island city, destroyed half of it, massacred many hundreds of the citizens, and sold the rest into slavery. It rose again, was taken again, passed under Julius Caesar into Roman dominion, during which it was embellished and entempled and flourished greatly as commercial port and manufacturer of dye, and Tyrian sailors still trafficked boldly round the shores of the Middle Sea, and beyond into the dangerous darkness of the Outer Ocean, where barbarians traded tin for amber and spices and silk. In the fourth century they still talked of Tyre's commercial greatness; by that time the temples of Melkarth had given place officially to the gods of Rome, and these to the churches of Christians. Flourishing richly under the Arabs for some centuries, Tyre when taken by the crusaders in 1124 was at the height of its prosperity, a noble city walled and towered on its promontory that had once been an island, with two fine harbours to north and south, as William, later Archbishop of Tyre, describes it in his chronicle. A very beautiful city, commented Benjamin of Tudela in 1163, "the port of which is in the town itself, and is guarded by two towers, within which the vessels ride at anchor. There is no port in the world equal to this. . . . If you mount the walls you may see the remains of Tyre the crowning, (Isaiah xxiii, 8) which was inundated of the sea; it is about a stone's throw from the new town, and whoever sails may observe the towers, the markets, the streets and the halls at the bottom of the sea."

Apart from this charming illusion about old Tyre, new Tyre was wholly admirable. Its beauty, its fabulous historic splendour, its almost impregnable strength, brought tears to the eyes of even those ruthless toughs, the crusaders. They held it for a hundred and sixty years, building double and triple lines of strong walls to withstand all attacks and sieges from land and sea by the infidels. Saladin himself assailed it twice in vain. Never captured, it was abandoned by the crusaders after the fall of Acre, seized by the Saracens and partly destroyed, its stones carried away for building. It continued as city and port, diminished but never quite abandoned; sixteenth-century pictures, perhaps flattering it, show a fine walled and towered little city. Yet the impression on travellers since the medieval period has always been of ruin and desolation William Lithgow got there in 1612 and found it "miserably brought to ruine".

"I and certain Armenians went to visit this decayed towne, and found the most famous ruines here that the World from memory can afforde, and a delicious encircling harbour, inclosed within the middle of the towne, fitt to receive small barkes, frigates and galleons: the compassing fore-face being all of

10 Arches in Alexandria Troas. Engraving by W H. Bartlett, 1836-8

11 Port of Caesarea, Syria. Lithograph after C Thienon, 1819

12 Remains of the port of Tyre Engraving by W H Bartlett, 1836-8

13 Turkish burial-ground and castle of Louis IX, Sidon. Engraving by W. H Bartlett, 1836-8

squared marble and alabaster stones; the houses used to stand on pillars of the same stones, the infinite number thereof may as yet be (above and below the sands) perspectively beheld. There be only 19 fine houses here, which are Moores."[1]

The Moors showed him a pillar lying on the ground, which they said was one of the pillars which Samson had pulled down in the house of Dagon. Lithgow said it could not be, as Samson died at Azath, "yet, howsoever it was, I brought home a pound weight of it and presented the half thereof to King James of blessed memory".

Through the seventeenth century it seems that Tyre became still more of a decayed town; the Reverend Henry Maundrell of Exeter College found it

"A mere Babel of broken walls, pillars, vaults, etc., there not being so much as one entire house left. Its present inhabitants are only a few poor wretches, housing themselves in the vaults and subsisting chiefly upon fishing; who seem to be preserv'd in this place by Divine Providence as a visible argument how God has fulfilled his word concerning Tyre, viz, *That it should be as the top of a rock, a place for fishers to dry their nets on.*"[2]

This fulfilment of Scripture was, indeed, the chief pleasure that Mr Maundrell enjoyed in Tyre. Dr Pococke, also Bible-minded, was rather puzzled to find any of the city standing at all; he had supposed, after reading Ezekiel's wishful thinking, that it would have been totally demolished. Through the eighteenth century it picked up a little; the Moslem tribes who occupied it after 1760 built the present town on the northern harbour; by the early nineteenth century, when Lady Hester Stanhope saw it, it was "a flourishing town" among its ruins. Lady Hester's physician companion, that despised but amiable man, enjoyed seeing under the sea a dozen fallen pillars among which men dived for fragments of carving and coins.

Tyre was then, and is now, among the most haunting of ruins. "Situated," as the crusader chronicler put it, "in the heart of the sea, and surrounded on all sides by walls. A small part of it, where it is not washed by the waves, is fortified by several lines of wall. It was once famous for its kings, and gave

[1] William Lithgow, *Rare Adventures and Painefull Peregrinations* (1632).
[2] Henry Maundrell, *Journey from Aleppo to Jerusalem* (1697).

birth to the founders of Thebes and Carthage." Now it has only one gate, vine-grown, which stands on the sandy isthmus, the causeway that Alexander threw up to join island and mainland during his siege, taking the material from abandoned Palaeotyrus on the shore. In the causeway people dug till lately for the débris and ruins of old Tyre In it are sunk fragments of walls, towers and great granite columns; you could trace the line of the buried walls. Sand has silted up and broadened the causeway; it is now covered by a road, at the end of it Tyre lies, narrow-streeted and close-built, and round it are strewn fragments of walls, towers and houses, some under and some above the sea, the ruins of medieval Tyre, lying among and above those of the Roman city. Phoenician Tyre seems almost utterly sunk beneath the accumulated wrecks of ages. The modern town stands on the harbour towards Sidon; in it is the ruin of the crusaders' great cathedral, with red syenite granite columns lying by it that were possibly part of the fourth-century church built by Paulinus. In the square harbour, closed by two old jetties, fishermen drag nets among the shattered fragments of a mole. Looking northward across the tumbling sea, you see a swarm of tiny islands swimming round; some say they were once joined by causeways now sunk. The whole harbour had, a few years ago, a wrecked and shattered air, its jetties, the protecting medieval walls that guarded it, lying among broken pillars at the bottom of the sea. Looking eastward, one sees the sandy shore of Phoenicia stretching north, strewn with ruined towers. Somewhere on it Palaeotyrus stood; its site was for centuries lost, and even Dr Pococke failed to find it; but now it is being excavated. In Tyre Phoenician and Roman lie mingled; a theatre has been dug out, and a forum; beautiful pillars of white and greenish marble and reddish granite lie tumbled. A great field of ruin, it slopes among thistles and coarse grass down to the sea; one may pick up stone eggs fallen from capitals, and fragments of Roman pottery and glass.

Tyre has always been a magnet to travellers. Past greatness, present desolation, the legend and the ruin—the contrast is irresistible. The questionable background of ancient cursing lingers on the air: young M. Volney, visiting Syria in 1782 and indulging his interest in ruined empires, quoted pages of scriptural prophesy in describing the fallen city; as also did Dr

Robinson, the American Biblical scholar, in the 1830s. Overwhelmed by the romantic beauty of the peninsula, its ruins and its drowned greatness, he was bored with having to stay with the American consular agent and his family (Syrians) who never left him alone; till on Sunday he escaped his hosts and "wandered out alone towards the south end of the peninsula, beyond the city, where all is now forsaken and lonely like the desert, and there bathed in the limpid waters of the sea, as they rolled into a small and beautiful sandy cove among the rocks". Then he walked round the peninsula, musing on the pomp and the glory, the pride and the fall, of ancient Tyre. "The sole remaining tokens of her ancient splendour lie strewed beneath the waves in the midst of the sea. . . . *Thou shalt be built no more*!" He looked with interest at the medieval fragments in the port, standing on the bases of antique pillars, at the red granite columns strewn about, and at the mean hovels that clung like swallows' nests to the old walls. Walking over ground uneven with buried towers and débris, he was so fortunate as to return without mishap; he had been warned that not everyone did so.[1]

Ruinensehnsucht has always affected strongly those who saw or even thought of Tyre. Ezekiel, breathing vengeance against the city, was nevertheless full of romantic sentiment about the fate he had arranged for it: it intoxicated him, and made of him a superb poet. "*O thou that art situated at the entry of the sea, which art a merchant people for many isles. . . . What city is like Tyre, like the destroyed in the midst of the sea*?" After reciting this poem, thoughtful visitors to Tyre, such as Mr William Howitt, the Nottingham chemist, are apt to compose meditations of their own, often in verse, and often something like this:

I thought I saw the palace domes of Tyre,
The gorgeous treasures of her merchandise . . .
I looked again, I saw a lonely shore,
A rock amidst the waters, and a waste
Of dreary sand . . .
She stood upon her isles, and in her pride
Of strength and beauty, waste and wave defied. . . .
Ruin and silence in her courts are met,
And on her city-rock the fisher spreads his net.[2]

[1] Edward Robinson, *Biblical Researches in Palestine* (1838).
[2] William Howitt, *Visits to Remarkable Places* (1840).

Turning from such musings, we may bathe, as Dr Robinson did, in a sandy cove, or among the fishing boats and ruins of the port and the islets beyond it, in a pearly dawn, a burning noon, or the deep violet and silver of a moon-drenched and star-glimmering night, diving among the marble foundations of the shattered piers of the crusaders' mole, among the sunk columns of Rome, among the fish and shells of drowned Phoenicia.

There is less point in the ruin-seeker's visiting Tyre's parent and famous rival in antiquity, Sidon, for the ancient remains of this, one of the several candidates for the position of oldest continuously extant city in the world, have been buried almost completely by prosperity, that foe so much deadlier to antiquity than destruction, plunder or abandonment. Sidon, Saida, destroyed so often, is, as she was in her Phoenician days, a thriving, trading port and town; a pleasant sea town, whose vaulted streets run above her ancient past. In 1840 her picturesque fortress towers were destroyed by European allies, for some anti-Mussalman reason. Her ruined thirteenth-century Château de Mer juts into the sea where once a Phoenician temple stood; the other crusaders' castle, standing dominatingly in the south of the town, was destroyed and rebuilt by Arabs; these ruins, as J. S. Buckingham observed in 1816, "tend to give the harbour a picturesque appearance". But even in 1697 Maundrell remarked that all the antiquities of Sidon were "perfectly obscured and buried by Turkish buildings"; he might have added that most of them lay at the bottom of the sea, choking the port, so that the main pleasure to be found in Sidon ruins is diving among them.

3

The ruin-seeking traveller pushes on to Antioch. He is exalted, almost intoxicated, by the magnificent mountain path through the oleandrous glen of Daphne, whose gushing streams and aromatic odours and smiling ghosts from the richly licentious past, when this Cintra-like suburb was "a perpetual festival of vice", set the right mood for the ghosts of the glory and luxury of ancient Antioch. We approach Antioch from Daphne along the broad valley of the Orontes, and there on the right Mount Silpius, that held the citadel, climbs craggily to the sky, and the stupendous Byzantine wall zig-zags up it. On the left the modern Arab town lies, with its close huddle of red-tiled roofs; high above them stands the desolate splendour that was Golden Antioch, the Seleucid and later the Roman Antioch, of rich temples, noble palaces, opulent living, the pleasures of the idle, dissolute and cultivated rich. Later, of course, it had also the sterner, purer pleasures of the early Christian church; but (say the books, which have copied one another down the ages for some eighteen hundred years or more)

"even the high-toned morality and powerful influence of Christianity were unable to eradicate the vices and follies for which Antioch had long been celebrated. Its beautiful climate and delicious environs attracted to it the votaries of pleasure from Greece and Rome. Some elevating thoughts are here and there associated with its schools; some noble names are found in its history; but its population was for the most part a worthless rabble. The amusements of the theatre were the occupation of their life. Their passion for races wasted their time and dissipated their energies. The Oriental element of superstition and imposture were not less active. Licentiousness seemed to triumph over all. At Daphne, under the glorious sun of Syria and the patronage of imperial Rome, all that was beautiful in nature and art had created a sanctuary for a perpetual festival of vice."

It all sounds fascinating. "Suburban" in Antioch must have had a very different connotation from that which it has somehow acquired to-day. Alike in suburb and city, life must have fleeted happily away, in that salubrious mountain air; and something of the atmosphere lingers even now that the temples, the palaces, the forum, the theatres, the racecourses, and the great baths are all gone. Gibbon tells of the sad seduction of crusaders by this atmosphere when they had captured Antioch from the Turks in 1098.

"The grove of Daphne no longer flourished; but the Syrian air was still impregnated with the same vices; the Christians were seduced by every temptation that nature either prompts or reprobates . . . and sermons and edicts were alike fruitless against those scandalous disorders, not less pernicious to military discipline than repugnant to evangelic purity."[1]

"See," adds Gibbon in a footnote, "the tragic and scandalous fate of an archdeacon of royal birth who was slain by the Turks as he reposed in an orchard playing at dice with a Syrian concubine." How many archdeacons and deacons had in earlier days, during the meetings of the great church councils in Antioch wearying of homoousion and homoiousion, slipped out of the conference rooms to meet Syrian beauties in orchards with their dice, we shall never know. But even to this day, the visitor to Antioch and Daphne is conscious of raised spirits and a heightened sense of readiness for life's enjoyments, and this is one of the high pleasures to be derived from the ruins of Antioch. The great wall, which it is the tourist's duty and pleasure to walk round, will have, with its seven-mile circuit over crag, mountain and ravine, a bracing, tonic effect, counteracting the enervating mood of voluptuous luxury; it takes five hours of hard going. Broken and despoiled, shaken by repeated and tremendous earthquakes, plundered of its stones by Turks, Egyptians and Antiochians, nevertheless this wall of Theodosius and Justinian, raised by the crusaders to a height of fifty or sixty feet, set all its way along with strong square towers, remains one of the world's most sensational walls. It has amazed all travellers. "A most extraordinary building," Dr Pococke commented in 1738. Much of it, he said, was fallen down, and lay in large pieces on the ground, witnessing to the great shock that had overturned them: but on the western side it stood intact, "not the least breach in it, and from this one may judge how beautiful all the walls must have been". There was a walk on the top; they used, it was said, to drive chariots with four horses abreast along its summit; that is as may be; it is impossible now to drive even one horse or one baby Austin far along it, because of the rents and chasms. It strides and zigzags over mountain and gorge, and across one tremendous deep ravine; its castle-like towers are many of them destroyed or half-destroyed; the walking on it is definitely bad; it gapes like the teeth of some formidable giant; it is a wild and dizzying sight. Eighteenth and nineteenth-century travellers have found in this half-ruined grandeur a magnificence nobler than its original form.

[1] Edward Gibbon, *Decline and Fall of the Roman Empire* (1776).

What must these walls have been, they ejaculate: but they prefer them as they are, tremendous wrecks of Golden Antioch and its splendour whose ghost marches across the ages, Seleucid, Roman, Byzantine, pagan, Christian, immortal.

The wall and the great pile of the aqueduct, and the ruined bridge near it, are all the ruins of Antioch considerable enough now to impress, though the whole site of the vanished city is strewn with occasional fragments of pillar and pediment, lying sunk in orchards, vineyards and olive-groves, and excavations have lately uncovered a great crop of mosaic pavements. Few cities have been more often and more catastrophically ruined than Antioch, during the last two and twenty centuries. Frequent and horrible earthquakes, still more frequent and only little less horrible Seleucid kings in a passion (usually well-justified), Persian generals in victorious orgies of destruction, Saracens and Ottoman Turks in anti-Christian hate, crusaders in anti-Saracen rage, Bibars the Egyptian and the Mamelouks, who sacked and smashed the city almost to pieces in 1268—all these ruin-makers have done their part; and finally the Turks, after their custom, let it moulder to decay, while their new town Antakia rose, full of mosques, from Antioch's quarried ruins. Two centuries ago there was rather more to see: Dr Pococke, though he found few remains of ancient buildings, saw a ruined castle on the eastern hill, with vaults under it for water cisterns, the remains of a bagnio, and a round basin fifty-three paces wide; "they have a tradition that the Roman emperors used to divert themselves here in boats". There were the remains, too, of what was said to be the palace of the emperors. Some of what Pococke thought Roman, later archaeologists have attributed to the thirteenth century; he had that additional pleasure. He had, too, a few ruined Christian churches (all that remained of that great Christian city that had, in Justinian's day, been called Theopolis) and the alleged house of St John Chrysostom. But the great wall and the great aqueduct were, then as now, the ruins that people came to Antioch to see. Antioch itself is a ghost, not to be seen but felt.

"Is this Antioch, the queen of the East, the glory of the monarch, the joy of the evangelist? brought down even to the dust. . . . On every side is the silence of ruin and the dimness of despair: yet how beautiful and exulting is the face of nature. . . . The soil is rank with the violet, the anemone, the rose, the myrtle. . . . No sound comes up the hill from the lost city, of the merchants and their companies and their going to and fro. . . . On the side of this hill, on one of these fragments, it is impressive to rest a while, ere the traveller enters the city, which is stretched silent and in darkness at his feet: domes, minarets, masses of ruin, low ill-built homes. . . . Were the homes of the Christians of old still there, how beautiful it would be to seek their roof—to talk of the time when Antioch was called the City of God; still later, when it contained 360 convents, and its numerous churches were the finest in the world! Church, convent, home of the faithful, are all gone. . . ."[1]

This was the pious note of the early nineteenth century. In our own age, so wistfully on vanished pleasures bent, Antioch visitors are apt to look nostalgically back on her voluptuous past. They explore in vain the woody groves of Daphne: "*Daphne demeure la promenade de prédilection des habitants d'Antioche*", but the temples of Apollo, of Daphne, of Hecate, that made this suburb so richly, ritualistically devout, are ghosts among those fragrant cypress groves. Where to-day, the traveller muses, in our impoverished and scrannelled world, are there such voluptuous pleasure cities, where the Antioch way of life may be led? Wandering about the site of fallen Antioch, the votary of pleasure enviously asks this question, and gets but a dusty answer. Once, how many such cities, according to report, there were. Sybaris, Antioch, Alexandria, Corinth, Constantinople, Persepolis, Cadiz, Bagdad, the great cities of Persia and India, the palace colonies washed by the sea round the gulf of Parthenope, the bay of Baiae, and all along that coast where Roman gentlemen made holiday; and Pompeii, they said, but this town of little houses under the mountains does not look as if one could have done much there, outside the narrow provincial round of the games, the plays, the gossip in the forum, the tavern, the brothel, the dice; even the finest villas do not suggest great luxury or the perpetual festival of vice.

Turning his back on seductive Antioch, one of the disciples of St Simon Stylites set up his pillar residence some miles to the east

[1] John Carne, *Syria, the Holy Land, Asia Minor, etc.* (1840).

of the city, and there sat for eight years in austere disapproval of the Antioch way of life: could he now see its desolate site, his ruin-pleasure would be great.

Dr Pococke, indefatigable ruin-explorer, rambled happily among the ancient sites, cities and churches that lie strewn about the country round Antioch: Laodicea, with its port, its cisterns, its churches, its grottos by the sea; Gabala, Balanea, the castle of Merkab, Tortosa, the island of Ruad, Seleucia, a hundred anonymous ruined buildings many of which he diligently identified. The sight of these romantic and famous Syrian ruins did not intoxicate him; he approached each with his scholarly calm, identifying, measuring, comparing what he saw with the descriptions of Strabo, Polybius and other historians; he found everything of interest, and for a single ruin would go miles. Under his composed manner and measurements, one detects the excitement of the ardent connoisseur, the romantic pleasure of *Ruinensehnsucht*. Faced with Seleucia, Antioch's ancient predecessor, no traveller can easily keep his composure. A place of a most extraordinary situation, says Pococke; and describes every detail with studious and loving care; the strong fortified acropolis city, the towers, the gates, the walls, the great stones joined together by cramps, the extraordinary tunnel pierced through the mountain-side in the time of Vespasian, diverting the torrent that ran through the town into a new channel to the sea. The citadel and the lower city at its foot are both overgrown with fragrant trees and shrubs; so too is the precipitous cliff-face above, hollowed and honeycombed with sepulchres and caves. Within the city walls few remains are to be seen; Pococke saw only a few fragments of pillars, a few levelled sites where buildings once stood. "This is all that is to be seen of those magnificent temples and buildings of which Polybius makes mention" He went down to the mouth of the Orontes to see the ancient port, long since shattered and abandoned; a broad, rocky, sandy beach lies strewn with fragments; from it two ruined jetties jut into the sea. A tower stands above them, and the barren precipitous peak of Mount Casius rises to the south "Pliny, with the exaggeration to which the ancients were so prone, makes it four miles in height". It is actually about seven thousand feet. Ruined ports make a peculiar impact on the imagination; the present loneliness, the vanished ships, the broken quays that once echoed with the chaffer of merchants, the cries of sailors; the eternal rustle and beat of the sea. Under the Seleucids, the Ptolemies and the Romans this port of Seleucia and Antioch was a world mart. It was still thriving in the fifteenth century; it decayed under Moslem rule, and by the seventeenth century was in ruins. Travellers to Antioch have always visited it, calling it the Ostia of Antioch, exploring the underground channel, recalling St Paul, who embarked from this beach on his first missionary journey. "On this solitary beach," they muse, "covered here and there with ruinous heaps, is the very spot where St Paul embarked . . ." and the moving contrast is drawn between

"Seleucia covering the declivities with its temples and columns and palaces; and now the solitary shepherd, reclining on one of the fragments, watching his scanty flock that seek a miserable herbage on the sea-beat shore: the dilapidated tower, on its rocky pile, can scarcely afford shelter from the rain and wind: the sea breaking on the poor memorials of pagan greatness advances with a louder murmur on the broad beach. . . ."[1]

What with the old port and the high-bastioned citadel behind it, the honeycombed cliff with its sepulchres (pleasant retreats, paved, dry, aromatically-shrubbed, delightfully placed and commanding beautiful views, so that they have served as grottos for hermits and to-day, it is said, as homes for artists who live in them and paint)—what with all this, and with its background of impressive and romantic history, Seleucia has always been among the most pleasurable of ruins.

4

Of the chain of royally-founded ruined sea cities that lie like beached and shattered galleons down the Syrian coast, one of the most romantic is Ascalon. Ancient Philistine stronghold, taken and re-taken down the ages by Egyptians, Jews, Assyrians, Macedonians, Romans, Moslems, Christians, Moslems again, and now Jews, nothing of it is now left but ruins lying among orchards and pine woods and mimosa on a sandy cliff. Cursed continually by Jewish prophets, who desired all that coast for

[1] John Carne, *Syria, the Holy Land, Asia Minor, etc.* (1840).

the Israelites—("For Gaza shall be forsaken, and Ashkelon a desolation. . . . And the sea coast shall be dwellings and cottages for shepherds, and folds for flocks, and the coast shall be for the remnant of the house of Judah; in the houses of Ashkelon shall they lie down in the evening")—spoiled by Samson, conquered by Egypt, Sennacherib, Alexander, adorned beautifully by Herod, whose native city it was, home of the mermaid goddess and of Byzantine rhetoric, seat of bishops, stormed over and dismantled by Saladin and by the Crusaders, it fell finally at the barbarous hands of the sultan Bibars in 1270, and Moslem darkness descended on it, till it attained the desolation long wished for it by vengeful prophets. It was once one of the most solid of strongholds. "Situated on the sea", wrote the crusading archbishop William of Tyre, "it has the shape of a semi-circle. It is surrounded by ramparts and flanked with towers, and exceedingly solid. It has four gates—the gate of Jerusalem, the gate on the sea, the gate of Gaza, the gate of Joppa." The crusaders built there a castle of great strength, of which little stands. D'Arvieux, in 1659, found the place a ruin; its fallen walls and towers were of a thickness that showed it to have been one of the strongest fortresses in Palestine. It curved in a half-moon shape round the cliff's edge; its site is covered with lemon groves, vineyards, pinewoods, mimosa. Among them lay broken pillars of granite and marble, all the magnificent débris of great shattered cities: they have now been collected into enclosed spaces. "Innumerable red granite pillars and long streets" were seen in the early nineteenth century. Streets can now be scarcely traced; excavations have revealed fragments of baths, peristyles and temples of a Byzantine and a medieval church. Ascalon was spoiled of much material to build the ramparts and mosques of Acre; Turkish torpor and neglect let what was not stolen lie as it fell. Occasionally there were spasmodic and unmethodical hunts for buried treasure, for tradition had it that Ascalon, that once rich trading city, had somewhere in its bowels hoards of wealth: but not even the hope of treasure (and they hope for it from all ruins—it is their third great ruin-pleasure; the others are building houses in the ruins, and quarrying in them for materials to embellish newer cities) can make Turks seek diligently or long. But they firmly believed that no visiting Franks came to Syria for any other purpose, for what else could they desire, and for what other reason should they nose about ancient ruins, measuring, making plans, copying inscriptions?

When Lady Hester Stanhope came to Ascalon, in April 1815, the Turks were for once right: she was looking for treasure. Armed with an Italian version of what was alleged to be an ancient document from a Syrian monastery, and a permit from the pasha, she and her physician arrived from Baalbek, with a great escort of cavalry, laden camels, donkeys, water-carriers, wheelbarrows, dragomans, interpreters, cooks, musicians, dancers, workmen and women, and a colourful assembly of tents, blue and green and elegantly patterned, twenty of which were presented by Soliman Pasha. Lady Hester herself drove behind a pair of white mules in a crimson velvet palanquin. The hunt was organized with every circumstance of elaboration and drama. The tents, some as large as marquees, were pitched round the mosque; one was set aside for a meal tent, and an excellent kitchen was established there. Lady Hester took up her quarters, with her women, in two cottages in a small village north of the ruins, and sat by day in a tent halfway between the cottages and Ascalon, receiving visits from important local personages. At two o'clock every afternoon she rode over on an ass to watch the workmen, who greeted her with a shout and renewed their digging. About a hundred workmen a day were employed with picks and mattocks, delighted with the excellent meals and wages, and with the treasure that they hoped to come on every moment. They worked with the greatest animation, while pipe and tabor played, and they sang and danced in time. The scene, wrote Dr Meryon, had a showy gaiety almost as lively as that of a racecourse; no doubt bets were placed on where the first gold would be struck. Crowds of astrologers and magicians gathered round with helpful divinations and crystal globes.

But no gold appeared. Pillars, marble pavements, fragments of statues, were dug up; one day appeared the foundations of a great building, on another a magnificent Roman, probably Herodean, statue of a warrior, of beautiful shape and colossal stature, scarcely broken. After that they found cisterns, which they hoped contained the treasure, but they were empty. The site had been already dug, and cleared of everything of value, probably by

Gezzar Pasha when he embellished Acre. The doctor tried to persuade his employer that the noble statue she had found was a finer and more notable treasure than any gold. Lady Hester knew better; the statue would not recoup the ruinous expenses of her expedition: in anger she ordered it to be broken up and thrown into the sea. It was carried away, but not, apparently, thrown into the sea; its fragments were seen years later on the pavement of a temple.

Nothing more was found; the search was called off. Everyone had enjoyed it while it lasted. The blue and green tents were taken up, the workers dismissed, the expedition, with its ostentatious escort, retreated to Mar-Elias, where Lady Hester stayed to rest and muse sadly over the state of her finances, the unhelpfulness of her country's government, and the illusory nature of buried treasure.

Since then, Ascalon has been excavated by the Palestine Restoration Fund; Herod's cloisters, mentioned by Josephus, have been uncovered, some statues, the remains of a Byzantine theatre, some Philistine pottery; no treasure. The site of the primitive city has been located: its precise age is obscure; the earliest signs of habitation are about 1800 B.C. They have put up a museum, for the pottery and the statues; unfortunately no one knows where the fragments of Lady Hester's warrior have got to.

The orchards among the ruins are a perpetual pleasure; for those who like either melons or shallot onions they offer good eating; from any point of view they are picturesque, lying in Syrian sunshine in the shattered Phoenician city above the sea. The word of the prophet has at last come to pass; the coast is now for the remnant of the house of Judah; and in the houses of Ascalon they lie down in the evening. But the houses are the huts of a small *kibbutz*, where the children of Israel dwell together and toil. On a Sabbath afternoon autobuses and cars converge on Ascalon, and more children of Israel emerge from them with cries of joy, to gaze on the enclosed fragments of the lost city of the Philistines and bathe in the breakers on the beach below.

If Lady Hester and her retinue visited Caesarea Palestina, further up the coast, they found, as Commanders Irby and Mangles found in 1817, the ruins of a Saracenic wall and a bay strewn with great pillars of granite which had supported a Roman temple. The promontory which ran into the sea and had closed Herod's huge harbour (as large as the Piraeus, Josephus said it had been) was also set with great columns; the naval gentlemen thought they had enclosed a landing-place for merchandize. Remains of aqueduct arches marched along the shore. There had been no inhabitants there since the Middle Ages; its ruins had been spoiled down the centuries by the dwellers on the coast. Josephus describes its sumptuous building by Herod. Strabo, describes this bay as nothing but a landing-place, with a castle called Strato's tower; Tacitus and Pliny, eighty years later, told of a great city, the head of Judaea. Herod, restoring and beautifying all Samaria at incalculable expense and in a style of unsurpassed magnificence, observed among the maritime towns the dilapidated little village, Turris Stratonis, saw its potentialities as a harbour, and rebuilt it grandiosely in white stone, with palaces, theatres, temples, aqueducts, sewers, every possible amenity for body and mind. Above all he built the great harbour, sinking in it huge stones to make a curved breakwater. A stone mole encircled the harbour, on which tall towers stood; the tallest, which replaced Strato's Tower, was called after Drusus, Caesar's stepson. Vaulted halls also rose on the mole, to receive merchandize from the ships and the merchants who landed. At the harbour's mouth stood three enormous statues. Behind it was the city of white stone, with straight streets running through it. At its gate rose Caesar's temple, adorned with two colossal figures of Caesar and of Rome; amphitheatre, theatre and market place were worthy of the city's style; Herod named it Caesarea.

Assaulted and destroyed and plundered and rebuilt by successive races down the ages, the ruins of Caesarea are an epitome of history. Taken by Moslems in the seventh century, it was still described as a beautiful city in the eleventh. A fine town, said a Persian writer in 1047, with running water, and fountains gushing through it. But by the end of the thirteenth century it was a ruin; the Crusaders, Saladin, a sultan of Egypt, had besieged it, taken it, lost it in turns; at last, after a thousand years, the irrigation system had decayed. The fruit trees were destroyed by King Baldwin. In 1265 an Arab geographer described it as "of old a fine city, the very mother of cities, but now more like a village"; it was finally destroyed by Egyptian mamelukes. It became malarial; sand drifted and silted over it, covering all the city but a small stretch, which includes the crusader citadel; the fertile fields and gardens are covered with dunes; the sand lies on the city two and a half metres deep; surf eats into and erodes the stones. Beneath the sand lies history piled in rich layers; visible until the end of last century, to-day they have to be sought for. Caesarea was colonized by Bosnians in the 1880s, and these ingenuous barbarians built their houses out of the materials they found, as better than Bosnians had done for centuries. Mosques grew out of Christian churches which stood on the foundations of Roman temples, palaces or castles, themselves built on Macedonian substructures. A century ago travellers saw the views engraved by Tipping, the great breakwater curving round with its tottering ruins of towers, the toppling masses of brick, from which buried columns had been dug out, groups of Bedouins camping among ruins, and washing their steeds in the waves that broke against the formless chaos of arches, gateways, fallen walls, overgrown with a tangle of shrubs. Forbin, in 1817, wrote of the ruins as entirely deserted and marvellously strong.

On y trouve des rues, des places, et en rétablissant les portes de ces hautes et terribles murailles, il serait facile d'habiter et défendre encore Césarée,[1]

which must have been in a state far less devastated than a few years later. Caesarea looked, said Forbin, as if some great disaster had slain or put to flight the inhabitants only a short time ago. The walls of the church were discoloured with the smoke of incense. The tombs were open, and only bones showed the past sojourn of men in the *solitude effrayante.* The silence was only disturbed by the noise of the waves breaking on the jetty and the quay; their force had shaken down great masses of granite; the door of the lighthouse was ajar; the stairs and rooms of the castle were exposed, and birds of prey made it their dwelling. The town still had superb columns, many of them entire; several had been used in the Middle Ages for the construction of the mole (apparently rebuilt); the richest materials had been used for its base; one saw among the ruins blocks of rose granite eight feet long, with Latin inscriptions too defaced to decipher.

[1]Comte de Forbin, *Voyage dans la Levant* (1817).

What Forbin saw was a medieval town, rebuilt and fortified by the Crusaders and the Saracens out of the material of the Roman city, and resting largely on Roman foundations, so that rich porphyry and rose granite were to be found beneath the sea, at the base of the medieval mole, as Mr Tipping found them in 1842.

"The finest remains of Herodian magnificence are in all probability under water, the sea having manifestly gained upon the land to a considerable extent. On examining the crusading remains, which are not to be compared with the noble ruins of Athlite, I found nothing worthy of remark, except that I detected in some places vestiges of ancient rubble serving as a basement to the more modern walls and towers. . . . I examined as far as the surf would allow me to do so . . . the foundations of this mole; and to my great satisfaction I found at, or rather below, the sea level, a very different class of masonry."[1]

No lover of medieval architecture, Mr Tipping was saddened by the "squalid and *morne* desolation" of Caesarea. "Almost engulphed by the sea, and half entombed by the sand, nothing but the unstoried remains of barbarous times now rescue the site of the splendid Caesarea from utter obliteration".

Other travellers found pleasure in the records of history preserved in these successive strata of buildings. As the Reverend R. D. Traill commented, in his edition of Josephus,

"Remains such as those which mark the site of the ancient Caesarea—once the glory of Palestine, now the haunt of jackals and wild boars—and from which obtrude the costly materials of a succession of structures, furnish a sort of condensed commentary upon that series of historical evidence which we derive from books. . . These tottering masses, so heterogeneous in their materials, might be described as the archives of four empires, which, on this soil, have in their turn blazed into brief splendour and sunk into darkness."[2]

He would have liked to make a chronological investigation, assigning to each fragment its period; but such a task was not then feasible. It would have taken years; and the neighbourhood, overgrown with grass and thistles and peopled with hideous reptiles

[1]Tipping.
[2]R. D. Traill, *The Works of Josephus* (1847).

and wild animals and remorseless Bedouins, seemed to Mr Traill not favourable to research. To track down the vanished splendours of ancient Caesarea one would have to explore the buildings of a whole region, for it had served as a quarry, furnishing costly shafts and ready-made blocks and capitals for not only the builders of the Middle Ages but for recent Pashas, who had used the vast remains within their reach to rear palaces, fountains and mosques, blasting the medieval buildings to extract from them the antique marbles and columns embedded there.

Exploration is now being carried out. Air photographs have shown theatres and the line of the semi-circular city wall. Columns are seen to protrude from the sand; they are perhaps part of that temple of Caesar whose beauty and proportions were praised by Josephus, and which was visible from afar. A Roman villa has been found, with a marble floor, an amphitheatre and two great statues. "Herod built a theatre with rock-cut stones in the town," said Josephus, "and behind it an amphitheatre which could accommodate a large crowd and had a wide view over the sea; from it a road is seen running down to the shore." Excavation will reveal more buildings. Meanwhile, tours to Caesarea are made from Telaviv. "Come and see," says the tourism office to American and British visitors, "a Roman pleasure city 2000 years old, with theatres, circus, hippodrome. . . ." I do not know what hopes are raised by this exhortation: what we do see is this great stone desolation of a harbour, some Roman and medieval walls thrust through with ancient columns, the waste of ruins that was a sumptuous city spreading above it. Certainly a pleasure city still.

So is Dor, the ancient Mantura, a little northward up the coast. But Dor was in ruins when St Jerome deplored it as a mighty city destroyed; now even the ruins are gone; nothing is left to the eye but a remote reef-bound bay, beyond which the sea sweeps and breaks. Mantura, the great city, rears its towers only in the mud.

Caesarea and Dor are examples of the process which has been going on in Syria and Palestine and all over the world for some two thousand years; everywhere about deserts, valleys, mountains and shores lie the ruins of ruin, plundered to build what turned to ruin again. Everywhere the age-old destruction, the

6

age-old, almost organic growth of the rich, improbable medleys that make travel so rewarding to some, so exasperating to others. Caesarea Philippi, near Damascus, is another example; a cave dedicated to Pan, a temple to Augustus, the new Roman city to Tiberius, castles and churches to Christ, mosques to Allah; a grand Roman city once, now a poor Moslem village with one of the finest crusader castles in Palestine, and the Roman city beneath the soil.

5

A more showy and exciting pleasure, indeed one of the most showy and exciting ruin-pleasures in the world, has, for several centuries, been Palmyra, that ancient Arab settlement in the Syrian desert. City of legend more dubious and remote than some, it has lost a few centuries of age and prestige since it began to be suspected not, after all, to be that Tadmor which King Solomon built in the wilderness, but to have grown from an Arab caravan halt on an oasis to become later a trading settlement on the merchant route across the desert from sea to sea. After the decline of Petra in 105 A.D. it largely took Petra's place; the merchant caravans went that way, carrying their silks and spices, ivory, ebony and gems, to the rich Arab desert city, which was to grow under the empire into such political importance, such dazzling grace.

What we see to-day, the fabulous golden-ochre colonnades, the Temple of the Sun with its pillared court, the great field of ruins like a garden of broken daffodils lying within the long low shattered line of Justinian's wall, is Syrian Graeco-Roman of the more florid period, and has excited, perhaps, a more startled ecstasy in beholders than almost any other of the world's wrecked cities.

Even the Arabs of early centuries made poems about it when it passed into their possession; and to the medieval Jews who made their homes there it seemed of palatial magnificence. True, a very few visitors, like Captains Irby and Mangles in 1844, saw little in it, finding the ruins on the small side for so long and arduous a journey, and

"not a single column, pediment, architrave or frieze worthy of admiration, and we judged Palmyra to be hardly worthy of the time, expense, anxiety and the fatiguing journey. . . . We suspect that it was the difficulty of getting to Tadmor, and the fact that few travellers have been there, that has given rise to the great renown of the ruins."[1]

The naval gentlemen were, no doubt, hot, exhausted and cross. The ejaculations of most visitors have been very different, even when, like the first English travellers to go there since its decline in prosperity, they suffered on their journey not only inconvenience and fatigue, but considerable danger. These visitors were English merchants of the Aleppo factory, who set out from that city in hot July weather in 1678, a company of sixteen, with servants and muleteers. Approaching Palmyra, they were met by an alarming Arab galloping at them on a camel with levelled lance, convinced that they were disguised Turks come to seize the Emir. He could scarcely be expected to credit the story that "we travelled thus in the desert only out of curiosity". He galloped back to tell the Palmyrenes about them; the merchants, prepared for the worst, rode on with guns at the ready. Still, they kept cool enough to observe the aqueduct running underground, and, on gaining the hill above Palmyra, to admire "these vast and noble ruins, having a plaine like a sea for greatness to the southwards of it". Arrived at the Arab town, they pitched their tents under its walls, "in the ruin of a great palace, the wall standing very high, the town within but small, and the houses, except two or three, no better than hogstyes". There they waited for a friendly message from the Emir. Since none came, some of the party went to visit him, with a present of coloured cloth. He fed them with coffee, camel and dates, and asked why they had come, since never had Franks done so before. They told him their unconvincing story about being curious to see the ruins; unable to believe this, he informed them that they were looking for treasure, and, now that they knew the way, might tell the Turks, who would come and destroy Palmyra. He then demanded a large ransom, frightened them a good deal, and finally got fifteen hundred dollars out of the party, in money and goods. Next day the merchants retreated for Aleppo in haste, the ruins scarcely seen.

Such were the pleasures of visiting Palmyra in 1678. 1691 was better. This time (the avaricious Emir having been opportunely

[1]Captain Irby and Captain Mangles, *Letters* (1823).

massacred) the merchants, having made the arduous journey across the desert again, enjoyed four days of sightseeing, staying in the Sheik's house.

"Having tir'd ourselves with Roming from Ruin to Ruin, and Romaging among Old Stones, and more especially not thinking it safe to linger too long . . . on October 8 we left Tadmor, being well satisfied with what we had seen, and glad to have escaped so dreaded a Place, but else with some regret, for having left a great many things behind which deserv'd a more Particular and Curious Inspection."[1]

Among the party was Dr William Halifax, a close and careful observer, who copied the inscriptions, counted and measured columns, and rhapsodized over the lost city—

"—such Magnificent Ruins that if it be lawful to frame a conjecture of the Original Beauty of that place by what is still remaining, I question somewhat whether any City in the world could have challenged precedence of this in its glory."[1]

Particularly he admired the great Temple of the Sun (turned into a mosque) standing in massive magnificence in its many-pillared court. He deplored the Arab hovels that nested in the court—

"The present inhabitants, as they are Poor, Miserable, Dirty People, so they have shut themselves up, to the number of thirty or forty families, in little Hutts made of Dirt, within the walls of a Spacious Court which enclosed a most magnificent Heathen Temple. . . . Certainly the world itself cannot afford the like Mixture of Remains of the greatest State and Magnificence, together with the extremity of Filth and Poverty."[1]

The pleasure of building houses in the ruins of antiquity has usually annoyed those who do not live in them, but who observe the strange and impertinent incongruity of the results. Still more Dr Halifax was outraged by the pleasures of destruction which had been enjoyed by the Turks, those "enemies to everything that is splendid and noble", who "out of vain superstition purposely beat down those beautiful cornices", and but for whom "we had seen the most curious and exquisite carvings in stone

[1]William Halifax, *Philosophical Transactions* (1693).

which perhaps the world could boast of, as here and there a small remainder which has escaped their fury, does abundantly evidence".

It was the Aleppo merchants' account in the Philosophical Transactions of the Royal Society that put Palmyra on the map as a goal for British travellers; ever since, it has been the marvel and admiration of all who could get so far, gleaming like a desert mirage before dazzled western eyes.

> Palmyra's far-extended waste I spy,
> (Once Tadmor, ancient in renown)
> Her marble heaps, by the wild Arab shown,
> Still load with useless pomp the ground,[1]

wrote a wistful English poet (who had only spied Palmyra with the eye of his mind) at the beginning of the eighteenth century. Fabulous city, its prestige heightened by its difficulty of access, by lying in the middle of a vast intractable desert, a very long way from anywhere else. To reach it was a job, entailing a great fuss of camels, dromedaries, tents and escorts—all the expensive paraphernalia of desert expeditions. Those who made it usually had some high intention, such as counting and measuring columns, making drawings and plans, copying inscriptions, stealing a few carvings and sculptures, or meditating on the ruins of greatness and composing a book. Yet they all found many pleasures on the way, even apart from the breathless delight of beholding what they held to be the first and most extensive ruins in the world. "The ruins were there. . . . What joy and what pleasure there is in the discovery of dead cities! Those places which were the theatre of events which distance has rendered extraordinary belong to the traveller. He is able at his pleasure and for some hours to recover the colonnades which the sand smothers, to finish Justinian's wall, to people the fallen temples and the mortally wounded tetraphylles with the shades of those he particularly admires . . ." This, which might be called the approach evocative, has been very usual at Palmyra. Particularly is Zenobia evoked: Volney had a long conversation with her spirit as he meditated there in 1792, composing his work on the Ruins of Empire. The more scholarly and less fanciful Dr Wood and Dr Dawkins, in

[1]John Hughes (1735).

1738, thought less about Zenobia and ruined empires than about the ruins themselves. Like all travellers, they were staggered by the first view, when the pass between the mountain ridges opens suddenly, dipping down between tall tomb towers, under the hill crowned with its massive brown Saracen castle, and discloses the pale golden-white vista of a colonnaded city, with its valley of ruined tombs stretching beyond it.

"The hills opening discovered to us, all at once, the greatest quantity of ruins we had ever seen, all of white marble, and beyond them to the Euphrates a flat waste, as far as the eye could reach. . . . It is scarce possible to imagine anything more striking than this view. So great a number of Corinthian columns, mixed with so little wall or solid building, afforded a most romantic variety of prospect."[1]

They spent a fortnight there, and produced the magnificent set of plans and drawings, described with diligent detail, that has been the standard work on Palmyra ever since. Though this fully engrossed their time, they had leisure to notice occasional pleasures, such as the appearance of the Palmyrenes, which seems to have been more startling then than now.

"The inhabitants, both men and women, were well-shaped, and the latter, though very swarthy, had good features. . . . They paint the ends of their fingers red, their lips blue, and their eye-brows and eye-lashes black, and wear very large gold or brass rings in their ears and noses. They had the appearance of good health."[2]

The only drawback to their visit was some feeling of apprehension about possible Bedouin attack. For they were loaded with treasures acquired on their travels. All over Greece and Syria they had appropriated what they could—"we carried off the marbles whenever it was possible, for the avarice or superstition of the inhabitants made that task difficult and somewhat impracticable." They took many manuscripts from the Maronite churches, and returned by no means empty-handed from the vast Tom Tiddler's ground which, for all enterprising Europeans, ringed their own territories about.

[1]Robert Wood, *Ruins of Palmyra* (1753).
[2]*Ibid.*

The first sight of Palmyra seen through the dust-haze of the desert, the pillared city, elegant beneath the dark Saracen fortress on the hill above it, has made poets and artists of nearly all tourists. Already keyed up by the long journey across the shimmering waste of lilac and fawn, indigo, silver and green, all the pure cold shadowy tones of the desert, and by fears of attacking Bedouins, travellers arrived at the ledge of mountain

"in whose curve lies the plain on which Palmyra is built. . . . What words can describe it as we saw it then? . . . In a square mile or so of fawn-coloured earth, lay the city in all its beauty and in all its sadness. Over the whole expanse, broken masonry of white or orange limestone was scattered in endless confusion —a tumultuous sea of stony fragments. . . . Across the centre ran one straight line, the line of the ancient colonnade."[1]

Dr Kelman, who thus describes it, adds that what distinguishes Palmyra from so many other ruined cities is that its ruins have never been built over; as it fell, from the violence of man and of earth, so it has lain, unencumbered with later débris or with any modern buildings. "The pillars lie complete, as an earthquake overturned them, and the whole neighbourhood is one pathless maze of exquisitely-carved cornices and pediments". Destroyed inadequately by Aurelian and Diocletian, more successfully by many earthquakes, the ancient city still stands and lies there in its beauty, and there really is nothing quite like it. The emotional author of Murray's Handbook was deeply affected by the magnificent sight, as he rode in one a dromedary.

"Ruins so extensive, desolate and bare exist nowhere else. . . . We are so much astonished that we cannot believe it to be real. While we wonder, our dromedary sweeps on, ascends what seems to be a flight of steps in ruins, passes a massive but shattered gateway, and, winding through some filthy lanes, kneels before the wretched dwelling of the Sheik of Tadmor."

Some, like Peacock, have been stirred to verse. He composed an ode, in a brisk, chirpy metre, reflecting that Death soon sweeps man from the world, the noblest works of human power in vain resist the fate-fraught hour, Oblivion's awful storms resound, and darkness veils its memory. Mid Syria's barren world of sand,

[1]Dr Kelman, *From Damascus to Palmyra* (1908).

where Tadmor's marble wastes expand, where desolation on the blasted plain has fixed his adamantine throne, I mark, in silence and alone, his melancholy reign. These silent wrecks more eloquent than speech full many a tale of awful note impart; truths more sublime than bard or sage can teach, this pomp of ruin presses on the heart. Peacock saw in the air a majestic crowd, among whom he recognized Zenobia, which led him to outline the tale of Palmyra's destruction by Aurelian. Having done this, he pictured ancient Palmyrene revels, and heard a solemn voice intone a moral about the shortness of man's day and its proper employment.

Peacock's thoughts were ruin-commonplaces, ill-expressed, but it was a pleasure to him to express them. Volney soared higher, and, sitting on a stone above the city, assembled his thoughts on the Ruins of Empire: his book on this subject germinated there, as did Gibbon's *Decline and Fall* before the ruins of the Forum. The intellectual stimulus of ruins is perhaps a theme worth pursuing; it must be accepted, anyhow, as a fact. "*Je vous salue, ruines solitaires*," Volney apostrophized them. "While your aspect repulses with secret fear the gaze of the vulgar, my heart finds in contemplating you the charm of a thousand sentiments and thoughts. How many useful lessons and touching reflections do you not offer to the spirit which knows how to consult you!" He relates how he wandered among the ruins, visiting the monuments, and how one evening he climbed a height, sat on the trunk of a broken column, that familiar seat of meditation, and looked over the desert city at sunset. Here, he said, flourished once a rich town, the seat of a powerful empire; lively crowds moved about those deserted streets, uttering "*les cris d'allégresse et de fête*"; there were palaces, arts, rich commerce, Tyrian purple, Kashmir silks, Baltic amber, perfumes of Arabia . . . and look at it now, "*un lugubre squelette*", the silence of death, squirrels in the palaces, reptiles in the sanctuaries. Thus perish the works of empires, nations and men. He proceeded (the course of thought is normal in ruin-viewers) to reflect on the destruction of past greatness—Assyria, Chaldea, Persia, Jerusalem, Phoenicia, Nineveh, Babylon, Tyre, Sidon and the rest, all fallen. "*Grand Dieu! d'où viennent de si funestes révolutions?*" One day, perhaps, some traveller would be sitting on the banks of the Seine or the Thames among ruins equally silent, and would weep alone over the ashes of nations and the memory of their grandeur. At this point Volney's own eyes filled, and covering his head with his cloak, he gave himself up to sombre meditations on human affairs. Presently there arrived to him a phantom, and conversed with him on the condition of man in the universe and the philosophy of human history. Other beings, shadowy but eloquent, arrived to take part in a long conversation on Life: in fact, by the time he descended again into Palmyra, his book was practically written.[1]

Not so soberly did Lady Hester Stanhope, "that highly eccentric gentlewoman", as Kinglake called her—take her Palmyrene pleasures, when, against all advice, she rode into the desert city on a white Arab horse in 1813, accompanied by Mr Bruce, the faithful Dr Meryon, and her Arab suite. It was said with the inaccuracy of most Arab statements, that no European woman had made this journey before; it was probably the case that within Arab memory she had not. In honour of the aristocratic Englishwoman who stood so high in the esteem of sheiks and emirs, who was regarded as the white queen of the desert, the inhabitants of Palmyra sallied out to meet her cavalcade in the Valley of the Tombs; to entertain her, they galloped about, made mock attacks, performed "all sorts of antics", as she described the scene in a letter. "The chief and about three hundred people came out to meet us . . . upon Arab mares", dressed like Turks and armed with guns,

"surrounding me and firing in my face, with most dreadful shouts and savage music and dances. They played all sorts of antics, till we arrived at the triumphal arch of Palmyra. The inhabitants were arranged in the most picturesque manner on the different columns leading to the Temple of the Sun."

The pillars had pedestals which had once held statues of prominent Palmyrene merchants; now, white-robed like statues, there stood on them lovely garlanded Palmyrene girls.

"The space before the arch was occupied with dancing girls, most fancifully and elegantly dressed, and beautiful children placed upon the projecting parts of the pillars with garlands of flowers. One, suspended over an arch, held a wreath over my

[1]Comte de Volney, *Les Ruines. ou Méditations sur les Révolutions des Empires* (1792).

head . . . poets from the banks of the Euphrates singing complimentary odes and playing various Arabian instruments. A tribe of male Palmyrenes brought up the rear,"[1]

and the whole village, singing and dancing, processed with their visitors to the gate of the Temple, and to the dwelling which had been prepared for Lady Hester, a cottage standing against the pillars in the north-west angle of the court. Much moved at this queenly reception, Lady Hester spent a week there. After resting for a day, she mounted her horse and rode about the ruins, tiring out the elderly sheik who accompanied her on foot, examining everything, going over the interiors of the sanctuaries with torches, looking at reliefs, decorated ceilings, fragments of statues. In the evenings there were revels in the open space in the temple ruins, coffee-drinking, story-telling and dancing. Lady Hester's name was cut in a conspicuous place as a memorial. She had never reached before, she was never to reach again, these dizzy heights of glory, when Zenobia's capital acclaimed her as its queen. One may say that no one has ever enjoyed himself or herself more in any ruins than did Pitt's niece in Palmyra; it was *Ruinenlust* in its highest, its most regal degree.

More modestly, the doctor and Mr Bruce walked about the ruins with Wood's plans, comparing them with the originals and looking for statues. They did not, apparently, enjoy the pleasure which later visitors found agreeable, of bathing in the sulphur stream that flows underground from the hills through the ancient aqueduct. Dr Kelman and his friends took this bathe by night, swimming into a cavern with candles fixed on a floating board to guide them: in this way they swam to the cave's far end, within the hill, and found it very mysterious and delightful. This stream is to-day turned into a swimming bath. Then there is the occasional spectacle of great herds of camels coming in from the desert to be watered, "with a multitudinous roaring like a stormy sea". Indeed, in Palmyra a hundred pleasures offer themselves among those golden colonnades.

Through the eighteenth and nineteenth centuries Palmyra became increasingly a European cult. Models of it were built; one was used as a stage set in a Warsaw theatre; it was painted on back cloths and curtains on English stages; its colonnade and

[1] *Travels of Lady Hester Stanhope*. Related by her physician (1846).

temple frescoed the walls of tea gardens and coffee houses, and made vistas at the ends of garden walks; it filled the sketch books of young ladies, and decorated their fans. It became, with Baalbek, one of the most fashionable ruins of the world; and villas at Twickenham were named Palmyra Lodge.

Entering Palmyra to-day by car, you will observe a few changes. The French, during their twenty years' mandate, made it an aviation centre, with barracks and aerodromes. The mud huts of the Arabs have been removed from the Temple of the Sun; no more do those hovels cling to the glorious walls, the columns pushing through their roofs. ("Visitors to the ruins," Baedeker used to inform us, "need have no hesitation in entering these houses or climbing on their roofs".) There are now hotels in Palmyra—Zénobie, Balkis, du Désert, perhaps more; some are said to be very modest, and frequented by indigenous chauffeurs; one, according to the French guidebook, has modern comfort and a good table; but by those who have stayed there it is somewhat less enthusiastically spoken of. Zenobia would have thought little of it, and Lady Hester would scarcely have stayed there; she preferred to pitch her tent in the open, as the guide books used to recommend in the days before the French mandate produced Zénobie, Balkis and du Désert. "Tents, for which a guard of soldiers is indispensable, had better be pitched in the orchards, or at the gate of the temple near the mosque. Sheikh Muhammed Abdullah receives travellers in his house." But one would prefer the orchards, which, besides apricots, pomegranates and other fruits, contain still many small fragments of antiquity; some of these it has always been found possible to secrete in the course of a well-spent night. But orderly excavations are now in hand; the amphitheatre has emerged; the pleasures of pilfering are somewhat checked.

6

Baalbek, being less remotely placed in the desert than Palmyra, had always been visited and admired by travellers, long before it became a tourist resort with a railway station and hotels. Lying on the Aleppo-Damascus route, it was popular with both merchants and pilgrims. Its origins are lost in the mists of Phoenician antiquity; its great Graeco-Roman temples stand on the sites of temples to older gods than Jupiter, Venus or Mercury. The richly-decorated oriental late-Roman architecture is that of Palmyra; the colour a deeper gold, like that of marmalade or amber honey. The Greeks and Romans called it Heliopolis, the city of the sun; it became a magnificently decorated Roman colony. In the second century Antoninus Pius built the Temple of Jupiter (probably to replace a temple of Baal) "which," said a seventh-century writer, "was one of the wonders of the world," as indeed its ruin is to-day. The Baalbek ruins are not, like Palmyra, spread over the whole city; they stand on an acropolis apart, and one buys tickets of admission at the entrance. "At the south-west side of this city," wrote Henry Maundrell in 1697 (actually it was the north-west)

"is a noble ruin, being the only curiosity for which this place is wont to be visited. It was anciently a heathen temple, together with some other edifices belonging to it, all truly magnificent; but in latter times these ancient structures have been patched and pieced up with several other buildings, converting the whole into a castle, under which name it goes at this day."

It was the Arabs who had built the acropolis into a fortress when they took Baalbek in the seventh century. To Bertrandon de la Brocquière, who stayed there in 1492, it was "a castle, built with very large stones", with a mosque in it, he knew nothing of the Roman temples. He thought Baalbek "a good town, well enclosed with walls, and tolerably commercial"; but he cannot be counted, like Pierre Belon and von Baumgarten in the following century, among its early admirers.

Though the modern Levantine town detracts from the magnificence of the ruins, in themselves they are even finer than Palmyra's. They pile up on a hillside platform, screened by trees; the Propylaea (the great flight of steps that led up to it now replaced by a modern stairway), with its columned portico and corniced towers (Antonine, topped with medieval fortifications), a hexagonal forecourt, a great court with the remains of a Theodosian basilica, and the two magnificent temples, each standing on its terrace, the Temple of Jupiter (or of the Sun), the lovely Temple of Bacchus, and the third exquisite little circular temple in a grove of trees. The Temple of the Sun, with its six splendid pillars, is probably the finest of its period in the world; but the special beauty of the Baalbek acropolis is largely in the grouping of all the buildings, in their relation to each other and to their background; to build a model of the Temple of the Sun and set it by itself on a wooded hill, as Mr Henry Hoare did at Stourhead, gives no idea of the actual effect, enhanced by the mountain background, by the rise of the garden-circled acropolis above the plain, and by the field of enormous prostrate columns that lie strewn about it, columns whose size recalls that other earth-shaken ruin, Selinunte in Sicily. The position, the mellow golden colour of the huge stones, the towering citadel of pillared buildings, seen for miles along the valley of approach, the size and magnificence which has sustained, though with damage, the assaults of man and nature down the ages, the stagey splendour of the whole, make Baalbek unique. Wood, who saw and described it before the earthquake of 1759 further devastated it, called it "the remains of the boldest plans we ever saw attempted in architecture" Seeing it as a superb work of art, spectators have discussed whether sunset or moonlight is the more rewarding hour in which to gaze on it. Many discriminating admirers have upheld the moonlight view.

The pleasure enjoyed by visitors to Baalbek have always had a particular note of rapture. Lamartine, though a little confused, was overcome with delight. "We were content to gaze and admire, without understanding anything beyond the colossal powers of human genius and the strength of religious feeling which had moved such masses of stone and wrought so many masterpieces." He thought the ornament too rich and exuberant, and put it down to the decline of Greek and Roman art rather than to the orientalism of the sculptures. The stone groaned, he complained, beneath the weight of its own luxuriance, and the walls were overspread with a lacework of marble. But he stood in dumb admiration before the six gigantic columns, where great birds perched on the cornices. Like others of his period, he felt the insignificance of human creatures, who cannot hope to last so long. He stayed in the house of a Christian bishop, who, oddly, was the first living being he had seen in Baalbek except jackals and swallows. While he supped, seated on the fragments that were used for chairs in the court of the Bishop's house, he admired the sublime spectacle of the ruins by moonlight, and heard an evening service coming melodiously from the ruined church. "A hallowed emotion inspired us, and we joined with religious fervour in the sacred hymns." Another evening he spent differently, the Emir having invited him to an entertainment in his palace; here he sat on a divan and watched improper dancing for an hour. Even the Emir, no doubt observing the puritan attitude of his guest, blushed and made signs of contempt and disapproval. The people, however, enjoyed it greatly. Afterwards they had delicious refreshments. Lamartine did not waste his time at Baalbek; having his full share of the acquisitiveness which all true ruin-tasters bring to celebrated ruins, he collected fragments of sculpture too many for personal transport, and got the kindly Bishop to send them on a camel to meet him at Beirut.[1]

A good time, too, was had by that diligent antiquarian traveller, Dr Richard Pococke, in the 1740s. He found the Pasha particularly civil.

> "When I asked to leave to see the antiquities, he told me I might go where I pleased, and called a janissary to attend me. Sweetmeats and coffee were brought . . . in the afternoon I went to see the famous temple. In the evening I was elegantly entertained by the Secretary [the Pasha's] in an open mocot in his court, a fountain of water playing into a basin in the middle of the court. We had for supper a roasted fowl stuffed, pilaw, stewed meat with the soup, a dulma of cucumbers stuffed with forced meat, and a dessert of apricots, apples and mulberries both red and white. On the 16th I viewed the two other temples and went round part of the walls."[2]

The Pasha treated him with the utmost politeness, conversed about world affairs, asked him who was the greatest prince in Europe, and showed him a young tiger.

The pleasure of Baalbek to the redoubtable Lady Hester Stanhope was not quite so heady as that which she had savoured at Palmyra. It was cold, as everyone, except during the hot summer months, finds Baalbek; the first snows had fallen. Lady Hester and her suite pitched their tents a short way out of the town, in

[1] Alphonse de Lamartine, *Nouvelle Voyage en Orient* (1839).
[2] Richard Pococke, *A Description of the East* (1745)

the ruins of an old mosque, in a valley full of springs that bubbled into stone basins (probably Ras-el-Ain). A shady path led through woods to the town. In the distance towered the snow-topped peaks of Lebanon; above the encircling gardens rose the acropolis and the six columns of the great temple. Dr Meryon, when they visited the temple, took a piece of charcoal and wrote on the wall of the inner temple, which was covered with names, a Latin quatrain in his employer's praise, which ended "*Esther, si pereant marmora, semper erit*". But Lady Hester (a gentlewoman, even if eccentric) made him rub it out. In spite of the weather, they spent a week in Baalbek.

But perhaps the most delicious Baalbek enjoyment has been described by two enthusiastic ordinary travellers—Dr John Carne in the 1830s, and a lady tourist in the 1860s. Dr Carne's description was actually of Ras-el-Ain, where, like Lady Hester, he camped. Here several English visitors had assembled to enjoy themselves, dressed and turbaned *en Turc*. Dr Carne was transported by the occasion and the romantic surroundings.

"A night and scene such as this [he recorded], is deeply exciting . . . this brilliant night on the plains of Baalbek—the great temples dimly yet awfully rising at a distance—the shepherd and his flock faintly covered with the moonlight. . . . The traveller left gladly the straggling and ruined homes of the town of Baalbek. . . . Consigning his horse to the care of a servant and entering the tents, the party were reclining in great comfort in the Turkish style, and received him with an earnest welcome. How quickly men become intimate and feel at ease and at home with each other in a lonely spot like this! . . . A young English lady, Mrs. ——, was reclining on an ottoman, and, like her husband, was dressed à la Turque, in which she appeared to advantage. . . . Refreshments were served, of a nature and variety that brought the tables of England to memory, and were very unusual in this wilderness. The hosts being accomplished and well-informed people, the conversation was animated and interesting; the evening passed delightfully. . . . The English consul from Beirut arrived a few days after: another tent was pitched, the British flag put up, and the encampment assumed a very animated appearance. The repasts were gay and social. . . . The emir of Baalbek used to come in the afternoons, sitting with his retinue and friends in the shade of the tree on the other side of the stream, take coffee, and enjoy himself. His people were quite obstreperous: even the old white-bearded men were as playful as schoolboys racing with each other, flinging their slippers, etc. He invited the whole party to coffee; but they declined, the consul deeming his excellency no better than a thief. . . . Every one felt sorrow when the party broke up."[1]

If Dr Carne's enjoyment seems rather of the nature of an escape from the Baalbek ruins, let us turn to the unstinted enthusiasm of C. G., who travelled there in 1868, on a horseback expedition from a friend's house on Mount Lebanon, which she recorded in a diary for her sister Maria in England. She learnt a little Arabic to speak to her horse; then the little party packed their saddlebags with requisites for the journey,

"not forgetting my nice little spirit-lamp, with the apparatus for making tea, some preserves, sardines, biscuits, hard eggs, etc., with which dear considerate Mrs B. kindly provided us. I equipped myself in my cool summer riding-habit of brown Holland, which I made at Leghorn two years ago, purposely for the Holy Land; a light Leghorn hat with a broad brim, and a yard or two of white muslin wound about it with long ends to protect the head and neck from the sun.

Onward, then, right onward!
This our watchword still,
Till we reach the glory
Of the wondrous hill.
For the journey girded
Haste we on our way."[2]

So they set out for Baalbek, halting for the night at a wayside hut, where C. G. slept on the roof by moonlight and got *coup de lune*. Next day

"the columns of *Baalbek* came into view at a considerable distance, and appeared to me quite small. I felt a little disappointed, and ready to exclaim, Can *this* be *Baalbek*, the most imposing structure of Syria? . . . The fact is that the exquisite proportions of the columns give them the aspect of such airy lightness, even at a little distance, that one can scarcely credit their vast magnitude till actually standing beside them. Then indeed . . . the mind is

[1] John Carne, *Syria, the Holy Land, Asia Minor, etc.* (1840).
[2] C. G., *Extracts from my Journal in Syria* (1868).

14 Seleucia, Antioch Engraving by W. H Bartlett, 1836-8

15 Ruins of Baalbek Engraving by W H. Bartlett, 1836-8

16 The city walls of Antioch. Engraving after L F Cassas, 1799

17 Ruins at Ascalon. Lithograph after Carle Vernet, 1819

overwhelmed by the view, and words can hardly express its feelings of admiration and wonder."

They approached the village, which consisted then of about a hundred huddled houses, and paused for refreshment before entering on the great experience.

"Now for a cup of delicious tea, some fresh eggs and splendid grapes. A walk of ten minutes, stumbling over huge stones, leaping or wading through gushing waters, climbing dilapidated walls, entering by an arch, through which I am dragged up, and, all obstacles surmounted, I stood among the far-famed ruins of the three temples of Baalbek. Well! this is indeed one of the wonders of the world. See to what Liliputian dimensions I am suddenly reduced beside two of these gigantic columns! There are six of them. Only fancy when there were twenty such! Then look at those prostrate columns, those huge fragments of fourteen feet thick. I almost shudder at their colossal dimensions. And now I stand in the centre of the broad platform, and in front of the main entrance to the Great Temple. No disappointment *now*! I am lost in amazement and admiration. . . . These ruins stand unrivalled for gorgeousness of decoration, combined with colour and magnitude."

She wondered how the huge stones had been moved about, admired the richness of the sculptured friezes and portals, climbed the spiral stairway to the top of the Temple of Bacchus (which, following Murray, she thought was that of Jupiter) for the view, explored the vaulted subterranean passages, which were very dismal, plucked a white mallow and pressed it in a book for Maria, and resolved to see the ruins by moonlight, for

"Dr Stewart thinks that these ruins as seen by moonlight exceed in grandeur and solemnity the far-famed moonlight view of the Colosseum at Rome. So, as soon as we had discussed our evening repast, we proposed resting on the divan of the little room for a few hours, until the advent of the moon, and that we should then revisit the old Temples of Baal, whilst the queen of night would be sailing majestically at large, completing by her magic touch the weird-like scene."

Possibly they over-slept, for C. G. has no further entry on the matter. But she had absorbed enough pleasure from Baalbek to last her for her life.

That particular romantic pleasure, when the city was a jumble of unsorted ruins, and travellers pitched their tents in the court of the great temple, has faded since Baalbek became a fashionable modern Levantine town. But the acropolis remains, with its orange-hued temples, pillars, courts, basilica, and fallen columns; and the excavations of the last fifty years have revealed buildings more clearly. These, with the towered Arab walls and great ruined mosque, should be, for most travellers, enough; though the scholarly Dr Wood found a moment between his plans and descriptions to regret that the ancient female beauty and kindness for which Baalbek was once famous seemed to have vanished altogether. He noted that the Arab inhabitants took pleasure in speaking of the "hours of dalliance" which King Solomon, they said, had enjoyed in Baalbek; "a subject on which the warm imagination of the Arabs is apt to be too particular."

As to the modern Levantines of Baalbek, going about their business against the background of that huge and stagey acropolis, they too have something of its improbable glamour, haloing them a little meretriciously.

7

Improbable glamour is, even more precisely, the apt description of Petra, that strange, lovely and most famous dead city carved out of the rock cliffs of Arabia. Unlike most famous ruins, Petra has not had a long and unbroken stream of foreign visitors. Since Saladin drove the crusaders out of Palestine, there is no certainly identifiable account of Petra by any European traveller until J. L. Burkhardt, got up as an Arab Sheik, explored the desert in 1812, and thought it "very probable that the ruins in Wady Mousa are those of the ancient Petra". Arabia Petraea was not a tempting land to travel: "countries which are little known and but thinly inhabited", Carsten Niebuhr described it in 1762, "the inhabitants of which wander among dry sands and rocks, seeking here and there a few spots which afford some scanty food for their cattle. None but Bedouins haunt these deserts". Since Burkhardt, they have been haunted by a stream of explorers eager and intelligent and extremely courageous in the face of the apparently excessively alarming habits of the residents in and near the ancient Nabataean capital, who used to evince the strongest xenophobia against visitors. Burkhardt, having apprehended quickly that, though every prospect pleased, man was pretty vile, only spent there the inside of a day, his excitement over the wonders he had discovered giving way to prudence, for

> "I knew well the character of the people round me. I was without protection in the midst of a desert where no traveller had ever before been seen; and a close examination of these works of the infidels, as they are called, would have excited suspicion that I was a magician in search of treasures. Future travellers may visit the spot under the protection of an armed force; the inhabitants will become more accustomed to the researches of strangers; and the antiquities of Wady Mousia will then be found to rank among the most curious remains of ancient art."[1]

Considering the untoward circumstances, Burkhardt's description of what he saw was astonishingly brilliant. He approached Petra, as nearly all subsequent travellers have done, along the deep gorge of the Sik, where rock walls tower overhead, shutting the ravine into intimidating gloom; it was, as two English travellers six years later felt, a more than Salvator Rosa scene, a fit stage for the murders so frequently (report said) perpetrated there, darkened by the wild luxuriance of the trees and shrubs hanging from the steep cliffs, and enlivened by the screaming of eagles, hawks and owls. This romantic gorge is by now familiar to us; all travellers have described its incidents—the ruined arch (now unfortunately disappeared) spanning the ravine near its beginning, a fit entry to so noble a capital city, the sudden apparition, more than a mile further on, of a deep red façade ninety feet high, with pillars, statues, bas-reliefs—the two-storied temple of Isis, called by the Arabs El-Kazneh, or the Treasure of Pharaoh. The startling beauty of this building, with its rich carvings and rosy bloom in the morning light (for here the gloom of the ravine is opened by a chasm crossing it at right angles) is, as Burkhardt remarked, calculated to make an extraordinary impression on the traveller, and is "one of the most elegant remains of antiquity existing in Syria". It dates from Hadrian; it is the Syrian version of late Roman, the columns Egyptian-Corinthian, rich in ornament; its

[1] J L. Burkhardt, *Travels in Arabia* (1829).

impact of singular beauty gains power from its surroundings; if seen elsewhere it would be less admirable.

"Its position [wrote Dr Edward Robinson in 1838] as a portion of the lofty mass of coloured rock over against the imposing avenue; its wonderful state of preservation, the glow and tint of the stone, and the wild scenery around; all are unique. . . . There it stands, as it has stood for ages, in beauty and loneliness; the generations which admired and rejoiced over it of old have passed away; the wild Arab, as he wanders by, regards it with stupid indifference and scorn; and none are left but strangers from far distant lands to do it reverence"

The only part of the building which interested the wild Arab (treasure-minded, however stupid) was the urn high up at the top of the façade, which he believed to contain hidden treasure, and which was dented with the musket balls he had fired at it through several centuries to break it open.

Having duly inscribed his name on this lovely building as he had done on the tombs of Thebes and on the summit of the great Pyramid, Dr Robinson went his way along the Sik, coming presently on a large triclinium, and then to the Roman theatre, of the first century A.D., a semi-circle of thirty-three tiers of seats hewn out of the rocky side of a mountain and surrounded by tombs far older than the theatre; some of them climb up from the top row of seats. "Strange contrast!" observed Dr Robinson, "where a taste for the frivolities of the day was at the same time gratified by the magnificence of tombs, amusement in a cemetery; a theatre in the midst of sepulchres."

Beyond the theatre begins the town, Roman in period, lying on both banks of the Wady Mousa in a large irregular oblong. It was a fine populous city; the remains of buildings, public and private, are thick on the ground, covering about two miles; there are three market places, a forum, baths, gymnasia, shops, colonnades, private houses, all lying in this rock-guarded valley, whose mountain walls rival any flower garden in rich tints and shades; they have been compared to rainbows, and to the shifting hues of watered silk; though sandstone red is the prevailing tone, the "rose-red city half as old as time"

[1]Edward Robinson, *Biblical Researches in Palestine* (1838)

of a very bad Newdigate poem is inaccurate both visually and mathematically.

There were many temples in the town; the chief and largest is now called Kasr Faraun, Pharaoh's castle; it is a first-century building, with the remains of Roman columns, and stucco ornament on the walls. Near it are the ruins of a large peripteral temple. A great three-bayed gate gives access to a way still partly paved, leading to the city, of which the centre is an immense market place, with shops and galleries opening out of it. Here the caravans of merchants from east and west brought and sold their wares; it is a strange and ghostly scene, whispering with the echoes of chaffering Nabataean merchants two thousand years ago: up from southern Arabia they came, with their camel trains, their rich bales, their spices, ivory and amber, calling en route at Petra, crowding in the market places of the rock city, looked down on by steep rainbow heights wherein were carved something like a thousand sepulchres.

The various magnificence of these tombs is extraordinary. Some are façaded with pilasters, some have arches and cornices, some are plain pyramids, some have elaborate terraces, and lofty chambers within, some are built like temples, with altars and columns, one like a palace, with eighteen pillars, three stories, and four doors. Some, identified by name, are the tombs of Roman governors; many of the more ostentatious must have been built for rich merchants. The wealth poured out on this superb and decorated necropolis shows a taste for stylized magnificence in the tradition of prosperous trading cities; it recalls the hey-day of eighteenth-century Portugal, when the treasure fleets from Brazil enriched King John V beyond the dreams of avarice, and grandiose palaces, churches and dwellings luxuriated over the land. The hey-day of Petra was in the first and second centuries A.D., after annexation by Rome had turned Arabia Petraea and the old Nabataean kingdom into a Roman province. It was under Trajan and Hadrian and Alexander Severus that Petra assumed its Hellenistic-Roman air; the theatre was hewn in the mountain side, the city filled with substantial Roman splendour, the cliffs with Roman tombs. The development of the style in tombs can be traced; early to later Nabataean; then Gaeco-Roman, with still the oriental touch; sumptuousness growing steadily, until some time in the third century, when Palmyra stole Petra's caravan trade and the Persian empire engulfed its glory. A century later, it had dwindled to an unprosperous little town, a Christian bishopric until the Saracen conquest; the crusaders held it for a time in the twelfth century, and built on the top of a mountain south of the city a fine castle. After Saladin had swept them out of it, there is little more news of Petra until Burkhardt found it. Since when it has become news indeed, and the Mecca of romantic eastern travellers, for if ever a dead city held romance it is Petra. Wild, Arab-infested, hewn out of ruddy rock in the midst of a mountain wilderness, sumptuous in ornament and savage in environs, poised in wildness like a great carved opal glowing in a desert, this lost caravan city of Edom staggers the most experienced traveller. Even Sir Henry Layard, robbed and enraged by villainous Arabs in 1840, and taking a poor view of the architecture, which he found debased, of a bad period and corrupt style, and wanting both in elegance and grandeur, admitted that these ruins were unlike any other ancient city in the world. As to Captains Irby and Mangles, who had found Palmyra so little worth the trouble and fatigue of getting to, they were overcome with enthusiasm for Petra, when they visited it in 1818, oddly dressed as Bedouins (for dressing up as Bedouins used to be, perhaps is still, among the pleasures of visiting Arab ruins). The awful sublimity of the approach ("Salvator Rosa never conceived so savage and suitable a quarter for banditti"), the riches of the decoration contrasting with the wild scenery, the summits of the rocks presenting "nature in her most savage and romantic form, while their bases are worked out in all the symmetry of art", the whole hewn out of the living, glowing rock . . . it all made a most singular scene, wherein they dared spend only two days for fear of the residents. M. Léon de Laborde, ten years later, spent eight days, and wrote a detailed description with drawings: over his precision enthusiasm hovers like a winged spirit; he had never seen anything so remarkable and romantic, and nor, he persuades us, have we He added to his pleasures by extensive quoting from the Bible, for this is what the earlier visitors to Petra loved to do, reiterating the curses on Edom. *O thou that dwellest in the clefts of the rock, that holdest the height of the hill, though thou shouldst make thy nest as high as the eagle, I will bring thee down from thence, saith the*

Lord. Also, Edom shall be a desolation; everyone that goeth by shall be astonished.

Everyone, in fact, is; whether, like Burkhardt and Layard, they spend only a day in the city in the clefts of the rock, or, like Doughty, turn in disgust from "the mountainous close of iron cliffs, in which the ghastly waste monuments of a sumptuous barbaric art are from the first an eye-sore", or whether they stay long enough to draw the monuments and examine all the tombs and make the steep ascent to the monastery of El Deir on its mountain. Drunk with colour, beauty, strangeness, and all the peculiar excitement imparted by antiquity, they have sometimes ended a perfect day by supping and sleeping in one of the better tombs. This is what Mr Bartlett did, in the 1840s, when he, surrounded by a posse of Arabs, visited Petra in the course of writing his book, *Forty Days in the Desert.* Having made the El-Deir ascent, he directed his steps to the tomb he had chosen for his bedroom.

"It was indeed a very comfortable abode, the funeral chamber was large enough for the reception of a goodly company, and had evidently been used by former travellers; the rock was blackened with smoke, and we had apprehensions of vermin, but happily these fears proved unfounded. Komeh built up an excellent kitchen, near the ruinous door, and the adjacent splendid sepulchre, hewn for no less than royalty, served as a slaughter-house, in which a lamb received its quietus. . . . Such festive preparations in these chambers of death might well seem a mockery of human pride. Little could the merchant prince who hollowed out for himself this costly mausoleum anticipate how, after that commerce which had so enriched him should have utterly passed away, a stranger from a far greater emporium . . . should thus appropriate the chamber designed to preserve inviolate to the end of time his mouldering remains! So it was, however; and the satisfaction of having fully attained an object long desired, with all appliances and means to restore the fatigue of sight-seeing and clambering, made this evening among the desolations of Petra pass away with a sort of wild gaiety."[1]

Such are the pleasures afforded by Petra, "that extraordinary rock-hewn capital of Edom, which, by its singular wildness, even

[1]Bartlett, *Forty Days in the Desert* (1849).

yet seems, beyond any other place, to thrill the imagination and waken the love of adventure".

8

A different, less sensuous and facile, more purely imaginative type of pleasure is offered by the remains of Nineveh and Babylon. Petra, Palmyra, and Baalbek can be enjoyed by anyone with eyes. Nineveh and Babylon need imagination, and some knowledge. To put it bluntly, they are, in fact, little more than mounds.

Sir A. H. Layard, Nineveh's pioneer excavator, drew the distinction a century ago. No use, he pointed out, crossing the Euphrates to seek such ruins in Mesopotamia and Chaldaea as one finds in Syria and Asia Minor. Not here the graceful columns rising above myrtle, ilex and oleander, the amphitheatre covering a gentle slope and overlooking a lake-like, dark blue bay; not here the richly-carved cornice or capital among luxuriant foliage; instead, the stern, shapeless mound rising like a hill from the scorched plain, the stupendous mass of brickwork occasionally laid bare by winter rains.

"He has left the land where nature is still lovely, where, in his mind's eye, he can rebuild the temple or the theatre, half doubting whether they could have made a more grateful impression on the senses than the ruin before him. He is now at a loss to give any form to the rude heaps of earth upon which he is gazing. . . . The scene around him is worthy of the ruin he is contemplating; desolation meets desolation."

Yet, "These huge mounds of Assyria made a deeper impression upon me, gave rise to more serious thoughts and more earnest reflections than the temples of Baalbec and the theatres of Ionia."[1]

For Layard was that imaginative and enterprising being, an archaeologist, to whom a shapeless mound in Mesopotamia suggested limitless discoveries, infinite pleasures and palaces through which he might roam. And so it turned out. There is no more zestful narration in the exciting history of archaeology than Layard's of his excavations of Nineveh and Nimroud.

No great city had ever gone more utterly underground than the huge ancient capital of Assyria since its destruction in the seventh

[1]A. H. Layard, *Nineveh* (1849).

century B.C. Its ruins crumbled gradually; as they covered a space of many miles, it was before long impossible to identify the site of the actual city; and which were the ruins seen by Cyrus's army as it marched by them in the fifth century, is doubtful. The whole business of Nineveh is confused: Lucian wrote (A.D. 150) that no trace remained, and that no one could say where it had stood; yet the ruins either of Nineveh or (more likely) of some city built later on its site were visible through the Middle Ages; an accepted, anchored, ambiguous tradition. Ibn Batuta saw and described them; so did all travellers who passed that way. As late as 1674 John Evelyn was assured by "certain strangers, not unlearned, who had been born not far from Old Nineveh", that the ruins were still extant, "and vast and wonderful were the buildings, vaults, pillars and magnificent fragments". Six years later Evelyn met Chardin, the French explorer; he described Nineveh as "a vast city, now all buried in her ruins, the inhabitants building on the subterranean vaults, which were, as appeared, the first stories of the old city; there were frequently found huge vases of fine earth, columns, and other antiquities". Chardin had made drawings of the ruins; so did some eighteenth century visitors; Nineveh was becoming less anchored, more speculative. By the nineteenth century, the great sprawling plain of city, suburbs, gardens and parks that lay along the Tigris opposite the town of Mosul was silted over by desert, and only mounds indicated where walls, palaces and ramparts stood.

The sensational first explorations were the work of M. Botta, the French consul at Mosul, who attacked the mound of Kouyunjik with vigour but with little expertize or success, was told by inhabitants that, if he desired sculptured stones, he had better dig in the neighbouring village of Khorsabad, and here came on gypsum-slabbed chambers carved with bas-reliefs which fell to pieces when exposed to the air. M. Botta, no expert, scarcely knew what it was he had found, but rather supposed it to be Nineveh; he succeeded in removing some sculptures and inscriptions and took them home to France. Mr Layard (as he then was) was fired with eagerness to explore the other mounds and uncover the true Nineveh; financed by Sir Stratford Canning, he set out from Constantinople in October, 1845, "gallopped over the vast plains of Assyria, and reached Mosul in twelve days". After cautious and secretive parleyings with the villainous Mohammed Pasha, he managed to depart for Nimroud under the pretence of boar-hunting (since excavations were viewed with deep suspicion), floated down the Tigris on a small raft, with a British merchant of Mosul, and arrived at the ruinous village by the mound of Nimroud, where they passed the night. "Visions of palaces underground, of gigantic monsters, of sculptured figures, and endless inscriptions, floated before me", through a night too exciting to be restful. In the morning, with Arabs engaged to dig, the party walked to the mound of Nimroud, which "broke like a distant mountain on the morning sky". Broken fragments of cuniform-inscribed pottery were strewn on all sides; among them were fragments of a bas-relief, and a piece of alabaster stuck out from the earth. Encouraged by this, Layard began to dig; soon they uncovered large inscribed slabs, and found that they had entered a chamber, of which the slabs were the walls Layard was now convinced, but wrongly, that he was digging up Nineveh. Henceforth the excavations proceeded with exhilarating success, handicapped only by the sharp and rapacious attention which the Pasha at Mosul kept on these obviously treasure-hunting Franks, who were doubtless trying to steal precious metals. Inspired by cupidity, more helpers offered their services. More mounds were dug; more finds brought in daily. Encamped in a mud hut three miles away and riding to the excavations every morning, Layard entered a magic world of slabbed chambers, inscriptions, carved scroll work, burnt bricks, bas-reliefs of warriors, chariots and horses, winged bulls, better than anything which M. Botta had found at Khorsabad. The work was unfortunately interrupted by the suspicious Pasha, who told Layard that he could no longer risk the anger of the Arabs at having their tombs disturbed. No use to protest that there were no tombs; the Pasha had had grave stones carried by night from the village and placed among the ruins. Layard left Nimroud for a month in charge of agents, returning when the cunning Mohammed had been replaced by a new and more agreeable Pasha. Troubles still broke out from time to time, when the age-old suspicion of foreigners stirred, and the Arabs' resentment rose against all this digging into their land, they were certain, too, that not stones but precious metals were actually the treasure sought, and that the Franks' ultimate design was to seize their country. Layard had to proceed cautiously, though the excitement and garrulousness of his workmen made public news of all his doings. He found walls carved with bas-reliefs of a period belonging to the second Assyrian empire; there were human figures, gods, warriors, kings, animals, flowers, eagle-headed men, winged bulls, human-headed lions, adorning the chambers of palaces of the ninth century B.C. After a particularly sensational find—two huge human-headed winged lions—Layard celebrated the discovery by a slaughter of sheep, of which all the Arabs partook; wandering musicians arrived, and there was dancing through the night. On the following day great crowds assembled on the mound to see what would turn up next. More winged lions rose from the bowels of the earth; apparently they had guarded the portals of a temple. Layard, delighted with their grand appearance, contemplated them for hours; he thought they looked noble and sublime, and the reflection that they had been, perhaps, hidden from the eye of man for twenty-five centuries overhelmed him.

Spring arrived, turning the desert into a flowery plain. Layard, with an imposing caravan party of camels, horsemen who galloped round and round firing pistols in the air, ladies in blue veils riding mules, Mosul gentlemen, armed servants, greyhounds in leashes, and Mr Rassam, the British vice-consul at Mosul, set out to pay a visit to the western bank of the Tigris to see an important sheik and the famous ruins of El-Hadr. They rode over the desert carpet of flowers in high exhilaration, chasing gazelles and wild boars as they rode. After a sumptuous visit to the Sheik, they pushed on to the great circular walled city of El-Hadr, its yellow stones golden in the sinking sun, arriving there in a furious storm. "The lightning played through the vast buildings, the thunder re-echoed through its deserted halls.... It was a fit moment to enter such ruins as these. They rose in solitary grandeur in the midst of a desert, '*in mediâ solitudine positae*', as they stood fifteen centuries before, when described by the Roman historian." They pitched their tents in the great palace courtyard, and spent three days there, measuring the ruins and making plans, and examining the rich sculptured stones of the magnificent building.

Returning to Mosul, Layard hastened back to Nimroud and continued to dig. People crowded in from neighbouring places to see the now famous sculptures; Layard, a genial and hospitable man, invited everyone in the district to a party. It was a noble entertainment: white pavilions were pitched on a lawn near the river for the ladies and the Sheiks; black tents were provided for other guests and for the kitchen; an open space was left for dancing. The chief Sheik arrived early in the morning, so as to miss nothing; dressed in red silk and yellow boots and riding a tall white mare, he was welcomed by a band of Kurdish musicians with pipes and drums; dismounting, he took his seat on the sofa prepared for him; his women folk repaired to the ladies' tents to eat sweetmeats and parched peas. A dinner of fourteen sheep was served to the assembled crowd; dancing followed, with other entertainments; the festivities lasted three days: "they earned me a great reputation and no small respect".

The summer came on; fresh discoveries were made daily. Sir Stratford Canning secured a letter from the Grand Vizier authorizing the continuation of the excavations and the removal of the objects found; "I read by the light of a small camel-dung fire the document which secured to the British nation the records of Nineveh, and a collection of the earliest monuments of Assyrian art". Layard was delighted; he could now pursue his researches in secure confidence, and their fruits would adorn the British Museum. He turned his attention for a time to the great mound of Kouyunik, close to Mosul, which had always been believed by travellers to mark the actual site of the city of Nineveh; he opened a few trenches in it, and returned to Nimroud to dig further into the north-west palace, where every day turned up richly-carved bas reliefs of figures, animals, monsters, sacred trees, and scenes of solemn ritual or adventure. The life they indicated was one of hunting, battle, religious ceremonies celebrated by king and priest, and the participation in all these activities of winged creatures of dubious biological category. The Arabs were highly interested in these figures, greeting them with extravagant gestures and cries of surprise. The bearded men they distrusted, believing them to be idols of jinns. The eunuchs they took for beautiful females, and kissed or patted them on the cheek. Excited by each fresh find, they would rush like madmen into the trenches, throwing off their clothes and shouting the war-cry of their tribe.

The business of transporting some of the sculptures to England now began; they were, with difficulty, packed on buffalo carts, taken to the Tigris, and floated down to Baghdad on a raft. They reached London in due course, and formed the first collection of Assyrian bas-reliefs to be shown in the British Museum. Meanwhile the Pasha and his armed retinue visited the excavations; terrified and amazed at the strange figures they saw, they pronounced them idols constructed by magicians, and concluded that in England they would be used as a gateway for the queen's palace; unfortunately this did not occur; they would have looked very well outside Buckingham Palace.

As many bas-reliefs of winged lions, bulls and kings as anyone could wish turned up; sphinxes too, and a black marble obelisk. The Arabs entered into the work with zest; Layard gave them frequent feasts and dances, and his enthusiasm was shared by all; at Christmas he sent another cargo of sculptures floating down the Tigris for London, then galloped back into Mosul to celebrate the festivities of the season. By April, twenty-eight rooms of the chief palace had been opened; one cannot, from seeing the sculptured slabs standing coldly in the Assyrian collection in the British Museum, get any idea of the richness and glory with which they dazzled the eyes of the explorers who found them lining the walls of the long buried palaces in the desert. The reliefs, the painted ornaments, the coloured frescoes on the walls, the rich friezes of animals, men, castles and ships, the pottery and the tombs, adorned for Layard's keen imagination the many-chambered palaces; his only disappointment was that the British government would not allow him more money, and directed him not to attempt the transport to England of winged bulls or lions until a more favourable opportunity. Layard, however, could not submit to this; he selected a lion and a bull from the great central hall, had a strong wooden cart built, and, after much careful contrivance, lowered the bull with ropes, pulled on by Nestorians, Chaldaean and Arabs, while Kurdish musicians played their drums and pipes, Arabs shouted war-cries, women screamed incessantly, the ropes strained and creaked, and finally broke. The bull, fortunately, was unhurt by his fall, and the music, the cries and the dancing rose more ecstatically than ever; indeed, they continued all that night. The Arab Sheikh commented, "Wonderful! Wonderful! In the name of the Most High, tell me, O Bey, what you are going to do with those stones. So many thousands of purses spent upon such things! . . . For twelve hundred years have the true believers been settled in this country, and none of them ever heard of a palace underground. But lo! here comes a Frank from many days' journeys off, and he walks up to the very place, and he takes a stick and makes a line here and makes a line there. Here, says he, is the palace; there, says he, is the gate; and he shows us what has been all our lives beneath our feet, without our having known anything about it. Wonderful! Wonderful!"

Mr Layard too thought it was wonderful, and so did all the Arabs. They killed and devoured sheep, feasted and danced all night, then "after passing the night in this fashion, these extraordinary beings, still singing and capering, started for the mound", and hauled the bull, with immense difficulty and continuous drumming, fifing and tilting horsemen, on to the buffalo cart which was to drag it to the river. The cart sank in the sand, had to be left all night, was attacked by wild Arabs who indented the bull with a bullet, but was safely next day placed on the banks of the Tigris. Later the lion joined it, and later still both creatures, with other sculptures, were embarked on two great rafts of six hundred blown-up sheep skins for the long voyage to Busrah.

Shortly after this the place became dangerous from Bedouins; the workmen protested against remaining there, and the excavations were suspended. The Nimroud palaces and sculptures were covered up again with earth, after their excavator had traversed the chambers again and recorded in fond detail their beauties and the subjects of their sculptures.

"We may wander through these galleries for an hour or two [he ends], examining the marvellous sculptures. Here we meet long rows of kings, attended by their eunuchs and priests, there lines of winged figures carrying fir-cones. . . . Other entrances, formed by winged lions and bulls, lead us into new chambers. In every one of them are fresh objects of curiosity and surprise. At length, wearied, we issue from the buried edifice . . . and find ourselves again upon the naked platform. We look around in vain for any traces of the wonderful remains we have just seen, and are half inclined to believe that we have dreamed a dream, or have been listening to some tale of Eastern romance. Some, who may hereafter tread on the spot when the grass again grows over the ruins of the Assyrian palaces, may indeed suspect that I have been relating a vision."[1]

And so, standing on the brown mound, hummocked with ridges and honeycombed with the holes of past digging and trenching, which to-day covers the Nimroud, they might; were it not that here and there a fragment of a winged Assyrian creature pushes up above the soil. Such a creature was unearthed by surprised British soldiers during the Old War, and, since the soldiers could not take it with them, it was buried once more where it belonged.

Layard went off to the mound of Kouyunjik. Kouyunjik had been quarried through the ages for building material; Mosul had been built out of it, and other neighbouring towns, which travellers had perhaps taken, after they had fallen into ruin, for Old Nineveh. Layard did not suppose that complete palaces could remain. He then believed Kouyunjik, Nimroud and Khorsabad to be different quarters of the same immense city, that city whose ruins were described by Diodorus and Xenephon and Strabo as lying in a great quadrangle along the Tigris, each quarter being separately fortified and walled. Nimroud was, Layard believed, the earliest, the original Nineveh. He was wrong. Settling in Mosul, he began to dig Kouyunjik, and was rewarded far beyond his hopes. Palace chambers emerged, their portals guarded by the ubiquitous human-headed winged bulls; there were huge bas-reliefs of battles, castles, ships and warriors; elegant gigs, drawn by plumb, caparisoned horses, carried triumphant, parasol-shaded kings along palm-bordered rivers full of fish; bland-faced, tasselled horses with riders who resembled them ambled along in pursuit of fleeing foes; women, children and beasts were led captive away. By the end of a month, nine chambers had been uncovered. It was the beginning of the emergence of the eighth-century palace of Sennacherib, who had made Nineveh his court at the zenith of Assyria's power. As time went on, the glories of the palace, and of other palaces and temples round it, were gradually revealed: the mound of Kouyunjik had covered the finest achievements of Assyrian architecture. Not only palace rooms and sculptured walls were discovered, but the royal library, its shelves packed close with clay tablets and cylinders, inscribed in cuniform

[1]A. H. Layard, *Nineveh* (1849).

letters with works of history, religion, grammar, astrology, legends, laws, hymns—all the lore and learning of ancient Assyria. Campaigns and conquests were described in detail; the reigns of kings recorded; the great flood rolled by. A dazzling light was suddenly turned on what had been mysterious darkness. "A few years ago," wrote James Ferguson in 1851, "a small packing-case could have contained all that Europe knew of the ancient kingdom of Assyria. . . . Now her palaces are laid open to us, and we know more of them than we do of Greece or Rome . . . the records of a history lost for centuries." Dynasties and people sprang to life; their history was deciphered in European museums; their palaces reconstructed in pictures and words, down to the lighting and the drains; the magnificent buildings took on the brilliant colours and decoration of remembered dreams—inlaid ceilings, rich friezes, gold and silver leaf on cedar beams, brightly painted walls, everywhere the winged monster gods with calm bearded faces guarding portals, chambers paved with alabaster slabs inscribed with royal doings. Never had finer palaces soared up from the bowels of the earth. No wonder that the Arabs, at Layard's parting feast, danced and sang all night.

"Is not Nineveh most delightful and prodigious?" wrote a young lady to her brother in India. "Papa says nothing so truly thrilling has happened in excavations since they found Pompeii." Nor, on the whole, had it. Visitors flocked out to see it; archaeologists wrote books reconstructing the palaces; more and more year by year was uncovered. Many travellers, rashly braving the Assyrian summer, succumbed to fever; recovering and returning home, they half-suspected that the strange underground world they had seen had been part of their delirium.

More than ever they might think so to-day, standing on the bare, unrewarding mounds of Kouyunjik and Nimroud, with the desert spreading round, and nothing to hint at buried palaces except ridges and trenched earth, and, at Nimroud, here and there a fragment of a winged bull (those creatures so little loveable to any but Assyrians) pushing up a bearded head, to be made a target for the shots of British marksmen.

The other Nineveh mound, Nebi Yunis, is protected from any but casual and amateur examination by its village and its mosque. In the mosque (they say) lies Jonah in his tomb, and on the wall

18 The Parthenon with the mosque erected in it by the Turks. Engraving after Wm. Pars, 1787

19 Palmyra. Engraving by I P. Borra, 1753

above him hangs part of his whale. It is a shrine for Moslem pilgrims.

Other pilgrims to Nineveh must rely now on the pleasures of imagination. They can roam about the mounds, treading on twenty centuries of Assyrian history; they can quote Zephaniah the prophet, who, like all prophets, rejoiced over the ruin of great cities, confident that they had richly deserved their fate, for prophets have believed all large cities to be given over to wickedness, and an abomination in the eyes of the Lord, and no doubt they are right. They have been the most single-minded of ruin-lovers, having no use for cities until they fall, and then rejoicing over the shattered remains in ringing words.

"And he will stretch out his hand against the south, and destroy Assyria, and will make Nineveh a desolation, and dry like a wilderness. . . . The cormorant and the bittern shall lodge in the upper lintels of it, their voice shall sing in the windows; desolation shall be in the thresholds. . . . This is the rejoicing city that dwelt carelessly, that said in her heart, I am, and there is none beside me: how is she become a desolation, a place for beasts to lie down in; every one that passeth by her shall hiss and wag his hand."

It may be questioned if Zephaniah would have approved the excavations which have brought the wicked palaces to light, to be marvelled at by future generations who neither hiss nor wag their hands, but carefully steal decorations and graven images and store them in museums for the admiration of the world.

9

Babylon, too, that "golden cup in the Lord's hand, that made all the earth drunken", Babylon "shall become heaps, a dwelling-place for dragons, an astonishment and an hissing, without an inhabitant"; neither shall the Arabian pitch tent there, but wild beasts of the desert shall lie there, and their houses shall be full of doleful creatures, and owls shall dwell there and satyrs shall dance there, and the wild beasts of the islands shall cry in their desolate houses, and dragons in their pleasant palaces.

Thus the triumphing Jewish prophets, starting the career of the ruined Babylon with the sensational press that it has maintained ever since. For Babylon, unlike Nineveh, has always been much visited and described in her ruin. The curious thing about her visitors is the dissimilarity of the accounts they have from the first given, almost as if they had seen different ruins. The Hebrew prophets, those grandiosely fantasticating ruin-builders, contrived owls, dragons, dancing satyrs in the pleasant palaces, every macabre circumstance of ruined cities that ruin-lovers have in all ages devised and sought. They liked to picture the resplendent edifices as caves for howling beasts, the temples and palaces hissing with serpents, the hanging gardens, once the wonder of the world, now its trample and spurn. It grieved them to see, half a century after the destruction of the wicked old Babylon by Sennacherib, a new Babylon arise, more resplendent, and very probably more wicked, than the old, to grow wealthier and more magnificent than all the cities of Asia and Egypt, not excepting Thebes. They must have been disappointed that Cyrus when he conquered it did not destroy it, but cherished and embellished it and made it a great Persian city, and one of his court residences: though he had a great massacre of citizens, he did not even destroy the walls. Darius, and after him Xerxes, apparently wrought more destruction, but even this cannot have come up to prophetic standards, for Herodotus, describing Babylon fifty years later, mentions the walls and the great temple of Belus and other buildings and towers as being there in his time. Ruin is always over-stated; it is part of the ruin-drama staged perpetually in the human imagination, half of whose desire is to build up, while the other half smashes and levels to the earth.

Alexander, entering Babylon a century after Herodotus wrote, found it still a fine city, though, according to Arrian and Strabo, much of it, including the Temple of Belus, lay buried in rubbish that it would have taken ten thousand workmen two months to clear. Accounts as usual, differ; one is inclined, from experience, to believe the less ruinous and spectacular, and not to accept such statements as that a little while after Alexander only two fortresses remained, or that under the Seleucids the city was a deserted wilderness. Long after this, anyhow, Jews were being persecuted in it under Caligula, and fleeing from it to the new city of Seleucia, and a century later Lucian spoke of it as a city which would soon disappear. After the beginning of the Christian era, tourists (who continued assiduously to visit or pass it) were of many minds about its precise condition. Eusebius in the third century thought it completely a desert, Jerome in the fourth had a notion that the walls had been repaired and enclosed a park of game which the Persian kings hunted, Cyril of Alexandria that the place had become a marsh, Theodoret in the fifth century that it was inhabited by a few Jews, Procopius in the sixth that it had for a long time been completely destroyed, Ibn Haukal in the tenth that it was a small village, Benjamin of Tudela in the twelfth that "it now lies in ruins, but the streets still extend thirty miles. The ruins of the palace of Nebuchadnezzar are still to be seen; but people are afraid to venture among them on account of the serpents and scorpions with which they are infested." Some of the ruins were still, apparently, well above ground in the sixteenth century, when a German and an English traveller described them. Rauwolff, the German, saw no houses, and would have doubted whether such a great city could have stood there, but that he knew it by its situation and several ancient and delicate antiquities that were still standing in great desolation. There was an old bridge, the ruins of a castle, and of the tower of Babel, half a league in diameter and so full of vermin that one could not get within half a mile of it. John Eldred, an Elizabethan merchant, travelling between Aleppo and "the new city of Babylon", often saw "the old mighty city, many old ruins whereof are easily to be seen by daylight", including those of the old tower of Babel, above a quarter of a mile in compass, and almost as high as St Paul's steeple—but he is thought to have seen the wrong ruins, and to have confounded Babylon with the ancient Seleucia on the Tigris. Pietro della Valle in 1616 got, as might be expected, to the right place, and was the first visitor to describe the ruins as a mound, a heap, a mountain of confused débris. He saw a high, irregular mass of varying heights, built of bricks, with no shape to indicate particular buildings, though he thought that he identified the tower of Babel. All that was visible to him of Babylon was this mountain of confusion, and it was difficult to believe that the proud city had stood on the site. His account is interesting as being the first to show Babylon going or gone to earth; henceforth it was what Jeremiah had called "heaps". What the Italian Carmelite, Father Vincenzo Maria, saw in 1667 seems doubtful; greatly harassed and over-excited by heat, lions, Arabs, dysentery and mosquitoes, he arrived at Zillah and saw the ruins of magnificent buildings for many miles round, including of course, the Tower of Babel; for fear of robbers, however, he did not like to go too near them.

The confusion of visitors on the spot was reflected by complete ignorance on the part of the untravelled,

> But where is lordly Babylon? where now
> Lifts she to heaven her giant brow?

the poet John Hughes enquired, and remained unanswered. During the next half-century, however, Babylonian travellers became more precise in their identifications.

Henceforth archaeologists took up in earnest the task of identifying the different mounds; it is when ruins have gone underground that research into them eagerly begins. Finally the German excavations, begun fifty years ago, scientifically and thoroughly uncovered what remained of a city used as a building quarry for some two thousand years. What was revealed was the New Babylon, the Babylon of Nebuchadnezzar and Belshazzar; of the more ancient city destroyed by Sennacherib practically nothing remained. Nebuchadnezzar's palaces, the Mene-Tekal throne room where Belshazzar feasted, the site of the Hanging Gardens, the temples, the walls, the gates, the quays, the great citadel, the Sacred Way, were unearthed, labelled, argued over, mapped and planned, written about, admired by countless visitors, covered up, and only excavated again lately; now one can see the Ishtur Gate and a mass of broken, clay-brick walls, and pick up enamelled bricks from the great processional way. Though it still looks a mess, it now repays a visit.

Apart from the excavations, Babylon has its rewards. The view over the undulating, ruin-strewn desert, with its shifting colours in the changing light, the long city site lying along the palm-fringed Euphrates, the waters of Babylon; the knowledge that among and underneath the mounds lies the jumbled débris that was three thousand years ago the greatest city of the world, the capital of the Assyrian and Babylonish empires, should be enough for the romantic ruin-fancier. Travellers no longer think they see the Tower of Babel rising among the lesser ruins; but still they can enjoy the familiar meditations on fallen cities which engrossed Dr Rauwolff in the sixteenth century when he viewed

"that so famous kingly city, which now with its magnificence and glorious buildings is quite desolated and lies in the dust, so that every one that passes through it has great reason to admire with astonishment when he considers that this which has been so glorious, and in which the greatest monarchs that ever were have had their seats and habitations, is now reduced to such a desolation and wilderness that the very shepherds cannot abide to fix their tents there. So [he concluded, having read his Bible], here is a most terrible example to all haughty tyrants, who may be sure that if they do not give over in time and leave their tyranny . . . God the Almighty will also come upon them, and for their transgressions punish them in anger."[1]

Being interested also in botany, he found among the ruins some rare plants.

Dr Rauwolff's feeling about deserved punishment was shared by Mrs Rich, the wife of the archaeologist who first scientifically began to excavate Babylon, about 1811.

"The rod strikes [wrote Mrs Rich], and from time to time lets itself be seen, and this is principally what we ought to observe as regards Babylon. . . . With difficulty does the traveller of modern times find out the remains of this Queen of Cities; he turns them over with astonishment and contempt; and seems to triumph over her, in carrying away some fragment of her remains. Thus has everything concurred to accomplish most literally that prophesy of Jeremaiah regarding the final ruin of Babylon—Her cities are a desolation, a dry land and a wilderness, a land where no man dwelleth, neither doth any man pass by."

Those who do not feel like joining Mrs Rich in the pleasures of triumph and contempt can unite themselves instead with the triumph of Alexander, riding into Babylon, his conquered capital, seeing above him the mighty walls, the pinnacles and palaces, the hanging gardens rising in tiers above the city, seeing before him the processional way paved with coloured tiles, that led through the triumphal gateway of Ishtar to Nebuchadnezzar's palace glittering in the sun.

[1]Dr Leonhart Rauwolff, *Travels into the Eastern Countries* (Ray's *Collection of Travels*, 1693).

The ghosts of Nineveh and Babylon, those mighty cities gone down into the immensities of the desert, have haunted men's minds with a sense of fearful hugeness, with their winged man-headed bulls guarding majestic gates, their improbable Assyrian grandeur. Vanished Assyria is no part of our western heritage; its ruins, uncovered, speak of an alien world in alien tongues; they stun us with aloof astonishment; Sennacherib and Sargon, Nebuchadnezzar and his court, seem as strange and remote as the winged bulls themselves. Not there, as in Greece, do we meet the legends and the myths we know; the ghosts that haunt those deserts are not the familiars of our childhood tales.

10

Nor yet are the ghosts of Thebes. Egyptian Thebes: enormously huge, enormously old, so old that no one knows its beginning; the massive, magnificent sprawl, lying along both banks of the Nile with its temples and palaces, prehistoric halls, great avenues of sphinxes, colossal statues, obelisks and sculptures, miles of immemorial tombs, Pharaohs and treasures, is outside the coverage of imagination. The scale is too vast, the antiquity too prehistoric, the gods and the Pharaohs too mysteriously of the Nile. All down history Thebes, both before and after ruin, has imposed itself on the human mind as a wonder of the world. "Egyptian Thebes," as Achilles said to Odysseus, "where the houses are full of treasure, and through every one of a hundred gates two hundred warriors with their chariots and horses come"—that was the Theban reputation among the Greeks. Diodorus tells of its magnificent temples; fabulous wealth poured into it under the Pharaohs; it was enriched continuously with noble buildings and sculptures by almost every king who reigned over it; plundered and assaulted, it was raised again, until finally destroyed under Augustus, after which it remained a collection of ruined villages. But the ruins include four of the most remarkable temples of the world. Karnak, with its gigantic columnar halls, courts, propylaea, temples and sculptures, its immemorial age, and its immense extent, staggers the imagination. It is possibly the most impressive assortment of ruins anywhere. The Roman emperors visited Thebes in awe and covetous cupidity; the colossal statue of the Memnon moaned for them, the avenues of sphinxes and the great halls of sculpture invited plunder; here was the finest affair that they had, in all their perambulations of the world, set eyes on. Hadrian got hints from it for his villa. Lying among ranges of mountains, it sprawled on both sides of the Nile; all fabulous, monstrous Egypt was evoked. For four thousand years travellers have flocked there to gaze and marvel. It was, one would imagine, a great deal finer before it was ruined; it is not among those ruins which gain by decay. But, in decay, it has been generally exalted to the position of chief ruin of the world. "The ancient city of Thebes," wrote Dr Pococke, on a fine note of exaltation, after measuring everything he saw and describing each temple and hall with a wealth of detail in which one loses one's way, "celebrated by the first of poets and historians that are now extant; that venerable city the date of whose ruin is older than the foundation of most other cities; and yet such vast and surprising remains are still to be seen of such magnificence and solidity, as may convince anyone that beholds them, that without some extraordinary accidents they must have lasted for ever. . . ."[1]

In their less articulate way, British royalty, over a century later, no doubt felt much the same. The Prince and Princess of Wales, touring the east in 1869, processed on asses from Luxor to Karnac, among the cheers of a multitude. The beautiful Princess rode a milk-white ass, caparisoned in red velvet and gold, the Prince a darker animal. Round them cantered nobility and gentry, dragomans and fellaheen, on horses, asses and camels, "some two hundred people, all in full cry and merry as the morn. And the solemn grandeur of the ruined temples came on us at last! Well! It is in the idea of 'what must have been' that much of the impression produced by these ruins is based. They are the only works of human hands that I know of which produce the effect of awe", for these stones were erected by men "in the nonage of the world".[2] So reflected Dr William Russell, physician to the royal party. They walked down the Avenue of Sphinxes, saw courts, pylons, inscriptions, palaces, halls built in 1380 B.C., obelisks, labyrinths of ruins, found it extremely hot (104 inside the ruins), lunched in the great Hall of Rameses, consuming a

[1]Richard Pococke, *A Description of the East* (1743).
[2]Dr William Russell, *Diary in the East* (1869).

banquet which would have astonished even that luxury-loving monarch. There followed pipes, coffee, conversation, more ruin-seeing; the heated Princess cantered about on her white donkey, protected by parasol and veil from the violent sun. They returned to Luxor; "we were sated with ruin, and the works of Amunoph and Rameses began to pall." But, "what joy to have seen them when perfect, when priest-kings went along sphinx-guarded avenues to Karnac!" It was a relief to get back to the royal ship, where, surrounded by an illuminated flotilla, they banqueted yet again.

II

Turn from the alien and mysterious Nile, that gigantic serpent that winds so fabulously, so ungraspably, back through history. Turn, then, to Mycenae and Tiryns; enter the world of ancient gods and heroes and their fearful yet familiar doings, the world that dips and shifts, anchorless and chartless, behind the dawn of history. One is not sure when history dawned; anyhow Mycenae was founded by Perseus, was powerful fifteen centuries before Christ, and was destroyed in 468 B.C. That is enough to stir us, as it stirred Pausanias eighteen hundred years ago. The attitude of that garrulous, precise, placid tourist towards the ruins he saw and described seems, on the whole, unemotional; but he dearly loved the legends that surrounded them. Genuine ruin-feeling was, we must assume, faint in this admirable traveller; historic reverence and inquisitive legend-hunting were with him major impulses. He looked back on Perseus building Mycenae, noticed the Lion Gate in the citadel wall constructed by the Cyclops, the fountain among the ruins called Persea, the tomb and treasure house of Atreus, the tombs of Agamemnon, Electra, Clytemnestra, and the infant twins born to Cassandra; then off he went to Argos, examining the remains of temples on the way. He was not concerned, as later visitors to Mycenae have been concerned, to search among the ruins of this Homeric city for antiquities, for relics of the ancient Aegean civilization; he does not mention (indeed, he seldom does) picking up and examining pottery or metal ornaments; the singular incuriosity of our ancestors of the first and second centuries with regard to such things is striking, when one compares it with their intense interest in legends and in the doings of men and gods. They were fascinated by tombs, since heroes and kings were buried in them; by treasuries, because kings had stored their treasure there; by temples, because gods had made these their abode; by statues, because these were of gods or persons; types of ancient art and architecture as such impressed them, it would seem, less. Even the elder Pliny's inquiring mind did not induce him to dig much for antiquities. Pausanias's deep interest in the Mycenae ruins sounds a different note from that of the learned seventeenth-century travellers and nineteenth-century archaeologists: but the difference may, after all, be mainly in the sound. To-day, like Pausanias, we observe the Lion Gate, and fancy the spring that rises near it to be the fountain that Perseus found among the mushrooms, admire the fragments of the Cyclopean walls, the Treasury of Atreus, the tombs, the remains of palace and temple, muse on the terrible family life led by the royal house of Pelops, as Edmond About mused at the Lion Gate on a Sunday morning a century ago, with the shocked pleasure of one reading the more sensational Sunday papers. Through the great gate, he recalled, King Agamemnon had gone out with Iphigenia whom he intended to butcher; by the same gate, when he returned from conquering Troy, his dark wife and her lover awaited him, with the shirt in which she enveloped him while her lover clove his head with an axe. Through this gate came Orestes her son, who was to murder his mother and her lover. Within these walls Atreus had killed the children of his brother, making of them "*cette abominable cuisine qui épouvanta le soleil. Mycènes a tout l'air de ce qu'elle a été, un nid d'horribles sacripants*". Its walls, About thought, had a peculiarly villainous physiognomy.

Indeed, to reflect on the extraordinary goings on that occurred when the ruins we survey were in their hey-day must ever be among the pleasures they afford us, and such reflections have profoundly moved those who have gazed on ruined cities, castles, palaces and abbeys. But even had Mycenae never harboured the stormy family that gave its name to the Peloponnese, had Agamemnon, Clytemnestra and Orestes played out their furious drama elsewhere, still its ruins, set on their hill in a mountain-guarded glen, must engage the emotions by their fame, their ancientness, and the splendour of the fragments of a dimly-divined cultural past.

"I approached the Cyclopean city of Perseus [wrote Dr Dodwell a hundred and forty years ago] with a greater degree of veneration than any other place in Greece had inspired. Its remote antiquity, enveloped in the deepest recesses of recorded time, and its present extraordinary remains, combined to fill my mind with a sentiment in which awe was mingled with admiration. I was not so forcibly impressed at Athens, at Delphi, or at Troy! With my thoughts thus wandering back to the earliest ages of antiquity, and engrossed with events of more than three thousand years past, I approached the royal and venerable capital of Agamemnon.[1]"

Dodwell, living before the Schliemann and later excavations, could not see all of Mycenae that we see to-day. He saw the long irregular triangle of the pre-historic acropolis rising above the lower town of the sixth century, the walls, the celebrated Treasury of Atreus, which he describes, with drawings, stone by stone. But he could not see the tombs of the royal cemetery where the Schliemanns found skeletons adorned with golden masks and gems, or the Homeric palace on the acropolis, with its great hall, the bases of columns, its staircase to a higher floor. The acropolis wall is fourteenth- or fifteenth-century, that of the lower town sixth-century. Over the main gate crouch the lions which have given so much pleasure to visitors for some three thousand years. From the gate climbs the paved ramp whereon chariots drove to and from the palace: along it went festal processions, royal triumphs, marches, the comings and goings of the rich Myceneans in their opulent broad-streeted city, as Homer called it. How did they live, in this city rich in gold? What were their daily doings? We know the general social scheme of the Bronze Age Aegean civilizations, led by Crete; the king in his palace on the citadel, with a few good-sized mansions grouped round and a crowd of little dwellings; we know the structure of the palace, the high civilization of the rooming and sanitary arrangements, the domed tombs, the style of the pictorial and ceramic and metallurgic arts, of the sculptures, friezes and reliefs. All this we know from Crete, from Mycenae, from Tiryns, from Hissarlik. The rest we may imagine; we get little help from history or from legend, for legend is too early, history too late. These intriguing gods, those storm-

[1]Edward Dodwell, *A classical and topographical tour through Greece* (1811)

ing royal persons, those bloody vengeances—they seem to bombinate in a vacuum, passions without habitations, so that the fifth-century dramatists even forgot where Agamemnon and his family had lived long ago, and placed them in Argos. In any case they are not fifth-century Hellenes, and are hard to know, both for Aeschylus and ourselves. Standing within those broken walls, beside the royal tombs now rifled of their treasure, among the scattered ruins of small dwellings, one drops through thirty centuries into a rich, great-walled city of broad paved streets where chariot wheels grind and creak and, over the vine-grown slopes below, the mean huts of peasants sprawl, and the singing in the mountains is in a strange Aegean tongue.

"And so this city, which in ancient times had enjoyed such felicity, possessing great men and having to its credit memorable achievements, met with such an end, and has remained uninhabited down to our own times."[1]

An over-statement, of the kind usually made about destroyed cities, which are seldom quite abandoned by their citizens; ruined Mycenae had been slightly inhabited through the four centuries of which Diodorus wrote, since its destruction by the jealous Argives in 468 B.C. In the second century A.D., when Pausanias saw it, it was probably still lived in, by those tenacious humble locals whose insubstantial dwellings cling like swallows' nests to the broken columns of temples, or burrow like fox-holes among the foundations and shards of wrecked palaces, or rise like mushrooms in waste places inside what is left of city walls, pasture their herds on the sprouting grass, watering them from the still springing fountains. There is no need to assume Mycenae empty when two second-century poets from Mitylene bewailed her as a total loss. This birthplace of heroes, wrote Alpheius, was now scarcely above ground.

"So, as I passed thee by, did I see thee, unhappy Mycenae, more waste than any goat-fold. The goat-herds pointed thee out, and an old man said, 'Here stood the city rich in gold, the city that the Cyclops built.'"

And Pompeius,

"Though I, Mycenae, am but dust here in the desert, he who

[1]Diodorus Siculus, *History*.

looks on the glorious city of Ilion, whose walls I trampled and emptied the house of Priam, shall know how mighty I was of old."

However that may have been, Mycenae seems to have been pretty well abandoned and gone to earth in the middle ages, and when the golden age of tourism dawned in the seventeenth century, its ruins were certainly not a home except for shepherds and their flocks. It has fascinated the imaginations of eighty-odd generations since it fell; only the Turks, "that host of dull oppressors, who have spread the shades of dense ignorance over the land once illuminated by science, and who unconsciously trampled on the venerable dust of the Pelopidae and the Atridae",[1] have remained unmoved by it. Chateaubriand to whom it was pointed out by "*un enfant tout nu, un pâtre*", went into one of his usual rhapsodies, described the Lion Gate with such *empressement* and inaccuracy that his recent critical commentator, M. Emile Malkis, wrote in a note, "*Il semble que le voyageur ne se soit guère approché de ces ruines*", and congratulated himself in a characteristically exuberant and often derided passage, on having discovered for himself the tomb of Clytemnestra. However near or far he got to his ruins, no one could say that Chateaubriand did not enjoy them and make them sound enjoyable; his frequent illusion that he was a pioneer in the field added both to his pleasure and that of his readers. As to Gabriele d'Annunzio, he was stirred by Mycenae to a drama of immense passion and incest, inspired by the passionate and incestuous Atridae who had reigned there.

I do not know if Tiryns, Mycenae's neighbour and predecessor, has inspired any modern plays. It is even more ancient than Mycenae, its walls still more Cyclopean (the most Cyclopean walls in Greece), its palace more Homeric, in fact the star Homeric palace on the Greek mainland. Homer admired the citadel walls, Pausanias was shown the bedrooms of the daughters of Proetus, the first Tirynthian king, Schliemann excavated the palace on the acropolis, and the sixth-century town, of which Dodwell reported that "time has not left one vestige". Still, he annoyed the suspicious Turks by taking a view of the ruins with his camera obscura. It has always added to the pleasure of Tiryns sightseers that Hercules lived there for a time; it would add to it further

[1]Edward Dodwell, *Tour Through Greece* (1811).

could they be shown his house; but even Pausanias, who was shown so many legendary habitations in the towns he visited, was not shown this. Destroyed at the same time as Mycenae, Tiryns seems to have harboured for some time after its debacle a continuous life, and a Byzantine city flourished there; probably a later Middle Age city too. Gradually, or suddenly, it became a group of noble half-buried ruins, until the great excavations of the last hundred years committed our vague Homeric imaginings so dramatically to history.

12

Most dramatically in Crete, where, after the speculations and partial explorings of travellers had groped for two thousand years after the ruins of a mighty civilization whose ghost has always haunted the mountains and shores of that mysterious island, and of the Greek mainland, the legend at last took shape, rising from the earth in the shape of cities, palaces, and the rich decorations of a culture that was a thousand years before Homer, seventeen centuries before the age of Pericles, over two thousand before the Christian era. The legends became real: Minos in his great palace, the minotaur in the labyrinth that Daedalus had made for him, Theseus, Ariadne, the birth of Zeus, even "Europa, a young lady, swimming into Crete upon a prestigious bull"; they all sprang to life, among palaces and pleasures, corridors of huge Aladdin jars, vivid frescoes of flowers, sea creatures, bull fights, youths and maidens, huge-pillared courts, labyrinthine mazes of rooms, subterranean dungeons, and the most admirable plumbing *à l'anglaise*. In 1898 Sir Arthur Evans bought a plot of land from the Turks; within two years there had been uncovered the prehistoric palace of Knossos, its great Throne Room, its frescoes, its vast warren of chambers, corridors and courts. Sir Arthur, their discoverer and presiding genius, threw up a skeleton tower from which to survey the ruins, and settled near them in the Villa Ariadne, lunching his friends under the olives, while wine flowed and mandolins played and Cretans danced; a brilliant showman, having conjured a civilization out of the earth he enjoyed it so much, and made everyone else enjoy it so much, that there was never a dull moment. From excavation he proceeded to reconstruction, building sham ruins on to ancient ones, causing to be painted gaudy frescoes of bulls, erecting columns with a downward taper that greatly vexes many archaeologists, throwing up bulls' horns over porticos, making the palace so nearly habitable that it has been one of the pleasures of tourists staying at the Villa Ariadne (lately the Cretan headquarters of the British archeaological school in Athens, now handed over to the Greek government) to roam about the ruins assigning the various rooms to themselves and their relations for dwellings. The Minoan civilization has been brought across the threshold of the western modern imagination, to become part of the familiar landscape of our minds, like the Hellenic and the Roman, only still with that mysterious and monstrous strangeness which lends to pre-Hellenic ages something of the dissolving, uneven quality of dreams. It is almost too much for us to take.

For now all Crete has sprung into ancient life, its soil everywhere yielding up traditions and legends of antique myth, carved in stone palaces, cities and streets. No sooner had Sir Arthur Evans uncovered Crete than Miss Boyd of the American Exploration Society saw a ridge at Gournia, near the bay of Mirabello, suspiciously strewn with ancient potsherds; losing no time, she got thirty diggers to work, and in three days got down to a Bronze Age city—houses, paved streets, vases, a palace—and had found the most complete pre-Hellenic town yet discovered. Middle Minoan, it was built before the great palace period of the Cretan golden age; its small palace, less pretentious than Knossos or Phaestos, was more like a country manor house later enlarged and adorned into a palace. In the centre of the town was a shrine with its goddess idol, twined with snakes and doves. Italians meanwhile discovered Gagia Triada, and the most impressive palace in Crete, Phaestos, standing on the spur of a hill range. A contemporary and rival of Knossos, with Gortyna, one of the three chief Cretan cities, Phaestos must have been almost as magnificent; its general effect to-day is more so, and its different periods less confused. It has the same intricate jumble of corridors, courts, stairways, chambers, cellars, terraces, walls, bathrooms and lavatories, brilliant frescos and precious inlay. No reconstruction has been done on Phaestos, which stands bare and stark on its hill, a ruin for three thousand years, stripped now of the Greek and Roman and later habitations which once hid it.

Homer said in the Iliad that Crete had a hundred cities, in the Odyssey he made them ninety: these cities never perished; destroyed, they were re-occupied by new inhabitants, lived on under successive layers of fresh cultures. Strabo, writing fifteen centuries after Minoan Knossos had fallen in ruin, spoke of the city (with which he had family connections) as a going concern, occupied by a Roman colony. The Knossos palace had never been re-inhabited after the Greek invasion of Crete; it remained, while still visible, a ghost-haunted labyrinth, mysterious and dark, possibly the legendary labyrinth of the minotaur; but the region round it was colonized and occupied, like most of the island towns, till they decayed away into villages, the homes of pirates, finally the "wretched heaps of stones" observed by early travellers. It is largely this strange succession that gives the keenest pleasure to the ordinary ruin-viewer who is not a single-minded Minoan; there is something excessively romantic in seeing the Achaean culture imposed on the last Minoan, the Dorian on the Achaean, the Roman on the Hellenic, the Byzantine on the Roman, then the Saracen, the Venetian, the Turkish, and the Cretan of to-day. Until the excavations of the last half century conjured up from the bowels of the earth the pomps and splendours of Minoan and pre-Mycenaean, these later layers of ruin were all that enquiring travellers had to enjoy; with complacent pity we read of their search for inscriptions and marbles, their false identifications of sites, their interminable wrangles, their discoveries of the labyrinth (for this, in one place or another, they one and all found), and of the birth-cave of Zeus. Of the famous ancient cities they found little. Pococke speaks of "the small remains of old Cnossus"; Andrea Cornaro, a century before him, of marbles, "*infinità di rovine*", and a long wall; Savary, in 1728, writes that "*ces monceaux de pierres, d'anciens murs à moitié démolis, et le nom de Cnossou, que cet emplacement a conservé, font connaître, d'une manière certaine, le lieu qu'elle occupait*"; while Dr Robert Pashley, the learned and contentious tourist of 1833, said that "all the now existing vestiges of the metropolis of Crete are some rude masses of Roman brickwork", since Cnossos under Venetian and Turkish rule had "dwindled down into this miserable hamlet, and the few shapelees heaps of masonry which alone recall to the remembrance of the passing traveller its ancient and bygone splendour". And so it was all over the fabled island, which has since blossomed into such pre-historic grandeur. Where there were rubbled mounds, palaces have risen; heaps of stones, shovelled aside, have uncovered city streets. Turn but a stone and start a palace, the amazed onlooker may feel. But archaeologists do not altogether care for this easy view. "Minoan sites are so plentiful," one of them wrote, "that the impression may have gained ground that excavators had only to walk up to a spot and dig, to find what they sought. This is by means the case." They had, in fact, quite a long search before they came on Phaestos. All the same, city and palace hunting in Crete seems so rewarding that one inevitably gets an impression of an earth teeming with buried buildings, and not alone in Crete. The mainland too may conceal under its deserts and hills a stony maze of ancient towns, which may one day in this atomic age be uncovered, taking history back yet again, beyond Minoa, beyond Egyptian Thebes, to who can say what unrealizable antiquity and pre-neolithic dawns of human life?

But those early travellers in Crete, who entertained no such grandiose dreams, greatly enjoyed what they could see. They went about probing ruins, copying inscriptions, digging up and stealing statues, condemning the superficial accounts and errors of previous observers, from Strabo, Ptolemy, Diodorus, Pliny and the other ancients, to the medieval and sixteenth and seventeenth century tourists, and the almost equally fallible visitors of the eighteenth and nineteenth centuries. "This is another fatal objection to Professor So-and-So's hypothesis," Dr Pashley of Cambridge kept declaring. With tenacity and through many pages they argued about sites. "The position of Aptera being once settled, we shall soon determine that of Berecyntos." All this determining of positions must have been a charming employment. But to have them already determined saves time, and sets the traveller free to enjoy what he sees.

Then, of course, there was the exciting, awful pleasure of the Labyrinth, which all visitors found in different places. William Lithgow, in 1609, saw its entry but dared not penetrate into it.

"We durst not enter, for there are many hollow places within it, so that if a man stumble or fall he can hardly be rescued. It is cut forthe, with many intricating wayes, on the face of a little hill,

20 Lady Hester Stanhope's arrival at Palmyra. Lithograph, 1846

21 Goethe resting in the Campagna. Oil painting by Joh. H W. Tischbein, 1788

22 Petra Lithograph by Léon de Laborde, 1830

joyning with Mount Ida, having many doores and pillars. Here is where Theseus by the help of Ariadne the daughter of King Minos, taking a bottome of thread, and tying the one end at the first doore, did enter and slay the Minotaurus."[1]

The blood froze and curdled, the hair rose, at the thought of entering such a place. And how much more now, when Theseus and the horrid Minotaur have risen from the interring ages to confront us, and the dark and haunted labyrinth is a mazy sprawl of courts and endless corridors, its walls painted with fierce bulls; from which, if we venture solitary, we may not return. *Plerique enim dii ex Creta prodierunt*, and they were not, for the most part beneficent gods: they still brood unexorcised over the pillared lanes and courts of the restored palace of King Minos, where holiday-making Cretans throng at week-ends, unintimidated and unawed, making festival among those brooding, decked-up ruins.

13

How different the effect on the mind of ruined Corinth!

Corinthian ruins, catastrophically created, dramatically wholesale, had from the first a fine press. The rich proud ancient city, Homer's *ἀφνειόν τε Κόρινθον*, treasury of art, emporium of wealth, so expensive to live in that the saying ran "not everyone can go to Corinth", its citadel poised so grandly on the craggy mountain above, the two blue gulfs spread below, its walls fortified with such extravagant strength—this superb city came crashing down in flames, and Mummius's Roman soldiery hacked their way about streets, temples, rich villas, sepulchres, great warehouses stored with merchandise, galleries set with marble and bronze statues and bright with paintings, smashing, looting, destroying and massacring, in philistine triumph and greed. They left behind them chaos, piled corpses, an almost razed city. Undestroyed statues, bronzes and paintings were given away to anyone who asked, looted by anyone who liked.

The dramatic contrast between the city of blackened ruins and broken stones and the magnificence that had been, stirred for a century the pity and the imagination of all who passed that way.

[1]William Lithgow, *Rare Adventures and Painefull Peregrinations* (1632).

9

Poets elegized it: Antipater of Sidon, writing soon after the destruction, over-stated it.

"Not a trace is left of thee, ill-fated city, but war has seized and devoured all."

This, of course, was not so; even to-day part of the Temple of Apollo stands, seven of its Doric columns upright and supporting a fragment of entablature; and visitors as late as the sixteenth, seventeenth and eighteenth centuries saw more. Cicero, visiting the ruins a century after the destruction, and just before Caesar built Corinth again, was deeply distressed by the sight. Melancholy pleasure and pity for the broken ancient magnificence stirred his humane and scholarly mind.

Wrecked Corinth lay thus derelict, lived in by a few, but uncleared and unbuilt, from 146 to 44 B.C. Then Julius Caesar, who knew the importance of its position, set to work to rebuild it, clearing away the hundred years of ruins and building up a fine Roman town. The freedmen he sent to colonize it opened and rifled the tombs, taking from them to Rome a wealth of bronzes, marbles, terra-cottas. The Roman town sprang up on the Greek foundations; a Roman temple on a Greek market, Roman theatres on Greek, a two-storied façade on the ancient fountain of Pirene. Roman merchants and gentlemen came and grew rich on the once-more flourishing sea trade; they built their villas where those of rich Corinthians had stood; digging about, they came on beautiful objects buried in débris; in their theatres they had gladiatorial shows; they soon became licentious enough to qualify for the diatribes of St Paul; perhaps they absorbed it from this ancient site of libertinism; and such influences may be numbered among the pleasures of ruins. From Acrocorinth the debauched residents looked complacently down over the incomparable view—Parnassus and Helicon, snow-clad, to the north, the gulf of Corinth to the west, the Saronic gulf and its islands to the east. At the foot of Acrocorinth the great piles of scattered ruins became Colonia Julia Corinthos, the smart Roman town, to be later embellished by beneficent emperors and rich merchant patrons in their turn.

How much of Greek Corinth Pausanias, two centuries after the rebuilding, saw, he did not himself seem to know, he has much to say of the Roman monuments, temples and statues, and as always (and this is where Pausanias is often boring) more of the legends connected with them. The ruins that had moved travelling Roman gentlemen to pity long ago were for the most part gone to ground beneath the new town; though there still stood visible a few Greek buildings, of which the chief was the great Doric temple of Apollo, built somewhere about 600 B.C. Pausanias merely mentions it—"on my right hand, a temple and brazen statue of Apollo"—before going off after the fountain of Glauce and stories of Medea; as he does not call the temple ruined, it was presumably whole, either undestroyed by Mummius or restored by the Romans. But after Pausanias's time, Corinth was sacked by Alaric, thrown down by earthquakes, quarried and spoiled by Byzantines, Venetians, Turks; in what state it was in in 1173 when Benjamin of Tudela visited it, we cannot say; Benjamin counted three hundred Jews there, but did not count the columns. Probably the worst damage was done by the Turks, who, during over three centuries of occupation, quarried incessantly; this has been, so far as appears, the main pleasure afforded to them by the finest ruins. The Latin princes and dukes of Achaia and the Morea, on the other hand, found a romantic and chivalrous pleasure in the citadel, which they fortified with stronger walls and towers.

Among the more romantic descriptions of Corinth is Chateaubriand's: his story that he went there himself has been thought to be among "*ses illusions grecques*". He admits that he could not get Turkish leave to ascend to the citadel, the view from which he describes largely in the words of his predecessors, but with added enthusiasm of his own; as to the monuments of Corinth, "*ils n'existent plus*". He could not recollect seeing any columns standing; he suggested that the English had carried them off. "*C'est à se demander si C. a vraiment été à Corinthe*", or if he yielded to that insidious temptation of travellers. . . . From its lack of celebrated ruins, he found the city dull; he had to fall back on those legends of history and poetry which he could associate with Corinth without going there—Jason, Medea, Pegasus, the fountain of Pyrene: he recited lines from the Odyssey, remembered St Paul and his letters to the somewhat lax Christian citizenry, and departed for Megara by a road which did not go by the Isthmus and its temple ruins. To divert attention from all that he had not seen, he mused on his native land; would it ever be devasted like this? It is supposed that actually he rode straight from Argos to Megara without turning aside to Corinth at all. It is pleasant to think of the great romantic envisaging classical ruins thus in his eloquent imagination.

Greatly as travellers have always admired Corinthian ruins, whether or not they have seen them, the keenest pleasure in them was reserved for the American archaeologists who started excavating in 1896, uncovering the buried fountain of Pirene, whose clear spring was first struck out of the rock by the hoof of the drinking Pegasus, and which still waters the town to-day. To find Roman Corinth below the centuries of later building, they had to dig twenty feet down; and five or ten feet below Rome lay Greece. From the topographical account of Pausanias the agora was located, and the long straight street that led to it, and the bordering colonnades that were portico to a row of shops. It was, said the director of the excavations, "the most ecstatic moment of my life" (and an archaeologist's life abounds in ecstatic moments), when part of the road intersecting the Straight Road was laid bare, for at their intersection would be found the agora; "we had hit the bull's-eye and settled the whole topography of Corinth". The diggers too knew ecstasy: one of them, having fallen through loose earth into a suddenly disclosed corner of the agora, emerged crying "*Eureka kolomais*! *Eureka agalmata*!" for he had found columns, found statues. The rewards of Corinthian excavation are rich: Roman basilicas, imperial and Greek sculptures, marble façades, fountains, a Roman odeum, a Greek and Roman theatre, vases, potteries, inscriptions, emerge. Only a small part of the temples and statues seen by Pausanias have yet been unearthed: probably few remain; but this methodical tourist's sober and detailed account of the glories to be seen in and around Corinth in A.D. 170 keep excavators at a high pitch of excitement: almost anything may turn up. And also in the Isthmian regions, where Pausanias saw statues of athletes victorious in the Isthmian games, a theatre and a stadium of white stone, and the temple of Neptune, adorned with brazen tritons, statues of marine deities in a sea of brass, gold horses with ivory hoofs, Amphitrite and Neptune standing in a chariot, the boy Palaemon on a dolphin, Venus, entouraged by nereides, rising from the sea, a horse half a whale, all the delicious marine incidents appropriate to a temple of Poseidon; besides Bellerophon and Pegasus. Other temples Pausanias saw about the Isthmus and on the road to Corinth, where there was no dull hundred yards. To be in this Isthmian sanctuary region, to imagine it holy and glittering with the temples and altars of its ocean gods, set about the shores of the deep blue Saronic gulf and about the long line of the Isthmus wall, where the young athletes strove for the corruptible crown, is to start wistfully searching for traces of this past beauty, so admirably seen, so carefully recorded, eighteen centuries ago. Searchers in the seventeenth century found ruins of walls, temples, theatres, many superb buildings, a half-buried inscription with the name of a Roman restorer and builder. Dr Chandler, in 1765, found some broken fragments of Doric pillars lying on the site of the temple of Neptune, a ruinous Christian church stood there, with the base of a column for its holy table. Most of what Wheeler had seen in 1676 was gone; quarried away to build fortresses and repair the Isthmus wall. Goatherds took Dr Chandler about, but could show him neither theatre nor stadium; the inscribed marble slab seen by Wheeler had been removed to the Verona museum. Dr Dodwell, forty years later, searching the Isthmus with "Pausanias, as usual, my only guide", does not mention the sanctuary precincts; he went straight from Corinth to the port of Cenchrea, seeking sepulchres and the temple of Diana; he found stone quarries and some wall foundations, and, a mile from the sea, the Bath of Helen gushing, salt and tepid, from its rock. The French excavators of later years have located the remains of the theatres. What more may turn up, either in Corinth or about the Isthmus, is any archaeologist's guess. Cicero's *lumen totius Graeciae* is effectively extinguished; only shattered fragments of that bright lamp emerge.

14

Sparta was never a lamp; when Alaric's Goths sacked and destroyed it, little perished that greatly mattered, though in those latter days it was a handsome enough Roman town. Stern Dorian city, it had, when Thucydides wrote of it, nothing splendid, no noble temples or other fine buildings; it resembled rather a straggle of undistinguished villages. It had a theatre, temples, a few sculptures, but no splendour, nothing to show, nothing to indicate the power and prestige of the Peloponnese capital; posterity, looking on its buildings, would scarcely credit its prestige. Six centuries later, Pausanias saw the Romanized town, and one gathers that by then it looked very well; he praises the market-place with its council chambers, its portico made from spoils of the Persian wars and altered in course of time "until it is as large and splendid as it is now", its temples to Caesar and Augustus, its statues of gods, its sanctuaries and tombs. The streets leading from the market place were also well adorned; there was the theatre, "made of white marble and worth seeing", and by it the tomb of Leonidas, with a slab inscribed with the names of those who fought at Thermopylae; the whole city was peopled with statues and holy with shrines and tombs. Many of these monuments were pre-Roman. But their ruins are inconsiderable, and lack that wrecked magnificence that moved Cicero looking on Corinth. "We entered in the Easterne Plaine of Morea, called anciently *Sparta*," wrote William Lithgow in 1614, "where that sometimes famous Citie of Lacedemon flourished, but now sacked, and the lumpes of ruines and memorie only remayne." The lumps of ruin have grown steadily less down the centuries, attacked by earthquakes and Turks, quarried to build medieval Mistrá and modern Sparta. Dr Dodwell added to these normal agents of destruction the dilapidating fury of the Abbé Fourmont, who, sent to Greece in 1729 by Louis XV to copy inscriptions, embarked (according to himself) on an orgy of destruction, not only destroying many inscriptions after copying them with, said his critics, the most mendacious inaccuracy, and fabricating many others, but boasting also of his worse than Gothic demolitions of whole cities, "*Vandalisme*," says his biographer, "*qu'on ne saurait attribuer qu'à l'esprit d'intolérance religieuse, qu'il avait pris parmi les solitaires d'Anjou*" (where he had once spent eight years in a hermitage). Apparently a maniac, he claimed to have destroyed five Greek towns.

"For over a month thirty, and sometimes forty or sixty workmen have been knocking down, destroying and exterminating the town of Sparta. . . . I have only four more towers to demolish . . To tell you frankly, I am astonished at this expedition. I have never read that, since the revival of letters, it has come into anyone's head to throw down thus whole towns. . . . At this moment I am occupied with the last destruction of Sparta. Imagine, if you can, in what joy I am. It is one of the greatest joys; but it would be extreme had I been allowed more time,"

for many other ancient cities of Greece awaited his attentions. In future, he hoped, the very site of Sparta would be unknown, but he would be able to make it known, and "I had only this way of making my journey illustrious". There is no evidence but his own that he actually did much damage to anything but inscribed marbles. Fifty years before he was at Sparta, the English traveller Vernon reported it "a desert place", with the walls of the towers and foundations of the temples remaining, and the theatre entire, but columns demolished. Successive depredations through the eighteenth century produced what Dodwell described as "the state of total ruin to which the Laconian capital is at present reduced." He, in those pre-excavation days, found the ruins "almost unintelligible"; but he always found pleasure in ruins, even in "heaps of large stones tossed about in a sort of promiscuous wreck". He saw the theatre, its marble coating gone, a sepulchral chamber which he half accepted as the tomb of Leonidas, "many other detached ruins," and several inscriptions, which he copied. Having taken a panoramic view from a hill, he went on to see the remains of Amyclae. The best thing about Sparta, he thought, was its magnificent setting and scenery;

"all the plains and all the mountains that I have seen are surpassed in the variety of their combinations and the beauty of their appearance by the plain of Lacedaemon and Mount Taygeton. . . . This scenery is enlivened by the lucid current of the Eurotas gliding close to the ruins, and gently meandering towards the south."[1]

But the happiest Spartan visit (setting aside the triumphantly-destructive Fourmont's) was probably Chateaubriand's. He spent there in 1806, animated by the combined joys of antiquity and coxcombry, a most delicious two days. Beginning his visit in some confusion, caused by the misleading statements of some romancing travellers that the site of ancient Sparta was Mistrá, he climbed

[1]Edward Dodwell, *Tour Through Greece* (1819).

up to the great Frankish castle that crowns this romantic place, and surveyed the view of the Laconian plain, trying to discern the contours and landmarks of the city of Lycurgus in a town

"whose architecture offered me nothing but a confused mixture of the Oriental manner, and of the Gothic, Greek and Italian styles, without one poor little antique ruin. . . . Sparta was overthrown in the dust, buried in the tomb, trodden underfoot by Turks, dead, dead, quite dead!"[1]

After much vain questioning of native guides, however, he discovered his mistake, and hastened away from Mistrá, whose Byzantine charms were not for him, to seek what the guides pointed out as "Palaeocherzi". Leaping on to his horse, half an hour before daybreak, he set off at full gallop for Lacedaemon. With the first light he "perceived some ruins and a long wall of antique construction; my heart began to palpitate". Then he saw the ancient theatre, and

"I cannot describe the confused feelings which overpowered me. The hill at whose foot I stood was, then, the hill of the citadel of Sparta. . . . I dismounted, and ran all the way up the hill of the citadel. As I reached the top, the sun was rising behind the Menelaion hills. What a beautiful spectacle! But how melancholy! . . . I stood motionless, in a kind of stupor. A mixture of admiration and grief checked my steps and my thoughts; the silence round me was profound. Wishing, at least, to make echo speak in a spot where the human voice is no longer heard, I shouted with all my might, 'Leonidas'! No ruin repeated this great name, and Sparta herself seemed to have forgotten it."

His agitation a little subsided, he began to examine the ruins, measuring, counting, trying to identify what he saw with what Pausanias had described. Looking at the ruins visible above ground, he named them as he fancied, calling one of them Helen's Temple. "In two others I fancied I beheld the heroic monuments of Aegeus and Cadmus". North, south, east and west he gazed, discerning or imagining landmarks. The whole site was desert: the new rectilinear Sparta of King Otho was still thirty years ahead. Lacedaemon lay dead.

"The sun parches it in silence, and is incessantly devouring the marble of the tombs. Not a plant adorned the ruins, not a bird,

[1]Chateaubriand, *Itinéraire de Paris à Jérusalem* (1811).

not an insect, not a creature enlivened them except millions of lizards, which crawled without noise up and down the sides of the scorching walls. A dozen half-wild horses were feeding here and there upon the withered grass."

Descending at last from the citadel, he reached the river Eurotas, overgrown with reeds and rose laurels, from which he drank abundantly, and plucked blue lilies in memory of Helen, before taking a walk along its banks. It was all romantic, all delightful. He pictured the river rejoicing, after centuries of oblivion, in the footsteps of a stranger on its shores; little as he cared for Spartan manners, he was not blind to Spartan qualities, and was moved by strong emotion as he trampled on their dust. After his walk he returned to the citadel to lunch off bread and dried figs in the theatre, and then disappointed his janissary, who had hoped they were about to depart, by settling down to write his observations for two hours. He then wandered from ruin to ruin, seeking the tomb of Leonidas and occupied in pleasing reflections about the illustrious dead, and about how (for he was unceasingly a patriot) nearly all the previous information about the ruins of Greece had been provided by his own countrymen; the English travel reports had been comparatively unsatisfactory, and many of them, thought Chateaubriand, had probably been taken without acknowledgment from the French. As to his own researches, "at least I have joined my name to Sparta's, which can alone save it from oblivion; I have, so to speak, rediscovered that immortal city, giving about the ruins details till now unknown". (As a contemporary critic remarked, when this vaunt was published, never had one day been so well spent by any traveller, and M. de Chateaubriand might well rejoice in a success which had escaped researches infinitely longer and more laborious.)

Night drew on, and the traveller reluctantly tore himself from "these illustrious ruins, from the shade of Lycurgus, the memories of Thermopylae, and all the fictions of legend and history. . . . The sun sank behind Taygetus, so that I had seen him begin and end his course on the ruins of Lacedaemon. It was three thousand five hundred and forty-three years since he had first risen and set on this just-born city" (which would make it 1737 B.C., comments his acid annotator, "*la date est incompréhensible, mais C. copie La Guilletière*"). "I departed, my mind full of the objects I had just seen, and given over to inexhaustible reflections: such days enable one to bear many misfortunes with patience."

He rode with his servant up the bank of the Eurotas for an hour and a half; then they lit a fire, supped off a gigot of mutton, wine, and water from the Eurotas (for Chateaubriand always made a point of drinking from famous rivers), and passed the night under a laurel tree, watching the Milky Way reflected in the stream. Remembering the pleasure he had felt in youth while sleeping out in American forests, he decided that to a man in mature life the ancient lands were more enjoyable—"old deserts which give me at will the walls of Babylon or the legions of Pharsalia, *grandia ossa!*"

It may be supposed that no visitor to Sparta since Paris ever got more pleasure out of it. Gifted with a double vision, he was enabled at once to peruse and profit by all the previous accounts of travellers, and to say, with complacence, "*très-peu de voyageurs ont pénétré jusqu'à Sparte; aucun n'en a complètement décrit les ruines*", and to boast himself "*le premier auteur moderne qui ait donné la description de Laconie d'après la vue même des lieux*". His vanity, "which, bye the bye, is not less entertaining at Sparta than elsewhere," as Sir William Gell wrote of him in 1824, tempted hoaxers; one of these published a description of a magnificent temple that the poet had incomprehensibly missed, though it stood only five hundred yards from him; such teasing could not deflate his pleasure in his glorious experiences and achievements. The more down-to-earth precision of his predecessors and contemporaries in the Laconian field did not daunt him; he drew on them, used their maps, plans and descriptions (often to his own detriment, for they were sometimes wrong and he sometimes did not get near enough to what they described to correct them), then blew them away with his airy "*très-peu de voyageurs . . .*". It is reasonable to believe him happier at Lacedaemon than La Guilletière, Le Roy, Spon and Wheeler, Mr Vernon, Dr Dodwell, Sir William Gell, Mr Leake, Edmond About, or even the nineteenth- and twentieth-century excavators: much happier than those emissaries from Sybaris who, having paid a visit to Sparta, declared themselves no longer surprised at the courage in battle of Spartans, for, after all, what life had they to leave? One of hard seats, wretched food, comfortless beds, everything of the most disagreeable.

Sybarite ghosts, revisiting its site, might be imagined to triumph over the plight of the odious city, reduced, though not to their own nothingness, at least to a jumble of scarcely recognizable wrecks. It would be useless for them, it is useless for us, to search Sparta's suburb Therapne for the Sparta of which Homer wrote; of the great vaulted hall, the gleaming palace where Menelaus and Helen held their court, not even shards remain. The pleasure of Homeric Sparta must feed wholly on imagination.

15

So, very nearly, must that of Boeotian Thebes, whose legend, like Troy's, has haunted man's romantic mind for over twenty-five centuries. There is little left of ancient Thebes; on the site of its Cadmeia, or acropolis, stands the present small town which is its ghost. The Acropolis itself has not been since the eleventh century In 1173, when Michael Akominatus wrote of it, there was, it seems, no more of it than we see to-day. Archaeologists have found their pleasure in tracing the extent of the ancient city, and the line of its walls—those walls which rose when Amphion played his lyre and sang—*movit Amphion lapides canendo*. The seven celebrated gates have been a difficulty. Pausanias said he was shewn seven; archaeologists say this is improbable, as the gates were destroyed by Demetrius in 290 B.C. Still, in A.D. 396, when Alaric stormed through Boetica, Thebes was still too strong a fortified city for him to take. No doubt the local guides shewed the seven gates, or what passed for them, to Pausanias, who was shown a good deal more everywhere than we are. The Thebans showed him delightful things—the ruins of Pindar's house, which Alexander spared when he destroyed Thebes, and which must, when Pausanias was there, have been over six hundred years old; but older still were the ruins of the palace occupied by Amphitryon after his expulsion from Tiryns, and Alcmene's bedroom in it where Zeus visited her, and where, presumably, Heracles was born, and the house of Cadmus, with the bedroom of Harmony his wife, at whose wedding the muses sang, and that of his daughter Semele, which was wrecked by Jove's thunderbolt, and which visitors were not allowed to enter. All these Pausanias was shewn, and all the tombs and sanctuaries of the city and its environs, and the tomb where Hector's bones, removed from Troy, had been laid. His legend-filled mind reflected on Cadmus, on the fate of Oedipus, on the Thebaïd, on Amphion's walls, built with such facility, enduring so long, on Heracles, Dionysus, the unfortunate Dirce and her well, the Seven against Thebes, the city's shifty behaviour during wars, its massacre by Alexander, its rebuilding, and its whole remarkable history down to his own time. Even though he could not see the magnificent castle built up by Nicholas of St Omer in the thirteenth century on the ruined city walls, and knew nothing of the fine life to be led in Thebes by the Frankish dukes of Athens, it must be supposed that the pleasure derived by Pausanias from Thebes was greater than ours. For we cannot even believe that we are seeing Pindar's house, whose ruins are, or were, said by Thebans to lie hard by Dirce's fountain. John Cam Hobhouse went, with his usual thoroughness, into this matter in 1809, and decided that the alleged fountain (tepid, he discovered by bathing in it) was really the stream of Ismenus, that Dirce sprang more to the west, and that Pindar's house was not to be identified. Hobhouse, writing before there had been much excavation, found few traces of the ancient city; he slightly disdained the romantic fantasies of Dr Clarke, who perceived vestiges too readily, and who doubted

"whether in any part of Greece there can be found a nobler association of sublime and dignified objects than was here collected into one view: the *living* fountain—the *speaking* sepulchre—the *Cadmoean* citadel—the *Ogygian* plain—overwhelming the mind with every recollection that has been made powerful by genius and consecrated by inspiration—where every zephyr breathing from Helicon and Parnassus over the mouldering relics of Thebes seems to whisper as it passes the names of *Epaminondas*, *Pindar*, *Homer* and *Orpheus*."[1]

Rather insubstantial, as Hobhouse comments. He himself got his pleasure from topographical explory, and from the fragments of ancient marble built into the ruined church of St Luke on the site of a temple to Apollo. As he remarked, "the Greeks have done a service to antiquarians by heaping up into the composition of their churches all portable remains"; some of these fragments had inscriptions. Of Nicholas de St Omer's great castle of Santa-

[1] Dr Clarke, *Travels* (1810-23).

meri, of which one tower remains, lordly feudal relic of the Latin conquest, Hobhouse has nothing to say.

But there is no doubt that ruined Thebes was most enjoyed by the residents in that palatial castle, the medieval Dukes of Athens who held their court there. It is permissible to suppose that these historically ignorant but zestful dukes were powerfully inspired by the mighty past that then lay more perceptibly about them than now—the Cadmeia, the broken walls of Amphion, the seven gates, the ghosts of the warriors of Thebes (they would know the Theban romances), all the traces of "*les géants*", of whom they knew so little, but whose presence must have haunted their devastated acropolis with disturbing dreams.

The ruinous dreams that haunted the Franks and Venetians who, in the middle ages, turned Nauplia into a strong fortress city, piling their towers on the two steep hills above the little town, using the ancient walls as foundations, were inspired by *géants* of a pre-classical age; (though the Franks would not grasp the difference); Mycenaean tombs have been found there; Nauplius was an Argonaut. Classical remains are scarcely visible; Pausanias saw ruined walls, and a temple of Neptune, and the fountain called Canathus, where Juno annually regained her virginity. To-day we see the great medieval castles, Palamidi and Itsh Kaleh, with their Venetian steps and walls. This superimposition of medieval on ancient, modern on medieval—one finds it all over Morea, Arcadia and Messenia, where the great Frankish castles thrust up on craggy heights from Byzantine or classical foundations, the ghosts of dead ages sleeping together; as among the ruins of Daulis, with its precipitous acropolis, over which these sad birds, the hoopoe, the swallow and the nightingale, have twittered and mourned their wickedness for three thousand years; a medieval tower flanks the gateway. To many ruin-fanciers these medleys give an enhanced sense of the rich mosaic of the ages. Others, more classic, less romantic, prefer their ruins pure; resenting the jumble of the centuries, they are enchanted to the uttermost only by a pure Doric or Ionic temple, a pure Mycenaean or Achamenid palace, Greek theatre, Byzantine church, Norman castle, Seljuk mosque, Romanesque cathedral, Gothic abbey, baroque convent, Victorian chapel, Chinese pavilion of one dynasty—anything so long as it is all of a piece.

16

It is true also that there are different tastes in degrees of ruin. Some prefer the merest faint traces of what has been, to intrigue and titillate curiosity, to make romantic contrast with the new, to free the mind for speculation; others like to be stunned by antiquity, and are impressed only by a great field of ruins, a huge waste of broken stone, like Merv or Balkh or Sumarra. From travellers who have written of Balkh, the mother of cities, that ancient city of Afghanistan, reputed old when Nineveh was young, an almost audible gasp of amazement goes up. Marco Polo mentions that Balc was a great and noble city, ravaged by Tartars and others, so that only the ruins of fine marble palaces remained; he adds that here Alexander took for wife the daughter of Darius, and, attempting no further description, ends abruptly, "Now let us quit this city and I will tell you of another country called Dogana." One supposes that Marco never got to Balkh, as was so usual with him. It seems unlikely that Balkh was a "great" city in 1275 or so, in anything but extent of ruins, after its destruction fifty years earlier by Jenghiz Khan. Ibn Batuta, about 1335, said the whole city was in ruins, and uninhabited. "The remains of its mosques and colleges," he said, "are still to be seen, the painted walls traced with azure." Twenty or thirty years after that Timur destroyed what still stood, or what had been built up again since Jenghiz Khan. Clavijo, the Spanish envoy in 1403, describes the great earthen wall, breached in many parts, the city within it very extensive (the walls were six or seven miles round) and largely sown with cotton. People partly reinhabited the area, and later built two towns within the walls; but buildings wasted away, the dead city was unhealthy; in 1858 most of the inhabitants were moved. To-day Balkh is a huge desolation of ruins with a small colony of people and a great maze of jumbled streets; above it stands a fragmentary citadel on a hill. For those who like completeness in ruin, Balkh is their city. But rebuilding is now beginning; the "vast metropolis of ruins"[1] may be one day again a thriving city.

Ancient Merv on its oasis on the river Durghab will not be this, for the Russians when they took it built a new Merv for their

[1]Osbert Sitwell, *Escape with Me* (1939).

purposes. Old Merv, the Queen of the World (and possibly, they say, the site of Eden) is an immense wilderness of ruined desolation—"crumbling brick and clay walls, towers, ramparts and domes stretching in bewildering confusion to the horizon".[1] Fifteen square miles of it, and the ruins of at least three ancient successive cities, each glorious in its day, each overrun and destroyed. Zoroaster haunts it, and Alexander, and Persia, and Antiochus Soter, and the Seleucids, and the Nestorian Church, and the Arabs in their great centuries, and then the Seljuk Turks, and after them the Mongols, who performed, in 1221, one of their familiar wholesale butcheries. Later it passed to Timur, then to the Uzbegs and then to Persia again; till, in 1787, it was utterly destroyed by Bokhara; the Russians took the oasis in 1883. Now ruined Merv lies about, fragments of the buildings of nearly all these ages, and nothing intact. Pieces of wall, tumbles of brick, shattered citadels, mosques and tombs. Some of the ruins are identifiable; the successive ages can be vaguely traced. But the wilderness is a clueless maze, the archaeologist's challenge or despair, the layman's bewildering confusion. He gazes in stunned amaze; it is too much. Great names and great epochs haunt this waste; he does not know in which corner to find them. Twelve hundred years before Christ, and more; but there is nothing of that, and nothing of Paradise; this is no ruined garden city. On the whole, ruin-lovers have found Merv, and such other vast "heaps of ruin", excessive. Wrecked civilization on wrecked civilization; no grace, no form; only antiquity and immensity.

17

Almost better, some have thought, to have to seek out antiquity where it hides smothered in modernity, as in Carthage. Punic Carthage, even Roman Carthage, is an elusive ghost to be sought for in the unlovely heart of a great modern city. Generation after generation has sought for all the Carthages—Punic, Roman, Byzantine, Saracen, each destroyed in turn. After Scipio had done his job and deleted Carthage, massacring and razing, and after Roman Carthage had bloomed on the ruins and cinders into a magnificent imperial city, its inhabitants and visitors still

[1]Lord Curzon, *Russia in Central Asia* (Hodder & Stoughton, 1889).

rummaged about it for Phoenician relics, identifying Dido's palace and the port where Aeneas landed, building up a great Carthaginian legend that undermined the loyalty of Roman colonists, and turned their eyes backwards to the great Punic past. St Augustine, visiting Carthage in his unregenerate days, let his fancy play over Dido and her supposed palace, as fancy has played ever since. Chateaubriand liked to envisage the bevy of princesses who accompanied their husbands on Louis IX's second crusade, settling themselves, when Louis took Carthage from the infidels, in the ruins of the palace of its foundress, "by one of those revolutions produced by the lapse of ages". How much pleasure the princesses got out of it, the chroniclers do not tell us.

One may assume, even after the last half century of rewarding research into the great Punic tombs, that far most of the pleasure of the ruins of Carthage has been afforded by the Carthage Rome built, that fine colonial city called by Solinus the second wonder of the world after Rome, beautified by successive emperors with temples, theatres, aqueducts, baths, arches, cisterns, statues, mosaics, cemeteries, basilicas, villas. This new Carthage, imperfectly wrecked by the Vandals in the fifth century, taken by Belisarius in the sixth and beautifully Byzantinized for another century, wrecked once more, and better, by the Arabs in 698, has lain in noble ruin through the centuries, plundered steadily for the building of the cities down the North African coast, robbed of columns for Genoa, Pisa, Tunis, and any of the palaces and cathedrals of Europe which needed masonry, ploughed in and quarried by forty generations of greedy and ignorant Arabs, so that, until systematic excavations began last century, almost all that was to be seen of Roman Carthage was its site, and the remains of Hadrian's aqueduct, "that noble aqueduct," wrote Lady Mary Wortley Montagu in 1718,

"which carried the water to Carthage over several high mountains, the length of forty miles. There are still many arches entire. We spent two hours viewing it with great attention, and Mr M. assured me that of Rome is very much inferior to it. The stones are of a prodigious size, and yet all polished, and so exactly fitted to each other, very little cement has been made use of to join them. Yet they may probably stand a thousand years longer, if art is not used to pull them down."

23 Achaemenid Relief at Moor Amb Water-colour by
Sir Robert Ker Porter, 1817-20

24 Nicholas Revett drawing the Theatre of Dionysos, Athens. Engraving after Wm Pars, 1787

25 Tomb of Virgil, Pozzuoli. Water-colour by Pietro Fabris, *c.* 1760

In 1859 the aqueduct was restored. For the rest, Lady Mary, "half broiled by the sun", but refreshed by some milk and exquisite fruit brought her, climbed up the small hill where once stood the castle of Byrsa, and admired the view of Carthage on its isthmus. "Strabo calls it forty miles in circuit. There are now no remains of it but what I have described."

Chateaubriand made a tour of such ruins as he could see: uncertain what any of them were, he knew they were Carthage, so enjoyed them.

> *Devictae Carthaginis arces*
> *Procubuere, jacent infausto in litore turres*
> *Eversae*

he quoted, and set to work on them, riding along the shore, finding jetties under the water, and on his left a great quantity of ruins, and a basin which he thought must be the Cothon, or inner port; he also thought he saw parts of Scipio's dam. Leaving the sea, he returned to the ruins of the city, scattered over the hills. He found the remains of a palace or theatre, some prodigious cisterns, and the hill of Byrsa, with fragments of marble on its top which seemed to have been a palace or temple: the palace of Dido? The temple of Aesculapius? Gazing on the extensive but ill-preserved ruins of Carthage, he reflected on Dido giving herself to the flames, on the wife of Hasdrubal throwing into them first her children, then herself, when Scipio was at the gates. The view was beautiful, with green thickets growing among fragments of coloured marble, and in the distance the isthmus, the double sea, distant islands; he saw forests, aqueducts, Moorish villages, the white buildings of Tunis. Thus surrounded by beauty he thought again of Dido, Sophonisba, and Hasdrubal's wife, of Vandals and of Moors, and finally on St Louis expiring on the ruins of Carthage. With a long account of this affecting deathbed, he ends his tour and embarks in an American schooner for Spain.

He missed most of the now excavated and identified antiquities that we can see to-day. He did not see the Augustan wall built of amphorae, the Theodosian wall, the Forum, the sites of the theatres, the ruins of the baths, the Christian basilica, the mosaics, the Byzantine house, the museum full of finds from tombs. On the other hand, neither did he see modern Carthage, which is a smart suburb of Tunis, reached by tram, in which traces of the ancient city lie hideously masked by pretentious villas and streets, and Arabs trade beneath a brand new Colosseum. He had the best of it; he and Tasso, who saw in Carthage only the grass and sand that hid its ruins.

Giace l'alta Cartago; a pena i segni
De l'alte sue ruine il lido serba.
Muoiono le città, muoiono i regni,
Copre i fasti e la pompa arena ed erba. . . .

Flaubert, re-visiting Carthage for fresh inspiration when he got stuck in *Salammbô*, found it less in the ruins (few were identifiable in 1858) than in the gay streets and noisy cafés of Tunis, and the singular appearance and behaviour of its residents.

The Carthage of to-day gives little pleasure; far less than most of the long chain of Roman cities and buildings that line the coast and hinterland of Roman Africa. Timgad, for example (one of the most magnificent), was never built up or built over; Trajan's city remains in its dignified beauty. All this Roman life imposed on the disorderly apathy of the Numidian desert and the Barbary coast, hidden often in jungles and the great folds of mountains, all this civility of majestic broken theatres, imperial arches, porticoes, temples, baths, the commanding, luxurious, formidable and for ever legible signature of the governing power, asserting lordship over savage lands that cannot be held, that are doomed to slip back into apathetic barbarism, has a moving quality of wrecked distinction, like that of the dead Graeco-Roman cities of the Syrian and Mesopotamian deserts; a distinction blurred and dulled when surrounded by the modern accretions of streets and shops and industry. Where now is the pleasure of the bays of Baiae and Puteoli, that were, within living memory, so deliciously strewn with wrecked palaces of emperors, with sunk foundations of the villas of fine Roman gentlemen, with broken piers jutting out beneath the sea, and all against the background of grand mountains and majestic rocks? The ruins still are there, but have to be sought for among factories, dock works, and the mean houses that line tram-run streets; their charm is gone.

18

But all along the Barbary coast, all along Mediterranean Africa, from Egypt westward to Morocco, Rome lies, a chain of broken stone, between the sea and the wild hinterlands of Cyrenaica, Libya, Tunisia, Algeria, Morocco and Mauretania. And not Rome alone; Greece, both classical and Hellenistic, has adorned these cities with the late flowering of Antioch and (occasionally) the fifth century grandeur of Magna Graecia. Beneath all lies Phoenicia, mysterious, secret and remote. Cyrene has its sixth century temple of Pythian Apollo, where priestesses inebriated with sacred laurel leaves gave tongue as at Delphi; Cyrene stands on a mountain, ten miles from the sea, and was founded in the seventh century at the command of the Delphic oracle by Battus from the island of Thera, who built on a hill this divine city, seen by strangers from far, planted the groves of the gods, and cut a level street out of the rock for the chariots, so that on the festival of Apollo their victories might be celebrated with song in the glorious hall. For such a victory won by a descendant of Battus in 462 B.C., Pindar wrote his fourth and fifth Pythian odes, to be sung in the palace of Cyrene at the victory banquet. The palace is destroyed; it stood, says Pindar, beside Apollo's fountain; the fountain still gushes from its cave, and there remain the ruined town, the paved way, the Greek theatre, the temple of Apollo with a few pillars erected, the sites of other temples, and of agoras, and the great necropolis of rock-cut tombs that terrace the hill-side, where rest, says Pindar, the holy kings whose lot is in Hades. The whole stance and pose of this high field of haunted ruins looking across mountain country to the sea is of incredible beauty. The architectural detail, mostly of the second century (when the city was rebuilt) is charming to those who enjoy Graeco-Roman second-century decoration; others have found it somewhat florid, second-rate and lush, as if nosegays of artificial flowers had blossomed about severe Doric ruins.

Cyrene was destroyed by the Vandals in the fifth century, after a thousand years of riches and fame. From its Alpine airs one descends with pleasure to Apollonia, Cyrene's ancient port, "a group of shining columns standing against the azure sea"; here a temple of Apollo made way for a Roman and Byzantine basilica; the Corinthian columns of this have been re-erected, and the effect is altogether delightful. To some minds, Cyrene and Apollonia are among the most beautiful ruins of Graeco-Roman Africa. Others prefer the Hellenistic-oriental sophistication of Sabratha, which was, with Leptis Magna, one of the three cities giving its name to Tripoli. The lovely elegance of its theatre on the seashore has been restored and reassembled after thirteen centuries of burial under the sands; so complete is the reconstruction that the theatre is now a brilliant pastiche. Nothing could be happier than this sea theatre, the waves lapping at its walls, the detail of frieze, cornice and capital rich with the decorative luxuriance of orientalized Greek, reminiscent of Baalbek. Here too are temples to Jupiter and to Phoenician Tanit, and two great basilicas, Roman Christian, later Byzantinized; both originally pagan temples; in one of them was the magnificent Byzantine mosaic floor—peacocks, trees and flowers—now in the museum. "The fatal activity of the Byzantines", all this Christianizing and rebuilding of Roman work has been called, by one who preferred the neglect of the Arabs and the preserving immersion in the drifting sand. But, whether Hellenized, Romanized, or Byzantinized, or, as is so usual, all three, Phoenicia lurks ambushed at the heart of most North African ruined cities. Certainly in Leptis Magna, that magnificent Tripolitanian city founded from Sidon a thousand years before Christ, tributary of Carthage before the Roman conquest, the native town of Septimius Severus, that enterprising and imaginative Caesar, who rebuilt and beautified it after inspecting with interest the monuments of Alexandria down the coast, "while looking at its ruins," writes Mr Sacheverell Sitwell, "this proximity to Alexandria must never be forgotten."[1] Leptis has the rich, decorated, Ptolemaic touch that makes Baalbek and Palmyra so exquisite, so sophisticated, so *fin de siècle*, it combines with the firmer Roman conception; the magnificent triumphal arch is richly sculptured; on the arched porticoes that border the huge and splendid forum sphinxes are carved and Egypt looks in; the great Christian basilica has pilasters delicious with Dionysus and his train, with centaurs, nymphs and vines; the Christians could take over the pagan past where the Moslem Arabs would hack it to

[1]Sacheverell Sitwell, *Mauretania* (Duckworth, 1940).

bits, and the Byzantine pulpit is the capital of a column. Leptis is (or was) full of some of the finest marbles anywhere; its great fountain has a stately grandeur unsurpassed in Rome; the apsed thermae have mosaic pavements and porphyry pillars. Through the city runs the Roman-paved way, sunk now so low beneath the level of the surrounding sand that it is reached by flights of steps. Even severely classical archaeologists, censorious about the late period, its decadent architecture, its inferior sculptures, melt into a mood of romance before Leptis.

"We went on to the Baths, the Palestra, and the Nymphaeum—truly imperial, even in their ruins, or perhaps especially in their ruins, for one suspects that ruins suggest sublimities that the completed building may not have attained. In their present state they are evocative and romantic to a degree that it would be hard to exaggerate. One wants to look and dream, and dream and look."[1]

Thus Mr Bernard Berenson, and thus, in effect, every traveller to Leptis, since the Arabs assaulted it thirteen centuries ago. After that, *andò rovinando*: sand drifted over the ruins, deepening century by century; it seems likely that it never wholly disappeared, but there is little mention of it between the seventh century and the seventeenth when, in 1687, the French consul at Tripoli began dragging its columns out of the sand to send to Louis XIV for his constructions in Paris. Over six hundred marble columns were dispatched to the Grand Monarque, and from the correspondence between the consul and the French ministers we get our main information about the Leptis of that time. From then on, it was a quarry for European consuls and merchants; in the early nineteenth century the French consul was still at it, describing and despatching, and the British Captain Smith took a hand, sending marbles to Windsor and Malta as a present to his sovereign from the Bey of Tunis. Some of Leptis Magna stands to-day at Virginia Water, built up into an imposing folly. Regular excavation was begun by the Italians in 1920; since then Leptis has emerged piece by piece, prostrate columns have found their feet; there is much still buried, but the beauty of the golden-grey columns and arches, temples, forum and nymphaeum rising

[1]Mary Berenson, *A Vicarious Trip to the Barbary Coast* (Constable, 1938).

above the sea, and above the ancient ruined port and mole where the rich commerce of Leptis flowed in and out, is more moving than any one building to be seen there. As with all these North African ghosts of cities, the beauty lies partly in the scene, its lonely solitude and remoteness.

All along the many hundred miles of coast they stand, each with its individual character, its own beauties, its own history, but all with the unmistakable Roman stamp, the proud domination of the ruling race in savage lands. Beneath the disguise of the small French-Arab town of Cherchel, west of Algiers, between the Atlas mountains and the sea, is the ancient Caesarea, "the Athens of the west", once the furthest western outpost of Rome in Africa; earlier, the Phoenician Jol, a great and prosperous trading harbour under Carthage. Rome set over it King Juba II and his queen Selena, the daughter of Antony and Cleopatra; they ruled in cultured glory and power for half a century; the Phoenician city became Graeco-Roman; palaces and temples covered twelve hundred acres round the harbour; copies of the best Greek statues filled the colonnades and halls. The white and coloured marbles were superb; after the Arab destruction they were quarried and plundered till little was left. But ancient columns from the thermae fill the Great Mosque, now a hospital; the walls of a Roman palace stand; the theatre and amphitheatre are to be seen. Four miles away a tremendous three-tiered aqueduct spans a great gorge. Outside the museum, there is not very much to be seen in this charming place, but long-ago grandeur and present beauty brood over its stones. In Tipaza, too, twenty miles east down the coast. Tipaza was a Phoenician port like Caesarea, but much smaller; its ruins lie picturesquely on three low promontories above the sea; on the middle promontory and round its bay stood the Roman town, massive temples which became Christian basilicas; a forum, baths, slight remains of a theatre. Above the other little bay palaces and villas stood, apparently of elegant sophistication and comfort; outside the town is a mosaic-floored mansion close above the sea, mountains and vineyards behind it. The stones of Tipaza have been plundered for fourteen centuries, and the sea has washed at its foundations; the neat little modern town stands charmingly outside the ruins like a dolls' house perched on a quarry.

And so along the Algerian coast, and the Tunisian, and on where, after Carthage, Africa bends steeply south towards the Gulf of Gabes and Tripolitania. All the way the Roman ruins stand like outposts of a ghostly world, forming the frontier of a crumbled empire whose legions march the paved streets through the arches of triumph, whose colonists murmur in the stone theatres above the sighing of the waves, and splash in the great baths and fountains of the broken cities, and chant in the columned temples of Isis, of Diana, of Christ. Here are cities once great and magnificent, cities small and beautiful, cities that spread over many acres, cities that are a few pillars by the sea; cities which hold their Phoenician origin deep and barely visible in their foundations and their rocky harbours; their Roman pride in their forums and temples and colonnades, their aqueducts, arches, streets and baths; their Byzantine conversion in their transformed, mosaic-paved, still classical basilicas, while Greece and Egypt luxuriate in their rich carved sculpture, in the weathered amber of columns and colonnades. There is grace and civility in these ruins of palaces and villas that lie on the hill slopes above the sea; even when only the sites remain, an air of luxury haunts them, as at Mersa Matruh, where Cleopatra's villa stood above the harbour on the edge of the sandy bay; visitors and bathers for three centuries have hunted round about it for finds, and, when identification was less scrupulous, have assigned to the queen and her lover villas and flights of rocky steps leading down to the rock-bound sea.

If these coast ruins are the most delightful in scene and setting, some of the best are inland, among desert and mountains and plains. Timgad, for instance, at the foot of the Aures mountains, in the wild hinterland of Numidia, is the most complete and the largest of the Roman cities. Buried progressively since Vandals and Byzantines and Arabs successively destroyed it, deeper and deeper sunk in sand and débris, it lay deserted and forgotten and preserved until excavators dug it out last century, almost as entire as Pompeii. It has much of what one wishes, this Roman outpost city of the second century and the Third Legion, but by no means all; paved streets rutted by chariot wheels; a paved and colonnaded forum; halls and courts and little shops, temples, theatre, mosaic-floored thermae (hot and cold, every convenience), the ruins of a huge capitol; a Byzantine basilica and monastery, built partly out of the Roman stones; the whole effect is of stark dignity; forests of columns, a maze of streets and buildings in a wilderness. It has not the charm of painted walls that ravishes the eyes in Pompeii and Herculaneum; fauns and nymphs and *amoretti* do not disport themselves in loggias, it was built for soldiers, not for rich villa-dwellers, and has a certain Roman harshness. Timgad is not lovely, like Sabathra, Djemila, or Dougga with its graceful architecture and its villas for men of taste; but it has a firm masculine beauty, the lonely and formidable pride of the pioneering Empire in a savage desert land. Passing from one to another of these relics of Rome in North Africa, one is inclined to think unrivalled each ruin in turn; so strongly the impressiveness of their merely being there, being visible, startles the imagination. Actually, the Roman-Greek cities of Syria have, on the whole, more beauty. It is significant of the change in human apprehension that most of the seventeenth-century travellers in North Africa are silent and incurious as Arabs about such ancient stones as were then visible, and there were very many. Late in the century foreign diplomatists were busy digging them up to despatch to their governments; but tourists such as the enterprising Jacobean Mr Lithgow, who fell into ecstasies before the ruins of Troy and Alexandria Troas, when he travelled in Morocco and Tunisia and Libya was interested only in their modern life and extraordinary inhabitants; Troy he had heard of, but not, it appears, the Roman colonial empire. On the other hand the Reverend Dr Thomas Shaw, in 1730 or so, being well versed in Roman history, did take notice of its ruins. He discovered Corinthian capitals supporting a smith's anvil, inscriptions and mosaic pavements under ragged carpets; "a great many capitals, bases, shafts of pillars, and other ancient materials, lie scattered all over the ruins". Coming to Cherchel, he knew it for Phoenician Jol, Roman Caesarea. He tells us that in 1738, a few years after he saw it, it was entirely thrown down by earthquake, but in 1730 it was a flourishing industrial town that made steel and tools. The ruins on which it had been built were, said he, as extensive as Carthage, and its former magnificence we may judge from the fine pillars, capitals, cisterns and mosaics that are everywhere to be seen.

Guided by Ptolemy, Strabo, Tacitus and Pliny, Dr Shaw

pursued his learned way along the coast, identifying such ruins as he saw, quoting the Roman poets, copying inscriptions. It would seem that most of the cities excavated during the last fifty years were partly visible in 1730; the sand that covered them did not entirely hide them; there was enough above ground to move and occupy antiquarians, and enough sculptures lying scattered about for them to carry away as trophies. The enchanting business of reconstruction was still to come: Dr Shaw and his contemporaries never saw the theatres with their columns re-erected, the forums with upright statues, the capitals in place; and the paved streets now laid bare were then deep-buried under débris. All this they had to imagine, as now we imagine the resurrection of the cities still buried under the drifting sands.

One day, if ever there is money and time, reconstruction may be carried much further; the Barbary coast may be adorned all the way along with fine Roman cities, with their forums, theatres, basilicas, arches, colonnaded open spaces, porticoed houses, noble baths, all inhabited by colonists again; and the desert hinterlands may blossom like a rose with flower-like golden columns set in gardens on the wild slopes of hills. Rome in Africa may yet resurrect, an imposing revenant, putting modern cities to shame.

19

The crowded grandeurs of Rome in Italy, of Athens, of Constantinople, dazzle and bewilder after these lonely ghosts. Constantinople, for instance, that great modern city, its beauties largely replaced by hideously smart new structures; the Stamboul which ravished Gautier is gone beyond recovery; but the ghosts of Byzantium and ancient Islam still haunt its ways, refusing to be laid. Half old Stamboul was thirty years ago destroyed by fire, which periodically assaults the largely wooden city; the rebuilding has been vile. But from the Sea of Marmora to the Golden Horn stretches for four miles the Theodosian wall, broken, crumbling, magnificent, set with its gates all the way, "this crown of ramparts, which yield nothing to those of Babylon", a fourteenth-century Byzantine boasted (but it seems that he can have had small acquaintance with those of Babylon, which were then a heap of ruins), it must be, except for the Great Wall of China, the most spectacular wall in the world, better than that of Antioch. It was still more beautiful before much of the greenery was torn from it; trees no more spring from the ramparts, nor ivy creep about the scarred stones. A reach of the doubly-arcaded fourth-century aqueduct strides from one great mosque to another, crumbling beneath its shrubs; columned Byzantine cisterns stretch beneath the city—the cistern of the thousand and one columns, the cistern of the basilica. The Basilica Cistern—called by the Turks the engulfed palace—still has water; one can row in a boat among the pillars; in the mysterious gloom it is like a drowned cathedral. The destructive crusaders, who sacked and took Constantinople in the thirteenth century (holding the Greek church to be unsound on the Trinity), fortunately, hydrophobes though they were, let the cisterns alone; they were too busy burning half the city down, looting its treasures, desecrating St Sophia's, and massacring the inhabitants. Constantinople never recovered from the Crusaders. The Turks, in their five centuries of occupation, did much less damage to the Byzantine marvels which they could never have emulated. The ruin of most of the palaces and churches reported by Clavijo, the Spanish visiting ambassador, in 1403, was crusading work.

All these destructive people, who destroyed so much, left the framework of the Roman hippodrome, the cisterns, a few columns, and the ruins of the great jumbled city within a city which was the Imperial Palace and its buildings, smothered and overbuilt with mosques, for here on the curved tip of the horn, looking on to the Bosphorus, the Ottoman sultans established their imperial seat, using for their great Seraglio the Byzantine palace buildings, climbing on those huge substructures, razing many to the ground, where they lie under gardens and parks. The histories of the Byzantine palace are confused; fire and excavation has revealed much that had been buried for centuries; in the tenth century the palace was seen intact; by the thirteenth, two centuries before the Turkish conquest, parts of it had been pulled down by the Crusaders, while other parts fell later into ruin; by the sixteenth Gyllius reported there was nothing of it to be seen. Since recent fires, some ruins have been uncovered; little care is taken of them, and decay and new building imperil them without cease.

The deserted Seraglio, the sumptuous great mosques, the ruinous mosques that were Greek churches, vanished Byzantium below Islam, the spacious gardens, the storks, the whole crumbling magnificence standing above those shining seas—in spite of the encroaching vulgarity and modernity of the occidental city, there is still nothing like it. The ancient imperial pomp, remote, ceremonious, Byzantine and strange, whispers like a proud, undefeated ghost among the mosques; the old pomp of Islam, as extravagant, luxurious, fastuous and fantastic, rises like a garden of tulips before our dazzled eyes, among the verdure, terraces and streams of that abandoned, cypress-grown quarter where the Sultans reigned among their viziers, janissaries, harems and pleasure gardens for four sumptuous centuries, before they deserted it for their modern palace on the Bosphorus. Once the capital of imperial Rome; later the greatest city of Christendom, the richest city in the world, the spiritual head of the eastern Church, the treasure house of culture and art; then the opulent capital of Islam; this sprawl of mosques, domes, minarets, ruined palaces, and crumbling walls, rising so superbly above three seas, looking towards Europe, Asia, and ocean, oriental, occidental, brooding on past magnificence, ancient rivalries and feuds, modern cultures and the spoils of the modern world, Constantinople has ruin in her soul, the ruin of a deep division; to look on her shining domes and teeming streets is to see a glittering, ruinous façade, girdled by great, broken, expugnable walls.

20

There is no such division in Persepolis; it is pure ruin and legend. The very name has a rich, magical, incantatory sound, suggesting Persian pleasures, palaces, pillars, playing fountains, pealing bells, dancing girls, luscious gardens of ripe pears, apples, plums, persimmons, and purling waters. Christopher Marlowe, haunted by it, made it the centre of Tamburlaine's martial dreams, though in Tamburlaine's day the ancient Achaemenid capital was a ruinous, almost abandoned city of no account. Unhampered by this, the Persian lord speaks to the Persian king of "your merchants of Persepolis", who trade with western lands, and Tamburlaine breaks into wishful thinking—

> Is it not passing brave to be a king,
> And ride in triumph through Persepolis?

"O my Lord," his follower agrees, "'tis sweet and full of pomp." And so, indeed, kings had found it, during the centuries from its building by Cyrus, Darius and Xerxes to its eclipse as Taphet-i-Jamshid (for the Persians would have it that the huge palaces had been built by Jamshid, who in them gloried and drank deep). But in 322 Alexander and his Macedonian army, chasing the Persians over the pass, rode down into the great valley a-lust for the fabulous city where the Persians stored prodigious treasure. In the palace halls on the great terrace they feasted with their courtesans, and then, so the tradition ran,

> Alexander, Thais, and the Macedonian soldiers,
> Reeling with their torches through the Persian palaces,
> Wrecked to flaring fragments pillared Persepolis. . . .

by way of vengeance for Athens. Alexander's "frolic at Persepolis", John Evelyn tolerantly called it; the French traveller, Chardin, more sharply, "*sa brutale débauche, par où il commença de brûler Persépolis*". But this legend, put about by Greek and Roman historians, is no longer so well thought of; even Chardin doubted it. There are traces of fire; but the wreck of Persepolis, the throwing down of so many hundreds of columns, so many halls and sculptures, could scarcely have been Alexander's work. Earthquake, time, enemy attacks, the vandalism and neglect of the Arabs, worked together on Persepolis which seems, by the end of the tenth century, to have been pretty well a ruin. A ruin always famous in legend, and always a sight for tourists, who described and drew its buildings from the middle ages down to to-day. "Those famous ruins called Chehil Minar, of the forty columns, the illustrious remains of the ancient Persepolis, which I so ardently and so long had wished to see," della Valle wrote. Pitching his tents on the margin of a stream, he settled down for several days to make a minute survey and description. Every sculpture, every relief, every portal, he examined and recorded;

designs of strange creatures, tombs, pillars, pedestals, carved battle scenes, he copied and described with loving care.

Sir Thomas Herbert, in 1628, admired it even more.

Let us now (what pace you please) to Persepolis, not much out of the road: but were it a thousand times further, it merits our paines to view it; being indeed the only brave Antique-Monument (not in Persia alone) but through all the Orient. . . . A Citie so excellent that Quintus Curtius and Diodorus Siculus intitle it the richest and most lovely Citie under the Sunne.[1]

He describes it as it had once been: the triple wall, of delicate polished marble entered by burnished gates; the temple of Diana, of rich marble and porphyry and refined gold ("a bait Antiochus the avaricious Atheist long had nibbled at, but could not swallow it"); the royal Palace, cut out of the marble rock, with roof and casements of gold, silver, amber and ivory; inside it gold and glittering gems; in one room a vine presented by Pythias, the stalk pure gold, the grapes, pearls and carbuncles; the treasure everywhere fabulous, and the Macedonian spoiler must have carried away many millions, on three thousand mules.

"But why stand we gaping at these prodigious sums? . . . For my part (by Gods help) I intend rather to admire the anatomy of this glorious ruine."

And admire it he did, and described it with detailed interest; the black marble stairway, so broad that a dozen horses could ride up it abreast, the carved animals, the pillars, whereon storks nest, the rooms, with their polished walls and a majestic monarch graven over each door, whom the silly inhabitants name Jamshyd, Aaron, Samson, and Solomon. Whether the fabric was Ionic, Doric or Corinthian, he could not judge; but it should be exactly and fully drawn, for every day the barbarous people (nowhere did Sir Thomas care much for the locals) defaced it and clove it asunder for grave-stones and benches.

"Alas! [he pleasurably lamented], this rich and lovely city, yea the palace itself . . . at a drunken feast. . . . Thais, an infamous strumpet. . . . Nothing now remains save what the merciless fire could not devour—I mean the walls and pavement, which, being of marble, have hitherto resisted air and weather, so as it is not

[1]Sir Thomas Herbert, *Travels* (1638).

defaced by barbarous hammers, it probably will remain a monument to express the old Persian magnificence unto all succeeding generations."

Chardin, fifty years later, gives a pictorial account of the city, once the most delicious on the earth; little rivers of clear water flow about the fertile valley, from which rises the magnificent terrace hewn out of the dark grey rock of the mountain side, and the huge double stairway climbing up to it; from the terrace rises the forest of great columns, massive in form, delicate in work, carved with fine designs on stone harder than marble. All about them felled columns lie strewn. The effect is rather grand and astonishing than lovely. "*Ce pays de merveilles*," wrote Chardin, "*où l'on aperçoit je ne sais quelles ombres de la grandeur des Perses, qui paroit si étonnante et si incroyable.*"

Astonishing, unbelievable, the greatness of the Persians; it is this fantastic, incredible past that haloes what Herbert calls the "ribs and ruins" on their high platform, so that it is less these that are seen and enjoyed than "the old Persian magnificence" that haunts them. Indeed, the pleasure of Persepolis is more a pleasure of ideas and imagination than of actual visual delight. Here are the courts (or so the silly inhabitants say) where Jamshyd gloried and drank deep; the lizard still keeps them, but the lion, shy of archaeologists, has retired. But, anyhow, here was Elam, here was Persia. Here were the palace halls, with their cedar and silver roofs, their coloured hangings fastened by silver rings to pillars of marble, their mosaic pavements, their great blocks of richly-carved stone; here reigned Darius; here the Macedonian victor feasted, Thais at his side; here the ghosts of slain Greeks cried vengeance, tossing their torches as they routed through the banquet hall, till

> The king seized a flambeau with zeal to destroy,
> Thais led the way,
> To light him to his prey.
> And, like another Helen, fired another Troy.

Yet students of architecture as well as of history and legend have found rich rewards in the study of what Thais and all the later destroyers have left. For the last two centuries they have poured forth praises and drawings in volumes comparable in size with the huge ruinated palaces beneath the mountain side. Of all the reminders of past greatness in Iran, said the admirable Dieulafoys in 1887, not one had impressed them more vividly than these skeletons of palaces. Architects are gratified by the finding of new elements in the Achaemenid style—Pharonic Egyptian, Chaldaeo-Assyrian, Ionic Greek. The ruins are a rich medley; reliefs, friezes and capitals suggesting Assyria surmount Graeco-Egyptian pillars—"the columns of the Nile on the plains of Persia". There are unattractive, un-Persian monsters, half-man, half-beast. The decoration is at once rich and formal; the polished dark grey stone gives it a grave air; the pillars of Persepolis have not the golden grace of Palmyra, the deep orange glow of Baalbek, the changing rainbow hues of Petra. And they have the air, from a distance, of an unusually fine row of ninepins. The general effect of the great rocky terraces with the grey roofless colonnade, backed by the mountainside honeycombed with tombs, and approached by the great double flight of shallow stairs, so suitable for horses, has been thought by some travellers just a little short of superb. Perhaps by Mr J. S. Buckingham, who, visiting the ruins in 1823, found them difficult to describe "without being tedious". It was all broken and detached fragments, admittedly extremely numerous, but so scattered and disjointed as to give no perfect idea of the whole. It was "an assemblage of tall, slender and isolated pillars and separate doorways and sanctuaries, spread over a large platform, elevated like a fortification from the level of the surrounding plain".

Mr Buckingham was right: this is somewhat tedious language for Persepolis. The *ombres de la grandeur* have slipped from his grasp. "The task of describing such remains in any connected or striking manner" was too difficult; he fell back on "Some of these monuments are quite perfect, and might be easily brought to the British museum".[1] Fortunately this was not attempted.

Sir Robert Ker Porter, in 1821, had the pleasure of riding the stairs. "I invariably rode my horse up and down them during my visits to their interesting summit."[2] Of the buildings on the interesting summit he made admirable drawings and descriptions; previous travellers he found inaccurate. Nor did he approve the

[1] J. S. Buckingham, *Travels* (1823).
[2] Sir Robert Ker Porter, *Travels* (1821).

vulgar way in which they had inscribed their names on the polished walls of the great portal. Easily corrupted, however, he would appear to have done the same himself; Dr Ainsworth, surgeon and geologist of the Euphrates expedition of 1836, found his name carved, together with those of Pietro della Valle, Niebuhr, Chardin, Rich, and many others, on a wall: this self-recording is, indeed, one of the last infirmities of noble, as of baser, minds.

Dr Ainsworth himself got immense excitement and delight out of Persepolis. Approaching it, his heart beat with anxious expectation, succeeded by surprise. His companion, Colonel Shee, "amused himself during the heat of the day practising with his rifle. He was a wonderful shot, and would, lying on his back, knock the head off a little bird sitting on some adjacent tree". Both gentlemen finished a well-spent day by sleeping "among the ruins of Persepolis, undisturbed by wild beasts".

William Francklin, fifty years earlier, had found the ruins depressing.

"Whilst viewing them [this child of his century had remarked], the mind becomes oppressed with an awful solemnity. When we consider the celebrity of this vast empire, when we reflect on the various changes and revolutions it has undergone . . . we must consequently feel the strongest conviction of the mutability of all human events!"[1]

As to what the main ruin had been—temple or palace—he felt less conviction. Now that we can identify everything, now that the site has been explored and labelled, it has inevitably lost some of its romance. Robert Byron, for instance, was annoyed and disillusioned; Persepolis was in the hands of German excavators

"In the old days [he complained], you rode up the steps on to the platform. You made a camp there, while the columns and winged beasts kept their solitude beneath the stars, and not a sound or a movement disturbed the empty moonlit plain. You thought of Darius and Alexander. You were alone with the ancient world. You saw Asia as the Greeks saw it, and you felt their magic breath stretching out towards China itself. . . . To-day you step out of a motor, while a couple of lorries thunder by in a cloud of dust. You find the approaches guarded by walls. You

[1] William Francklin, *Tour from Bengal to Persia, 1786–7* (1788).

enter by leave of a porter, and are greeted on reaching the platform by a light railway, a neo-German hostel, and a code of academic malice compiled from Chicago. These useful additions clarify the intelligence. You may persuade yourself, in spite of them, into a mood of romance. But the mood they invite is that of a critic at an exhibition. That is the penalty of greater knowledge.[1]"

It is the familiar tragedy of archaeology—the sacrifice of beauty to knowledge. Burckhardt wept over it on re-visiting the de-mossed Greek temples of Sicily after twenty years; Augustus Hare over Hadrian's cleaned-up villa; we to-day over all the excavated, tidied up monuments of the world. Robert Byron, looking on Persepolis, was put out of conceit with it altogether. He found the columns surprising but meaningless, the stairs only fine because so many of them, the terrace of buildings impressive because so massive, the crenellations on the parapet ugly, the cold, shining grey stone repellent and like an aluminium saucepan. It is possible not to be transported by Persepolis; perhaps, to approach it in the right mood, one needs a horse to ride up the stairs; motor cars take them less well. It was after scaling the great stairway on his sixteen-hand steed that Colonel P. M. Sykes, in 1914, was overwhelmed with admiration of what he saw at the top.

But some recent travellers have found the old Persian magnificence still haunting the column-strewn terrace like a ghost. "Xerxes and Darius haunted us that evening", one of these wrote. He saw in the moonlight, among the litter of broken pillars,

"the invisible causeways, staircases and triumphal processions of men in gold armour, royal bed-chambers and the golden throne, all lost and gathered in the dust. . . . You heard music. . . .[2]"

It was, this traveller remarked, like being drunk, to see all this ruinous beauty under the moon. Pacing the reconstructed harem, a young Persian archaelogist recalled the glorious Achaemenian past, while in the deep ditches the excavators dug for what more of this past they might find.

But, at Persepolis, the ghosts of lost splendour are better than anything dug from the earth.

[1]Robert Byron, *The Road to Oxiana* (1937)
[2]Robert Payne, *Journey to Persia* (1951).

21

Still more so at Susa, where Shushan the palace of Darius, and the earlier city of the Elamites, that the Assyrians destroyed, and the stone age settlement, are represented by mounds, out of which are dug pottery and enamelled bricks and coloured friezes of lions and archers. Here, in Shushan the palace, young Nehemiah the cup-bearer served wine to Artaxerxes the king, before going off to his city of Jerusalem to build up the walls; here Ahasuerus, who was Xerxes, sat on his throne and made a feast to all his princes and his servants, showing the riches of his kingdom for a hundred and eighty days; and in the court of the garden of the king's palace were white, green and blue hangings, fastened with cords of fine linen and purple, and the beds were of gold and silver, upon a pavement of red and blue and white and black marble, and they drank from vessels of gold, all different, and Queen Vashti refused to come at the king's command, and Esther found favour in his sight, and got her uncle Mordecai into power. On the banks of the river Choaspes the city stands—"that city of Susa," said Aristagoras the despot of Miletos to Cleomenes of Sparta, "where the great king has his residence, and where the money is laid up in treasuries. After you have taken this city, you may then with good courage enter into a contest with Zeus in the matter of wealth". To Susa came the joyful news that Xerxes had taken Athens, and they strewed all the ways with myrtle boughs and offered incense and continued in sacrifice and feasting. There followed the news of Salamis, and the Susians tore their garments and gave themselves to crying and lamentation without stint.

But of Susa, which was a fortified city in 3800 B.C. which became the seat of the Babylonian viceroy, which was razed by the Assyrians in 640, and rose again after Assyria fell to become a Persian capital, of Susa nothing remains but mounds and pottery and bronze ornaments and enamelled bricks.

Yet the spectacle and the exploration of this mighty site has always given acute pleasure to its beholders. To it across the Persian plains came, for the second time, the enthusiastic M. and Madame Dieulafoy in 1884, he to begin his great work on the site, she to rejoice with exuberant animation in all they saw and found, and to write two immense volumes about it. As they approached, Susa was revealed by a flash of lightning. "Chouch! Chouch!" the guides cried (for that was what they called Susa). And "*Dieu soit loué!*" ejaculated Madame Dieulafoy, "*nous touchons au but vers lequel nos esprits et nos cœurs tendent depuis plus d'une année.*" They arrived first at the Tomb of Daniel, where they passed the night in the shelter of an arcade in the wall of this Moslem building, exposed to wind, rain and insects; they woke to see, in the morning sunlight, the great green mass of the citadel of Susa, the Kalehè Chouch, rising like a ravine-ridden mountain, with goats climbing its steep paths. Weary, bruised, starving, afflicted with lumbago, as they were, the Dieulafoys explored the ground and pitched their camp on the northernmost tumulus. There, when night came, they lay in peace and joy. The moonlight bathed the desert; all was silent but for the jackals' cries; no wind moved; Madame Dieulafoy lay and reflected on what remained of the empire of Elam and of its capital, the ancestor of cities. To the south, the pointed crest of the mound of the citadel; to the north west, the river Chaour, black in the shadows, glittering like metal where the moonlight touched it; to the north, on the horizon, that snowy chain which was disturbed neither by Darius nor Alexander, and which, in its immoveable majesty, sees with equal indifference the passing of centuries and men. "The earth beneath my feet is made of the dust of Asiatic monarchies; the vanished generations seem to rise from the depths of Memnon; their ghosts contemplate the sons of Japhet come from the ends of the western world for the conquest of their age-old secrets, then they vanish in the mists of the river.

"No more apprehension! No more cares! To have reached this land of Susa, to camp on the ruins of the palace of the great kings, is it not already a victory? You will open your sides, jealous mountains which guard the history of the past! You will yield up your treasures, inviolate tombs! Are we not the heirs of the victors of Salamis?"

Next day began the happy months of excavation, following in the tracks of the English excavators of thirty years before, General Williams and W. K. Loftus. Going further than Sir Loftus (who had been chased away by fanatical clergy), M. Dieulafoy discovered what was left (it was not much) of the great palace of Darius. Enamelled bricks, a frieze of wild beasts, fragments of columns and of a marble bull, these delighted them and their Arab workers. "*Venez, venez! On trouve des faïences! Cinq corbeilles de briques émaillées . . . Le cœur bien ému, nous courons à la tranchée. . . .*"[1]

It is not much, in the end, that has been recovered from the mounds of Susa, where it was hoped that all Shushan the palace lay hid, like the Assyrian palaces at Nineveh and Babylon. But Shushan had been quarried away; stone by stone, brick by brick, column by column, it had been taken centuries since, to build other cities, that now stand about the desert enriched with its fragments, based on its foundations. After the Arab period, the palace and the citadel grew slowly into earthy tumuli. The Dieulafoys' hopes of vast structures, huge treasures, hidden in the mountain's scarred sides, dwindled into delight in enamelled bricks, the beauty of the frieze of lions.

And Madame Dieulafoy mused always on the past, on the huge destruction first of the Elamite, then of the Persian city; and on the marching of two hundred generations about that desert, horizoned by those snowy crests.

Susa is one of the huge ramparts of the ancient world gone to earth: nothing to be seen of it but pots and shards and mounds, its ruins are deep buried. But the fairy-tale cities of Persia—Shiraz, Kazvin, Isfahan, that shimmer through the centuries like golden fruit, stand ruining and mouldering before our eyes. Isfahan, ancient in history but made glorious by its Shahs, embellished with hundreds of palaces and gardens and mosques by the great Shah Abbas in the sixteenth century, who made it capital of Persia, filled it with art, luxury, and admiring foreigners, and laid out the Chahar Bagh, that tremendous avenue of approach bordered with gardens, terraces, palaces, pavilions and running, cascading water—Isfahan, "the porches shining with gilded foliages, architrave and marble pillars, as all the palaces of their nobles do", as John Fryer wrote of it in the seventeenth century, is to-day a quarter ruined and abandoned, palaces and mosques shaken down by earthquake and Afghans, or crumbling to decay, the great avenue a derelict road running through a desolate, waterless, ruinous wilderness. The Chehul Situn palace of the Forty Pillars still stands, and the Shah's royal mosque in the great square, so singularly embellished, said visitors, that it glittered

[1] Jane Dieulafoy, *Assyrie, Journal des Fouilles* (1888).

like the sun at noon; many times restored and re-tiled, it is still decaying. Round the twenty square miles that was the city a ruinous mud wall runs. Isfahan still has splendour shining out of squalor; looking on its squares and its forlorn great avenue of approach, one imagines it as all the travellers described—the entrance between two fair rows of trees planted by crystal streams, reaching a long way through a broad street whose paved causeways led to the river, where on the bridge there waited to welcome eminent visitors the several European residents with their trains, trumpeters, horses richly trapped, and pages.

"Thus attended, we were brought over a most magnificent bridge with arches over our heads, and on both sides rails and galleries to view the river, the cloisters whereof were paved with broad marble, in which were several niches and open portals. . . . Which led us to a stately large street, continued on the other side with equal gallantry of buildings and trees, till we were carried under their lofty-ceiled and stately-erected Bazaars. . . ."[1]

With such fine hearsay bravery and glitter we can fill Isfahan at will. Kazvin, also once a capital, and also ruined by time, earthquake, Afghans, Turks, and rain which disintegrates the mud walls, is in worse state. In 1627 it was, said Shirley, equal in grandeur to any other city in the Persian empire except Isfahan. By 1674 the walls, said Chardin, were in ruins, and the town had "lost all those perquisites that set forth the pomp and grandeur of a sumptuous court". To-day it has lost more: the Royal Palace stands in ruin, and the great mosque of Harun al Raschid, its blue minarets broken. All over Persia the mud cities moulder, the tiled mosques decay, the blue towers fall, the Shahs' brilliant palaces crumble to earth. They are houses of clay, whose foundation is in the dust, between morning and evening they are destroyed, they perish for ever without any regarding it. But the gardens blossom, the fountains play, in the bazaars round the great squares the merchants chaffer; the fairy-tale cities live on in the mind like the chiming of bells.

22

But, in the ruin-loving dreams of western man, Persia cannot compete. It is Greece and Italy which have always mainly

[1] John Fryer, *A New Account of East India and Persia* (1698).

enshrined those wistful, backward-gazing dreams. Perhaps because it was there that our civilization was cradled and grew; we yearn back to these vestiges of our past. Perhaps because we have been bred in a classical culture, given from our youth up to understand that there was the glory of the world: hypnotized, our eyes dazzle with it. Here were Socrates, Plato, Pericles, Praxiteles; here was Troy, here Athens, the Islands, there Magna Graecia, and the tremendousness of Rome. Nothing can compete.

The traditional emotions of gratification and learned excitement experienced by those who have looked on Athens in her long ruin were summed up by John Cam Hobhouse, when he first beheld the city with Lord Byron, in 1809. "Not Thrasybulus himself could from these hills have surveyed his own Athens, the object of all his patriotic efforts, with more ardour and effection, mixed with a not unpleasing melancholy" than was felt by Hobhouse. For it was

"most gratifying to behold the stupendous monuments of the magnificence of Pericles and the skill of Phidias, still standing on the very spots. . . . These noble masterpieces still retain their grandeur and their grace, and towering from amidst their own ruins and the miserable mansions of barbarians, present a grand but melancholy spectacle, where you behold not only the final effects, but the successive progress of devastation, and, at one rapid glance, peruse the history of a thousand ages."[1]

The problem of tracing back these emotions through history is complicated by some uncertainties and gaps in our knowledge of the various ruin dates. How many, for instance, of the Acropolis buildings were destroyed and burnt by the Persians in the fifth century? "Set fire to the whole of the Acropolis," says Herodotus; and Thucydides too implies total devastation. But contemporary comments are scarce; the planning and rebuilding of a more glorious citadel was quickly put in hand, and there was little time to sentimentalize. Socrates, as a young man, must have philosophized among those blackened ruins; among them, but not about them; his thoughts were on other, less material, matters. He and his contemporaries saw the wrecked city and its resurrection, but have left no comments of the kind usually elicited by noble ruins. So we have no record of the emotions roused by the ruined

[1]Lord Broughton, *Travels in Albania, etc.* (1854).

Acropolis at the end of the fifth century; all we know is that fragments of the broken monuments were often incorporated into the new buildings, as foundations or decoration; these may have afforded a melancholy pleasure when shown to the next generation. But fifth-century Athens lacked such mourners as Archbishop Michael Akominatos, who was to bewail the ruined city of the twelfth century.

We have more comments on the destructions and depredations of Sulla four centuries later; but the Acropolis suffered much less from these than the surrounding cities; it was not laid utterly waste. Pausanias has less to say of ruins in Athens than anywhere else in Greece; he describes the ancient monuments as being on the whole well preserved; the barbarian and Byzantine ravages were still to come.

Beyond the gulf of two centuries, a gulf stormy with barbarian raids and violence, lies the Athens visited by Synesius of Cyrene in 395. He, a lamenting and exaggerating tourist, complained that nothing sublime remained in Athens but its famous name—

"as with a victim burnt in the sacrificial fire, there remains nothing but the skin to help us to reconstruct the creature once alive, so, ever since philosophy left these precincts, there is nothing for the tourist to admire except the Academy, the Lyceum, and the Decorated Porch (no longer decorated, for the pro-consul has taken away the panels). . . . The bee-keepers alone bring Athens fame."

But of the actual state of the buildings he says nothing. Nor did Procopius when, two hundred years later, he bewailed the state of Greece under Justinian, yearly ravaged by barbarians and become like the deserts of Scythia. The Byzantine emperors spoiled Athens, as they spoiled Rome, to enrich the new Byzantium. The temples became Christian churches; but the Parthenon, as St. Sophia, fitted up with altar, screen, apse, and other ecclesiastical decor, and deprived of the great bronze Athene, remained essentially intact. The Propylaea, transformed into a castle, lost its character but not its walls, the Erectheum and other buildings were hacked and hewn into churches. Time, the barbarians, and the Byzantines worked together on the citadel through the long dark ages; gradually the city that crowded its lower slopes fell into ruin.

Before the end of the twelfth century Michael Akominatos, the last Metropolitan before the Frankish conquest, complained to the Byzantine praetor, "Look at the most famous of cities. It has been turned into a small village, known only by its venerable ruins."

The city was, in fact, by then a wilderness; its walls were in ruins, many of the streets rocky lanes; villas and palaces crumbled about them. The Acropolis buildings were in better case; many were ruined, but in the main, though transformed and looking very peculiar, they stood upright. Twenty years after Michael's complaint, Frankish dukes of Athens reigned from Thebes, and further fortified the Acropolis, which they regarded, wrongly, as an impregnable citadel. Those enterprising buccaneers, the Catalan Grand Company, followed them; they further ruined the town and fortified the citadel; with towers and walls they strengthened the Propylaea; they called the Acropolis the Castle of Cetines, and greatly esteemed it, not merely on military but on aesthetic grounds. King Peter sent orders from Barcelona that a guard of twelve men-at-arms should always defend the Cetines; he added, with characteristic Catalan appreciation of foreign architecture, "This castle is the richest jewel in the world, and such that not all the kings of Christendom together could make anything like it." But how far those who had reported on the Cetines to him felt admiration for its ruined buildings, we do not know.

From the fourteenth century on, under the troubled succession of Catalans, Florentines, Venetians and Turks, the increasingly ruinous city had no lack of commentators; every few years some traveller or pilgrim would record his impressions of its monuments, whose fascinating ruins drew tourists like a magnet. They have left between them a pretty thorough account of what they saw, and of its effect on their surprised minds. One of the first was the Italian notary, Niccolo de Martoni, stopping off at Athens in 1394, on a pilgrimage to Jerusalem. "The city of Athens," he wrote, "as it shows by its ancient buildings, was at one time a great city, and great buildings were in it, for we saw many columns and many marble stones which now lie where that city was built." The note of naiveté was struck. Uninformed but fascinated by these spectres of a mighty unknown past, the notary made his eager tour of the antiquities, describing them in delighted detail. He was the forerunner of a long line (still unbroken) of foreign Athenians, who made their visits, wrote their accounts, drew their pictures, some anonymous, some named, so that we have no excuse for not knowing how Athens has looked every twenty years or so from about 1400 till to-day. The Renaissance wind, stirring and gathering force, blew every scholar to worship at the shrines of ruined classical antiquity. The commentators swing between admiration and lamentation. There was the "*O rerum humanarum miserabiles vices! O tragicam humanae potentiae permutationem!*" of the civilized and travelled Pope Aeneas Sylvius—"Go to Athens and see, instead of the most magnificent works, broken fragments and lamentable ruins":—moral, do not trust in your own strength but in God's. But the Pope had not actually seen Athens; he had heard the pessimistic descriptions of those who had not seen it either, and he hated the Turks and their infidel occupation of Greece; he saw them mosquing the church of the Parthenon, making the Propylaea their palace, the Erechtheum a harem, building their mean hovels over the lower slopes of the Acropolis—*O tragicam permutationem!* Others of his time asserted that nothing of Athens was left but a miserable village, infested by foxes and wolves. It was left for a German professor, Martin Crusius, to publish in 1584 accounts of Athens as it actually was, collected from Greeks who knew it. These accounts give a much better impression; the extant famous buildings, some of which had been said by earlier writers to have perished, are described, and others which fifty years later were only seen in ruins. Marble palaces and pillars rose again; the Parthenon, though misnamed, was lofty and beautiful; the city was divided into three parts, the citadel, inhabited by Turks, the second part, where Christians lived; and "The Ancient City of Theseus", where there were still some inhabited houses; the whole city contained about twelve thousand people, and was six or seven miles in circumference. The inhabitants, though fallen into barbarism, still remembered something of their former greatness.

Fifty years later Deshayes gave his pleasant and intelligent account; more than half the city was in ruins, he said; he described the mosqued and minaretted Parthenon as entire and unimpaired by time, as if recently erected; he made no scientific archaeological examination of the ruins. As time went on, the travellers became more informed and exact, their plans and drawings more careful, their guesses at identification more plausible. During the seventeenth century enthusiasm reached its height; pilgrims and capuchins, oriental scholars and ambassadors, historians, antiquarians, artists, and collectors of antiques, fell over one another to make the Athens visit and write their Athens book, illustrated, if they could not themselves draw, by an attendant artist. There was, for instance, the Marquis de Nointel, Louis XIV's ambassador to Turkey, who took with him to Athens in 1674 the Flemish painter who executed the twenty-one charming but incorrect drawings that were formerly thought to be by Jaques Carrey. The eager activities and curiosities of M. de Nointel are described in a journal kept by one of his suite; in Athens he let nothing go by him; he saw everything of interest, and picked up anything of antiquarian value that he could come by, whether manuscripts, coins, or fragments of antique buildings and sculptures. He spent much time exploring "*le temple ancien qui sert à présent de mosquée, lequel reste encore assez entier dans le lieu qu'on appellait autrefois Acropolis*", examining its friezes, sculptures and statues, questioning the Athenians about their history. There was not a dull moment for the ambassador or for his artist in the presence of these stupendous relics. It was understood, too, that it was part of his ambassadorial duties to get hold of anything interesting that he might find among the ruins and send them to Colbert for his collections, as well as any valuable manuscripts he could acquire, for "*ce serait orner notre France des despouilles de l'Orient*". After his first month in Athens Nointel sent a despatch full of reverent enthusiasm over what he had seen—"all these riches of art, of which I can say of those round the temple of Minerva that they are superior to the most beautiful of the reliefs and statues of Rome". He had again and again gone to admire the exquisite objects, ruined and whole, that his artist was drawing. No one had been before allowed, he said, to make such drawings. As to the originals, he could not say anything higher of them than that they deserved to be placed in the cabinets or galleries of Sa Majesté, where they would enjoy the protection that the Grand Monarque gave to arts and sciences, and be sheltered from the injury and affronts put upon them by the Turks, who, in their extreme distaste for idolatry, thought to do a meritorious work by breaking off noses and other excrescences from the statues.

As we know, the Grand Monarque and the French art galleries and museums did remarkably well out of their eastern embassies, and Lord Elgin and the British Museum had little on them in the end.

One of the best accounts of the Acropolis was written by a Jesuit, Père Jacques Babin, in 1672. He deplores the denigrating descriptions of some of his predecessors, who had not, he thought, properly looked at the place, but had called it merely a castle above a wretched village, run over by wolves and foxes, containing nothing but hovels. But "you will see", he says to the abbé to whom his letter is addressed, "that it is still a large enough and beautiful enough town, despite its extremely decayed age and all the wars by which it has been so often ruined". He has a passage of moralizing on the inconstancy of human affairs which can so reduce great cities, and another of thankfulness to Providence that Athens should survive after so many vexatious revolutions which threatened to destroy her. His description, the most detailed since Pausanias, begins with a faint note of apology—"I hope that this relation will not be disagreeable to you, and that your piety and curiosity will find in it some satisfaction"—for he will describe the ancient churches, and the temples of the false gods, the lantern of Demosthenes, the Academy of Plato, the Lyceum of Aristotle, the palaces of Theseus, Themistocles and the Emperor Hadrian, columns, triumphal arches and the other superb remains of antiquity which still survive in this afflicted country. If the abbé likes to hear of savage countries like America and Canada, how much more should he be interested in news from a city which was once called the eye and the sun of Greece, which was the most enlightened country in the world, and called all other nations barbarians. So he will describe Athens as she is among her ruins to-day. Enthusiastic over every building and fragment that he saw, he regretted only that he could not find all that Pausanias described—"*on ne voit plus tous ces Temples, tous ces mausolées, et toutes ces statues dont parlent les historiens*".[1]

Athens-enthusiasm was now in full cry. Account followed account; many were illustrated by engravings, all were painstaking labours of love; they have varying degrees of value. Those of the French antiquary Spon and the English clerical

[1] Jaques Babin (1672).

botanist, Sir George Wheeler, describing a month in Athens in 1676, have great detail and some inaccuracies; Spon gives more information, while Wheeler acquired more marbles and inscriptions. They corrected some of the mistakes made by their predecessors, and made some of their own; they became for a time the standard authorities on the subject. More learned, they were less emotionally moved than Guillet de St Georges, who, probably without having been there, had the year before lamented the ruins described by earlier writers.

"We passed through the *jardinages* which cover the ruins outside the Academy. When we arrived at the famous school, what was our grief, and what desolation did we see? There were only heaps of great stones, and marble débris hidden by earth and grass. Everywhere were clusters of fig trees and olives, gardens, and huts where the gardeners lived It is not possible to dig into six feet of earth without finding some precious antique. Four or five years ago a gardener digging found a white marble Pallas Athene which he sold for two crowns."[1]

Meanwhile, in the hands of the destructive Turks, changes occurred on the Acropolis; besides mutilating and breaking up sculptures, and building their hovels of (and over) fragments of antiquity, they stuffed the Propylaea with gunpowder and let it blow up in 1656, and, during the attack by the Venetians in 1687, similarly stuffed the Parthenon, so that a bomb aimed at it exploded the gunpowder and shattered, for the first time since it was built, its form. The Venetian commanders, like most others, put military aims before aesthetic, they had contemplated mining and blowing up the whole Acropolis, but found this too difficult. They had, however, their own love of fine architecture, and would have liked to see it in Venice; when they left Athens after a brief occupation, they tried to take with them from the Parthenon the horses of Athene's chariot and the statue of Poseidon; unfortunately they were dropped and smashed while being lowered. Athens was left again to the Turks, and continued its long career of progressive ruin and spoliation, noted and recorded with increasing learning and care by visitors throughout the eighteenth century. Societies such as the Dilettanti were formed to increase the knowledge of ancient art; they sent their envoys to draw and

[1]Guillet de St Georges (1675).

describe Athenian antiquities, and to bring back samples. This was easily done. Valuable objects could be picked up from anywhere on the Acropolis, lying neglected on waste ground, or found built into houses in the town. "We purchased two fine fragments of the frieze of the Parthenon", wrote Dr Richard Chandler in 1776, "which we found inserted over the doorways in the town, and were presented with a beautiful trunk which had fallen from the metopes and lay neglected in the garden of a Turk." In spite of Chateaubriand's assertion that the British kept taking sculptures, they seem to have been no more successful at this than the French; Athens became an international thieves' kitchen, from which ruin-tasters of all nations abstracted what they could, and the museums and galleries of the more cultured European countries became rich in Hellenic treasures. "You have the best sculptures; we want them", they in effect said British and French ambassadors to Constantinople made the collection of "pieces" from Athens a regular part of their official duties. The Dilettanti Society's agents were particularly adventurous, climbing up to positions from which they could draw the Parthenon frieze, and at the same time, overlook the houses of the Turks, so that their female inhabitants had to be confined or removed. Fashionable visitors followed the artists and antiquarians; the spirited Lady Craven enjoyed herself there greatly in 1786, observing the habits of the Turks, the nests of the storks on the roofs of the temples, those of the hermits on the summits of pillars, and the magnificence "of the superb temple of Theseus", on which she inscribed her name; "there is no such thing as tearing me away from this charming building," she wrote As to Mr John Morritt of Rokeby, an enterprising Yorkshire squire, he made a brave attempt to carry off the centaurs and Lapithae from the Parthenon frieze for his sculpture gallery at Rokeby, but fortunately failed. A few years later Lord Elgin set to work on his famous plunderings on behalf of his government; bought and paid for, the sculptures were roughly dragged off, and damage done that has never been forgiven by envious rivals and shocked travellers. Chateaubriand who preferred Athens antiquities to be taken by the French, found it "cruel to think Alaric and Mahomet II respected the Parthenon, and that it was demolished by Morosini and Lord Elgin". In exonerating Alaric he differed from Lord

Byron, who made the goddess of the temple say "Know, Alaric and Elgin did the rest," and blame both "the Gothic monarch and the Pictish peer," but the latter most. Indeed, Lord Elgin had an extremely poor press from visitors to Athens. "Everything relative to this catastrophe," wrote Edward Dodwell, who was in Athens at the time, "was conducted with an eager spirit of insensate outrage, and an ardour of insatiate rapacity, in opposition not only to every feeling of taste, but to every sentiment of justice and humanity."[1] Hobhouse and Byron, going about Athens, found everywhere the gaps the Pictish peer had made where he had removed columns, capitals and sculptures; once they came on the shaft of an Ionic column, of very white marble, lying entire in a wooden trough on the beach, waiting for exportation: it belonged, they were told, to the English.

With the English all about Athens (in 1813 there were ten times as many Britons there as there were French or Germans), it is interesting to trace differences in their ruin-approach. Hobhouse, for example, came to the Acropolis as a scholar; everything recalled to him the relevant passages and events in classical literature and history; without this association and learning, he would not have taken great pleasure in the buildings as such. He liked to "peruse the history of a thousand ages" in the noble monuments on which he gazed. When he acquired relics, as, like everyone else in Athens, he liked to do (for no visitor was without some share of "insatiate rapacity"), he cherished them from scholarly motives, and his "look what I picked up in Athens" was always intelligently uttered. Byron, who knew and cared much less about classical history and literature, was a romantic, not a scholar: he enjoyed the ruins for their beauty and their romance; feeling a "preference of the wild charms of nature to all the classic associations of art and history". He disdained "the paltry antiquarian and his despicable agents", ostensibly because they looted, but perhaps partly because Hobhouse rather bored him with too much archaeology. He was fascinated, but unlearned. "Here let me sit upon this massy stone", and muse and poeticize about the buildings above me, but I do not want to be bothered with antiquarian details, which anyhow hamper poetry. He passed his time in Athens in a rapture of poetic emotion about Greece; and for the

[1]Edward Dodwell, *Tour through Greece* (1819).

rest, enjoyed all the minor pleasures of Athenian ruins, such as cutting his name on the more famous buildings, writing poetry in the monument of Lysicrates, seeing the dwellings of stylite hermits on the tops of pillars, inveighing against Lord Elgin, and appropriating marble fragments and ancient skulls out of tombs.

While archaeologists examined and identified fragments of columns, and artists made drawings of the sculptures, and poets mused and wrote, the ordinary visitors (including the midshipmen from frigates stationed in the Piraeus) gaped at the monuments, fitfully recalled their classics, pocketed fragments of antiquity, and cut or wrote their names on ancient columns. These were the typical English travellers mentioned in a contemporary poem, "He comes to Athens, and he writes his name". Some of them knocked the noses off statues as mementoes; all enjoyed their introduction to Athenian culture; many, on returning to England, built model temples in their gardens or parks. Princess Caroline, who was there with her suite in 1816, enjoyed herself greatly, directing excavations to be made everywhere where she hoped to come on buried objects, and was hospitably entertained by the antiquarian French consul, M. Fauvel, the cicerone of all distinguished visitors. He had embellished his house *en grecque* with fragments of Athens—parts of columns and capitals for seats, antique tiles for roof, tombs and inscriptions all about. The house stood between the Temple of Theseus and the ruined library of the Ptolemies; from its terrace, one of the Princess's suite records, they listened to the singing and dancing of Egyptian slaves on the Acropolis. Of the Parthenon and Propylaea he wrote,

"these admirable, these venerable marbles are much defaced by the obscure names of the different travellers who have visited Athens for some centuries past. The impression on the mind amidst these sacred ruins is so intense, that we feel a diffidence, a solemn awe, which seems to deprive us of a great measure of the power of utterance: we speak in half whispers."[1]

At sunrise the diarist, a man of sensibility, sat on the marble walls of the Parthenon and imagined victorious fleets in the Piraeus, songs of triumph, festivals and feasts, the assembled multitude,

[1]Dr Byron, *Travels of Princess Caroline* (1845).

the orators. "When I awakened from my reveries, I could not but feel myself overwhelmed with melancholy: I looked around me, but could perceive nothing besides immense heaps of ruins, sterile plains, and a deserted sea." To console himself, he said, "Everything passes away, everything must have an end in this world . . . I too soon shall be no more, and other mortals, transitory as myself, will make the same reflections on the same ruins." Such reflections were set, as it were, to music by the beauty of the scene, by the golden hue of the Acropolis under the rising sun, and by the wind that whistled among the tall columns as among palms in the ruins of Alexandria. Then there were the pleasures of walking about the town, where hardly a house was without "some little marble fragment of ancient sculpture stuck in its front". Visitors to Athens enjoyed, according to their capacities, all the great ruin-pleasures, and the small delicate entertainments to be found among shattered temples and palaces, among the lovely débris of the ages.

The beauty of Athens as a whole, with all its layers of Periclean, Hellenistic, Roman, Byzantine, Frankish, Turkish, has often been obscured by a too exclusive concentration on the classical. Perhaps the best description of Turkish Athens in the early nineteenth century is Chateaubriand's.

"Its flat roofs interspersed with minarets, cypresses, ruins, detached columns, the domes of its mosques crowned with large nests of storks, produced a delightful effect in the sun's rays. But, if Athens might still be recognized by its ruins, it was obvious at the same time, from the general appearance of its architecture, and the character of its buildings, that the city of Minerva was no longer inhabited by her people."

Athens gave him, nevertheless,

"a kind of pleasure which deprived me of the power of reflection. . . . Sparta and Athens have, even in their ruins, kept their different characters; those of the former gloomy, grave and solitary, of the latter light, pleasing and social."

At Athens

"you are enchanted by the magic of genius, filled with the idea of the perfection of man, considered as an intelligent and immortal being. The lofty sentiments of human nature assumed at Athens a degree of elegance which they had not at Sparta. . . . In a word, as I passed from the ruins of Lacedaemon to the ruins of Athens I felt that I should have liked to die with Leonidas and live with Pericles."[1]

He went walking with the charming and learned M. Fauvel, who showed him antique fragments at every step. Crowds of children capered before them, as they wandered from broken monument to prostrate column and delicately carved capital. Chateaubriand noted the mellow golden colour of the buildings, the harmony of their proportions, the strength of the Parthenon. They ascended by the minaret stairway, sat on the broken frieze and looked at the view—the great spread of ruins on the hill's slopes, the waste heath, the olive groves and vineyards, the white walls and the gardens, the Albanian women carrying water. All was illumined by brilliant light, and the buildings had the soft colour of peach blossom, struck by the golden ray of sunrise. On the horizon of the light-bathed sea the citadel of Corinth glowed like purple fire. In short, the view was magnificent.Chateaubriand mused on the past, pictured the Athenian fleet in the Piraeus, the orations of Demosthenes, the voices chanting from the theatre. But all was silence, and he fell into the usual ruin-meditations—everything must have an end in this world, where are fled those divine geniuses, I too shall be soon no more, and others will make the same reflections on the same ruins, our lives are in the hands of God.

So musing, he descended from the citadel, picking up as he went a piece of marble belonging to the Parthenon. He had also preserved a fragment of the tomb of Agamemnon, for "I have made a practice of taking something with me from the monuments I have visited. Not such splendid memorials as Lord Elgin's and M. Choiseul's; but I preserve them with care. When I look at these trifles, they remind me of my pilgrimages and adventures".

He rode away from Athens in a daydream of what he would make of it were it his.

Chateaubriand, for all his clichés, got something from Athens that both the learned researches of archaeologists and the dreaming raptures of poets missed—the actual contemporary Athens, lying in its picturesque beauty, squalor and ruin in the Aegean sunshine. An Athens that was to pass with the lethargic Turks who

[1]René de Chauteaubriand, *Itinéraire de Paris à Jérusalem* (1825).

misruled it, and has been too much neglected and disdained, its huddle of medieval dwellings cleared away like rubbish to uncover the classical Athens beneath them, its mosques largely destroyed, its Byzantine churches decayed, while the classical Acropolis was stripped, excavated, austerely ordered and labelled, and the streets of the great modern capital superseded the village at its foot.

With the expulsion of the Turks in 1833, the era of the archaeologist in Athens began. Excavations, reconstructions, the clearing away of débris and of medieval accretions, the removal of mosque and minaret from the Parthenon and of the Frankish tower from the Propylaea, the establishment of archaeological schools, the digging up of statues and sculptures, the placing of fallen columns where they did or did not belong, the storing of moveable exhibits in museums, the shoring up of unsteady edifices, the discovery of ancient foundations, the repairing of broken friezes and columns, the speculations of rival professors, the new and the abandoned theories, the disputes, the learned volumes written, the Hellenic cruises, the pilgrimages of scholars and tourists eager to breathe the glorious air of Hellas, have made Athens during the past century the very centre of ruin-pleasure. Some possible pleasures were rejected: a German proposal of 1835 to build on the Acropolis a huge castle surrounding a restored Parthenon was not carried out; nor have the temples been painted to look as they looked in the days of their glory. There are those (such as Mr Osbert Lancaster) who think that the archaeologists have carried their peculiar pleasures too far, deplore the laying bare of the Agora by the pulling down of the old Turkish quarter which covered it, and admire the sound judgment of the Duke of Wellington, who, on being informed that a Roman pavement (Silchester) had been laid bare on his estate, at once ordered it to be covered up again without delay.[1] It is all a question of point of view. There are antiquarians; there are also romantic wanderers such as Chateaubriand, Byron, Goethe and Lamartine, meditating on past glories and transported by the view of the Aegean from the Acropolis; there are cheerful tourists pocketing mementoes and writing their names on temples and being photographed outside the Parthenon. All these classes of traveller have agreed

[1] Osbert Lancaster, *Classical Landscape with Figures* (John Murray, 1947).

that "much greater hardships and perils than it can be the lot of any traveller . . . to undergo would be at once recompensed and forgotten in arriving at Athens", such is the power of majestic ruins over the astonished mind of man.

23

But much more extensive has always been the effect of the ruins of Rome. Rome is accessible; its progressive ruining has been observed closely, and without intermission, by citizens and travellers for nearly two thousand years. Rome's fame, her power and glory, her secular and religious authority, created a mystique necessarily unique; Rome in ruins is a symbol of a lost world; the emotional impact is intense. Age by age, piece by piece, history falls with Rome; age by age, piece by piece, history rises as Rome rises; it is the tale of western historical man.

Historical man: for, coming to Rome, one moves into history. Rome is a city comparatively modern; Romulus was, it seems, not building on the Palatine until seven hundred years after the fall of Knossos; by the side of Mycenae, Tiryns, Troy, Athens, and the Egyptian, Babylonish and Assyrian cities, Rome is a parvenu. Even Romulus left little enough trace; there is not much ruin to look at before the Republic. What there was, was honoured and cherished by later generations, as the cradle of their glory—

> "*praeterea disjectis oppida muris*
> *reliquas veterumque vides monumenta virorum*"

has been uttered by Roman voices even through all the ages of plundering, looting, transformation and destruction. The hallowed shrines, the temples of the gods, the sacred source of Rome's beginning, the broken lines of her earliest walls, these were honoured by proud Roman piety, while the palaces, temples, triumphal arches, huge baths and theatres, of Imperial Rome magnificently covered all the Seven Hills, and the palaces of the Caesars sprawled glorious beside the thatched house of Romulus.

But in ruins as such there was not then much sign of interest; indeed, before Constantine there were not many ruins in imperial Rome. After that, ruin-sensibility, such as it was, did not lack food for its growth, what with Constantine's plunderings of Rome for

Constantinople, the turning of many temples into churches, the neglect and destruction of others, and the rapidly developing habit of quarrying the new buildings from the old. Even before the sackings, Rome's external glory was dwindling, under the assaults of Christians and the desertion of noble families who followed the emperor to the gorgeous capital in the east. Jerome, seven years before the first barbarian sack, put it too strongly, breaking into a paean of triumph over a Capitol filled with mire, all the temples tottering and defiled with dirt and cobwebs, paganism banished into the wilderness, and the gods dwelling with bats and owls among the desolate house-tops. Like the Hebrew prophets, he always over-wrote ruin. Damage there was; but even after the suppression of paganism by Theodosius, the pagans still celebrated their rites in their ancient temples, and Christian assaults on these were held in check. The topographical registers of the fourth and fifth centuries show a Rome still nearly intact: temples, amphitheatres and circuses, the great baths, the triumphal arches, the palaces and gardens, still for the most part stood in splendid perfection, while the basilicas of the new faith sprang up among them, sometimes, like St Peter's, quarried from the pagan walls. A little later Alaric and his Goths, then Genseric and his Vandals, sacking and plundering the city and massacring its inhabitants, found themselves unable, perhaps disinclined, to destroy its massive ancient buildings; taking everything portable of value, they left few ruins, except the Romans themselves, who, wandering penniless about their sacked dwellings, or seeking refuge abroad, hated the very word ruin. There was certainly, in the fifth century in Rome, no inclination towards ruin-petting.

Nor were the foreign visitors of that time much interested in the ruins of pagan buildings, or, indeed, in pagan buildings intact, if we are to judge from their letters and utterances. For the influx of tourists to Rome had, by the fifth century, assumed the character of religious pilgrimage; after Jerusalem, Rome was the most rewarding objective (and cheaper and easier than the Holy Land), to the seeker after absolution, improved devotions, health, and the other benefits conferred at the tombs of martyrs and saints. "*Innumeros cineres sanctorum Romula in urbe vidimus*," said Prudentius; and the Roman guide-books, which at first added a short section on Christian buildings and shrines to the itinerary of places and objects contained in the *Notitia* and the *Curiosum Urbis Romae*, soon omitted everything else, and became an enumeration of gates, churches, tombs of martyrs and sacred relics. As,

"The first is the Cornelian gate, which is now called the gate of St Peter. Near it is situated the Church of St Peter, in which his body lies, decked with gold and silver and precious stones; and no one knows the number of the holy martyrs who rest in that church. On the same way is another church, in which lie the holy virgins Rufina and Decunda. In a third church . . ."

and so on, all round the walls. Are we to imagine that the throng of pilgrims, arrived at the church of the chief apostle by the Cornelian gate, passed with unconcerned or unseeing eyes the great Circus of Nero on whose northern wall the basilica was built, the Pantheon, the Baths of Agrippa, the Forum of Trajan? Sunk in devotions, eager to attain the sanctuaries which they had travelled so far to see, which were to do them so much good, did they ignore these majestic pagan monuments, turning on them vague, incurious, lack-lustre eyes? Or did they regard them with the contemptuous, the shocked distaste, the angry aversion, felt by Richard Ford in Spain for baroque, or the negligent inconcern which travellers seeking baroque may feel for Gothic, or the impatience with which those who are all for classical architecture dismiss Byzantine, and vice versa? The Christian barbarians were not conditioned to Pagan culture; further, they knew it to be irreligious. They must, nevertheless, have turned their heads to stare at the mighty objects, the tremendous, richly wrought, sometimes crumbling monuments to a perished and wicked civilization, as they hurried on their way to holiness "to pay worship to the most blessed apostle St Peter". The streets they trod were haunted by alien gods, whose broken habitations loomed sinisterly over them; something of that ghostly past may have chilled and haunted their credulous souls, hinting at horizons more mysterious than those they knew. They have left on this matter no communications; no utterance concerning Rome's ruins has come down to us from these early tourists. No word of the ravages committed by the barbarian invaders, and being even then committed by predatory barons and clerical and civic authorities on noble buildings; nothing about the stripping of bronze roofs from temples, or the quarrying of marble to build churches or palaces or to transport to the east. Nothing of the Capitol, or the condition of the Palace of the Caesars, or the great baths, or the triumphal arches. Incurious travellers, the pilgrims pressed on to their goals; to them the greatest city of the world was simply Holy Rome, spiritually resplendent on her seven hills, triumphant over defeated paganism, whose monuments yet stood intimidatingly grouped around her churches; and what more they thought they have not left on record.

More exasperatingly, Sidonius, the amiable bishop of Lyons, gives, in his letters from Rome in 467 and 8, no account of the architectural state of the twice sacked city. It is cheerful and bustling, there are festivities for the wedding of the patrician Ricimer with the emperor's daughter, it is (still) "Rome, the abode of law, the training school of letters, the fount of honours, the head of the world, the motherland of freedom, the city unique upon earth, where none but the barbarian and the slave is foreign", and every one should visit it; but the extent of the damage done by the Vandals a dozen years ago passes unnoted; he does not even mention the stripping by Genseric of the statues and the gilded tiles from the Temple of Jupiter on the Capitol. Yet one cannot think that so cultivated a cleric of the world was oblivious of such matters, or that, though he fell prostrate at the *limina apostolorum* before entering the city, deriving from the apostles' protection new health and vigour after his journey, such devotions filled his interested mind.

Though Sidonius has not left on record any laments for it, imperial Rome was rapidly becoming a quarry, where marble columns and carvings were torn from temples and theatres and burned into lime for churches and new houses, and deserted temples were demolished for gain. The intelligent and public-spirited emperor Marjorian, disgusted at the destruction, issued in 458 a ferocious edict against it. He was determined to

"put an end to the abuses which have long excited our indignation. . . . Public buildings, in which all the ornament of the city consisted, have been destroyed with the criminal permission of the authorities on the pretext that the materials were necessary for public works. The splendid structures of ancient buildings have been overthrown, and the great has been everywhere destroyed in order to erect the little."

Builders of private houses, he went on, had despoiled public buildings, whereas all such buildings should have been preserved by the loving reverence of the citizens. It was forbidden in future to damage any ancient buildings, under the intimidating penalty of being flogged and losing both hands. What had been appropriated was to be returned, the restoration of old buildings was to be taken in hand, and what could not be restored should at least be used for the adornment of other public buildings.

It was a brave but fruitless effort. Three years later Marjorian fell. Under successive rulers, the secular glories of Rome dwindled with her secular power, and the pleasures of ruin, for nobles and plebs alike, consisted in pillage and greed. Only the churches flourished, ever more lavishly adorned, shining sumptuously in the gathering darkness. The Roman empire in the west fell to the Ostrogoths in ecclesiastical splendour and secular decay. Theodoric, the letterless but culture-admiring Gothic king, doing his best to save Rome's magnificence, fought the relentless tide of greed and ignorance with edicts and threats and the flow of eloquent denunciation that poured from his minister Cassiodorus. "*Gothorum laus est civilitas custodita*", the Goth-praising Cassiodorus wrote; but not even the care of these disgusting savages who roamed over Europe sacking other people's cities, who are so praised by German historians, and who ought never to have left the Vistula, could save Rome's monuments.

The Rome of Justinian was taking already the pattern it was to keep through the Middle Ages—classical antiquity mouldering into picturesque decay, grass and shrubs, ivy and trees, pushing through and covering its stones, its ghosts stalking almost forgotten about the cloistered and monkish and baronial city, where a world of new churches and monasteries grew unceasingly out of ancient spoiled magnificence. Ruin came into its own, harbouring in its mouldering corners beggars, robbers and the destitute, who led in its crumbling recesses such domestic life as they enjoyed, lurking in the shadows of falling palaces and dilapidated walls, till the stones that sheltered them were little by little quarried away by enterprising builders, or the deserted temples of the old gods transformed, rebuilt and redecorated for the new.

One must believe that there were, both among Romans and visitors (and the pilgrim tide swelled year by year) some, even through those ages of incurious ignorance, who knew and cared for classical Rome, even before Hildebert, with his "*Pars tibi, Roma, nihil*". But the church preached triumphantly of its downfall, adding, inevitably, that what the prophet had said about the destruction of Nineveh had been in Rome fulfilled.

The pilgrims, swarming in to the city like crowds at a cup final, suffocated and trampled to death (as they were in the first Jubilee year) must, in their less urgent moments, have felt pressing on their consciousness the ghostly, the even sinister, weight of old Rome. Bede, at the beginning of the eighth century, mentioned a proverb popular among Anglo-Saxon pilgrims, "*Quamdiu stat Colysaeus, stat et Roma*; *quando cadet Colysaeus, cadet Roma, cadet et mundus*"—a saying made famous by an English poet twelve hundred years later. Then and ever since, English travellers have been Colosseum-minded.

The pilgrims' admiration was instructed only by topographical handbooks, crude medleys of legend and fact, such as the *Mirabilia Urbis Romae*, the *vade mecum* of Roman sight-seers for some centuries. Interest in Roman ruins rose like a swelling tide; but archaeological studies were still rudimentary when Cola di Rienzo, in the middle of the fourteenth century, took them up. He was the first ruin-enthusiast to make a close study of classical inscriptions. "Every day he would walk among the ruins, scrutinizing every piece of sculptured marble. No one could decipher inscriptions better than he". Actually this was to say little enough; Rienzo made grave mistakes in his deciphering, as everyone, for many years after him, did. "Formerly there were many wonderful inscriptions", a thirteenth-century scholar had written, "with letters which to-day we are not able fully to read or understand".

To Rienzo belongs the credit of being the first scientific inscriptologist. But in him, interest in Rome's past was less a scholar's than a patriot's; set on reviving Rome's grandeur and authority, he called in her ruined stones as witnesses, extracting from an altar in the Lateran a bronze tablet inscribed with a fragment of the Lex Regia, and having it built into the wall behind the choir, surrounded by a painting of the Senate. Then, clad in white toga and hat, he summoned a meeting in the Lateran and delivered an oration on the Lex Regia and Rome's present degradation.

Like other future dictators, he passionately praised the Rights of the People. There is no doubt that his antiquarian studies went to his head and made him a little mad. His imagination became intoxicated, he developed delusions of grandeur; like Caracalla before ruined Troy, he began to think himself one of the mighty figures from the past, until imagination, bursting its bounds, swept him into action. To be surrounded by great ruins is seldom safe; they have a singular effect on the mind. The Romans, always thus surrounded, were never safe, and life was for them an unsteady affair. To live among all that strange broken grandeur was more than any but equable spirits could endure tranquilly, and few Romans have had equable spirits. Excitement, turbulence, rivalry and greed stirred them incessantly. Those who could afford it rushed at the ruins hacking them to pieces to build themselves palaces and churches; the destruction wrought on Rome between the fifth and the sixteenth centuries was so appalling as to invoke curses and denunciations from its more civilized contemporaries in each century, but no one had the power to stop it. Had Rienzo, during his years of power, devoted himself to saving Roman monuments, he might have temporarily checked the assaults on them; but no such attempts had a lasting effect. Popes and barons went their own way, knocking down, throwing up, building medieval Rome from classical; a score of cloistered convents and churches blossomed where a porticoed temple had stood, palaces and towers sprouted luxuriously or menacingly from the broken walls of great theatres and baths. Those, on the other hand, who could not afford to build new habitations nested in the old, burrowing into crannies like rabbits, plastering their hovels to the walls like swallows' nests, and setting up their dark low shops between column and column. What no one in Rome did with the ruins was to forget them and leave them alone, whether they were prelates and noblemen using them for building or beggars and criminals lurking in the ivied gloom of their vaults. Each noble family seized on some noble ruin for his fortress; the Savelli family took the Theatre of Marcellus; the Frangipani erected their castles on the Palace of the Caesars, the Colosseum, the arches of Titus and Constantine; the Colonna took the Temple of the Sun, the Crescenzi the baths of Severus, the Orsini the theatre of Pompey, and so on. Everyone took what he liked from the Colosseum, regarded as the universal quarry—

> "A ruin—yet what ruin! from its mass
> Walls, palaces, half-cities, have been rear'd. . . .

Petrarch, Rienzo's friend and admirer, did his best to save Rome from her predatory citizens. Not a scientific archaeologist, he approached her as a poet. At his first visit he was stupefied by her magnificence, as he wrote to Giovanni Colonna from the Capitol on the Ides of March, 1337.

> "I do not know what to say; so many great things cause in me astonishment and stupor. . . . You used to dissuade me from coming on the grounds that at the sight of the city in ruins . . . my enthusiasm would be lessened. . . . Truly Rome is greater, and its ruins are greater, than I had supposed. I marvel now not that the world was conquered by this city, but that it was conquered so late."

From this promising starting-point he proceeded to explore Rome, *Mirabilia* in hand, uncritical, enthusiastic, delighted, and accepting all he saw and read, the Christian legends of the *Mirabilia* together with classical history. Like Rienzo, he attempted no deciphering; he was that familiar figure, the romantic poet straying at large through Rome, passionate both in admiration and in rage at the wilful destruction. He paid five short visits, and left on record a kaleidoscope of impressions, musings, denunciations, catalogues of things seen, and glorifications of the great past as compared with the decadent and squalid present. On many of his walks about the city he was companioned by his friend Cardinal Giovanni Colonna di San Vito, and for long afterwards they corresponded about these delightful rambles, during which the conversation had sustained a remarkable level. After listing seventy-seven notable objects seen, Petrarch continues,

> "After the fatigue of wandering over the immense circuit of the city, we used often to stop at the Baths of Diocletian. Sometimes we climbed on the roof of that magnificent building, to enjoy, more than in any other place, wholesome air and a spacious view, silence and friendly solitude. We had under our eyes the spectacle of all those great ruins. We talked of history and of moral philo-

sophy and of the beginnings of the arts. One day I spoke at some length of the origin of the liberal and mechanical arts. You ask me to repeat it, but without the place and the day and your rapt attention, I cannot."

The spectacle of ruins had played its familiar historic role of stimulus and inspiration: it induced him to write to another companion of his rambles, Paolo Annibaldi, a letter in Latin hexameters, recalling the ruins they had seen together and exhorting his friend to try to keep the peace between the turbulent factions of noblemen and check the spoliation of the precious relics of antiquity. Annibaldi, for excellent reasons, had already been trying to put a check on this; his family was of the Colonna faction, and the Colonna had succceeded in expelling the Frangipani from the Colosseum and had made it one of their own many strongholds, protecting its walls, so far as possible, from the determined quarrying of their fellow noblemen. In some of the Colonna castles Petrarch had stayed, getting from their square, fortified towers fine views of the prospect of ruins that was fourteenth-century Rome.

"Rome resembled a huge field, encircled with moss-covered walls, with tracts of wild and cultivated land, from which rose gloomy towers or castles, basilicas and convents crumbling to decay, and monuments of colossal size clothed with verdure; baths, broken aqueducts, colonnades of temples, isolated columns, and triumphal arches surmounted by towers; while a labyrinth of narrow streets, interrupted by rubbish heaps, led among these dilapidated remains, and the yellow Tiber, passing under broken stone bridges, flowed sadly through the ruinous waste. Round the city, within the ancient walls of Aurelian, stood tracts of land, here waste, there cultivated, resembling country estates in their extent. Vineyards and vegetable gardens lay scattered like oases through the whole of Rome. . . . Baths and circuses were overgrown with grass, and were here and there absolutely marshy. Everywhere that the eye rested might be seen gloomy, defiant, battlemented towers, built out of the monuments of the ancients, with crenelated enceintes of most original form, constructed of pieces of marble, bricks, and fragments of peperino. These were the castles and palaces of Guelf or Ghibelline nobles, who sat thirsting for battle in ruins on the classic hills. . . There was not a single nobleman in Rome at the time who was not the owner of a tower. In deeds of the period the possessions of the Romans in the city are occasionally specified as 'towers, palaces, houses and ruins.' Families dwelt among ruins, in uncomfortable quarters, barred by heavy iron chains, with their relatives and retainers, and now and then burst forth with the wild din of arms, to make war on their hereditary enemies."[1]

And among the ruins noblemen and prelates and popes ravaged, wrecking and looting, burning marble into lime, throwing up new palaces, castles, churches and convents out of ancient buildings, stripping marble from Rome to adorn, as Petrarch bitterly complained, the court of Naples, as five hundred years ago Charlemagne had stripped it for Aix-la-Chapelle. "*Impietas*," cried Petrarch, and "*heu scelus indignum!*" leading a swelling chorus of indignation, which, though it had singularly little effect on the marauders, who continued to maraud without a blush, induced in visitors to Rome a growing attention to the classical grandeur which stood, a tremendous wrecked background to the modern scene. Cultivated travellers came "*per vedere quelle magnificenze antiche, che al presente si possono vedere in Roma*". In Fazio degli Uberti's *Dittamondo* (1360), Rome is personified as an ancient Sibyl in torn clothes, pointing out to strangers the ruins of the city, "*che comprender potrai quanto fui bella*". To Petrarch this ancient Rome was an obsession. "It is scarcely to be believed," he wrote to Colonna, "how great in me is the desire to contemplate that city which, though a desert, is the effigy of antique Rome . . . Rome, I say, that city unique in the world, to which there neither has been nor ever will be anything similar". Over its ruining he mused with melancholy pleasure.

> "*Passan vostre grandezze e vostre pompe,*
> *Passan le signorie, passano i regni;*
> *Ogni cosa mortal Tempo interrompe.*"

It was a pleasure that, as life went on, took on a slightly sanctimonious quality. His lament over lost ruins is interesting as showing what, in his time, was largely or wholly gone, but has plenty of rhetorical exaggeration, as when he enquires of the baths which he and Colonna had so often visited and conversed in, "*Ubi sunt Thermae Diocletianae?*" His "*Ubi sunt tot luxurias*

[1]Gregorovius, *History of the City of Rome.*

principum palatia", where are so many luxurious palaces of princes, has also a spurious ring, going on as it does, "You will find their names in books, but seek through the city and you will find no remains at all, or else only the most insignificant". He put these doleful enquiries in his later-life mood of "Nothing endures, only God".

Petrarch's was the most famous voice before Raphael's that mobilized foreign opinion against the wrecking of antique Rome; it became a world atrocity; the Romans were held up to execration for their vandalism. Popes were besought to stop it; the Popes, themselves tremendous offenders, issued minatory decrees, quietly pillaging the while. The fifteenth century, protesting still more, also ravaged still more, and new Rome went up in increasing splendour. Or, as Gibbon sternly put it,

"If the forms of ancient architecture were disregarded by a people insensible of their use and beauty, the plentiful materials were applied to every call of necessity or superstition, till the fairest columns of the Ionic and Corinthian orders, the richest marbles of Paros and Numidia, were degraded, perhaps, to the support of a convent or a stable."[1]

But the new classical humanism was also in full flower. Poggio the Florentine had none of the religious considerations which had half consoled Hildebert three centuries before him; he was the pure pagan, overcome by the greatness of the ruined buildings and the collapse of so much splendour. His *De varietate fortunae urbis Romae* includes a survey of monuments which it is interesting to compare with Rienzo's of the last century. One observes that the vegetation has grown, concealing more of the buildings and inscriptions; there was considerably less of the Colosseum, on which the assaults had been redoubled during the past fifty years; the Forum Romanum was completely overgrown, and a pasture for cattle and pigs; the Capitol a mass of vineyard-covered ruins, the Palatine a shapeless wilderness. Many of the fortresses of the nobles were in ruin, and more of the churches; swamps encroached everywhere. Even medieval Rome was largely in ruins. Poggio, sitting on the Capitoline hill with a friend and surveying the desolation spread beneath them, conceived there his "elegant

[1]Edward Gibbon, *The Decline and Fall of the Roman Empire.*

moral lecture" *De varietate fortunae*, as Gibbon, who reports him, was three centuries later to be inspired on the same spot to his history of the fallen fortunes of Rome. So many true and imposing reflections are bound to occur to the visitor gazing on this stupendous and melancholy prospect, and Poggio had them all.

"The hill of the Capitol on which we sit was formerly the head of the Roman empire, the citadel of the earth, the terror of kings, illustrated by the footsteps of so many triumphs, enriched with the spoils and tributes of so many nations. This spectacle of the world, how is it fallen! how changed! how defaced! the path of victory is obliterated by vines, and the benches of the senators are concealed by a dunghill. Cast your eyes on the Palatine hill, and seek among the shapeless and enormous fragments the marble theatre, the obelisks, the colossal statues, the porticos of Nero's palace: survey the other hills of the city, the vacant space is interrupted only by ruins and gardens. The forum of the Roman people, where they assembled to enact their laws and elect their magistrates, is now enclosed for the cultivation of pot-herbs, or thrown open for the reception of swine and buffalos. The public and private edifices that were founded for eternity, lie prostrate, naked and broken, like the limb of a mighty giant, and the ruin is the more visible from the stupendous relics that have survived the injuries of time and fortune."[1]

Poggio's list of these remaining relics became the indispensable travellers' guide to Rome, superseding the *Mirabilia* ("*Poggius noster saepe mecum est. . . .*"). There were rival guides: Biondo's *Roma Instaurata*, a good and accurate topographical description; Pomponius, the antiquary and founder of the first Roman Academy, so devout a Rome-worshipper that the sight of an antique monument moved him to tears; Giovanni Dondi of Padua, who measured ancient buildings and copied inscriptions. To describe Rome became a fashion; to admire its ruins was the hall-mark of a civilized mind. Poggio searched them daily, recovering from the surrounding rubbish statues and sculptures, "the offspring of Grecian art, which the refined rapacity of Roman generals had selected from amongst the spoils of Greece as ornaments worthy to adorn the temples and palaces of the capital of the world", as Gibbon put it. Poggio wrote to a friend, "I see

[1] Poggio Bracciolini, *De Varietate Fortunae* (1430).

you desire to visit the city, and nothing shall prevent me from encouraging you to look at the relics of that city which was once the most splendid light of the world. For my part I have been for several years from my youth employed in this; but every day, like a new inhabitant, I am stupefied with admiration."

A few years later, Sigismundo Malatesta is alluding, in a letter from Rome to Isolte, to the prevalent fashion of ruin-enjoyment. "But to me," he adds, "wonderful ruins can hardly give pleasure, when you are nowhere to be seen in this place."

Through the century war was waged between the ruin-preservers and the ruin-destroyers, the archaeologists and the builders. Some of the more ardent among the former demanded the death penalty for the latter; and this line was approved by the popes, who saw no reason why anyone but themselves and those to whom they gave permission should quarry the precious marble and travertine. Nicholas V took from the Colosseum alone 2500 waggon loads in one year, and almost demolished the Servian wall. Pius II, the cultivated and sight-seeing Aeneas Silvius, issued a bull decreeing penalties against those who injured the monuments that he loved and used for his own purposes. "It delights me, Rome," he wrote, in enthusiastic Latin verse, "to look on thy ruins, out of whose fall ancient glory shines. But thy people dig into thy ancient walls, and out of hard marble prepare hard lime. If this impious people goes on plundering for three hundred years more, there will be nothing left to indicate nobleness."

So saying, Pius quarried away at ancient Rome to build the new. He was himself an enthusiastic ruin-fancier; he tried, he said, to interpret the fragments, and in imagination to restore what they had been. No aesthetic bigot, he admired both the ruins and the new buildings; unlike a critic of his time who called the manufacture of lime "a shame, because the new buildings are pitiful, and the beauty of Rome is in its ruins." Pius, like the other Renaissance popes, was in love with the new Rome, the dazzling palatial and ecclesiastical Rome, that was covering the old ruins as with new garments. "*Roma vetusta fui, sed nunc Roma nova vocabur.*" Antiquarians yearly published new topographies, plans, descriptions, drawings and imaginary reconstructions of the ancient buildings; ruin-worship was in full swing, and knowledge of which ruin was which daily increased. Petrarch's mistakes of identity, and even Poggio's, were, by the beginning of the sixteenth century, less likely. Ruin-tending became a science; each building was measured and drawn and compared with the descriptions of ancient writers. Raffaelle Sanzio, appointed superintendent of antiquities in 1516, drew up a magnificent plan of restoration; archaeology, patriotism and sentiment combined in a happy fusion of enthusiasm; but his illustrated plan of the city was interrupted by his death. His famous letter to Leo X remains one of the most urgent of the many protests against the destruction of monuments, which continued, though at a decreasing pace, through the century.

A new type of foreign visitor became frequent as the century went on, and the pilgrim, earnestly proceeding from shrine to shrine, gave place to the enquiring tourist interested in pagan ruins. In 1510 arrived Martin Luther, not yet anti-papal, still apostrophizing Holy Rome made holy by the martyrs. But he did not like what he saw of the Vatican, and does not seem either to have taken much stock of the ruins; Rome to him had no virtues. He was, no doubt, of those who grimly rejoiced in the awful sack and massacre by the Imperialist troops in 1527. This shattering event and its consequences, while increasing the number of Roman ruins, for some years kept visitors nervously away, as well as driving into exile and beggary hundreds of the noble families and the scholars. But by the 1540's tourism seems to have been in full swing. English travellers came and wrote descriptions of the antiquities; Sir Thomas Hoby grieved over vanished splendours—

"the wonderful majesty of buildings that only the roots thereof do yet represent the huge temples, the infinite great palaces, the immeasurable pillars . . . the goodly arches of triumph, the bains, the conduits of water . . . and a number of other things not to be found again throughout an whole world; imagining withal what majesty the city might be of when all these things flourished; then did it grieve me to see the only jewell, mirror, mistress and beauty of this world that never had her like nor (as I think) never shall, lie so desolate and disfigured."

So,

"after Mr Barker, Mr Parker, Whitehorn and I had thoroughly searched out such antiquities as were here to be seen from place

26 Temple of the Olympian Zeus, Athens Etching by D. Le Roy, 1758

27 Roman ruins with figures. Oil painting by Guardi

28 Campo Vaccino (Forum Romanum). Etching by G. B. Piranesi, 1772

to place, having bestowed all this time of our being here about the same, we thought it but loss of time to make any longer abode here,"[1]

and off they went to Naples, a pleasanter and less disfigured city. One gets from all these writers the impression of a Rome less evident than formerly, a Rome whose ancient remains were more shattered and gone to earth. Montaigne, later in the century, declared that nothing was to be seen of ancient Rome but its sky and the outline of its form; "those who said that the ruins of Rome at least remained said more than they were warranted in saying", for nothing remained of Rome but its sepulchre.

This sepulchre obsessed the poets. The approach became more subjective; personal gloom, alarm and despondency were transferred to the ruinous fragments that spoke to the beholder of their death and his. The desire for some mighty catastrophe that should bring the world crashing down, annihilating personal sorrows with all else, is occasionally evident. Joachim du Bellay's lovely lament for the antiquities of Rome is a medley of regret, hope, and self-consolation.

> "*Tristes désirs, vivez doncques contents:*
> *Car si le temps finit chose si dure*
> *Il finira la peine que j'endure.*"[2]

As to Rome, neither flames nor swords nor sackings nor the envious centuries nor the spite of men or gods have so abased her that "*la grandeur du rien qu'ils t'ont laissé*" does not still confound the world. And she will rebuild herself; her ruins serve the builders as models; the Roman genius will "*ressusciter ces poudreuses ruines.*"

> "*O merveille profonde!*
> *Rome vivant fut l'ornement du monde,*
> *Et morte elle est du monde le tombeau.*
> *Nouveau venu qui cherches Rome en Rome,*
> *Et rien de Rome en Rome n'apperçois,*
> *Ces vieux palais, ces vieux arcs que tu vois,*
> *Et ces vieux murs, c'est ce que Rome on nomme.*
> *Voy quel orgueil, quelle ruine: et comme*

[1] Sir Thomas Hoby (1545–61).
[2] Du Bellay, *Antiquités de Rome* (1557).

Celle qui mist le monde sous les loix
Pour douter tout, se douta quelque fois,
Et devint proye au temps, qui tout consomme.
Rome de Rome est le seul monument,
Et Rome a vaincu seulement.
Le Tybre seul, qui vers la mer s'enfuit,
Reste à Rome. O mondaine inconstance!
Ce qui est ferme, est par le temps détruit,
Et ce qui fuit, au temps fait resistance . . .
Rome n'est plus; et si l'architecture
Quelque ombre encore de Rome fait revoir,
C'est comme un corps par magique sçavoir
Tiré de nuit hors de la sepulture.
Le corps de Rome en cendre est devallé,
Et son esprit rejoindre s'est allé
Au grand esprit de cette masse ronde. . . ."[1]

The sack of 1527 had given a morbid stimulus to ruin-feeling, and later generations, who could not remember Rome before it, attributed to the imperial army of German and Spanish toughs much that was the wreck of time and of the Romans themselves Tasso and many others found religious consolation in the ruin of man's mighty works—

"*Muoiono le città, muoiono i regni,*
Copre i fasti e le pompe arena ed erba,
E l'uom d'esser mortale par che so sdegni:
O nostra mente cupida e superba!"

The annihilation of Rome, a tragedy to the renaissance humanists, was to the new poets of the reformation and counter-reformation, a triumph of God over proud man: it was the anti-humanist mystique of Augustine creeping back from the Dark Ages, a grim revenant never exorcised, though largely demoded by the pagan-minded scholars of the fourteenth and fifteenth centuries.

"*Confessez que le temps tout ruine et consomme,*"

Jaques Grevin exhorts the former masters of Rome. Rome

"*crie en déclarant sa ruine publique*
que rien n'est éternel que la grandeur de Dieu."[2]

[1] Du Bellay, *Antiquités de Rome* (1557)
[2] Jaques Grevin, *Le Bruit Ruineux* (1570).

Meanwhile the grass grows longer and the creepers climb in a denser jungle over broken columns and marbles: in vain the pilgrim seeks for Rome through *le ruine herbose*, Marini at the end of the century declared. He added that Rome, though now a phantom, would lead the spiritual universe. What he did not mention, nor anyone, was that the ruins were growing, beneath their jungled verdure, all the time more beautiful, more picturesque, and that a new kind of pleasure in them was developing, a pleasure neither antiquarian nor philosophical nor religious, but aesthetic. To gaze on the great ivied fragments was charming in itself, even though the purity of the emotion they aroused might be coloured with self-pity, and the tragedy of Rome's fall might form a sympathetic background to the visitor's personal sorrows. There were already, in fact, advance ripples of the great tide of pleasing romantic *Weltschmerz* that was to sweep over ruin-gazers a century later. It was scarcely, in the earlier seventeenth century, recognized as pleasure; James Howell, for instance, thought it wholesome medicine for the soul.

"Truly" (he wrote from Rome), "I must confess, that I find myself much better'd by it; for the sight of some of these ruins did fill me with symptoms of mortification, and make me more sensible of the frailty of all sublunary things, how all bodies, as well inanimate as animate, are subject to dissolution and change, and everything else under the moon."[1]

The Roman Catholic traveller, Richard Lassels, at Rome in the 1640's, enjoyed the ruins more frankly, when he had leisure to spare for them from his tour of the churches.

"Though Rome be growne again, by her new pallaces, one of the finest Cyties of Europe, yet her very ruines are finer than her new buildings," he said. "And though I am not ignorant how Rome, since her Ladyship governed the world, and was at her greatness, hath been six several times ruined and sacked by the envy and avarice of barbarous nations (*Visegoths*, *Wandals*, *Erules*, *Ostrogoths*, *Totila* who set fire on Rome 18 dayes together, and the *Germans* under *Bourbon*) whose malice was so great against Rome, that of thirty-six *Triumphal Arches* once in Rome there remained but four now visibly appearing; of ten *Thermae* anciently, but two remain any way visible; of seven *Circos*, but

[1] James Howell, *Epistolae Hoelianae* (1645).

one now appeares; yet as of fair Ladyes, there remain even in their old age fair rests of comelinesse, so the very ruines of Rome which malice could not reach to nor avarice carry away, are yet so comely, that they ravish still the beholders eye with their beauty, and make good the saying of an ancient author, that *Roma jacens quoque miracula est*, *Rome is a miracle even in its ruines*. But to returne to the *Coliseo*, its another wonder of the world: and I wonder indeed how such prodigious stones could either be layd together in a building, or being layd together, could fall."[1]

Rambling delightedly about, he turned his ravished eyes on baths that looked more like towns than bathing places, the Campo Vaccino, various triumphal arches, the Arch of Severus, half of it buried under ground, the other half sore battered with the air ("but why do I accuse the *Ayre*, when its onely *Time* that hath battered this *Triumphal Arch*, and moultered even marble?") and the Palatine hill with "the goodly ruines of the *Emperors pallace*, called *Palazzo Maggiore*. It possessed almost all the *Palatin hill*, as the ruines shew. Stately ruines I confesse: but ruines, and *Imperiall ruines*. And here I could not but wonder to see the pallace of the persecuting *Emperors* ruined quite, and the Church of the poore *Fisherman* standing still, more glorious than ever." Lassels was intelligent and knowledgeable about the ruins; he had guide-books, and knew the measurements even of the vanished Circus Maximus, and how in its vaulted caves or *fornices* prostitutes had carried on their business, which took from the *fornices* its name (another ruin-pleasure). So the pleased tourist "made Hue and Cry after every little thing which time seemed to have robbed us of", as well as after churches, palaces, convents, fountains, catacombs and gardens, before moving on to Naples. He had something of the universal curiosity of John Evelyn, with much less expertise, learning and taste. Evelyn also explored all the sights of Rome with delight; to him noble villas, gardens, palaces and churches were the supreme pleasure (ornamental gardens particularly his "elysium of delight"), but ancient Rome claimed his interest too, and he describes the more famous ruins with admiration and detail. The connoisseur in quest of objects of art and vertù was now frequent—Inigo Jones; the magnificent Earl of Arundel bringing back marbles

[1]Richard Lassels, *The Voyage of Italy* (1670).

and inscriptions, the cultured Evelyn with his pleasure in all forms of beauty except mountain scenery, his informed antiquarianism, and his Dilettante Royal Society intelligence. To such travellers, the great ruins were not what they had been to the renaissance classicists, the tomb of fallen Rome; Rome to them flourished most richly and gracefully in her new buildings. Evelyn's phrase, "heaps of ruins", has sometimes a touch of regretful impatience.

Meanwhile the artists were at work, painting broken arches and porticos as backgrounds to their religious or secular scenes, setting the fashion that was to rage so soon and so long, bringing Roman ruins into every cultivated home. The popularity of Claude, Poussin and Salvator Rosa achieved what the earlier Italian religious ruin-painters had not—they made ruins the fashion, hung them on English walls, built them in English gardens, and introduced them into the sketches of amateur artists abroad, so that by the end of the seventeenth century the average visitor to Italy sought first, and rhapsodized most, over

"The ruins, too, of some majestic piece,
Boasting the power of ancient Rome or Greece,
Whose statues, friezes, columns, broken lie,
And, though defaced, the wonder of the eye."

More Rome than Greece sprang up in British gardens, when the time arrived for that delightful craze. Addison, touring Europe in 1701, felt

"Immortal glories in my soul revive,
And in my soul a thousand passions strive,
When Rome's exalted beauties I descry.
Magnificent in piles of ruins lie
An amphitheatre's amazing height
Here fills my eye with terror and delight. . . ."[1]

And so on, the magnificent aspect of the ruins blending in his mind with all the superb history of Rome, for Addison had been classically bred. So Roman was his taste that he thought nothing of Gothic by comparison.

"Let anyone reflect," said he, "on the disposition of mind he finds in himself at his first entrance into the Pantheon at Rome,

[1] Joseph Addison, *Persia*

and how his imagination is filled with something great and amazing; and at the same time consider how little in proportion he is affected with the inside of a Gothick cathedral, though it be five times larger than the other; which can arise from nothing else but the greatness of the manner in one, and the meanness in the other."[1]

But also, in Englishmen, from the frequency of English Gothic, for our admiration for ruins, said Addison, arises mainly from their uncommonness.

"There are indeed many extraordinary ruins, but I believe a traveller would not be so much astonished at them did he find any works of the same kind in his own country. Amphitheatres, triumphal arches, baths, grottos, catacombs . . . are most of them at present out of fashion," he wrote at the turn of the century, "and only to be met with among the antiquities of Italy."[2]

In Italy, he was an indefatigable ruin-hunter. He preferred pagan to Christian ruins, for their legends recalled the ancient authors, and "a man who is in Rome can scarce see an object that does not call to mind a piece of a Latin poet or historian." Antiquities roused interesting reflections, though, in so beaten a subject, one could scarcely hope that these would be new. But his greatest ruin-pleasure was statue-seeking; he thought the Palatine should be thoroughly dug up and searched. People in Rome often bought land, gardens and vineyards in order to dig in them for sculptures and ancient bricks, "as they do for coal in England". Who knew but that they might not be rewarded for their labours by coming on some lovely column of porphyry, alabaster, jasper or agate, like that broken alabaster pillar, the colour of fire, which had been found in the ruins of Livia's portico, and was now over the high altar of Sta Maria in Campitello, with the light shining through it from a hole in the wall? So Addison assiduously searched.

British poets were rushing abroad, to enjoy and celebrate in verse "the resistless theme, imperial Rome." The scene they beheld was delicious; far more delicious than to-day. Sheer ruin-pleasure was drunk in intoxicating draughts; the head swam and the steps reeled with it. All those ruins. . . .

[1] Joseph Addison, *Remarks on Italy* (1701, 1702 and 1703).
[2] *Ibid.*

"Fall'n, fall'n, a silent heap; her heroes all
Sunk in their urns; behold the pride of pomp,
The throne of nations fall'n; obscur'd in dust;
Ev'n yet majestical; the solemn scene
Elates the soul, while now the rising Sun
Flames on the ruins in the purer air
Towering aloft upon the glittering plain,
Like broken rocks, a vast circumference;
Rent palaces, crush'd columns, rifled moles,
Fanes roll'd on fanes, and tombs on buried tombs."[1]

Thus John Dyer in 1740, in his long rhapsody *The Ruins of Rome*, which he impatiently begins with, "Enough of Grongar and the shady dales of winding Towy." Nothing but Roman ruins would now do for him; he felt, beholding them, that revolt from what Britain could offer which is familiar to most visitors to Italy. Transported, though fatigued, he made "the toilsome step up the proud Palatine", among cypress groves, big ruins, numerous arches, dreadful chasms breathing forth darkness, vases, huge inscriptive stones, vines, figured nymphs, tombs, dells, mouldering shrines, old decay, nodding towers, and all else that makes the perfect ruin-scene.

"A solemn wilderness! with error sweet
I wind the lingering step,"

over maimed sculptures, idols of antique guise and horned Pan, preposterous Gods, unfortunately still worshipped in the guise of saints: a moment of superior protestant pleasure over this, and he is off again in raptures over the statues of Roman statesmen and the view from the top of the hill of ruined antiquities, including the Colosseum, the site of the vanished Capitol, the Pantheon, and the Temple of Concord, which reminded Dyer of the Catiline conspiracy and of how Britain, though inferior to some nations in tuneful airs, masque and dance, sculpture, and the use of the pencil, is better than all the others at government, liberty and trade. He then noticed the Temple of Peace, the tomb of Cestius, the baths of Caracalla, so huge that

"The stately pines that spread their branches wide
In the dun ruins of its ample halls
Appear but tufts,

[1] John Dyer, *The Ruins of Rome* (1740).

and other noticeable objects in the *Trummerwelt*. From a heap of mouldering urns he saw a serpent glide down the green desert street, and sank into a pleasant muse, a *Ruinensehnsucht*, which he tries to explain—

"The solitary, silent, solemn scene,
Where Caesars, heroes, peasants, hermits lie,
Blended in dust together; where the slave
Rests from his labours; where th'insulting proud
Resigns his power; the miser drops his hoard;
Where human folly sleeps.—There is a mood,
(I sing not to the vacant and the young)
There is a kindly mood of melancholy,
That wings the soul, and points her to the skies . . .
How musical! when all-devouring Time
Here sitting on his throne of ruins hoar,
While winds and tempests sweep his various lyre,
How sweet thy diapason, Melancholy!"

Descending the hill, he delighted in the fallen sculptures strewn about, reflected how apt travellers are to take them home, and how, consequently, every country is now rich in them, yet Rome seems no poorer; and sought the temple of Romulus, which inspired a long reflection on Rome's birth, decline and fall. The last he attributed to luxurious decadence, Goths and Vandals, whom he credited with more destruction of buildings than historians have allowed. As to luxury—

"O luxury!
Bane of elated life, of affluent states,
What dreary change, what ruin is not thine?
How doth thy bowl intoxicate the mind! . . .
Dreadful attraction! while behind thee gapes
Th'unfathomable gulph where Asher lies
O'erwhelmed, forgotten; and high-sounding Cham;
And Elam's haughty pomp; and beauteous Greece;
And the great Queen of earth, imperial Rome."

That luxury goes before a fall, and deserves it, has always been among the axioms of ruin-lovers, whose moral sense seeks judgment, retribution, and a balance of fortune; whose aesthetic sense likes the sharp contrast, the heightened colours, of such a then and such a now. The same sense cries up the former power and greatness of the fallen. John Hughes (1735) was typical of ruin-tasters in all ages when he broke out

"O Cyrus! Alexander! Julius! all
Ye mighty lords that ever ruled this ball!
Once gods of earth, the living destinies
That made a hundred nations bow!
Where's your extent of empire now?
Say where preserv'd your phantom glory lies?
Can brass the fleeting thing secure?
Enchain'd in temples does it stay?
Or in huge amphitheatres endure
The rage of rolling time, and scorn decay?
Ah no! The mouldering monuments of Fame
Your vain deluded hopes betray. . . ."

And again—

"In Rome herself behold th'extremes of fate,
Her ancient greatness sunk, her modern boasted state!
See her luxurious palaces arise
With broken arches mix'd between!
And here what splendid domes possess the skies!
And there old temples, open to the day,
Their walls o'ergrown with moss display;
And columns awful in decay
Rear up their roofless heads to form the various scene."[1]

Thus "melodious Hughes", and thus some scores of other versifiers, and some thousands of tourists to Rome. James Thomson, who once declared that he had no taste for smelling old musty stones, devoted the first section of his long and tedious poem on Liberty to fallen Rome, for whose desolate state he found nothing but condemnation, and in the lively streets only "a deep unanimated gloom". One gathers that, if Roman ruins gave him any pleasure, it was the pleasure of priggish disapproval and of patriotism; he was worrying all the time about corruption, lethargy, and lack of British, and what he fondly believed to have been ancient Roman, liberty. A stern moralizer, he did not long, like Pope, to

"repose where Tully once was laid,
Or seek some Ruin's formidable shade."

[1]John Hughes, *Poems* (1735)

The ripe, rich, herbaceous exquisiteness of Rome in decay was not to him the warm and enervating bath of melancholy sensuousness that it was to the romantics who followed him. Rome-worship in Britain was such that the Romans by 1730 were saying: "Were our amphitheatre portable, the English would carry it off".[1] What they did carry off from the ruins were marble fragments, sculptures, inscriptions, and ideas. Horace Walpole for instance, in Rome with Gray in 1740, got from the ruins of the Temple of Minerva an idea for a villa and grounds.

"Figure," he wrote to West, "what a villa might be laid out here. 'Tis in the middle of a garden: at a little distance are two subterraneous grottos, which were the burial places of the liberti of Augustus. . . . Some of the walks would terminate upon the Castellum Aquae Martiae, St John Lateran, and St Maria Maggiore besides other churches; the walls of the garden would be two aqueducts, and the entrance through one of the old gates of Rome. This glorious spot is neglected, and only serves for a small vineyard and kitchen garden."

Horace was "persuaded that in an hundred years Rome will not be worth seeing; 'tis less so now than one would believe. All the public pictures are decayed or decaying; the few ruins cannot last long; and the statues and private collections must be sold, from the great poverty of the families".

Gray's great pleasure in Rome was its historical associations: "our memory sees more than our eyes in this country", he quotes Walpole as saying.

If Walpole got from Rome ideas for villas and grounds, Gibbon was the greatest of the long succession of writers who got an idea for a book. It was the culmination of a week of overwhelming rapture.

"I am now, Dear Sir, at Rome," he wrote to his father on October 9, 1764. ". . . I am really almost in a dream. Whatever ideas books may have given us of the greatness of that people, their accounts of the most flourishing state of Rome fall infinitely short of the picture of its ruins. I am convinced there never never existed such a nation, and I hope for the happiness of mankind there never will again."

[1]E. W. Manwaring, *Italian Landscape in Eighteenth-century England.*

Then, in his autobiography—

"My temper is not very susceptible of enthusiasm, and the enthusiasm which I do not feel I have ever scorned to affect. But at the distance of twenty-five years I can neither forget nor express the strong emotions which agitated my mind as I first approached and entered the *eternal City*. After a sleepless night, I trod with a lofty step the ruins of the Forum; each memorable spot where Romulus stood, or Tully spoke, or Caesar fell, was at once present to my eye; and several days of intoxication were lost or enjoyed before I could descend to a cool and minute investigation."

The great moment of conception is recorded in almost identical words in the various drafts of the memoirs.

"I must not forget the day, the hour, the most interesting in my literary life. It was on the fifteenth of October, in the gloom of evening, as I sat musing on the Capitol, while the bare-footed fryars were chanting their litanies in the temple of Jupiter, that the idea of writing the decline and fall of the City first started to my mind."

And it is one of the chief beauties of the great work that it is implicitly ruin-haunted: the physical breaking to pieces of Rome runs parallel to the long political and military decadence, and the mighty shattered monuments form a sombre background to the tale. Never, in fact, is Gibbon more marmoreally imposing than when he describes the desolate field of ruins stretching to and beyond the Aurelian walls; his baroque pleasure in it is like that of Poggio or Gregorovius.

William Beckford's enjoyment was, as can be imagined, more purely aesthetic. He took Rome in his Italian tour of 1780, and took it as an exquisite picture, enjoying it capriciously in his own manner.

"I absolutely," he wrote, "will have no antiquary to go prating from fragment to fragment, and tell me that were I to stay five years in Rome I should not see half it contained. The thought alone of so much to look at is quite distracting, and makes me resolve to view nothing at all in a scientific way, but straggle and wander about, just as the spirit chuses. This evening it led me to the Coliseo, and excited a vehement desire in me to break down and pulverize the whole circle of saints' nests and chapels which disgrace the arena. You recollect, I dare say, the vile effect of this holy trumpery, and would join with all your heart in kicking it into the Tyber. A few lazy abbots were at their devotions before them, such as would have made a lion's mouth water, fatter, I dare say, than any saint in the whole martyrology, and ten times more tantalizing. . . . Heavens! thought I to myself, how times are changed! Could ever Vespasian have imagined his amphitheatre would have been thus inhabited?"[1]

Then beauty caught him.

"I passed on, making these reflections, to a dark arcade, overgrown with ilex. In the openings which time and violence have made, a distant grove of cypresses discover themselves, springing from heaps of mouldering ruins, relieved by a clear transparent sky strewn with a few red clouds. This was the sort of prospect I desired, and I sat down on a shattered frieze to enjoy it. Many stories of antient Rome thronged into my mind as I mused; triumphal scenes, but tempered by sadness, and the awful thoughts of their being all passed away. . . . When the procession was fleeted by (for I not only thought but seemed to see warriors moving amongst the cypresses, and consuls returning from Parthian expeditions, loaded with strange spoils and receiving the acclamations of millions upon entering the theatre) I arose, crossed the arena, paced several times round and round, looked up to arcade rising above arcade, and admired the stately height and masses of the structure, considered it in various points of view, and felt as if I should never be satisfied with gazing, hour after hour and day after day. Next, directing my steps to the Arch of Constantine, I surveyed the groups of ruins which surrounded me. The cool breeze of the evening played in the beds of canes and oziers which flourished under the walls of the Coliseo."[2]

Returning by the Campo Vaccino, he leaned against a column of the temple of Jupiter and watched the peasants fetching water, kindling a fire among the shrubs and trees of the Palatine hill. He noted the vaults and arches peeping out of the vegetation, and mused on the splendid palaces of the Caesars which had stood

[1]William Beckford, *Dreams, waking thoughts and incidents* (1783)
[2]*Ibid.*

there, and left only confused fragments of marble and walls of lofty terraces.

"A wretched rabble were roasting their chestnuts, on the very spot, perhaps, where Domitian convened a senate to harangue upon the delicacies of his entertainment. The light of the flame cast upon the figures around it, and the mixture of tottering wall with foliage impending above their heads, formed a striking picture, which I staid contemplating from my pillar till the fire went out, the assembly dispersed, and none remained but a withered hag, raking the embers and muttering to herself."

By this time, Roman *Ruinenstimmung* was enjoying a lush growth all over Europe. Germans were peculiarly susceptible to the delicious disease. Reproductions of the ruin pictures of Piranesi, Pannini, Rosa, Poussin and Claude, and the host of lesser artists who flocked to draw Rome, adorned German homes; families such as the Goethes had themselves painted against a background of ruined pillars and temple; ruins ornamented the backdrops of theatres and the settings of stages. The emotion could be voluptuous: "when one looks on ancient buildings," wrote Heinse in 1780, "one has always the kind of feeling that one has before a beautiful naked body." Goethe's passionate love of Rome held something of this voluptuousness; his original title for his *Romische Elegien* was *Erotica Romana*. Rome turned him, at his first visit, from the Gothic to the classical, from the romantic confusion of *Sturm und Drang* to an ardent appreciation of what remained of the Latin inheritance. "These men worked for eternity," he wrote, admiring the massive broken fabrics of walls, tombs and circuses. He roved about Rome with Tischbein, picking up fragments and minor objects out of the ruins, and enjoying picturesque effects. So strong was his desire of acquisition that he had sculptured ornaments moulded and cast in gypsum to take away. "It is necessary to acquire these invaluable treasures," he wrote. "I am modelling them in clay, in order to appropriate everything." He was also sketching the monuments, and writing down descriptions of all that struck his taste. He noted the hermit and the beggars who had made their homes in the crumbling arches of the Colosseum, and how the fires they lit in the arena shone through the openings, while the smoke drifted out and the moon lit up like a cloud: "the sight was exceedingly glorious".

Sometimes music added to the scene; he would visit a piano-playing lady friend, and

"it was an inestimable enjoyment to listen to an excellent lady pouring herself forth in the tenderest tones at the pianoforte, and in the same moment to gaze from the window into the most unique landscape in the world, and then with a little turning of the head to survey in the evening sunset glow the grand picture which to the left stretched from the Campo Vaccino to the Temples of Minerva and of Peace, with the Colosseum towering behind. Next, turning the eye to the right, you pass by the Arch of Titus and lose yourself in the labyrinth of the Palatine ruins, its solitude gladdened by horticulture and wild vegetation."[1]

Then there was the great and more restful pleasure of being painted by Tischbein. "He paints me life-size, dressed in a white cloak, in the open air sitting on ruins, and in the background the Campagna of Rome. It is a beautiful picture." Tischbein too liked it. "I have begun his portrait," he wrote, "and shall make it life-size, as he sits on the ruins and reflects on the fate of human works." In the background are the Alban hills, in the middle the arches of an aqueduct, and before it the tomb of Cecilia Metella; beside the ruins of a temple and an ivy-grown sculptured relief, Goethe rests in elegant dignity on the block of an obelisk. In spite of his aesthetic and historic appreciation of the past, and his deep *Schönheitsempfindung*, he looks as if he believed in progress, and was perhaps echoing Schiller's "*Wir, wir leben! Unser sind die Stunden, und der Lebende hat Recht*".

By the beginning of the nineteenth century, Roman ruin-pleasure had grown still more aesthetically luxurious. Such an incredible mass of ruins, wrote Wilhelm von Humboldt in 1804, makes one feel excessively happy. Beauty of shape, greatness of appearance, richness of vegetation, beauty of outline and colour . . . But it is a delusion to wish we had been inhabitants of ancient Athens or Rome, for the romance of antiquity must be in the past. We are, he said, even vexed when a half-buried building is dug up; it is a gain for learning at the expense of imagination (one compares this period sentiment with the Renaissance desire to build up the ancient ruins into their glorious first state, and to

[1]Goethe, *Travels in Italy*.

lament their ruin as wreckage of perfection). Humboldt, regretting excavations and complaining of the building up of the Campagna, and the policing of Rome, so that men could no more with impunity draw knives, carried romanticism into the coming century, the century of Chateaubriand, Corinne, Lamartine, Byron, Shelley, Stendhal, Dickens, all the eager host of dreaming wanderers over the grass-grown Campo Vaccino and the *mondlichtübergossene Kolosseum*, whose ghosts must drift to-day with protesting shudders about the stark new Rome of the excavators and the destroyers and the tearers out of shrubs, less happy than the great shades whom Chateaubriand pictured as wandering among monuments and tombs. He agreed with Byron that those with no human ties should come to live in Rome, where the very dust is full of great dead lives. Seated on the step of one of the altars in the Colosseum, he watched the setting sun throw golden waves over the galleries where once the people surged, while dark shadows lay in the corridors. Above the massive broken walls he saw the garden of the palace of the Caesars, adorned by a palm tree which must have been placed on the ruins for the delight of painters and poets. Instead of the ferocious cries of the vanished spectators of the savage sports, one heard only the barking of the dogs of the hermit who guarded the ruins, and the chiming of the bell of St Peter's. The thought of these two great monuments of pagan and Christian Rome caused in him a deep emotion.

"I dreamt that the modern building would fall like the ancient one, and that monuments follow one another like the men who build them; I remembered that the Jews, who in their first captivity toiled at the pyramids of Egypt and the walls of Babylon had, during their last dispersal, built this enormous amphitheatre. The vaults which echoed the sound of the Christian bell were the work of a pagan emperor marked in the prophecies for the final destruction of Jerusalem. Are there here high enough subjects for meditation, and do you think that a city where such effects are produced at every step is worth seeing?"[1]

Returning to the Colosseum next winter, he found that the hermit had died.

"It is thus that we are warned at each step of our nothingness; man goes to meditate on the ruins of empires; he forgets that he

[1]Chateaubriand, *Génie du Christianisme* (1802).

is himself a ruin still more unsteady, and that he will fall before these remains."

His meditation wanders from ruin to mortality, from mortality to the Christian church which had begun in the Roman underground and had flowered into its splendour in Roman basilicas; and through it all the moon roved her pale solitudes amid the solitudes of ruined Rome.

The pleasure of realizing the past from its ruins was the strongest emotion roused in the breast of Madame de Stael's serious young Scot, Oswald, when, under the agreeable tutelage of the lovely and learned Corinne, he was taken on his daily conducted tour of Rome. "After having seen the ruins of Rome, one believes in the ancient Romans as if one had lived in their time." On the Palatine hill they thought of Livy and Augustus. Corinne was full of information; the pleasure of lecturing on ruins was hers, and she did it with unflagging zest.

"*C'est là que se promenaient les orateurs de Rome en sortant du Forum; c'est là que César et Pompée se rencontraient . . . et qu'ils cherchaient à captiver Ciceron.*"[1]

Wherever one turned one found history; modern Rome was built out of ancient, and its fragments adorned new walls. Columns from Hadrian's tomb and the Capitol stood in churches; an ancient portico supported a humble roof; a tomb was a home for a rustic family; these mixtures, new upon old, old into new, produce "*je ne sais quel mélange d'idées grandes et simples, je ne sais quel plaisir de découverte, qui inspire un intérêt continuel.*" A broken column, a half destroyed bas-relief, remind one that there is in man a divine eternal spark. "*Ce Forum,*" Corinne and Oswald thought, "*est une preuve frappante de la grandeur morale de l'homme.*" About the Colosseum they differed. Oswald, with his strong Scottish moral sense, could not overlook the luxury of its masters and the blood of their slaves. Corinne told him that he must not bring the rigour of his principles on morality and justice into the contemplation of Italian monuments. Romans even in decadence were imposing; the death of liberty filled the world with marvels. Look, said she, at those huge baths, at the circuses

[1]Mme. de Stael, *Corinne* (1807).

29 The so-called tomb of the Horatii and Curatii, Via Appia, Rome. Engraving by G B Piranesi, 1764

30 Basilica, Paestum. Wash drawings by G. B. Piranesi

31 Allegorical representation of Roman Britain in the 1st century A.D. Engraved frontispiece, from William Stukeley *Itinerarium Curiosum*, 1724

32 The Greek Theatre, Taormina. Etching after L. F. Cassas, 1785

where elephants fought tigers, at the arena which aqueducts turned into a lake, where ships fought and crocodiles lazed in the place where lions had roared. Look at the obelisks from Egypt, at the population of statues: there is something supernatural in all this magnificence, and its poetic splendour makes one forget its origin and aim. But the eloquence of Corinne did not convince Oswald, for whom the magic of the arts was not enough, he looked always for a moral sentiment. Corinne had to remind him of the Christian martyrs before he could think the Colosseum justified.

On the whole, however, Oswald found the ruins, as shown him by Corinne, extremely delightful. He saw them in more agreeable circumstances, no doubt, than Dr Byron, of Princess Caroline's suite, who recorded his melancholy impressions in 1814. What he and the unhappy (though cheerful) Princess saw was, "extended in disordered heaps before him, the disjointed carcase of fallen Rome. . . . To a contemplative mind, the survey is indeed awful and impressive." In the Via Sacra a herdsman sat on a marble pedestal while his oxen drank from a marble fountain; silence and solitude reigned; the place seemed returned to its original wildness, abandoned once more to flocks and herds of cattle.

"So far, in fact, have the modern Romans forgotten the theatre of the glory and the imperial power of their ancestors as to degrade it into a common market for cattle, and sink its name, illustrated by every page of Roman history, into the contemptible appellation of Campo Vaccino."[1]

The disapproving doctor described the mass of ruins, covered with weeds and shrubs, vaults opening on more ruins, a vast collection of magnificence and devastation, grandeur and decay. The Palatine hill now presented two solitary villas and a convent, with deserted gardens and vineyards; its numerous temples, palaces, porticos, and libraries, once the glory of Rome and the admiration of the universe, were heaps of ruins. On the columns of Trajan and Antoninus, which once held these emperors, now stood St Peter and St Paul, very improperly, as the profane scenes on the shafts were ill adapted to the characters of these

[1] *Voyages and Travels of Princess Caroline.* By a member of her suite (1821).

apostles. He was all for excavation. "The classic traveller may entertain fond hopes that the veil which has so long concealed the beauties of this ancient city may be in part removed. . . ." Dr Byron, unlike Humboldt, would have welcomed modern Rome without regretful nostalgia for the green veil torn from its stones.

The rage of Lord Byron at the new Rome might have produced some furious vituperative verse: fortunately he did not see it, and the Roman stanzas of *Childe Harold* are perhaps the finest poetry he ever wrote. He saw its beauty subjectively; its tragedy of ruin as transcending his own, and therefore softening it.

> What are our woes and sufferance? Come and see
> The cypress, hear the owl, and plod your way
> O'er steps of broken thrones and temples, ye
> Whose agonies are evils of a day!
> A world is at our feet as fragile as our clay. . . .
>
> Then let the winds howl on! Their harmony
> Shall henceforth be my music, and the night
> The sound shall temper with the owlets' cry,
> As I now hear them in the fading light
> Dim o'er the bird of darkness' native site,
> Answering each other on the Palatine,
> With their large eyes, all glistening grey and bright,
> And sailing pinions.—Upon such a shrine
> What are our petty griefs?—let me not number mine.
>
> Cypress and ivy, weed and wall-flower grown
> Matted and mass'd together, hillocks heap'd
> On what were chambers, arch crush'd, column strown
> In fragments, choked-up vaults, and frescos steep'd
> In subterranean damps, where the owl peep'd,
> Deeming it midnight;—temples, baths or halls?
> Pronounce who can; for all that learning reap'd
> From her research hath been, that these are walls—
> Behold the Imperial Mount! 'Tis thus the mighty falls.
>
> There is the moral of all human tales;
> 'Tis but the same rehearsal of the past;
> First freedom, and then glory—when that fails,
> Wealth, vice, corruption, barbarism at last.

Morals, human tales, and his own griefs apart, Byron felt passionately the romance of ruined Rome.

> She saw her glories star by star expire,
> And up the steep barbarian monarchs ride,
> Where the car climbed the capitol; far and wide
> Temple and tower went down, nor left a site :—
> Chaos of ruins! who shall trace the void,
> O'er the dim fragments cast a lunar light,
> And say, 'here was, or is,' where all is doubly night?

His descriptions, in *Childe Harold* and in *Manfred*, of the moonlit Colosseum, are objective enough.

> "The trees which grew along the broken arches
> Waved dark in the blue midnight, and the stars
> Shone through the rents of ruin; from afar
> The watch-dog bay'd beyond the Tiber; and
> More near from out the Caesar's palace came
> The owl's long cry. . . ."

And so on. But it was as his city of the soul that he turned to Rome with such wistful passion and lost desolation, finding his own sorrows symbolized by her devastation.

Shelley wrote of Rome as a beauty-intoxicated poet. His description of the wooded and flowering ravines and arches of the Baths of Caracalla is an exquisite rhapsody. In them he wrote most of *Prometheus Unbound*.

> "This poem," he says, "was chiefly written upon the mountainous ruins of the Baths of Caracalla, among the flowery glades and thickets of odoriferous blossoming trees, which are extending in ever-winding labyrinths upon its immense platforms and dizzy arches suspended in the air . . . the new life with which it drenches the spirits even to intoxication, were the inspiration of this drama."

Competition for the inspiration of literary works has always been keen among Roman ruins: does it go on to-day? One can believe that the unpicturesque gauntness and bareness of the vegetation-stripped stones ("out of this stony waste what branches grow?") might suit with the stark contemporary muse, even as Shelley's more lyric temper was intoxicated by the "towers and labyrinthine recesses hidden and woven over by the wild growth of weeds and ivy", and the shattered heights

"overgrown with anemones, wall-flowers and violets, whose stalks pierce the starry moss and with radiant blue flowers . . . which scatter through the air the divinest odour, which, as you recline under the shade of the ruin, produces sensations of voluptuous faintness, like the combinations of sweet music."

The Roman ruins of to-day are so unvoluptuous that Lamartine, for instance, would find small pleasure in his poetic meditations "*sur les murs dentelés du sacré Colisée*", where, listening to the sighing and moaning of the wind about the vast ruin, he felt that he was hearing the torrent of the years rolling its waves beneath the arches.

"*Rome, te voilà donc ! O mère des Césars,*
J'aime à fouler aux pieds tes monuments épars;
J'aime à sentir le temps, plus fort que ta mémoire,
Effacer pas à pas les traces de ta gloire!
L'homme serait-il de ses oeuvres jaloux?
Nos monuments sont-ils plus immortels que nous?
Egaux devant le temps, non, ta ruine immense
Nous console du moins de notre décadence.
J'aime, j'aime à venir rêver sur le tombeau,
A l'heure où de la nuit le lugubre flambeau,
Comme l'oeil du passé, flottant sur les ruines,
D'un pâle demi-deuil revêt tes sept collines. . . ."

It was the Colosseum, too, that captured most wholly the enthusiasm of Stendhal. One must be alone there, he said; but one is not, one is annoyed too often by the pious murmurings of the devout who make the stations of the cross, or by a Capuchin preaching, or by masons in their perpetual work of repairing. One must climb up to the highest galleries, and see the view of the Forum, the arches, and the churches. The effect on the mind is emotionally immense; these great walls, ruined by time, make an impression like the music of Cimarosa, which makes sublime and touching the vulgar words of a libretto. To read about the Colosseum without seeing it is to find the description exaggerated. His own detailed account of it should, he instructed, be read aloud, after midnight, in the house of an amiable woman, in good company, and first a lithograph drawing of the Colosseum should be studied—("*cet édifice immense, plus beau peut-être aujourd'hui qu'il tombe en ruines, qu'il ne le fut jamais dans toute sa splendeur*", for then it was only a theatre, to-day it is the most beautiful ruin of the Roman people). Nothing so magnificent, he supposed, has ever been: the ruins of the east, of Palmyra, Baalbek and Petra, astonish without pleasing; they are strange to us, for the civilizations which created that beauty have disappeared, and they recall despotic memories of thousands of slaves dying of fatigue while they worked. But the Colosseum is sublime for us because it is a living relic of those Romans whose history engaged all our childhood, and the greatness of whose enterprises it symbolizes. Then there is the contrast between the cries of a hundred thousand spectators, and the silence now.

"What happy mornings I have passed in the Colosseum, lost in some corner of the huge ruins! From the higher galleries one sees below in the arena the *galériens* of the pope sing as they work. The noise of their chains mingles with the song of the birds. . . . The peaceful fluttering of the birds which sounds faintly in the vast building, and the profound silence which from time to time follows it, help the imagination to take flight into ancient times. One arrives at the most lively joys that memory can procure. This reverie, of which I boast to the reader, and which will perhaps seem to him ridiculous, '*c'est le sombre plaisir d'un coeur mélancolique*' (La Fontaine). To tell the truth, this is the one great pleasure that one finds in Rome. It is impossible for early youth, foolish with hope. . . ."[1]

It is possible that Beyle made himself something of a bore to his travel companions about the Romans and about the Colosseum; anyhow one of them, Paul, complained that these ruins fatigued him and made him ill. The tendency of visitors to pay disproportionate attention to a few of the Roman ruins—the Colosseum, the Palatine, the arches in the Forum, the Pantheon, the great baths—is an old tradition. Of these, the Colosseum has usually come first. Its huge size, its shape, its tiers towering above one another to the sky, the trees and creepers which in old days embellished it, its historic prestige, and the memory of the bloody spectacles seen in it by such vast crowds, have acted on the nerves like an intoxicant. One is not surprised that the Anglo-Saxon

[1]Stendhal, *Promenades dans Rome* (1829).

pilgrims of the early centuries looked aside at it from their pious ecclesiastical itineraries and sang of it, or that more than a thousand years later Charles Dickens wrote his exuberant paean—

"They who will may have the whole great pile before them, as it used to be, with thousands of eager faces staring down into the arena, and such a whirl of strife and blood and dust going on there as no language can describe. Its solitude, its awful beauty, and its utter desolation, strike upon the stranger the next moment like a softened sorrow; and never in his life, perhaps, will he be so moved and overcome by any sight not immediately connected with his own affections and afflictions.

"To see it crumbling there, an inch a year, its walls and arches overgrown with green, its corridors open to the day; the long grass growing in its porches, young trees of yesterday springing up on its rugged parapets and bearing fruit . . . to see its pit of fight filled up with earth, and the peaceful cross planted in the centre, to climb into its upper halls and look down on ruin, ruin, ruin, all about it, the triumphal arches of Constantine, Septimius Severus and Titus, the Roman Forum, the Palace of the Caesars, the temples of the old religion, fallen down and gone; is to see the ghost of old Rome, wicked, wonderful old city, haunting the very ground on which its people trod. It is the most impressive, the most stately, the most solemn, grand, majestic, mournful sight conceivable. Never, in its bloodiest prime, can the sight of the gigantic Coliseum, full and running over with the lustiest life, have moved one heart as it must move all who look upon it now, a ruin God be thanked: a ruin."

The Colosseum's is (or was) an obvious and flamboyant appeal, needing for its success little aesthetic or intellectual training in appreciation; the highest intelligences and the lower have felt it. Even the despicable English, according to Stendhal, admired the building, if only because they supposed it a fine new stadium going up, for the English could not be supposed to know any better. And Christians, before Rome's secularization, liked to kiss the cross which commemorated the martyrs of their faith, make the stations round the little chapels that encircled the arena, and listen to the fervid preaching of a Capuchin monk.

As to the view from the top storeys, it was, in the nineteenth century, all that could be desired of romantic grandeur. Dr Arnold, in 1827, was transported by it.

"I sat and gazed upon the scene with an intense and mingled feeling. The world could show nothing grander. . . . I never thought to have felt thus tenderly towards Rome; but the inexplicable solemnity and beauty of her ruined condition has quite bewitched me, and to the latest hour of my life I shall remember the Forum, the surrounding hills, and the magnificent Coliseum."

So said they all; the appeal is irresistible. It was so much the correct thing to feel it that even egotists like Marie Bashkirtzeff, who was really interested only in her personal affairs, had to make gestures of appreciation. When first she reached Rome, in 1876, she could think only of Nice, and of what they were perhaps saying about her there. Seeing the Colosseum, she evaded comment by writing in her journal, "What can I say after Byron?" and her subsequent entries concerned her love affairs, her painting, and the men she met. Her personal romances, as usual, slew the larger romance, and though she wrote that "the beauty and the ruins of Rome intoxicate me," all she found to say of the Capitol was about a masked ball there and "the piece of ivy he gave me." A year later, before visiting Rome en route for Naples, she wrote brightly, "The heroes, the folds of the toga, the Capitol, the Cupola, the *bal masqué*, the Pincio . . . O Rome" But she was annoyed by having to waste a whole day there before the Naples train. Not for her the romance of wandering about Rome, finding its charming corners and by-ways, of tracing classical fragments and columns built into later palaces and villas and even hovels, of finding pagan pillars and friezes in Christian basilicas, of following the fascinating story of ruin and plunder down the thievish years.

This pleasure persists, even in the tidied, de-shrubbed, excavated, built-up Rome of our day, the Rome which has given such pleasure to archaeologists, such wistful pain, exasperation and rage to others. For, in the last eighty-odd years, Rome has been spoilt. By 1905 Augustus Hare, that passionate Rome-lover, was writing his lament—

"The thirty-five years of United Italy, if they have done well by archaeology, have done more for the destruction of the artistic beauty of Rome than all the invasions of the Goths and Vandals. They have done for the City what the sixteenth-century Popes did for the Forum. . . . Except for definite archaeologists, much of the old charm is gone for ever, the whole aspect of the city is changed, and the picturesqueness of former days must now be sought in such obscure corners as have escaped the hands of the spoiler . . . the pagan ruins have been denuded of all that gave them picturesqueness or beauty. . . . The Palaces of Caesar have been stripped of the flowers and ivy which formerly adorned them . . .. The Baths of Caracalla, which, until 1870, was one of the most beautiful spots in the world, is now scarcely more attractive than the ruins of a London warehouse. . . . Even the Coliseum has been deprived not only of its shrines, but of its marvellous flora, and in dragging out the roots of its shrubs more of the buildings was destroyed than would have fallen naturally perhaps in five centuries."[1]

He quotes an angry *Times* leader of 1888 on the vulgarity of the hideous new town—"Rome might and should have been made the most beautiful city in the world"—and D'Annunzio—"There passed over Rome a blighting blizzard of barbarism, menacing all that greatness and loveliness which were without equals in the memory of the world". Even in 1873 Henry James could write of the Colosseum that its beauty had pretty well vanished, since the high-growing wild flowers had been plucked away by the new government. More flowers were to go, the shrubs, the trees that so charmingly sprouted from arches and walls. The Forum was to be cleared, excavated, de-mossed, the cattle and swineherds expelled, each ruin cleaned and scrubbed. The great baths, those forested mountains of arcaded vaults, became as neat and bare as bombed swimming baths; but still huge, still vaulted, still belonging to emperors, to the echoing corridors of the imperial past. Shelley would have been disgusted; the archaeologists have won; it is the eternal battle between those who love ruins for their beauty and their poetry, and those who love them for their antiquarian past. But now in the baths and the amphitheatres they have concerts and opera in the warm summer nights. "*Dopo la Roma di Augusto e la Roma dei Papi del Rinascimento, la Roma Mussoliniana*", and that was a Rome that not even Hare, D'Annunzio, or Henry James, could in their most pessimistic moments have foreseen.

"Rome's past beauty," writes a modern artist, "has all but

[1]Augustus Hare, *Walks in Rome* (17th edition, 1905).

vanished. . . . The books of engravings and pink-washed aquatints that the young men came home with from the Grand Tour showed galaxies of enormous whiskered ruins half obscured by a profusion of picturesque houses. Then, Rome was before all else a city of visual poetry. To-day it has been turned into a city of antiquarian interest and political propaganda. . . . We must establish the appreciation of ruins and decay, *visually*."[1]

Yet much of the poetry does remain: still in every street you may come on ancient Rome built into medieval, into renaissance, into baroque, and feel that lift of the heart which imperishable beauty, persisting through changes, brings, the pleasure of ruins perpetually re-ruined, perpetually re-formed, perpetually old-into-new. Still you may climb the arboreal Palatine, among the ruined palaces of emperors, the golden house of Nero, the crumbled, gone-to-earth villas of patrician Romans, the thatched hut of Romulus, the shattered strongholds of medieval barons, the convents and churches, the terraced stairways, the subterranean vaults, the fig-trees in the sun. Still ruined Rome sprawls about us between her Aurelian walls, and beyond these the spoilt, the progressively spoilt, the now almost unbearably spoilt, Campagna rolls. And from this great ruin-field, this stupendous *Trümmerfeld*, rises a combined shout of pleasure, the mingled ecstasy of archaeologists, poets, artists, historians, aesthetes, scholars, tourists, the voices of Rienzi, Petrarch, Raphael, Poggio, Piranesi, Claude, a hundred quarrying popes, several thousand building barons and Renaissance plutocrats, Goethe, Gibbon, Byron, Shelley, Chateaubriand, Stendhal, Ruskin, Pater, Lanciani, Gregorovius and all; besides many milliards of joyful unknown travellers, wandering from ruin to ruin, guidebooks in hand, wrapped in a dream, almost in a trance, bemused and transported with a deep and stirring pleasure that has endured for a millennium and a half, and will ensure for how long now? Perhaps until the imperial city becomes a shambles, radio-active, plague-struck, sickening to sense and thought, her temples and palaces smouldering on the shattered ground.

And even after that. The command *delenda est Roma* will itself in time start a new era of ruin-pleasure, and posterity will for ever rummage among ashes for Rome, laid waste and flat in the

[1] John Piper, *Buildings and Prospects* (1947).

desolation of her Campagna, that wilderness of ghostly cities that rolls about her like a sea.

24

In that sea lies drowned a past far older than Rome's; there lie the dead cities of Etruscans, Volscians, Sabines, founded by gods and heroes before history. Of Tusculum, high in the Alban hills, till its defeat at Lake Regillus the most important Latian city, a summer resort under the empire, a great stronghold of the Middle Ages, utterly destroyed by the Romans in 1191, there remains on the high grass-grown citadel only the ancient theatre, built into the hillside. The city site was excavated and explored for sculptures over a century ago, covered up again and left in amorphous confusion; scattered about are a few medieval ruins (for here the Dukes of Tusculum had a fortress); but, except for the theatre and the seatless amphitheatre, ancient Tusculum has gone to earth, Cicero's villa and all. It lies beneath one's feet, supporting the angular hill with the buried, broken stones of its streets and walls and temples. Standing on that wind-swept citadel, or sitting in that small rock-hewn theatre, with the campagna rolling below from the Alban hills to Rome and the misty sea, one may see the centuries of buried history rise and stalk like ghosts; behind Rome they stalk, and back and back, to who knows what of primeval dreads? Tusculum, Veii, Alba Longa, Praeneste, Tibur—these fastnesses saw Rome rise, and were in the end by Rome conquered and destroyed.

Of all the Campagna pre-Roman cities, Praeneste is, in history and imagination and present ruin, the grandest and most imposing. Its fabulous origin and magnificent early history, its cyclopean walls piled by the hands of giants, its tremendous, commanding site, its temple of Fortune so grandiosely rebuilt by Sulla after he had destroyed it, have drawn visitors, settlers and archaeologists from the days of imperial Rome to the Middle Ages, from the Middle Ages until now. But, among the mass of Roman allusions to it, none seem to refer to the ruins that underlay the rebuilt city and temple; no archaeological zeal prompted the owners of the summer villas to describe the so recently ruined ancient Praeneste. Yet the great terraces climbing the hill with their cyclopean walls, the high ruined fortress of the citadel above, connected with the city by a causeway, were the startling background of the fashionable villadom that sprang up about the hill slopes, where emperors summered, where Horace read Homer, where the younger Pliny and other villa-owning Roman gentry built themselves houses to reside in as a change from their other villas at Tibur, Tusculum, Laurentum and Sorrento, and everyone came to consult the oracle of the temple. No one has left a precise picture of how the ancient Praeneste mingled with the new, and how the gigantic enclosure of the temple of Fortune encircled the old town. Nor did the medieval counts who later made it their stronghold take much notice of the ancient ruins; they fortified them, threw up their castles on them, guarding the town that grew up within the huge temple; Praeneste (by then Palestrina) was the most important fortress outside Rome, and the most coveted; it changed hands between the Colonna and the Popes, it was captured and recaptured, destroyed (less completely, as in most destructions, than was ordered) by Boniface VIII in 1300, rebuilt by the Colonna, destroyed and rebuilt again, passing to the Barberini in the seventeenth century. To-day we see the ruins of all the ages piled like a pyramid, terrace above terrace, up the hill: the cyclopean walls of the ancient city, the acropolis at the top, antique fragments of old Praeneste built into walls and streets and gates, the vast ruin of the temple of Fortune that Sulla rebuilt, enclosing the medieval town, the Colonna-Barberini palace standing on the highest terrace of the original temple, the tangle of terraces, colonnades, sanctuaries, halls, that cover the hill. Since the Renaissance, Palestrina has been the delight of artists, architects and archaeologists. The reconstruction of the temple of Fortune, the exploration of its ruins, the tracing of the walls of the sixth century B.C. among the mazy halls, galleries, arcades, chambers, fountains, porticos, and terraces of Sulla's temple, the finding in 1638 of the great Alexandrian mosaic of the Nile on a floor, which the Barberini moved to their lately acquired palace, the climbing of medieval streets and steps, coming at every turn on ancient columns buried in walls, engaged Corinthian arcades, Renaissance wells, fragments of polygonal wall, arriving at last at the seventeenth-century palace into which antique columns and sculptures are so richly built (for the Roman nobility knew well how to use the ruins of their past)—to climb through Palestrina thus, and to look from its summit over the Volscian, Alban and Sabine hills and their white towns, the stretch of the Campagna with its ruined towers and aqueducts, villas and farms, Rome and its dome floating in a summer haze, the silver gleam of the sea beyond, has always been to experience the finest ecstasy of ruins.

To seek later for the Praeneste villas of Horace, Hadrian, Pliny and the rest is an exercise charming but unrewarding; there is, it seems, no knowing which was whose. Still there the sites and ruins stand, eloquent with echoes of Roman gossip, cultured literary discussions, long cool sojourns away from the heat of Rome (for it seems that they all found Praeneste chilly).

But archaeologists for long deplored the picturesque medieval hill town that for centuries obscured the upper part of the temple site; in 1944 the town was bombed, with characteristic insouciance, by allied airmen; the cobbled streets, the little climbing houses partly built out of Sulla's masonry, that sprawled over the terraces and ramps, and what had once been the open colonnaded space at the top, were smashed up. Directly the war ended, the archaeologists seized their chance; exiling and rehousing elsewhere the unlucky inhabitants, they set to work to clear and expose the site. To-day the top terraces, Doric colonnade, ramps and walls, central stairway flanked by two great hemicycles, and the open court in front of the rotunda, are all visible. The Barberini palace that crowns the sanctuary site was not bombed; next time Palestrina is assaulted it too may be smashed to pieces, and then, say the archaeologists, we shall know more of the secrets of the top terrace, which may have been the approach to the shrine and statue of the goddess. Meanwhile restoration is going on, or nearly finished; walls are repaired, columns re-erected; the whole effect has a grandeur which possibly compensates for the loss of the medieval houses; or possibly not. One had thought that Palestrina as a spectacle could not be improved, and one was perhaps right. But Praeneste, however one may miss the jumble of the ages, is emerging in greater magnificence; if the reconstructions are carried much further, it will be a spectacular and dazzling affair indeed. It might even be given a coat of paint. The Renaissance architects would have liked the new discoveries: so, one feels sure, would the Roman villa owners under the empire.

The identification of the villas about Tivoli is more successful than round Praeneste; that is, more ruined buildings and fragments of buildings are ascribed to their late owners; no doubt wrongly, but one has the gratification of being told that here summered Horace (when not at his Sabine farm), there Maecenas, (whose huge and splendid mansion is believed really to have been the famous Heracleum, but no matter, Maecenas can have it if we prefer, and we do prefer); here too in these ruins scattered over the hillside resided Catullus, Brutus, Cassius, Sallust, Propertius's brilliant mistress Cynthia, Zenobia, retired from fallen Palmyra to Tiburtine villadom, a succession of emperors, Varus, whom Horace bade grow vines, Statius's friend Vopiscus in his luxury villa that looked on the murmuring Anio in front, on the silent woods behind, a villa rich in statues of ivory, bronze and gold, with bright mosaic floors, with a cherished tree growing up through the roof, with hot baths built on the stream's bank, the furnace heating the river water: such a villa springs up as we look on the jumble of broken stones above the river, and on all the ruined piles and fragments strewn round Tibur. Just as the perfect round temple with its eighteen Corinthian columns, forms itself when we look, as we have looked for ten centuries, and probably more (the date of its ruin is not known) at the celebrated broken rotunda of the Sibyl, or of Vesta, that stands so picturesquely on the top of the shaggy cliff above the steep gorge of the foaming Anio. This little temple has possibly given more joy to ruin-tasters and artists than any other single ruin except the Colosseum and the Parthenon. "This singular ruin has been too often engraven to need description," wrote Joseph Forsyth; need it or not, it has always got it. Probably because of its picturesque position, which has enshrined it in so many hundreds of paintings and drawings for four centuries or so.

"In its delicate form and its rich orange colour" (wrote the susceptible Augustus Hare), "standing out against the opposite heights of Monte Peschiavatore, it is impossible to conceive anything more picturesque, and the situation is sublime, perched on the very edge of the cliff, overhung with masses of clematis and ivy, through which portions of the ruined arch of a bridge are just visible, while below the river foams and roars."

Every British, French and German tourist has joined Italian

artists and poets in rhapsody over Tivoli and its temples. Cascades, hills, steep wooded cliffs, graceful ruins, join to form a landscape by Claude, Poussin, Rosa, and by a million lesser artists. Many visitors to Tivoli have given their hearts to its natural beauties, the grottos, the waterfalls, the rock caves, the ruins of nature rather than of art—"*un désordre grandiose*", said George Sand—"*une ruine du passé autrement imposante que les débris des temples et des aqueducs*"; it made her think pleasurably of "*scènes effroyables*", "*craquements*", "*rugissements*", "*bouillonnements affreux*" and the great convulsions of Nature beside which man's ruinings are puny efforts. But most visitors have centred their emotions on the Sibyl's temple (since no one knows whose temple it was, we may as well use the old ascription). John Evelyn, in 1645, was too full of the "artificial miracles" of the Villa d'Este and the prodigiousness of the cascade to give more than a mild tribute to "the Temple of Sibylla Tiburtina, or Albunea, a round fabric, still discovering some of its pristine beauty"; but the temple's fame spread through Europe, and was perhaps more often reproduced in the parks and gardens of England than any other.

"Without doors all is pleasing: there is a beautiful (artificial) river, with a fine semi-circular wood overlooking it, and the temple of Tivoli placed happily on a rising towards the end."[1]

It became a common object in the English landscape, and a still commoner one in miniscule (marble or bronze) on the chimney pieces and chiffoniers of returned travellers. This pretty little rotunda captured, in fact, once and for ever, the fond European heart. It has always been the fashion to read Horace before it, as, before the ruins of Troy, Homer.

Though, naturally, Horace has been still more read and quoted on the site of his farm, fifteen miles or so to the north-east, lying in the valley of the stream which was Horace's Digentia, and below the slopes of Mount Lucretilis. The site, once only guessed at, has been in the last two centuries identified, though undug and overgrown with woods and vineyards until the last forty years or so of excavation. Only fifty years ago the guide books could say "Nothing now remains of the villa but a mosaic floor, grown over

[1]Horace Walpole, *Letter from Wentworth Castle* (1756).

with vines". Byron, more doubtful, was content with: "It seems possible that the mosaic pavement which the peasants uncover by throwing up the earth of a vineyard may belong to his villa." Byron was no lover of Horace, who had ill-treated him at school; he was not going to join in the Horace-quoting.

"May he who will his recollections rake
And quote in classic raptures, and awake
The hills with Latin echoes: I abhorred
Too much to conquer for the poet's sake
The drill'd dull lesson, forc'd down word by word
In my repugnant youth. . . .
Then farewell, Horace, whom I hated so,
Not for thy faults, but mine. . . ."

Nevertheless, he made his pilgrimage to the Sabine farm, the knoll covered with chestnut-trees, the vineyard, and the mosaic floor. To others it was "a holy spot". George Dennis, in 1842, spent rapturous weeks tracing the Horatian landscape round it, identifying streams, hills, villages, arriving at the knoll crested with chestnuts which rose above the stream and marked "the site of the much-sung farm".

"A few remains of brick wall, a scattered fragment or two of columns . . . of ordinary travertine, and a small piece of mosaic pavement, mark the exact site. These are the sole traces now visible, but my host tells me that within his memory—some fifty years ago—the mosaic floors of six chambers were brought to light, but were covered again with earth, as nothing was found to tempt to further excavation."[1]

Twenty years later Ampère wrote that nothing marked the site but a few buried stones and bricks; Augustus Hare, however, found the contadini still at their profitable, if fitful, work of throwing up spadefuls of earth to expose the tesselated floor to tourists, with "*Ecco la villa d'Orazio*". It would seem that they believed that Horace must have been an Englishman, so great was British enthusiasm for the scanty traces of his one-time residence. The pleasure derived from ruins by the locals has never been negligible. When asked by English visitors where were the remains of the villa, they had great delight in replying "At your

[1]G. W. Dennis (1842).

feet", and setting to work with the shovel. The visitors, gazing with rapture at the Horatian scene, got out their Horaces and read diligently about the various features of the demesne, scarcely knowing whether they rejoiced more in the poetic associations or in the wild beauty of the rough landscape, so rich in chestnut-trees, vines, olives and figs, with the running line of Mons Lucretilis behind the *gelidus rivus* of the Digentia below. "*Hic in reducta valle Caniculae*," they would repeat, in their strange Anglican accents; then go off up a hill path to explore for the Fons Bandusiae.

But, since 1911, the villa of the Sabine farm has been excavated; we can see the remains of Horace's walls in reticulated limestone—about twelve rooms—and those added in brick in the second century; there is a large quadrangle, with a portico, a bathing establishment, the remains of a fountain; the rooms have mosaic floors, the walls were frescoed. In the Middle Ages a church and monastery, now disappeared, were built over the west side Whether these ruins, now visible, but no great sight, give more gratification to visitors and Horace-lovers than the knoll with the one mosaic floor which was all we had of the villa in former centuries, is questionable. Anyhow, it is now a national monument, and well laid out with box-trees and marble busts.

There are those who may be called ruin-snobs, who despise such popular exhibits as Tivoli, Praeneste, Tusculum, and the Sabine farm: these roam the Campagna in search of ruinous places less (as they believe) hackneyed; such they hold many of the ancient, often pre-Roman, hill towns to be; Etruscan, Hernican, Latin, Volscian, and Sabine, standing grandly and medievally on their mountain slopes, encircled by ruins of vast polygonal pre-Roman walls, that enclose the space, larger than the existing town, where the ancient city stood. They have often, at the top of the steep winding streets, an acropolis, with traces of an earlier acropolis, an amphitheatre, the remains of colonnaded porticos, a forum, temples, either mere ruins or built up into Christian churches, Roman and pre-Roman gates, cisterns, the stumps of Roman villas scattered round. Here we may find some of the earliest Latin temples, sometimes having served as capitols, enclosing the ruins of later Christian churches, as at Segni. At the Etruscan Veii, that city which was old when Rome was new, which was larger than Athens, as fine in buildings, says Dionysius, as Rome, her ancient enemy and final conqueror (in B.C. 396, after an eight years' siege) there are the remains of huge walls, Roman and Etruscan bridges, gates, *thermae*, a cistern, magnificent foundations of a great Etruscan temple. Through the ruins of the later Roman city we climb to the citadel, and, looking down over the desolate hill country, meet history, pre-history, and legend, which brood among these broken stones. These are, indeed, the deepest pleasures of the Campagna ruins; the everlasting wash of air, Rome's ghost since her decease, bears on its tide the tales, told and untold, of seven and twenty centuries. At Gabii, that ancient colony of Alba, standing on the rim of a long-dried lake, with its acropolis and tower, and its temple of Juno standing, a lonely fragment of tawny tufa, on the wild grass-grown plain, Romulus and Remus were, we remember, sent for their schooling; false Sextus betrayed it to Rome; it declined into desolation and nothingness as the centuries rolled by. The lake of Albano is haunted by the ghost of Alba Longa, brooding tremendously among the ruins of the Roman colony built on its razed site. Here are the remains of the great imperial villas, and of Domitian's huge palace that sprawled over the hill where the Villa Barberini now stands; those who are well-informed quote Juvenal as they explore the ground. Here, too, one may trace the walls of the great camp that Severus built for his legionaries; and here stand the great vaults and arches of the huge baths, holding houses, churches, convents in their shelter. The legionaries had every amenity; the amphitheatre, cut out of the rocky hillside, a complicated and broken maze of arcades, corridors, small rooms, stairways, subterranean passages, arena and seats jungled over with a tangle of green, is a huge affair. This picturesque ruin, with the jumble of *thermae* and medieval houses, the great vaulted cisterns, the terraces of Domitian's villa and its fragments that underlie the Villa Barberini (including a nymphaeum and a small buried theatre) and the Papal palace built in the ruins of the castle of the Gandolfi and mirrored in the lake below, have always been felt by painters and sketchers, professional and amateur, to be among the most promising subjects for the practice of their art.

But, wherever they ramble in the Campagna, and whatever their style and medium, they can erect their easels with confidence; interesting ruins can scarcely be avoided. Archaeologists, too, have no dull moment. They are often, when not excavating, engaged in acrimonious disputes about the age of polygonal walls, pieces of which are to be seen about most of the ancient hill cities: the great divide is between those who hold that they can be as late as Roman, and those who cling to a more exciting antiquity. Lesser but more unhappy differences obtain on the topic of who excavated what first; all the acute, though dignified, wranglings which animate the practitioners of this great and arduous profession. A more tranquil happiness pervades the souls of the amateurs, who may hold whichever theory they prefer, and who do not care who dug up what. These innocent enthusiasts roam the ruinous Campagna delighted and excited with all they see, or rather, with all that modernization and commercializing and smart new building have left them. There is a case for holding that the greater the ignorance (so long as it stops short of the incuriousness of the peasant and the wild buffalo) the greater the joy. "*That's a fine tower, look.*" "*Torre degli Schiavi, that's called. Where they used to put the slaves, I suppose.*" "*No, I should think the Schiavi were a Roman family. Or perhaps medieval, should you think?*" "*I don't know, and I don't care. But isn't it grand, standing up all alone like that against the sky?*" "*Look, this must have been a temple. Eight pillars left, all broken. Tempio di Giunone, it's carved up there. Who was Giunone?*" "*Don't know. But isn't it a beauty? And just look at the view from between these pillars. You can see the sea . . . what are you doing?*" "*Just writing my name on this pillar. Sort of way of saying thank-you to old Giunone.*" "*Think of those old Romans, all that time ago, saying their prayers there. . . .*"

The poetry of ancient ruins thrills like music in the blood. Someone fishes up from his ill-stored memory some lines of verse—

> "From the gigantic watch-towers,
> No work of earthly men,
> Whence Cora's sentinels o'erlook
> The never-ending fen; . . ."

Who shall say which experience the greater pleasure, these innocent viewers or the diligent scholar peering at fragments of wall? Both are happy. And there is room for all approaches in that ruin-wilderness, where the antiques lie sunk like galleons in a heaving sea.

25

Further south, where the glories of Magna Graecia toll like drowned bells all round the Tarentum Gulf, from Taranto to Croton and beyond, visible ruins are few, and ignorant enthusiasm is apt to encounter, except for one or two splendid eye-catches such as Metapontum, a chill and discouraging void. To enjoy the ruins of Sybaris, for instance, destroyed and drowned two thousand four hundred and sixty years ago, and now lying buried deep in rich river mud, requires not only imagination but a little knowledge of what Sybaris was like when it was to be seen. That opulent ancient city, once the capital of Magna Graecia, once so happy in its vast prosperity and elegance, was destroyed by its rival Croton, and drowned by the diversion of the river Cratis over its razed temples and courts, theatres, streets and baths, and lies fathoms deep beneath the marshy plain, sunk without trace. Archaeologists take pleasure in looking for its site; ordinary people gaze with admiration at the great curve of the gulf scooped from the Ionian sea, beneath Italy's heel and toe, where the Greeks set their chain of cities twenty-six centuries ago—Tarentum, Metapontum, Siris, Locri, Croton, Ciro, Sybaris, carrying eastward from Cumae on the Mediterranean coast the plantations of their culture. The new cities they set among rivers, in an alluvial plain, the circle of steep forested Calabrian mountains at their back; down to the shore runs a carpet of bright flowers. There, between the Cratis and the Sybaris, the Achaeans built Sybaris in the eighth century B.C., and the circuit of its walls was fifty stades; there, in the sixth, its enemies the Crotonians assaulted and drowned it utterly. No trace of its ruins remains above ground; no one is certain of the site. We know nothing of ruined Sybaris; all the records are of the city in its rich florescence, that scented, delicate hot-house bloom of luxury. It is on this Sybaris that we muse as we stand above the sunk city preserved in river mud, the city whose broken temples must resemble those of her daughter city, Paestum; her marble baths and great fora perhaps surpass any others in beauty. The sense of grandiose ruin is sharpened by the dreams we have of those who inhabited there; those Sybaritish Achaean Greeks, the envy and derision of their neighbours, a legend down the centuries that followed their dispersal, with their exquisite meals, their silken garments, their prolonged matutinal slumbers that must not be disturbed by cocks, their horses that caprioled and danced to music, their wanton pleasure-seeking that has made of them for twenty-six centuries a legend, "those prodigious prodigals and mad Sybaritical spendthrifts", as Robert Burton sourly called them—imagining those sunk and viewless ruins of their city, we can see them still, strolling languidly about their wrecked streets, carefully shaded from the sun, followed by pet dwarfs and leading costly little dogs from Malta, saying to their friends, "You must dine with me a year from to-day" (so great an occasion was a Sybarite dinner), turning away their eyes in distaste (or even swooning) if they saw a labourer at work, going to the baths leading slaves in chains, in order to punish them if the water should prove too hot or too little perfumed, lying on beds of rose petals, complaining in anguish if any were crumpled, discussing new and exquisite sauces for fish (for in this matter of sauces they were excessively ingenious, bestowing especial rewards on those who invented anything recherché, such as roe pickled in brine and soaked in oil and sweet wine, which was, it seems, something like anchovy sauce), crowning with gold crowns those who were judged to have given the most sumptuous public dinners. Reclining on the turf so far above the lost city, we can almost see those marble-pillared arcades and courts where elegant Sybarites drank together (women, too, for this happy and admirable people practised sex equality in pleasure, shocking their less advanced neighbours such as the sour puritan Pythagorean citizens of Croton who barbarously destroyed them in the end.) There the magnificent city lies, wrecked and drowned, but safe from quarrying, protected these thousands of years by river mud and earth, as Pompeii and Herculaneum by ashes and lava; its fallen columns lying lovely and intact, its buildings worthy of the greatest and richest city of Greater Greece; its temples were perhaps as huge as Selinunte, huger than Paestum. A complete civilization lies beneath our feet as we tread the marshy ground through which the Cratis winds. What sculptures, lavish in beauty, decorate this city, what baths, what plumbing, what heating, what beds! None of those hard bedsteads used by those of Herculaneum: the beds of the Sybarites would have, we may be sure, beneath the withered rose petals (potpourri by now) admirable springs. When Sybarites visited Sparta, the hard benches they had to sit on at meals, and the frugal food, caused them to exclaim that they no longer wondered at the courage of these people in battle, for what regret could attend the leaving of so harsh a life, so different from that of Sybaris, where, lapped in rose-leaves and silken sheets, Sybarites lay late in exquisite chambers?

Seventy years ago M. Lenormant uttered an impassioned plea for bringing Sybaris to light. He believed that he knew its exact site; only it lay so deep. Its discovery, he thought, would be more rewarding than that of any other city. Were it dug up and set in order, a unique way of life would rise before our envious and applauding eyes; it would be the most titillating of ruin pleasures. And sprouting, no doubt, with that lush vegetable and aquaceous life, water weeds and deep moss (since the Cratis mud is of a teeming fertility) which, to romantic eyes, adds beauty to the bare bones of noble ruins. It would need much scraping.

But Sybaris lies too deep. To reach it would be too costly. Shallow digging and drilling has produced no results. Unless someone should put up a fabulous sum, the kind of sum only put up in these days for the manufacture of deadly weapons and military expeditions, we shall not see the first Sybaris. Nor the second, built sixty years later out of its ruins, for the Crotonians, who had sworn *delenda est Sybaris*, destroyed this almost at once. The third, built on higher ground, round the spring Thurii, with strong defending walls, which became a Roman colony and was wiped out of history by Saracens, has left a few fragments of wall and aqueduct, a buried necropolis, and a spring. The site of the fourth and last Sybaris, founded by Sybarites who fled from Thurii, having made themselves odious to the other Thurians, was found lately near Castiglione, three miles from the Trionto valley. There is a large acropolis partly surrounded by a strong wall of huge squared blocks. There is a grotto which probably led to an underground aqueduct; fragments of a Doric capital, many tiles, and some shards of black glazed pottery. It seems that we must accept this precipitous, wood-grown rock as all that is left of the last Sybaris. But did the Sybarites in their fourth city, after so much destruction, exile, quarrelling, massacre and resettlement, lead still the happy life which has made them famous? Are we to picture them, on and around this rocky acropolis, still at it, during the century before the new city was destroyed by the barbarian Brutti from the interior and no more known? We may not know: all we see is a barren mountainy country, where Sybarites, forlornly expatriate ghosts, seem to wander, murmuring of rich sauces, far from home. So that all our Sybaritish ruin pleasure is in the ecstatic contemplation of the unseen, in wistful meditation on beauty wrecked and perished from our view and lying far below our feet.

But this may well be the profoundest ruin pleasure of the Tarentum Gulf. There is little of Greek Tarentum, and Croton is a modern city; the great walls described by Livy are gone, and the acropolis is known only by its site and shape, rising high above the sea and built over with the later town. All that is left of Achaean Croton is one tall lonely Doric column of the great temple of Hera Lacinia on the tip of Cape Colonna. The rest of the temple, famous as late as the Roman Empire, was destroyed and pillaged long since for building (the sixteenth-century Bishops' Palace, the fortified castle of the Duke of Toledo, the great mole), and battered to pieces by sea and earthquake. The one column, standing in lonely prominence above the beating sea, has an extraordinary effect of lost grandeur. It haunted George Gissing, who saw it through field-glasses from Cotrone, and never got there.

"It is a Doric column, some five and twenty feet high; the one pillar that remains of the great temple of Hera. . . . I planned for the morrow a visit to this spot, which is best reached by sea. To-day great breakers were rolling upon the strand, and all the blue of the bay was dashed with white foam. . . . "[1]

Kept in Cotrone, he looked in vain for the ruins of old Croton.

"Yet a city bounded with a wall of twelve miles circumference is not easily swept from the face of the earth. . . . Nearly two

[1]George Gissing, *By the Ionian Sea* (1901).

hundred years before Christ the place was forsaken. Rome colonized it anew, and it recovered an obscure life as a place of embarkation for Greece, its houses occupying only the rock of the ancient citadel. Were there at that date any remnants of the great Greek city?—still great only two centuries before? Did all go to the building of Roman dwellings and temples and walls, which since have crumbled or been buried? . . . Could one but see in a vision the harbour, the streets, the vast encompassing wall! From the eminence where I stood, how many a friend and foe of Croton has looked down upon its shining ways, peopled with strength and beauty and wisdom! Here Pythagoras may have walked, glancing afar at the Lacinian sanctuary, then new built."[1]

Developing a fever, he tormented himself through sleepless nights with the thought that he should never see Colonna. To turn his back on the Lacinian promontory, leaving the ruin of the temple unseen, seemed to be a miserable necessity, which he would lament as long as he lived. So near and yet so far: tossing in delirium, he seemed to be in a boat on wild waters, the Column visible afar. Then falling into "a visionary state", he saw pictures of ancient Croton—thronged streets, processions, carved marbles and vases, the promontory with its column, the strand where Hannibal slaughtered Italian mercenaries for refusing to follow him to Carthage. Over this scene of two thousand years ago lay "an indescribable brilliancy which puts light and warmth into my mind whenever I try to recall it." These visions never returned.

"That gate of dreams was closed, but I shall always feel that for an hour it was granted me to see the vanished life so dear to my imagination. . . . Tell me who can by what power I reconstructed, to the last perfection of intimacy, a world known to me only in ruined fragments."[2]

Such visions are the not infrequent reward of the frustrated and delirious ruin-seeker. Indeed, in Magna Graecia they must remain his chief reward.—"*Magnamque Graeciam, quae nunc quidem deleta est, tum florebat,*" wrote Cicero, with his scholarly nostalgia for the past. But at Metapontum he saw the house of

[1]George Gissing, *By the Ionian Sea* (1901).
[2]*Ibid.*

Pythagoras (or so he supposed), and must have seen the walls, theatre and temple. Pausanias, two centuries later, said that nothing was left of this famous city but the theatre and walls; the temple he does not mention; nor did he know, apparently, how or when Metapontum had been destroyed. Pausanias's reflections on ruins are seldom either enthusiastic, full, or morbid; he retains, before the most noble wrecks, his dry tourist urbanity. Later travellers have been stirred by thoughts of Pythagoras, of Metapontum's greatness and wealth among the Magna Graecia cities, by the ruins scattered about the farm of Sansone, and chiefly by the fifteen magnificent Doric columns left standing from the sixth century temple, and named the Tavole Paladine by generations who had heard of paladins, but not of Greater Greece.

As to Locri, its remains are rather an archaeologist's pleasure than a layman's. You may walk about the great site within the vanished walls, and inspect its plan. It has been a collector's paradise, a treasury of terra-cotta fragments, mostly of the fifth century, and (if we are to believe Mr Norman Douglas) a temptation to sculpture-fakers. The traces of temples about the city site are too slight to please greatly any but the learned. But they enhance the beauty of the paths that wind about the olive-grown hillside and of the shore where the foundations of a temple lie. The excitement of Locri is partly this natural beauty; partly the finds of the last hundred years—the Ionian temple, the marble figures of the Dioscuri, the terra-cotta fragments, the sanctuary of Persephone—one feels that anything may still turn up; and partly the haunting of a splendid history, the praise of Pindar, the famous victories, the grandeur under Dionysius. All this is unobscured by the later cities that conceal Croton and Tarentum; the impact of ancient Locri is unconfused; it comes with a thin, ghostly clarity from that sun-baked hill site.

26

Cumae too is unspoilt by modernity; though recent excavations and clearance have diminished the romantic glamour of the cave-tunnelled, forested hillside, with its hundred mouths to transmit the Sibyl's utterance. The impression, of course, remains tremendous; as ruin-feeling, it is muddled by legend, by the aura of poetry and tradition. None seeing it can escape pious Aeneas and the

> "*arces, quibus altus Apollo*
> *Praesidet, horrendaeque procul secreta Sibyllae,*
> *Antrum immane. . . .*"

When Virgil knew Cumae, the cult of the Sibyl, abolished for a time, had been restored by Rome; he saw the caves, the tunnelled paths, the ruins of the Greek temples of Apollo and Zeus, before they were rebuilt by Augustus, the Roman city lying at the foot of the Acropolis, the broken walls that circled it. The Greek, the pre-Greek legend confronted him in that riddled tufa mountain side, as it has confronted all later travellers, strengthened and enriched by his tale. They have thought of the oracle, of the cave that ran through to Avernus, of Aeneas among the shades, of Odysseus, of the Cimmerians dwelling underground. The Roman city covered the ancient site; the forests were cut down; "all these stories have been proved to be mere myths," wrote Strabo; yet Statius, nearly a century later, refers, as one of the pleasures of the bay of Baiae, to the haunted shrine of the inspired Sibyl; and brings her out, white-haired and laurel-crowned, to celebrate with song and lyre the emperor's new road to Cumae. Possibly the cult never quite died. The temples were adapted to Christian basilicas; in the caves beneath them the oracle still brooded. The Saracens, burning the Roman Cumae in the tenth century, added mysterious haunting to her ruins; the Neapolitans, more completely destroying her four centuries later, so that she lay henceforth deserted, could not destroy the memory and the ghosts. The greatest, the oldest, Greek city of Italy; a sacred shrine; it is such heady prestige as this that confuses the visitor in his capacity as ruin-gazer. Through the centuries of abandonment the ruins of Cumae lay visible, dug among for statues and treasures, diminishing gradually as they were plundered and taken for building, yet never losing their prestige.

"From hence" (wrote in 1645 John Evelyn, who always thought ruins rather a pity), "we ascended to that most ancient city of Italy, the renowned Cuma, built by the Grecians. It stands on a very eminent promontory, but is now a heap of ruins. A little below stands the Arco Felice, heretofore part of Apollo's temple, with the foundations of divers goodly buildings, amongst whose heaps are frequently found statues and other antiquities, by such as dig for them"[1]

Such as dug for them dug, until the nineteenth century, with complete lack of system or coherent purpose. For the last hundred years systematic excavations have spasmodically occurred, and the Cave of the Sibyl is now exposed. To-day we may enter it, penetrate all the tunnels; we can distinguish the Greek, Roman and later work in the Temple of Apollo, and in the fragments of the wall. The Grotto of the Sibyl, so romantic and mysterious to our nineteenth-century ancestors, has been cleared and exposed, and is now, someone has said, "about as picturesque as a railway tunnel". There is no more groping in the dark into the "*antrum immane*", or scrambling about a hillside overgrown with shrubs and woods. But there remains the stupendous view from the acropolis top, the tunnels and caves that riddle the mountain, one running through to the Lake of Avernus, the temple ruins, and the amphitheatre, and the many Roman remains scattered about vineyards and slopes. The ruins are still excessively romantic; no human effort can turn them into prose.

They were one of the goals of the romantic ruin-seekers of the eighteenth century, who, ardent with the *Ruinenlust* inspired by Salvator Rosa and his south Italian crags, broken arches, and brooding banditti, rushed to Italy to feed their melancholy cravings with this stimulating fare. There they found the desolate grandeur that their souls sought, greatness crumbled, or vanished wholly. They wandered entranced about the recovered cities of Pompeii and Herculaneum; they brooded over the Sibyl and read the Aeneid at Cumae; they roved down the richly ruin-strewn bay of Naples, seeing the amphitheatre and the Serapeum of Puteoli, the Temple of Hercules beneath the sea, the wrecks of noble Roman villas that have foundered on Baiae's coasts or been long drowned in the encroaching sea. They marvelled at Paestum: Goethe took his artist Kniep there, in 1787; a countryman led them through the "remains of temples and other buildings of a once splendid city". Goethe was critical.

[1]John Evelyn, *Diary*.

"The first sight excited nothing but astonishment. I found myself in a perfectly strange world; for, as centuries pass from the severe to the pleasing, they form man's taste at the same time. . . . Our eyes, and through them our whole being, have been used to and decidedly prepossessed in favour of a lighter style of architecture; so that these crowded masses of stumpy conical pillars appear heavy, not to say frightful. But I soon recollected myself . . . and in less than an hour found myself reconciled to it—nay, I went so far as to thank my genius for permitting me to see with my own eyes such well-preserved remains. . . ."

Henry Swinburne, that enthusiastic traveller, had ten years earlier experienced a more unadulterated delight, in spite of the "perniciousness of the air". Arriving by boat from Salerno, and walking over a sandy down, he arrived at the west gate of the desolate city, and felt that "few cities have left such noble proofs of their magnificence". The town wall was almost entire; a great street could still be traced from north to south; the temples, whose pillars he carefully measured, belonged to the noblest style of the Doric order; though "an eye that brightens only with the view of nice Corinthian foliage will perhaps receive no delectable impression from the sight of such massive proportions, such simple and solid parts as these". He was discouraging about the theory of Mr Brydon, who, visiting Paestum in 1770, had accepted the romantic notion that it had been lost to view for many ages, until a few years ago "some of its lofty temples were seen, peeping over the tops of the woods", after which intriguing sight "curiosity and the hopes of gain soon opened a passage, and exposed to view these valuable and respectable relics".

Not so, said Mr Swinburne, for Paestum was never surrounded by woods, but stood on a bare sandy down, and its pillars had always been a landmark for sailors. He threw cold water on Mr Brydon's hopes "that some magnificent heap of ruins will hereafter be discovered among the forests of Calabria", for the situations of almost all the Greek cities had been ascertained, and the natives, who were "well acquainted with the recesses of their wildernesses", declared that they harboured no such things. So Mr Brydon's charming dream of impenetrable Calabrian forests concealing monuments of ancient magnificence received no encouragement; Mr Brydon's hunting-ground would more suitably be the jungles of Central America or Ceylon.

Ruin excitement is fed by forests, modified by open ground; but the astonishment of ancient Poseidonia and its temples has triumphed over its visibility to the whole gulf of Salerno.

27

The discovery of Sicily by the eighteenth-century tourists was an inevitable sequel to their romantic excitement in the ruins of the southern mainland. The island had always had its visitors; but it was not regarded as very accessible or very agreeable travelling. It required the classical antiquarianism of the mid-eighteenth century and the romantic poeticism of a few years later to send the enthusiastic addicts of the picturesque and of Salvator Rosa to the very home of picturesque ruin. Ruins were scattered about Europe and Asia; but in Sicily there were ruins everywhere, and ruins set in landscapes of wild mountain scenery, against seascapes of startling loveliness, overrun by banditti and pirates and liable to be destroyed by convulsions of the earth without parallel. Sicily was obviously the spiritual home of those who loved convulsions, the mouldering of past greatness, desolation, the lizard among the ancient stones, as well as of those who loved classical history and art.

Sir William Hamilton, visiting Sicily from Naples in the 1760's, was of these last; he and his lady returned delighted and laden with those objects of antiquity that tourists then picked up wherever they went. Brydon, a year later, thought the island highly dangerous and comfortless, being full of mountains, forests, bogs, and the most daring banditti in Europe; he stayed in wretched hovels with nothing to eat; "if we had not brought some cold fowls with us," he wrote at Syracuse, "we might have starved." But the spirit triumphed over such discomforts, and he explored with intelligent interest. Syracuse, "the largest of Greek cities and the loveliest of all cities", as Cicero had described it, praising it not only for its beauty but for its size and great strength, was "now reduced to a heap of rubbish, for what remains of it deserves not the name of a city". Great spaces grown with vineyards and orchards lay where once the city stood; the walls of the vineyards were built with broken marbles carved with inscriptions and reliefs, most of them defaced and spoiled. He saw the theatre and amphitheatre, many sepulchres, the quarries, the ear of Dionysius; he fell into the melancholy musings on decay usual before such sights.

"It is truly melancholy to think of the dismal contrast that its former magnificence makes with its present meanness. The mighty Syracuse, the most opulent and powerful of the Grecian cities, which, by its own strength alone, was able at different times to contend against all the power of Carthage and of Rome. . . . This haughty and magnificent city, reduced even below the consequence of the most insignificant burgh!—*Sic transit gloria mundi.*"[1]

Mr Henry Swinburne suffered similar reactions at Syracuse, but with more detail in his historical reflections. He recalled Cicero's description, he thought of the successive occurrences which since then had combined to make this description inapt; he thought about the destructions by Vandals, Goths, Byzantines, Saracens, earthquakes, Sicilians; of the five ancient divisions of the city, which Strabo had said was twenty-two miles in circuit, only Ortygia remained, oblong in shape, about two miles in circumference; the rest of the most magnificent city in the world had become the habitation of wild beasts and birds. Such thoughts produced

"a melancholy impression on the mind. . . . I had already viewed the desert sites of many great ancient cities, and had as often mourned over their remains; but never did I feel the impression of pity and regret so strong as in wandering among the ruins of Syracuse."[2]

He wondered, as all visitors to Syracuse have wondered, what forces can have so utterly annihilated so great a city and the very dust of the materials of which it had been built, and left what Gregorovius was later to call "the vast plain of the dead Syracuse". It was characteristic of the eighteenth-century travellers to spend almost more time and emotion over the contemplation of vanished Syracuse than of the remains of its temples and theatres. But they took great notice of the Greek theatre, for it

[1] P. Brydon, *Tour Through Sicily and Malta* (1770).
[2] Henry Swinburne, *Travels in the Two Sicilies* (1783).

made a wonderfully picturesque scene; its steps were still half-buried and overgrown with bushes and trees; and water from the ancient aqueduct turned the wheel of a mill and fell in cascades over the first two stages, "adding to these great ruins an accident of the most picturesque and agreeable effect". Even as late as the middle of the nineteenth century the stage was unexcavated, and was a heap of ruins overgrown with brushwood. Gregorovius derived his pleasure from imagining the view seen by the Greeks —temples, halls, sumptuous buildings, the harbour filled with masts; and most from the vision of the Hellenic past; "here, on these grass-grown steps once sat Plato, Aeschylus, Aristippus, Pindar; here Timoleon discoursed . . . the entire history of Syracuse from its most brilliant period was enacted here in speeches and affairs of state".[1] The great articulate past of Greek Sicily fought for dominance in the souls of travellers with the sense of the romantic ruined present: the Marquis de Foresta at Syracuse, in 1805, surrounded himself with the shades of great men and mythological phantoms, meditated on history and philosophy, quoted classical writers, and came back to "*la délectable mélancolie du contraste entre la ruine des oeuvres humaines et la nature toujours vivante; entre le passé splendide et le présent sans gloire*"[2] and the also not unfamiliar conceit of some traveller of the future finding the ruins of the Louvre buried in the grass. All those past passions, and now silence and peace, flocks pasturing among the porticoes of destroyed temples, columns and capitals lying among acanthus bushes. In that silence the Marquis imagined the playing of antique lyres and Aracadian pipes.

The "*entêtement de l'antiquité*" possessed all, or nearly all, these classical and romantic travellers. Like Chateaubriand (who was never in Sicily) they gazed on ruins by moonlight, deriving from the silence of vanished cities a delicious melancholy. Some ruins, such as the Temple of Concord at Agrigentum, they found too well kept to please; they preferred disorder, thrown columns, roots and shrubs and flowers thrusting up between the stones, thistles, nettles, hellebore and bindweed, snakes and lizards, adders on the one-time altars, columns blackened by shepherds' fires, hawks nesting on friezes, broken pavements where lean

[1]F. Gregorovius, *Sketches of Naples and Sicily in the Nineteenth Century*.
[2]Marquis de Foresta, *Lettres sur la Sicile* (1821).

flocks browsed on sparse yellow grass. They adored most of all the grand desolation of Selinunte; painters and poets and travel-writers found something sublime in so many gigantic pillars so completely upset. Not yet were the temples labelled alphabetically; all was confusion, a huge destruction entwined with wild vines, ivy, figs, rhododendron, pomegranates, aromatic plants that served as incense on the broken altars; a carpet of greenery roved over the paved floors, where rabbits and goats wandered. In a watch-tower lived a few inhabitants; two old men and a young woman. People called the temples the pillars of the giants. Below them lay the foundered port; under the sea one saw streets and houses; sometimes a storm would sweep over them drifts of sand and seaweed; then the sea swept them bare again, and one saw a labyrinth of broken pillars crusted with shells, and walls green under moss. One tower, the Torre dei Forti, stood lonely on the desolate beach. Such complete desolation had, said the travellers, inexpressible charm. Three of them, brothers, decided to spend a night in the tower, for ruins must be contemplated by moonlight. The tower was half-ruined, its base was washed by the sea; they supped in an ancient chapel, kindling a fire on the altar, then climbed to the top storey of the tower and slept, lulled by the murmur of the waves and the cries of sea birds.[1]

Gregorovius, returning to Selinunte in 1886, after thirty years, was vexed by its tidied, excavated appearance. In 1853 the ruins still were beautifully desolate in the wilderness, grown with shrubs and palms and full of those spotted snakes so dear to ruin-lovers. In 1886

"the excavator, at war with the savagery of nature, is again victorious, and as almost everywhere in the classic ruins which learning has recovered, the poetry of these ruins has been utterly destroyed. Instead of vegetation clothing the overthrown temples . . . burying the ruined splendour under flowers, the artistic or poetic feeling of travellers sees with sorrow only bare cleansed architraves, metopes, triglyphs . . . and it only requires numbers or labels on the blocks to persuade him that he has before him a well-arranged archaeological museum. The gain to learning is occasionally a loss to imagination, for poetry and art derive their inner life from the mysterious."

[1]Hélène Tuzet, *Voyageurs Français en Sicile au temps du Romanticisme* (1945).

Further reflection, however, reconciled the mystical but learned German to the advance of archaeological science and the necessity of making ancient monuments accessible to students.

So the romantic travellers roved over the ruinous island, with pen, pencil and paint-box, transported by all they saw. Segesta towered lonely on its wild mountain over a desert, surrounded by long grass and forests of thistles, nettles growing in the cornices and the beloved adder creeping about the floor; lovely in its hues at sunrise, standing flanked by black ravines at night. Some artists sought to improve their drawings of Segesta by surrounding it with trees; Forbin, in 1820, made an acid comment on this; for his part, he drew the temple with great care and without fanciful embellishments, and sat in the shade of the columns, not knowing or caring to whom they were dedicated, but enjoying the delightful sight, the sparrow-hawks that screamed from the summit, the emerald lizards darting from the crevices, before climbing the hill to the ruins of the theatre and the heaps of loose stones that lay about where Segesta the city had stood. Forbin's ruin-passion was intense, like a lover's; his drawings caress and illumine his subject. He fell in love, on first landing in Sicily, with the ruins of Tyndaris on its sea promontory, ruins placed picturesquely half way up a hill, surrounded by wild vines and carobs, with a view of all the Aeolian islands; he would gladly have spent days there. Selinunte overwhelmed him with emotion. The ruins of the theatre at Taormina he called the finest sight in the world, and imagined what it must have been when the fires of Etna lit it, matching with the passions of nature the passions on the stage. He pictured evenings of the utmost excitement, the lava pouring down to the shore, the volcanic flames lighting the theatre, the soul and eyes struck simultaneously by the convulsions of mountain and sea, and those of the Atrides on the stage. "Where could one better represent the Cyclops of Euripides than with Etna vomiting smoke behind?"[1]

Not all travellers to Sicily have been ruin-lovers. There were anti-clericals, such as Gourbillon, who disliked temples on principle, even in ruin, and approved of antique columns being used, as the Turks used them, to construct moles; this he considered better than degrading them further by turning them into churches,

[1]Comte de Forbin, *Souvenirs de la Sicile* (1823).

33 'The Sibyl's Temple', Tivoli. Pencil drawing by Maria Lady Callcott, 1819

34 The Temple of Hercules, Agrigentum. Water-colour by J. P. Hackert (1737-1807)

35 Remains of an Ionic Temple on the road between Tyre and St Jean d'Acre
Engraving after L. F. Cassas, 1799

like the Temple of Athena at Syracuse. Others were interested in Roman ruins but not in Greek, and were put off by having to climb up and down ravines to reach either. Others again had an antipathy to all ruins, believing that buildings, to be worth looking at, should be entire. These did not care for the past, or for dangerously tottering stones, or for the vegetation that sprouted among them, or for scrambling about débris under a hot sun in order to see such discouraging objects. It was of no use to speak to such travellers of the flight of the centuries, or to remind them of ancient cultures; like Dumas *père*, they had no taste for ruins, and in buildings in pieces saw no grandeur.[1]

This was unusual. But very usual in the eighteenth and early nineteenth centuries, among the French, was distaste for Gothic and Norman and "*le goût barbare et dégénéré du Moyen Age.*" In consequence, the Norman Saracen churches of Palermo and its environs got less than their share of enthusiasm, in spite of Forbin's descriptions and drawings. The classically minded thought these churches built by ignorant hands, with their short pillars and massive capitals, so different from the Greek. But, after Forbin, interest increased; by the thirties and forties the French admirers of classical ruins were including medieval buildings, and writing monographs on Norman architecture.

28

While many travellers flocked to the ruinous island, there was a more ambitious, laborious and learned and equally enthusiastic rush (if rush can be the word for the, on the whole, dignified cavalcade by mule, horse and ship) to the stupendous antiquities of Greece and the east. Athens, of course, had always been visited by foreigners; its purloined marble fragments had adorned British, French and Italian homes from the fifteenth century on; books about it, learned, fanciful, conceited, packed with the most improbable detail and the most well-known facts, and illustrated with the most charming drawings, had trickled with regularity in all the civilized languages from the press for almost as long. Nor had the other well-known Greek splendours been neglected. To Corinth, Sparta, Argos, Thebes, the site of Troy,

[1] Hélène Tuzet, *Voyageurs Français en Sicile* (1945).

Olympia, Delphi, Epidaurus, Eleusis, Bassae, Mycenae, Tiryns, Nauplia, Aegina, Sunium, Delos, the phil-Hellenes, the phil-ruin tourists made, when time and means allowed, their pilgrimage. Many pushed further east and south to Constantinople, Syria and Alexandria. They made drawings and plans, they measured and reconstructed, they brought out large learned books of description and engravings. The stately homes and parks of England burgeoned with models of the broken majesty of Greece and the Levant, copied with a certain patrician looseness from these careful designs. Pausanias, that proto-tourist, led the way; firmly clasping his itinerary in their hands, together with Strabo, Pliny and a great deal else to inform them and afford matter for dispute, the long queue followed, inspired by various curiosities and desires; some among them, ignoring ruins, travelled to see countries and their natives, others, such as Benjamin of Tudela, went to count the Jews in each city, others to trade, some to throw up castles on such foundations of ancient buildings as were suitable and reside there in feudal state; others again went on pilgrimage to the Holy Land, passing on their way the broken relics of a majestic pagan age. But not until the Renaissance did the great stream of ruin-lovers, obstructed at every point by suspicious Turks, begin to pour over Greece and the east. The artists got under weigh with Francesco Giambetti in 1465, becoming increasingly articulate in their descriptions through the next century, disposed to concentrate most of their attention on Athens, but roaming at large over Turco-Graecia, the islands, Albania and the Levant, growing in learning with the savants, French, English and Italian (Deshayes, Spon, Wheeler, Francis Vernon, Chishull, Stuart, Leroi, and the rest), all of whom sought and faithfully or fancifully recorded famous ruins. The task became more exacting as informed antiquarianism grew, and the learned societies sent their emissaries abroad. Dr Richard Pococke, who made his scholarly and extensive tour of Egypt, Palestine, Syria, Mesopotamia, Asia Minor, Greece and the islands, between 1737 and 1740, describes the ruins he encountered with a learned excitement that makes this future Bishop of Ossory one of the most endearing of travellers. At Alexandria he took a boat and peered down through the calm sea round Pharos and saw pillars in it; they might be, he thought, the remains of "that superb building" the lighthouse. He did not detect that fragments of the Pharos pillars were built into the fifteenth century Turkish castle. But "my observing so nicely, and so near the castle, was much taken notice of, and, as I was informed, several soldiers, who were that day on guard in the castle, were punished for permitting me to examine the port so exactly." Having observed the Pharos, he paced round and measured the city walls, counting the towers thereof, examined the site of the Ptolemy Palace, saw along the shore "great remains", pieces of porphyry and fine marble, and tells us of those submerged ruins in the sea which it was so often his delight to surmise and to detect.

Practically everything ancient in Alexandria is destroyed long since, by assault, quarrying and decay. Much was ruinous before the Arab conquest of 641; yet, when the Arab leader marched in he wrote to the Caliph that he had captured a city containing four thousand palaces, four thousand baths, four hundred theatres, and forty thousand Jews. How and when the palaces perished is not certain; the Arabs did their share, and the walls and later city were built out of the destruction of the ancient buildings. English Elizabethan voyagers reported the promontory of the Ptolemy palaces to be built over with houses of Jews; there were Arab castles and walls and Turkish mosques, but deep under the water of the harbour ancient ruins lay, "great sepulchres and other buildings, out of which are dayly digged with engines Jaspar and Porphyrie stones of great value, of the which great store are sent to Constantinople for the ornament of the Mesquitas or Turkish temples." "Alexandria," wrote another, "is an old thing decayed or ruinated, having bene a faire and great citie"; and a third estimated the destroyed part of the city to be six times greater than that which stood. "Such," wrote George Sandys, who called there in 1610, "was this Queen of Cities and Metropolis of Africa . . . who now hath nothing left her but ruins, and those ill witnesses of her perished beauties."

This ruinous state suited the antiquarian temper of Dr Pococke. The old city, he said, was entirely ruined, and the material carried away to build the new, "which makes a very mean appearance." But much of the ancient outer walls remained, besides the Arab walls within them; the old walls, he thought, must have enclosed all the city but the palaces to the north east.

He knew much less than we know now about ancient Alexandria, the city, the palace, the Mouseion, and the Pharos; but he built them up in his imagination, the old magnificent streets, the porticoes, of which ruins and red granite pillars still stood, the forum, the gates. Of the thousand years of Arab rule, during which the city and the Pharos fell gradually into ruin, he knew less, and did not greatly care. But he would have liked the picture of Ptolemaic Alexandria evoked by a writer of the twentieth century, looking down in imagination from the lantern of the Pharos as it stood in its first splendour, a glittering beacon to the sea:

"Let him delete the mosques and the ground they stand on, and imagine in their place an expanse of water crossed by a dyke; let him add to 'Pompey's Pillar' the Temple of Serapis and Isis and the vast buttressed walls of the Library; let him turn Kom-el-Dik into a gorgeous and fantastic park, with the Tomb of Alexander at its feet, and the Eastern Suburbs into gardens; and finally let him suppose that it is not Silsileh that stretches towards him but the peak of the Ptolemaic Palace, sheltering to its right the ships of the royal fleet and flanked on the landward side by the tiers of the theatre and the groves of the Mouseion—then he may have some conception of what Ancient Alexandria looked like from the summit of the Pharos—what she looked like when the Arabs entered in the autumn of 641."[1]

Dr Pococke's mind may have groped after this view as he rambled, inquisitive and measuring, among the ruins of ancient Alexandria, for he was not only a scholarly but an imaginative man. Exploring eastward along the coast beyond Alexandria, "to see what remains there were of antiquity", he came everywhere on enchanting ruins, which he identified with zest and knowledge and constant reference to Strabo: theatres, temples, cities, statues, rose in his imagination and stored memory as he inspected these tiers of broken stones. He saw wonderful things beneath the sea, which, as he said, had gained much on the land. There were ruins of an ancient temple in the water, and broken statues of sphynxes in yellow marble, and the grey and red granite pillars of a portico. "All along the shore are many ruins,

[1]E. M. Forster, *Alexandria* (1938).

and the rocks at the bottom of the sea seem cut out in such a manner, as shews there have been great buildings there." Sailing up the Nile, he saw great ruins right and left; Heliopolis, Memphis, Antinoopolis, Old Cairo, "the heaps of ruins of the ancient Arsinoe", the heaps of ruins that were ancient Egypt, littered the ground for his pleasure, and his pleasure was great. Sheiks entertained him, enquiring what it was he came to see; he replied, the ruined cities; they presented him with sugar canes, coffee, and large sheep; or sometimes some soap and a lamb. By the time he got to Thebes, he must have had a sizeable flock of sheep pattering after him, or else have consumed a surfeit of mutton. Every ruin he met he measured with the utmost care, somewhat to the annoyance of the locals, who suspected sinister designs. The antiquity, the beauty, the ruinous condition, the celebrity, the legends, the measurements, combined to fill him with "the greatest satisfaction". He met with the same satisfaction all over Palestine, Syria, Mesopotamia, Cyprus and Greece, measuring, counting columns, copying inscriptions, tracing walls, identifying fragments, recalling history, chasing aqueducts over the mountains, peering for submerged ruins in the sea (unlike us, he never failed to find them), examining the various layers of culture and history in Cyprus, the "four or five heaps of ruins about the little plain" of Knossos in Crete, tasting all the hot springs of Mytilene, pacing "the remains of that mole which was esteemed one of the wonders of Samos, and is said to have been two hundred and fifty paces long", admiring the half buried columns and statues of another of the Samos wonders, the temple of Juno, searching for the third wonder, the canal cut through the mountains, mentioned by Herodotus, then, leaving the islands, exploring Asia Minor, recording the most careful, intelligent, and painstaking description of the ruins of Ephesus as they were in the middle of the eighteenth century that any traveller has set down. Dr Pococke was among the great ruin-travellers: his exact, detailed investigations, his highly intelligent deductions and surmises (his "I suppose", "I should conjecture", "I take this to be", are based on much learning and reason, as well as imagination) and the breaking out now and then, through the dry facts, of enthusiastic visions of the past (as "When all these buildings were standing, they must have made a most glorious appearance") give to his pages a learned luminousness that makes them delightful reading. Undeterred by physical fatigue, plague, high mountains, oppressive weather, dangerous inhabitants, huge distances, he pursued his way over the Troad, through great heaps of ruin, broken pillars and pieces of marble, to the various supposed sites of old Troy ("the site of it was not known seventeen hundred years ago"), the ruins of the ancient cities of Mount Ida, the magnificence of wrecked Troas; then off again to the islands, before returning to Asia Minor. Unexhausted, he explored thoroughly the antique remains of Nicaea, Ancyra, and the other ancient cities of the Anatolian peninsula. The distances were immense, the pace unflagging, the energy and interest unabated. He traversed Anatolia, Great Phrygia, Bithynia, Lydia, Caria, the islands of the Sea of Marmora, the Bosphorus, Thrace, Thessalonica, and so down into Attica. Oddly, both he and Dr Chandler twenty years after him, only allude to Pergamum, and do not mention Pteria. Pergamum they most probably did not, for some reason, and in spite of its tremendous reputation, visit; it would have been interesting to hear how much of it was to be seen in the mid-eighteenth century. Pococke's descriptions of all he saw are admirably precise, and his plates very beautiful, if sometimes over diagrammatic. He has a passion for detail. Here, for instance, is his long footnote about the walls of Smyrna:

"The city wall went up what they call the windmill hill, on the top of which there are the foundations of a small castle; from this hill the wall runs about a furlong to the north, turns again to the east, and goes up a summit of the hill, which is to the south of the Circus, from which turning north, and going east of the Circus, it afterwards turns to the east for a little way, and so joined the south-west corner of the castle: the northern wall began from the north-west corner of the castle, descends to the north west, in which direction I suppose it went to the sea, through the middle of the present town, near the Armenian street, where there are some remains of a wall. . . . "[1]

And so on. Doubtless Dr Pococke kept his head clearly throughout all these turnings; into them he will drop pleasant pieces of information, such as that the modern city of Smyrna

[1] Dr Richard Pococke, *A Description of the East* (1745).

is called by the English Pegg's hole (but Chandler says this applied only to the roadstead). Chandler's account of Smyrna is rather more romantic, less precise. It has been styled, says he, the lovely, the crown of Ionia, the ornament of Asia, this Turkish town built of ancient marbles, columns standing in the market, antiquities thrown up in digging, to enrich the collections of the curious. In the country round, "cameleons and lizards are commonly seen about the rubbish of old buildings, basking in the sun." Both writers add to their text admirable plates (Chandler's, executed by Revett and Parr, are in a separate folio); and they bear in mind, besides the ancient cities gone, the modern cities that stand among the ruins. There is ruined Magnesia on the Meander, and there is, to improve the prospect, says Pococke, a modern city with courts and gardens, orange and cypress trees, and trees planted also in the streets, so that it appeared like a city in a wood. Pococke never loses sight of the aesthetic aspect. The Reverend Edmund Chishull, chaplain to the Turkey Company in Smyrna, who visited Magnesia in 1699, was mainly interested in its mosques, seeing few relics of antiquity except the columns and ancient inscriptions that he observed to be built into these mosques. More than the ruins, Mr Chishull enjoyed the "delicious situation" of Magnesia, and the pleasure house lent to him and his party by a hospitable effendi, which offered a diverting prospect over the plain of the Hermus. His search for antiquities was apt to be side-tracked by such amenities.

Dr Pococke, on the other hand, was immensely painstaking and single-minded. We are lucky in having from him a description and plate of the temple of Augustus and Rome at Mylassa, "a most exquisite piece of architecture"; soon after his visit it was demolished, and a large mosque has risen, dressed in its marble. Dr Chandler missed the temple by a few years; it was taken down sometime between 1740 and 1760. The mosque in its stone vesture stood on the mountain above, and on the temple's site was the house of a Turk, harem and all, so that no entry was permissible. All we have of the temple is Dr Pococke's plate; the colonnade had twenty-two fluted pillars, the design of which caused him to complain. What happened to the frieze of bulls' heads and tripods? It would not have done for the mosque; perhaps the Turk had it in his house.

No others of the Mylassa temples mentioned by Strabo and Pausanias were to be seen, except as stones in the Turkish town buildings. A Corinthian gateway remained, three fluted columns, and a small mausoleum; but "this city, in every way beautifully adorned with porticoes and temples," as Strabo described it, had been all but quarried away. But Dr Pococke saw more than we do, and more even than Dr Chandler did; ruins are always on the wing, piece by piece they crumble away, or are transformed into something else, we stalk them down the centuries, surprising them at intervals, pinning them down stage by stage, and in each stage they are less. This is more than usually so in Asia Minor, where antiquity is so huge and so ubiquitous and the inhabitants, on the whole, *ἰδιῶται* (as Strabo called those who inherited Aristotle's books and hid them in a trench to be spoilt by damp and moths).

Having done, for the moment, with Asia Minor, Dr Pococke went to Greece. Confronted with the Parthenon, he was not at his best; he did not much care for its "plain Doric", exaggerated the Venetian bomb damage, and surmised that the outer pillars were Hadrian additions; his greatest pleasure was in the frieze. The other acropolis buildings delighted him; he measured them in detail and counted the pillars. Having done Athens, he went ruin-hunting to Megara, Corinth and Patras, then sailed for Sicily and Alexandria. Returned at last to his clerical duties, he recorded his travels in two magnificent folios, and proceeded to investigate the sadly inferior ruins of the British Isles.

Other antiquarians followed him in Asia Minor; Dr Robert Wood in 1750; Dr Richard Chandler in 1764, sent by the Society of Dilettanti, in "the cause of Virtu", accompanied by Messrs Revett and Pars to draw the pictures and plans. They were directed to make Smyrna their headquarters, and visit from there such remains of antiquity as lay within eight or ten days' journey. They were to make accurate drawings and measurements and copy all the inscriptions they saw.

Thus directed and backed, Dr Chandler's account of his travels has weight and a certain solemnity of style. A careful ruin-explorer, he is less graceful than Pococke. But the romance of desolation, its contrast with past greatness, surges through his sometimes stilted periods. As at Teos, where he devoted himself mainly to the recovery of the Temple of Bacchus.

"It might reasonably be presumed (he decided) that the Teians did not fail to provide a temple worthy to receive so illustrious an inhabitant as this profitable God, and that his shrine was most richly adorned,"

in spite of

"the present, though inconsiderable, Remain, consisting of a confused heap of prostrate marble, now too continually diminishing,"

for the Turks melted down, "indiscriminately and without regret", such marble as they did not take for building or grave stones.

But he saw all round the ruined temple the desolation of great vanished Teos, and poetry seized him.

"We found this city almost as desolate as Erythrae and Clazomene. . . . Instead of the stately piles, which once impressed ideas of opulence and grandeur, we saw a marsh, a field of barley in ear, buffaloes ploughing heavily by defaced heaps and prostrate edifices, high trees supporting aged vines, and fences of stones and rubbish, with illegible inscriptions, and time-worn fragments. . . . The heap of the temple of Bacchus, which was visible from the theatre . . . lay in the middle of a corn field, and is overrun with bushes and olive trees. It was one of the most celebrated structures in Ionia . . . a beautiful portico has been erected at the seat of the Right Hon Lord Le Despenser, near High Wycombe, under the inspection of Mr Revett, in which the exact proportions of the order are observed.

"The town has long been deserted. . . . The site is a wilderness; and the low grounds, which are wet, produce the iris, or flag, blue and white. . . . We saw cranes here stalking singly in the corn and grass. . . ."[1]

The poetry of ruin haunted this conscientious and learned emissary of the Dilettanti all the way, as he moved about the fragments of ancient grandeur that littered the plague-stricken coasts of Asia Minor. At Ephesus he brooded over

"The condition to which that renowned city has been gradually reduced. It was a ruinous place when the emperor Justinian

[1]Richard Chandler, *Travels in Asia Minor* (1765).

filled Constantinople with its statues, and raised his church of St Sophia on its columns. Since then it has been almost quite exhausted. Its streets are obscured and overgrown. A herd of goats was driven to it for shelter from the sun at noon; and a noisy flight of crows from the quarries seemed to insult its silence. We heard the partridge call in the arc of the theatre and of the stadium. The glorious pomp of its heathen worship is no longer remembered; and Christianity, which was there nursed by apostles and fostered by general councils, until it increased to fullness of stature, barely lingers on in an existence hardly visible."[1]

At Miletus the remains of the largest theatre of Asia Minor are, at first, described with dry formality:

"The principle relic of its former magnificence is a ruined theatre, which is visible afar off, and was a most capacious edifice, measuring in front four hundred and fifty-seven feet. The external face of this vast fabric is marble, and the stones have a projection near the upper edge, which, we surmised, might contribute to raising them with facility. . . . The vaults . . . are constructed with such solidity as not easily to be demolished. . . ."

But, when they crept into a vault, behind an Armenian with a paper lantern, "innumerable large bats began flitting about us", and the authentic ruin atmosphere surrounds them. Thereafter they explored the city, which was overrun with thickets, growing over pieces of wall and broken arches and marble urns; lying among bushes near the theatre was a pedestal which had held a statue of the emperor Severus, and was inscribed, "The senate and people of the city of the Milesians, the first settled in Ionia, and mother of many and great cities both in Pontus and Egypt and in various other parts of the world." Comparing its past glory with its present desolation, "we may justly exclaim," said Dr Chandler, "Miletus, how much lower art thou now fallen!"

The poetry of ruin; the bats of ruin; the moralizings of ruin: undoubtedly the doctor had the root of the matter in him. Every little while, as before the Temple of Apollo of the Branchidae, or the site of Myus on its rock-girt lake, he lets himself go into enchantment. Neither did he avoid the adventures and alarms of ruin, scaling perilous mountains, climbing frail ladders

[1] Richard Chandler, *Travels in Asia Minor* (1765).

to examine the ornament of gateways (the local Turks thought this courageous but brainless), fleeing from savage natives, dogs, bulls and plague, in pursuit of his romantic quarry. Indeed, the party must have been extremely happy, riding about that historic coast, coming every few miles on the remnants of broken greatness, of theatres, walls, pillars, temples, all the splendid relics of Greece in Asia Minor, but more magnificent, in their prime, than the buildings of Hellas. Engulfed by Persia, Macedonia, Seleucia, Rome, Byzantium, Islam, they were by turns fortified, cherished, adorned, plundered, ruined, new built, annihilated. Barbarians from the east swept over them; Saracens, Turks, Armenians, Greeks, living in dying cities, let them die; their marbled ruins were robbed to build mosques and mean medieval villages. The tumbled columns, the Greek and Roman inscribed entablatures, such western travellers as went that way found thrown among thickets and wildernesses, eyed with apathy and ignorance, taken for drinking-troughs, steps and seats, by a local peasantry as far below understanding or wonder as their own camels.

Such was the romantic and delightful road trodden by the feet of the Dilettanti emissaries of the eighteenth century and their fellow tourists. Besides its rich rewards, it had its sorrows. Temples had disappeared; marbles had been melted away for lime; thickets proved impenetrable; so did the hareems, which were paved and walled, the seekers believed, with valuable inscriptions; the ancient names of places were sometimes undiscoverable; Strabo was too often misleading; Spon and Wheeler, and even at times Pococke, confusing and unreliable. The nights grew cold, the janizary was ill, sleep was disturbed by frogs, owls, jackals and dogs. In one ancient, nameless city the people were luxurious and gluttonous, it was full of gnats, scorpions and female minstrels. Plague raged about the travellers; sometimes they were pent up in small chambers among doves and Turks, devoured by myriads of insects, and suffering from extreme heat and chagrin. But these misfortunes were forgotten when, hidden at the foot of a mountain, they "discovered the solemn ruin of a temple", and, with Strabo's help, could conjecture its name, or, on a mountain ridge, came on a colonnade with columns standing, a broken aqueduct, remains of a theatre, a city wall. Then they would come to a formidable mass of ruin—

amphitheatre, theatres, stadium, odeum, gymnasium, great nameless piles—Laodicea and Lycum, whose inhabitants, though lukewarm, it seems, in matters of religion, had lived such a noble social life; and Hierapolis, whose huge vaults struck a pleasing horror as the travellers rode underneath them, whose marble theatre seats bore inscriptions to be copied ("Hail golden city Hierapolis; the spot to be preferred before any in wide Asia; revered for the rills of the nymphs; adorned with splendour") but whose greatest pleasures to visitors were the hot springs and the stalactite cliff and the causey as white as driven snow. The exotic and magnificent settings, the imposing histories, the formidable fragments, of these noble, often conquered, long-destroyed cities that lay like wrecked ships about the Asiatic plains and mountains, stirred in Dr Chandler every emotion that grand ruins may be supposed to evoke. Sardis, for instance ("of great antiquity, though posterior to the war of Troy"), once the capital of Lydian kings, lying in wreckage on Mount Tmolus—"the site of this once noble city is now green and flowery", but the broken arches and walls had echoed to the feet of Gyges and Croesus, Xerxes and Alexander, Antigonus, the Seleucids, Antiochus the Great, Goths and Byzantines; among the ruins stood, thought Dr Chandler, the palace where Croesus had reigned and prospered; actually this was a Byzantine fortress. Between this citadel and the mountain stood columns of the Ionic temple of Cybele; "it was impossible to behold without deep regret this imperfect remnant of so beautiful and glorious an edifice"; it lifted Dr Chandler's heart with the joy of wrecked civilizations. These civilizations, that had ridden the seas of time and foundered, one behind another, for thirty centuries and more (far more, but some were sunk without trace), can be met all over Asia Minor. Hittite rock cities, sculptures, inscriptions and tombs, mark the Royal Road of the Cappadocian kings; the ruin-seeker in Anatolia, armed with the utensils of his trade, such as blotting-paper, clothes-brush and sponge, or merely pencil and paper and determined impudence, can imperfectly reproduce the more than incomprehensible utterances inscribed in stone by those loquacious, perambulating and highly articulate pre-Aryans. But for ruined buildings he must wait for the Greeks, who peopled Anatolia with their colonies, built their cities and temples and theatres and harbours all down its indented coast. He can travel from ruin to ruin, as Dr Pococke and Dr Chandler did, with Homer, Herodotus, Strabo, Pausanias, and several Greek poets in hand; if he feels unable to follow these explorers in their close and learned attention to the antiquities, he can still muse over the great Ionian cities, weep for the cruel fate of Miletus, trace the lines of its theatre, stroll among the fallen columns of Apollo Branchidae, the greatest of Ionian temples, named for a family as singular in its way as the Pelopidae of Mycene, climb the Acropolis of Priene and look down on the city ruins, and on those of Miletus beyond. Assos and Pergamum, Cnidus and Adalia, await him; all raise the ancient question, has ruin given to such cities more than it has taken away? Their marred, piled and jumbled beauty now, their crowded, bright-hued glory then, steeply towering into the same Aegean sky; the centuries have added Byzantine churches, Turkish forts; satiated with ruin, one looks back to the glorious Pergamese city of the Attalid kings, "the throne of Satan", as the author of the Apocalypse called her; (for, pre-occupied by Zeus and the deified Augustus, Pergamum looked askance on the new religion). There stood the temples, the great theatre, the high altar of Zeus, the library of two hundred thousand books which Antony, that extravagant gallant, presented to his highbrow Egypt, but to whom did she bequeath them? And where now is the glorious frieze of agonist gods, men and beasts that cavorted so grandly, with such noble baroque animation, round the base of the great Zeus altar, and which, resurrected and installed in Berlin, cavorted again for seventy years in that melancholy metropolis, but, if the Russian conquerors did indeed remove them as spoils, where now do they cavort?

In Ionia, the mind hankers after the resplendent past; these proud Greek cities and shrines were too good to be thrown down, to be taken by Croesus, Cyrus, Darius, ruled by Ptolemies, misruled by Seleucids, engulfed by Rome, ravaged in turn by Arabs, earthquakes, Turks, Crusaders, Mongols, Turks again; too great to lie ruining where once they stood triumphing. One wants to see Cnidus towering on its Triopian headland over the deep gulf of Kos between its two harbours, its acropolis precipicing steeply to the sky, its temples terracing down to the sea, the shrine of Aphrodite with the statue by Praxitiles which strangers crossed the world to see; so lovely was it, says Lucian, that he and his two friends, having put in at Cnidus to see it, fell into a rapture before it, one, as if bereft of his senses, springing forward to kiss it repeatedly, the other, who normally hated the sight of women, standing lost in admiration, and all three discussed it with delight until their ship sailed. A few centuries later it was taken, with many more, by Theodosius to Constantinople; fourteen centuries after that, the British Museum got Demeter and an outsize lion, and very noble they both look there. Cnidus was one of the most glorious of Greek cities in Asia; in 1765, when Chandler saw and drew it, a great extent of walls, citadel, temples and streets were still to be seen.

There is, and will be, no end to the disinterment of ruined antiquity in Asia Minor, for more, no doubt, is under the ground than above it. In Anatolia, and particularly in Pamphylia, between the Taurus mountains and the sea, cities are being extricated from the deep layers of drifted sand, grown over with shrubs and trees, that has buried them for a thousand years; Greek and Roman cities, with their temples and paved streets and shops and great theatres so deep sunk that only their top seats show, and Thermessos impregnable on its high mountain ridge, to which the eighteenth-century Dilettanti never climbed. But as to that, these travellers missed much that one would suppose they would have visited; even the immense site of the great Hittite city of Pteria in Cappadocia, of which there was even then what Dr Chandler would have called a considerable remain to be seen. Nor did they, the Dilettanti, visit the island of Rhodes, possibly put off by the most inept utterance ever made by their learned predecessor, Dr Pococke, who landed there in a gale, spent five or six days (but not in Rhodes city, where plague obtained) and summed it up with, "There is nothing worthy of the curiosity of a stranger on this island." This of the island of the Sun God, settled by Tlepolemos, son of Heracles, its three ancient cities sung by Pindar and Homer, which united in the fifth century to build the new city of Rhodes, praised by all beholders, magnificent in its walls, harbours and buildings. True that fifth-century Rhodes and the still more ancient cities have disappeared to make way for the medieval Rhodes of the Knights, so that Greek remains have to be sought for; but fragments can be seen in gardens and orchards and in the crusaders' castle at Lindus and a whole Greek world lies hidden beneath the island stronghold of the Middle Ages. The Middle Ages meant little to Dr Pococke; he classed their buildings, with the Byzantine, as "mean modern edifices", so he would not care for Rhodes.

29

Syria is a better ruin hunting-ground. "This kingdom," wrote William Lithgow, mooning about Syria in 1612, "this kingdom hath suffered many alterations especially by the Persians, Grecians, Armenians, Romans, Egyptians, lastly by the Turks, and daily molested by the incursive Arabs." The incursive Arabs, now in possession, have not had the energy or the means to build their own world upon the ruins of the old; they accept the dead cities as nothing strange, the dead cities of Greece, Seleucia, Rome and Byzantium, brooding like ghosts over desert and mountain and fertile valley, from Antioch and Aleppo in the north to Wady Araba in the far south, while among them the great crusaders' castles ride the desert like moored battleships. Here are the ruins of Graeco-Roman culture imposed on ancient Semitic sites, as at Baalbek and Palmyra and Petra; here are the Seleucid-founded towns, Apamea on the Orontes, Dura Europas on the Euphrates, the latter city besieged for ten years, like Troy, by archaeologists, who have issued annual reports on what they call "the campaign", and are now enjoying an armistice while the spoils of excavation are digested. Dura-Europas is likely to be an archaeologists' pleasure for many years to come. Apamea, the Seleucid military centre on the Orontes, with its herds of martial elephants and horses, its school of philosophy, its long colonnaded street, was destroyed by Persians and earthquake, its remains quarried for centuries, a crusaders' castle built on its acropolis. A century ago one saw more—Corinthian columns lying on either side of the main street; houses and public buildings, also prostrate; part of the wall and north gate, groups of columns all about the city, marking the sites of temples and forums; a statue of Bacchus lying drunk in the middle of the street. Much of all this has been quarried away; but excavation is revealing more. Within the ramparts of the thirteenth-century castle has grown up a Syrian village, full of ancient fragments and inscriptions; the French guidebook calls it the most picturesque part of Apamea. Murray's guide of a hundred years ago puts this citadel in its proper place, as "a modern castle, not older than crusading times. It stands on the top of a mound, and possesses nothing of interest." And again, "Now the only representative of this great and beautiful city is the rickety castle of Mudik, and the few wretched huts that cluster in and around its walls."

Since the crusaders threw up castles all over Syria, almost wherever they found an ancient site, this rivalry in ruin-appeal is common enough. The castle is apt to be the more picturesque, imposing, wearing its legendary and intimidating panache; the remains of the ancient city have to be sought out and identified, even if not dug for. The castle ruins have made, down the centuries, an irresistible appeal to home-seekers, who squat among their guarding walls, building their village colonies out of the stones they find or can detach. They are "modern castles, not older than crusading times", and have a formidable fairy-tale cosiness lacked by the ruins of Greece and Rome which lie around them.

But it is ruined Greece and Rome which occupy Syria. The dead Byzantine cities, the dead outposts of Rome, these lie crumbling on mountain, desert and plain, lost in time and in the oblivion of barbarians, but invincibly in occupation.

"The ruins of the Roman past remain, preserved to some extent by the very depopulation and misery of the centuries that have intervened. Had an organized civilization been maintained in these hills, the mark of Rome would have been overlaid. No such civilization lingered on, and for over a decaying millennium the ancient buildings have crumbled uncomprehended. . . . Rome rises among hovels, and the ancient sites are honeycombed with the shapeless structures of the peasantry. It is a strange irony to find baths and theatres in such a country, or triumphal avenues down which only a flock of ragged goats are driven out and back at dawn and sunset."[1]

This was written particularly of the Jebel country, where Roman cities, baths, markets and theatres stick strangely out of

[1] Robin Fedden, *Syria* (Hale, 1946).

36 An artist drawing Roman columns built into a house in Barcelona. Lithograph by F. J. Parcevisa, 1843

37 Acropolis, Emerita Augusta (Mérida). Lithograph by Don Ivo da Cortina Roperto y Corochano, 1868

the rocky basalt wilderness: Chahba, which became Philippopolis after the emperor Philip who was born there; Kanouat, full of ruined streets, Roman temples, Byzantine churches, vaulted cisterns; Bosra, once the capital of Roman Arabia, succeeding Petra, preceding Palmyra, as the most important of the caravan trade cities of the desert. Bosra is to-day one of the happiest of the ruin-hunters' Syrian haunts; it has everything.

"Bosrah stood up, black and imposing, before us for miles before we arrived, a mass of columns and triumphal arches with the castle dominating the whole. I went up the square tower of the minaret and looked out over the town—columns and black square towers over every ruined church and mosque, and the big castle, and the countless masses of fallen stone. I had been joined by a cheerful, handsome person, the Mamur . . . who climbed with me in and out of the little churches and the fallen walls and the ruined houses. Such a spectacle of past magnificence and present squalor it would be difficult to conceive. There were inscriptions everywhere, Latin, Greek, Cufic and Arabic, built into the walls of the Fellahin houses, topsy turvy, together with the perforated slabs that were once windows, and bits of columns and capitals of pillars. . . . At last he took me to the top of the castle and introduced me to the head of the soldiers, who produced chairs and coffee on his roof-top, and subsequently glasses of arack and water in his room below."[1]

Such are the amenities: coffee on roof-tops, views of the great jumble of medieval ruin, arack and water with cheerful handsome Mamurs, the general sense of magnificence. Behind these the ghosts of Roman legions stalk Trajan's streets between ghostly columns; a Roman triumphal arch still stands; ruins of temples, colonnades, baths, lie about. Somewhere there sits the ghost of the Prophet who was to overturn the east, studying Christian theology.

Jerash, Gerasa, that once great city of the Decapolis, now one of the most beautiful columned ruins anywhere, had a briefer heyday than Bosra, but more greatness, more brilliant a prosperity, and has left far more to show for it. Lying in a remote valley among the mountains of Gilead, with the small river Chrysorrhoas running through it, it was once called Antioch,

[1]Gertrude Bell, *Letters*.

which suggests a Seleucid origin of the second century B.C.; but there are earlier attributions, notably to Ptolemy II, who changed Amman into the Hellenistic Philadelphia in the third century, and even to Alexander the Great. It is supposed that each of these and general prosperity may have helped in "the emergence of Jerash from the chrysalis village of mud huts to the brightly coloured butterfly of an Hellenistic town".[1] But most of the buildings we see now date from the magnificent Roman rebuilding of the first and second centuries A.D. A new Temple of Zeus, a portico, propylaea, and pool added to the great Temple of Artemis (the presiding goddess), the widening of the paved Street of Columns, and changing its Ionic pillars to Corinthian, the colonnade round the forum, ornamental tetrapylons, theatres, huge baths, a triumphal arch that commemorated Hadrian's stay there in 129–30, a richly decorated nymphaeum—all these we see to-day, as well as the ruins of several Byzantine churches. Approaching Jerash by the rough road from the south, one sees the triple triumphal arch ahead, its columns acanthus-based; beyond it the south gate, the colonnaded oval of the forum lying within it, and from there the paved main street drives straight across the city to the north gate, deeply rutted with the wheels of chariots. Drive cautiously along it in a car or jeep; you will pass on your left the glories of Roman Jerash, the cathedral with its second-century façade and its great flight of steps, and the majestic Temple of Artemis behind it. By the edge of the street is the delicious, decadent, conch-decorated nymphaeum, with a sprawl of little Arabs in the fountain basin. Excavated Byzantine churches group east and west among the baths. To the right, across the wooded river, there are more baths, more churches, a mosque, and the mud-built, flat-roofed Circassian village.

You pass excavators at their work, with pick-axe and spade, while others haul up great blocks or capitals into position, and set prostrate pillars on end, for reconstruction proceeds; we may have in the end a Gerasa of the second and third centuries, and very beautiful it will look. Somewhat shaken by Gerasa's paved street, you arrive at the archaeologists' house, and, from the cool shade of its terrace, have a magnificent view over the tawny, columned city, whose wall was two miles round. Here once was

[1]G. L. Harding (Department of Antiquities, Amman), *Jerash* (1948).

luxury, culture, drama, amusement, gladiatorial sport, flourishing commerce, religion, all the amenities of a prosperous Roman colony: the sheer beauty of that well-appointed, seemly city lying above the oleandrous-banked river breathes like a memory about its broken ruins. Destruction, step by step, slew it. The Byzantine Christians built their churches from the pagan shrines; the Persians invaded it in 614, the Arabs in 635, earthquakes shook it, eighth-century caliphs destroyed images and mosaic floors; by the twelfth century it had been long abandoned, and the Artemis temple was turned into a fortress, captured by crusaders, and burnt down. The city became a ruin-field. "To this day Arabs as far afield as south Palestine, when they wish to speak of something as extremely ruinous, say: 'It is like the ruins of Jerash'."[1] Yet, surveyed from the terrace above it, the colonnaded, paved, templed and fountained town, grass-grown and shrubbed but laid out in streets with tetrapylons and the remains of arcaded shops, and set about with graceful shattered buildings, does not wear an air of desolation. These courts, these steps that climb up to noble Christian and pagan shrines, these baths and play-houses, those columns rising up as from a long sleep, the whole set in the green solitude of the circling ruin-sprouting hills; this fragment of Rome in the wilderness has a lovely civility. More of it is emerging month by month, more going up; even the mud village which has during the past century lain at its gates and expedited its ruin, cannot spoil this beauty.

Amman, on the other hand, the capital of Transjordan, has not only Circassians but a modern town to spoil it: nevertheless, the Graeco-Roman city stands on its hill above the river with almost an excess of assertive history and pride. Through the storm-driven ages one plunges down and back, through the Arab centuries to Byzantine Christianity, past that to Philadelphia of the Decapolis, built by Ptolemy Philadelphus the Second on the ruins of old defeated Rabath Amman, the stronghold of the children of Ammon, at the siege of which by King David's army Uriah the Hittite met his planned end. Defeated again and again, Amman kept recovering its prosperity after its constant buffetings. Saul cut down the Ammonites for a whole morning, until the noon heat caused his fatigued troops to pause;

[1]G. L. Harding, *Jerash*.

David besieged and conquered them and looted their city; they were defeated by everyone in turn, but still thundered at by Jeremiah for their wealth and luxury, and for cutting the corners of their hair and dispossessing Gad and boasting of their valleys; Amman should become, said the prophet, a desolate mound, its villages burnt with fire, like the other desert cities that had set themselves against Israel; but "afterwards I will restore the fortunes of the Ammonites, says the Lord." And so it came to pass: Rabath Amman, ruined and desolated at last, rose up again as a new Ptolemaic city, of extreme beauty and great strength, its high citadel rose on three terraces on the mountain top, with a great temple of Hercules or Zeus at its side; fragments of this lie prostrate. Near it stands the beautiful ruin of a Sassanian or Ummayad palace, domed and arched and alcoved, richly panelled and sculptured and delicately arcaded. Looking down on the lower city, one sees to-day, strange and beautiful and incongruous in the bustling modern town, a Roman theatre built into the hollow of a steep hill above a main street. Rose-hued tiers of grass-grown seats climb high, among arches and vaults; in the evening light they glow pink, and are enormously beautiful. The vaults have been found useful by the population for the stabling of horses and families; children play about the theatre, and at the end of Ramadan it is gay with swing boats and a fun-fair. Before it runs a colonnade of eight Corinthian columns. Those who stay in the hotel opposite enjoy a vision of great felicity.

Jerash, Bosra, Amman, are only specimens. Ruined Ptolemaic, Roman and Byzantine cities, or isolated fragments of temples, arches, columns, paved streets, are strewn about the desert as milestones or sheepfolds are in lands of less high pedigree. Entering some Arab village of squalid hovels, we are in a Roman colony, among temple columns, triumphal arches, traces of theatres and baths which no one has had the intellect or the cleanliness to use since the Arabs expelled the civilized Graeco-Roman-Syrian inhabitants and squatted among their broken monuments, stabling their horses in the nave of a Christian basilica, their camels in a richly-carved pagan temple, their families in mud huts clustering about the proscenium of a theatre: the broken heirlooms of the race that ruled stand like desolate ghosts among the squalor. Or they stand alone, lonely outposts in the desert, with perhaps a Syrian herdsman and his lean flock lying in the shade of what was, a millennium and a half ago, a marble colonnade. This shade, those fallen capitals for seats, those broken shafts for tethering, this enigmatic but familiar suggestion of a mansion in the desert spaces, may be all the ruin pleasure the oblivious herdsman gets; unless some travelling enthusiast chances by, and, like Dr Pococke, starts measuring each pillar and surmising past magnificence from the broken stones. Familiar, perhaps, from hearsay or experience, with the strange ways of Franks (who have always pretended this unaccountable interest in ruins, but in reality, as all Arabs know, are looking for treasure) the herdsman may reap an immediate reward for civility and officiousness, or, when the inquisitive Frank is off the scenes, he may do a little groping and digging himself about the sand drifts that hold those fallen temples and arches; for a while the pleasures of brief hope may be his. No more ruin-excitement than this, we believe; unless that of quarrying away the ancient stones for houses and folds. But there is no being sure that, throughout the long centuries of apathy and destruction and greed, there has not been a haunting awareness of the stone signatures of those extraordinary, unknown, mysterious races who once dominated and held the desert, building in it an alien culture, setting it about with alien fortresses and gods, leaving it with the débris of a whole civilization strewn about its face.

The dead Byzantine cities, too; Justinian's magnificent Halebiyah on the Euphrates, which sets even experts speculating on the precise quality of its appeal—

"a pair of foxes that live in the ruins are now the only inhabitants. . . . The perpetual silence, the sombre grey walls, the Euphrates sucking and dragging at their feet. . . . Halebiyah is in fact one of those confusing places which demand a careful examination of conscience, since as the traveller leaves the ruins he is hardly sure whether the impression that remains is really due to the original Byzantine achievement or to the dramatic desolation in which the ruins stand."[1]

such doubts drift like a pleasing mist between the spectator and most of the best ruins. These dead late Greek cities of Syria are

[1]Robin Fedden, *Syria* (Hale, 1946).

nearly all dramatically set; this, and their silent desertion, together with the romantic greatness of their past, would be enough without the splendour of their Byzantine walls and gates. There is no need for them to have the exquisite grace and distinction of Rasafa, that almost melodramatically beautiful caravan and pilgrimage city glorified by the martyrdom of St Sergius, Syria's patron saint, or the rich sculpture and decoration and magnificent proportions of Kala'at Seman with its apsed basilica of St Simon Stylites, or the colonnaded dignity of Deir Seman, or of a hundred other sites of Byzantium scattered about that rocky land. The placing is enough, and the ruin, and the wild coloured desert spreading like a wind-tossed sea. Syria, Mesopotamia, all the far spaces of Arabia, from the Turkish frontier southward to Palestine and Transjordan, from the Lebanon eastward to the Euphrates and across it, are the ruinous paradise of archaeologists and romantics (the former class are always the latter, the latter but rarely the former). While the eye delights in the stupendous Rakka, that great Abbasid caliphs' city whose horseshoe walls, opening on the Euphrates, enclose a field of ruins—palace, mosque, minaret, gates—imagination evokes Haroun Al Raschid who for a time held his court there, and greed digs for Rakka pottery in the grass-grown ruin-field, dug for the same purpose by Arabs for five centuries (in fact, they and others have probably by now got it pretty nearly all out). This treasure-seeking was seen through by the Reverend Henry Maundrell, Fellow of Oriel and chaplain to the British Factory of merchants at Aleppo, who penetrated into ruinous sepulchres near Tortosa in 1697.

"It cost us some time and pains to get into them; the avenues being obstructed, first with briars and weeds, and then with dirt. But, however, we removed both these obstacles; encouraging ourselves with the hopes, or rather, making ourselves merry with the fancy, of hidden treasure. But as soon as we were entered into the vaults, we found that our golden imaginations ended (as all worldly hopes and projects do at last) in dust and putrefaction."[1]

To console themselves, "we took as exact a survey as we could of those chambers of darkness", and made some excellent drawings.

Mr Maundrell, a cultivated and enthusiastic traveller, enjoyed

[1]Henry Maundrell, *Journey from Aleppo to Jerusalem* (1703).

all aspects and amenities of ruins, but did not take the morbid view. He liked to picture the fine buildings the ruins once had been. Fallen pillars and carved marble capitals lying in gardens at Gabala, or tumbled into the sea, "testify in some measure the ancient splendour of this city"; "the remains of a noble theatre" suggest its original grandeur ("this monument of the Roman love of Pleasure", a more disapproving traveller called it). The cleanly don did not like to see the houses with which the Turks had filled its arena, or Tortosa church used as a stall for cattle and full of dirt and mire, or Jericho "at present only a poor nasty village of the Arabs"; he lamented, in his composed way, "that general ruin which the Turks bring with them into most places where they come". The Turks spoiled the antiquities that he travelled to see; at Sidon, "whatever antiquities may at any time have been hereabout, they are now all perfectly obscured and buried by the Turkish buildings," he complained. What he liked was to see "remains of antiquity, from which it may be assuredly concluded that here must needs have been some famous habitation in ancient times", though he was not always sure which. He got to Jerusalem, carrying with him his decent, donnish curiosity and admiration all along the caravan way; in the Holy Land itself, his feeling for antiquities was almost submerged by his reverence for the holy places. Indeed, the Holy Land has been down the ages somewhat bemused for us by the religious exuberance of many of its visitors, including the truculent Crusaders, who cared nothing for ruins except for making them and taking them, and including the long procession of Christian pilgrims, whose interest in archaeology has been slight, but whose reverence for the great story so fervently believed in by many, so wistfully yearned after by more, has carried them about the Holy Places in a trance of pleasure, devotion and grief, a kind of *delectatio morosa* before the broken shrines.

30

More disengaged, probably more satisfied, are those ruinologers who have taken for their province that island whose eastern end points like a hand at the Syrian coast. In this compact island, strewn with the relics of almost three thousand years, thronged with the ghosts of immemorial ages of foreign occupation, layer upon layer of intruded civilizations stand wrecked. Ruin on ruin they stand: on pre-historic sites rose Phoenician temples, classical temples and theatres; on the pavements of Cypriote palaces stood Greek and Roman columns; Phoenician shrines of Aphrodite gave place to Graeco-oriental courts and Roman colonnades; Mycenaean, Egyptian, Persian and Ptolemaic *bijouterie* lies in layers under Byzantine church pavements; towering above the Byzantine rise in Gothic magnificence the Latin palaces, churches and abbeys of the Frankish crusaders, the Lusignan princes who for three centuries made Cyprus luxurious and glorious, the Venetians who threw up great walls and forts, and did little more for ecclesiastical and domestic architecture than to stamp it with their lions. Then, among and above the Greek and Latin churches, mosques and minarets swelled like bubbles and spired like cypress trees into the clear sky: ruins are composite, the wrecked faiths and cultures of the centuries jostling one another in inimical, jumbled beauty. In the towns stand the ruined Lusignan palaces; in the desolate sites (such as Salamis, Kouklia, Curium, Vouni) Phoenician and Greek cities and shrines have gone to earth, sand-strewn, shrub-grown, sea-washed, earth-shaken, crumbling on cistus-grown hill-sides above foaming shores; on the mountains, among carob and olive woods and vineyards, rear the ruins of grand crusader castles and of the Gothic abbeys and churches of the Lusignans. On a spur of cypressed, olive-grey hills with a white arcaded village straggling about its walls, stands the huge Premonstratensian Bella Paise, before which travellers have stood entranced for centuries; its grey magnificence is set in and enhanced by a glory of oranges, palms, cypresses, myrtle, oleander, and the silver sea of olives, and beyond its ranging mountains gleams the Cyprian sea and the desolate line of the Anatolian coast. There it stands, and there the other great abbeys and the huge feudal castles stand, western architecture in a Greek island, monuments of Frankish culture, of Catholic piety, of feudal tyranny, thrown up in this alien conquered mountain land, ruined Gothic cloisters twined with Cypriote blossom and besieged by Mediterranean trees and scented shrubs, the bastions and barbicans of tremendous palace castles set steeply on high peaks, seeming part of the mountain cliffs; both abbeys and castles wear that strange alien grandeur, hard, tough, feudal, dominant, austere. In Bella Paise, handed over to the Orthodox clergy by the Turks after 1570, the Greeks now worship; their eastern softness barely impinges on the hard western pattern. The monastery itself, so wrecked and so commanding, has stood untenanted for four centuries: "a most magnificent uninhabited convent, which is almost entire, called Telabaise", Dr Pococke described it in 1738. The huge fourteenth-century refectory, the broken cloisters with their plundered traceries, the chapter house and dormitories and vaulted undercroft, the battlemented gateway and quadrangular court, impose on the imagination that feudal Lusignan world of which the great castles are the other symbol; the Latin occupation, greedy, tyrannous, knightly, romantic, cruel and proud, remains, a haunting Frankish ghost.

In Nicosia and Famagusta ruined Latin and Greek churches crowd together among Gothic cathedrals now mosques, escutcheoned palaces now offices, medieval chapter houses now garages, a Turkish market house once a Greek cathedral, its rich carved doorway facing the Latin St Sophia across the road. There has been much mending of ruins during the last years. Famagusta is a city of ruins in hiding, ruins restored, the glory and the luxury, the Latin pride and the Latin praying, broken to pieces or disguised. Many of the Gothic churches are now mosques, wearing the incongruity of misapplication, having the air of catholic churches gone wrong, altars destroyed and wall paintings white washed out. All about lie ruined palaces and the houses of chevaliers, set with Lusignan and Venetian coats of arms, strewn with broken fragments of classical friezes, Gothic columns rising out of classical drums. The massive citadel wall encloses the old town—an exquisite group of tawny Gothic churches, set about with palms in an arcaded square, a few Turkish streets. Odd bits of carved and inscribed Greek stones are set in medieval and modern houses or lie foundered in Famagusta Bay, beneath whose waves much of old Salamis too lies drowned. Most of the rest of the ancient Greek capital, such of its ruins as were not quarried away to build Famagusta, is buried with the ruins of Constantius's fourth-century city of Constantia (destroyed by Arabs) beneath sand dunes and wattle forests, from which columns, fragments of arches, the broken white marble pillars of a small Roman forum and the stone pillars of the earlier agora, emerge, still half-overgrown with thorny scrub. In this huge market place, earthquake-shattered, one may see part of a temple, and of the enormous cistern into which the water flowed into the city from the mountains through the great aqueduct of which a few arches still stride across the country. There is a smaller cistern with Byzantine paintings; and underground rooms with Christian inscriptions; there are rows of broken granite columns of the huge basilica built by Constantius for his new city; a tourist's pleasure here has long been picking up the scattered cubes of mosaic that once paved the floors. There are ruins of Roman villas and baths, of Byzantine churches, of temples and statues and walls. Two centuries ago Pococke saw "great remains" of the walls both of the older city and of the city of Constantius; he inspected the ruined city site with less knowledge of it than excavation has given us, but with the same pleasure. The scene is of immense and mysterious beauty—the great, renowned, powerful city gone to earth, destroyed, quarried, shaken down, Arab-smashed, become a wilderness drifted over with sand dunes and grown with a tangle of scrub, golden fennel and wattle running down to the shore. Salamis is still possibly the most beautiful city in Cyprus, its ruins the most impressive. It is better than Paphos, Aphrodite's haunt at the island's western shoulder, where the village of Kouklia holds the excavated ruins of her oldest temple, already a ruin in the fourth century. Phoenician Astarte, Arcadian Aphrodite, Roman Venus: her courts and chambers, built *à la fénicienne*, are marked by a few pieces of low thick wall, a few huge cyclopean blocks of stone, some inscribed stones and pediments, (many are built into the Byzantine village church) lying on the desolate shoulder of a hill. Most of the stones are Roman; Old Paphos was cherished as a shrine through the imperial centuries, built and rebuilt by enthusiastic emperors. Here the worshippers of the goddess made pilgrimage from New Paphos by the sea, to enjoy the divine orgies. "Profligate processions crowded the road between the two towns", after purifying and disporting themselves in the seaside pleasure resort in preparation for the religious rites. Pleasing memories haunt Paphos; Christian apostles, arriving at New Paphos, converted its governor in his palace, and in the foamy waves below Old Paphos the goddess made her lovely shell-borne landing that would have so shocked St Paul. New

Paphos, once the magnificent, richly-templed port where the pilgrims landed, the luxurious city of merchants and princes and priests, is Mycenaean in origin, but destroyed and rebuilt, so that most of its few visible ruins are Roman or medieval. From it the road runs round the coast eastward to Episkopi Bay set with ruined or transformed Byzantine churches, tombs, and, dominating the scene on its high rock peak, the royal Argive city of Curium, a jumble of Greek, Roman and Byzantine ruins, beneath which the bold and successful General Cesnola found (or so he said) the gold and silver treasure now in the New York Museum; a story found by most archaeologists too odd. Standing in the Acropolis among the tumbled stones of lost streets, walls, palaces and temples, looking over the heave of hills, carob grown, olive-grey, strewn with the ruins of Islam, Byzantium, Rome and Greece, and with squalid Turkish and Cypriote villages (fragments of the great temple of Apollo lie in a wood near by) and over the sweeping curve of Episkopi Bay, one is caught into the eternally receptive mood of the perpetually violated, perpetually vanquished island, where ruined civilizations lie tumbled and crumbled on hill and shore, cultures *engloutis*, their broken symbols held in the amber of Cypriote sunshine. There they lie, the one-time cities, forums, theatres, temples, castles, churches, monasteries, palaces, decorating coast and mountain and plain, or foundered and sunk and no more seen. On the north-west coast, looking across to Turkey, is the great royal palace of Vouni, built for the kings of Cyprus in the fifth century B.C., majestically elaborate, luxurious and profuse in plan, destroyed in 400 B.C.; near it the remains of a temple of Athene crown another hill. From east to west the huge medieval fortresses and castles and monasteries stand in tremendous ruin; between them, hidden all about the mountains, crouch the broken shells of Byzantine churches, with their wall paintings and mosaics. No island comparable in size carries so many ruined religious buildings. Of the ruins, only the great castles and monasteries are in the first class of their type: the enchantment of ruinous Cyprus is cumulative rather than individual.

31

The individual ruined Roman splendours stand for our admiration all about the known world, environed by modern buildings, as at Merida, as in countless cities of Roman Spain, Roman Gaul, all over Italy. Or they startle the eye in country landscapes; great walls extend (even in spoilt Britain), broken bridges span rivers or gorges, the arches of aqueducts march in grandeur, almost everywhere huge theatres and amphitheatres lie, Roman and Greek, their tiers of stone or marble seats circling open to the sky. To many these theatres are what they know of Rome and Greece; the better preserved have been for years used for their ancient purposes, and one may see Greek drama on the Syracuse stage, *Romeo e Giulietta* in the huge Verona theatre, Seneca's agonists ranting in their mortal throes before the entranced sympathy of his fellow-countrymen in Merida; everywhere the ancient stones echoing to music, song and resounding line.

Thus, pleasure-seeking in the theatres, repairing the broken bridges, even, perhaps, running water along the aqueducts, thus we link the stupendous past with our smothering, runagate, unlovely present, appeasing our eternally nostalgic appetite with its desperate reaches beyond the horizon to where stretch the limitless, only partly charted, dimly seen and largely obliviated civilities and deserts of time.

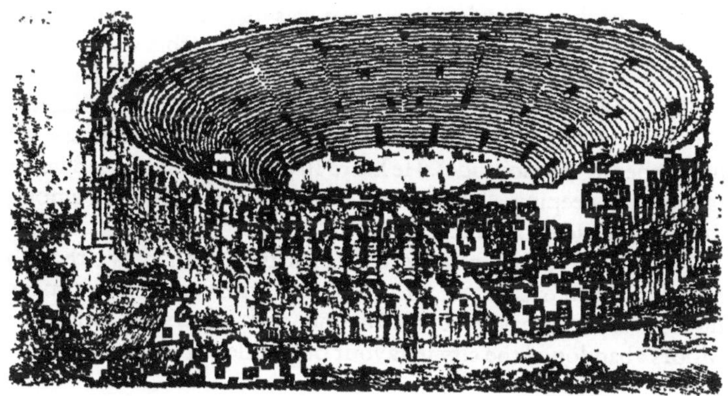

III

GHOSTLY STREETS

I

OF all ruins, possibly the most moving are those of long-deserted cities, fallen century by century into deeper decay, their forsaken streets grown over by forest and shrubs, their decadent buildings, quarried and plundered down the years, gaping ruinous, the haunt of lizards and of owls Such dead cities stir us with their desolate beauty, in contrast with their past greatness and wealth. As the ruins of Roman Italica, near Seville, stirred the Spanish poet and archaeologist Rodrigo Caro, when he visited them at the end of the sixteenth century and addressed an ode to his friend Fabio. These fields of loneliness which you now see, he wrote, were once famous Italica; here was the victorious colony of Scipio; demolished on the earth lies the fearful glory of the wonderful wall, and the only relic of its invincible people. . . . This plain was a plaza; there stood a temple; of the whole scarcely any traces remain; the towers which soared into the air have given way under their great weight. This broken amphitheatre is covered with the yellow jaramago. . . . Oh fable of time, showing how great was its greatness and is now its ruin. Here came Trojan and Hadrian; the marble and gold of palaces, the laurel and jasmine of gardens, are now brambles and lagoons; the house built for Caesar is now dwelt in by lizards. The poet went on to reflect on Troy, Rome, gods, goddesses, all now ashes in vast solitudes. He heard in the warm night a sad voice that cried, weeping, "Italica fell!" and groans whispered among the noble shades of ruin.

There was probably more of Italica then than now; though more has been excavated, what has been uncovered cannot make up for the centuries of destruction and quarrying since the Moors abandoned the city in favour of Seville in the sixth century.

Medieval Seville, indeed, was largely built out of Italica, which, from being a great and prosperous military Roman city, fell into decay; in the Middle Ages it stood a ruin, neglected and overgrown. Even when Borrow visited it first, he had to force his way into the vaults of the great amphitheatre through wild fennel and brushwood among hissing adders. He spent several hours there, imagining how "the gladiator shouted and the lion and the leopard yelled", and the human and bestial combatants darted into the arena by their several doors. Very soon after this, systematic excavations must have been begun, for when Colonel Napier, who travelled and drew so busily about Europe, went there in 1838, the foundations were exposed, mosaic floors brought to light, and statues, pedestals and columns lying about —"and no doubt, should the enterprise be prosecuted with the spirit which has characterized its commencement, many interesting relics of antiquity may be discovered." So they have; many too have disappeared, and no mosaic floors are to be seen to-day. Excavations have proceeded fitfully, and Italica is still a picturesque, not a tidy, ruin. It has had the usual ill treatment; in 1774 a large part of the amphitheatre walls was blown up and the stones used for road-making. It was in such a mess when Napier saw it that the chance companion he had met in Seville (apparently George Borrow), seated on a fragment of the broken wall, was moved to quote Byron, "with great emphasis and effect."

"Cypress and ivy, weed and wallflower, grown,
Matted and massed together, hillocks heap'd
On what were chambers, arch crushed, column strown
In fragments, choked up vaults, and frescoes steep'd
In subterraneum damps, where the owl peep'd,
Deeming it midnight:—Temples, baths, or halls—
Pronounce who can; for all that Learning reap'd
From her research hath been, that these are walls."

After this the two visitors descended among the wild beasts' dens and conversed with the gypsies who lived there, with whom Borrow had a great social success.

To-day the outline of streets can just be traced, the forum, and the remains of some houses. Outside the town stands the huge shattered amphitheatre; on the slopes of the valley around it are fragments of mosaic, of columns, the ghost of old Italica haunting the land where it stood.

There are, of course, far older ghost cities in Spain than Italica. There is, for instance, Ampurias, that little Greek trading settlement of the sixth century, founded by Phocaeans from Marseilles hard by an Iberian village in the Catalan Gulf of Rosas, close above the sea: on the Greek settlement grew up a fifth-century Attic town, then a Hellenistic, then a splendid and ornate Roman one; magnificent with villas, mosaics, temples, baths, forum, stoa and fine plumbing. There was a gymnasium, an amphitheatre, tremendous walls (which divided the native population from the Greek and Roman): it was a trading port, where merchants from all the seas bartered and sold in the market-place above the singing sea. Then came the Visigoths and took possession; Ampurias became a bishopric. By the ninth century it was no more known; sacked, probably, by Norman or Saracen pirates, it disappears from history, silted over by sand and forgotten, to wait a thousand years for rediscovery, beside the ruinous medieval hamlet of San Martì, itself built over Palaeopolis, the earliest Ampurias of them all, which lies for ever hidden under that crumbling peasant village.

Ampurias is very lovely in its tranquil abandonment. Its intersecting streets and open spaces run between the vanished houses and tombs; columns of porticos and temples, sunken floors of villas, lie among dark cypresses and fig-trees that smell sweetly in the sun, red oleanders sprawl over the wall above the sea which breathes and murmurs through the silent city like a song.

2

Ampurias was founded two thousand five hundred years ago, and has been a dead city for a thousand years. Italica, created two thousand two hundred years ago, lived actively for under a thousand years. Portuguese Goa, the old Goa, founded in 1440 by the Hindus, to replace the ancient city of the same name, became the capital of Portuguese India when Albuquerque took it in 1510, flourished richly for one century, slipped downhill, fitfully and languidly, through the next, was abandoned, little by little, in the third, and to-day is the most desolate of ghosts, a forest-grown deserted city, full of churches, convents and ruinous streets of houses. It has captured the imagination of all travellers, first as the rich and beautiful Portuguese colonial capital, where churches and convents and elegant houses crowded the streets and squares, and the commerce of the Oriental empire filled the harbour with shipping and the market-places with trade. Albuquerque, having conquered and massacred the Mahometan population, filled Goa with Hindus and Portuguese, and set to work to build and fortify a noble and Christian commercial city; Goa grew in beauty, luxury and religion like a flower, rivalling Lisbon, people said, in magnificence and grace. St Francis Xavier, who lies buried there, described it thirty years after its conquest—"Goa is a beautiful town, peopled with Christians; it has a magnificent cathedral and many other churches, and a Franciscan convent." There were more convents soon, and more churches, and more fine buildings; into Goa flowed all the riches of the east, gold, ivory and ebony from Mozambique, carpets from the Persian Gulf, silver, pearls, indigo, sugar, silk, pepper, spices, opium and wax; there seemed no limit set to its opulent career. The princes of the east came to visit the brilliant court of the Viceroy and went away dazzled; the saying arose, "who has seen Goa need not see Lisbon"; the luxurious city was even compared to Rome. The triumphal entries of victorious viceroys were pagan in their splendour; from the balconied seigneurial houses, typical of the late Renaissance in Spain and Portugal, with added Oriental decoration, flowers were flung down before the horses and chariots of leaders and of distinguished guests.

From its zenith, Goa's wealth and high fortune had begun by the end of the sixteenth century to decline. It had formidable and harassing trade rivals in the Dutch; cholera and hostile Deccan neighbours occurred; the population, interbred with the natives, weakened physically and mentally in stamina; luxury and a tropical climate softened their energy; their military fortifications and defences were outgrown by the city's spread. The accounts of visitors through the seventeenth century trace its gradual decadence; they speak at first of markets continually busy, of slaves and Arab horses sold, of the Portuguese who all claim to be fidalgos, shun work, go through the streets on horses or in palanquins, followed by servants on foot, of the excessive number of churches, convents, priests and religious orders, of rich food, dances and masques, of women in covered palanquins; later they write of the rich become poor, of many houses ruinous, of unhealthiness, of the removal of the viceroy to a palace in the faubourgs. In 1759 the seat of government was moved to Panjum; the houses and public buildings of Goa were abandoned and allowed to slip into decay; the population had fallen to a few hundred. Old Goa was presently deserted and used as a quarry for the new town. It lingered on in decay, a dwindling, dying city, full of churches and convents ringing their bells across empty streets. As early as 1710 a Jesuit wrote that it was so ruined and deserted that its ancient grandeur could only be guessed from the magnificence of the convents and churches, which were still preserved with great veneration and splendour. A century later, people spoke of the shapes of streets and squares just distinguishable among ruins covered with coconut trees; the houses were a few wretched buildings in a vast solitude. In 1835 the religious Orders were dispersed, and their convents abandoned or destroyed; the last spark of life in the city was extinct; Goa was, wrote Fonseca in 1878, a wilderness infested with snakes, in which it was hard to trace the overgrown buildings. Sir William Russell, who went there with the Prince of Wales in their tour of 1877, wrote of it with melancholy interest. "The river washes the remains of a great city; an arsenal in ruins; palaces in ruins; quay walls in ruins; churches in ruins; all in ruins. We saw the site of the Inquisition, the Bishop's palace, a grand Cathedral, great churches, chapels, convents, religious houses, on knolls surrounded by jungle. . . . We saw the crumbling masonry which once marked the lines of streets and enclosures of palaces, dockyards with weeds and desolate cranes." The quays lay deserted. "Instead of the bustle which once prevailed there, a complete silence now reigns, broken only by the wind whistling through the branches of the palm trees which grow luxuriantly on the spot."

So, but with more detail, have all travellers to Goa written of it for the past hundred and fifty years. Its buildings have been described, its forest-grown streets traced out and reconstructed, so that we can explore the ghost of the city, knowing where we are, identifying the green streets, the embosked churches, convents and palaces, noting how the sea road runs up from the deserted quays through the graceful curiously-shaped Viceroy's Arch, erected in 1599, still bearing the arms and statue of Vasco de Gama and surrounded by coconut palms, into the jungled phantom city of Velha Goa. Near the arch stood the immense Viceroy's Palace, described by so many early visitors as of grandiose magnificence; all that remains of it is one great portal, which was cleared from the smothering forest early this century. Beyond it we enter the strange tree-shadowed city of churches and convents and roofless houses with window-panes of sliced oyster-shell. There is the great Inquisition Palace, once the largest building in Goa, with its cells and winding corridors: it was, wrote Jean Baptiste Tavernier in 1676, one of the most beautiful buildings in all the Indies; in 1827 the abbé Cottineau spoke of its "*façade de toute beauté*", but said that the palace had been falling into ruin since, at the demand of England during the peninsular war, the Inquisition had been abolished in the Portuguese dominions; it is now a pile of jumbled stones; there is less of it left than of the great hospital, beautiful still in its vine-grown, palm-thronged dilapidation. But the glory of Goa was and is in its churches and convents; a group of these stands in the largest square, whose outlines can be traced in the dense greenery. There is S. Caetan, modelled on St Peter's; bats hang from its chancel roof. S. Augustine's towered façade is of great beauty and dignity, the body of the church is destroyed; the gaping windows and doors are wreathed with vine and ivy. All these broken masks, these gaping façades, where trees thrust through windows and shrubs creep round doors and the hot sky burns beyond, give an extraordinary effect of a city enspelled, magicked, sunk in a green ocean. Around the crowd of churches and convents lie coconut groves that were city squares, wind green alleys that were streets, criss-crossing among the jungle, running, faintly traceable, beside roofless houses. The sweet scent of frangipani drifts on the warm air. A few Goanese priests come in by day to say masses in one of the mouldering churches; they do not spend the night in the ghostly, malarial city, but return to New Goa at sunset.

Old Goa induces in those who wander in it a strange form of

enchanted and dream-like trance. *Dilettevole molta e poco sana*: so said an Italian traveller of the seventeenth century. Its historian, the enthusiastic and erudite Sr da Silva Correia, maintains that its solitudes are heavy with the ideas and feelings of those who dwelt there once, and that these move us more greatly than the ruins themselves. "*Il est toutefois vrai*," he wisely adds, "*que chaque voyageur éprouve des sentiments personnels en face des ruines. . . . Mais le seul mot, ruine, est capable d'éveiller des idées étranges et mystiques dans la pensée surexcitée des touristes érudits.*"[1] Exploring the green streets where once merchants thronged with the rich wares of the Indies, where luxurious and lazy *fidalgos* rode abroad in ornate palanquins, where their slaves were bought and sold in the market squares, where heretics walked in dire procession to that other square with its piled faggots, where, among the tangle of coconut palm, liana and vine, the ancient bells still ring out for mass, where, at every step, lies the broken, crumbling baroque beauty of old colonial Portugal, the erudite and over-excited tourist is indeed moved to the most delicious melancholy. He may feel, with Sr Correia, that old Goa should be taken in hand by archaeologists, its decay arrested before it entirely crumbles away, that buildings should be restored and roads defined before all traces are forest-drowned, that it should become a celebrated goal for travellers. Or he may feel that this would be, as nearly always, to rub the bloom from a fruit in exquisite decay, and that Velha Goa thus taken in hand would lose the peculiar rotten-ripe flavour that now enspells its phantom streets. A day will come, fears its patriotic Portuguese champion, when, if it is left abandoned and uncared-for, its ruins will be swallowed up in the earth, entirely lost in the vegetable ocean which is choking them. He is, of course, right: such a day will come, and Old Goa, the glory of colonial Portugal, will be only a memory and a forest of mounds. On the other hand, it may become a museum piece, tidy, labelled and bare, the encroaching jungle thrown back, the grass plucked from the streets and squares, the trees cut down from the church windows, the slumbering bats sent flying. Whichever of these destinies awaits it, it may be said that it is having to-day its finest hour. Would that it might be for ever thus preserved, caught and held in the amber moment.

[1] G. da Silva Correia, *La Vieille Goa* (1937).

3

Another of Albuquerque's conquests, another city which, but for how disconcertingly brief a period, enjoyed the lovely Portuguese luxury, the gorgeous Portuguese rewards of eastern commerce, as well as those, still richer, of Persia trading from her gulf—another such rich lost city, but now more lost, more sunk into the engulfing earth, was Ormuz, the ancient Hormuz, once standing on the mainland of the Persian Gulf, transferred medievally, because of Tartar raids, to the island five miles off shore where now its remains lie. The remains of the ancient mainland Hormuz, too, have been traced in the last century; extensive ruins, said Colonel Pelly, the British Resident at Bushire, who identified them, several miles up a creek, largely obliterated by cultivation; he collected from them a few ancient bricks. The sea has receded from that one-time great commercial port, the emporium of Arabia, Egypt and the Indies, whose long wharf is still faintly to be seen. Ormuz, a well-known gulf trading city from the second century A.D., had later its own dynasty of small kings, its palaces and mosques and harbour. About 1300 the new island city was built; well fortified and full of costly merchandise, but hot, and the island was waterless. Ibn Batuta described it, a fine city, a great mart, on an island made of rock salt, rich with great pearls from its fisheries, spoken of through the next centuries as the world's emporium, as if it were a modern Tyre. The greedy eyes of Portugal fell on it; Albuquerque with his Portuguese squadron swooped on it, and the Persian king yielded, becoming a tributary to Albuquerque's master. The Portuguese commander built a strong fortified castle, bastioned and ramparted, on the island; it still stands there, ruined but spectacular.

"There is standing near the water side a very fair castle, in the which the captain of the king of Portugal is always resident with a good band of Portugals, and before this castle is a very fair prospect. . . . In this city there is very great trade for all sorts of spices, drugs, silk. . . . This land has a Moor king of the race of the Persians, who is created and made king by the captain of the castle, in the name of the king of Portugal."[1]

But in 1622, after over a century of subjection, the puppet

[1] Hakluyt, *The Voyage and Travel of Cesare Frederici* (1563).

Persian ruler revolted, called in the East India Company to help him (trade rivals of Portugal, and resenting the Inquisition's burning of English merchants and seamen at Ormuz, they were also heavily bribed by "the Duke of Shiraz"), and, after a ten weeks' siege, the Portugals surrendered castle, city and island to Persia. Plundered and spoiled, from then on, Hormuz dwindled and decayed; the Persians transferred their main trade to the new royal port at Gombroon on the mainland, and Hormuz died. It was to its past glories that Milton looked back when he wrote of

"the wealth of Ormus or of Ind,
Or where the gorgeous East, with richest hand
Showers on her kings barbaric pearl and gold."

Not many years after the Persian reconquest Sir Thomas Herbert wrote a melancholy obituary.

"At the end of the isle appear yet the ruins of that late glorious city, built by the Portugals" (Herbert corrected this in a later edition), "but under command of a titular king, a Moor. It was once as big as Exeter, the buildings fair and spacious, with some monasteries and a large bazaar or market. Of most note and excellence is the castle, well-seated, entrenched, and fortified. In a word, this poor place, now not worth the owning, was but ten years ago the only stately city in the Orient, if we may believe this universal proverb—*Si terrarum Orbis anulus esset, illius Ormusium gemma decusque foret*. . . . The poor city is now disrobed of all her bravery; the Persians each month convey her ribs of wood and stone to aggrandize Gombroon, not three leagues distant, out of whose ruins she begins to triumph."[1]

A wretched hot salt island; but the Portuguese city had had many churches and friaries, stately houses, a fine bazaar, and as gallant a castle as any other in the Orient. But a ruin Ormuz became and remains. Even the bastioned castle, so much admired for so long, is now falling into decay, ravaged by the sea, its deep moat silted up. Of the city, nothing stands but a minaret; of other buildings, all the stately houses, palaces, churches and monasteries mentioned by sixteenth and seventeenth-century writers, only foundations remain. There is a small sea-faring and pearl-fishing population living in huts on the eastern shore;

[1] Sir Thomas Herbert, *Some Years Travels into divers parts of Asia and Afrique* (1638).

otherwise Ormuz has sunk into fantastic desolation, a ghost city haunting the strange island of red ochre ridges and low purple hills, above which tower a few high sharp peaks of gleaming white salt, as in a Doré picture. The Portugals who lived and traded and built and fortified and grew rich there cannot have enjoyed it, though in its strange tawny desolation and burning heat Castilians might feel at home.

4

The Portuguese and the Spanish strewed their now abandoned cities all about the world; they lie on coasts, in dense green jungles, in wildernesses, in river swamps. Round some, such as the ruined Antigua in Guatemala, twenty-five miles from the present capital, a new town has grown up, and the ruins have to be traced and trodden among modern streets and hotels. The pleasure of Antigua, therefore, is not what it was even fifty years back. It was then a ghostly town. Wrecked by earthquake in 1773, it was rebuilt more or less, abandoned for the new capital, Guatemala, wrecked again in 1874, and left deserted in its ruin. It had itself replaced the Conquistadores' town of 1527, which was destroyed by the volcano of Agua in 1541. Antigua, founded forthwith on its site, became the glory of colonial Spain, leading for two hundred and thirty years a brilliant and resplendent life, architecturally exquisite in its Spanish colonial magnificence, with over a hundred churches and convents, two learned universities (Bernal Diaz lived and died there), the seigneurial houses of hidalgos, the great arcaded palace of the Captains-General whose word and sword ruled Central America, enforcing the discipline and the religion of the Conquistadores on an alien and enslaved people from Mexico to Costa Rica. Except Lima in Peru, there was no Conquest town to stand with Antigua for might, beauty and wealth, and ecclesiastical and military power. Thomas Gage, the ex-Jesuit, described it in the seventeenth century: beautiful and wealthy, with magnificent houses and churches and many palaces, the finest cathedral in Central America, scores of monasteries, a great plaza set round with colleges, hospitals, jails, it had sixty thousand inhabitants. "*Antigua Guatemala de guerreros y de clérigos, de conquistadores españoles y de*

Capitanes Generales. . . ." It is the ghost of this that one sees, as one enters Antigua from the mountains and walks the flagged streets between the ruined walls of over seventy churches and convents, between the carved façades, the coloured tiles, the coats of arms, the twisted pillars of gate-posts, of deserted eighteenth-century palaces and houses, gaily coloured, often roofless, with grass and flowers and trees sprouting from the stones. The predominant colour is a soft yellow. There are magnificent palace gateways, the great broken arcades of convents, within which markets are held and women do their washing, cloister gardens with fountains in cracked stone basins, roofless churches where birds nest on the altars and shrubs sprout from flagged chancel floors, the great double-tiered arcades of the Captain-Generals' palace, round which the town park now grows; the old plaza with its cracked arcades, the ruined viceroys' palace overgrown with vines, the arched and sculptured portal to what was the largest cathedral of Central America, the plazas lined with eighteenth-century palaces and broken gates, the carved pillars of the Mercéd church, richly decorated with fruit and leaves, the double row of great ruined arches of the convent of Santa Clara, the ruinous façade of the church of Belén with the mountains towering behind, the busy, shouting market within the walls of the Church of Recolección, the sweet, heavy, tropical smell of fruit, the earthy smells of manure and cattle and goats. But Antigua has become self-conscious. Anglo-Saxons, English and American, cast on it the picturesque-seeking eyes of their race, and started to buy, roof, and inhabit the ruined houses. It began with an Englishwoman and her husband, who turned their house into an antique Spanish-Indian model. Their example caught on, and to-day Antigua is full of such houses; there is a smart hotel in the park, and consciously picturesque streets. From the antique arcades, radio incongruously blares. And over the town brood the high mauve peaks of the twin volcanos Agua and Fuego, which have destroyed Antigua before and will perhaps destroy it again, so that even the ruins will perish. This brooding, waiting menace gives to ruined Antigua a sinister doomed fascination; the new, growing town which one resents will pass too, and in the end, perhaps soon, will lie wrecked together with the churches and palaces of old Antigua, and with that ancient Ciudad Vieja of the conquest which perished four hundred years ago. Meanwhile, the gaping colonnades, fallen domes, broken arches and derelict plazas of Antigua give to American tourists that nostalgic pleasure which their race finds in the ancient airs from Europe that drift darkly and strangely to their nostrils from half-remembered lands, and the Maya Indians, finding the city of their conquerors decadent about them, pad about its ruined ways and make it their home, as its hutted site was their home five hundred years ago.

5

All about Central and South America the green dusk embosks the lost cities of Americans, not the Americans our late colonists, our present benefactors and defenders, but the Americans before them, who built in the deep heart of great forests, built carved stone cities, palaces, temples, tombs, abandoned them and moved on to build fresh cities somewhere else, leaving cities, temples, palaces, tombs, to sink into the jungle, to become part of that encroaching green, often to be no more found or seen, sometimes to be discovered by travellers of other races many centuries later. The lost cities in the mountains of Peru were not the settlements of these wandering tribes, but the mountain fastnesses of the Inca chiefs, who built themselves eyries in the high sierras above the Cuzco valley and the basin of Titicaca, impregnable against their enemies and against the encroaching grasp of the invading Spaniards. So high and so steep their cities stood, so hidden in the forested, precipitous folds and canyons of the rocky sierras, that it has been possible to climb and walk the mountains about them for weeks and months and never come on them, until suddenly round the turn of a cliff a startling mass of stone towers on a plateau above a vertical jut of precipice. Such a lost city an American archaeologist, Mr Hiram Bingham, set out to seek some forty years ago; such a city he at last found, among the high peaks of Machu Picchu. He had read of it in Peruvian chronicles: the palace city built by the Inca Manco, fleeing from Pizarro's army, which had taken Cuzco, the Inca capital; this new royal city and shrine was hidden away in the inaccessibility of the great forested precipices.

"The royal city of Vilcapampa was completely lost. It was a sacred shrine hidden on the top of great precipices in a stupendous canyon, where the secret of its existence was safely buried for three centuries under the shadow of Machu Picchu mountain."

Many expeditions had sought it in vain; its existence had been rumoured since 1875; it seemed untraceable and inaccessible. But Mr Bingham and his expedition traced it, setting out up the steep Urabumba valley, climbing past Inca ruins, passing a sugar plantation whose manager could not direct them, but who had heard it said that somewhere in the great forests there was an Inca city.

Then at last they came to the ruins of an Inca temple, standing by a dark, intimidating pool; this they took to be Vitcos. They pushed on through the great wild forest, climbing precipitous ravines and canyons, and always above them towered the snow-capped peaks. They came, after much mortal effort, to a small farm, where two Indians lived alone. From this place great green precipices fell away to the foaming rapids of the Urubumba below. Before them was a great granite cliff, two thousand feet high; thousands of feet above that rose the snowy mountains. Round a promontory was a great flight of beautifully made stone-faced terraces, which the Indians had lately cleared of forest. Following along one terrace into the uncleared forest beyond, they suddenly saw them, the Inca ruined houses, covered with the trees and moss of centuries; and, in the shadow of bamboo thickets and tangled vines, there rose walls of white granite ashlars beautifully fitted. Scrambling through the dense thickets, they came to a cave lined with cut stone—it seemed a royal mausoleum. Above it was a semi-circular building which reminded them of the temple of the sun in Cuzco; but it seemed to the delighted Mr Bingham even better than this Inca marvel, and as fine as any stonework in the world. "It fairly took my breath away. What could this place be?" Near a clearing where the Indians had planted a small vegetable garden, stood two of the finest and most interesting structures in ancient America, built in Cyclopean blocks of beautiful white granite. They were roofless temples, twelve feet high.

Mr Bingham gazed with amaze on the beautifully constructed granite city, with its hundreds of terraces and stairs. Could this, he asked, be the principal city of Manco and his sons, that Vilcapampa where was the "University of Idolatry" which the Spanish friars had tried in vain to reach? He photographed it, and they made a map.

Later, expeditions to Vilcapampa were organized; the site was cleared, roads made. The members of the expeditions were tough men; they climbed precipices, fell down them, tore the muscles of their arms, and never flagged in the desperate work. Now Vilcapampa is one of the great sights which draws South American tourists, who approach it by the new road. Four hundred kinds of bird have been found in the place, twenty snakes, ten lizards, and a variety of fishes. While naturalists pursued these creatures, Mr Bingham mused over his city's past.

"Surely this remarkable lost city which had made such a strong appeal to us on account of its striking beauty and the indescribable grandeur of its surroundings appears to have had a most interesting history."[1]

Mr Bingham was one of those explorers whose high romantic feeling seems to have lacked somewhat its adequate expression.

Not so other seekers after the ghostly lost cities buried in the green dusk of trackless jungle. The Maya forest cities and temples have not lacked their inspired reporters and artists, and to peruse the nineteenth century volumes of ruin-seeking in Central America is like reading a series of illustrated epic poems. Excitement ran high, as well it might. For, hidden in these wild green wildernesses, lay glorious Indian cities and temples and palaces built of massive sculptured stones, once densely peopled, once the shrines of religious devotion and pilgrimage, then abandoned, who knows when, to ruin and decay, while the forest drifted over them and trees grew from windows and roofs and vines bound them about, and jackals laired in their temples, and the bright birds of the jungle whistled and hooted in their mossy halls. Either the inhabitants moved on, in the ancient Indian manner, driven by their gods or their fears, to make new settlements elsewhere, or, in many cases, they fled from their cities to escape the cruel invading Spaniards who pressed in from the coast with slaughter and slavery and the white man's power of

[1]Hiram Bingham, *A Lost City of the Incas* (1911).

making life intolerable to the indigenous races whose homes he seized. "Apparently abandoned soon after the conquest"—again and again this is the presumption about the deserted cities discovered, after three or four centuries of abandonment, by explorers. When they were built is usually a matter of dispute among archaeologists; some say early, some say late; the dating of the inscriptions has still a long way to go. Explorers have come on these forest ruins after tremendous battling with the intimidating jungle, perhaps inspired by the accounts of other explorers, perhaps almost by chance, perhaps by the identification of sites with the descriptions given by post-conquest Spaniards who had seen the cities in their full glory, or in their early ruin, as Copan in Honduras was seen and described by a Spanish officer in a letter to King Philip in 1576. The fashion of exploring to Copan was started by John Lloyd Stephens of New Jersey, who, in 1839, having seen various references to it, set off with the artist Frederick Catherwood to struggle through the most painful tropical jungles and swamps in search of the fabulous ruins. Having fought through the green, stifling, thorn-set, poisonous and mosquito-infested hell, they at last came on the extraordinary stones—richly carved steles and pyramids, as fine in workmanship, thought Stephens, as anything in Egypt, idols, great solid walls thickly overgrown with green, temples, altars and shrines, terraces and flights of stairs, strange monuments scattered over a wide tract of forest, half buried in throttling trees; a city long lost, built when, abandoned when? Except that it was Mayan, Stephens did not know. None of the local Indians took any interest in it; one of them informed him that that part of the jungle was his land (though neither he nor anyone else had seen the ruins), and showed signs of being obstructive; Stephens bought the ruins from him for fifty dollars, celebrated his purchase with a gala party for the village, and proceeded to explore it. Later they went on into Guatemala, Chiapas and Yucatan, finding Mayan buildings scattered all about the jungles. In 1842 Stephens published his sensational account of his discoveries, illustrated by Catherwood's drawings, and Mayan ruins broke dramatically into the world's imagination. Stephens was not the first white man to visit and describe them; indeed it seems that there is seldom a first discovery of anything. Henri

Mouhot's finding of Angkor was preceded by another Frenchman's; Stephens' Mayan journey had been anticipated by de Waldeck's a few years earlier, and by other travellers and writers during the past three centuries; Columbus was anticipated by Norsemen; the Spanish Conquistadores by less sensational and showy colonists; the excavators of all buried cities by wandering tourists and their random spades; we too easily use the word "discovery" when a little earth, a little vegetation, a drift of sand, has temporarily obscured buildings from view and someone takes a spade and uncovers them.

But, if there are few (and untraceable) pioneers, there are followers; after Copan and the other Central American cities and temples entered the news, explorers were drawn to the scene, excited by this extraordinary and beautiful unknown architecture. A. P. Maudslay was one of the most able and determined of these; he did not have the great pleasure, as Stephens had, of acquiring ruins by purchase, but he enjoyed himself at intervals for years, settling down by Copan with his wife and Indian workmen, pitching a tent in the shade of a large tree, and digging. Nothing could have been more pleasurable than the surroundings; fruit and brilliant birds in the trees, richly carved buildings beneath the matted forest growths, the great plaza,

> "studded with strangely carved monuments and surrounded by lofty mounds and great stone stairways, moss-grown and hoary with age, broken by the twisted roots of giant trees. . . . The huge mass of squared and faced building stones, the profusion of sculptured ornament, boldly carved human figures, strangely grotesque imps, half human and half animal. . . ."[1]

—much of all this had been explored fifty years before by Stephens, but there remained dense scrub and thicket to be cleared. Maudslay dug into the great mounds and uncovered temples within them. Mrs Maudslay meanwhile kept house in the tent, doctored the villagers, watched the birds, for which she had a passion, acted as admiring spectator of the work in the plaza, and dreamt romantically of ancient Copan and its ways. They went on to Quiriga, where the monuments were so thickly covered with vegetation that they looked like dead tree trunks;

[1] A. P. and A. C. Maudslay, *A Glimpse at Guatemala* (1899).

moss had to be scrubbed from the carvings, and sculptured monoliths disinterred from the roots of trees. A splendid altar was uncovered; rich doorways revealed; all about stood great mounds and terraces, with flights of stone steps. There were huge stone animals, with great trees growing from their backs; one, a turtle, carved all over with figures, weighed nearly twenty tons. Maudslay felled trees, cleared away earth, took photographs and mouldings in plaster and paper, some of the party got fever, and the work was broken off. Mrs Maudslay, more and more obsessed with animals, bought a baby squirrel; her great disappointment at Quiriga was that she did not see a monkey. At Ixcun Maudslay discovered ruins of which no one knew; they were hidden under thick vegetation, and the site was impenetrable with wood and liana vine. He got twenty mozos working on them with machetes, and presently foundations of temples and houses, chambers, and sculptured monoliths appeared; an unimportant town of a good period. In some places there were no ruins visible, only conical mounds into which they dug, and, like magicians, resurrected a town. They proceeded over the Great Pine Ridge and down the Belize River into British Honduras, floated downstream on a raft, shot alligators, found an alligator's nest with thirty eggs, ate the eggs and shot the mother, reached Belize, and were soon off for the famous Chichen Itza, where, in 1842, Stevens and Catherwood had found a hacienda built among the ruins; forty years later Maudslay found the ancient city and the ruined hacienda covered in dense jungle. He engaged his workers and clearance began; he took up his residence in the Casa de Monjas, a fine Maya Nunnery raised on a solid block of masonry and approached by a magnificent stairway; there was a broad terrace round the house, from which one looked over the vast rippling sea of the untouched forest. To the north the ruins stretched, and the sunk, rock-walled lake which supplied the water, and the magnificent Castillo on its high, stairwayed pyramid. Westward of the Castillo were colonnades and temples still unexcavated, and the great walled Ball Court, with its beautiful little tiger-friezed temple in one corner. Through that spring and summer Maudslay lived in the Nunnery and worked at surveying, clearing, and making casts, in that "ghostly grandeur and magnificence which becomes almost oppressive to one who wanders day after day amongst the ruined buildings." Less fortunate in his lodging had been the French archaeologist, Désiré Charnay, who in 1881 made his headquarters in the open gallery of the Castillo, and found it exposed to a continual *courant d'air*. Nevertheless, M. Charnay fell under the spell of the dead city and its glorious surroundings, and spent much time evoking and musing on its extraordinary past. The Spanish had used the Castillo as a fortress; they had whitewashed over the reliefs of figures, which seemed to them irreligious; much time had to be spent in chipping away the whitewash. In its prime, Chichen Itza had been a great religious city of pilgrimages, temples, and sacrifices; devout processions had wound through the forest to worship at its shrines five and six centuries ago. It has become so again. Processions still wind through those dense forests, processions of explorers, archaeologists, and their assistants, making pilgrimage and doing reverence to those carved gods that have risen again out of the green wilderness for our amaze, seeking for temples still buried and lost. When they, the explorers, meet other explorers bound on the same quests, their ruin-pleasure may turn to bitterness, even to hate. Thus M. Charnay, camping on the river which divides Guatemala from Mexico and sighting a canoe rowed by white men:

"A horrible suspicion flashed across my mind that they were men belonging to another expedition, who had forestalled me"—

Presently the canoe's owner was encountered among the ruins that M. Charnay was hoping to make his own.

"We were met by Don Alvaredo, whose fair looks and elastic step showed him to be an Englishman. We shook hands; he knew my name, he told me his: Alfred Maudslay, Esq. from London; and as my looks betrayed the inward annoyance I felt 'It's all right,' he said, 'there is no reason why you should look so distressed. My having had the start of you was a mere chance. . . . Come, I have had a place got ready; and as for the ruins, I make them over to you. You can name the town, claim to have discovered it, in fact, do what you please."[1]

So, owing to Mr Maudslay's magnanimity, all turned out well that time; M. Charnay explored the ruined place, named it

[1]Désiré Charnay, *Ancient Cities of the New World* (1887)

Lorillard, and found it full of wonders—temples, palaces, richly sculptured lintels, idols. The neighbouring Lacandones had been used to performing their religious ceremonies in the ruins, until, a shy and diffident people, they had retired into the woods at the coming of white explorers. Mr Maudslay soon left Lorillard to the possessive Frenchman, and departed after other game. M. Charnay, a contentious man, had his own strongly held views on the dates, origins, times of abandonment, of all the Indian cities; most archaeologists are inclined to caution on these matters. But, whether Toltec, Aztec, Yucatan, Mayan, or whatever, whether dating from the seventh century or the fifteenth, whether deserted at the coming of the Spanish, or long before, or even after, whether dedicated to the cult of the Quetzalcoatl or any other gods, whether belonging to the "best period" or the less good, whether sunk and obliterated in dense jungle, or standing in clearings, whether on mountains or on plains or set round great lakes or on some almost unvisited sea coast (such as those found by turtle fishers buried in the drifting sands of a sickle-shaped bay on the Vera Cruz coast, and visited in 1927 by Dr Thomas Gann), whether magnificent like Chichen Itza, Palenque, Copan, Ixmal, Tula, Teotihuacan, Tikal, Menche, and others, or small palaces and temples of a poor period dug out of the jungle in fragments, all these American Indian medieval cities, so engulfed, so dendrofied, so mysterious, so massive and so ornate, so haunted by the ghosts of gods and men who still dwell there, so intent on hastening back into the reaching arms of the forest that stretch to hold them, have an attraction that is partly fear. They are beautiful in themselves; they must have been beautiful unruined, as described by the Spaniards who first saw them—"All the temples and palaces were perfectly built, whitewashed and polished outside, so that it gave pleasure to see them from a distance. All the streets and squares were beautifully paved . . ." and were still more beautiful when discovered again by travellers, with the forest growing on palace roofs and drifting into temple windows, with the rich carvings green with lichen and moss, with the ruins of Spanish houses tumbling about the monuments of the conquered races. Now that so many are cleared of forest and excavated from earth and dug out of mounds, they are still beautiful and delightful, and still haunted. To the temples, Indians still come to pray to their ancient gods. There must be hundreds of such cities still undiscovered, still unearthed, biding their time in the depths of the primeval, perhaps now quite impenetrable, forests; cities that may never, short of some earth-shaking catastrophe of natural or human destruction, be seen again by man. Meanwhile, the descendants, the disinherited heirs, of those who built these cities, build no more. Reduced and plundered, driven from their proud towns, palaces and temples by ferocious and possessive white men, they have abandoned dwellings of stone and for centuries have taken to the woods, living in wooden cabins, sometimes putting up these in the shadow of their ancestral ruins, sometimes in forest clearings, cultivating small patches of soil. They have become barbarous; persecution, slavery and fear stunned them into apathetic lack of initiative. How could these races have built those cities, we ask. In the same way, looking at the ignorant and destructive Arabs of the deserts, we ask, was it the ancestors of this race who once dazzled and led the world of thought in science, art, letters and geography? Where, for that matter, are the heirs of the fifth-century Hellenes, or of the Romans whose empire was the known world? Such questions are idle; races go up and go down; their ruined civilizations strew the earth. Even the Bantu negroes of Rhodesia, now living in huts and kraals, were, from five to eight centuries ago, building in stone and putting up fortified villages such as that known as the Great Zimbabwe, of which the granite ruins stand, in three groups, about seventeen miles from Fort Victoria. There is a large irregular elliptical enclosure, surrounded by massive, ill-constructed walls of unhewn granite, with chevron ornament and a cone at one end. It may have been a sacred enclosure; it was more likely a large fortified kraal. Trees grow within it. Above it is built . citadel, on a hill, the most impressive part of the ruins, with massive ramparts and parapets, and two supposed temples. There are signs of a large one-time habitation; the hillside is tunnelled with passages and caves; there are remains of balconies and walls. It is the best of many Zimbabwes in Mashonaland, and looks very impressive and mysterious, with its air of belonging to another age and another race. Its construction is not skilled; it has been now recognized as Bantu. Why the Bantus left it, why, if they could build houses of stone with chevron decor, did they prefer to live in huts, what was the religion practiced by their ancestors who lived in the fortified kraal, are unanswered questions. With regard to all these Mashonaland stone buildings, one must say, as Dr Johnson said about women preaching and dogs walking on their hind legs, that they were not done well, but that it was a marvel that they should be done at all.

6

Of the deserted cities of Asia, no one could feel any such thing. The people of India, Pakistan, Cambodia, Burma, Ceylon, China, carry their past cultures like heirlooms, with serene dignity. All those worlds of rich, sinister, decayed beauty encircle them like nimbuses as they go about their employs, eyes turned a little obliquely, as if they communed with a past just round the corner. Much of it is a bloody past enough; its ruins decorate the deserts and lakes and mountains of Rajputana, that battle-ground of ancient Hindu civilization with the waves of Moslem invaders. There wrecked Chitor, the ancient capital of the kings of Mewar in their glory, stands high on its hill, holding within its fortified broken wall the abandoned ruins of palaces, temples, streets and towers. The invaders sacked it from the fourteenth century on; Akbar took it in 1570, sacking and massacring and destroying, leaving it in ruin unrepaired, looking on the ruins with high victorious pleasure, taking away all its royal symbols, removing its gates for his capital at Akbarabad; henceforth the Mewar capital was Udaipur. Chitor lay desolate, a jumble of magnificent wreckage. Its tremendous tree-riven walls tower like a great ship above the new little town at its foot. A steep road winds up to the walls and town gates; entering in, one is in a stupendous murdered city. All about the rocky hill climb the empty palaces and temples. How fine and prosperous Chitor once looked is described in the ninth-century Khoman Rasa—

"Its towers of defence are planted on the rock, nor can their inmates even in sleep know alarm. . . . It is in the grasp of no foe. . . ."

But the foe Akbar grasped it and Jehangir installed there a traitor son of Chitor who had gone over to the Mogul foe, "to reign among the ruins." He did so for seven years, protected by a Mogul guard, while the wrecked city of his ancestors shamed his treachery, until at last he threw up his post and handed it over to a Rajput patriot.

If the Chitor ruins hurt this quisling, their beauty pleased the English embassy which Elizabeth sent out to Jehangir, and whose chaplain wrote of them,

> "Chitor, an ancient great kingdom, the chief city so called, which standeth upon a mighty hill flat on the top, walled about at the least ten English miles. There appear to this day above a hundred ruined churches and divers fair palaces, which are lodged in like manner among their ruins, beside many exquisite pillars of carved stone; and the ruins likewise of one hundred thousand stone houses. . . . There is but one ascent to it, cut out of a firm rock, to which a man must pass through four (sometime very magnificent) gates. Its chief inhabitants at this day are Zum and Ohim, birds and wild beasts; but the stately ruins thereof give a shadow of its beauty while it flourished in its pride."

Similar aesthetic pleasure was experienced by Colonel James Tod, learned annalist of the Rajput states, when he visited Chitor in 1822. His heart beat high as he approached the ancient capital with its reminiscences of glory, its shattered splendour. He climbed the jungled slopes which led steeply up to the rocky summit, passing through broken gates to the plateau strewn with tumbled fragments of palaces once lovely. He went over the ruined city, measuring and describing each building; until at last, "it is time to close this description, which I do by observing, that one cannot move a step without treading on some fragment of the olden times":

> "Columns strewn, and statues fallen and cleft,
> Heaped like a host in battle overthrown."

Above the city stand the richly carved Jain Towers of Victory and of Fame, intricately stairwayed, little ruined; one of them is crowned, insultingly, with a Moslem dome; from the top of either one may look down on the vanquished, silent city asleep within its broken walls, and the blue plain stretching beyond it. Kipling gives the best description of Chitor, in *The Naulahka* and in *Letters of Marque*; the Chitor of sixty years ago. His American, Tarvin, entered it through the torn wall before the dawn.

"The loom of the night lifted a little, and he could see the outline of some great building a few yards away. Beyond this were other shadows, faint as the visions in a dream—the shadows of yet more temples and lines of houses, the wind, blowing among them, brought back a rustle of tossing hedges. . . . Then, without warning or presage, the red dawn shot up behind him, and there leaped out of the night the city of the dead. Tall-built, sharp-domed palaces flushing to the colour of blood, revealed the horror of their emptiness, and glared at the day that pierced them through and through. The wind passed singing down the empty streets. . . . A screen of fretted marble lay on the dry grass, where it had fallen from some window above, and a gecko crawled over it to sun himself. . . .

"As he took his first step into the streets, a peacock stepped from the threshold of a lofty red house, and spread his tail in the splendour of the sun. Tarvin halted, and with perfect gravity took off his hat to the royal bird, where it blazed against the sculptures on the wall, the sole living thing in sight.

"The silence of the place and the insolent nakedness of the empty ways lay on him like a dead weight. . . . He rambled aimlessly from one wall to another, looking at the gigantic reservoirs, dry and neglected, the hollow guard-houses that studded the battlements, the time-riven arches that spanned the streets, and, above all, the carven tower with a shattered roof that sprang a hundred and fifty feet into the air, for a sign that the royal city was not dead, but would one day hum with men."[1]

Tarvin climbed this tower, then came down to the streets, disturbing the squirrels and monkeys that lived in the cool dark of the empty houses, and then, it will be remembered, descended a slippery rock path into a tangle of trees that concealed a tank of stagnant green, a sinisterly chuckling drip of water, a sacred crocodile, and a terrifying cave. It is more desirable than this to walk about the palaces, with sunlight streaming through walls and roof, and climb "crazy stone stairways, held together, it seemed, by the marauding trees", stepping delicately among the

[1]Rudyard Kipling, *The Naulahka* (1892).

fallen sculptures and the ghosts of the Rajput men and women who died in vain and could not save their city.

Another ancient Rajput capital, Amber, abandoned in 1728 for Jaipur, five miles away, is possibly the most beautiful of ruined cities. More famous people have written lyrically of it than of anything else in India; it is, indeed, itself a lyric. It has everything: picturesque position at the mouth of a pass, built on a rocky platform round three sides of a lake which (when not dry) holds its image in its stagnant and shining darkness, walls and streets climbing steeply up a hill crowned with forts, a fairy palace on a spur of hill, and round it the deserted city,

"nine-tenths of its stone dwellings tumbled and ruined as though by an earthquake, wild weeds growing over its mansions and temples, and the ancient streets choked with wild fig trees and broken blocks of carved marble and sandstone. In the midst of these silent ruins sleeps a large lake full of amphibious snakes and alligators."[1]

Completely picturesque, and ravishingly lovely with its shells of palace-like houses and summer pavilions, its wooded streets and terraces, and, above all, its ivory-coloured palace, rising in terraces above the lake. From the balconies, you look down on the desolate, domed, broken city, the tangled forest running down the streets, monkeys and squirrels and birds chattering in the gaping windows; all is a lovely desolation, guarded by the great fort that bastions the hill-top.

Amber was an old city in the tenth century. To explore it, says Murray, "will occupy a whole morning. A refreshment room has now been opened there": so coca-cola may doubtless be imbibed among the ruins.

Of Halebid, in Mysore, only one street is traceable in the ruined eleventh-century city, destroyed by the Mohammedan armies two centuries later. Sites can be identified, and there are two very beautiful temples; the larger and less ruined is entirely covered with carved scrolls and friezes, elephants, tigers, birds, horsemen, dancers, epics of conquest. The smaller temple, almost equally remarkable, was many years ago torn to pieces by a tree growing in its entrails.

[1] Sir Edwin Arnold, *India Revisited*.

7

The question arises, why have so many beautiful Indian cities, ruined by enemies or abandoned by caprice, been left in their ruins through the centuries? Money has not lacked: the rich Rajahs who ruled the provinces spent lavishly on their new cities, their palaces, their courts, their queens, their pleasures, their caparisoned elephants, their armies. The traditional jewels the size of eggs, gold and silver and ivory, were tossed about like annas and rupees; Amber, Chitor, Halebid, Vijayanagar, Gaur, Mandu, a score of other exquisite ruined towns full of costly palaces and noble temples could have been restored and inhabited, had their rulers or their conquerors been so minded. Instead, they were left to decay in beauty, the wild trees and long grass taking possession year by year, decade after decade, century after century, while only the jungle creatures and pigeons and peacocks walked the marble floors of the palaces and spread their tails on the roofs. Was it inertia, or distaste for the shattered and discarded, or for the towns of the conquered foe, or was it something subtler, the half-conscious, eternal love of ruin, *plus beau que la beauté*? Indians cannot tell you; perhaps they do not know. The Mogul invaders from the north ruined great Vijayanagar, the magnificent capital of a great kingdom, the glory of south India; its magnificence, wealth and state were the talk of Asia and Europe, its buildings, secular and profane, of fabulous splendour and grace, the kings and their thousands of elephants and wives. The city, stretching south from the river Tungabhadra, covered many square miles, a resplendent glitter of palatial glory, temple towers, baths, fountains, pavilions, gardens and lakes, and streets thronged with elephants and men. Sacked and battered by the Moslem armies in 1565, Vijayanagar fell; fleeing inhabitants escaped with much gold and jewellery, many elephants, and as much of their portable property as possible; most of the citizens and most of the wealth went down with their city before the ravening Mogul army. The great area of the populous capital became a desolate space, strewn with the ruins of buildings once splendid, now mostly past identification, fragments of Dravidian architecture in rich profusion. Hampi, the old original core of Vijayanagar on the river, is still lived in and is full of temples, and a place of pilgrimage. But no one, in the four centuries of its ruin, has tried to rebuild Vijayanagar, nor, it seems, will.

Nor did anyone rebuild the ancient cities of Delhi which lie in ruins to the south of the present city. Hindu and Moslem, forts, palaces, mosques and streets, their vestiges, covering about fifty square miles, bear broken witness to the predatory, destroying, building, massacring races which descended on Delhi at intervals between the eleventh and the ninteeenth centuries. Given to continual motion, they would desert their newly built cities, with their forts and palaces and temples, for reasons now lost to history, and move their capital a few miles north, or a few miles south, and start to build forts and palaces and mosques all over again. Perhaps it was the nomadic instinct, working on a royal scale; whatever it was, it surrounded the Mogul capital with abandoned ghosts from the Mogul and Hindu past. Here are many-gated city walls, there a ruined palace, such as the great palaces at Tughlakabad and Ferozabad, the last burnt by Tamurlane. Only the mausoleums of the Mogul emperors remain whole. Environed by these ghost cities, the modern seventeenth century Delhi, with its great fort and palace, often assaulted, besieged, sacked, massacred, has so far survived, though the fort was turned after the mutiny into a British barracks, and the palace plundered of much of its beautiful ornament, which no restoration (and Lord Curzon did his best) can make good.

Many abandoned cities, such as Gaur and Pandua in Bengal, Mandu and Chandravati in Central India, and probably hundreds more, have gone down into the jungle, some to be recovered in our present age of tenderness to ancient ruins, others to be lost for ever. Gaur, one of the most magnificent in India (which is to say in the world), was, both before and after its Mohammedan conquest in 1198, the capital of Bengal, a celebrated city of beautiful buildings and high learning, splendidly walled, ten miles long, with great stone embankments. Its huge brick citadel, set with four corner towers and gate, now encloses desolation. The Golden Mosque, with arcaded corridor and brick domes, has been long since wrecked by trees growing up between its bricks, tearing it to pieces; other smaller but delightful mosques are also partly shattered; their courts grown with trees. The tall minaret, from which the muezzin was called, stands erect, shrub-grown, broken-domed; the immense walls of the palace look, in the nineteenth-century pictures, like vertical forests, a-sprout with trees; they would make easy climbing. The Dakhill Gate, in the same pictures, also supports a grove of trees on its square lintel. Broken marbles and fragments lie everywhere. For centuries deserted Gaur was plundered of its stones; scarcely a village, city or building in all the Maldah district but was largely built of Gaur's ruins; Pandua, twenty miles away, which succeeded it for a time as capital is full of its sculptured stones with Hindu carvings, turned face inward and built incongruously into mosques. For their restless rulers alternated between the two capitals; always, as usual, they sought a city. Finally in 1575 Akbar's governor, struck with Gaur's charm, moved back into it with his court and people; too many people, for the density of the inhabitants caused plague to break out; flinging the corpses into the moat and lake only made things worse, and everyone who was left moved on, and that was the end of Gaur as a going concern. Pandua too, for the plague raged all around. Both cities, and all the district, were abandoned, and jungle enveloped them. Tigers roamed the grassy streets of Gaur, and lurked in the forests that edged the road to Pandua; approach was dangerous. All about lay a wild country, uneven with buried ruins. Across a forest path stands a lonely carved lintel, like a stile; ornamental bricks and marbles lie scattered in deep, dangerous grass among the snakes.

This is how dead Gaur stood for three centuries and more. The jungle is now largely cleared and ploughed; and tigers no more pad about the tree-grown streets or leap from silent mosques. The preservation of ancient cities, so foreign a western notion, is at work; Gaur's antiquities can now be better seen, but are less becomingly clothed.

This is so in very many of the deserted cities. Mandu, that great walled town stretching for eight miles along the high ridge of the Vindhya hills, full of glorious memorials of Pathan architecture, has suffered much the same processes—Hindu and early Moslem magnificence, noble buildings, fame in the east and the west, conquests, destruction, desertion, vegetation, twentieth-century care and protection. One may have one's own preference for any among its stages; one may look back nostalgically to the days before the Moguls took over and destroyed much of the city, rebuilding it with Hindu materials; or to the two glorious Moslem centuries of fame, learning, conquest and wealth, the age of the Jumma Musjid mosque, the tomb of the great ruler Hosgang Ghori, the Column of Victory, the Palace of the Ship, that stood in water, the immense seraglio, and the Amazon guards; or later, the days of the great Jehangir, when Sir Thomas Roe came to Mandu and admired its magnificence. Or one may wistfully hanker after the three centuries of picturesque and dendrofied ruin; or one may opt for twentieth-century clarity. The dendrofied ruin is not to be preferred by the clear and intelligent mind; yet it stirs the imagination as no tidied up and labelled antiquities can. When we read, about the ruined, the long lost, the almost vanished, city of Chandravati near Ahmedabad,

"Nature herself, so prolific in these regions, is rapidly covering the glories of the Pramaras with an impenetrable veil. The silence of desolation reigns among these magnificent shrines, and the once populous streets, which religion and commerce united to fill with wealthy votaries, are now occupied by the tiger and the bear, or the scarcely more civilized Bhil"—[1]

the heart leaps up to hail tiger and bear and Bhil and prolific nature; one is delighted to read further that

"the city itself is now overgrown with jungle; its fountains and wells choked up, its temples destroyed, and the remains daily dilapidated by the Girwur chief who sells the marble materials to any who have taste and money to buy them."[1]

That was in 1824. The gifted discoverer and explorer, Colonel Tod, never penetrated to the ancient city he had identified with much research as the city out of whose transported materials Ahmed had built Ahmedabad, on the banks of the Sahermaty. The Colonel himself, being unwell, never got to Chandravati (it is called Chandola now on the map) but he "sent a party" there to report on the ruins. The party "spoke in raptures" of what they had found, mentioning

"Columns strewn on the waste sand,
And statues fall'n and cleft,
Heap'd like a host in battle overthrown,"

[1]Lt.-Col. James Tod, *Travels in Western India* (1839).

and beautiful marble edifices, of which twenty had been seen by them. The drawing of one of these marble edifices, a Brahmin temple, by the talented Mrs. Colonel William Hunter Blair, that accompanies their description is, indeed, very lovely; its arcaded façade is elaborately and richly carved with figures; it is crowned with three small domes; from one of them a tree springs. The hilly ground before it is strewn with fallen capitals and friezes; two sculptured columns, part of a fallen colonnade, stand among the grass to one side, and in the foreground two peacocks pace with spread tails. Marble, said the reporting party, was strewn about in great profusion, and columns, statues, cornices, tossed in heaps all around. Becoming lyrical again, they added that

> "many a proud
> Contemporary pile the wilderness
> Environs with her solitary waste,
> Where mortal visits rarely—save the step
> Of Eastern Bandit over the deep wild
> Tracking the Beast of Deserts."

This was the magical ruined place that had lain for four centuries unseen by Europeans, run over by the jungle and its beasts, quarried and plundered of marble by builders and thieves, and that Colonel Tod had located with such diligence and now contemplated and described with such enthusiasm. So far as he was concerned, the pleasure of this ruin was in the imagination, in the research he gave to its history, and in the delight of identification. He enjoyed similar pleasures all about India, resurrecting lost cities out of old chronicles, from the contemporary reports of Arabian travellers, and from local tradition. He discovered Anulwarra, by the Gulf of Cambay, that ancient Jain capital founded in 740 and growing at once into magnificence, great in trade, schools, learning, temples, palace, and a "sea of men"; in the eleventh and twelfth centuries it dominated eighteen countries. Every Jain and Brahmin temple was destroyed by convert Moslem rulers. Anulwarra lost its independence in the fourteenth century to the ferocious scourge of Rajputana, Alla-u-din; its importance sank, its towers were levelled, and finally its name perished. When Colonel Tod visited it, he saw only a fragment of its high walls, the two strong towers of Kali, a gate with Hindu

Saracenic arch, the remains of a palace and of one out of eighty-four market squares; the temples had perished. Ruins of the town itself lay three miles outside the inner wall. "The sanguinary Alla", who had razed walls, temples and palaces, had even ploughed up the ground. Anulwarra lingered on, its power and prosperity dead. "With its discovery," Colonel Tod exulted, "years of anxiety terminated" (for his life was passed in these anxious quests, these happy finds); "here is the site of the first city of Vansraj".

8

All Colonel Tod's deserted cities were, however densely jungled, above the ground. There are, all over north India, more ancient cities still, buried layer below layer, town below town, to be dug up almost by chance by archaeologists in search of early civilizations. The great Indus valley is the centre of such a pre-Aryan civilization, perhaps flourishing there five thousand years ago, building cities and temples of brick, laying out streets, nearly four thousand years before the Aryans flooded in. Excavation during the last thirty years has exposed one of these cities—or rather a pile of such cities, each climbing on the wreckage of the city below it. Mohenjo-Daro, the Indians call it, "the city of the dead"; it lies in the dreary wastes of Sind, on the borders of Baluchistan. It is an impressive sight: great grass-grown streets thirty feet wide and three-quarters of a mile long, bordered with huge blocks of brick that were walls and houses, stupas and an enormous bath. This top city perhaps dates from 2,750 B.C.; older foundations lie below it. From these jewellery, pottery, gold and silver, and terra-cotta toys have been reclaimed, and coins from far lands. It seems that trade flourished; as for the town drainage and water system, it appears to have been as efficient as that of Knossos. It became a Buddhist city, as the stupas show. The Indians of the Indus make pilgrimages to the ruins seeking treasure; there are still acres of mounds not fully excavated, and no one knows what will be revealed on the deepest levels. Mohenjo-Daro is no object of beauty; its antiquarian interest is immense.

So also is that of Taxila in the Punjab, a much more modern city, traceable only to the fifth century B.C. When Alexander entered the Punjab, Taxila was already a great trading city, and a city of learning and civility; Alexander, with his attraction towards Indian culture, made friends with these civilized, rather snobbish, Aryan Buddhists; he ordered games and sacrifices in the city to mark their friendship, he enlisted some of their horsemen to serve with his Macedonian cavalry, the Companions, though the Macedonians did not go down very well with the more sophisticated Indians, who found them tough and barbarous. But Alexander they accepted as lord. Greek culture mingled with Indian, producing that Graeco-Buddhist art familiar in northern India. Taxila was soon merged in the Mauryan empire; it became a Buddhist centre and stronghold, full of stupas and monasteries; after many vicissitudes and a thousand years of importance, it was destroyed by Huns in the fifth century A.D. and became a deserted, ruined city. So it stayed till the 1860's, when the site was explored and excavated. The ruins cover a wide space; monasteries and stupas abound; they are described by the Chinese traveller Huain Tsaing, who visited them in the seventh century. There is much less of them now, but they can still be identified. Taxila was not only a great monastic centre, but was full of residential houses, which would appear to have been neither convenient nor good, and small shops; there are also the remains of walls, and of a large palace. All these vestigial remains have, necessarily (except the great stupa), a stumpy look, pretty dull to the eye after the great enjungled medieval cities; the interest lies in the imagination, for here is one of the cradles of Hellenistic-Indian-Buddhist culture; and here came Alexander to conquer, as he hoped, India.

Vanished, ruined, or decaying cities lie all over India, in their varied stages of decadence or all-but disappearance. Some, once great and prosperous, have dwindled into villages, with the shells of palaces tumbling on noble flights of steps above some lovely lake where pilgrims bathe or women come from mud hovels to wash their clothes; some, sunk in river mud, moulder on the banks of the great rivers, and crocodiles wallow in the deserted ports. Magnificent houses, stately mosques, falling yearly into deeper ruin, stand among palm-roofed huts; the mouldering palace halls shelter hovels, the jungle creeps about the streets, and the bazaars are carpeted in green.

9

The famous deserted Roman towns of Italy—Pompeii, Herculaneum, Ostia and the others—unlike those crumbling tropical ex-capitals which contend against the encroachments of forest and modern building, present to the world an aspect less brittle, more established and secure. They have achieved ruin; they have been disinterred, set in order, we know where we are with them. More will be excavated; they will not go to earth. (Unless, indeed, Vesuvius, now so quietly brooding without a puff, should once again boil over and detain its neighbouring towns and villages in lava and ashes for another spell.) To that fortunate disturbance of nearly nineteen centuries ago we owe an infinity of pleasure. As Goethe remarked, "Many a calamity has happened in the world, but never one that has caused so much entertainment to posterity as this one." Competition in this field is keen: but on the whole he may be right. From the first hour of chance rediscovery in 1743 (thirty-eight years after Herculaneum had, piece by piece, begun to yield up its treasures) Pompeii captured and held the world's imagination. The melodramatic manner of its disappearance, the surprise of its resurrection, the miniature completeness of its streets and houses, and shops, the gay and sometimes noble paintings on its walls, the pretty elegance of many of its courts, peristyles and gardens, the stony streets with their deep wheel-ruts and great stepping-stones, the grim casts left in the lava by its victims, the disinterring, year by year, of fresh houses, theatres, temples, forum, kept attention fastened on the fascinating discovery as on some slowly and spasmodically unrolling picture-reel. From the first, Pompeii was written of, talked of, painted, modelled in miniature; its different houses and streets became household names. Everyone liked to picture its destruction, the stream of lava and ashes, the sudden overwhelming of the gay city, its houses, inhabitants, soldiers, dogs. It was all so remarkable, it could scarcely be believed.

"*Je suis tout étonné de me promener de maisons en maisons, de temples en temples, de rues en rues, dans une ville bâtie, il y a deux mille ans, habitée par les Romains, exhumée par un roi de Naples, et parfaitement conservée,*"

wrote a French visitor some years after the discovery; and

pictured, with more pleasure than accuracy, that entertaining calamity, when Pompeii

"*fut ensevelie toute vivante, en un quart-d'heure, avec Herculanum, avec Sorrente, avec une foule de villages et de villes, avec milliers d'hommes, et Pline. Quel réveil pour les habitants! Ils maudirent sans doute mille fois le Vésuve et sa cendre et sa lave. Hommes imprudents, qui avaient bâti Pompéia au pied de Vésuve, sur sa lave et sur sa cendre!*"

This is the kind of reflection which Pompeii has from the first inspired. The unfortunate elder Pliny was, no doubt, engaged in such thoughts when he returned all too near the fatal scene and was himself caught in it. Contemporaries of the catastrophe deplored it with horrified fascination. Vesuvius spouting destruction down the happy slopes of Bacchus, burying everything in ash; they delighted to contemplate such ruin. The Jews regarded it as judgment for the destruction of Jerusalem. But on the buried cities themselves there was little detailed comment. Herculaneum had disappeared utterly, under a solid mass of lava mud; Pompeii was not so deep under its ashy blanket, but that here and there the taller buildings pushed up their heads. When the ashes cooled, those parts of the Forum which could be reached were searched for valuables; statues and pictures and marble were removed; and the Pompeiians returned to look for what they could rescue from their homes. Breaking through walls from one house to another, they salvaged what they could; like the rescue workers in more recently destroyed cities, they took anything of value that they saw. Then, abandoned to ruin, the visible tops of walls and towers were quarried away, and Pompeii lay level, sinking more profoundly beneath earth and ashes, on which greenery and vineyards and cultivation rose layer on layer, while above Herculaneum, more stonily sealed, a village grew up. None concerned themselves much with the covered cities; the emperors had other affairs on their hands. Severus Alexander, in the third century, ordered some digging to be done round the site of Pompeii, which turned up marble fragments; after that no one bothered; the sites were almost forgotten, Pompeii having its city status vaguely commemorated by the local name of Civitas. From the incurious, unarchaeological minds of our ancestors, the memory faded, vaguely haunting later ages like a forgotten ghost, while Vesuvius, every century or so, boiled again over Campania's smiling fields.

Still, a memory it was, never quite laid. Jacopo Sanazzaro, writing his *Arcadia* in 1502, is conducted by his Nymph below ground, on the Vesuvian slopes where, he recalls, in time past flames and ashes covered the land and even now testify to those who look on them that people and dwellings and noble cities are buried beneath. Without doubt, said the nymph, there is the celebrated city called in your lands Pompeii, and suddenly engulfed by earthquake. "And already, with these words, we were close to the town of which she spoke, of which the towers, houses, theatres and temples could be discerned almost intact."

The ghosts still haunted; the sites were still approximately known; the names still persisted on maps. At the end of the sixteenth century a conduit was ordered by the Spanish viceroy to be constructed through the hill of Civita; passing over the tops of the Pompeiian buildings, it turned up a few marbles and coins, enough to be noted by historians; but no excavations were undertaken; for one thing, Vesuvius had again broken out and was devastating the land. But scholars began to dispute about sites; layers of stone were dug up, and small relics to which people assigned different origins. Those who were sure they were Pompeiian had no chance of starting thorough investigations; nothing happened but more eruptions until 1710, when a peasant, digging a well on his land near Resina, came on valuable marble fragments and sold them to a marble-merchant; in this way they came to the notice of the Austrian Prince d'Elbeuf, who was building a summer villa; he and his architect were delighted with the *giallo antico* and fragments of coloured alabaster. Still not recognizing Herculaneum, the prince bought the peasant's field and had it dug into; beautiful statues emerged, alabaster pillars, a great inscribed slab of B.C. 38. The enthusiasm of Prince d'Elbeuf increased with every object found. He sent three statues, repaired, to Prince Eugene of Savoy in Vienna, whom he desired to please, and went on digging, decorating with his finds his house in Portici, until after a few years he left the neighbourhood and the excavations ceased. His house passed in 1734 to the new king of Naples and the Sicilies, young Charles of Bourbon; it was full of statues and other Herculaneum finds.

Incited by his young wife from Saxony, a great art enthusiast, Charles got excavations going again; they grew more and more rewarding. Statues, bronze horses, pillars, a theatre inscribed "Herculaneum" that put the identity of the discovered town beyond doubt, were wrested out of the solid lava stone that covered them; some were taken to the king's villa at Portici. Houses near the theatre were discovered, many of them with delightful frescoes; these were also removed to Portici, where a museum for the finds was made. Then a magnificent villa came to light, with a great pillared peristyle, loggias and verandahs, a bathing pool, a set of fine bronze statues and busts, shelves full of carbonized papyrus rolls inscribed with writing, showing that the villa had been a library. Difficulties in unrolling the papyrus without destroying the leaves were almost insurmountable, and were, in fact, not well surmounted; the frescoes and statues were more satisfactory. Fresh delightful objects turned up continually, they included the oddest things, such as eggs, nuts and almonds, carbonized vegetables, fossilized doves on nests, and vases still holding water. The whole civilized world was enchantedly agog. Herculanean successes excited hopes of finding whatever lay beneath the hill of Civita; excavations here began in April 1748, and at once struck into houses and streets, frescoes, skeletons and coins, and a villa which was labelled by its finders Cicero's. The frescoes were cut out, after the usual barbarous manner of the day, and taken to the king, who had them copied. The centre of interest shifted between Civita and Herculaneum. Society, led by the Neapolitan court, thronged to admire the museum with its rich collection of treasures. Entering the subterranean site under Portici was difficult for visitors, and needed special leave. The early accounts discourage. Lady Mary Wortley Montagu, in 1740, wrote from Naples, "There was a theatre entire, with all the scenes and ancient decorations; they have broke it to pieces by digging irregularly. I hope in a few days to get permission to go, and will then give you the exactest description I am capable of." Mr George Shevocke, a few months earlier, had better luck. He succeeded in penetrating into the ruins, which were very dangerous going; one crept through holes from house to house, in a darkness only lit by torches. "The ruin in general is not to be expressed." But he saw rooms with paintings of birds and beasts on walls of deep red; one large room, painted with temples, houses and gardens, divided by palm trees, was "represented in so very picturesque a manner that I think it one of the most pleasing ornaments I ever saw."

Horace Walpole visited Herculaneum in the same year; he wrote of it with enthusiasm to West, calling it, rather surprisingly, "something that I am sure you never read of, and perhaps never heard of."

"Have you ever heard of a subterraneous town? a whole Roman town, with all its edifices, remaining under ground? Don't fancy the inhabitants buried it there to save it from the Goths: they were buried with it themselves; which is a precaution we are not told that they ever took. You remember in Titus's time there were several cities destroyed by an eruption of Vesuvius attended with an earthquake. Well, this was one of them, not very considerable, and then called Herculaneum. Above it has since been built Portici, about three miles from Naples, where the King has a villa. This underground city is perhaps one of the noblest curiosities that ever has been discovered. . . . You may walk the compass of a mile; but by the misfortune of the modern town being overhead, they are obliged to proceed with great caution, lest they destroy both one and t'other. By this occasion the path is very narrow, just wide enough and high enough for one man to walk upright . . . except some columns, they have found all the edifices standing upright in their proper situation. There is one inside of a temple quite perfect. . . . It is built of brick plastered over and painted with architecture: almost all the insides of the houses are in the same manner; and, what is very particular, the general ground of all the painting is red. Besides this temple, they make out very plainly an amphitheatre: the stairs of white marble and the seats are very perfect. . . . They have found among other things some fine statues, some human bones, some rice, medals, and a few paintings extremely fine. . . . There is nothing of the kind known in the world; I mean a Roman city entire of that age, and that has not been corrupted with modern repairs. . . . 'Tis certainly an advantage to the learned world that this has been laid up so long. Most of the discoveries in Rome were made in a barbarous age, where they only ransacked the ruins in quest of treasure."

The age was still pretty barbarous, and the quest for treasure went briskly on. The excavations were carried out with the utmost

38 Maya archway, Casa del Gobernador, Uxmal, Yucatan.
Lithograph after F Catherwood, 1844

39 The Gymnasium at Troas. Engraving by Wm Pars, 1747

stupidity, clumsiness and greed; marbles and frescoes were torn from the walls, statues removed, houses and courtyards and gardens ruthlessly damaged. The directors of the early excavations, wrote a scornful German later, "knew no more of archaeology than a crab does about the moon." All the same, buildings little by little emerged, during the fitful spasms of endeavour; the beautiful city, plundered and injured as it was, took gradual shape.

Pompeii, too. Here, in 1764, the Temple of Isis was discovered. Paintings were copied, paintings were faked, experts were tricked. Everyone was eager to secure treasures; Sir William Hamilton, lately arrived in Naples, made secret finds and deals of his own. The skeletons lying about Pompeii were often decked in valuable jewellery, presumably caught up before attempted flight; silver and gold lay spilt round them. The greatest interest in the excavations was shown by the clever young queen of the backward Bourbon king Ferdinand of Naples, who relieved the tedium of her matrimonial life by spending much time in the fascinating ruins; often she took parties of guests, and special discoveries were organized for them; the queen would take away with her as much as would go in her carriage. Treasure-looting, both from Pompeii and Herculaneum, was a flourishing industry; the ruins were treated as Tom Tiddler's grounds for picking and stealing, when it could be done unobserved. People wrote to one another, "If you are visiting Pompeii or Herculaneum, bring me back some small statue or ornament." Lady Holland brought Horace Walpole, in 1767, a bust of Caligula from Herculaneum, "the finest little bust that ever my eyes beheld." Any traveller of enterprise did well out of both the delightful revenant cities, which it became increasingly the fashion to include in one's European tour. Goethe and Tischbein were there in 1787. Goethe found the Pompeiian houses too small—more like dolls' houses than real buildings; the streets were straight, the ground-floor storeys of the houses had no windows, but were lit only by doors opening on atrium or street. The painted rooms and bright frescoes he found delightful, but on the whole "the impression which this mummied city leaves on the mind" was not altogether pleasant. He should have seen it later; his romantic mind would have relished the eloquent and vivid reconstructions of houses, gardens and peristyles.

It is true that much of the town was crowded and rectilinear, the small plain windowless houses lining the streets monotonous and unornamental; to live in them must have been like living in one of a row of bathing huts. Yet the better houses must have been delightful, with their colonnaded courts, flowering gardens set with statues, mosaic floors, and charmingly illustrated walls. The Pompeiian and Herculanean frescoes, when they still decorated the houses to which they belonged (most are now in the Naples museum) must have been the loveliest sight imaginable, Hellenistic art at its prettiest. Mythology bloomed round the walls with gods, nymphs, satyrs, fauns and heroes; scenes from legend and history (such as Europa on her bull, Polyphemus sitting among his flocks while Galatea teased him from a dolphin's back, Theseus slaying the minotaur), alternated with pastoral scenes, shepherds piping to their sheep among broken columns and arches (for the painting of ruins was a common Pompeiian decoration; from shattered shafts of pillars trees sprout, bare of leaves; the wooden horse is pushed into Troy in a landscape of twisted trees and broken walls); while on other walls the personified Alexandria walked, a tiny parasol held over her head, or garlands of fruit and flowers looped from arch to arch, or still life lay piled on tables, lemons, lobsters, rabbits, dead birds. Or there were Watteau-like rural scenes, with railed bridges over water, figures strolling, a pretty house behind; and landscapes with little temples, gates, summer houses, country altars, buildings falling or fallen; or streets seen in perspective through painted windows. Cupids played their games together, or were sold by pedlars like birds in cages; fauns piped and capered; satyrs chased nymphs; when they caught them, love of the most practical type ensued. But such scenes as this were promptly removed to the more secluded rooms of palace museums, and eager antiquarians were frustrated in their attempts to view them.

The excavations, in spite of interruptions due to changing political régimes, were carried on with enthusiasm. Murat and his wife Caroline were delighted with Pompeii; clearing, uncovering and rebuilding were eagerly planned and executed. It became Caroline's hobby to look on at the excavations, and everything that she fancied taking from them was hers. Interesting discoveries were planned, and made in her presence. Jars, amulets, skeletons, jewels, painted dining-rooms with stone couches, everything pleased her. "I have had excavations made, and that, my dear Hortense, is my pastime," she wrote from Portici. She took parties of guests to enjoy the spectacle, and everything was prepared for their pleasure; the skeletons which were found decked in jewellery and surrounded by gold coins were covered up again until Caroline's next visit. The queen was delighted with the finds; she had a donkey attached to her coach, laden with spoils to take back. All this royal interest was also a pleasure to the excavators, for Caroline, a generous and lavish young woman, was apt to hand them out money on the spot for their efforts; no wonder that they continually discovered fresh skeletons dressed up in fresh jewels. Pompeii had been a rich town; or at least had had a top social layer of rich citizens, of jewelled women and moneyed men. In the skeletons of the rich there is great pathos; the pictures called up of these unfortunate beings fleeing in vain, laden with all they could take, and caught and smothered in ashes before they could get out, plunged their rich Neapolitan successors who looked on their remains into the most pleasing melancholy. Caroline Murat could hardly drag herself away. Reveries on the gay life led by the Pompeiians delighted many minds, even among those who had not yet visited the scene; they have produced much literature, from Bulwer Lytton's historical fantasy to the Chancellor's Medal poem of young Tom Macaulay in 1819. He liked to muse on these gay unfortunates, who

> "To death, unconscious, stray o'er a flowery way . . .
> And sport and wanton on the brink of fate",

and on the panic flight in which they trampled one another to death—

> "See, trampled to the earth th'expiring maid
> Clings round her lover's feet and shrieks for aid. . . ."

The excavations were followed by the British with the greatest interest, particularly after the expulsion of the French enabled them to visit Naples again and see the enchanting resurrected cities for themselves. The Murats were, of course, gone, but Pompeii was still a show place for the Bourbon king Ferdinand and his visitors, who drove through it in their coaches, having first had the great stepping-stones removed Foreign visitors arrived in great numbers. King Ludwig of Bavaria was so delighted with some of the houses that he had one built for him in Aschaffenburg, peristyle, atrium, frescoes and all. In England, small models of them sprang up in gardens and parks, to be used as summer-houses, and fountains were adorned with Drunken Fauns. No one, however, could attempt to reproduce successfully the magnificent mosaics; Alexander at the Battle of Issus, a huge floor-piece made with a million and a half of tiny coloured stones; crocodiles and ibises and creatures of the Nile; fish, sea-horses and tritons of the Mediterranean; all the charming fantasies of Hellenistic mosaic art.

Though the pleasure and renown of such discoveries was great, money lacked, and the work went only fitfully on; still more fitfully at Herculaneum, where it was a matter of cutting away solid lava rather than of clearing ashes.

Excavations, such as they were, were interrupted by Garibaldi and the unification of Italy and resumed after the expulsion of the Bourbons. After the brief episode of the directorship of Alexandre Dumas, who was for making Pompeii a hunting-ground for French archaeologists, it was put in the charge of the brilliant Fiorelli, and from that time the work was systematized. Scholars from all nations crowded in, writing articles and books, making plans for raising funds, or merely watching in breathless admiration while the buried marvels of both cities were resurrected. Herculaneum did not really come into its own until the twentieth century.

Under Mussolini its excavation was carried on continuously until the war; the hard tufa was drilled and cut away, revealing a city more beautiful and elegant than Pompeii; houses larger and less regular in plan, with peristyles, atria, gardens, columned porticoes, piscinas, floors of marble and giallo antico, mosaics and beautiful wall paintings, and marble and bronze statues. Herculaneum, it is evident, was a good resort, a charming provincial town, where cultured Roman gentlemen had their villas and lived in artistic luxury. In Pompeii there are fewer such spacious houses and gardens, few such good frescoes and sculptures. The new *scavi* have revealed buildings more decorative than almost any found earlier. To walk about Herculaneum is a feast of pleasure; we pass through spacious triclinia with mosaic floors and marble tables and porches painted with vines, peacocks, and deer; bedrooms with real beds; bathrooms with marine mosaics; everywhere colour, form, elegance. The courts and gardens open, colonnaded and tree-grown, from the porticoed entrances. In one house there is an inlaid nymphaeum, with a fountain in the middle; nothing could be more charming. Indeed, this delightful little city, with its riches of sculpture and painting, suggests a life of ease, culture, and appreciation of the arts which recalls its Greek origin. Like Pompeii, Herculaneum, when overwhelmed, had only lately been built up again after the earthquake of 63. When Cicero had his Pompeiian villa, Pompeii was a town more ancient and Greek; restored, it must have looked very bright, gay, new and Roman; perhaps even here and there a little vulgar. But beneath and beside the new houses was the core of the ancient city, Etruscan, Doric, Samnite, Hellenistic, republican, imperial; temples, forum, baths, amphitheatre, theatres, shops, houses, taverns, brothels, streets, showing the amenities of the Pompeiian way of life through some four centuries. It is this that has always been the charm of both these ruins and the reward of their study, this looking as through a telescope at a remote past incredibly brought close to us, a bright, unfaded miniature, clear and eerie like a dream, of the daily life of those classical ages familiar yet so far. It is this that pleases and excites when we see, say, the houses of the Vettii and of Loreius Tiburtinus and of Argo, with their rooms and colonnades decorated with graceful paintings, their courts and gardens, fountains and cascades and pools, the little shops and taverns with their marble counters and their wine jars, the paved streets with their deep wheel-ruts and great stepping-stones, the graffiti on the walls announcing coming spectacles in the theatre, the vulgar graffiti and facetious paintings and sculptures that a more modest age locked discreetly away from public view, to be shown to signori while their signore waited tantalized without; all "the little familiar tokens of human habitation and every-day pursuits; the chafing of the bucket-rope in the stone rim of the well . . . the marks of drinking-vessels on the stone counter of the wineshop; the amphorae in private cellars, stored away so many hundred years ago. . . "

So wrote Dickens, then turned to a macabre pleasure even more to his taste—the impressions of the bodies of victims in the hardened ashes, evidences of the desperate struggle against suffocation and death. His mind, too, was always on Vesuvius.

"Stand at the bottom of the great market place of Pompeii, and look up the silent streets, through the ruined temples of Jupiter and Isis, over the broken houses with their inmost sanctuaries open to the day, away to Mount Vesuvius . . . and lose all count of time and heed of other things in the strange and melancholy sensation of seeing the Destroyed and the Destroyer making this quiet picture in the sun. . . . The mountain is the genius of the scene . . . we look again with an absorbing interest to where its smoke is rising up into the sky. It is beyond us as we thread the ruined streets: above us as we stand upon the ruined walls; we follow it through every vista of broken columns, we wander through the empty courtyards of the houses; and through the garlandings and interlacings of every wanton vine . . . the doom and destiny of this beautiful country, biding its time."

In short, no one would have been more pleased than he, had Vesuvius spouted forth again and destroyed a fresh group of towns.

There is still much excavation to be done in both cities. In Pompeii it is proceeding slowly, after the interval of war; but the best of Pompeii, and the larger part, has been uncovered. In Herculaneum, which is harder going, the best, and almost certainly the most, is still underground, beneath the town of Resina. Till the Resina houses can be shifted, and till a great deal of money is available, the work is almost at a standstill. Infinitely precious treasures and discoveries no doubt lie down there, safely cased and covered in hard tufa, which preserved them from salvaging by their owners after the disaster, as so many Pompeiian valuables were salvaged. The concealing land stretches away, with its streets, its houses, its cultivated ground: what lies beneath it? What further riches of villas and gardens, basilicas, arches, temples, baths, spacious streets, colonnades set with sculptures, rooms blooming with legendary paintings in rich colours, undulating floors in mosaic, little taverns where wine jars stand in rows?

It is a pleasure to speculate: it would be pleasure more satisfying if the enterprising nations, now set to spend their all on destruction, were to combine in devoting a few millions to the rewarding task of uncovering more of these subterranean paradises. For, who knows, there may be many miniature Herculaneums, many village Pompeiis, lying sealed in their buried beauty beneath the Campanian lands where the destroyer, now mute and smokeless, slopes down to the sea.

10

Sadder than these abruptly slain cities now half resurrected are the ruins of ancient Ostia, for Ostia died slowly, of abandonment, pillage, malaria and decay, and Ostia had more greatness in its day. Strolling through its silent streets, among the houses of republican and imperial merchants, pillared courts, great warehouses and granaries and store houses for salt, baths (the Ostians must have bathed more than anyone since the Sybarites), forums, temples, large blocks of apartments, one mourns for Ostia, regrets the passing of its trade importance to its neighbour Portus, regrets its exposure to barbarian raids from the sea, its malaria, its desertion, its ruthless quarrying (out of it medieval cathedrals were built), its decay. This must have been a noble town, a rich mercantile town, with every amenity. They have now identified and named (rightly or wrongly) every building; they have, during the last fifty years, cleared the city from the vegetation that made it once so beautiful, turned it into a clean archaeologist's delight, whereas once it was an artist's and poet's dream, lying half choked with earth and wilderness in a malarial waste. The beauty of the old Ostia of the nineteenth century must have been staggering. There was the deserted, ghostly ancient city, half unearthed: "thistles flourish everywhere, and snakes and lizards abound, and glide in and out of the hot unsladed stones. . . . The ground is littered with pieces of coloured marble, and of ancient glass tinted with all the hues of a peacock's tail by its long interment. The banks are filled with fragments of pottery, and here and there of human bones. The whole scene is melancholy and strange beyond description." A quarter of a mile away was the fifteenth-century castle, dominating the tiny town that grew up in the middle ages, when Ostia was fortified and used as a defence against the Saracens and other raiders from the sea.

To-day Ostia is less picturesque. But it has extraordinary interest; and many of its details are very beautiful, in particular its frescoes, and some of the mosaic floors, decorated with marine scenes—sea horses, chariots driven by Neptune among mermen and sea creatures, battles and myths and dolphins. There are theatres set round with masks, shrines of gods, shops with marble tables where fish lay for sale, granaries, peristyles, courts and gardens, streets paved with great blocks, walls of solid brick. It all gives an impression of firm solidity and intelligence; Roman merchants lived there, and lived well. The ghosts that walk the Ostia streets, and pace those pillared atria, seem the ghosts of merchants, not of the luxurious holiday-makers and leisurely gentlemen who lived in and decorated many of the houses of Herculaneum and Pompeii. One hears the cries of sailors unloading their freights in the long since land-locked port, the washing of the sea, now slipped back a full half mile, against the city walls, the creaking of wheels in the deep ruts in the paved streets, as carts carry cargoes of salt and of Ostia melons down to the harbour, those melons which Pliny praised.

Or, if you prefer it, you may think of St Augustine talking to St Monica five days before her death in an Ostia inn. Or, if given to more intellectual pleasures, you may go about Ostia with a plan and guide-book, identifying each building, distinguishing those of the republican period from the imperial, making out the inscriptions and the dates of the paintings, examining the heating arrangements for the baths, discovering which are the *frigidaria*, the *tepidaria* and the *calidaria*, and which are the remains of the Christian oratory built among them, identifying the temples, the statues and the shrines, walking each street, entering each house and shop, and climbing each stair. Or you may visit the necropolis of Isola Sacra, and the reedy basin that was Trajan's harbour, and the ornate ghost of Portus beside it, and in the evening, if you are fortunate, attend a classical play in Augustus's theatre. A short way off, along the shore that was once strewn with the villas of Roman patricians (one of these was Pliny's capacious winter villa near Laurentum; in Ostia he did his major shopping) is Ostia Marina, the modern Lido di Roma, where Romans all

July and August bathe noisily in the sea and sun, while Ostia Scavi lies silent behind them, deserted alike by Ostians, Romans and the sea itself.

II

Forty-five miles from Rome, in the Pontine marshes, lies Ninfa, that strange little abandoned ramparted green city round a stream, at the foot of the steep height on which the citadels of Norma and Norba are poised. Ninfa, like Goa, and unlike Pompeii, Herculaneum and Ostia, is sprawled over with greenery: unlike Goa, the greenery, once a wild thicket, has been, during the past century, taken in hand and turned into a very beautiful wild garden by its ducal owners, the Gaetani family. It is exuberantly, fantastically lovely and strange. An early Middle Age town (it seems to enter history in the sixth century), it played a part in the feudal, papal and imperial wars of its time, passed from hand to hand, was made a fortress in the eleventh century, was sacked by Frederick Barbarossa, in the twelfth, presented to the Gaetani by a pope in the thirteenth, and steadily declined, owing to the malaria of its marshes, from the fifteenth on. Between 1670 and 75 there were reported to be a few inhabitants still living in it, no doubt very ill. In 1681 it was seen to be deserted and invaded by trees, ivy and shrubs; the inhabitants had all fled from its miasmas to more healthy airs, carrying their possessions in ox-carts. For some years its buildings were quarried for stone, then finally abandoned to invasion of the woodland growths; the ivy, the vine, the creeping plants, covered them up; the young trees sprouted from their walls. In spite of an attempt a century later to exorcise its fevers, Ninfa remained a malarial swamp. A garden was made of the ruinous town; a new palace built, a mill set going; it was no use. Ninfa lay crumbling and deserted between its crenellated medieval walls, its ruined churches, noblemen's castles and houses, streets and dwellings and monastery walls, disintegrating beneath their mantle of green, beside the clear cold stream and little lake where once had stood a temple of the nymphs. The stream runs, swift and strong and clear, through the jungled town; beside its banks rise square, green-wreathed towers, castle keeps, the vaulted walls and broken apses of Romanesque churches with peeling, overgrown frescos; among them wind green lanes that were streets (their names have been recovered) and round them stand the old battlemented walls, for the most part still upright beneath their ivy coats, with their moats of running water beside them. The main street ends in an open space that was once a market place, is now a meadow. In the walls are still some gates, over the stream still two ancient bridges. One of the little palaces has been restored and is now lived in by the Duke and Duchess of Sermoneta. All the garden town is a mass of tangled sweetness and crowding shrubs and flowers.

This strange and charming place has always given intense pleasure to visitors. Among those who have surrendered themselves to its sensuous attractions are Augustus Hare and, before him, the great Gregorovius, whose enthusiastic German mind and sensibilities were wholly captured; even, it could be said, overturned. He felt the most delicious *Ruinenempsfindung*, from the moment when, looking down over the Pontine marshes from the romantic heights of Norma, he caught a view of

"a great ring of ivy-mantled walls, within which lay curious mounds and hillocks, apparently made of flowers. Grey towers stood up out of them, ruins, all garlanded with green, and from the midst of this strange circle we could see a silver stream hurrying forth and traversing the Pontine marshes. . . . I asked, amazed, what that most puzzling great garland of flowers, that mysterious green ring, could be. 'Nympha, Nympha,' said our host. Nympha! then that is the Pompeii of the Middle Ages, buried in the marshes—that city of the dead, ghostly, silent. And this afternoon we would wander through it, at the hour when fair Selene rises behind the Cyclopean stones of Norba.

"After a good midday meal and a refreshing rest we sallied out, and hurried down the mountain. And this is Nympha, this unreal semblance of a town—its walls, its towers, its churches, its convents all half buried in the swamp and entombed beneath the thickest of ivy. Assuredly it has a more charming aspect than Pompeii with its staring houses, like half-decayed mummies dragged from amongst volcanic ashes and set up all around. But a fragrant sea of flowers waves above Nympha; every wall is veiled with green, over every ruined house or church the god of spring is waving his purple banner triumphantly. . . .

"Flowers crowd in through all the streets. They march in procession through the ruined churches, they climb up all the towers, they smile and nod to you out of every empty window-frame, they besiege all the doors . . . you fling yourself down into this ocean of flowers quite intoxicated by their fragrance, while, as in the most charming fairy-tale, the soul seems imprisoned and held by them. . . .

"Wondrous are the churches to behold . . . such fantastic ruins as I never before have seen. How can I describe them? . . . From their walls, from here and there a tribune smothered with greenery, peers forth some early Christian saint or martyr, his palm branch in his hand. . . .

"The lake might have come out of the world of shadows of the Iliad or the Aeneid. The dark tower and others cast their trembling images down upon the still waters of this pool. The reeds rustled sadly. . . .

"You should sit here when evening bathes, first in purple then in gold, these ivied halls and ruins. I will say no word about it, nor will I try to describe it when the moon rides forth across the sky and the fairies dance in circles. . . ."

An acute case of ruin-pleasure to the head. This romantic place found its spiritual home in the romantic soul of the learned, picturesque and ivy-loving historian of the Middle Ages. Some other visitors have found it just a little too lush. But, if you like crumbling medieval ruins overgrown by wild greenery now tamed into a beautiful garden, then Ninfa is precisely what you will like. In winter and by night it has been said to be both melancholy and alarming; mist swathes the phantom town, reptiles and rodents glide about, pursued by rapacious and hooting owls, and the atmosphere is eerily bewitched. The careful and orderly guardianship of the last years may, however, have modified this effect. It may, too, have reduced the apprehension felt formerly that weather and vegetation would in time totally disintegrate the ruins, dragging them down to moulder in the damp earth until they become one with it.

A final warning: the stream Nymphaeus, besides being rapid, is excessively cold, and should (as Baedeker would say) be entered with caution, and only in really hot weather.

12

There are other dead towns in the Campagna, other towns which have died of malaria, and more lately than Ninfa. There is Galera, twenty-one miles north of Rome, in the Orsini country, on the way to Bracciano. Galera, too, is medieval; there is no mention of it before the eleventh century; but some Roman remains exist, and it is built on the site of the Etruscan Galeria. It was not abandoned till the middle of the nineteenth century. A high citadel, on a lava rock above a woody ravine, its walls and towers and castle, struggling above the invading forest and shrubs, can be seen from the via Clodia; one turns off at a medieval farm-house, and crosses the valley by a deep, densely grown lane, ending in a meadow running down to the river Arrone, which circles the citadel. At the foot of the meadow rises a great rampart based on the rock and crested by ivy-draped trees, behind which show a church tower, a town gate, the great walls of a palace. You cross the stream by a bridge carpeted with greenery, and climb to the town up a paved road, ivied and brambled, which goes under two gates to a piazza bordered by roofless buildings. On the right is the high wall of the Orsini palace; enter it by the piazza gate and wander through huge empty ceilingless rooms. The streets are now almost impassable brambled paths; in the crumbling houses, many of them of the fourteenth century, trees grow. Galera is falling; there is less of it upright now, and more of it gone to earth and forest, than when Hare described and drew it eighty years ago. He found it "absolutely deserted except by bats and serpents . . . a bewitched solitude, with the ghosts of the past in full possession. All is fast decaying: the town walls, some of which date from the eleventh century, are sliding over into the thickets of brambles." More of them has now slid; Galera gives the melancholy pleasure of a lost city which can never be reclaimed. Malaria must, indeed, be counted as the ruin-tasters' friend, for it gives him the gradual and gentle ruin of abandonment and decay: the desolation of an undamaged city standing at first whole and empty and silent, then sliding piece by piece to earth. Cities dead in this manner, even when in life they have been of no great importance, take a peculiar hold on the imagination; even those deserted hamlets of loosely piled stone falling to pieces on the barren Highland mountains from which their inhabitants drifted long since in search of a better life, are moving. The imperial streets of Numantia, Italica, Ostia, Timgad, the green streets of Goa and Antigua, those exotic colonial capitals, move by their wrecked greatness; these small ghostly-streeted deserts, by their abandonment to solitude and decay. Many deserted citadels are of such grand poise and such turbulent history that they carry us by storm; of these are the ruins of ancient Saguntum that proudly crown the steep hill above the later town that climbs it; all Iberian pride and fierceness, all Punic savagery, all Roman conquest, cry silently from that steep crest. And of these, too, is Norba, the Roman citadel in the Volscian hills, half a mile from the medieval village of Norma that succeeded it and high above the Pontine marshes where the towers of Ninfa thrust up through their tangle of green. Norba, a Roman military colony of the fifth century B.C., was destroyed by Sulla's generals—or destroyed itself, like Numantia and Sagunto—during the Marian wars; it was, it seems, never rebuilt; it has stood deserted and ruinous for close on two thousand years, guarding the highest point of that rocky ridge with its tremendous Cyclopean walls seven thousand feet round. It scarcely can be said to have streets; its ghosts haunt only the walls, the faintly discerned gates, the razed citadel in the centre of the enceinte, the foundations of houses and of what must have been a temple, an ancient square cistern, a few subterranean grottos. From the wall that falls sheer down to the precipice on the southern side, the whole seaboard is seen spread below, from Antium to Monte Circeo, with the anti-Saracen martello towers guarding the coast along. But the noblest aspect of Norba is seen from below; the circle of its walls crests the mountain ridge in the stark grandeur of its Roman pride, and is enormously impressive.

13

In the category of Ghostly Streets one must put the Provençal mountain stronghold of Les Baux, whose ruins sprawl, a robber's nest, over a spur of the Alpilles, overlooking three valleys, its ruined dwellings, churches and castle cut out of the living rock, towers, walls and boulders intextricably mixed, the whole a fantastic Doré scene of infernal nightmare. Pleasure has been given to many by the legend that Dante made it a model for some of his Circles; unfortunately this tale seems insubstantially based. Still, it is enough in its own right, this shattered mountain citadel hewn out of pale soft limestone, sprawling over its high escarpment, with the crazed air of an extinct moon. Through its ruins runs a little street called the Grande Rue; the ruins are so many and so ruined that, before they were neatly labelled in this century, it was impossible to know which was what, except for the great feudal castle, a few churches, the Hotel de Ville, a palace or two. It is a jumble of medieval houses, with Romanesque or Renaissance façades, of towers scooped out of cylindrical rocks, arches and vaults, battlements, underground passages and chambers, fallen columns with rich carving, great shapeless fragments and massy boulders lying everywhere, the rock-based castle itself tottering and falling, a few tiled roofs and inhabited small houses, where the tiny population makes its living out of guiding tourists: "of the present inhabitants of Les Baux it were better not to speak" says the guide sold on the postcard stalls. This population is a recent growth. Dumas, in the 1850's, found Les Baux empty but for a few beggars; Prosper Mérimée said that "*une demi-douzaine de mendicants composent toute la population*", but the pleasures of ruined Les Baux were gradually discovered, both by tourists, and by those who made money out of tourists, and in 1906 the number of inhabitants was a hundred and eleven; one gathers that all of these competed fiercely for the profitable job of showing the tourists round, and that blood on occasion flowed mong "*ceux des Baux*". Possibly it still does; but in these days, as the ruins are labelled, guides are less required. The guides, if you employ them, will bore you by telling you about the Courts of Love, the least interesting phenomena of Les Baux's romantic history, though apparently regarded as the greatest pleasure for tourists. For the history of Les Baux *is* romantic; very early it seems to have been a refuge for those who fled from the Visigoths who had captured Arles; three centuries later, we hear of a Count of Les Baux, and through the Middle Ages these enterprising and turbulent counts and seigneurs and princes played their stormy feudal part, terrorizing neighbouring baronies and cities, waging war against Barcelona, acquiring fresh lands by treaty, by intrigue, by marriage, till they had half Provence at heel. They did not lose their heritage until the fifteenth century, when it passed to the royal family of Anjou. It played a war-like part in the wars of religion, and its fortress castle was demolished by Richelieu. After this its inhabitants drifted out of it; at the Revolution it was taken over by the nation, and crumbled year by year into wilder desolation, until the thriving industry of tourism has of late years turned the desolation to profit by making it a show place. Show-place though it be, it remains fantastically, excitingly grand; a crater of the moon set with thirteenth-, fourteenth- and fifteenth-century houses, Romanesque churches and chapels, fine renaissance dwellings, with their family arms. Over the ruins towers the extraordinary, huge castle, more than half in ruins and looking most insecure. Below the citadel is Beaumanoire, the renaissance pleasure garden of which remains one lovely round pavilion. Among the ruins nestles the "squalid little village" which feeds on them. But neither this nor the placarded labels have wholly taken from Les Baux the strange, frightening air of doom that broods among those grotesque shapes. "You feel," wrote Theodore Cook half a century ago, "as if a blood-stained band of medieval cut-throats were lurking behind every crag, or slowly retreating, as you mount, to lure you on to final, irremediable fate." As well you may, for the Seigneurs des Baux, who must still haunt their eyrie, were precisely this.

Pleasure in Les Baux has been, at least since the romantic revival of the eighteenth century, keen and growing. It had everything that the ruin-tasters could desire—antiquity, abandonment, decay, a magnificent and forbidding site. It was indeed

> "an awful pile. . . .
> Waste, desolate, where *Ruin* dreary dwells",

with in addition, the romance of troubadour Provence, courts of love, and all the rest of the medieval feudal trappings beloved of the public. It has inspired novels and poems, not all of which have seen print; no nineteenth-century *Rambles in Old Provence*, illustrated with little drawings, was complete without it; and from the walls of Victorian drawing-rooms discreet pale water colours looked down, entitled in flowing scripts, "A Robbers' Eyrie in Provence", and painted by great-aunts. To-day, though grown vulgar, it still makes its flamboyant dramatic effect.

14

There are ghostly streets of ruins which do not pass through cities. Outside the gates of Rome the ancient Roman highways run into the Campagna—Via Appia, Via Tiburtina, Via Latina, Aurelia, Prenestina, Tuscolana, Laurentina, all taking their way through what was until lately a beautiful wilderness, strewn with the ruins of ages. Leave Rome by the Porta San Sebastiano and tread the Via Appia Antica that runs out to Albano in the hills: it is not what it was when Dickens trod it, when it was "long since ruined and overgrown", and one walked for twelve miles to Albano

"over an unbroken succession of mounds and heaps and hills of ruin. Tombs and temples, overthrown and prostrate; small fragments of columns, friezes, pediments; great blocks of granite and marble; mouldering arches, grass-grown and decayed; ruin enough to build a spacious city, lay strewn about us. . . . Now we tracked a piece of the old road above the ground; now traced it underneath a grassy covering, as if that were its grave; but all the way was ruin. In the distance, ruined aqueducts went stalking on their giant course along the plain. . . . The unseen larks above us, who alone disturbed the awful silence, had their nests in ruin; and the fierce herdsmen, clad in sheepskins, who now and then scowled upon us from their sleeping nooks, were housed in ruin. . . . I almost felt as if the sun would never rise again, but look its last, that night, upon a ruined world."

The Campagna, alas, is very different now. The Appian Way is weeded and levelled; it became long since a carriage road, and is now a motoring road; much of the Via Appia Nuova flares with garish advertisements. Fierce herdsmen no longer scowl, but give amiable greetings; the fallen fragments of ruin have been tidied up. As well as the giant aqueduct, giant pylons stalk along the plain; and aerodromes adorn it; among the ancient towers, tombs and farm-houses (in 1874 Hare wrote that *all* buildings were

40 Ruins of the Pyramid of Xochicalco, Mexico Lithograph from C. Nebel, *Voyage Pittoresque, etc.*, 1836

41 Broken Maya idol, Copan, Guatemala. Lithograph after F. Catherwood, 1844

42 Ruins of Gaur on the Ganges. Aquatint by Thomas Daniell, 1795

43 Strada dell'Abbondanza, Pompeii. Water-colour by J. H. Ramberg (1763-1840)

medieval or classical) have sprung up modern villas, factories, new unsightly suburbs of ancient hill towns. The Campagna, then, is, to a large extent, spoilt; any one of middle age can remember the indescribable, so often described, beauty and desolation that it had before the old war; anyone who has seen it since the newer war must mourn it. But it is still a sea of shifting colours, set with tombs, towers, medieval farm-houses, shattered fragments of Rome, and the paved highways along which the legions marched out to conquer, marched back victorious, along which, for over two thousand years, ox-carts have creaked, bearing in wine to the city from the Alban and Sabine hills, and along which Roman gentry drove or rode up to their villas in Albano, Nemi and Tibur, fleeing from the Roman summer. The highways were cut through a country immeasurably older than Rome, and about them spreads a land of buried cities, a land of ghosts; Etruscans, Volscians, Sabines, all the ancient dwellers on that mountain-circled plain which the Latin conquerors took over. Still the grass and thistle and asphodel carpet swells in mounds and tussocks over sunk towns; still nameless towers and tombs line the roads and strew the reedy earth; Orsini towers, Colonna towers, all the strongholds of the fighting Roman lords of the middle ages; all the tombs of noble Romans, some of them later fortified and towered, and the columbaria honeycombing brick walls, and the catacombs under the earth where more tombs lie hid, and the thousands of fragments pushing up through grass and marsh and farm land. It is still a land of ghosts—"*une terre composée de la poussière des morts et des débris des empires,*" said Chateaubriand. "Dead generations lie under your feet wherever you tread. The place is haunted by ghosts that outnumber by myriads the living." It is this sense of the immense past, of walking through a "desert where we steer, stumbling o'er recollections", of the timeless surge of time, of the blue hills where Veii and Tusculum and Praeneste stood, and a myriad of ancient cities drowned long since in this swelling sea, of a world beneath our feet as fragile as our clay—it is this, as well as the sense of Rome, as well as the Campagna's desolate beauty, now so blurred, which haunts the traveller who treads its ruin-lined streets.

15

There are some streets so ghostly as to be only faintly discerned, shadows darkening and paling to the rippling of the wind, barely apprehensible hints of the hidden streets below waving corn or grass. Such are the streets of Roman Calleva, lying in Silchester under a Hampshire field, buried deeply beneath meadow land and cornfield, crossing one another from north to south and from east to west, glimpsed now and then during the past two hundred years, when enquiring archaeologists started excavating, but each time covered up again, the fields replaced over the city's face, for the land was wanted for cultivation. The sixteenth-century antiquaries, who have left accounts, did not penetrate below the field; they describe the wall—enclosing, says Leland, eighty acres, enclosing, besides fields, the manor house and the church; a wall with four gaps where gates stood, six or seven feet high, and large oaks grew on its top, incorporated, says Camden, with the stones. The inhabitants told him that they could trace by the corn's thinness where the streets of the old city had run. The country people constantly dug up Roman coins and tiles and inscriptions of which their ignorance robbed the world. There was a spasm of excavation in the 1740's; parts of a forum and of a basilica were uncovered; a paper was read to the Royal Society about it. Then no more uncovering until the nineteenth century, when it proceeded at intervals of a few years, becoming systematic and thorough from 1890 on; the field was stripped off each summer and replaced for the season's crops. Plans were made, showing the foundations of houses, baths, dye-works, three temples, a fourth-century Christian Basilica—the only Roman Christian church yet found in Britain—an amphitheatre without the walls, streets and remains of gates. In the centre of the town were the forum and basilica, with colonnades and wide ambulatories. The houses had had painted plaster walls, imitating marble; paintings of the Pompeian type have been pierced together; the mosaic was in bright colours, the windows were glazed; there was the usual hypocaust, so essential in Britain; on the whole the houses must have been commodious and fair-sized, with pillars and porticoes. Leland judged the south part of the city the most considerable; near the south gate was a tesselated pavement which suggested the floor of a palace; the palace, Leland believed, where King Arthur was crowned, and where emperors, princes and the great used to lodge when they visited this strong-walled city built in the woods out of regard for the British, who, "like the Gauls, delighted to have their buildings seated within woods." They were pleased also with the oaks which sprang from the thick walls, for oaks have a beneficent power.

What with the oaks and what with the walls, Silchester should have been safe, but was not. Camden believed it destroyed after 900, by the Danes. But there is no mention of it in the Anglo-Saxon Chronicle, though it had been a bishopric; it looks as if the destruction was by the Saxons, who burnt and threw down cities everywhere in their savage vandalism, sometimes building others in a manner "more agreeable to their rude and unpolished education." But walls they sometimes left. Silchester's must, thought Leland, have been once twenty feet high. After the city's destruction, its ruins must have gradually perished. The marks of fire on the mosaic mansion floors may show where herdsmen sheltered there, lighting their fires among the broken courts; as time went on the ruins were levelled and the stones carried away, and the site ploughed up for corn. Nothing now lies within those strong walls but the Elizabethan farm house and the medieval parish church and the hundred acres of pasture and crops, and below these the hidden fragments of Rome built on a Celtic site sixteen centuries ago.

Silchester evokes romantic pleasure both for its Roman city and for the beautiful lie of its concealing landscape. Not only poets and artists, antiquarians and romanticists, but such a hard-headed judge and lord advocate as Lord Jeffrey, writing to his friend Lord Cockburn in 1833, grew lyrical over it.

"It stands upon a high lonely part of the country, with only a rude low church and a single farmhouse in the neighbourhood, but commanding a most lovely and almost boundless view over woody plains and blue skyey ridges on all sides of it. It is about the most striking thing I ever saw, and the effect of that grand stretch of shaded wall, with all its antique roughness and overhanging wood, lighted by a low autumnal sun, and the sheep and cattle at its feet, makes a picture not soon to be forgotten."[1]

[1]Lord Cockburn, *Works* (1872).

The Reverend Joseph Jefferson saw it less picturesquely, but more morally—

> "O VINDON! (Silchester thy later name)
> Thou once could'st call a royal grandeur thine;
> An Arthur crown'd reflects thy wonted fame,
> When ancient BRITONS saw thy glories shine.
> Alas! thy fam'd magnificence is lost!
> Thy once fair streets now yield the farmer's grain!
> 'Tis but a moment bounds our latest breath;
> A span hath well describ'd the narrow space.
> O! . . . be it thine that read'st to think of death,
> Be it thy prayer to know the Saviour's grace."[1]

And so to the Last Trump, the Awful Day, and the Dread Tribunal of the Skies, topics to which Mr Jefferson's muse readily turned. And all the time, as the Lord Advocate admires the picturesque view and the clergyman mused on mortality, the streets of the Romans below rise up through the fields, rectilinear and straight, trodden by the legions and by the urban Romanized British and by King Arthur and his knights, and "towards harvest, when the corn is ripe, it is not difficult to discover the very traces of the streets of the city, by the different conditions of the corn, that which stands where the streets were, quite decaying."

So the ghostly streets have, in the end, their way.

[1] Joseph Jefferson, *The Ruins of a Temple* (1793).

IV

THE HAUNTING GODS

I

THE time-struck abbeys and ruinated churches of Europe, the broken, pillared temples, Doric, Ionic, Corinthian, that decorate the mountains and islands of Greece, Greater Greece, Asia Minor, the Byzantine domes that climb the mountain-sides like figs, the mouldering mosques and fallen minarets, the great abbeys of Cyprus, the huge halls of Thebes, the drowned sanctuary of Philae, the shining grey pillars of Persia, the Assyrian, Roman and Oriental temples that stand beautifully about Mesopotamian deserts, the richly-wrought, terraced, jungle-drowned palace-temples of Central and South America, of Burma and Ceylon, the Hindu and Mogul splendours of India, the eaved exquisites of China—all these are haunted by their gods, as the fallen palaces by their kings and courts, the streets of abandoned cities by the ghostly treading of feet, wrecked ports by the swish of keels in slipping waves, the clanking of anchors, the chaffering of merchants on the quays. It is not really possible to assess the various elements: the beauty, the ruination, the contrast of present desolation with former grandeur, the backcloth of some gorgeous or dim mysterious ancient past, the haunting of the gods.

In Greece, perhaps, less possible than elsewhere, since the Greeks built their temples in places of the wildest beauty, and since their divine and secular history are so inextricably entangled together. Who can say, looking on Paestum, Segesta, Selinunte, Agrigentum, Delphi, Bassae, Aegina, the temple of Zeus at Olympia, the mountain sanctuaries of Greek Asia Minor, what nerve is touched?

Coming by sea to Cape Colonna, sailing from Asia Minor into the Saronic Gulf, Dr Chandler perceived from afar "the ruin of the temple of Minerva Sunias" (for such the temple of Poseidon was still held to be) standing on its precipice, shining, white marble, Doric, dominating the deep blue gulf. The Cape was still a nest for pirates, as Herodotus had related, and as all since had found. The waves broke gently, with a hollow murmur, at the foot of the rock beneath the temple. They anchored within the cape, and climbed to the ruin, while the sailors bathed. Fifteen columns were standing. Spon, in 1667, had seen nineteen. They searched diligently for inscriptions, but the only inscriptions they found were modern, for it has, it seems, always been the habit to cut or write one's name on these columns or walls. Dr Dodwell remained four days, sleeping in a cavern in the side of the precipice, making drawings, entranced with the view, and scrambling down the precipice to examine the columns and metopes which had fallen down the cliff-side. Did Dodwell carve his name? Nine years later, Byron, of course, did so. He was enraptured by the spot.

"Place me" (sings Don Juan) "on Sunium's marbled steep—
Where nothing, save the waves and I
May hear our mutual murmurs sweep;
There, swan-like, let me sing and die."

Byron thought it the most interesting place in Attica except Athens and Marathon. "To the antiquary and artist sixteen columns are an inexhaustible source of observation and design; to the philosopher, the supposed scene of some of Plato's conversations will not be unwelcome, and the traveller will be struck with the beauty of the prospect." Byron himself was the traveller; Hobhouse, who accompanied him on his first visit there, was the antiquary, and wrote his usual exact description of each part of the building. Neither Pallas Athene nor Poseidon stirred for them among those white columns, neither trident nor feather of owl.

2

But Athene usually, Apollo always, have haunted and dominated their ruined shrines. At Delphi, Apollo is not to be escaped; he is still the living centre of the sanctuary, the god behind the oracle, the guardian of the great plundered ruined precincts that lie steeply high beneath Parnassus with their stumps of vanished temples and treasuries, all votive offerings to the god from his cities of Greece. Nothing stands of the great temple itself; only foundations, and the great quadrangle set with the treasuries, some quite ruined, some less. The precincts were robbed of their statues and their treasures for five centuries before Theodosius finally closed the business down. Apollo's power gradually waned; Nero and others tried to drive him out; he held his ground with diminished credit down the centuries; his oracle commanded the continuance of the offerings, but they became increasingly unearned. Read Pausanias's description of their richness, and imagine them set in their places round the sanctuary. Imagine, too, the Pythian priestess at her job, bathed and purified by the cold Castilian springs, frenzied by the sacred laurel between her teeth, seated on the tripod over the intoxicating air that welled up from the deep till she spoke what she received from the oracle, sending men to death or conquest, loss or victory, or (often) merely confusing or deceiving them, for Apollo, though usually succeeding in saving his face, was full of wiles. Long since expelled from his dubious, rewarding job, he still, we may assume, haunts his sanctuary, brooding among his broken treasuries, hiding his face among the goats and crags, or breaking out with radiance that lights all the great jumbled mass of mountain peaks and the Gulf of Salona below. He is inescapable; when his sanctuary lay buried deep through the centuries under the village of Kastri, the Kastri locals felt the uneasy shuddering of unseen powers; now, from a safe distance, they watch the rising again of the broken pedestals and fragments that were once those rich treasuries. The beauty and magnificence of Delphi, where sanctuary and ancient town, theatre, stadium, stoa, sacred way, the Castalian springs, climb among the wild olive-grown hills and gorges below the peaks of Parnassus, are perhaps the greatest beauty and magnificence in Greece. For many centuries the ruins of the Sacred Precincts lay unseen beneath Kastris; Spon and Wheeler, and the other early visitors, had to guess where they stood. Spon and Wheeler, guided to Kastri as a village which had some antiquities, recognized it at once for "*les restes de la celèbre ville de Delphes*," though unable to find any particular remain, and not realizing that

Delphes lay buried below. They could not imagine where the temple had stood, and found Pausanias confusing. However, they were glad to find outside a small church a heap of marble fragments, one of which bore an inscription, and which they decided to purloin. Their Greek guide thought it sacrilege, but "*nous nous moquâmes de son scrupule, qui luy était commun avec les autres Grecs,*" and put the marble in their luggage. Though bothered by their failure to identify the site of the temple, they fell enthusiastically under Delphic influence, enjoyed the Castalian water, which, said Spon, made people poets and inspired enthusiasm in all who drank of it. He himself, inspired by the pure air and the thought of being so close to the dwelling of Apollo and the Muses, suddenly was delivered of a song he had composed in modern Greek, which he had not thought he knew. In French it ran, with happy ingenuousness,

"*Donnez moy de grace une plume,*
Que je compose une chanson,
Puisque nous avons la fortune
De voir la maison d'Apollon."

There followed all the antiquarians, Pococke, Wood, Chandler and the rest, studying Pausanias, making drawings, copying inscriptions, musing on Apollo and the oracle and the Pythian games, imagining what they could not see of Delphi. Dr Chandler, washing his hands in a bath of cold, limpid water probably used by the Pythia, was taken with a violent tremor, which rendered him unable to stand without support. This shivering probably, he speculated later, overtook the Pythia after her bathe, and she ascribed it to the god. There was no doubt that Dr Chandler was under the influence too. Dr Dodwell, though deeply aware of the presence of the god—("The very locality breathed the presence of Apollo") was sceptical about the magical effects of the spring water on Spon and Chandler. It was, he found, an "excellent beverage." The approach to Delphi was "awfully grand and strikingly picturesque". He asked himself the ancient questions about the emotions excited. Delphi's "grand and theatrical appearance, combined with its ancient celebrity, its mouldering ruins, and its fallen state, form such extreme contrasts, that it is difficult to decide whether more regret is excited by its deserted splendour, or more satisfaction felt in still beholding some remains of its former magnificence". He quoted Justin—"*Prorsus ut incertum sit utrum munimentum loci, an majestas Dei plus hic admirationis habeat?*" Probably it was the majesty of the god. Dodwell, more learned than his predecessors, having sought in vain for any traces of the great vanished temple, decided that they lay under the village of Kastri, which must occupy the whole site; he had no authority to move the village, so had to be content with stray marbles, fluted columns built into walls, and inscriptions. These had to satisfy also Colonel Leake and the determined Hobhouse; Hobhouse, one feels, given half a chance, would have had the "small mud town" blown up. He roamed happily, however, about the crags and "the immortal rill", inspected Pythia's basin, and found scratched on a marble column supporting the roof of a tiny chapel "ABERDEEN, 1803", and "H.P. HOPE, 1799". Hobhouse felt that "there is something agreeable in meeting even with the name of a fellow countryman", and preferred these inscriptions to those more ancient and Greek. On the whole, Hobhouse was disappointed in the situation of Delphi; he thought it "hidden in a nook", but was happy enough pottering about it looking for inscriptions and guessing at sites. Byron, archaeologically ignorant and unconcerned, meanwhile rode his mule up Parnassus and dreamed.

All these travellers were at Delphi too soon. To-day we can see, where the small mud town once stood, the excavated and labelled sacred precincts of the god, the temple partly restored, the Votive Offerings standing round in their shattered fragments, as Pausanias had named them. No one since Sulla's siege of Athens has seen Delphi in its full glory. Now more reconstruction might well be done, and the Museum might return many of its treasures to be placed in situ Apollo, who continues through all his changing guises, would doubtless prefer his temple and his votive offerings to rise again in his greatest sanctuary.

3

Delos, too. That abandonment, that lonely desertion, pitied by poets since the island was sacked two thousand years ago, is more complete than that of Delphi. The native island of Apollo and Artemis has lain, swinging at anchor in the eye of the sun, its sacred precincts for many centuries unexcavated, while history, once so active in and round it, passed it by. To-day, though so little is to be seen of temples or monuments, except pedestals and sites, to walk among these to the high terrace where Apollo's temple stood, surrounded by what were treasuries, colonnades, courts and temples to other gods, has the excitement almost peculiar to the sanctuaries of Phoebus. Baedeker, with the fatuous inapprehensiveness that on occasion overtook this great man, remarks of Delos "The excursion is interesting only to archaeologists". On the contrary: Delos is, of all places, calculated to capture the imaginations of those who do not know an exedra from a metope, Doric from Corinthian, and could not care less what columns in antis are. For here is the grotto where Apollo and Artemis were born; and I have seen a stout American lady galloping up the hillside to it, at full speed, calling to her daughter, "Alice, Alice! Come and see the house where Apollo lived!" The cistus-grown, craggy island, so full of religious and secular history, with its sacred harbour silted up below it, its sanctuaries dominated by the high cone of Mount Kynthos, its barren, shrubbed, sweet-smelling solitude washed by the splashing or murmuring or tempest-driven sea, is poetry to the least informed. These, however innocent of Greek, can wordlessly cry

"But how shall I praise thee, Apollo, whom songs so many praise? . . .
Shall I tell how Leto, resting on Mount Cynthus, gave thee birth,
There in the rocky islet, to thee, the joy of earth,
Alone in sea-girt Delos, while round on beach and cove
Before the piping sea wind the dark blue billow drove?"[1]

Sometimes the sea wind pipes too hard, the billows drive too wildly, and it is impossible to land or leave; it is then that travellers have before now had enough of sea-girt Delos. This occurred to Spon and Wheeler in 1676; their boat could not set out again to join the fleet; they were left marooned, with a penny loaf, a few morsels of biscuit, and no water, for which they dug in vain,

[1] F. L. Lucas, Translation of the *Homeric Hymn to the Delian Apollo* (*Greek Poetry for Everyman*. Dent. 1951).

until at last one of the party discovered a cistern over a spring. While they were waterless and apprehensive, Apollo's ruins lost charm, though they had found, among a vast heap of marble, the trunk of the great statue of the god, whose head and limbs had been broken off three years before by some thieving sea captain (English or Venetian, they were told) and carried away. So, roaming over "a world of ruins", they waited uneasily for rescue.

Even more than at Delphi, a reconstruction of temples and statues is called for. Purists would be shocked; romantics deeply delighted.

4

The sun god's temple at Bassae, high in the wild Arcadian mountains, calls for no restoration beyond the return of its frieze from the British Museum. The great statue of the god is gone, and might be replaced by one of the many now in galleries. The aesthetic impact of Bassae, standing in broken Doric splendour lost in wild hills, so solitary, so lost, that it remained unknown to any but local shepherds through centuries till it was discovered by chance in 1765—the effect of Bassae is stupendous. To come on it unexpectedly on a mountain excursion, as the French architect did, must have been a ruin-pleasure unique in kind. He was travelling the mountains to see an ancient building, when he perceived, says Dr Chandler, who heard it from him soon afterwards, a ruin, two hours from Vervizza, which prevented his going any further. Chandler went to see it himself, and wrote of it.

"The ruin, called 'the Columns', stands on an eminence sheltered by lofty mountains. The temple, it is supposed, was that of Apollo Epicurius, near Phigalia. . . . It was of the Doric order, and had six columns in front. The number which ranged round the cell was thirty-eight. Two at the angles are fallen; the rest are entire, in good preservation, and support their architraves. Within them lies a confused heap. . . . These remains had their effect, striking equally the mind and the eyes of the beholder."

Through the quiet, formal words, the ecstasy of the beholder strikes. Bassae, designed by the architect of the Parthenon, set in its wild and lonely hills, has excited the passions of visitors ever since.

5

The scanty, in fact stumpy, ruins of Olympia, the great altis with only the foundations of the many temples, altars, treasuries and statues described with such elaboration by Pausanias, the stadium, the hippodrome, the gymnasium, the Pelopian, and, above all, the earthquake-thrown, prostrate temple of Zeus, the centre of this citadel of sport, politics and religion, must excite that peculiar medley of emotions which is evoked by silence, desertion and ruin where has been long ago a thousand years of glad and triumphant clamour. Thus might posterity feel surveying the site, centuries hence, of Newmarket or Epsom Downs. Closing one's eyes in this sun-drenched wilderness, one may hear the shouting crowds, the thudding feet of men and horses, the creak of the racing chariots, the shouting of the odds, the political chatter, the chanting of the priests as sacrificial victims bled. One may almost see, on the trodden turf that was once mosaic pavement, the wine-gourds, the spat-out olive stones, the scattered ashes, the entrails of boars and goats. Still on the honeyed air hangs the sense of a great and brilliant occasion, the greatest social occasion of Greek life.

"There are many things, indeed, in Greece which call forth admiration both when seen and related; but the Eleusinian mysteries and the Olympic games must be particularly admirable to such as are endued with divine solicitude about religious affairs."

This may, as Pausanias suggests, be the reason for our Olympian emotion. It would, anyhow, seem certain that, if the gods are anywhere, they are here.

6

Also, presumably, at Eleusis. But Eleusis is less impressive, partly because the view is spoilt by factory chimneys, partly because its occasions were less delightful, more mysteriously occult, and are less precisely known to us, though described often enough since the days when who revealed them was liable to death. Opinions have differed as to these rites "*quae frustra cupiunt audire profani*". Were they morally edifying, as Cicero and many more have maintained, or quite otherwise, as has been surmised by others? There is an unpleasant suggestion of revivalism, of religious hysteria, in the accounts which have come down to us. Yet a favourable view has, on the whole, been taken. "It produced sanctity of manners, and an attention to the social duties," says Dr Chandler, after describing the strange excitements, terrors, and illuminations undergone by the mystae. Chateaubriand thought it highly respectable. "*Eleusis est, selon moi, le lieu le plus respectable de la Grèce, puisqu'on y enseignait l'unité de Dieu*", and because it lies hard by Salamis, where had occurred the "*plus grand effort . . . que jamais les hommes aient tenté en faveur de la liberté*". Anyhow the Athenians, and with them pilgrims from the world over, continued the mysteries until Alaric destroyed Eleusis. Along the Sacred Way the flower-crowned, singing, cymbal-crashing processions capered from Athens to the temple of Demeter at Eleusis, fourteen miles away. The road was set with sumptuous monuments, temples, altars, statues and sepulchres; it can, according to Pausanias and others who have described it in detail, have had no dull half mile. At every point of the way Demeter, Proserpine, Triptolemos, or Pluto had left their traces. But the Sacred Way has been plundered and despoiled, and now a motoring road runs along its course. Wheeler, in 1675, still passed many ruins of temples and shrines; through the eighteenth century, the time of the great looters, they dwindled away, as in Eleusis itself. Wheeler saw better ruins than we do. He saw

"the stately temple of Ceres, now laid prostrate on the ground . . . all in a confused heap together: the beautiful pillars buried in the Rubbish of its dejected Roof and Walls. . . ."[1]

The stones carved with wheat-ears and poppies, "the remains of the state of Ceres", we can still see. And excavation has made clear the construction of the great temple of the mysteries, where now we see mainly pedestals and bases. The fragments and statues and capitals that earlier travellers saw lying about have been either stolen or removed to the museum. We are left to gaze

[1]Sir George Wheeler, *A Journey into Greece* (1676).

at the labelled and cleared design of the temple and, if we can, raise in imagination those elevating, intoxicating mystic rites which so delighted the most religious people of the world. Here again, what a case for reconstruction! Were those temples, grottoes, altars, halls of mystery, to be raised again according to their ancient designs, and were the Mysteries again to be celebrated in them, with those orgiastic fervours and strange pomps that resulted of old in increased sanctity of manners and attention to the social duties, what pilgrimages, we may be sure, would stream to Eleusis from every quarter of a mystery-starved world! What processions, what chantings, what social joys, what special correspondents, what spiritual delights, what lavish exploitation of a more magnificent Lourdes! Here is a ruin-pleasure that is called for. We have, all over the world of ruins, plays acted in the great ruined theatres, concerts held in the great ruined baths; surely the Mysteries should be enacted again at Eleusis.

7

One would like, too, to see more going on in Ephesus. The great temple of Artemis, that wonder of the world, destroyed first by Goths then by Christians in the third century, lost to view for so long, rediscovered eighty years ago, the site where successive temples had been built, each on the foundations of the temple before it, between the seventh century B.C. and Augustus, can never be built again; its gorgeousness was incomparable, and not for our drab days to emulate. It has been for the past half century a neatly laid out site; so neat, so labelled, so tamed, that the goddess can scarcely haunt it. But in the grassy spaces of the great theatre, every full moon, the Ephesians might assemble in worship of their goddess, and shout for two hours, as they did two thousand years ago, when missionaries arrived with the message of an alien god, "Great is Diana of the Ephesians."

One must be glad that the temple has been traced, though there was romance in its long pursuit. The Reverend Edmund Chishull, chaplain to the Factory of the Turkey Company in Smyrna, who visited Ephesus in 1699, was sure that he had located it—two broken pieces of a massy wall in marshy ground between the haven Panormus and the ancient city. Under the wall were passages and subterraneous arches, commonly visited by travellers with a candle and a clue of thread, which was called, "by we know not what fancy, the labyrinth of Diana's temple."

"Returning from this cavity, the traveller has nothing else in view but venerable heaps of rubbish, and uncertain traces of foundations, and must be forced to supply his curiosity with considering, that this was the place, where once stood and flourished that renowned wonder of the world."[1]

But the renowned wonder of the world was not so easily traced. Dr Chandler supposed that it might have been, as the Sibyl had prophesied, swallowed up by the opening earth. Pitching his tent in the great gymnasium, he spent three days exploring, measuring, and speculating.

"What is become of the renowned temple of Diana? Can a wonder of the world be vanished like a phantom, without leaving a trace behind? . . . To our great regret, we searched for the site of this fabric to as little purpose as the travellers who had preceded us."[2]

The glorious temple rose in his mind, as described by the historians who had seen it or heard tell of it: the fifth, or Hellenistic, temple, the carved Ionic columns sixty feet high, the polished cypress wood doors, the cedar ceiling, the steps cut from a vine's single stem, the treasure given by kings, the incomparable works of art, the Phrygian marble banqueting hall, the portico, the unimaginable sanctity and wealth. There Alexander had come and done reverence; there Antony, living in love and luxury with Cleopatra at Ephesus, had gone to church; there the kings of the earth had sent their costly and magnificent treasures, and the wise and simple from all lands had come to gaze and tell the tale of fabulous glory. The temple glowed for Dr Chandler more luminously than if he had been shown, as we are now shown, its fragments and pavements, shorn of their beauty. He remembered the Sibyl's words: the earth, said she, would open and quake, and the temple be engorged, like a ship in a storm, into the abyss.

For all anyone knew, even a century later, this fatality might well have occurred. Travellers could see no trace. "Its remains,"

[1]Edmund Chishull, *Travels in Turkey and back to England* (1747)
[2]Richard Chandler, *Travels in Asia Minor and Greece* (1764).

they said, "are to be sought for in medieval buildings, in the columns of green jaspar which support the dome of St Sophia, even in the naves of Italian cathedrals."[1] Then, in 1869, it was discovered, by the pertinacious, obstinate and irascible Mr J. T. Wood, who, after digging about the tobacco fields of Ephesus for six years, found the site, struck the pavement of the fourth temple of the sixth century, and laid bare during the next few years both this and the Hellenistic temple above it. The eleven years of Mr Wood's toil were to him passionately exciting; stinted of money by the British Museum, frustrated by Pashas and Beys and Turkish workmen, robbed by burglars, stabbed by local maniacs, haunted by brigands, injured by falls, prostrated by sickness, visited by tourists who only cared for their food and ignored his ruins, and by others who picked up and pocketed valuable fragments, he indomitably kept at it, digging up the Odeum, the Great Theatre, and hundreds of inscribed slabs, before coming on the temple itself; entertaining Prince Arthur of Connaught, the Bishop of Gibraltar, and large parties of Greeks, copying inscriptions and drawing plans, sending packing cases full of marble to the British Museum, writing reports for the *Times*, finally returning to England with most of the excavations still to be done, and publishing his book about them, to be told by Sir James Fergusson that his drawings showed a temple too mean and small; the building which had the ancient world in raptures must have been on a grander scale; such amenities between archaeologists are a permanent ingredient in ruin-pleasure. Anyhow, it was clear where the great temple had stood, and visitors need no more roam over that swampy plain seeking the site of the building which Pausanias said surpassed all others raised by human hands, and Philo, "Whoever examines it would believe that the gods had left their immortal regions to come down and live on earth."

Ephesus and the neighbouring Turkish village of Ayasoluk (at the foot of whose hill the Artemiseon had stood) were more picturesque before they were excavated; in the days when Wheeler and Pococke and Chandler and Hobhouse and Byron and Conybeare and Howson roamed about and found their own ruins, in the wild wide basin mountain-rimmed, golden with angelica and

[1] W. J. Conybeare and J. S. Howson, *Life and Epistles of St Paul* (1854).

yellow iris, surrounded by mosques, wild rocks, and forest trees. "I never," said Mr Wood, "became weary of the scenery by which I was surrounded."[1] His own excavations added to the grandeur of the scene; in one of his illustrations a majestic rubble of drums, capitals and walls strews the mountain-surrounded site, on which Mr Wood, in tail-coat and fine beard, Mrs Wood and two other ladies in bonnets and pelisses, and a few Turks, stand with satisfaction among the noble débris. Later excavators dug up more, and the site is now arranged with systematic neatness; visitors stay near it in hotels. Gone are the days when Hobhouse and Byron put up their beds "in a most miserable han" at Ayasoluk and partook of cold provisions on a stone seat by a fountain near a cypress-shaded mosque, and rambled about the ruins, climbing up to the Turkish castle and to the mosque built over Justinian's great church of St John, overrun with weeds and with shrubs shooting from the broken walls. A ruined minaret rose over the west door, a stork had made her nest in it; the broken columns of a portico stood in the court. Other ruined mosques stood near, the minarets of which might have been taken for the columns of some Grecian temple. The whole scene was desolate, and, said Hobhouse,

"cannot but suggest a train of melancholy reflections. The decay of three religions is there presented at one view. The marble spoils of the Grecian temple adorn the mouldering edifice once dedicated to the service of Christ, over which the tower of the Mussulman is itself seen to totter and sink into the surrounding ruins."[2]

All the gods, in fact, had been, as usual, betrayed; but all the gods still haunt their broken temples.

8

It is the god of the elevated order of the Stylites who may be presumed to haunt the great ruins of Kalat Siman, the monastery built round the pillar of the proto-stylite in the fifth century. They are perhaps the best church ruins in Syria, lying high on a plateau in the wild Jebel Barakat, the mountain country north-

[1] J. T. Wood, *Discoveries at Ephesus* (1877).
[2] Lord Broughton, *Journey through Albania, etc.*, 1809-10 (1813).

east of Aleppo. Inside the remains of towered Moslem fortress walls the huge ruined church stands, in shape like a Greek cross. In the centre of the ruin-littered octagonal court is the base of the pillar (perhaps) on which the saint so long and so publicly dwelt; in the middle of a quadrangle court outside lies another candidate for this honour; one may take one's choice. The Moslem destroyers left the shape and plan of this lovely Antiochian church unspoiled; a wealth of pillars still stands among the jumbled ruin; the ornateness of the decoration is lavish. Round the church stand the remains of monastery buildings, covering the slope, and at the hill's foot there are more basilicas and a wrecked hostelry for pilgrims. From all parts of Christendom the pilgrims came, both to gaze at St Simon on his pillar and later to worship in his church; female visitors, whom he would never permit to approach the pillar, for they were occasions of temptation even to one elevated so high in the sky above them, now visit his column and seat themselves on its base.

In extent, and in the richness of its sophisticated Antiochian beauty, Kalat Siman is unrivalled even among the marvels of fifth and sixth century and Seleucid architecture that lie Arab-wrecked about the deserts and mountains of North Syria. There is enormous variety of style. From one end of Syria to the other the sanctuaries blend and merge, ruin on ruin, each carrying forward some of its character and style into the next metamorphosis. The Roman temples become Byzantine churches, with Greek-Oriental ornament; they develop in style right up to the Arab invasion, till such late sixth-century buildings as Kalb Lozeh among the mountains of Barisha are nearly Romanesque. The Arabs either doomed or destroyed them; in either case they stand now in ruin, tranquil and harmonious, a part of the wild landscape in which they seem natural growths, like the olive trees. There seems no strangeness in the wrecked Syrian and Palestine shrines, only a quietly brooding desolation.

9

A much stranger melancholy broods over the drowned island of Philae, the ancient sanctuary of Isis and Osiris on the upper Nile. A sanctuary, it seems, from at least the sixth century B.C.;

but its main temple was Ptolemaic, with sculptures and decorations added continuously under the Caesars. How lovely a building it is, with its complicated, irregular maze of porticos, columns, corridors, stairways, shadowy halls and courts, has been recorded by artists and travellers for over two thousand years; the palmy island, covered with ruined temples and churches, is familiar. We have Prince Pückler-Muskau's account of it in the 1830's—

"an emerald isle of an almost perfect oval, shaded with palm-trees and entirely resembling an Hesperian garden, supported by lofty quays, and covered from one end to the other with an unbroken series of the most splendid buildings which appeared more like the etherial dwelling of some fairy than the work of human hands. It was Philae! certainly one of the most lovely wonders in the fabulous kingdom of the Pharaohs. . . . The fanaticism of Persians and Christians have hitherto only half succeeded in their attempts on these gigantic works; and the combined efforts of religious fury, self-interest, and the iron tooth of time, have not been able to accomplish it in the lapse of thousands of years. . . ."[1]

He spoke too soon. Since the end of the last century, the Nile has flowed over Philae's temples and palms, having been turned into a reservoir by the British, to increase the fertility of the cotton land, so that now only from July to October, when the waters are undammed, do the temples arise from them, like the world resurrecting from the flood.

To the cry of "Vandalism" that rose when this strange project was initiated, the British replied blandly, "Dear me no. Water is good for the buildings. We have underpinned them with tons of cement, and no temple in the Nile valley is more secured against collapse than those on Philae Island. Indeed, submersion does them good, removing saline efflorescence. Beyond the usual decay of old age brought about by atmospheric influences and water action, no special general destruction of the temple is taking place. . . ."

The French, full at that time of anti-British malice, took a different view; the view expressed by Pierre Loti in *La Mort de*

[1]Prince Puckler-Muskau, *Egypt under Mehemet Ali* (1836).

Philae (1908). Loti's account of his visit to the submerged island is a dirge for the *temples engloutis*, rich with melancholy emotion and anger; through its phrases Philae arises like a lovely drowned ghost. The sanctuary of Isis, on its hill covered with colonnades and statues, emerges (he writes) alone. We row over the artificial lake to the island; the boatmen sing. The sacrilegious lake has enveloped in its waters ruins beyond price—temples of the gods of Egypt, early Christian churches, it is over these that we pass, whipped in the face by the foam of little waves. Palms, dying with their stems under water, still show their heads. We touch at the kiosk; we enter in our boat; it is a strange port, with its sumptuous antiquity, its nameless melancholy; but how adorable it is! Its columns seem slimmer and taller, carrying high their capitals of stone foliage; one feels them about to disappear for ever under the waters. Leaving the kiosk, our boats make a detour among the drowned palms by the road that pilgrims used to take on foot to the temple. Still magnificent, still bordered with colonnades and statues, it lies wholly drowned; we row between double rows of columns, at the level of the capitals, which emerge above the water so that we can touch them with our hands. We arrive at the temple. Above us are enormous pylons, ornamented with personages in bas-relief; a giant Isis, and other divinities with mysterious gestures. The gate in the wall is low and half flooded; we row in to the sanctuary. And, as our boat passes the sacred threshold, the boatmen interrupt their song and raise the new cry that they have learnt from the tourists: *Hip! Hip! Hip! Hurrah!* Oh the effect of coarse and imbecile profanation that this shout of English joy gives! It is darker inside, and the icy wind whistles more lugubriously; there is a penetrating dampness; one hears only the plaint of the wind and the clapping of the water against the columns—and then suddenly the noise of a heavy fall, followed by eddies without end; some great sculptured stone has plunged in its turn to rejoin in the black chaos those already disappeared, the temples already drowned, the old Coptic churches and the town of the first Christian centuries—all which was once the isle of Philae, the pearl of Egypt, one of the wonders of the world.

Let us shelter somewhere to wait for the moon. We land in the holy of holies, the highest part of the temple. Our steps seem noisy on the great flagstones; owls fly out. Deep darkness; the wind and damp freeze us. Three hours before moonrise; to wait there would be mortal; we return to Chelal, find a cabaret in the horrible village where they sell absinthe; one warms oneself over a smoky brazier. The landlord is a Maltese, who has pictures cut from our European pornographic magazines. At moonrise we get into our boat again. Cradled always by the Nubian song of the boatmen, we reach the Kiosk, and the great disc lights everything in discreet splendour.

We follow a second time the drowned way between the capitals and friezes of the colonnade. In the ante-temple, still in darkness, we fasten the boat to a wall. And then a luminous triangle grows little by little on the huge wall, descends to the base of the temple, showing us by degrees the intimidating presence of bas-reliefs, gods and goddesses, persons who make signs among themselves. We are no more alone; a whole world of phantoms has been evoked round us by the moon, phantoms who suddenly begin to talk in dumb show, with expressive hands and raised fingers. Now begins to appear also the colossal Isis. But she seems astonished and disturbed to see at her feet, instead of the flagstones she has known for two thousand years, her own image reflected in the water upside down.

And suddenly, in the middle of the calm nocturne of this temple in a lake, again there breaks a melancholy rumbling, more precious stones which detach themselves and fall, and then on the surface of the water a thousand circles form and disappear, troubling this mirror shut in granite where Isis sadly regards herself.

To this dirge Loti adds a bitter postscript. The drowning of Philae had increased by millions of pounds the annual return of the land. Encouraged, the English planned to raise the barrage by another six metres. The temple of Isis would then be completely immersed; more of the ancient temples of Nubia would be under water, fever would infect the country. But how good for the cotton plantations!

The half century of immersion has turned the temples from their tawny hue to a pale seaweed green. And at last the steady pressure of the water has broken down the beautiful little temple, Pharaoh's Bed, whose capitals were, said Pococke, among the most beautiful in Egypt. Philae's age-old career as a shrine for pilgrims and tourists is nearing its end; it has assumed the status of an aquatic resort, a submarine curiosity. A melancholy end to so much pleasure and devotion, which not all Justinian's anti-pagan efforts could stop; and, indeed, it was succeeded by Christian pilgrimage to Christian shrines. Visitors to the island used to rely on being fed by the priests of Isis, till at last Ptolemy excused them from so intolerable a burden. After that, pilgrims had to bring their own provisions, and picnicked joyfully beneath the date palms. Napoleon was there in 1799; the Prince and Princess of Wales in 1869. After wandering very pleasantly about the ruins and the prostrate slabs and columns of the temples, the royal party banqueted in a tent, afterwards hearing Arab music by moonlight. Royalty has always taken particular pleasure in Philae. We should have kept it as it was; to drown it was one of the more sordid enterprises of utilitarian greed.

10

It would have been less harmful to have drowned the ancient sanctuary of Jupiter Ammon on the palm-grown Lybian desert oasis of Siwa. The sanctuary is even more ancient than Philae; but it is not a group of beautiful temples; all that now remains of the fabled shrine is one upright ruined fragment and some tumbled blocks and slabs beneath the palms. The famous oracle has been dumb for nearly two thousand years; the Romans, said Strabo, thought little of it and neglected it; a century later Pausanias declared it dumb. Its great days were far behind it; the days when Medea spoke of it, when the great of the earth crossed deserts and seas to consult it, Cambyses and Croesus and Alexander and Lysander, and Pindar wrote to it an ode which Pausanias, five centuries later, saw inscribed on a slab of the temple. The temple was built in the sixth century; there were formerly two, but now only a fragment of one, and that the smaller one, standing alone in the palm-groves. In itself it does not look much or very good; but there, standing a lonely relic on the palmy oasis among sand dunes in the great desert, with the extraordinary, crumbling clay-built jumble of Aghourmi village behind it, roofless houses, broken mosques, dark maze of alley streets, all climbing up the hill (as at Siwa, two miles away)—in this startling setting, the tall, shapeless fragment has a hypnotizing fascination. One is stirred by desire to ask foolish questions of the oracle so long neglected and now, it is said, dumb; enquiries whisper themselves on the sand-blown wind. If I march into the desert, shall I conquer Libya and Egypt? Do great cities, treasure-laden, lie beneath the sand? Where is the army of Cambyses, lost in the sands, sunk without trace? Will the oracle utter if sufficiently bribed, as Lysander vainly supposed? Who were the last to walk in chanting procession through the palm groves, bearing rich offerings to the god? Will the Fons Solis, the sacred spring, boil and cool, boil and cool, in rhythmic progression all day and night, as of old? Jupiter Ammon, Zeus Ammon, the Libyan sun-god, and so back and back in the awful succession of desert gods, to who can say what of dark and monstrous incogniti. The dark heritage of the oracle gods seems to brood over Siwa, its huddled labyrinth of hidden lanes, its steeply piled jumble of clay houses, its ruinous domeless mosques. Always Siwans have disliked foreigners; the oracle has made no hospitable gesture to visiting explorers since it flattered Alexander; perhaps it is avenging itself for the neglectful Romans, who, said Strabo, were satisfied with the oracles of Sibylla and the Tyrrhenian prophecies. Among the caves and the tombs and the ruins, evil jinns lurk.

II

After the sad, morbid and charming pleasures of drowned Philae, and the mysterious intimidations of Siwa, we turn to the temples of Greece to be exalted and braced. Climb, like Poseidon, to the topmost peak of the rugged mountains of Samothrace; from that craggy hillside look down on the broken marble columns of the Doric temple of the Cabeiri, on the rotunda built by Queen Arsinoe, on the Cyclopean wall that still lies tumbled about the sanctuary; picture the winged Victory still standing on her prow above the stone-banked basin on the mountain-side, her companion Victory, discovered three years ago, facing her from the rock of the Doric temple, the sacred hall where the ancient mysteries were celebrated by Pelasgians six centuries before Christ, the Alexandrian temples, the Greek and Roman devotees thronging across the Aegean to the wild mountain island to celebrate the Cabeiri who passed into Greek and Roman gods. Over the windy mountain-side the ancient chanting seems to rise; every now and then archaeologists dig up another fragment of the exiled Victory residing in Paris, or a vase or two, or another headless statue. They could, they say, reconstruct the temples, replace the two Victories on their sites, looking over the wind-swept Aegean. Then, from the peaks above, we should see a finer Samothrace than Poseidon saw, marble temples and halls, statues and colonnades, and the Cabeiri, lolling vine-crowned among maenads and Bacchae, would come into their own again, while the archaeologists went on digging for fragments; they might even find the Victories' heads.

12

On the other hand, it would not do to restore Aesculapius's clinic near Epidaurus; the sacred grove, the abaton and the temple would again be filled with patients, the Tholos with votive offerings, the theatre with *malades* seeking distraction from their ills, the ground would crawl with yellow serpents eager to lick the afflicted (one of which might well be the "blameless physician" himself, so it would not do to kill them). Instead of picturesque ruins, arrived at after fatiguing struggles up a rocky gorge and mountain-side, the place would have the air of a spa, or of Lourdes in a holy year, crowded with the credulous sick seeing visions and awaking healed, or bathing in the curative waters. There would also be the valetudinarian seekers after entertainment, gossipping in the halls and colonnades of the abaton, taking the waters, reading the inscriptions in the Tholos which related miraculous cures, attending the play in the evening, exchanging the news of the cities from which they had come, betting on how long one another's cures would last, and whether they would have to come again next season. Meanwhile the less *mondains*, the simpletons and the neurotics, would be evincing symptoms of hysteria in the great temple, recounting their dreams (as approved a cure for sickness in the Aesculapian clinic as now in a Freudian one), and leaving with broken bones miraculously joined, blind eyes opened to the light, rushing in a state of happy auto-hypnosis to the tholos to cast their thankofferings into its pit. Or, a few centuries later, grown a trifle more scientific and less gullible, so that Aesculapius and his staff of priest-physicians would feel obliged to provide some more substantial treatment than magic, they would be crowding about the dispensaries to receive the hieroglyphics illegibly handed to them, hurrying away to the hot springs, or to gather roots and medicinal leaves from the Sacred Grove. We should see the dying and the prospective mothers carried hurriedly outside the sacred precincts, where none might die, none be born; there would brood over the whole Hieron, behind the social amenities and the valetudinarian recreations, the nervous, uneasy malaise that characterizes all clinics and spas.

Indeed, something of this clinical air still actually hangs about the beautifully excavated Hieron, lying grey and shrub-grown up the rocky valley between the mountains, with its almost perfect theatre. Was Dr Dodwell sensible of it, during the day he spent there in 1801? There had been then no excavation; he saw a jumble of ruins, occupying "the space of a city". It had been, thought Dr Dodwell, "a splendid hospital—this useful establishment, in which superstition assisted the purposes of benevolence", with Aesculapius himself dispensing his remedies "for those numerous maladies which shorten the days or embitter the existence of man". So he wandered with approval about the ground "strewed with elegant fragments of the Doric and Ionic orders", searching for the temple of Aesculapius, and for the great ivory and gold statue which had been removed after Pausanias saw it, no one knows when or where, but the Hieron has been plundered for some two thousand years.

12

No ruined temple is more beautiful, more heroically and exquisitely poised in the wild heights of a mountainous island, looking over the Saronic Gulf to Attica and Athens, the wild pine woods climbing to its platform, the precipitous slopes falling below to the port and sea, than the temple of Aphaea, goddess of the woods, the moon, and the underworld, which stands on Aegina, its two and twenty golden Doric columns gleaming like pale honey, roofless and luminous against the sky. It is hard to find and to reach, climbing up over hills and valleys and vineyards, medieval ruins and steep mazes of paths, from the port and ancient town; its goddess loved solitude and the green woods and chose precipitous ways. Standing there, breathing the pine-tanged wind, looking through the mellow weathered fifth-century columns across the sea to Salamis and Attica and Athens the ancient foe, one feels the surge of Aeginetan history, the island pride and defiance, the valour that won glory at Salamis, the independence crushed without mercy by the bully of Attica, the decline into the long centuries of unimportance, a rocky island washed by the blue Aegean, with Zeus, the sky-god, brooding on its topmost peak. For, climbing high above Aphaea's temple, you come at last to the high terrace where once stood the sanctuary of Zeus Panhellenios; and above that to the Oros, the highest summit of the Gulf, where his great altar was, and terraces supported a pre-historic town. But nothing is left; only a small Christian chapel represents the gods on the high sanctuary of Zeus. Descend again to Aphaea's temple; there, among the golden columns, the asphodel and the wild woods, the huntress goddess dwells apart.

As is suitable, Aphrodite dwells below, practically in the port. But all that is left of her temple is one tall broken column. The island belongs to Aphaea.

13

All over Greece and her islands, Greek Asia Minor, Greece in Italy, the ruined temples stand. The most religious race in the world except the Jews (and more religious than the Jews, for they had many more gods, and therefore many more shrines), they built temples out of all proportion in number to their palaces, their castles, their triumphal arches, even their theatres. They stand about the mountains and valleys in their broken beauty, their classical perfection, haunted by their gods and by that uniquely magnificent past that is instilled into the mind of every literate child. That past is inescapable; it commands our spirits. Take it away, and what have we left? Finely proportioned buildings, usually in fine situations, in varying stages of ruin; the soul is gone. Another question: what does ruin add to their beauty and our emotion? If they stood to-day as they stood when first built, in all the glory of fresh paint, dazzling whiteness, polychrome sculptures, polished marble floors, roofs fraught with brightly hued godlike forms, should we admire them as much, or should we feel a faint suggestion of garishness, even of bad taste, in those brilliant, accomplished, flawless places of worship set so opulently in the barren mountain land above seas the vivid blue of posters? Now, mellowed, weathered, roofless and broken, their gay colour flaked away, half their columns prostrate on the ground around them, assaulted by the centuries, by enemies, by robbers, by the shaking of the earth, but still standing in their wrecked beauty among herbs and rocks and the encroaching wilderness, defying time, symbols of a lost civilization unparalleled in our history, they have achieved a unique emotional grandeur.

They are exquisitely foiled by the crumbling Byzantine churches that nestle like clustered fruits about the hills and valleys and cities of Greece. Too often in the undulant history of artistic taste, admiration for classical, Byzantine, Gothic or baroque architecture has been contemptuously exclusive, and visitors to Greece have exalted one mode of building to the detriment of others; actually the different styles set one another exquisitely off, each enhancing the beauties of its rivals, like contrasting colours and shapes in a flower-bed. But the eighteenth-century Dilettanti, in search of classical architecture, thought little of the ruins of Byzantium that strewed their way: Dr Richard Chandler, passing the eleventh-century monastery of Daphni on the road to Eleusis in 1764, called it "a mean and barbarous edifice, inclosed within a high wall;" the church he owned to be "large and lofty", but what mainly interested him (he gives the mosaic Christ under the dome an indifferent mention, saying it was much injured) was the fact that the church stood on the site of a temple of Apollo, some of whose columns were immured in a wall. Having given Daphni (then much less ruined than to-day) this cursory attention, the classically-minded doctor proceeded along the Sacred Way to Eleusis. So much for what has been described since as perhaps the most beautiful of all the Byzantine churches in Greece, containing under its dome a mosaic (lately restored) which now draws visitors away from Athens, away from Eleusis, to gaze on its hieratic glory. Looking at the ruined Byzantine churches of Greece, Turkey and Asia, one compares the pleasure of these crumbling clustered Christian domes, often touchingly pretty and small, with that of the shattered glory of the Greek temples standing superbly on their olive-silver hills, or rock-strewn Sicilian forest slopes, or above the ruined shores of Tyrrhenian and Ionian bays; or with the more austere pleasures of the time-struck gothic abbeys of western Europe; the charm of the broken Romanesque churches built into farm-houses and barns that stand among the fig-trees and olive-groves of Spain; of the broken baroque Cartujas that successive revolutions have shattered and that poverty and cynical apathy have left to moulder away; of the jungle-grown ancient temples of Mexico and the Maya country and Cambodia and Ceylon; the medieval Arab mosques that bear witness to the Islamic glories of Anatolia and of East Africa; the Assyrian temples lying buried, or piece by piece emerging, from under the medieval cities, villages and castles of Mesopotamia; and all the uncountable broken places of worship that stand or lie like defeated prayers about the world. That air of defeat the ruined temples and churches all wear in common. One concludes, on the whole (perhaps this is a view purely personal), that classical temples gain by moderate breakage, but should not be entirely prone, and that their partial and skilful reconstruction is not amiss; that Byzantine churches are more exquisite when entire but a trifle decayed; that there is a quality peculiarly emotion-stirring in ruinous baroque, built for such graceful elegance and fallen on barbarous days; that the barbaric temples of the jungles need no ruining to enhance their mysterious awe, though an extra intensity of delight is given by the thrust of trees through roof and walls. In fact, enjungled ruins, religious or secular, are in a class apart. There are few now in Europe; one does not now have the excitement of pushing through the Kentish weald or a Devonshire combe or the Forest of Arden or the great wild woods of Roncevalles or the Black Forest of Bavaria or the woody crags of the Apennines where Romans chased the boar, and finding in the heart of dense jungle some lost forgotten city, or tree-grown palace, or broken temple with boughs pushing greenly through window, door and roof. True, the boughs push and the shrubs grow and the creepers sprawl across smashed altars in modern cities now; but these derelict shattered relics stand in the open for all to see; no jungle swallows them into its green dusk.

14

Our ruined abbeys and churches are, as a rule, only too well tidied up and cleared, losing in the process who can say how much of mystery and nostalgic awe. Many were built up long since into manor houses or farm-houses or barns, so that one may see chancel arches and fragments of carved stone and Gothic windows in the most incongruous places, in a thousand farm buildings standing about the countryside, as in the seventeenth-century farm-house which has incorporated great fragments of Halesowen abbey, so that hay-waggons, cattle and horses are stabled within church walls set with cloister doorways, and lancet windows look down on munching carthorses. But this is among the ordinary vicissitudes of English abbeys, nearly all of which have contributed less or more to neighbouring buildings; all over the country manor houses, farms and cottages are haunted with strange intimations from shadowy vanished worlds; long refectories are piled with hay and strewn with agricultural tools, and in cow-house walls are niches where once saints stood.

But, when too much ruined to be tidied up, still the foundations and fragments of the great abbeys lie neglected in fields and commons, among thrusting woods and trees, like the Cistercian abbey of Quarr, whose ruins lie above Wootton Creek within their great circle of massive broken wall; the gate-house has been "deformed into a farm-house"; ancient trees grow through more ancient chapels and arches; a wilderness of grass, forest and stone with the flowing sea creek at its edge; strange contrast to the handsome brand-new pink Benedictine Abbey and church built on to a nearby mansion by monks from Solesmes early this century. There are, of course, many other wooded abbey ruins (as Netley, Beaulieu, Melrose); but wholly embosked ruined churches are usually small chapels which no one has bothered to clear, like the little rapidly disappearing fourteenth-century chapel of St Nicholas near Minsden, once the chapel of the Knights of St John of Jerusalem; from its vanished altar those knightly adventurers set out to capture and loot Jerusalem's holy towers. Still smaller is the ancient chapel of Knowlton Circles, nestling among earthworks and trees near Crichel in Dorset; both are heirs, no doubt, of an age-old sequence of religious buildings standing on the same sites, in the same sacred thickets, through who knows how many wild centuries of strange cults? As Evander said to Aeneas about the Tarpeian rock, the awful religion of the place had always alarmed the local rustics, who dreaded the woods and rocks; "*hoc nemus, quis deus incertum est, habitat deus*"; the Arcadians often thought they saw Jove himself there, particularly during thunder-storms. The tradition of hallowed ground persists: Christian church on pagan, mosque on Christian church, until the last church is fallen and built into secular houses which remain faintly, disturbingly, haunted. Needless to inscribe on plaques "The place whereon thou standest is holy ground", as at the entrance to the ruined Gothic arches and roofless walls and grass-grown chancel of the old church at Ayot St Lawrence, left to decay away among encroaching trees after the lord of the manor, wearying of Gothic, had partly demolished it and commissioned Messrs Stuart and Revett, of Athenian fame, to erect on the hill above it a new Palladian church in the smart Grecian manner, looking like something on the Acropolis. That was in 1779; since then the ancient church in the woods below has fallen into dilapidated sanctity, hallowed and haunted; Christ among the dryads and fauns of the coppice that pushes round it. Comparing the atmosphere of the two churches, one must share the pro-Gothic predelictions of Mr William Woty—

"*Gothic* the stile, and tending to excite
Free-thinkers to a sense of what is right . . .
Not like Saint Paul's, beneath whose ample dome
No thought arises of the life to come.
For, tho' superb, not solemn is the place. . . ."[1]

Solemnity, if not a sense of what is right, is certainly increased by surrounding woods. "The pointed ruin peeping o'er the

[1] William Woty, *Church Laryton* (1770).

wood" is less commonly observed to-day than once it was. But here and there one finds, in the heart of a dark and shadowy thicket, such ruins as those of Bindon Abbey, the twelfth-century Cistercian monastery near Lulworth; fragments of wall, a few bases of columns, indications of the cloister court and refectory, everything grown with ivy and becoming one with the devouring woods. Round the abbey lie dark, shadowed fish-ponds. The monastery was pulled down at the Dissolution; "a faire monasterie of White Cistercian monks", wrote the antiquarian Dorset parson Mr Coker a few years later; and "out of the Ruines that faire house which stands there" (Lulworth Castle?) was raised by Viscount Bindon, a Howard, who should have kept better faith with his church. What he left was quarried away for later buildings: it probably supplied the Jacobean parts of the old manor house at Wool, where the Angel Clares honeymooned, and the barn with its ecclesiastical Gothic details. Bindon's utter desolation and mournful bosky twilight, through which the perceptive are aware of rambling, breviary-reading, or angling monks, have deepened century by century. Just above the Cove is the small farm-house whose Early English window marks it as the only relic remaining of the earlier and unfinished abbey, Little Bindon, abandoned for the more spacious site near Wool.

Much pleasure was given to antiquarian visitors to Dorset between the Dissolution and the later eighteenth century by the majestic and romantic remains of Milton Abbey (Benedictine), standing in its woody valley surrounded by the old town of Milton Abbas. But in 1752 the abbey was bought by Mr Joseph Damer, who, on becoming Lord Milton, demolished most of it to erect on its foundations a new mansion. The ancient town he destroyed (for it was annoyingly near his mansion), and built for its inhabitants the new and neat model village some way off which still thrives there. To-day "those who stroll over the smooth lawns around the Abbey Church" (which was not destroyed) "will hardly realize that they are walking over the site of the ancient town of Milton." The enterprising Mr Damer had just begun his activities when Dr Pococke passed that way in 1754.

"There are great remains of the Abbey," he wrote, "as a hall with a fine carved skreen, a date on it of about 1428; a room called the Starchamber, from the wooden cieling in compartments adorn'd with gilt stars; most of the other rooms are alter'd, but some of the old building, which was very fine, remains. Lord Milton is casing it round in a beautiful modern taste. The town is a very poor small place."[1]

Dr Pococke thought better of Lord Milton's activities than we think now. But in the imposing grey mansion are still the old abbey hall with its carved screen; the abbey church beside it is untouched, and the two stand together in their wooded green peace. The ruins (of town and abbey) are both unseen, both hidden away by beautiful modern taste, but they haunt the green lawns and the fine mansion still.

A much more wild and wood-embedded abbey ruin was, till thirty years ago, Cistercian Netley; which rivals Tintern and Melrose and Glastonbury in the number of poems it has evoked.

"But how shall I describe Netley to you?" wrote Horace Walpole to Richard Bentley (September 1755). "I can only do so by telling you that it is the spot in the world for which Mr Chute and I wish. The ruins are vast, and retain fragments of beautiful fretted roofs pendent in the air, with all variety of Gothic patterns of windows wrapped round and round with ivy—many trees are sprouted up against the walls, and only want to be increased with cypresses! A hill rises above the Abbey, encircled with wood: the fort, in which we would build a tower for habitation, remains with two small platforms. This little castle is buried from the Abbey in a wood, in the very centre, on the edge of the hill: on each side breaks in the view of the Southampton sea, deep blue, glistening with silver and vessels. . . . In short, they are not the ruins of Netley, but of Paradise. Oh! the purple abbots, what a spot had they chosen to slumber in!"

Horace took a less melancholy view of monastic life than did many of his contemporaries; the slumbering purple abbots, like those whom Pope pictured in "happy convents bosom'd deep in vines", had obviously enjoyed life at Netley, and had not passed the "long unvarying years of lonely deep despair" only enlivened by "many a secret rite", which fed the imaginations of some who gazed on "the sinking towers and mouldering walls" of ruined religious houses. Netley, according to all reports but those of Henry's visitors, had been a good and happy community;

[1]Richard Pococke, *Travels through England* (*Camden Society*, 1888).

its situation was delicious, among beautiful woods that sloped down to Southampton water, "a dense, impervious screen of luxuriant foliage"; as its chief elegist, George Keate, wrote of it in 1764, its prospects of land and sea were most agreeable, its fishponds abundant Mr Keate prefaces his poem with an account of its luckless career after the dissolution, when it "descended through the hands of various owners . . . and bears the marks of the several depredations of them all." Depredations indeed. Its

first possessor, Sir William Paulet, Marquis of Winchester, adapted part of it to form a dwelling-house; it passed later into the hands of the Marquis of Hertford, and was assaulted by parliamentarian soldiers during the civil war; some years after this it belonged to the Earl of Huntingdon (Netley seems to have been passed from hand to hand of the covetous aristocracy, and no wonder, for it was an enormously desirable residence), who enjoyed the pleasures of ruin to the full by turning the nave of the church into a tennis court, the choir into his private chapel, the chapter house into a kitchen, and other parts of the abbey into stables. In 1700, this earl having fallen on evil days through his support of James II, the next owner sold the church to a Southampton builder, who was to remove it wholly. Uneasy at the sacrilege (against which he was warned in dreams), but greedy for money, the builder began his demolitions, and had done considerable damage before he was crushed to death by the fall of the west window, and serve him right. This awful judgment for some time stayed the hands of demolishers. Some time in the eighteenth century abbey and church were acquired by an enterprising pair who had the north transept removed in order to put up a ruin in it. A good idea while it lasted; but the end of all these fantastic uses of Netley was at hand; it came into the hands of a more conventional owner, who treated what was left of it with propriety. In 1764, when Keate wrote his poem on it, such a happy issue was not looked for; he wrote it

"to preserve the memory of an ancient ruin, which has alternately suffered from weather and the ill taste of its owners, to such a degree that they who seek it a few years hence may find it only in the following description of its beauty."[1]

Fortunately, though weather has continued, ill taste has been partly stayed, and the abbey ruins now stand among their woods, stripped of ivy, encroaching trees, and fallen masonry, and wearing an aspect somewhat stark and neat—a Ministry of Works aspect—but preserved. As to the ivy, "most people prefer it without", says the abbey keeper; while as to the trees, "Well, you don't expect to find trees growing inside a church, do you," he unanswerably points out. Though really one does, when the church is part of Netley Abbey. One wonders what Mr R. A. Cram, who wrote of it in 1906, would think of it to-day.

"The treatment has been absolutely judicious; it has not been furbished up into smug neatness, as has been the case with Tintern and Kirkstall, it is not abandoned to cumulative decay, like Rievaulx. The trees and luxuriant ivy are kept well within bounds, the débris has been removed, the disintegration stopped. As a result, Netley is a faultless ruin, a thing of almost unimaginable beauty . . . a living poem . . . it is perhaps the most wholly lovely thing amongst all the abbeys of Great Britain."[2]

[1]George Keate, *The Ruins of Netley Abbey: A Poem* (1764).
[2]R. A. Cram, *The Ruined Abbeys of Great Britain* (1906).

So also, in his day, thought Mr Keate, whom it inspired to many edifying thoughts. He liked to reflect (as we do)

> "How pious Beadsmen, from the world retir'd,
> In blissful Visions wing'd their souls to Heav'n,"

and to enquire

> "Where burn the gorgeous Altars lasting fires?
> Where frowns the dreaful Sanctuary now?"

to muse on the charity of old dispensed at the gates, on the early call of the Matin bell that woke up the Fathers, on the guilty Southampton builder who had sought to destroy and had been himself destroyed, and now lies crushed beneath the Monument of Wrath, on the monkish shades that seem to walk the violated groves, on the melancholy decay, the bleak wind howling through the shattered pile, the reeling Gothic pillars and walls rent by growing trees; and finally he wished that the neighbouring young and fair should visit the ruin and learn from it that beauty is wrecked by time and that they would do well to cultivate instead Reason and Sense.

The Netley pleasures of Mr William Sotheby, who had been used when young to visit it at midnight, seem to have been less improving and more eerie; reclining upon a mossy stone, his habit had been to "call the pale spectres forth from the forgotten tombs", and to hear upon the passing wind

> "Melodious sounds in solemn chorus join'd,
> Echoing the chaunted vesper's peaceful note,"[1]

as a visionary procession floated down the vaulted aisle. Returning in his maturer years, he heard no more vespers, saw no more monks; nothing but the sea, the waving grass, the melancholy bird. He regretted the vespers and the ghostly processions; they had been the pleasures of youth, imparting the same delicious tremors that agitated those who visited Melrose Abbey by night, when

> "Strange sounds along the chancel pass'd,
> The banners wav'd without a blast . . .
> Yet somewhat was he chill'd with dread,
> And his hair did bristle on his head."

[1] William Sotheby, *Netley Abbey: Midnight* (1790).

The Netley poets and Sir Walter Scott were in more sympathy with the monastic life than many of their contemporaries; they made no reference to Superstition, a bogy liable to haunt even the most ardent fanciers of ruined monastic buildings. Even the Reverend Joseph Jefferson, in his enthusiastic verses on the little roofless and broken sixteenth-century Chapel of the Holy Ghost, standing forlornly among long grass and weeds in the old disused burial ground at Basingstoke, after his suitable reflections on mortality, vanity and time, the frailty of man and his works, and the once beauteous temple that now was mouldering walls, remarks with something less of nostalgic regret, that

"No more the cowl or rosary is known;
The Monkish garb and worship are no more;
Those walls are moulder'd where the list'ning stone
Heard Superstition frame its solemn roar."[1]

15

How soon after the destruction of the abbeys did this melancholy pleasure in their ruined grandeur and pathos begin? As regards buildings, the sixteenth and early seventeenth-century poets were still a little inexpressive; they preferred to write of pastoral scenes, when they could for a few hours detach themselves from the human species, from religion and mythology, and from the emotion of love. None the less, they and their more prosy fellow-creatures cannot have ignored the hundreds of broken monastic buildings that strewed the land; it was not only the antiquarians who observed them. Some, of course, were taken over at once, with less or more of adaptation, for private mansions; most decayed gradually into ruin, serving as quarries for builders; parts of them were incorporated into farms and barns; many stood broken and mouldering away for all to gaze on. Poor people made their homes in the ruins; two and a half centuries after the Dissolution, William Gilpin described the settlers in the great ruins of Tintern as a whole hamlet, which lived mainly by begging, or acting as guides to the ruins, "as if

[1]Joseph Jefferson, *The Ruins of a Temple* (1793).

a place once devoted to indolence could never again become the seat of industry" (Dr Gilpin, it would seem, inclined towards the "slumbering purple abbots" view of monastic life). "One woman showed us the monks' library, a place overgrown with nettles and briars, with the remains of a shattered cloister. It was where she lived—her own mansion".[1] It seems likely that such a use of abbey ruins began early, though no mention of these colonists is to be found in the pages of Camden, Leland, Stowe, or the other sixteenth-century antiquarian writers. As the memory of the living monasteries faded, and a generation grew up which had never known them but as shattered piles of lost magnificence, the homes of bats, owls, ghosts, and the homeless poor, they must have been regarded with a certain eerie dread; for one who, like the Gothic soldier, strayed from his troops "to gaze upon a ruinous monastery", there must have been hundreds who preferred to give the doubtless haunted piles a wide berth, not knowing what dubious shapes and shades might emerge from those wrecked gateways and broken cloisters. Some might have been taught that the monkish inhabitants were a good riddance, having led lives not only of sloth and superstition, but of the greatest immorality; others would have mourned them as holy men and sources of charity to the poor, and anyhow as part of the immemorial British scene and way of life. Of these last was the anonymous author (possibly, but from internal evidence improbably, Robert Southwell) of the passionately bitter lament for the wrecked shrine of Walsingham—

"In the wrackes of Walsingham
   Whom should I chuse
But the Queen of Walsingham
   to be guide to my muse;
Then thou Prince of Walsingham
   Gaunt me to frame
Bitter plaintes to rewe thy wronge
   bitter wo for thy name,
Bitter was it so to see
   The seely sheepe
Murdred by the ravening wolves
   While the sheephardes did sleep,

[1] William Gilpin, *Observations on the River Wye, etc.* (1770).

Bitter was it oh to vewe
  The sacred vyne,
While the gardiners plaied all close,
  rooted up by the swine,
Bitter bitter oh to behould
  the grasse to growe
Where the walles of Walsingam
  So stately did shewe,
Such were the workes of Walsingam
  While shee did stand,
Such are the wrackes as now do shewe
  of that holy land.
Levell Levell with the ground
  the towres do lye,
Which with their golden glitteringe tops
  Pearsed once with the skye,
Wher were gates no gates are now,
  the waies unknowen
Where the presse of peares did passe
  While her fame was blowen.
Oules do skrike wher the sweetest himnes
  lately weer songe,
Toades and serpentes hold ther dennes
  Wher the Palmers did thronge.
Weepe weepe o Walsingam
  Whose dayes ar nightes,
Blessinges turned to blasphemies
  Holy deedes do dispites,
Sinne is wher our Ladie sate,
  Heaven turned is to Hell.
Sathan sittes wher our Lord did swaye;
  Walsingam oh Farewell."

No ruin-pleasure here; we only need to compare it with the eighth-century Saxon's richly romantic dirge over the long-destroyed and fantastically imagined city of Bath, to be aware of the different note, the knell of personal grief and loss, the anguished sense of outrage.

Indeed, this sense of outraged loss still to-day mars our pleasure in abbey ruins. We look on Cistercian Beaulieu, foundered like a noble skeleton ship by its deserted port, its stones plundered for fortifications and castles, little left standing but a few walls, a few beautiful chapter house arches, the Conversorum, the refectory, converted into the remains of a fine cloister lavatory, a church, and the great Gatehouse, kept for a dwelling-house and so remaining to-day. We remember the great abbey church, whose foundations are marked in chalk, whose columns by mounds of stone, the vast stretch of the monastic buildings over forest and sward, the seven manorial gateways, the vineyards where the monks grew sour Hampshire wine, the grange farm in the forest where a ruined chapel and a huge ruined barn still stand to-day, the three centuries of prayer, work and trade that passed up and down the tidal river, the first abbot, who got into trouble with the mother house of Citeaux for drinking wassail with three earls and forty knights and being guarded in bed by a watchdog on a silver chain. *Sic transit gloria monasteriorum.*

Looking on Bellum Locum, on Tintern, on Glastonbury, those majestic shells of splendour and grace, on Rievaulx lying magnificent in its broad glen under steep green terraced cliffs, on Fountains striding across its river, on Kirkstall, demeaned into the pleasure park of a hideous Leeds suburb, on the desolation of Whitby, disintegrating in the wild salt winds on its high cliff between moor and sea—looking on these, and on the ruins of all the lost abbeys and priories that once so richly bejewelled Britain, one is moved to rage; the rage, only more bitter and personal, that assaults the mind at the sight of the churches and monasteries of Spain destroyed in periodic fits of Iberian anti-clerical fury. The destruction of the British abbeys was a crime for which there was not even that excuse, cold greed and rapacity are motives less respectable. The reports by episcopal visitors, commissioners and spies, throughout the middle ages, of monastic scandals and shortcomings are impertinent in both senses of the word; those of Henry's inquisitors are, of course, negligible. What lives were led by individual monks matters little; like lives led elsewhere, they were, no doubt, mixed. What matters is the enshrining of an idea, the splendour and incomparable grace of the buildings, the libraries, the manuscripts, the fishponds, the vineyards, the grange barns, the ordered beauty of the religious services, the hospitality, the charity at the gates, the great bells that pealed over the countryside.

It would have been possible, in our past centuries of wealth.

to have restored and rehabilitated many of the abbeys; to have filled them again with communities, of one sex or another, of one or another branch of the Christian church (it matters little which; they might be shared out, Anglicans to get most) and to have converted others into cathedrals or churches. It is not possible now; we are a ruined nation; the time may (improbably) come again, when we can afford such exquisite expenditure by ceasing to spend our all on weapons, so brittle and barbarous, of war. Losing the beauty of ruin, we should regain that of abbeys; a few ruins—perhaps Netley, Riveaulx, Glastonbury, Beaulieu, Fountains, and those which have been irrevocably and beautifully merged in secular houses—might be kept as they are, to satisfy our appetite for ruinous beauty. Nothing can restore the lost libraries, the illuminated manuscripts that after the dissolution flew about (says Aubrey) like butterflies; but the fabrics themselves could be repaired and used, appeasing thus our sense of loss.

Oddly, this sense of loss seems to have steadily grown with the passing of time. The sixteenth-century antiquarian writers show little of it. Leland and the rest describe with interest, curiosity and learning what they saw; neither regret, nor aesthetic pleasure in ruin as such, is discernible. If they admired or deplored the ruinous state, they concealed an emotion so morbid and unscholarly with carefully cool antiquarian language. They did not exclaim with delight on seeing windows wrapped in ivy, trees sprouting from walls, or end their rhapsodies, "In short, they are not the ruins of Netley, but of paradise." They examined the wrecked piles with equability, and no eighteenth-century cries of joy or grief were wrung from them by the pointed ruin peeping o'er the wood. Not like later writers did they "meditate on this world's passing pageant and the fate" of all mortality; or anyhow they did not commit such meditations to paper; they did not even admit in print, like Anthony à Wood on seeing Malmesbury, "I had a strange veneration come upon me to see the ruins of such a majestick and gigantic pile". And again at Eynsham, in 1657—

"A. W. . . . was wonderfully strucken with a veneration of the stately, yet much lamented, ruins of the abbey there, built before the Norman Conquest. . . . He spent some time with a melan choly delight in taking a prospect of the ruins of that place. . . .

The place hath yet some ruins to show, and to instruct the pensive beholder with an exemplary frailty."[1]

Such emotions, though doubtless always present in the breast of man, found little voice among English antiquarians until the seventeenth century, though English poets, and the Renaissance ruin-fanciers of Italy and France, had not been dumb to proclaim them. From the later seventeenth century on, they sound in the ears with the inevitability of the lover's sonnet to his mistress, and every ruin, religious and secular, is decorated with garlands of eloquent sensibility, garlands that get to wear, as we grow used to them, a somewhat faded and accustomed air. Only rarely, for instance, has it been given to the beholders of Glastonbury, one of the most magical of the great abbey ruins, to say of it anything new. Visitors have repeated the legends, overcome by St Joseph of Arimathea, the Holy Grail, the blossoming thorn, King Arthur, the mystique of Avalon, the martyrdom of the last abbot, and the forlorn grace and grandeur of the arches and columns on the green sward. Poems have been written on it, ghostly bells heard to ring, ghostly monks seen to walk the vanished cloisters. It was, in 1750, still mourned by the local population; Dr Pococke wrote with disapproval

"The people here seem to have learned by tradition to lament the loss of the support they had from this abbey. . . . But it is much better the poor should earn their bread by labour than be maintained in idleness."

This reflection has the air of being a defence against too deep a submersion in regret for lost beauty. Dr Gilpin, twenty years later, deeply as he admired the picturesque buildings, expounded a view of the life he believed to have been led in them when intact which afforded him considerable gratification.

"When we consider five hundred persons bred up in indolence . . . great nurseries of superstition, bigotry and ignorance; the stews of sloth, stupidity, and perhaps intemperance," and so forth, "we are led to acquiesce in the fate of these great foundations, and view their ruins not only with a picturesque eye, but with moral and religious satisfaction."[2]

[1]Anthony à Wood, *Life and Times*.
[2]William Gilpin, *Observations on the River Wye, etc.* (1770).

Similar satisfaction filled the poet who mused over Halesowen Abbey; when he saw

> "the mould'ring pile
> Where hood and cowl devotion's aspect wore,
> I trace the tottr'ing reliques with a smile
> To think the mental bondage is no more."

This strand in the complex pattern of ruin-pleasure has lamentably weakened; a century after Dr Gilpin, a cultivated visitor to Glastonbury from our late colonies across the Atlantic felt nothing of it; he saw only the ruins, beautiful in shape and colour.

"The dainty weeds and wild flowers overlace the antique tracery with their bright arabesques, and deepen the gray of the stone-work as it brightens their bloom. . . It has often seemed to me in England that the purest enjoyment of architecture was to be had among the ruins of great buildings. In the perfect building one is rarely sure that the impression is simply architectural: it is more or less pictorial and romantic; it depends partly upon association. . . . But in so far as beauty of structure is beauty of line and curve, balance and harmony of masses and dimensions, I have seldom relished it as deeply as on the grassy nave of some crumbling church, before lonely columns and empty windows where the wild flowers were a cornice and the sailing clouds a roof."[1]

Not, as he supposed, simply architectural, but more or less pictorial and romantic after all, even though he did not wander through the ghostly cloisters by night and listen for the screech-owl's note. But the essential difference between ruin-tasters of earlier centuries and those of to-day is that we appear to be less moved by what we see to moral reflections. "Its awful ruins; which, Good God! were enough to strike the most hardened heart into the softest and most serious Reflexion", commented Mr Gent on Kirkstall Abbey in 1733. Hearts are perhaps harder now, reflections less soft and serious, which may be a pity. Nevertheless, the essential feeling is the same, the impact on the senses and imagination of ancient and forlorn beauty. However great the "moral and religious satisfaction" experienced by the Reverend William Gilpin before ruined monasteries, what he

[1]Henry James, *English Hours* (Heinemann, 1905).

primarily sought and found was the picturesque. As at Brecknock—

"Amidst the gloom arose the ruins of the abbey, tinged with a bright ray, which discovered a profusion of rich Gothic workmanship, and exhibited in pleasing contrast the grey stone of which the ruins are composed, with the feathering foliage that floated round them. . . . The imagination formed it, after the vision vanished."[1]

"The imagination formed it": that is the constant and eternal element, behind all the pleasures supplied by architecture, associations, history, the grandeur of the monastic past, its supersititions, vices and corruptions, moral satisfaction over its destruction, religious lamentations over the same, investigation into the several strata of building, comparison of Benedictine, Cistercian, Augustinian, Carthusian, Premonstratensian, indignation, awe, ghosts, screech-owls, vespers whispered down the wind, the protestant view, the catholic view, the antiquarian view, the common sightseer's view of these marvels of the past (compare the Frankish awe of the ancient Greek buildings among which they settled and reared their castles—those ruins were obviously the work of "*les géants*" of some dim past, to be reverenced with half superstitious astonishment and uneasiness). But beneath all these feelings, a constant sentiment was pleasure in picturesque beauty. Dorothy Wordsworth at Riveaulx—"Green grown hillocks among the ruins . . . wild roses. I could have stayed in this solemn quiet spot till evening . . .", and at Dryburgh—"a very sweet ruin, standing so enclosed in wood. . . ."

So we have all felt and feel. The tremendousness of Fountains, flung across its smooth river, with its complex jumble of periods, stuns the imagination with magnificence; Riveaulx, too, even more actually beautiful in situation, lying in the bend of a deep river valley, beneath climbing terraces cut in the precipitous hill, and fronted with steep woods. These two great Cistercian ruins rival each other in grandeur. Fountains has the charm of rising in its ruined splendour from smooth, charming, artificially laid out pleasure grounds, constructed in 1720 to surround the abbey,

[1] William Gilpin, *Observations on the River Wye, etc., relative chiefly to Picturesque Beauty, made in the Summer of* 1770.

with every device of their style and period except artificial ruins; who could forbear not to use such heaven-given actual ruins as a centre for the landscape garden? To lay it out was a delicious pleasure, increased no doubt by the handsome Jacobean mansion that had been erected in 1611 in the abbey grounds. A huge thirteenth-century ruined abbey; an old-world mansion; a planned landscape park; the ensemble was, and is, both elegant and sublime.

Riveaulx's stance is even finer. The abbey itself has been left to progressive decay; it belonged to the first Duke of Buckingham, whose castle of Helmsley is near by. The second duke sold the abbey and grounds to Sir Charles Duncombe; it was his nephew who saw their capabilities (as Brown would have put it) as a landscape, and cut the fine terraces on the hill that rises sheer above the glen, building a circular temple at one end of the high ridge, and an elegant pavilion, adorned with paintings, at the other. From the temple one has a superb view of the abbey, standing far below. The landscape is completed by the handsome Vanbrugh mansion, Duncombe Park. In the middle of all the eighteenth-century elegance, the great thirteenth-century ruin moulders, grass-grown and tree-grown, the Gothic romance of those who gazed down on it from the belvedere on the high ridge.

> "Ah then most happy, if thy vale below
> Wash, with the crystal coolness of its rills,
> Some mould'ring abbey's ivy-vested wall,"

as one of the greatest of landscape gardeners ejaculated. Indeed, it seems odd that still more ruined abbeys have not been made the centres of planned landscapes, since an ecclesiastical touch has always been held to improve a gentleman's park, and some have set up on their estates ancient arches from some ruined church, and even a font, to add a Christian note among classical porticoes and groves of trees.

There are, besides the immense aesthetic pleasure in a good ruined abbey, a hundred minor enjoyments to be found there. There are services, pageants and mystery plays performed in many a ruinated abbey church (as annually in St Mary's, York), pilgrimages made from and to them (most enjoyably the barefoot processional walk over wet sands at low tide from the Northumbrian coast to Holy Island and Lindisfarne Priory, where Mass is celebrated among the broken pillars of the Priory church, and at the next low tide the procession paddles back.) Ruin creates sanctity, sets up shrines. Then, there are a number of pretty things one can do to ecclesiastical ruins—place saints in empty niches, hang bells in the tower, plant shrubs on broken walls, make herb gardens in cloister garths, turn vaults into grottos, paint frescoes on walls, build kirks in the nave, as the Scotch did to their dissolved abbeys, or classical temples, as did Mr Wood of Bath in 1732 in Llandaff Cathedral a century before it was restored; or imitate the young lady mentioned by Horace Walpole at Battle Abbey—"a Miss of the family has clothed a fragment of a portico with cockle shells." Other Misses have been known to swing censers and chant hymns before moss-grown altars. "Mr Chute says, what charming things we should have done if Battle Abbey had been to be sold at Mrs Chevenix's, as Strawberry was."

Thus Horace Walpole; and indeed the Abbey would, in his hands, have become something very rich and Gothic As it was, parts of it became a very fine dwelling-house; this, indeed, is one of the greatest abbey ruin-joys, and has been practised with enthusiasm for many centuries. Battle was ill-treated; its first owner after the Dissolution destroyed the church entirely, turning it into a barn and coach-house; the Abbot's Lodge is the present dwelling-house.

Much more grievously treated was Malmesbury, whose ruins impressed Anthony à Wood with a "strange veneration", and of which Aubrey lamented "Where the choir was, now grass grows, where anciently were buried kings and great men." Wood amplified this with "In place of the choir is now a garden belonging to a gentleman's house." This Saxon-built, Norman-rebuilt, Benedictine monastery, founded by Aldhelm in the seventh century, was said by William of Malmesbury in the twelfth to be larger and more beautiful than any other religious building in the country. It was, besides, a centre of learning, and produced more scholars, valuable manuscripts, and a finer library, than any of its English contemporaries but Canterbury. It was obviously a good spoil for Henry; it was suppressed, the library destroyed or sold, the abbey buildings and church sold to a rich clothier, Mr Stumpe.

"The whole lodgings of the abbey be now longing," wrote Leland in 1540, "to one Stumpe. . . . At this present time every corner of the vast houses of office that belong to th' abbey be full of looms to weave cloth in, and this Stumpe intendeth to make a street or 2 for clothiers in the back vacant ground of th' abbey that is within the town wall."[1]

This Stumpe's only merit was that he gave, or sold, the nave of the abbey church to the parish for their services, for which it is still used to-day. Otherwise he was, after Henry and his commissioners, the villain of the Malmesbury tragedy. The library was destroyed or scattered; we have Aubrey's account of how in his grandfather's days

"the manuscripts flew about like butterflies. All musick bookes, account bookes, copie bookes, etc. were covered with old manuscripts . . . and the glovers of Malmesbury made great havoc of them. Before the late warrs a world of rare manuscripts perished hereabout."[2]

The great-grandson of Mr Stumpe the clothier in Aubrey's day had some Malmesbury manuscripts still, with which he used to stop the bung-holes of beer barrels and scour guns. Many were shipped overseas for sale; the ruin was more complete than that of the abbey and church. Of that we have left nine bays of the shattered nave, "an abbreviated trunk, shorn of its towers, choir, transepts, chapels and west front"; it is ill-kept, and has a deformed appearance, though it still stands with a certain magnificence on its hill above the town; the monastic buildings, after Mr Stumpe and his cloth mills had passed, were used as a stone quarry; according to precedent, the Abbot's Lodge became a dwelling-house.

In 1662 Anthony à Wood, visiting Abingdon,

"saw the ruins of the most ancient and stately abbey that once stood there; but these ruins are since gone to ruin. A great scandal it is, that that most noble structure should now have little or no memory of it left."[3]

[1] John Leland, *Itinerary*.
[2] John Aubrey, *Natural History of Wiltshire*.
[3] Anthony à Wood, *Life and Times*.

What Wood saw was more ruinous than what we see to-day. There was the great gateway, used then as a prison, now as part of the Borough Council chambers, the porter's lodge, now gone, the old hospital, used by the Corporation for their meetings, and one wing of it for the grammar school, the Elizabethan cottages along the millstream, built in the old granary, bakehouse, and malt houses; the cottages were pulled down a few years ago, and the ancient buildings reconditioned. In one of them a gaily-painted little theatre now flourishes. The thirteenth-century Checker, with lancet-windowed chimney, the Long Gallery, with its arched, timbered roof, were both used in the seventeenth century in various disguising ways, their doors and windows knocked about, the whole structure maltreated. Now, in the hands of the Friends of Abingdon, they are being excavated and restored, so far as funds permit, to something nearer their original form. The last war was a set-back, for, urged on by the strange mania for hiding stores of food about the country, as a dog hides bones (to be consumed in what emergency, the God of battles alone knows), the authorities knocked to pieces two beautiful fourteenth-century doors to admit loads of tinned nourishment. This vandalism was, it seems, permitted by the Borough Council, which now talks of destroying and carting away as unsafe the elaborate Victorian Gothic ruin folly in the public gardens near by. It is said, however, that better advice may prevail, and lead instead to the labelling and identifying of the various parts of these ruins; some were taken from St Helen's church when it was restored.

The jumbled medley of the fragments that remain of one of our greatest, most ancient and most famous Saxon-founded Benedictine abbeys, has a tranquil and sedate appearance, standing in its quiet corner above the millstream beside the spirited little town that always hated and fought and sometimes partly destroyed it. The tranquillity of these adapted, transformed, disguised monastic buildings is very admirable and touching; they stand as if awaiting some future rehabilitation, patient, regretful, proud in their shorn dignity, achieving a mellow beauty of their own.

There is no mellow beauty in the savagely ruinous, cliff-like fragments that stand in a corner of the public gardens at Reading; the only compensations they offer are dignity and pride; the same dignity and pride with which their last abbot, Hugh, refusing meek surrender to royal rapacity, was dragged to the gallows outside his mighty abbey. Taken by the same royal rapacity for use as an occasional palace, "the monastery", says Camden, "was converted into a royal seat, adjoining to which stands a fair stable, stored with noble horses of the king." All the same, plundering and demolition began at once, and continued; lead and timber from the roofs, stones for building bridges and streets and churches; the great church was soon roofless, and the painted windows without glass. Henry often stayed there, with his horses; in 1625 when the plague raged in London, Charles I spent the Michaelmas term there, using the monastic buildings for law courts. In 1643 the royalist troops garrisoned the abbey with much damage, setting up a fort across the cloisters and nave; while the parliamentary army banged away at its walls. Surprisingly after all this—but abbeys are tough—a survey made in 1650 shows a great deal left of it, and a good part of the church. The abbey lands were parcelled out among those who built small houses and kept dove-houses in the gardens. Among the ruins was built a new county gaol. Through the eighteenth and much of the nineteenth centuries the abbey stood as a quarry for the town. A town hall was built which demolished the refectory; in 1835 the site and the ruins were sold to the town corporation, which promptly allowed a Roman Catholic church to be built, destroying one transept of the church; a gaol and Baptist schools destroyed the other transept. In all the neighbouring walls one may see bits of the abbey built; indeed, the abbey stones largely maintain the bridges and streets of Reading and its environs; hence the quarried ruin we now see.

In the dull modernity of the biscuit town, in the most banal of public gardens, these massive towering vestiges of greatness strike an alien note of fear and gloom; they loom with a menacing majesty which suggests that the visits to it, in its palace phase, of the royal robber and his successors may have been haunted with unease; the abbot done to death at his gates can scarcely have been a comfortable ghost. Anyhow, royalty abandoned it in the end.

44 The Temple of Poseidon, Sunium. Water-colour by Wm. Pars, 1764-6

45 Cave Temple, Elephanta. Aquatint by Thomas Daniell, 1799

46 The Churchyard in the snow. Oil painting by Caspar David Friedrich, 1810

16

Reading's fate was more dignified than that of many of the Scotch abbeys, assaulted in war by the enemy neighbour, in religious disapproval by Caledonian reformers, mutilated and deformed into Presbyterian kirks, bickered over by the local lairds, who quarrelled unceasingly and tartly for places for their burial and pews for their worship, built about with ugly houses and shops, falling gradually into decay. William Lithgow, a zealous protestant Scot who hated "the calumnious and vituperious Papists, the miscreant and miserable Atheists, the peevish and self-opinionating Puritanes" and "irreligious and disdainful Nullifidians" with a fine impartiality, complained sharply of what

"Mr Knoxe did with our glorious Churches of Abbacies and Monasteries (which were the greatest beauty of the Kingdome) knocking all downe to desolation; leaving naught to be seene of admirable Edifices, but like to the Ruines of Troy, Tyrus and Thebes, lumpes of Walls and heapes of stones."[1]

After Mr Knox had done his job, the forlorn abbeys became a prey to squatters, to quarriers, to citizens who divided the buildings and lands among themselves, and kept part of the church for a kirk. Shops, houses and mean streets sprang up round the great walls.

"Instead of lonely ruins hidden in shielding forests, forgotten often of man, we find the glories of ancient Scotland jostled by taverns, workshops and inns, rising sheer, not from green meadows or amongst tangled thickets of thorns, but out of unseemly assemblages of shops and houses crowding up into cloister and graveyard, obliterating every trace of chapter house, refectory, dorter, even in some cases of portions of the church itself."[2]

It would seem that, of the great Scottish ecclesiastical ruins, only Elgin and Dryburgh, standing among their woods, have been preserved from this squalid entourage. Yet there is dramatic pleasure in the towering beauty of Jedburgh, for instance, rising unexpectedly and improbably from its crowded surroundings, rather as the Forum of Trajan used to from huddled streets,

[1] William Lithgow, *Comments upon Scotland* (1628).

[2] R. C Cram, *The Ruined Abbeys of Great Britain* (Gay & Bird, 1906).

striking the eye with amaze. Melrose is less wholly surrounded, less sudden, can be approached on two sides from open space; but it too has the effect of a noble incongruity, apart from its rich poetic and pictorial elaboration of beauty. The haunted romantic gloom of Melrose as a ruin'd pile so worked on Scott that he transferred his sense of it to the medieval, still presumably unruined abbey visited by Sir William Deloraine; one must assume that it was this knight's peculiar mission of disinterring a skeleton that induced strange sounds in the chancel, caused the banners to wave without a blast, and Sir William's hair to bristle on his head. He never, anyhow, saw "the broken arches black in night" that impressed later visitors. The beauty of Melrose is largely in its rich architectural detail, and, as in all the Scottish abbeys, in the succession of one style on another, from Norman to perpendicular. Elgin cathedral and Dryburgh add to splendour of architecture the romance of forest setting. A good setting is, to the average ruin-seer, a good deal more important than interesting architecture; these need some background of knowledge; the pleasures of picturesque setting, only a simple sense of beauty. It was mainly the attractive mountain valley setting of the ruins of the twelfth-century Llanthony Priory (built for Austin canons, who, finding the Welsh country and countrymen barbarous, deserted it for Gloucester) which caused Walter Savage Landor to fall in love with it and buy it. He began to build in it a house for himself and his bride; in three years he had quarrelled with his neighbours, as the Austin canons had in a shorter time, and with the estate managers, and abandoned his scheme. When Turner drew the abbey a few years later, the half-built house was still there; afterwards it was replaced by a farm and by the Abbey Hotel, which stands in the prior's house. There is not much left of the monastic buildings; but dilapidated ruins of the church remain. There are fragments of walls and foundations; and, in a barn west of the church, a fine arch that was once the abbey gateway. The group of buildings has a beauty that even the hotel cannot spoil.

An extra-ecclesiastical aura of magnificence surrounds the noble ruins of episcopal palaces; they are haunted less by the gods than by the prelates and princes of the church who once habited there. Looking on the glorious shell of St David's palace, or on Wells reflected in its moat, or on any other of these shattered prides, one recalls the great line of lawn-sleeved church lords, all those whom Milton, who could not think of them without rage, called "swan-eating, canary-sucking prelates", soon to be, he confidently hoped, "the trample and spurn of all the damned." Less episcophobe gazers on these ruined habitations cannot view them without wistful regret for that lost feudal sanctity and grandeur; bishops feel a sad nostalgia.

17

There is no adequate account of all the vicissitudes in the careers of the dissolved abbeys that passed into private hands; historians are apt to record every trivial incident of their ecclesiastical history, which they ploddingly transcribe from monastic registers—("in 1182 the abbey granted 5 hydes to Roger Fitzbeef", and so on)—and deal with their even more fascinating secular development, if at all, in the cursory and chancy manner of those who have neither the skill nor the enterprise to look into it. There is here a wonderful subject awaiting its historian—abbeys into houses. Some were taken over with little alteration, like Rothley Temple, where the Templar's chapel remains unchanged in the Tudor house into which the temple was transformed after the suppression of the Knights of St John who had inherited it from the Templars in 1306. The then Turcpolier, a Babington, took it over for his private mansion; it has, until lately, been in the hands of this family. More often, most of the monastic buildings were pulled down, and the new mansion built on their site, with fragments of the ruin incorporated, as at Mottisfont Priory near Romsey, which was turned by Lord Chamberlain Sandys into "a goodly place," where he "intends to live most of his life", wrote a priest in 1538; but large pieces of the Priory were kept—a carved stone pulpit in the canons' choir that had become the back kitchen, a vaulted undercroft, beneath which tools and potatoes now lie, some medieval arcading, parts of the ancient arches in the eighteenth-century windows of the Georgian house, a piscina sanctifying a bedroom. Other priories, such as Gracedieu in Leicestershire, are mere ruins lying beside the new house.

Everywhere one sees traces of churches in village cottages and old inns and farm buildings; at Shaftesbury in 1754 Dr Pococke saw remains of the several vanished Shaftesbury churches in houses in the town, and at the Swan inn a painted glory going up to the roof at the east end. At Wharton in Lancashire "opposite the church is an old ruin they call the priory; it is now the Vicarage house." (Since then the vicarage has been improved.) Constantly Dr Pococke and other tourers of the country observe "Here Mr —— has a fine house, on the site of the old monastery, some of whose ruins are preserved": one might get the impression that more old mansions than not are monastic in origin or site, and that the monastic remains have always been considered to improve them. As the fine house built by Mr Aislabie and improved by Mr Hunter where Waverley Abbey had stood: "the grand front of the house is to the garden, which is laid out in lawn, wood and winding walks near the river. The ruins of the monastery add no small beauty to it. A building which seems to have been the refectory is pretty entire." Such abbey and priory houses abound; perhaps the best description of one of them is Henry James's of Wenlock Abbey, where he stayed with the owner.

"I returned to the habitation of my friend . . . through an old Norman portal, massively arched and quaintly sculptured, across whose hollow threshold the eye of fancy might see the ghosts of monks and the shadows of abbots pass noiselessly to and fro. This aperture admits you to a beautiful ambulatory of the thirteenth century—a long stone gallery or cloister, repeated in two storeys . . . with its long, low, narrow, charming vista still perfect and picturesque, with its flags worn away by monkish sandals and with huge round-arched doorways opening from its inner side into great rooms roofed like cathedrals. These rooms are furnished with narrow windows of almost defensive aspect, set in embrasures three feet deep and ornamented with little grotesque medieval faces. To see one of the small monkish masks grinning at you while you dress and undress . . . is a mere detail in the entertainment of living in a *ci-devant* priory. This entertainment is inexhaustible; for every step you take in such a house confronts you in one way or another with the remote past. . . . Adjoining the house is a beautiful ruin, part of . . . the magnificent church administered by the predecessors of your host, the mitred abbot.

. . It is but an hour's walk to another great ruin. . . . There . . . the round arches and massive pillars of the nave make a perfect vista on the unencumbered turf. You get an impression that when catholic England was in her prime great abbeys were as thick as milestones. . . . The abbey was in those days a great affair; it sprawled, as my companion said, all over the place. As you walk away from it you encounter it still in the shape of a rugged outhouse enriched with an Early English arch, or an ancient well hidden in a kind of sculptured cavern. . . . After spending twenty-four hours in a house that is six hundred years old, you seem yourself to have lived in it six hundred years. You seem yourself to have hollowed the flags with your tread and to have polished the oak with your touch. You walk along the little stone gallery where the monks used to pace, looking out of the Gothic window-places at their beautiful church, and you pause at the big, round, rugged doorway that admits you to what is now the drawing room. The massive step by which you ascend to the threshold is a trifle crooked, as it should be; the lintels are cracked and worn by the myriad-fingered years . . . you look up and down the miniature cloister before you pass in; it seems wonderfully old and queer Then you turn into the drawing room, where you find modern conversation and late publications and the prospect of dinner. The new life and the old have melted together; there is no dividing line."[1]

This may serve, with differences, as a description of many once monastic dwelling-houses in England. A few have preserved wall paintings, like Shulbrede Priory, hidden in the heart of Sussex woods, with its Nativity animals. All are excessively English: the medieval abbey or priory that has become the Tudor mansion or farm-house, later the Stuart or Georgian medley; there is, indeed, no dividing line. One friary, that of the Carmelites at Aylesford, turned after the Dissolution into an Elizabethan mansion, but having kept much of its medieval structure—the long refectory, the fine gatehouse, part of the cloisters, and a watergate leading to a quay beside the Medway—has been lately restored and returned to the Carmelites.

In the slums about Oxford railway station lies the site of the magnificent Osney, beloved of the sixteenth and seventeenth-century antiquarians, doted on by Aubrey, who had drawings of

[1] Henry James, *Abbeys and Castles* (1877) from *English Hours* (Heinemann, 1905).

the ruins made by a hedge-priest and presented to the Ashmolean and to Dugdale for his *Monasticon*, a few years before they were pulled down. "*Quid digni feci hic process viam?*" he asked himself when he was twenty-seven, and replied "Truly nothing; only umbrages, Osney abbey ruines, etc., antiquities." To-day there is nothing of them above ground; a cemetery, and a small chapel with a door apparently permanently locked, mark the site. Walk three miles to the north-west, and, lying among the fields by Godstow bridge, you will find all that is left of Godstow nunnery—a broken wall round a grassy space where farm cattle graze, the remains of a chapel, two windows; nettles and high grass grow round it; even the farm buildings which Godstow became are fallen to nothing. Passers along the field path sometimes turn aside and look for a minute at all that remains of the dwelling of Henry II's Rosamund, haunted now only by farm workers and farm animals.

18

Godstow in its fields, beside its little stream and ancient bridge, seems a ruin typically English Celtic ruins, usually in a wilder setting, wear another look. Ireland, that land of ecclesiastical and other ruins, is strewn every few miles with abbeys (mostly Anglo-Norman of the twelfth and thirteenth centuries, smaller, on the whole, than the English abbeys, and less fine in architecture), Franciscan friaries, and fifth, sixth and seventh century Celtic oratories and churches. These oratories and monastic buildings, small, solid, often beehive-shaped, founded by the Irish missionary saints, often escaped wrecking by the Danish pirates owing to their inaccessibility; built on rocky islands off the west coast or in lonely lakes, or on mountain-tops, they need resolute seeking. In these lonely, wild resorts, the early missionaries made their centres among sea birds and rocks; to reach St Finan's monastery on the Great Skellig rock, one crosses seven and a half miles of uneasy sea and climbs six hundred steps. Pilgrims have done penance by climbing the highest rock peak, above the ruined oratories and cells. It is this kind of setting that gives the early Celtic monasteries their peculiar, intimidating fascination. Most of the oratories and churches are tiny, desolate, remote: one remembers that from these hut-like monastery cells Christianity radiated over Europe, as well as from the centres of light and learning in the plains—St Columba's Kells, wrecked by the Danes, Clonfert on the Shannon, with its cathedral that succeeded Brendan's monastery, Clonmacnoise, that huddle of crumbling chapels and belfries, gravestones and crosses, to which Alcuin and Charlemagne did honour, and which founded houses in Europe that still live, St Kevin's Glendalough, desolate between mountains and lake, that miraculous group of buildings behind its gateway—a hermit's cell that grew into a monastery, into a college, into a town; Dane-destroyed, it keeps its ruined cathedral, its little ruined churches, its high bell-tower, the two-storeyed oratory; at week-ends it is dense with visitors. Of late years it has been furbished up, the cathedral restored, the Round Tower re-capped, little St Saviour's Priory built up into neatness; it no doubt looked better before; about a hundred and twenty years ago Mr and Mrs Hall wrote of St Saviour's that only two of its sculptured pillars were in good condition, the ruin being overgrown with brambles, and a mountain ash growing through a wall; their illustration shows a ruin indeed. They found Glendalough very gloomy and delightful—

"the bare mountains which so completely environ it, giving a character of peculiar gloom—in solemn and impressive harmony with the ruins of remote ages—churches unroofed and crumbling, oratories levelled to the height of humble graves; sculptured crosses shattered into fragments; broken pillars, corbels, and mouldings, of rare workmanship; gorgeous tombs of prelates and princes confused with the coarse headstones of the peasants; and the mysterious round tower . . . standing high above them all! In contemplating these worn-down and subdued relics of ancient power,

> "A weight of awe, not easy to be borne,
> Fell suddenly upon our spirit—cast
> From the dread bosom of the unknown past."

". . . Mr Nicholl, who searched the ruins with exceeding care and perseverance, informs us there is scarcely a stone in the vicinity that did not afford some subject for his pencil, although they were nearly all broken."[1]

[1]Mr and Mrs S. C. Hall, *Ireland: scenery, character, etc* (1841).

Now visitors throng Glendalough to admire, and to enjoy that "weight of awe" from the past, and the beauty of the ruinous vestiges among mountains and lake of five hundred years of monastic culture.

Cashel, too, is tourist-beset. The famous Rock towers precipitate over the shabby little town and the rich, treeless, mountain-bounded vale of Tipperary; the ruined thirteenth-century cathedral stands like a fort, a Gothic mass of stone, roofless and collapsed, a high Round Tower by its north transept, a castle in its west end, ruins of abbeys and walls lying round it, the beautiful little twelfth-century Cormac's Chapel nestling against its south wall. Here, in this small corbel-roofed, arcaded-walled chapel, is Irish Romanesque, that fleeting, lovely decoration that the Anglo-Norman invasion was to check, at its richest and most beautiful. The carved, zigzagged round entrance porch suggests in its exuberance a chaster manueline. Visitors complain that both the chapel and the cathedral were more romantic when they stood wholly ruinous among their old walls and abbey remains and nettles and weeds and piles of boulders; now they are rescued from decay, tidied up, pieced together, thronged about with week-end admirers, and preserved by the Ministry of Works. Even so, their beauty staggers and disturbs. Like other Irish ecclesiastical ruins and restorations, like Jerpoint Abbey, like Graiguenamanagh, both Cistercian (the latter disagreeably restored and vulgarized but still the remains of the great walls of the English abbey of Duiske rove round the little town in strange sadness), like the ruined abbeys and churches strewn every few miles over Ireland, in a profusion of beauty for the most part less architectural than picturesquely desolate, Cashel weighs on us with melancholy. This Irish melancholy—one can feel it in Kilkenny, the one-time capital of the English Pale, with its shattered old cathedral, its smart new one, its ruined abbeys and friaries along the Nore, its English-town and Irish-town, its alleys and lanes, where Gothic doorways and carved pillars support mean houses, its memories of the Kilkenny Statute that put the Irish in their place in the fourteenth century, of the parliament of Confederate Catholics of 1642, of Cromwell's siege of 1650, that smashed up the cathedral and its glass. Now Kilkenny has gone native again; the "mere Irish" are in possession; the descendants of the Pale could repeat in their own sense the Gaelic lament for the dispossessed MacCarthy lords of Killarney—

"The heart within my breast this night is wild with grief
Because of all the haughty men who ruled this place
From Cashel and from Thomond to the wave beneath
None lives, and where they lived lives now an alien race."

But it is the dispossession of the ancient Catholic glory of Ireland that gives Irish church and monastic ruins their grief. Here once was a Church that travelled the world, mixing on equal terms with the great Churches of Europe, intellectually at one with the great scholastic foundations of France, Germany, Italy, Britain, founding continental daughter-houses, peopling them with Irish monks, conversing at Charlemagne's court, illuminating manuscripts and writing poems, inventing its own architecture, building abbeys that held towns within their walls—here, its exquisite broken ruins behind us, was such a Church once. Among the ruins now rise the brash modern chapels and churches that represent the Irish Church to-day, bemeaned and deflowered by the bitter centuries of persecution which, though they could not crush it out of existence, plucked from it the proud flower of its intellect and breeding, reducing it to a devout provincialism. It is a fact that one cannot travel more than a few miles in Ireland without passing some broken abbey or church; they lie strewn along coast and river, hill and plain, island and lake-side, in ruinous profusion. Destroyed by Danes, by Normans, by Englishmen, by decay, by time, by poverty, vandalism and dissolution, their crumbling arches and portals and fragments of wall stand in reproachful witness to the passing of a murdered culture.

19

In Wales, too, church and abbey ruins abound. They always have. All through the middle ages the Welsh ecclesiastical foundations suffered rapine and assault; every Norman and English raid, every rebellion and its suppression, every baronial disturbance, every outbreak of Owen Glendower, left in its wake a trail of smashed and plundered churches and monastic buildings. The royal ruffians in turn took their will of them; the Edwards, Richards, Henrys and their agents looted and sacked; when the last Henry had his turn, the abbeys he dissolved and spoiled were many of them already in ruin, their revenues given away to English colleges. The native population disliked them as foreigners, as rich, as reputedly immoral, as pets of Rome, (for they claimed exemption from episcopal authority and to be subject to the Pope alone) above all, as bad neighbours, robbing the land from its owners, the tithes from the local parish priests, the very churches themselves. Gerald of Wales, who hated the Cistercians in particular, added a new clause to the Litany—"*A monachorum malitia, maxime vero Cisterciensium, libera nos, Domine*". Indeed, Cistercian avarice was extreme. Richard I, accused of having three daughters, Pride, Licentiousness and Avarice, replied, "I have already given them away: Pride to the Templars, Licentiousness to the black monks, Avarice to the white." If we are to believe contemporary comments, all monastic orders began well and soon declined. Whatever their moral errors, the Cistercians set their glorious houses beautifully about the wild glens and hills of Wales, often choosing sanctuaries already long hallowed by Celtic monastic cells. Still the ruins gape about glens and hills; Tintern, Valle Crucis, Strata Florida, Cwmhir, Margam, Neath, Whitland; others wholly gone to earth. Tintern has, one supposes, given as much high poetic pleasure to ruin-gazers as even the finest English abbeys. Valle Crucis, too; there is more of it than of any other abbey in north Wales, and its position above the Dee is magnificent. As to Strata Florida, once "the Westminster Abbey of Wales", with a church larger than St David's cathedral, with its granges scattered over many acres, there is little left but the west portal, two ruined small buildings, and some fourteenth-century tiles. Strata Florida was destroyed and despoiled many times before the dissolution; Henry IV and his destructive son sacked it, but it partly recovered, and died richer than most. Its stones were used for a seventeenth-century mansion afterwards turned into a farm-house; the abbey and lands later passed into the hands of an old Welsh family. The grandeur of the vanished abbey haunts the lonely site, where a small parish church now stands; here princes came, and bards, here wars and sieges raged, here are the graves of poets and great chiefs. To-day the curlews cry over the wild bog-lands of the Teifi, and the waters of the Teifi pools whisper against the reeds, and if you turn up the earth among the ruins you may come on some fragments of broken medieval tile.

To Dr Pococke, who enjoyed mansions, the ruins of Margam abbey, though beautiful and containing a fine chapter house, gave less pleasure than the great house which had been built out of the abbey by the Mansell family, with its beautiful orangery and its fine timbered park; the house, said Pococke, "might be improved into a very beautiful thing"; the fine stables were adorned with stucco fretwork and carved stalls, the summer-house with a grand walnut staircase, Corinthian balustrade, marble decoration and inlaid floors. Abbeys, the doctor thought, might, and often did, end much worse. Neath ended worse; some of its buildings, including the abbot's house, grew into a seventeenth-century mansion, but coal, iron and copper grew around them, and they lie in their beautiful valley blackened with smoke.

It would have been pleasant to see Llandaff cathedral two hundred years ago, when Pococke visited it. It had decayed into ruin during two centuries of neglect and robbery; its canons in 1540, excited by the general monastic pillage, had torn up its shrines and stolen its gold plate; in 1575 the Bishop told the chapter that it must be repaired forthwith, "lest it should perish utterly"; twenty years later it was still ruinous and decayed, the paving torn up and pits dug in the aisles, "more like a desolate and profane place than like a house of prayer", and no revenues to repair it with; at the beginning of the seventeenth century it was "tottering with age and threatening to fall". Parliamentary troopers during the civil war, calling in during the communion service on Easter morning to arrest the celebrating priest and drink the consecrated wine, did further damage. Repairs were never adequate, complaints of the ruinous state of floors, walls and roof continued through the century; at last, in the 1720's, much of the building was destroyed by storm. It was time to do something drastic; Bishop Harris decided to leave the west end of the roofless nave and the two towers in ruins, and to erect a very neat and elegant Italian-style church within the rest of the cathedral. The bishop thought it looked very well, and no doubt he was right. He had planned to "finish with a rustic porch" and a tower over the front of the nave, but funds ran out. Dr Pococke thought little of the "Italian temple". "Sash windows like a play-house", he severely commented, "and a modern front of Roman architecture, and the East end in the same style, with a Venetian window, so that altogether it is the most absurd improvement that ever was made." "A new church, in debased Italian style," say other critics, "was planted among the ruins." In engravings, the effect of the little classical church standing in the ruined thirteenth-century cathedral is peculiar but agreeable. Near it stood the gateway of the ruined Bishops' Palace; an inn was built over it, and the sign "The Bush Inn" hung above it. Later all the cathedral dwelling-houses became farm buildings, round them cows stood in the fields. All this was tidied up in the middle of the nineteenth century, when the cathedral was at last restored, and the little un-Gothic temple within it demolished; a few relics of it decorate the present episcopal garden. Llandaff is picturesque no more. In 1941 it became a bomb-ruin; it is now being repaired. Its bombed, roofless state induces comparisons. These modern war ruins have an air of painful futility that stirs anger; an anger less often roused by the no less criminal and futile catastrophes of the past. The destructive bestiality was the same; but usually the long years, the swathing ivy and the thrusting trees, the extreme beauty which the conditions of ruin can create, muffle the anger and the vexation. But the haunting gods hover about with reproachful sighs: one cannot forget.

In Wales particularly one feels disgust, turning from the lovely vestiges of greatness to what has replaced them: the mean, brash little conventicles that spatter the wild countryside with their ugliness. Most are dissenting chapels; some are Roman Catholic; in appearance there is little to choose. The Anglican churches are usually better, because older. But what must Wales have looked like with abbeys and priories, their granges and monastic buildings, rising in glens and valleys, on mountain and river side, all about its land? Hugh Latimer begged that a few religious houses might be left in each shire, "not in monkery, but so as to be converted to preaching, study and prayer"; but, since Henry's aim was neither to destroy monkery nor to encourage preaching, study and prayer, this would have seemed to him silly. It is an agreeable fancy, communities of clerkly scholars studying the reformed religion and the new learning in the libraries, halls and cloisters of Valle Crucis, Tintern and Strata Florida, dispensing the sacraments according to the reformed rite at their ancient altars, emerging to preach the word to their wild flocks on those wild hills.

20

What we most miss in British church ruins are the fragments of Rome. For these we must go to the countries where Rome left more lasting monuments. All about Italy we find them; dwelling-houses formed of monastic buildings that had been built on Roman foundations, built between Roman columns, circled by Roman walls. Like Sant Antonio at Tivoli, emptied of its monks in the last century and bought for seventy pounds by a Harrow master about fifty years ago; its cellar is an atrium with mosaic pavements and a perfect honeycombed nymphaeum; reputed, like so many ruined Tivoli and near-Tivoli villas to have belonged to Horace, it is surrounded by the sites or remains of the alleged dwellings of Cynthia, Maecenas, Cassius, Catullus, Quintilius, Varus; all the ruins anyone could ask to look at from his windows, with the Anio, the cascades, and the slopes of olive-grown mountains for background. All about the Campagna, all about Italy, such domesticated ecclesiastical ruins grow, seemingly as natural products of the soil as vines and olives. In Spain, too; to a less extent in France and Germany; French abbey ruins are more apt, when not left to decay away, to become public buildings, lycées, or factories, though many are used as farm-houses and barns, and some have been partly absorbed by châteaux and manoirs; among these last are the splendid and spectacular remains of Jumièges, which stand in private grounds, magnificently untamed, and Bec, whose towered gateway admits us to a modern château garden. The comparative fewness of abbeys-into-houses among a thrifty and utilitarian people is probably due to the fact that the revolutionary abbey destructions occurred in France when manors and manor-owners were under the same cloud as ecclesiastical institutions, in England at a time of lavish luxury mansion building. The most imposing use of a destroyed abbey is, perhaps, Cluny, whose Romanesque church of St Peter (the largest in Christendom before its Roman namesake was rebuilt) was almost demolished; all one sees of it to-day is fragments of a transept, an octagonal tower, a few fifteenth-century chapels, a ruined apse. The huge abbey was built into a town; the cloisters surround a public square, the abbot's palace houses a museum, other parts of the monastic buildings a school of arts and sciences, the church a breeding stud. Among these worldly modernities, the temporal and spiritual magnificence of the mother of the Cluniac order broods, a fallen, pillaged kingdom whose writ no longer runs, but whispers, broken and menacing, from the ghosts of the outraged feudal abbots who reigned there. One can believe that the proud abbots would have preferred, rather than to have their wrecked kingdom thus yoked to the activities of modern secular France, that it should have been left to moulder away in solitary abandonment, a vast derelict town. Or even that it should have disappeared as almost entirely as the Cistercian Cîteaux, or as Clairvaux, where all that is left of the original abbey is engulfed in a great eighteenth-century building that is now a prison, and affords little pleasure to anyone; though possibly the austere St Bernard might dislike this less than if his abbey had served as a hôtel de ville, a dance hall, or a stud, or even, like the cloister and abbot's lodge of Lanfranc's Bec, as a gendarmerie.

As in England, picturesque ruins of the smaller abbeys lie charmingly about among orchards, woods and villages; walking or driving about France, one is detained every few miles by one of these agreeably forlorn objects—a refectory and its kitchen standing on the bank of a stream, a portal with zigzag mouldings, the fragment of a chapel with a frescoed wall, a solitary tower rising up from a meadow, an old well and a few cloister arches in an orchard, part of a broken nave, a romanesque barn with apse, sheltering waggons in a lane, a farm-house with a rose-window, a towered gate-house, arcades built into a wall green with the weeds of a duckpond, a deserted chapel grown through with trees, the faint colours of a Judgment still showing on a white-washed wall, broken cloisters choked with thorns, renaissance windows looking out from a creamy mass of magnolia blossom, a roofless oratory a-hum with bees in a deep wood, a jumble of ruined buildings on a high rock above a ravine. The harmony of shape and colour with the landscape, the ancient distinction of these derelicts that were churches and abbeys, add a rich beauty to the scene: eye and imagination are at once engaged, while indignation at the ruining that seeks to deprive us of our heritage of beauty is tempered by the beauty involuntarily achieved. As in the case of Fountains, when the question of restoration and rehabilitation was recently raised, the mind is divided. Do we wish these dead stones to live, soaring into the skies, pealing with bells, summoning to prayer, humming with religion instead of bees, sweet with incense instead of wild flowers, dispensing charity at the gates, affording shelter to travellers, lives of piety to their inmates? So far so good: but there is no doubt that the shape and picturesqueness of the buildings would be greatly spoilt, as can be seen in nearly all the reconstructed and restored churches and monastic buildings of Europe. In Spain, the restored Cartujas (for instance, that outside Jerez, so long a lovely ruin, now built up in a smart style and lived in by monks) lamentably lack taste; Poblet, that majestic Cistercian monastery in the mountains above Tarragona, wrecked by the French fury of 1812 and the Spanish anti-clerical fury of 1835, was still, before restoration, a tremendous sight, with its battlemented walls and towered gateway, its great cloister on the model of Fontfroide, its wrecked abbots' palace and church. Augustus Hare, writing in 1870, called it

"the very abomination of desolation . . . the most utterly ruined ruin that can exist. Violence and vengeance are written on every stone. The vast walls, the mighty courts, the endless cloisters, look as if the shock of a terrible earthquake had passed over them. . . . Surely no picture that the world can offer of the sudden destruction of human power can be more appalling than fallen Poblet, beautiful still, but most awful in the agony of its destruction."

Hare looked on Poblet with fascinated horror; the local peasantry with triumphant delight in the ruin of the monastic tyranny they had hated and feared. Now that Poblet is restored and once more inhabited, it has lost that picturesque stagey air of grand tragedy that haunts great ruins, and particularly the ecclesiastical ruins of Spain, where the tragedy is sharpened by the angry hatred which impelled the destroyers. The lately ruined churches, in their raw, blackened, shattered desolation, give no pleasure, wear no dignity. Hare was perhaps too near to 1835, as the Elizabethans were too near the Dissolution; Ford, who wrote Murray's first Spanish Handbook, too near the horrors of the French occupation; Cicero and his friends too near the Roman destructions in Greece; all of us to-day too near the bombing that wrecked Caen and Monte Cassino and our City churches: passions have not cooled, the lichen has not grown. Ruin-pleasure requires a gulf of years; seeking it, we find enough.

All about the mountains of Spain the great ruined Benedictine abbeys tower, abandoned, wrecked and plundered, but indomitably majestic, seeming still to dominate and command the villages at their feet; like San Pere de Roda on its mountain above the little Costa Brava fishing port of Selva, brooding, a sombre solitary broken pile of magnificence, over Ampurdán and the sea. With variety of national and local idiom, the ruined abbeys brood thus about all the Latin lands. In Spain, Christian churches rise on Roman temples, which became Moorish mosques, then Christian churches again; ruin growing on ruin with the slow admirable rhythm of the centuries. In Italy and France, pagan churches developed with less abrupt transitions into Christian; a duomo is built in the ruins of a temple, its portico has Roman columns on medieval bases; Roman pavement lies together with twelfth-century mosaic. Roofless medieval abbeys stand (as at Falleri) among Etruscan walls and tombs, approached by cart tracks winding under Roman gates; a ruined Romanesque church stands on a mountain on the site of a vanished Etruscan village named after Hercules; through the piers of the famous imperial bridge over the gorge below Narni is seen a ruined convent on a rock; Volscian altars and columns, Etruscan and Roman, bear witness to the Etruscan temple of the goddess Norcia, in the city of miracles Bolsena, which is haunted by Christian legends and Etruscan and Roman gods; at Aquino a partly ruined twelfth-century church stands above a flight of marble Roman steps, on the foundations of a temple of Hercules; its façade, now restored and altered, had a portico of antique pillars; near it is a Corinthian arch; other Aquino churches are built out of temples to Diana and Ceres; above it towers Monte Cassino with its great abbey rising again from destruction. At Terracina the

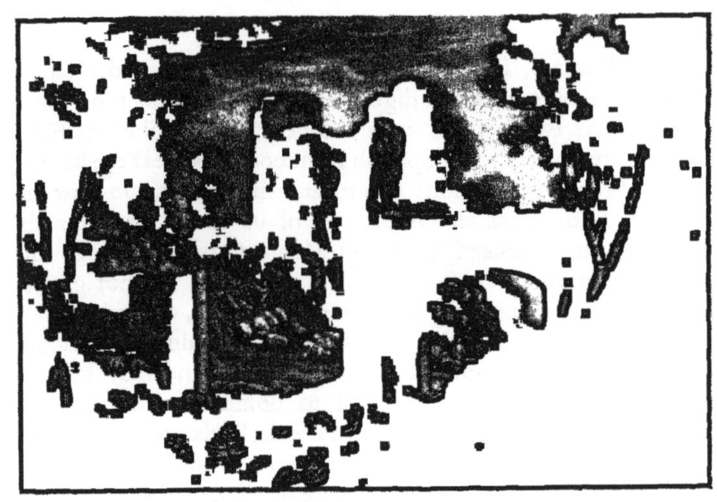

47 East Gate, Winchelsea, Sussex Etching by J. M W Turner, 1819

48 Church ruin, Bacharach on the Rhine. Water-colour by John Gardner (1729-1808)

49 Tintern Abbey Water-colour by J. M. W. Turner, 1794

cathedral stands on the ruins of a Roman temple and is full of its columns; at Syracuse the walls of the seventh-century duomo rose on the great Doric columns of the sixth century B.C. temple of Athene, once, says Cicero, the most magnificent building of Syracuse with its golden adornments that shone over the sea, a beacon to sailors. Now the cathedral walls rise between its columns, which stand also inside; the massive grandeur is in piquant contrast with the animated eighteenth-century baroque façade. Archaeologists, wrote Renan, were for freeing the ancient temple, and building a new cathedral. But "*quel temple savamment restauré vaut cette cathédrale bâtie dans un temple dorique? . . . J'ai vu peu d'effets d'un pittoresque aussi complet*".

One meets similar picturesqueness all over the lands that are heirs to Greece and Rome; everywhere the temples of the new faith climbing on and within the ruins of the old; or the old supports, with massive broken columns, some peasant's farm-house on an olive-grown hillside. Everywhere the ancient and the later gods meet together in the cities, on the mountains and in the wooded valleys. Even when the haunted relics of the ancient gods are unseen, they are felt; as in the shattered walls of the abbey of San Pietro in Palazzolo, standing solitary on its forested hill above the Masserella torrent, built on who knows what pagan site? Or those wild mountain church ruins in the Abruzzi, such as the broken tower, apse and walls of the Benedictine abbey of Santa Maria di Cartignano, standing among heath and olive-trees and rough grass, subject to Montecassino, ruined long ago, but preserving in its apse a thirteenth-century fresco of Christ between the Madonna and St John, which seems to uphold the Christian god against the beleaguering pagan deities of wood and hillside and river, who have through the centuries worked slowly to destroy the blessed place In the eighth-century Benedictine ruin of San Vincenzo al Volturno, near the source of that sinuous river, which serpentines round and round the monastery, the old gods have won a victory, for little more than the arches of the portico remain; the church was built partly out of the remains of a temple. The church of the abbey of San Leonardo, in the hills above Foggia, now a farm-house, is rich with cupola, apse, and magnificently sculptured portal; further on is the only slightly ruined though long abandoned church on the site of the vanished city of

Sipontum; it was once an archiepiscopal cathedral, built out of the stones of Sipontum, which a little later fell into complete decay when Manfredonia was founded. Santa Maria, with its Byzantine air, its rich portal, broken ancient columns, mosque-like interior, and twelfth-century crypt forested with pillars, stands solitary in the desolate Apulian landscape, above the port of Manfredonia and the green Adriatic. It looks Apulian, as the Cistercian abbey of San Galgano, progressively ruined since the seventeenth century, looks Tuscan. From north to south of Italy, one can identify the types, until modern restoration removes character and imposes a dull uniformity. To return, after years, to a ruined monastery remembered from childhood, beautiful among wild hills and rocks, torrents and woods, and find it a smart white building in a neat plateau, with cheerful monks gardening in its olive groves, is to lose a dream: the Deserto is now ruined indeed. On the whole, fine ruins should not be restored unless their use is necessary: they are part of the aesthetic kingdom of the eye and mind; like the poetry and painting of desolation, they fulfil a function. Occasionally some gay reconstruction may be made, as at Pompeii, Herculaneum, Crete; some of the Greek temples would look delightful in painted splendour on their hills. Gothic restores less attractively than classical; many of the columns of Roman temples that grow all about Italy like pine-trees, might with advantage be built up into temples again. How grandiose, for instance, would Tiberius's Villa of Jove, looming high on its Capri crag, appear, if it should be transformed from ruined Villa into the great temple of the god, standing against the sky above the pagan island.

21

Turn from the Mediterranean, the Ionian and Aegean seas, the clear, naked atmosphere of Europe, of Syria, of Asia Minor, the great temples standing in their shattered glory on pine-clad mountains, or buried in rocky valleys, or shining palely against golden deserts, or in Gothic grace among British and French landscapes, haunted by the gods of our Greek and Oriental cults; turn to the green dusk. Buried in deep jungles lie the hidden or discovered temples of the east and the west; Ceylon, Java,

Burma, parts of India, the great forests of Central and South America, the tropic swamps of Africa. The forest growths press in, swiftly, surely, stealthily, unstayably, like a sea; the trees circle around, take root in walls and roofs, thrust boughs through window jambs, finally engulf all, until, for centuries, no one can say where they once stood, where they now stand, enjungled in warm, trackless green. Then, after the lost centuries, the jungle may be searched, explored, a little cleared; and where some small settlement or village has alone been seen in the wilderness of vegetation, or not even a settlement, little by little some exquisite royal city of temples is uncovered, lying there as at the bottom of a deep, hot sargassum sea. This is what happened to the ancient Ceylon temple cities; Anuradhapura, Polonnaruwa, and other smaller groups of dagobas, many still forest-drowned. Anuradhapura is perhaps the largest ruin anywhere; it anyhow rivals Nineveh and Babylon in size. Founded in the fifth century B.C., it became the royal capital two centuries later, when it was converted to Buddhism, and received a cutting from the Sacred Bo Tree whereunder the Master had sat; the cutting grew and flowered into the sacred tree, and has flourished there for over two thousand years; if its continuity is authentic, it must be the oldest tree in the world. So Anuradhapura became a shrine for pilgrimage; magnificent monastic centre, as well as royal capital, its temples and dagobas were grouped about its green plain, and the Sacred Bo Tree has seeded and given birth to a host of lesser bo-trees. Before the precincts of the Sacred Tree is offered a mass of sweet-smelling blossoms; a monk clad in saffron yellow arranges them on an altar; the drums beat and the pipes shrill and monkeys skip about the grass. Near the Bo Tree is the collection of temple columns called the Peacock Palace, and the much larger group of the Brazen Palace—sixteen hundred columns standing together like slim tree trunks, the only remains of the great Mahawansa built in the second century B.C., which rose to many storeys, all roofed with brazen tiles, and encircled by gated walls. Inside were golden and pearl halls, an ivory throne decorated with the sun, moon and stars, and the most gorgeous furnishings in the world: it must have looked like the New Jerusalem. It was, however, not a royal palace but a monks' residence and temple. For Anuradhapura was one of the most religious cities that have ever been. The Brazen Temple has been thrown down and rebuilt, the last time in the twelfth century; the bo-tree has, they say, never been destroyed. The four great dagobas of Anuradhapura stand about it, solid domes, inverted bowls, some still grown with scrub, some containing relics, some merely commemorative; there are a crowd of smaller humps scattered over the green landscape, like a field of toadstools, and, no doubt, many more in the jungle, as yet undiscovered. For jungle stretches all round and about Anuradhapura, and in it are doubtless more temples, more forests of grey stone pillars, more humped dagobas, which camouflage themselves as tree-grown hillocks; possibly, too, the undiscovered walls of the city, and the royal palace and secular residential town. For Anuradhapura was a great city from the fifth century B.C. to the ninth A.D., when the turbulent Tamils invaded and caused it to be abandoned. What has chiefly so far been reclaimed from the jungle is the monastic settlement. Those great assemblages of pillars, the storied Mahawansa, the humped dagobas, are not excessively beautiful in themselves, in spite of carved balustrades, carved moon-shaped stone slabs, sculptured Buddhas and elephants; what gives them aesthetic charm is their situation, jungle-surrounded, barely reclaimed, the green sward on which they stand, the scattered lakes, the delicious stone baths, the clammy, swooning climate which lies like warm, scented flowers on forest and clearing, the frisking monkeys, and, above all, the long reaches of the mysterious, exotic past, winding like a dimly seen river through green enjungled silence to the gorgeous heyday of royal and priestly magnificence of two thousand years ago, and beyond that to the earliest beginnings, when the bo-tree took root. Long reaches of silence and desertion, of the slow green drowning of the insatiable jungle; following the thousand years of elegant, cruel, religious kingship, when the love of Gautama was preached and those who incurred royal displeasure were torn to pieces by elephants.

After the desertion of Anuradhapura, Polonnaruwa took its place as royal capital. It was abandoned at the end of the thirteenth century; more utterly abandoned, for not even a village marked its site; its ruins lay, and vast numbers of them still lie, unseen in the forest which engulfed them. Pushing through the eighty miles or so of jungle from Anuradhapura along the forest tracks (avoiding the road), is to journey through exotic beauty, strangely set with the half buried ruins of an ecclesiastical Buddhist world—temples and dagobas that sprout with trees, statues and carved sculptures partly seen among the rank undergrowth, groups of monastery buildings in all stages of ruin and clearance, hermitages enclosed in great tangles of twisting tree roots, hung with brilliant flowers and skipped about by monkeys, rock baths and cisterns and large pools bright with kingfishers and full of tortoises, stone portals carved with Buddhas, elephants and cobras, groups of richly-capitaled pillars, moonstone stair slabs carved with prancing animals, great monasteries of temples and pillars such as Jetawan-arama, built two thousand years ago and scattered for miles through the forest, the remains of palaces, rocky hills covered with terraces and steps, grass and scrub, and finally Polonnaruwa on its lake, with the great pleasure garden the Park of Heaven, laid out by King Parakama in the twelfth century. This must have been a glorious landscape park, set with lotus-grown pools, a dazzling and exquisite bathing hall with sandalwood pillars, a summer pavilion, a royal palace of great loveliness. All this is described in the Mahawansa in enthusiastic and beautiful detail; we can see the ruins of each thing described, and imagination rears the palace and park as they were. One of the loveliest things to be seen is the Lotus bath—five granite flower-shaped circular steps, lying one within another, until they enclose the rose-shaped bath itself. Such carved decoration as there is (the colossal Buddhas, the charming elephants, the naïve stone dwarfs that guard the sacred places, the animals and flowers) has an engaging Cingalese grace, in keeping with the swinging bells and the scented flowers. You will not encounter in Ceylon those barbaric winged bulls and lions and bearded ox-eyed men of Assyria; the sculptured youths have long painted almond eyes and delicate hands. These de-forested ruins of ancient Buddhism lack the finest architecture and art, but they have much compensating charm.

The ruined temples and pagodas of Burma are not comparable with these jungle felicities. They are more elaborate, ambitious, rich in ornament, fussier, more splendid individually; they do not sprawl in great groups about dense forest; they are tabulated and known. The great ruins of Pagan have given, through the past six centuries, much pleasure, and more particularly their general view as seen from the Irawaddy. Pagan had in its prime about thirteen thousand pagodas and monasteries; the effect of the crowd of bell-shaped, dome-shaped, pumpkin-shaped, or cross-shaped sacred buildings, standing above the great river, every variety of Buddha decorating their niches and their tiles, must have been very brilliant and glittering. Pagan, wrecked by Kubla Khan's army in anger, is still in its diminished ruins a place of shrines and pilgrimage. Since the Burmese are probably the most religious people in the world, their ruins are all sacred, even the palaces, and Buddha presides everywhere. There is a bland, smiling tranquillity about these temples and monasteries even in ruin; the Buddhas sit in their shrines unperturbed; the haunting gods are amiable, charming, even a little smug; there is no Gothic darkness, creeping ivy, bats, foxes, or melancholy owls to induce *Ruinenschmerz*, and the most shattered pagoda is still elegant and well-mannered, and not really morbid.

22

Sail across the Gulf of Siam to Indo-China: here, in Cambodia, Cochin China, Tonkin, Laos, Annam, you will find the great jungles and the hidden cities. They are possibly the most romantic in the world; none of the jungle temples or cities of Central America is as splendid as Angkor Wat and Angkor Thom; no piece of country more set with hidden beauties than the great green sea of forest that rolls over Cambodia and about the great river of Mekong. One may feel Angkor Vat too ornate, too crowded with decoration and sculpture, lacking the grand simplicity of Greece and the exquisite clustered-fruit curves of Byzantium; it may oppress with its many-coned prodigiousness, its seemingly endless stairways, corridors, towers, colonnades and fuss, its unpausing friezes of animals and men marching and capering in bas-relief, its lack of uncovered spaces, its redundancy of great bland faces of the god which have smiled so tranquilly and ironically down on all this animation for over a thousand years. One may feel this too muchness, or one may not: but, rising like a great galleon from the rolling sea, Angkor's splendour seems to belong to dreams. Indeed it has been part of men's dreams down the ages; the greatest city of that extraordinary race, the Khmers, capital of the Fu-Nan empire, holding subject a hundred and twenty kings, founded in the ninth century but destroyed and rebuilt in the twelfth, in the valley of Siem Reap, the magnificent heart of a kingdom glorious for four or five centuries; for magnificence there was nothing in the east to touch it. The golden city of lotus-crowned towers, described by Kublai Khan's ambassador, full of tombs, treasure, concubines, dancing girls, processions and religious shrines, monumental phalluses which also were religious, caparisoned elephants, palanquins, gods and slaves. The vast temple (or was it a funerary shrine of kings?) Angkor Vat, the many more whose wrecked piles stand about and around the city, all belong to those three centuries from the ninth to the twelfth; precise chronology is, archaeologists admit, guesswork, and they all contradict one another. There are Hindu influences; there is Buddha and Brahminism; and Angkor Vat suggests the great Java ziggurat of Borobudar; but the work is the characteristic work of the Khmers at the zenith of their creative pride, since fallen into such decadent and incurious simplicity. The great era declined; there was trouble with the barbarous invading Siamese; about the year 1400 they attacked and took Angkor and the other Khmer cities; the Khmers abandoned the cities and went under, and so, it seems, did the cities, drowning slowly in the jungle that flowed over them. Both Khmers and cities have been under ever since, forest-drowned. From time to time European travellers have seen strange visions of huge carved towers, cone-shaped, scarcely rising above the rippled green, submerged ships over which the swaying seas parted and closed. In the nineteenth century Angkor was discovered and explored. A French traveller saw it in 1850; the naturalist Henri Mouhot in 1861; ruins grander, he exclaimed in delighted amaze, than any Greece or Rome had left. The Cambodians regarded it with awed mistrust; it was the work of giants, they said, or of the King of the Angels, or of the Leper King; or it made itself; they know many legends, but, it seems, little history; in this they resemble many other commentators on Angkor. When Mouhot came it was deep in jungle; it has since been cleared but not stripped bare; it still has the air, or anyhow Angkor Thom has the air, of a great ship riding a swaying, surfing sea. Angkor Vat stands in a green clearing; deeper in the jungle lies the great city, once, it was said, larger than Augustan Rome, standing on a great trade route, passing commerce through its hands like ropes of gold, now for five centuries desolate, given over to its ancient gods, to the forest, and to a dark whisper of crowding bats.

No ruin has better illustrated the great cleavage between the two divergent schools of ruin-pleasurists, the romantic and the archaeological. Since the discovery of Angkor, many volumes and many articles have appeared, most of them conceived in poetic excitement and achieving romantic inexactitude. Almost everyone who has seen these prestigious prodigies becomes temporarily an intoxicated poet. The Chinese ambassador with his golden city and the great burnished lotus flower that blazed like a beacon on the highest tower of Bayon; the French naturalist who rhapsodized over the startling vision five centuries later; Pierre Loti, who described it with a felicitous beauty even greater than his normal lushness; nearly all the twentieth-century travellers, who fall suddenly into enchantment, intoxicated by the delirious maze that piles its complications to the sky, by the stone city and its palaces and temples foundered in the engulfing forest. Pierre Loti saw a picture of it as a child, great strange towers entwined with exotic branches, and knew that he would one day see them. When he did so, in middle age, the colossal temple seemed, in the hot glare of noon, like a mirage. It took a little time before he was caught in its spell, wandering enchanted and bemused through the maze of courts, terraces, corridors, twisting stairways, between walls carved with long processions of dancing Apsaras, lovely in their smiling grace, and battling chariots and elephants, and always the musing god, cross-legged and calm. To enter the great temple by causeway and lilied moat was to be caught into some delirious dream; by night a dream of darkness, wandering through endless galleries, climbing spiralling stairs grown with grass and slippery with centuries of feet, past great towered and arcaded terraces, tree-grown, one terrace above another till from the summit he looked down on the roof of forest that waved over Angkor Thom. By night the halls were windy with the swirling, squeaking multitude of bats that hung from the roof all day, spreading their musky smell, flapping and twittering about intruders' heads. In daylight the temple is also a fantastic dream, its splendours illustrated with a more than earthly light that gleams on the sculptured dancers, the warriors, the elephants, and the gods who occupy. Pierre Loti was caught in the strangeness, the melancholy, of the sanctuary of his childish dreams, the mystery of the enigmatic race who had built their empire in these forests, flourished there for a few centuries, and departed, leaving behind their gods to hold it. Looking down from the high terrace of the temple, he surveyed the jungle which hid Angkor Thom. If we could now, he mused, cut down those branches, we should see long paved avenues, bordered by gods, seven-headed serpents, bell-towers, all foundered now.

Darkness fell. The gods around him began to cause him uneasiness. A nameless horror issued from the dark recesses, trailing along the gallery; above him little rat-like cries chirped from stone ceilings. Mystery and fear enveloped him.

The Khmers too were a dark mystery; it has been the fashion to write of them as if they had no known origins and had departed into nowhere, like gods. This annoys more informed historians of Angkor, such as M. Coedès of the Ecole Française d'Extrême Orient, who has published learned articles on Cambodian inscriptions. "*Mais peut-être,*" he observes with acerbity of one such writer, "*notre écrivain a-t-il simplement cédé au goût romantique du mystère des ruines.*" He quotes with irony from Pierre Loti's *Pèlerin d'Angkor.* "See," said Loti, "where palaces stood, see where lived kings stupendously magnificent—of whom one knows nothing more, who passed into oblivion without leaving even one name graven on a stone or in a memory." How much more literary, remarks M. Coedès, is this fine period than the phrase with which H. Parmentier begins his little guide to Angkor Vat: "The temple of Angkor Vat is dedicated to the god Vishnu, with whom the king Suryavarman was confused after his death; this fact gives the approximate date of the building, which, unfinished, must have been built in the reign of this king (1113–45)." These, adds M. Coedès, are the amateurs of mystery who sometimes reproach us for despoiling the ruins of the vegetation which hides them, and making them accessible and comprehensible. Alas! Are we then obliged to choose between the forest which devours ruins and the conserving of the relics of the past, though it may not be impossible to reconcile the two; the example of Ta Prohm proves it, where the admirable frame of verdure and the tentacules of the cotton trees do not prevent people from visiting the monument, nor from knowing that it is a temple built in 1189 by King Jayavarman VII to the memory of his mother."

The exasperated scholar has more to say about the vague romanticism which ignores facts and heeds only the poetry of ruin and jungle. But the romantics, intoxicated with beauty, will go their way. Angkor Thom is even more to their taste than Angkor Vat—"the winding-sheet of a town, where every stone bears traces of an antique sculpture. Nothing in Angkor Thom is so elaborately magnificent as Angkor Vat; but the ruin is much greater; nearly all is shattered and jungle-grown, though the French have, since 1907, done some clearance and mapping of the city's plan. Cleared or uncleared, it is an extraordinary and stupendous sight. The great metropolis covered, with its palaces and temples and outlying buildings, many miles. Within the city walls a maze of wrecked beauty lies—temples, palaces, squares. Bayon, the huge step-pyramid temple, a mountainous mass of shattered terraces and high towers, god-adorned, is an architectural mystery. It has had the romantics in trembling raptures, and has baffled even archaeologists. Parmentier, the doyen of Indo-China archaeologists, admits that, before the forest had been cleared from it, Bayon was an incomprehensible maze, but of a poignant romanticism. Loti's lyrical description sprouts with huge destructive fig-trees, strangling roots, the forest waving its greenery from every crevice and gallery, quite impossible to see what was what. Recent work has despoiled Bayon of its green shroud and of much of its romantic aspect; there emerges, clear and bare, what has been called the greatest monument of Cambodia; but they have not learnt so much about it even yet; archaeologists, bemused by this mysterious splendour, talk mistily about the bizarre pile; they gaze on it by moonlight and refer to the Nagas, as if they were awed Khmer peasants. Round it lie strewn on the ground many more towers, and from each smiles the god, about whose identity much discussion has been held, much ink expended. Brahma, Buddha, Siva,

Locesvara; anyone may think what he likes. The date, too; latest opinion seems to favour the twelfth century, not earlier. But, confounding speculations, the intricate marvel climbs to heaven, with its galleries, terraces, deep courts, steep stairways, and the high central tower that, once gold-painted, held aloft, said the Chinese ambassador, the burnished lotus, shining like a beacon over the magnificent city; and on the front terrace stood two golden lions. All is now desolate, fantastic, and ambushed with ghosts; the erroneous opinions of archaeologists twitter among them like bats. From the third terrace can be surveyed the mass of shattered walls and towers and courts that were Angkor Thom's palaces, temples, baths, colonnades. There is a great central plaza, but no theatre; the Khmers, like the Ceylonese and the Maya, were untouched by Greece and Rome; and there are no remains of ordinary houses, for these were built of earth and wood and have gone to earth and wood again, leaving no trace. Palaces, temples, monasteries, shrines, tombs: these tiled, colonnaded and sculptured buildings make the huge wilderness of ruins that spreads for miles through the dense jungle. Between the Vat and the Thom rises the oldest shrine of the district, Pnom Bak Kheng, crowning a natural hill, sanctuary-topped, mysterious; north-east of it Ta Prohm strangles within its binding forest trees, for here destruction has gone too far; something has been attempted, but to tear up all the trees which spring from pavements and walls and thrust huge roots through vaults and roofs, tearing the stones apart, would be to wreck more completely the columned building—temple, treasure-house, hospital?—which is one of the most beautiful things in Angkor. Twenty years ago Ta Prohm was in danger of death.

"Trees eight and ten feet in diameter rise out of the pavements on the terraces. Roots pursue a snake-like course for hundreds of feet across the ruined courts. . . . Great trunks press down on the weakened vaults and tear great friezes apart to pile their wreckage amid the splinters of earlier destruction. . . . And yet Ta Prohm is beautiful in the chaotic *mélange* of its trees and in the isolated glimpses of desolated gods who peer out of its walls through the infrequent clearings . . . the trees are left to work as they will with Ta Prohm, the destruction must go on and on unceasingly."[1]

[1]R. J. Casey, *Four Faces of Siva* (Harrap, 1929).

The conservers of Angkor now believe that it has been checked, and quote Ta Prohm as a successful example of a compromise between the taste of the wild-woodland romantics and the austere archaeologists; enough forest for picturesqueness, enough clearance for safety and for lucidity. It is possible that the romantic visitors of twenty years back find Ta Prohm now less to their mind. Perhaps too the great wilderness outside the walls which was Pra Khan, "the temple of the green twilight", pleases less now that not only clearance but restoration has been at work on it. Twenty years ago

"Beyond the wall the path plunged down into a tangle of wild growths that enclosed us with ghastly suddenness. We had entered into a kingdom of twilight, a dark green twilight. . . . I felt a sense of utter terror. . . . In the gauzy apparition of the forest appeared a wall and shattered pillars, all struggling out of verdant disorder. . . In places entire trees had broken through the crumbling ramparts . . . Kim Khouan gestured toward the giant trees.

"'The gods,' he whispered. 'Trees hundreds of years old—with the souls of gods in them—angry gods. . . . They were a great people, the Khmers. . . . Some say they were gods. And when they were defeated by Siam their souls entered the mighty trees and destroyed the city they had built. . . .' The ruins seemed to stretch on interminably, like a vast drowned city."[1]

Pra Khan is in better order to-day, if less alarming.

The city within the walls has been also cleared and planned; no longer are the courts of the temples choked with forest, as till lately the huge Baphuon was choked. The hundred-foot high galleried and terraced pyramid temple is now almost cleared of its smothering green; it adjoins the great terrace of what was a royal palace, shattered and gone to earth and scarcely identifiable; between it and the main plaza of the city stands the high terrace wall, carved with its frieze of marching elephants and of eagle-men. The remains of smaller temples and palaces stand round about the plaza. In time, no doubt, everything will be given a name. Meanwhile, though many learned and detailed descriptions of the city and its entouraging forest suburbs appear, experts still differ: beyond their differences Angkor and its offspring incredibly

[1]H. Hervey, *Travels in French Indo-China* (Thornton Butterworth, 1928).

sprawl through miles of jungle, some of the most prodigious, exciting, intricately wrought and sensuously moving ruins in the world. All round Angkor lie exquisite sanctuaries, some on lake islands, some whose wrecked cloisters and columns hint at past glory as tremendous as Angkor itself.

Go on from Angkor through the great forests of Indo-China and the Malay Peninsula where the paddy fields have not yet pushed them back; jungle-buried Khmer cities and temples strew the way. According to travellers one comes on them like truffles in a wood, seductively decaying in green boskage, to be dug up and plucked by any white explorers who happen along. Travellers camp by suspected mounds, pitch camp among the lunatic fringe of monkeys, mosquitos, tigers and modern Khmers (intermittently helpful beings, but slightly alarmed at the work of their ancestors and something of a bore with their legends—unless, as one suspects, the travellers themselves get these out of books) and proceed to dig up ancient colonies mentioned by Ptolemy, ancient trading marts at the mouths of rivers silted up centuries ago. They find eighth-century stone images of Indian gods grown about by the trunks of huge trees; they discover in a remote valley the site of an Indian city built centuries before Angkor.

"We had reached the ramparts of Sri Deva. In the moat lotuses held up their gorgeous blossoms towards us . . it needed only a flash of the imagination to complete the picture of past splendours: a vision of painted parapets topping the ramparts, with here and there a gilded turret . . . while the murmur of an Eastern market within the city and the tramp of Indian soldiery without seemed for one moment to break the silence of the jungle . . . it was our realization of all that the discoveries awaiting us within the city might mean that which sharpened our curiosity to a pitch which that of the naturalist Mouhot can hardly have attained as he gazed uncomprehendingly upon the towers of Angkor."[1]

It must all have been great fun. The explorers, Dr and Mrs Wales, pitched their camp by this site, excavated and mapped it, and the oldest Hindu temple in Indo-China (early sixth century) was revealed. They were tracking Indian culture in the Khmer

[1]H. G. Quaritch Wales, *Towards Angkor* (Harrap, 1937).

empire of Fu-Nan; their exploration was a quest, not a casual ramble. Travellers in Indo-China have usually been committed to quests. M. Henri Mouhot looked for birds, beasts, fishes, insects and people, and found magnificent ruins by the way. Pierre Loti set out to substantiate a childhood dream. Mr Harry Hervey sought the lost city of Wat-Phu (it is not clear who had lost it, except, long ago, the Khmers) up the Mekong on the Siamese border of Laos. He found it; or rather its temple, which was all that remained; it was grander, he decided, than Angkor Vat, and more restrained; in high fever he climbed about it. Other explorers have discovered, after extremities of labour, jungle-conflicts, and physical exhaustion, hidden Khmer cities which they never found again. "Possibly," they muse as they gaze upon their find, "possibly no white man before me has looked upon this city," or this temple, or these columns, or that piece of frieze that lies split by tree roots on the ground, or those carved stones that monkeys are throwing at one another in the tree-tops, having apparently picked them out of the walls. Possibly not: but possibly on the other hand a series of men of this enterprising colour have stood and gazed as this last arrival is gazing, and have had the same gratifying thoughts. Some helpful romancing native had directed or misdirected them, egging on their eager souls to the quest. They seek a city; and, since there are so many cities, or fragments of cities, about, the odds are they find one, or perhaps several.

But they have not invariably been sure what it is; it may be an outlying fragment, a suburb, in the green belt of some city already known; can it, they uneasily wonder, have been after all only a part of Pra Khan, or Sambour, or Pnom Dek, or some other of the found cities? Can it even be, the newcomer to the business may fear, one of these cities themselves? Is it really a discovery? Was the city really lost, or is it only perhaps the traveller? These are riddles, and many of them must still remain so.

But should his city not, after all, prove a find, the explorer need not feel discouraged, for where that came from there are plenty more; it seems that one cannot come to the end of the lost cities of the jungles, in their various stages of dilapidation and decay. Were the Khmers of to-day as intelligent as their forbears, they would go in for the ruin-faking business in the remote fastnesses of their forests, and then lead their white visitors, who enjoy such things, to see their handiwork. Possibly they do.

Be this as it may, the excitement and rapture of coming on these delightful objects, so solitary, so richly carved, so religious, so ruinous, so like Angkor, so very Khmer (yet sometimes with strange alien touches, such as the little Doric-looking temple at Sambour)—the excitement of tracking down and looking upon one of these forest dreams is worth all the anguish of the quest, wherein the ruin-seekers have persevered in peril of tigers, peril of snakes, peril of mosquitoes, of crocodiles, fever, thirst, exhaustion, rival explorers, and the nightmare of the tropical green dusk. For there, at last, the broken walls rise, the tree-crushed towers rear, the columns peer from among strangling vines, the ghosts of the gods look down; here the mysterious Khmers built, perhaps before Angkor, perhaps after, a sculptured city of temples, palaces, tombs and shrines, part of their extraordinary empire that rose so stupendously and crumbled so utterly, leaving behind it these scattered groups of elaborately decorated stone and brick in the forest, set with the faces of their gods.

23

There is more excitement in these buried ruins than in shrines far more ancient but less obscured, and structurally much less beautiful, such as the great relic stupas at Sanchi in Central India, and the other Jain and Buddhist ruins scattered about that region. The Great Stupa is over a thousand years older than the Khmer buildings; its carvings, less dazzlingly elaborate and profuse, have sometimes been called the best Buddhist art in India. Sanchi was a sacred city, full of stupas and monasteries and monks, a centre of pilgrimage; deserted from the thirteenth century, it was overrun with jungle, but less densely and destructively than the Cambodian shrines; it is much better preserved; more damage has been done to it by European seekers for treasure than by vegetation. It is a less romantic ruin than those of the Indo-China forests; and since the hope of treasure was abandoned, British sight-seers have not flocked there, as they have flocked to Elephanta Island off Bombay, to see the cave temple and its remarkable statuary. The huge stone elephant no longer stands on guard at the landing-place, for its head fell off and it was carted away to the Victoria Gardens in Bombay. But there remains the temple cut out of the rock in the eighth century, some of its pillars still standing, the Lingam shrine with its stone door-keepers, and the huge magnificent wall relief of the versatile three-faced Siva; the whole temple is so impressive and odd that it has always been a favourite excursion from Bombay; tea is served in a bungalow near the landing-place, and the Prince of Wales was given a banquet there in 1875; it was the kind of place in which royalty takes great pleasure. Bishop Heber, too. The elephant was there in his day, three times as large as life. As he climbed up the path from the landing-stage, winding prettily through woods, he was reminded of his Hodnet rectory home. The sculptures, he complained, had suffered from the vulgar love of collecting knick-knacks and specimens which prevailed among the English more than among most nations. But the great cave, with its colonnaded portico, its temple hall, courts and shrines, its concourse of sculptured divinities, an animated *turba deorum* that gives an alarmingly populated feeling, together with the several surrounding caves, smaller but also polytheous, is truly magnificent. So, indeed, are the rock temples of Ellora in Hyderabad—Buddhist, Brahmin and Jain, hewn out of the hillside with their chapels, courts, columns, shrines, galleries, statues, carvings, elephants and gods, the finest of which, the Dravidian Brahmin temple of Kailas, is one of the most beautiful things in India, and unique in kind, being a monolithic temple from which the rock has been cut away; it stands in a great court, and is richly carved within and without. Battered by a millennium of years, by the quakings of the earth, and by the furious iconoclasm of Moslems, the firm embedding of most of these cave temples in their rocky matrix has preserved them largely intact; enough damage to qualify as ruin, too little to harm them. They are, of course, comparative parvenus among Indian cave temples; the solid permanence and near invulnerability which almost disqualifies them for these pages is even more noticeable in the cave temples of the first few centuries A.D. and the second and third centuries B.C., such as those of Ajanta and Karli and (most ancient of all), Barabar. One compares these rock-hewn sanctuaries with the temple of Buddh Gaya, probably the oldest sculptured building in

50 Tortosa Cathedral, 1836 Engraving by W. H Bartlett, 1836-8

51 Tántipára Mosque, Gaur

India, founded in the sixth century B.C., built at various times during the next four centuries, containing the sacred Bo-Tree beneath which the master sat, branches from which have been planted and have flowered over the Buddhist world. The temple, with its carved railings of the second century B.C., a holy shrine for world pilgrimage, was restored by Burmese Buddhists in the fourteenth century, and again and more destructively by them in the nineteenth; it could scarcely have been worse done. Much of it was knocked about and broken; Sir Edwin Arnold saw hundreds of broken sculptures, some exquisitely carved with the adventures of Buddha, lying about on rubbish piles.

But Indian ruined temples need a volume to themselves; they are strewn as thickly as a galaxy. Go, for instance, to where, at Konorak, the celebrated Black Pagoda stands magnificent in huge ruin, its great porch alone upright, a stupendous fantasy of carving (much of it erotic), tumbled horses and elephants, and piles of stone. Not far off is Bhuvaneshwar, ancient capital of Orissa, now to be its capital again, the centre of an immense district of temples mostly in ruin; round the sacred lake seven thousand temples once lay; there are now a few hundred, all ruinous, representing about six centuries of Orissan art. But all over the richly idolatrous sub-continent the ruined temples and monasteries stand. What ruins most gracefully is any one's choice. Some prefer the decorative sculptured pillars of the eighth century chaitya which is the most beautiful of the Ajanta cave temples; the richly worked shafts and capitals achieve an aesthetic effect more pleasing than the more primitive type of temple or monastery cell. Again, the delicate and profuse elaboration of Jain decoration takes on, in ruin, a peculiarly appealing melancholy grace. One may prefer the Indo-Aryan of the north, or the Dravidian of the south, or the pillared Buddhist stupa, or the verandahed and courted vihara. Till the Mogul conquest checked it, Indian architecture grew in grandeur and grace, and in a dozen different styles. Mountains are crowded with exquisite Jain temples in ruin; the more magnificent Dravidian vitamas stand about the south-east, in almost Assyrian splendour. Out of the temples they found, the invaders built their mosques; some they adapted, purging them, sometimes more, sometimes less, of idolatrous ornament, many they destroyed and rebuilt. The mosque of Quwwat ul near Delhi boasts in an inscription of being built out of twenty-seven Jain temples. The mosques in ruin now mingle, inimically and beautifully, with their destroyed victims; Jain columns, stripped of carvings, support Moslem domes. Sometimes carvings of flowers remain. The ruined mosques have, on the whole, less beauty; they did not flower from such animated idolatrous imagination, they are less rare and fantastic. They are fewer; they do not lie in disintegrated groups over mountain and plain, delighting the eyes with intricate carved creatures.

24

There is a case for thinking that mosques are all the better for a touch of ruin; it imparts to the bland and confident rotundity of their domes, the regularity of their colonnaded courts, the assertiveness of their minarets, that note of pathos which their triumphant builders themselves gave to so many thousands of the temples of other faiths. There might seem something a little smug, a trifle too perfect, about all those unflawed domes that curve like halved melons over pillared and glistening exquisiteness, tiled, marbled, mosaic-bright, neat and complete, or else solidly brick, with the latticed and tiered minarets springing to heaven beside them. Pearl Mosques, Golden Mosques, mosques of India, of Damascus, Aleppo, Syria, Persia, Egypt, Africa, Spain, Turkestan, Turkey, Constantinople, Greece, every part of the world where Islam penetrated and stayed—how firmly, solidly handsome they are. The carvings of living creatures, of men and gods and animals and trees which make many Hindu, Greek and Christian temples so animated and so enchanting, they hack away as blasphemies; the destroyers, who cannot trust themselves to look on sculptured forms or female faces without paying them improper attention, adorn their places of prayer with painted or mosaic circles, flourishes, scrolls, squares, abstract patterns, and cries of devotion and praise. Mosques, though they have spawned over the world a rash of vulgar and brash imitations, though their domes have been thought suited to museums, post offices, casinos, picture palaces, bathing establishments, town halls and railway stations (and indeed have often been converted to such uses by Christian conquerors), can be magnificent in their intact and fruity bloom. But a few gashes and schisms in their structure, a little decadence, a suggestion of passibility, a little evidence that something of the destruction their owners have, during the past millennium, dealt to others, has been in turn dealt to them, lend them a touch of the age-old insecurity that haunts their rivals. Actually, though they look, on the whole, nobly durable, mosques have been shattered and destroyed by their foes ever since the Prophet first put up his roofless house of prayer at Medina; destroyed and restored and enlarged and built anew, in ever increasing magnificence and style. So much magnificence, so much marble, such coloured tiling and arcading, that they astound and dazzle; while all over Persia and Turkestan the mosques, faced with brilliant tiles, are built of clay and brick, and crumble to ruin.

"The minarets topple over, the cupolas fall, the glazed facings peel off like torn wallpaper, great cracks and fissures appear in the walls. Of some of the most magnificent monuments only a few crumbling clay fragments remain."[1]

This was written by a Russian of the mosques of Samarkand, which, like the rest of old Samarkand, have stood long in ruins. Stripped and shattered, earth-shaken and gaunt, the dazzling mosques and tombs of Tamerlane, and the colleges that stand round three sides of the great square, are haunted by the ghosts of the Timurid glory, grandiose, showy, the rich bandit's dream of grandeur and pride: the Bibi Khanum, built by Tamerlane's Chinese wife, once fabulously brilliant and a-glitter with jewel-like tiles and gold, lifts its great clay arches and broken pillars above the tented chaffering chattering bazaar, bare and humped like a huge camel which may at any time fall finally to its knees. The glory of the Samarkand mosques and great mausoleums is long since wrecked by earthquake, time and man; Moslem sloth restores little; Tamerlane's great tomb outside the city, with its melon-shaped fluted dome, stands half ruined, its blue porcelain tiles strewing the ground, though some attempt is now made to protect it from further harm; one of the colleges that lie round the great square with its cells for mullahs has become a tourist's

[1] *From Moscow to Samarkand*, Y. Z. (Hogarth Press, 1934).

hostel and is kept in fair repair; this is the seventeenth-century Tillah-Kar, once covered with gold leaf and mosaic, now bare and gaunt. Behind the façade with its tremendous arched gateway and double-storeyed arcades is the tower of the mosque, and this, too, was gold-leafed without and gold-mosaicked within. All three madrasahs enclosed a fountained court, with cloisters and cells; each has its mosque. Those who came to Samarkand in the centuries of its glory, that Timurid renascence which flowered in the eastern world with such extraordinary synthetic Islam lustre, have borne witness to the extreme beauty of all these buildings—the mosques and colleges and tombs, the palaces and gardens, that then were a glittering splendour in the desert land and became a dusty dilapidation, "the great monuments that once made Samarkand the glory, and that still, in their ruin, leave it the wonder, of the Asiatic continent"[1] Such splendour, said visitors and ambassadors, such brilliance, such wealth, such learning, was not to be seen elsewhere; these mosques, these tombs, the progenitors of the mosques and tombs of the Moguls in India (Baber, who overran India, was fifth in descent from Timur), were perfect in symmetry, resplendent in colour and light, exquisite works of art. All are sinking to ruin; their way to dusty death is strewn with fallen tiles like jewels. It seems that their Russian governors are doing now more to save them than they were doing in 1889, when Lord Curzon, writing of the cluster of mosques and cupolas that make the mausoleum of Shah Zindeh, complained,

"A ruin unfortunately it is; for domes have collapsed, inscriptions have been defaced, and the most exquisite enamelling has perished. But still . . . at intervals in the masonry there open out small recessed mosques and tomb chambers with faultless honeycomb groining, executed in moulded and coloured tiles. Gladly would I expatiate upon the beauty of these Samarkandian tiles. . . . But it is more relevant to point out that, beyond having patched up the most glaring traces of dilapidation and made a few attempts, with deplorable results, to replace destroyed ornaments, the Russians have done nothing, and are doing nothing, whatever to preserve these sacred relics either from wanton demolition or from natural decay; and that, what with the depredations of

[1]Lord Curzon, *Russia in Central Asia in 1889* (Longman, 1889).

vandals, the shock of earthquakes, and the lapse of time, the visitor in the twentieth century may find cause to enquire with resentful surprise what has become of the fabled grandeurs of the old Samarkand. A Society for the Preservation of Ancient Monuments should at once be formed in Russian Central Asia. . . . But this is a step which can hardly be expected from a Government which has never, outside of Russia, shown the faintest interest in antiquarian preservation or research, and which would sit still till the crack of doom upon a site that was known to contain the great bronze Athene of Pheidias or the lost books of Livy."[1]

To-day, those Russians who write of Samarkand do so in terms of Five Year Plans and cotton crops; meanwhile, the mosques and tombs and colleges and minarets waste slowly like corpses and will one day sink into the desert.

It is much the same all over Turkestan and Central Asia; everywhere mouldering mosques and perishing pillars and broken beauty. At Herat, that ancient place of splendour, the British, in 1885, razed minarets and mosques to the ground lest the Russians should occupy Herat and use them for cover. Seven minarets remain.

"Seven sky-blue pillars rise out of the bare fields against the delicate, heather-coloured mountains. Down each the dawn casts a highlight of pale gold. In their midst shines a blue melon-dome with the top bitten off. . . .

"This array of blue towers rising haphazard from a patchwork of brown fields and yellow orchards has a most unnatural look. . . . It can be seen . . that they were originally joined by walls or arches and must have formed part of a series of mosques or colleges. What has happened to these buildings? . . . It is a miserable story."[2]

So it is, for the Herat Musalla was one of the loveliest groups of domes and minarets in Asia. It is lovely still, what is left of it. But it seems that most mosques of Central Asia are doomed to ruin, through earthquake, vandalism, or slow decay. Almost every town has a Friday mosque in ruin. Few can feel that mosques take ruin well; it lies like a blight on what should be,

[1]Lord Curzon, *Russia in Central Asia in 1889* (Longman, 1889).
[2]Robert Byron, *The Road to Oxiana* (1937).

and once was, a tranquil perfection; though a touch of it may soften and refine tile-work too brash, imparting a graceful negligence to that shining symmetry. All over Persia mosques crumble, forlorn symbols of a culture long since grown static, perhaps on its way out. The ruined mosques of Cairo, on the other hand, and of Mesopotamia, stand with a gaunter dignity; the western pointed arch strikes a different note, less beautiful, more adapted to good wreckage. The lonely tremendous grandeur of the great mosques of Samarra, and of all the desperate ruined shrines that strew that waste land, the beauty of the carved and arcaded Aleppo mosques, sometimes with a classical touch, often with acanthus capitals, transcend the rotund Persian exquisiteness of cupolas and fountained courts and gardens.

Among the ruined mosques to which "exquisiteness" has little application are those discovered lately on the coral islands off the Tanganyika coast, where the Kilwa kings ruled in East Africa between 1285 and 1505 when the Portuguese took over. An expedition was sent to examine and date the various ruins of this Islamic island empire—palaces, town settlements, mosques, fortifications. The Friday mosque on Kilwa island is the largest in East Africa; early fourteenth century, built of grey stone, with domes of white coral over semi-pointed arches; falling to pieces, grown over with scrub and trees, startlingly beautiful and romantic, it stands broken above the blue smooth sea of the harbour that was a medieval trade port for centuries. There is also a smaller domed mosque, even shaggier with forest, with fluted vaulting and, on another island, where a complete medieval deserted city was found, there stands, linked to the palace by a series of chambers, the remains of a mosque with a beautifully fluted demi-dome praying niche. There are further excavations to be made, other islands to be explored; out of the mangrove swamps more mosques may rise, and more palaces with Gothic arches.

25

If ruined mosques stand about Africa with the kind of intimidating savagery in which this distressing continent has its being, crumbling and smitten temples stand about China with an easy, debonair, light-come-light-go transience.

"Soaring, thousand-year-old towers of carved stone . . . are alien in spirit to the Chinese builder. . . . On the contrary, he accepts fate; fire, earthquakes, plundering by armies and the massacres they frequently inflict; and plans his edifices so that, when they have been burned down—which, the experience of four thousand years has taught him, happens every hundred years or so—they can very easily and precisely be repeated, and will seem, on the contrary, never to have been injured. (Indeed, a notable fault of Chinese architecture as well as a notable merit . . . consists in its transience: it can disappear, melt into nothingness as easily as, on the other hand, it can be renewed.)"[1]

There is, it seems, in China no Society for the Preservation of Ancient Buildings. There is possibly, though this is hard for foreigners to assess, little romantic ruin-feeling in this ancient civilization which so reveres antiquity, which abounds in magnificently romantic ruins whose imitations have decorated English landscape gardens so strangely and so often with their elegant and exotic charms.

There is nothing elegant about the temples and fortified monasteries of adobe brick that strew the mountains and deserts of Chinese Turkestan, often crumbling in ruin, often buried in desert sand, nor in the rock temples carved out of the mountain sides, hewn to endure. The ancient ruined cities of Chinese Turkestan are all religious settlements, nowhere is the determined religious nature of humanity more asserted. In the temples prayed Buddhists, Christians, Manichaeans (who in East Turkestan greatly flourished), Turks and Zoroastrians; there was no exclusiveness here, though from time to time a good deal of sectarian massacre. Here are Buddhist relics from the third century B.C., here are walled cities two thousand years old, sand-buried, destroyed by storm or flood or fire, dug up and explored, their ruinous temples yielding treasure of manuscripts (Manichaean and Buddhist and Christian), paintings, sculpture. The manuscripts are in exquisite script on exquisite parchment, silk and leather; the local peasantry have found them useful for window-panes, but have thrown many into rivers. The clay walls of the temples hold the remains of paintings; the locals, who know all about the varied pleasures to be obtained from ruins, have

[1]Sir Osbert Sitwell, *Escape With Me* (Macmillan, 1939).

used much of the clay for fertilizing their fields, the beams of the doors for fuel and building; treasure also was found and removed by these resourceful and far from simple people. There are painted floors and roofs, and in one domed building the corpses of a hundred Buddhist monks murdered by Chinese in the ninth century; anything may, it seems, turn up. There are innumerable stupas and temples; the gilded Buddhas that once stood in their niches were destroyed by anti-Buddhist races in fits of the odium theologicum that Buddhists, like other churchmen, have so frequently excited among rivals. In some of the temples goat-herds have settled themselves, in others archaeologists, who dig for manuscripts, paintings and pottery, finding complete fifth-century psalters, vaults stuffed with Christian and Manichaean documents, tablets inscribed with known and unknown scripts, Graeco-Buddhist carvings, Chinese paintings.

Similar treasure-hunts have been pursued also in the ancient churches that stand ruining about Armenia. Many even of those still in use are ruinous; the Armenians regret it with a shrug, but what would you have? There is little money for church upkeep. They are among the most ancient of Christian churches; many of them are extremely picturesque and beautiful in ruin, particularly the more Byzantine types, with their small conical tiled roofs and apses and broken columns, some from Roman temples. About them mutter the eccentric ghosts of the so tenacious, so wrong-headed anti-Chalcedon churchmen who maintained their monophysite rites and notions in them for so long, who have suffered so hideously from the savage Persians, Turks and Russians who entourage them. The ruins wear an air of stubborn, vulnerable, but invincible human frailty, none of the serene pride that gives a few columns of a Greek temple on a pine-grown mountain-side their look of tranquil eternity, and none of the self-confident hubris of mosques, or the soaring aspiration of shattered Gothic; these are, for the most part, small fallible buildings, that earth and man have shaken down, but which yet retain their crumbling obstinate existence down the centuries. There is something reassuring in their ancientness, their sturdy frailty, and their spirited, erroneous, martyred history. They do not shock and frighten, like the broken pillars of Melkarth and horned Ashtaroth that lie buried deep beneath the marbled streets of the Roman cities of Barbary, reminding us of the ancient gods who twine about the roots of the world, whispering "Before Zeus was, we were; after Christ passes, we shall be."

However this may turn out, the North African Roman temples, and the basilicas they were so apt to become, stand in their ruin with a truly Roman persistence. As in Djemila, the ancient Cuical, that fine Trajan city in the mountain country of Algeria, whose temple stands colonnaded and granite-pillared on a high platform, looking over the city of baths, fountains, theatres, arches and mansions that once made Cuical so magnificent; and near it a Christian basilica and a baptistery, on whose font an inscription remarks hopefully that in time all nations will be baptized.

26

Be this as it may, the valiant attempts to bring such a state of affairs about has strewn the habitable and unhabitable world with the most enchanting buildings in decay. The Jesuit order in particular, diving into fantastic jungles to baptize the most improbable beings, planted their baroque mission churches in clearings among dense forests and cannibal Americans whom they instructed in the faith against startling odds; the faith may not have deeply penetrated their anthropophagous flock, but when the missionaries departed, as Jesuits (an Order to whom expulsion has always been part of the periodic rhythm of life), will sooner or later do, they left behind them their charming edifices, to crumble away abandoned, to be slowly engulfed in greenery, to be lost in small clearings in wild forest. Thus they stand, it is said, in the deep forests of Paraguay, these civilized baroque constructions, the broken saints standing in tiers of niches up the façades, liana vines thrusting through doors and windows, jungle cats and snakes making their homes round the altars, which are also used for such sacrifices as Paraguayans affect, but upon these it is scarcely wise to speculate. To come suddenly out of savage forest into such a clearing, to see such a church embraced by the twining vines and figs, its civility mouldering and drowning in the wild growths of the centuries since its desertion, but still civil, still elegantly baroque in its ruin, would be an encounter of the most rewarding.

It would scarcely, however, have the "soothing and tranquillizing effect" produced by the shell of the Portuguese cathedral of Macao, which was burnt down in 1835, leaving only the great baroque façade standing high above the town at the top of a magnificent flight of stone steps, the sky behind its empty windows. The façade is complete; four stages of arched windows rising to the high pointed roof, niches with saints, four tiers of pillars with grass tufting on their carved capitals, grass also waving on the top of the façade; it very probably looks more charming than during the two centuries and a half when the cathedral stood behind it. A visitor to Macao in 1817 observed that the churches were not sufficiently remarkable to deserve being visited, the cathedral façade to-day is startingly beautiful against the sky. "The large and handsome church, milk-white, with a splendid flight of stone steps, and surrounded by trees and shrubbery," a young lady described it a few years before its destruction.[1] It withstood the great gale and sea that destroyed much of Macao in 1831, tearing away the quay and the roofs of houses and damaging churches; but Macao was always, even in its heyday, on the road to destruction, always on its way out; "formerly very nice and populous," said Lord Anson's chaplain in 1743, "but at present it is much fallen from its ancient splendour." William Hickey went on shore from his ship to see it, but found it a miserable place; Lord Macartney in 1794 commented on the neglected state of many large and costly buildings, and on the luxury which had enervated the Portuguese, giving the envious explanation of the decline and fall of foreigners. In 1857 Macao pleased Laurence Oliphant by its "air of respectable antiquity," which was refreshing after the parvenu Hongkong. "The narrow streets and grass-grown plazas, the handsome façade of the fine old cathedral crumbling to decay . . . the shady walks and cool grottos, once the haunt of the Portuguese poet . . . all combine to produce a soothing and tranquillizing effect."[2]

A little more, and Macao would slip into being a decayed city; drowsy obsolescence haunts its cobbled streets and verandahed, brightly painted houses, over which the great cathedral façade towers like a warning ghost, or like a particularly successful sham

[1]Miss Law, *My Mother's Journal*, 1829–34 (Edited Catherine Hilbard, 1900).
[2]Laurence Oliphant, *Lord Elgin's Mission* (1857).

ruin closing a vista in a gentleman'slandscape garden. It seems, indeed, a little curious that no English gentleman has ever, we believe, used it for a model: baroque Follies have been less used than one would expect; considering the admirable effect that a baroque, preferably churriguerresque, temple, arch or façade would produce in parks, it seems an opportunity neglected and an adornment overdue.

But the world is strewn with such missed opportunities; one marvels at the limits of the folly of our folly-minded forbears. Why, for instance, did no one set up in his grounds (I think they did not) some cluster of Byzantine apses, or a ruined Hindu temple with erotic carvings? Classical temples abound, and mosques, and Chinese pagodas, and rotundas, nymphaeums, arches, porticoes, broken columns, castles, Gothic towers. But, so far as I know, no baroque sham façade; certainly nothing like Macao.

V

PLEASURES AND PALACES

I

ALL over the world, palaces stand ruined. Crumbling palaces, shattered palaces, palaces engulfed by green forest, palaces drowned in the sea, palaces whose only remnants are a few prostrate broken columns, a sprawl of foundations, grass-grown, some mosaic floors, a swimming bath, fragments of wall painted in colours that were bright two thousand years ago. Palaces like Priam's, scarcely now to be identified among the rubbled trenches that were Ilium; palace castles like Santameri where the Frankish Dukes of Athens held their court at Thebes, of which one massive tower still stands, palaces like Sans Souci that a black king built at Haiti, palaces beneath the desert like Nineveh and Babylon, palaces beneath the sea like those of emperors round the Naples bay, palaces of the Caesars sprawled over the Palatine hill, palaces of Cyprus, where (says Dante) the Lusignan princes led a beastly life among the beastly Cypriotes, palaces huge and containing towns, like Diocletian's at Spalato, palaces at Delhi, Mistrà, Tiryns, Mycenae, Persepolis, Peking, palaces rising out of lakes all about Rajputana, palaces built by Norman kings for their pleasure in Sicily, palaces covering twice five miles of fertile ground with walls and towers and domes of pleasure at Xanadu. Palaces everywhere; and more beneath the earth that we shall never see, so deeply over them have piled and silted the sands of Syria, the river mud of Sybaris, the brittle but immobile cities of the world.

In ruined palaces there lies peculiar pleasure. The grandeur they had, the courtly life led in them, the banquets, the music, the dancing, the painted walls, the sculptures, the rich tapestries, the bright mosaics, the princely chatter, the foreign envoys coming and going, the merchants laying their costly bales before the royal treasurer—and now the shattered walls, the broken columns, the green trees thrusting through the crumbling floors. Fallen pride, wealth and fine living in the dust, the flitting shades of patrician ghosts, the silence where imperious voices rang, the trickle of unchannelled springs where fountains soared, of water where wine flowed. All this makes for that melancholy delight so eagerly sought, so gratefully treasured, by man in his brief passage down the corridor of time, from which, looking this way and that, he may observe such enchanting chambers of the past.

Of all palaces, the palace of Xanadu (one must keep Coleridge's euphonious name for it), that stately pleasure-dome on the river Alph, a hundred and eighty miles north-west of Peking, that miracle of rare device set in green forests and gardens of incense-bearing trees, with the sacred river meandering with mazy motion five miles through them to the sea, is the most dream-like. Indeed, all that most of us know of it comes through a dream. And, as Dr Livingstone Lowes has pointed out, tradition relates that the great Khan himself saw it in a dream before he built it If you travel to see it now, all you will find standing of the forest city of Xanadu or of its seven hundred years old palace that was the summer residence of the mighty Kublai Khan, will be one of the six thirteenth-century gates in a fragment of wall. Some years ago there was more. Two Englishmen from Peking visited it in 1872, they found a deserted site, overgrown with weeds and grass, standing above the marshy river's bed. The walls still stood, forming a double enceinte; the inner line defined the area of the palace; it had three gates, of which one, a great arch in the south wall, was intact. The outer wall had six gates. Within the walls were foundations of buildings, blocks of marble and fragments of sculptures; all the debris of a once flourishing city. It stood in a space which must have been a park, and which covered about five square miles. Inside the park, said Marco Polo, who served Kublai in his summer palace for years, there were fountains and rivers and brooks, and beautiful meadows with all kinds of wild animals; the woods and rivers and fountains are all gone; there only remain on the desolate land the wild animals and a small lama monastery.

And of the palace, a few fragments and a mass of buried

foundations. We can build up the palace in imagination, as Coleridge did, from Marco Polo's account. "You come to a city called Chandu, which was built by the Kaan now reigning. There is at this place a very fine marble Palace, the rooms of which are all gilt and painted with figures of men and beasts and birds, all executed with such exquisite art that you regard them with delight and astonishment. Round this Palace a wall is built, inclosing a compass of 16 miles. . . ." In the park the Khan had another palace built of cane, which could be taken down and moved from place to place; it was gilded all over, and rested on gilt and lacquered columns. Kublai spent three months of each summer at this park of his, dwelling sometimes in the marble palace, sometimes in the cane, and all the summer he drank the milk of his brood of pure white mares, and his enchanters, when he sat at table in the palace, caused cups of wine to be set before him without human hand. The palace stood among a throng of temples, courts, pavilions and domes, and the green forest arched about them.

Of course Coleridge has enhanced, partly created, our pleasure in Xanadu. No British traveller but, on seeing it, must recite the dream poem that we all learnt in childhood. "I on honey-dew have fed, and drunk the milk of paradise," a clergyman wrote in 1887. "I stood among the palace ruins and recited 'In Xanadu did Kubla Khan,' and truly thought that I saw before me 'the shadow of the dome of pleasure', the gardens bright with sinuous rills, the incense-bearing trees, and heard the murmur from the caverns measureless to man, and even fancied the Abyssinian maid performing on the dulcimer. I was rapt away. . . ."

A dream palace, seen through a dream poem.

2

In another mood—but we are still more rapt away, by the splendour of what we see and what once was there—we climb the hill on the road to Tibur, where Hadrian's Villa lies, among olive-groves and vines, with the high line of Monte Calvio behind. Its ruins are so extensive that it used, before excavation, to be thought by the Campagna peasants the remains of a town, a predecessor of Tivoli; they called it Tivoli Vecchio. Even after centuries of excavation and archaeological research, not all is clear in the magnificent *Trümmerfeld* of this great palace town, this huge Folly of the second century, which must have given its creator such infinite pleasure to construct. For Hadrian's Villa was a work of piety, a monument to what he had always loved best in the world—the beautiful things he had seen on his travels. Travelling abroad, seeing foreign sights, restoring and improving them, taking some of them back to Rome, building temples and theatres and arches and forums, and adding whole new quarters to Greek and Eastern cities (to be called Adrianopolis)—these were his noble and generous pastimes. He had, says Audrollet, "*la manie de la pierre et du ciment*"; he was accompanied on his travels by a legion of architects and masons, and sowed buildings all along his route. But most he liked to see things; it was his ruling passion, and what he called touring the empire was a labour of love, an enthusiastic adventure among the beauties of art and of nature (he was, among other things, an ardent mountaineer), and famous ruins, such as Ilium, Thebes and Nauplia sent him into ecstasies. He returned from his first empire tour in 125, and settled at Tivoli, where, upon a villa already in existence, he started the planning and building of his great rambling inconsequent palace. Yet, though it rather wears that air, inconsequent it was not; he had a definite scheme and plan for it; it was to reproduce the buildings, even the landscapes, that had given him so much pleasure in Greece and Egypt. He gave them the names of their prototypes abroad—the Lyceum, the Academy, the Prytaneus, the Poecile, the Canopus, the Vale of Tempe, with the Peneus flowing through; and by these names they are, rightly or wrongly, identified to-day. Whatever they are called, and whatever they were meant to resemble, to walk through them is an extraordinary experience of palatial life on its most imposing scale. Entering by a cypress avenue from the Tivoli road, one passes on one side a Greek theatre, on the other, in the distance, the Vale of Tempe and the Peneus; overlooking the Vale is a fine groved terrace. The path leads on to the Poecile, its walls painted after Polygnotus; only one wall now remains, and no painting. Off the Poecile is a decorated dining-room; then the olive-grown stadium, courtyards and colonnades, a tangle of small rooms and latrines, an immense number of baths of all temperatures, elaborate heating arrangements, vaulted and frescoed and mosaicked colonnaded halls, libraries, guests' quarters, the magnificent Piazza d'Oro, a moated island which was possibly an aviary, a cryptoporticus with mosaic vaulting, swimming pools entered by steps, and the imitation of the Canopus, that celebrated and popular Alexandrian pleasure canal bordered by hostelries and booths leading to the temple of Serapis. How far Hadrian's canal, bordered by amusement booths, and ending in the large vaulted temple surrounded with fountains and decorated with frescoes and statues, resembled its original, it is hard to say; but making it and using it for parties of pleasure on pretended trips to Serapis must have been the greatest fun, even if the orgies en route fell short of Alexandrian form. Beyond this fantasy the ruins straggle on—another smaller palace on a terrace, a theatre, subterranean passages supposed to be a mimic Hades, an olive farm strewn with ancient fragments. By the time one has walked the several miles of this palatial ramble, one has a great affection for its charming, eager, erudite, art-loving, pleasure-loving and immensely vain creator, who so expended his imagination and wealth in building images of the beauty he had seen, who collected the rich store of statues (many were of the drowned and beloved Antinous as a god) which were found and removed from the palace during the centuries of excavation; who entertained his friends on such a lordly scale, who built lecture halls, exquisitely decorated banqueting rooms, libraries, theatres, swimming baths, pleasure canals, who sought to bring Greece and Egypt, Elysium and the infernal regions, to his Tivoli hillside, constructing this great marble town of assorted and beautiful buildings and gardens, this stupendous and learned Folly.

The villa was added to after Hadrian's death, down to the time of Diocletian. It must have been largely destroyed by Totila when he sacked Tivoli; what was left of it stood decaying through the middle ages, and was pillaged for its sculptures and mosaics during the Renaissance, in the usual destructive manner, regardless of damage to structure. "Unfortunately for it," wrote Gaston Boissier, "Hadrian's villa turned out to be much richer in such things than all the other ruins that had been excavated.

52 Temple of Jupiter Panhellenius. Aegina Engraving by Wm Pars, 1747

53 Ruins of the Palace of Justinian, Byzantium

54 Ruins of the Bishop's Palace, Lincoln. Water-colour by Peter de Wint (1784-1849)

55 Robert Adam drawing the interior of the Palace of Diocletian, Spalato, 1764

56 Ruins at the head of the Knights Street, Rhodes. Engraving by W. H. Bartlett, 1836-8

It became for three centuries a kind of inexhaustible mine which furnished masterpieces to all the museums in the world. Thence came the Faun in *rosso antico*, the Centaurs in grey marble, and the Harpocrates of the Capitol; the Muses and the Flora of the Vatican. . . . The pillage lasted down to our days" (i.e. the late nineteenth century, when the villa was bought by the government). Many more statues and sculptures than these came out of the villa; in the eighteenth century a great number were seized for Lansdowne House; very few capital cities have not their share of the plunder; and since the first serious assaults under Alexander VI, over two hundred and sixty works of art have been extracted from the vast treasure-house. Indeed, even more pleasure has been derived from the villa in ruin than during the centuries of its glorious heyday. All intelligent sightseers have rejoiced in the unrivalled spectacle. That great enthusiast for travel and works of art and nature, including good ruins, Aeneas Silvius, Pope Pius II, visited Tivoli in 1461, on one of his many tours, and broke into a delighted dirge. "Time," said he, "has defaced everything. The walls which were once adorned by tapestries of bright colours and gold and by embroidered hangings are now covered with ivy. Thorns and briars grow where Tribunes used to sit in their purple robes, and snakes now inhabit the chambers of princes. Such is the fortune of all mortal things." Travellers through the sixteenth, seventeenth and eighteenth centuries never failed to be similarly impressed; except perhaps John Evelyn, who, a little dizzy with the glories of the Villa d'Este and its delicious "artificial miracles", pronounced the Hadrian Villa, which he was shown in passing, "only a heap of ruins". The French traveller, M. Guys, found that "*toute la magnificence des ouvrages et des bâtiments Romains respire encore dans ces restes*", but he preferred Tivoli, with its Sibyl's temple and cascades and its memories of Horace, Catullus, Maecenas and Zenobia. The romanticism of Chateaubriand was, on the other hand, richly fed by this immense ruin-maze, grown over with wild verdure that charmed the eye and saddened the heart; "never were heaven and earth, the works of nature and of man, better mingled in a picture." Wandering over the ruins, he felt himself transported to Greece and Egypt, Elysium and Hades. He was, in fact, the visitor for whom the villa was designed. He did not leave it without filling his pockets with small pieces of porphyry, alabaster, vert antique and mosaic, and noting how other people had written their names on the marble walls, hoping to prolong their existence by attaching to celebrated places a souvenir of their existence; but, he decided, they deceived themselves.

Before the ruins were stripped of their shrubs and flowers in the 1870's, they must have been fantastically beautiful—"a wide and wondrous wilderness of ruin, avenues dark with cypress, and steep banks purple with violets. The air was heavy with perfume. The glades were carpeted with daisies, wild periwinkle, and white and yellow crocus blooms . . . we found a sheet of mosaic pavement glowing with all its marbles in the sun, and close by, half buried in deep grass, a shattered column of the richest porphyry. . . ." And so on. Later, the destroying hand of the ruin-clearers got to work, and in 1875 Augustus Hare complained that, with the flowers rooted up, the ruins stripped of their creepers and of their fringe of lovely shrubs, the Villa Adriana was little worth a visit. He was of that school of romantics which likes its ruins picturesquely served up. But those who do not to-day find the villa beautiful, exciting and grand, sprawling over its olive and cypress slopes and valleys, the shattered, fantastic palace of a cultivated, pleasure-loving and whimsical emperor and patron of the arts, had better spend their Tivoli visit, as Evelyn did, in the ingenious gardens of the Villa d'Este, or looking at the cascades and the temples and guessing at the site of Horace's villa.

3

The Mons Palatinus, which gave its name to all palaces, is perhaps the most moving of the groups of memorials to imperial Rome. Roma Quadrata, the cradle of primitive Rome, once enclosed by the walls of Romulus, became a hill of elegant private houses and then of the palaces of the Caesars, climbing one above the other, sprawling over what is really three hills, Tiberius overshadowing with his great palace the modest house of Augustus, Caligula extending the Domus Tiberiana till it overlooked the Via Nova, Nero creating his gigantic Golden House after the fire, Vespasian beginning and Domitian completing the series of magnificent halls that toadying contemporary poets and admiring posterity have compared to Olympus, Hadrian building his exquisite palace that the mighty structures of Severus swallowed up—all of them fallen into ruin by the seventh century, progressively wrecked and buried deeper through the middle ages, whose writers called the whole lot collectively the *palatium maius*, and whose robber barons set on their foundations their castles and towers, till the Farnesi took them in the sixteenth century and laid on them great gardens; and all down the centuries they were battered to pieces, quarried, plundered, and buried in débris, until the hill was a shapeless mass of shrubbed ruin, to be at last explored and excavated in the nineteenth century. To-day the different palaces are identified and named, the identification varying from decade to decade, so that some confusion reigns. Of some there remain scarcely any visible vestiges; of others rows of magnificent arches and vaults, broken columns, massive sub-structures and terraces and fragments of wall, loom upon the hillside and valleys among the jumble of other ruins—temples, libraries, porticoes, houses and baths—in shattered majesty still beautiful in spite of their spoliation, and in spite of the stripping from them of much of the vegetation that gave them once the aspect of a jungle-buried city.

Behind the rugged beauty of the ruined arcaded piles standing formidably among greenery, there rise the shadowy palaces in all their glory, one imposed like a palimpsest on another as each age shifts into the next. There lies the Palatine of the late republic, the aristocratic quarter of Rome, the resort of rich and famous Romans, set about with commodious and elegant villas; here Cicero had his house, "*in conspectu totius urbis*", surrounded by his friends and enemies (Clodius had a house just above his, and Catullus was round the corner) and in easy reach of the Forum: Cicero's life, as we know, was spent in almost continuous travel from one of his villas to another and he pretended to prefer the country life of Tusculum, Antium, Tivoli, Cumae or Baiae, or the provincial gaieties of Pompeii, to the bustle of Rome; but in Rome he lived while engaged in public business, and on the Mons Palatinus he breathed good air and had a fine view of the city; his *Palatina praenesta* was "*in pulcherrimo urbis loco*", and we know pretty well where it stood and what it was like. Clodius destroyed it in malice, and its site was swallowed up later by the palace of Caligula. This cloud-capped palace stands, on the high arches we still see, looking over the Via Nova, sumptuously decorated with the glories of Hellenistic art. A flight of steps runs up from the street to the highest storey; a bridge is flung across the valley passing over the Forum and joining the Palatine to the Capitol; through the temple of Castor and Pollux the emperor passes from his palace to take his seat between the statues of the divine twins and receive the adoration of the crowds below; the palace, shining in marble and painted stucco ornament, is a warren of galleries, stairways, corridors and halls; about it Caligula capers and struts, mad, naked, or dressed up as a god, a warrior, or a charioteer; before he is thirty he is to be a shrieking, murdered ghost.

On the great arcades topped by Farnese trees, rises the shadowy image of the Domus Tiberiana, the earliest of the great palaces, for the house of Augustus was a modest, delicately lovely dwelling, scarcely to be called a palace. Tiberius's palace is a fine building, full of gracefully decorated rooms. But it is put in the shade by Nero's Golden House, built in the open spaces made by the great fire of 64. Like a country villa, it spreads over a huge region, surrounded by meadows, vineyards, woods full of wild creatures, "to resemble a wilderness", says Tacitus, and a lake as large as a sea, with buildings on its shores; it steals, complains Pliny, half Rome, lying across the plain between the Palatine and Caelian and the Esquiline. We see the palace as Suetonius describes it; triple porticoes a mile in length, its walls overlaid with gold, jewels and mother-of-pearl, banqueting halls vaulted with ivory ceilings which scatter on the guests unguents and flowers as they sup; the chief supper room is circular, and perpetually revolves like the celestial bodies. The baths are fed with water from the sea. At the entry to the palace stands a colossal statue of Nero, one hundred and twenty feet high. He should have died hereafter, for he had unfinished mighty works in hand, such as a pond into which should flow hot streams from Baiae, and he hoped to find in Carthage the treasure hidden there by Dido. However, he admitted to his architects that he now had a dwelling fit for a man. Alas that we can only see it with the eyes of imagination. As we gaze at the grandiose, arrogant, glittering structure, magnificently lying in its wooded spaces, it melts and changes into the great palace of the Flavians which replaced it. Domitian's palace is one of the most famous in history; it was not inferior, said the poets who were invited to sup there, to Olympus, but still inferior to the emperor who entertained them. As to Statius, his head was altogether turned after his first banquet in that noble hall.

"I seemed to be feasting in the heart of heaven with Jove, taking from the Trojan's hand immortal wine. . . . Ruler of the world, great father of the conquered globe, hope of mankind, darling of the gods, can it be that I behold thee as I recline? Is it *thou*? And dost thou suffer me to see thy face hard by at the board over the wine. . . .? Noble is the hall and spacious, not glorified with a hundred columns, but with so many as might bear up the gods in heaven were Atlas discharged. . . . So high the vault above, the weary sight can scarce strain to the roof: you might think it the ceiling of the golden heavens."

The tables were of Moorish citron-wood, set on pillars of ivory; but when we are hoping for further description of the decor of the supper room, the over-excited poet only raves of the glory and beauty of his god-like host. Bianchini, who excavated the hall for the Duke of Parma in 1722, gives more detail, telling of marble-inlaid walls, Corinthian columns wonderfully worked, colossal statues in basalt, columns of *giallo antico* on either side of the door (which were sold for a large sum), and a great marble threshold. The triclinium has a pavement of coloured marbles; the windows, with columns of red granite, open on fountains, cascading coolly for the pleasure of the reclining guests. Nothing more brilliant, says Martial, does the eye of day see in all the world, than this hall, of which all is vanished but a floor of polychrome marble, a few Corinthian columns and some fragments of wall. The decorations and statues which were still there when Bianchini made his excavations were taken and sold; the palace was a treasury of rich marbles and sculpture. An immense peristyle with pillars of porta santa and walls polished to reflect approaching enemies, where the emperor took his walks in well-justified apprehension, opens out of the chain of sumptuous halls. To the south east is the *domus augustana*, the part of the palace used as the emperor's private residence; it used to be supposed the palace of Augustus; its porticoed façade looks on the Circus Maximus. Its grandiose, complicated structure is still being progressively discovered. Beyond it is the great stadium, with its imperial box whence the emperors could watch the games. Those of us who grew up believing Octavius Augustus to have dwelt in this magnificence miss him from the pompous scene; one would rather see him there than Domitian catching flies. But Augustus, it now appears, dwelt in the *casa di Augusto*, that used to be *detto* the House of Germanicus, and after that was *detto* the *casa di Livia* (and indeed by some still is). If so, one likes him the better, and it is the better also for us, since this house is still beautiful, and the best preserved of the desirable residences on the Palatine. With palaces and temples perishing all round it, burying it, as time went on, under piles of earth and ruin, this exquisite dwelling was never quite destroyed, either by fire or by rebuilding emperors; when it was excavated by Signor Rosa in 1869 the lower storey, though mutilated, still had its wall paintings and its friezes, preserved in the darkness of centuries of oblivion. The painted decorations of the rooms are most lovely, even now, when blurred and defaced by mishandling, clumsy excavation and restorations, and the fading caused by exposure to bright light. When first excavated, the colours must have been radiantly beautiful; Hellenistic art in the second style of Pompeii, but even better than anything found there. There are graceful festoons of fruit and flowers, friezes of winged figures and arabesques, country views, gardens, fountains and Roman streets framed in elegant cheating windows, fluted pillars painted on red walls, and scenes from mythology. The sala di Polifemo has, on two of its walls, a painting of Io, Argos and Hermes, much blurred since its discovery, and another of Poyphemus pursuing Galatea through the sea; this has almost entirely disappeared; we only know it from photographs and paintings made just after the excavation; it is a melancholy loss, for its grace and spirit and colour must have been exquisite. Through a transparent blue-green sea, whose reaches wind back between hills, the burly Cyclops, a little Eros on his shoulders, wades breast-deep after the white-bodied nymph riding a prancing sea-horse and turning back on her lover a bland gaze of unconcern, while her two companion nereids, waist-deep, look on and mock the clumsy shepherd. It is the gayest and prettiest of Theocritan idylls; and to look at the poor reproductions which are all we have to recall it is a melancholy business; its death was so unnecessary. The pictures seem to have been by Greek artists, and were probably after famous Greek originals.

The whole house is the most attractive ruin imaginable; really to understand it one should read Dr Giulio Rizzo's beautifully illustrated *Casa di Livia* before seeing it, Dr Giuseppe Lugli on its probable origins, and Dr Jacquemont on *Les Peintures de Mont Palatin*.

After this enchanting house, the tremendous arches and vaults that supported the palace of Septimus Severus—or were they, as is now suggested, only baths?—seem clumsily magnificent, with a picturesque grandeur almost medieval. Here, indeed, the Roman barons of the middle ages, set their castles; and its ruins stood up through the centuries above the encroaching earth that buried the rest of the *palatium maius*. From the terrace above the arcades one can see all Rome, and half the Campagna; on a clear day, the Alban hills, Frascati, Castel Gandolfo. This—if palace it was—was the last of the imperial palaces. Beside it rose the Septizonium, that marvellous pretentious façade that Sixtus V destroyed. Engulfed among the huge structures of Severus are the few remains of the palace of Hadrian; and work is still in progress underground among the foundations of the Flavian palace, excavating a labyrinth of halls, mosaic pavements, rooms decorated with frescoes and arabesques. There seems, indeed, no end to the *palatium maius*.

But it is such stuff as dreams are made on, and, like the baseless fabric of this vision, the cloud-capped towers, the gorgeous palaces, dissolve as we look, leaving only wracks behind.

4

More substantial is the palace that Diocletian built at Spalato, and where he spent his last nine years living in luxurious retirement and growing cabbages. "Reason had dictated, and content seems to have accompanied, his retreat," as Gibbon observed. No one who has seen this magnificent palace can be surprised.

It has always, both before and after it took on (in the seventh century) its present eccentric and unique appearance of a town enclosed in a palace, produced a stupendous effect on those who have visited it. It has been, possibly, the most serviceable ruin in the world, for it contains several hundred houses and several thousand inhabitants, besides a whole medieval town of narrow streets and small squares, clustering about the few Roman buildings that remain. The refugees from the ruined Salona, after fleeing from the detestable Avars to the islands, crept back to shelter themselves behind the walls of the great abandoned palace, building their houses in the arches and between the columns, blocking up the arched windows of the long cryptoporticus that ran the length of the wall above the sea, destroying halls and courts and colonnades so as to fit in their little dwellings and streets, turning a Roman palace into a medieval slum, turning pagan temples and a mausoleum into Christian churches. With its backing of mountains and its long arcaded façade rising from the sea, and the wide bay of ships before it stretching east and west between sheltering juts of land, the square palace town lying amid its outer fortifications and the sprawl of modern town that has grown up outside its walls astonishes the eye and mind. "As we skirt its waterfront for about six hundred feet we gradually understand that there is no parallel to what we are seeing," a professor of archaeology from the new world wrote forty years ago; "a medieval city of nearly twenty thousand people built largely inside the walls of an imperial fortified villa-palace, planned like a military camp and yet a monument of luxury and magnificence." Visitors to Spalato have always said much the same of it, since the emperor Constantine Porphyrogenitus commented in the tenth century that it surpassed, even in its ruin, all powers of description. It was admired and described by sixteenth, seventeenth and eighteenth-century travellers; but the first accurate and detailed survey, that publicized it in Europe, was Robert Adam's monumental work of description and engraving. Adam, who had a great desire to "add the observation of a private residence of the Ancients to my study of their public works", and who, apparently, had not visited the recently discovered Pompeii or Herculaneum, travelled to Dalmatia in 1754 to inspect the palace of which he had heard so much, taking with him the French artist, Clerisseau, and two draughtsmen. What he wanted to see was one of the magnificent villas described by the Romans, such as Pliny's, with the additional grandeur given it by that noble and extravagant imperial architect whose structures he had admired in Rome and elsewhere; he undertook his expedition with the most sanguine hopes, rewarded by his first sight of the city, "so happily situated that it appears, when viewed from the sea, not only picturesque, but magnificent. As we entered a grand bay, and sailed slowly towards the harbour, the Marine Wall, and long Arcades of the Palace, one of the ancient Temples, and other parts of that building which was the object of our voyage, presented themselves to our view, and flattered me that my labor in visiting it would be amply rewarded.

"To these soothing expectations of the pleasure of my task, the certain knowledge of its difficulty soon succeeded." For the inhabitants who had made their home in the abandoned palace had, as they built up their town down the centuries, destroyed much of the Roman buildings, using the stones for what indignant visitors ever since have called their mean and paltry houses, their maze of narrow streets and squares. Medieval towers and walls, Venetian fortifications, destroyed arcades and colonnades, christianized temples, had made a confusion of the palatial scheme which needed great skill to sort out. But Adam's views and plans have admirable lucidity as well as beauty, and have been the chief guide to the palace ever since. Even the French archaeologist, Cassas, full of patriotic jealousy forty years later, who complained that Adam had seen everything with the cold egotism of his nation, plagiarized from him freely and without acknowledgment. Since Adam, there has been restoration, renovation and reconstruction, not all good: but in the main the palace-town is as he saw and drew it. There is the long arcaded cryptoporticus on the sea wall, its arches filled in with green-shuttered dwellings and shops; here the emperor took his walks, and from the chamber at the western end saw the sunset like a rose beyond the bay; of the fifty Doric columns between the arches, forty remain; of the four gates there are three. Entering by the Porta Aurea in the north wall, an arched portal beneath a row of arcaded niches where statues once stood (something in the style of Theodoric's palace at Ravenna) one walks between medieval houses and shops to where the residential part of the palace and the Roman buildings begin. Before us is the arcaded peristylium, now the piazza del Duomo, its arcades filled up with medieval and later houses and buildings; it is rich in sculptured decoration; its Corinthian pillars, mostly intact, are of rose granite and cipollino; the doors and balconies between them do not spoil the effect. Adam's engraving shows merchants selling bales of cloth, and women washing clothes, beneath the rich friezes and capitals, and marble lattices with shrubs pushing up through the pavement, and a sphinx couchant beside the steps leading into the portico of the vestibule. A colossal modern bronze statue of a bishop by Mestrovik stands incongruously there to-day. A great quadrangular atrium opens on to the crypto-porticus, that tremendous gallery above the sea wall, once decorated all along its length with statues and sculpture and paintings. Off the gallery is a row of large rooms; all the usual accommodation of a large Roman villa, but on the immense and majestic scale suited to an emperor. It is less ambitious and romantically exciting than Hadrian's villa; Diocletian, a century and a half later, had not that picturesque and world-embracing artistic taste; and architecture and sculpture had both begun to decline. But it is a better specimen of an imperial villa; to study its scheme and plan is to realize more precisely the Roman way of life. And it has the eternally attractive romance of the accretions of the ages; medieval built on to classical, pagan turning Christian; it is one of the best examples in the world of picturesque life in a ruin. Diocletian's octagonal domed mausoleum became a Christian church when the refugees from Salona settled there, then a cathedral, its original beauty and decoration visible under its fourteenth and fifteenth-century interior work and the recent unfortunate restorations. In spite of these, it is the only imperial tomb preserved almost intact. Outside, it is more beautiful; the medieval campanile erected in what was its portico is, though incongruous and much restored, attractive. To the west of it, almost entire, the heavily friezed and portalled baptistery, once a temple, with its waggon roof and rich carvings, is a beautiful example of its period and style. It is surrounded by charming sculptured fragments, and by a jumble of houses.

To walk about the nine acres or so of city between the palace walls is delightful. Everywhere about the narrow medieval streets are Venetian houses and palaces, balconies and windows, among modern shops and cafés, Roman colonnades, pretty courtyards, and stairs, fragments of ancient friezes and bas-reliefs on houses and gates; the medley recalls, as it should, the late empire with an Oriental touch, the Dalmatian Middle Ages, the Venetian and Hungarian régimes. Much of the imperial stone, pulled down by the settlers, is still to be seen in the medieval houses.

The town outside the palace walls sprawls westward between mountains and sea, Venetian towers and palace and a labyrinth of narrow streets round the great Piazza dei Signori and the smaller Piazza del Mercato down by the quay. Split is now a thriving capital city, full of hotels, modern shops, casinos, cafes, bathing beach, and all a capital should have. But, so long as its great palace stands there, holding the medieval town close within its arcaded walls, it will remain the *palatium*, the last great imperial palace, Diocletian's seaside villa outside his noble Roman city of Salona, the capital of Dalmatia.

5

Diocletian's is one of the few Roman imperial villas now standing moderately intact; it is also the largest. But it lacks, with its huge formidable military-camp air, the delicious amenities of the palaces and villas that crowd the gulf of Naples, the Phlegraean fields so beloved of patrician Romans, poets, statesmen and emperors, the *optandosque sinus*, the *blandissima litora*, of *aestuantes Baiae*, the Sorrentine hills beloved of Bacchus, the shores where Roman *honos* and Greek *licentia* so happily mixed (*deversorium vitiorum*, growled Seneca), and where every one in Rome who was any one had his villa or his palace to retire to from the Roman dog-days. We see their ruins now, or many of them; scattered down the mountains that run down to the sea, themselves too running into the sea, *villes englouties*, drowned as well as wrecked, for some who lacked enough room on the shore (so great was the competition for house-space) thrust out, as Horace jeered, into the sea, "and met there the freshness and salubrity of another element": but the cause of their drowning was that the sea of the bay, so often convulsed by volcanic commotions, rose twenty feet above its old level, so that, crossing the bay, "you will sail over ancient villas, you will discern deep under your boat, a branch of the Domitian way," wrote Joseph Forsyth a century and a half ago; and, as Lucretius wrote, nineteen centuries earlier,

> "*multae per mare pessum*
> *Subsedere, suis pariter cum civibus, urbes.*"

It is the case that the ruins of the villas have gradually or suddenly "tumbled over the rocks into the sea or else been submerged, and so if you take a boat beyond the Mergellina mole and look into the water in which the children are swimming like fishes, you can see the floors of Roman apartments in the seaweed twenty feet below."[1] Fynes Moryson, visiting the lovely bay in 1594, thought the ancient city of Baiae "most sweete":

> "but all the houses neere to the shoare are drowned, except the Baths, and the houses on the mountains are all ruined, . . . yet these ruines show the pride and magnificence of that old time. . . . Here bee the foresaid ruines of Caligula his bridge. . . . Here we did see the stately ruines of two senators' houses, where the excellent pictures did yet remaine upon the highest roofe . . . all this Territorie, on both sides neere this Creeke or Bay of the Sea, are so full of ruined Palaces, Temples, and Sepulchres, as a man would say, they were not several villages, but one great Citie. . . ."

as Pliny also remarked of the coast near Ostia where his Laurentum villa stood. One gathers that the whole Mediterranean coast of Italy was crowded with resorts and fine villas; the bays of the Naples gulf being the smartest. Here were the palaces, and here, as John Evelyn said, "the sweet retirements of the most opulent and voluptuous Romans." George Sandys, visiting the elegant bay in 1610, mused pleasurably on the ruins, the opulence, and the vice.

> "A declaration of the magnificency and riches of the Romans; but too much of their luxury; beautified with ample temples, multitudes of Bannios, Imperial Palaces, and the adjoining Mannor-houses of the principal Romans. . . . Egyptian Canopus was a school of virtue, compared to the voluptuous liberty of this City.

[1]Bernard Wall, *Italian Life and Landscape* (1950).

The Inn (saith Seneca) and receptacle for vices: where luxury taketh the reins. . . . What a sight it is to see drunkards reeling along the shoar; the banquetings of such as are rowed on the water, the Lakes reckoning their continual canzonets and the like. . . . One winter only here enfeebled Hannibal, and the delights of Campania did what the snow and the Alps could not do; victorious in arms, yet by vices vanquished. . . ."[1]

Harlots, he mused, sailed by in painted boats of diverse colours, the Lake was strewed over with roses, the night noises of singers would have displeased Cato. But see what happened to Baiae.

"*Baiae*, not much inferiour to *Rome* in magnificency, equal in beauty, and superiour in healthful situation, hath now scarce one stone left above another, demolished by War, and devoured by Water. For it would seem that the *Lombards* and *Saracens* in the destruction hereof had not only a hand, but that the extruded Sea hath again regained his usurped limits: made apparent by the paved streets and traces of foundations to be seen under water. The shore is all overgrown with bushes and myrtles, the vaults and thrown down walls inhabited by Serpents: and what is more, the air heretofore so salubrious is now become infectious and unhealthful."

Palaces, fishponds, lampreys, swimming-pools on the tops of houses, all were perished, leaving only their ruins under water or in caves. Here in these villas were held the house parties of the political and literary intellectuals; the gatherings and the topics discussed recall Falkland's house parties at Great Tew. Near Cumae are the ruins of Cicero's villa, and that of his friend Catullus, and a little way off was the house of Varro, which Cicero made the setting of the first Dialogue of his Academica; the second was held at Hortensius's villa at Bauli, of which we see the ruins beneath the sea; here Hortensius had his cisterns of lampreys, which, says Martial, came when called by name, and on which Antonia the wife of Drusus (who, says the elder Pliny, was never known to spit) hung golden ear rings. Here, too, wicked Nero planned the murder of his mother by drowning (which she foiled on that occasion by swimming too well), and here Cicero and Catullus and Lucullus, seated in Hortensius's colonnade, discussed philosophy, logic and what have you until it was time

[1]George Sandys, *Travels* (1636)

to sail for Naples and Pompeii across the smooth evening bay before the breeze from the peach-red west. The modern village of Bacoli is built among the vast scattered ruins of this villa. Those of Cicero's own villa are supposed to lie between Pozzuoli and the Lucrine Lake. But the ruins scattered all round the bay of Pozzuoli and Baiae down to the promontory of Miseno are mostly indistinguishable, a huge jumble of the patrician homes of the noblest Romans on holiday. The famed house of Lucullus, which later passed to Tiberius, sprawled over the cape in its huge and extravagent grandiosity, half of it under the sea.

"In the course of a few minutes," said Forsyth, "you sail past the highest names of antiquity. You see Marius, Sylla, Pompey, Piso, Tiberius, Nero, all crowding in for the most beautiful angles and elbowing each other's villas. Yet where are those villas now? Alas! nothing but masses of built tufo which you can hardly distinguish from the tufo of the hill."[1]

Evelyn, who wisely accepted what he was told by guides, had the pleasure of feeling sure which ruin had been which villa or palace; he "rowed along towards a villa of the orator Cicero's, where we were showed the ruins of his Academy, and at the foot of a rock, his Baths, the waters reciprocating their tides with the neighbouring sea;" he even believed that he saw the Elysian fields, "full of myrtles and sweet shrubs, and having a most delightful prospect towards the Tyrrhene Sea. Upon the verge of these remain the ruins of the Mercato di Saboto, formerly a Circus; over the arches stand divers urns, full of Roman ashes."[2]

But, though Virgil's traditional tomb on the cape of Posilipo has fallen into discredit, we can even to-day, climbing to the top of the promontory, see and accept without question Pausilypum, the great palace villa of Vedius Pollio, whose ruins cover the whole headland and drop down into the sea, jutting up from the water in huge fragments and blocks. It must have been the most palatial villa of all this palatial coast; it was bequeathed to Augustus. Vedius Pollio, despite his pleasure-palace, one cannot think of with pleasure, for he threw slaves into the lamprey stews to be devoured. Alas, there is always, or nearly always, something in the past of ruins which displeases, and probably

[1] Joseph Forsyth.
[2] John Evelyn, *Diary*.

one should not know too much of their late owners. Of the imperial palaces down this golden coast and on its islands, those of Nero, Caligula, Tiberius and the rest, there remain a few temples, great baths, cisterns, the fragments jutting from the sea, and the seaweed-green pavements dimly seen through clear blue water. You can still swim about among palace walls, though now you have to hire a cabin and swim from a crowded bathing beach or rocks brown with sprawling bodies. For more than ever crowds are drawn from the hot cities to the *blandissima litora* of *aestuantes Baiae*, where Boccaccio's Fiammetta was taken by him to be cheered when she was pining of love. He retailed to her its delights—

"by ancient Cuma and Pozzuolo is the delightful Baiae above the sea shore, than which there is nothing more beautiful or more pleasing under the sky. There are beautiful hills covered with trees and vines . . . the oracles of the Cuman Sybil, the lake of Averno, the theatre of the ancient games, the baths, Monte Barbaro, and the vain works of the wicked Nero; which ancient things, new to modern minds, are no small cause of joy to see and wonder at."[1]

Fiammetta, foolish girl, pining of love, cared for none of these things. But, all down the ages, Italians and foreigners have rejoiced in them, agreeing with Evelyn that here is "doubtless one of the most divertissant and considerable vistas in the world" and full of the most stupendous rarities. To the ancient Roman and Italian enthusiasm for scenery, hills, woods, coast and sea, there has been added a pleasure they did not know, swimming among ruined palaces; for—*mira fides*—they did not go in much for bathing in the open sea, and the palaces were not yet in ruins. On the other hand, the coast was far more beautiful, being unspoilt by tram lines, industrial towns, and the sordid spread of Naples. Bishop Burnet's comment in 1685 is ironically interesting to-day.

"Though anciently," he wrote, "this was all so well built, so peopled, and so beautifully laid out, yet no where doth one see more visibly what a change time brings upon all places. For Naples hath so entirely eat out this place, and drawn its inhabitants to it, that Puzzuolo itself is but a small village, and there

[1]Boccaccio. *Fiammetta.*

is now no other in this Bay, which was anciently built almost all round; for there were seven big towns upon it."[1]

The towns have returned, and Naples, instead of drawing the bay's inhabitants into itself, has spewed her own all round the bay. Yet one may still agree with Burnet that "it is certain, that a man can no where pass a day of his life both with so much pleasure, and with such advantage, as he finds in his journey to Puzzuolo, and all along the Bay."

6

The imperial palaces burgeoned into luxuriant flower on Capri, where Augustus spent so much time, and where Tiberius passed the wicked evening of his days in at least twelve villas, some of which had belonged to Augustus before him. They are scattered about the island, some on mountain-tops, some down by the sea. The largest and the highest up is the Villa di Giove, or Palazzo di Timberio, on the north-east heights. To reach it is a long steep climb from the town; Tiberius, according to a sculpture found on the island, did it by donkey; so do wise travellers to-day. Its ruins are immense; Gregorovius, who got much pleasure out of them in 1853, thought them "among the most considerable remains of Roman pleasure palaces yet existing."

"One strays in a labyrinth of vaults, galleries, and chambers, now partly used as vineyard-houses and stables. Capitals, bases, mutilated columns, and slabs of marble are strewn around. Several chambers still bear traces of stucco on their walls, and even the mural paintings in deep yellow or the dark red of Pompei are yet distinguishable. Several floors still preserve their mosaic of white marble with black bordering, and here and there the staircases leading to the lower apartments remain intact. . . . Added to its other glories was the incomparably beautiful situation, overlooking both gulfs. . . .

"Many an hour I remained seated on the ruins and allowed my fancy to rebuild Capri. What a prospect, if one imagines all these heights crowned with marble palaces, and the island covered with temples, arcades, statues, theatres, streets, and pleasure-grounds! And what a picture this would form, enlivened by the court of a Roman Emperor."[2]

[1]Gilbert Burnet. *Travels* 1687).
[2]Gregorovius. *Wanderjahre in Italien* (1881-2).

57 The Castle of Tiflis Water-colour by Sir Robert Ker Porter, 1817-20

58 The Borgia Castle, Nepi

59 Château of Mehun-sur-Yèvre. Illumination by Pol de Limbourg, 1409-16

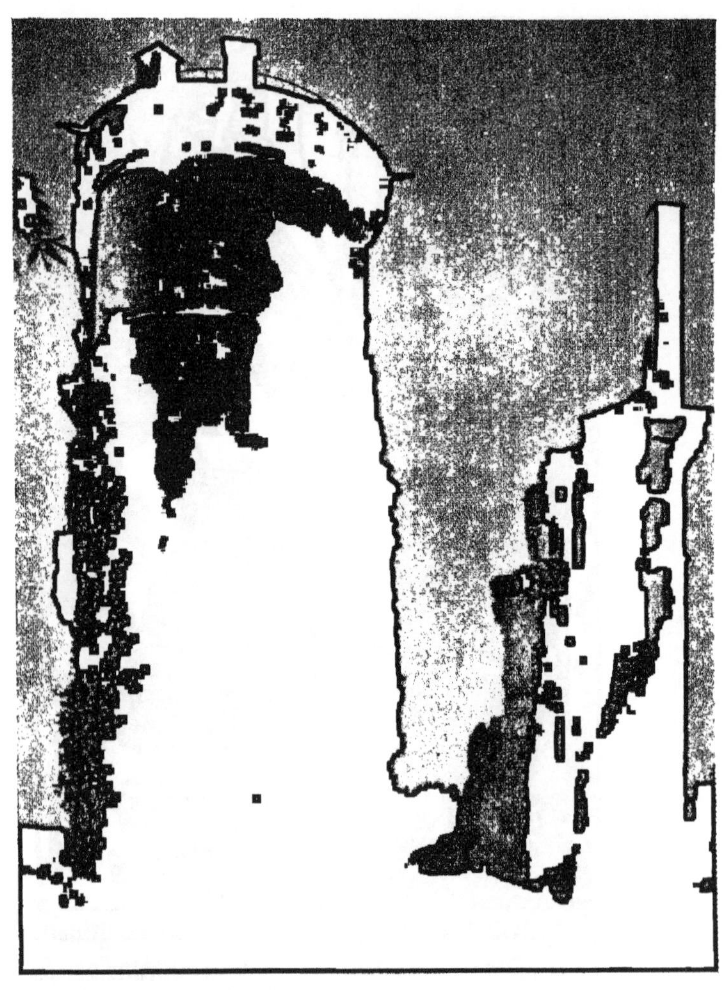

60 Château of Mehun-sur-Yèvre. Present condition

61 Walls of St Jean d'Acre. Engraving by W. H Bartlett, 1836-8

Yet, looking at a drawing of the Villa di Giove as imaginatively reconstructed by a German archaeologist, crowning the mountain, dazzlingly white, terraced and pinnacled, with hanging gardens full of toga'd statues, one may think that it looks grandiose, even a little vulgar, and is better in magnificent ruin, with the broken shafts of great columns standing among massive fragments of wall and vaulted roof on the mountain-top, behind the Salto di Tiberio, the cliff from which the as yet unwhitewashed emperor had his victims hurled into the sea a thousand feet below. Among this pagan wickedness, perhaps to sanctify it, the Caprenses have built a little Christian chapel, complete with hermit. There are ruins of the other villas elsewhere—the Villa Tiberiana, the Palazzo a Mare, one near the Blue Grotto, one at Fort San Michele; Tiberian ruins of this and that, villas, grottos, baths, litter the sea and hills.

The keenest pleasure given by Capri ruins must have been that of Dr Axel Munthe, digging the foundations of his new villa at San Michele near Anacapri on the site of another palace of Tiberius, or probably of Augustus. A yard below the surface he came on Roman walls,

"*opus reticulatum* as hard as granite with nymphs and bacchantes dancing on the intonoco of Pompeian red. Below appeared the mosaic floor framed with vine leaves of nero antico and a broken pavement of beautiful palombino, now in the centre of the big loggia. A fluted column of cipollino, now supporting the little loggia in the inner courtyard, lay across the pavement where it had fallen two thousand years ago, crushing in its fall a big vase of Parian marble, the lion-headed handle of which is now lying on my table. 'Roba di Timberio,' said Mastro Nicola, picking up a mutilated head of Augustus split in two."[1]

They found earthenware jars full of Roman coins ("*il tesoro di Timberio,*" said the peasants), the bronze hoofs of an equestrian statue, thousands of polished slabs of coloured marble, all which were used for the pavement of the new loggia and terraces and the old ruined chapel, which was being turned into a library. An exquisite agate cup was found, Greek vases, innumerable fragments of early Roman sculpture, Greek and Roman inscriptions, a tomb containing a skeleton with a Greek coin in his mouth,

[1] Axel Munthe, *The Story of San Michele* (1929).

all the ruin-finds one dreams of. Before Dr Munthe bought the land, an old peasant had dug it, planting vines, it had been full of "*roba di Timberio*", columns, capitals, marbles, which he had split up and used for his house and garden, throwing what he did not want over the precipice. He had come on a large subterranean room, with red walls painted with naked people dancing like mad, their hands full of flowers and grapes; it had taken him several days to scrape off the paintings and cover the walls with cement.

In the eighteenth and nineteenth centuries, the island was a happy hunting ground for diggers up of antiquities; Gregorovius tells of robbed marbles, mosaics, pillars and urns; well preserved chambers were discovered underground by the inhabitants and filled up again because the land was wanted; marble tablets with inscriptions were used as doorsteps, marble slabs paved roads, foreign collectors, such as Sir William Hamilton, Tischbein, and other connoisseurs from the barbarian lands, went home with rich spoils. Legends were repeated of how a peasant lad had seen underground somewhere, and forgotten just where, Timberio seated on a bronze horse with diamond eyes; perhaps the horse of which Dr Munthe years later found the hoofs. At Fort San Michele (on the other side of the island from Axel Munthe's San Michele) there are remains of a richly luxurious palace. The road climbs up on the roofs of vaulted chambers; gardens and vineyards stand on hollow ground; the mountain is covered with vine and olive terraces that mount the hill in steps above who knows what of palatial treasure, much was discovered and removed, much more covered up or left undug.

7

"The isle of Caprea," Burnet observed, "gave me a strange idea of Tiberius's reign." Indeed, many of the relics of emperors are liable to do this. They behave so eccentrically, catch flies, bathe in aqueducts, build such extraordinary bridges, moles, palaces, baths, proliferate into so many dwelling-houses. I do not know if Nero's, for instance, have been counted; (though for that matter he probably did not outdo Cicero.) He had a fine one at Subiaco, another on the Anzio shore, close to the port he had constructed. It contained some famous statues; the Apollo Belvedere and the Borghese gladiator were both found in its ruins. Some of its walls and corridors are still to be seen in the tufa rock. Antium was his birthplace, and he made it the fashion; the shore as far as and beyond Nettuno is strewn with the remains of Roman villas. To-day they are obscured by bathing establishments; it was nearly a century ago that the romantic Gregorovius described them.

"Out of the sea rise the foundations of ancient Roman water-palaces, and at a quarter of an hour's distance from Antium, the shore is nothing less than a ruin of continuous masonry. They look like masses of rock and the over-throwings of a cliff, and if one examines one finds that they are simply Roman walls of Peperino stone, and the imperishable Pozzolano, and delicate Roman reticulated work. Now the whole weird coast yawns with grottoes and halls of old baths and villas, and the foundations of temples, and palaces crop up along the edge of the shore. Here stood once the beautiful marble villas of the emperors. . . . Also in earlier days Antium was the beloved holiday resort of the Romans, Atticus, Lucullus, Cicero, Maecenas, and Augustus, had here their villas. . . . How this shore must then have shone with all the stones, the historic fragments, which the waves have constantly been tossing to and fro for centuries."[1]

Even in the present century Dr Lanciani saw more palace fragments in the sea than it is easy, without more imagination, than it is right to use, to see to-day. Sailing by the Antium coast through crystal-clear waters, he saw every detail of the bottom thirty feet below. "So perfect was their transparency that we were able to test for the first time the accuracy of the tradition current among the local fishermen about the existence of art treasures along this shallow shore." They saw a number of white marble columns half buried in sand, among weed, coral and sea lilies and thought that "those caverns of swaying submarine vegetation" contained works of higher value. Lanciani doubts the tradition that the Romans built villas into the sea; they were built, he says, on cliffs and headlands, which later got washed away, so that great masses of masonry lie out to sea, sometimes within a stone's throw of the shore, sometimes six hundred feet

[1]Gregorovius, *A Latian Summer*.

out; some of these can be seen, he says, in favourable conditions, off the promontory of Arco Scuro, and if proper search were made many works of art might be found. Bronze and gold objects had been recovered from the sand under Nero's palace, and columns from his harbour. Since Lanciani wrote thus, forty years ago, there has been a good deal of dredging, and a good many interesting finds: more will no doubt be made. Nero's palace is only to be seen in drowned fragments; the ruins of his mole, however, jut far into the harbour.

Anzio beach to-day has more recent ruinings than these, and Gregorovius's "delightful idyll of Antium" has become something of a mess; but these ruins too will put on beauty with time

One of the more dubious of ruined palaces is the palace that Trajan is said by some archaeologists to have built on the strip of land that divided his new Ostian port from that of Claudius. Others believe these remains to be of warehouses, or of some private dwelling. Whatever they were, their discovery was romantic, as recorded by M. Texier in an article at the time. In 1870 or so a workman chasing a badger found a hole. It was like the discovery of the Lascaux caves; how many more holes in the earth, if penetrated, will lead us to subterranean chambers of antiquity? One gets to feel that no hole should be left unprodded, and that a whole world of palaces, painted caverns, mosaic floors, pillared chambers, strewn perhaps with exquisite sculptures, bright with delightful mural paintings, lies beneath our feet awaiting our spades. Anyhow, this Ostian workman prodded his hole with a stick, removed a few large stones, and saw through the opening a spacious hall. Incurious contadino, caring only for badgers, he did not, it seems, penetrate further; but he gave information of his strange find, and M. Texier, who was studying the alluvium of the Mediterranean rivers for the French government, arrived and entered the underground hall and was overcome with wonder.

"Within this first ray of light, penetrating depths where darkness had reigned for centuries, fluttered a whole world of insects who had taken up their abode there; it illumined the bindweeds and the stalactites hanging from the roof, and the little pools of water shining on the floor. This hall led to another, and that to others again. There were so many, said M. Texier, and they were so vast, that in order to find one's way in the darkness one had to guide oneself by means of a compass, as one does in a virgin forest."[1]

Excavations were begun, but ill carried out, with the sole object of finding and removing objects of art for the museum; this done, the ruins were covered up. The only man allowed to see them before they were re-buried was Signor Lanciani, who described them as having splendid halls, baths, temples, a small theatre, and a huge portico. To-day, less romantically, it is described as a collection of different buildings, the principal ones being a bathing establishment, a small mithraeum, and a large portico with a number of vaulted rooms, probably a warehouse *Sic transit gloria palatium*: but, while its palatial status lasted, it gave extreme pleasure to M. Texier, Signor Lanciani, Prince Torlonia who had it excavated and extracted its objects of beauty, and "the rough peasant who guided Signor Lanciani", uttering cries of admiration the while.

8

For, there is no denying it, the ruins of palaces bestow a unique pleasure; greater than those of castles, temples, abbeys, theatres, warehouses, baths, or small dwellings. It is the haunting of past grandeur, the contrast betwen the vanished luxury, the rich grandiose living, and the shattered decay we now see.

> "Though he his House of polish't marble build,
> Yet shall it ruine like the Moth's frail cell."

Looking, for instance, on the solitary massive tower, with walls nine feet thick, that stands on the Cadmaea of Greek Thebes, the only remnant left of the magnificent palace-castle built there in the thirteenth century by a Frankish Duke of Athens, the fabulously rich Nicholas II of St Omer, one looks in imagination at that extraordinary pageant of medieval history, the reign of the crusading Dukes of Athens who governed Morea from their court at Thebes. And a court indeed it was. The palace is described in the *Chronicle of Morea*; it was called Santameri (St Omer), and was the finest mansion in all Greece. It had suites of

[1]Gaston Boissier, *Rome and Pompeii* (Fisher Unwin, 1896).

rooms enough for an emperor and all his court; round the walls were painted frescoes of the victories of the crusaders in the Holy Land; its banqueting halls were gorgeous and splendid, and in its outer courts tilted and jousted all the chivalry of Frankish Greece. Embassies came there from all lands; never was more magnificent ceremonial and pageantry than in this alien feudal western court lording it in a conquered eastern land.

"Here . . . a society which retained all the religious and feudal usages of the West was able, thanks to the absence of any threat from a cowed but industrious native population of serfs and the far higher standard of material comfort prevailing in lands which had once been ruled from Byzantium, to cultivate the politer arts of the Middle Ages, minstrelsy, jousting, the courts of love, to a pitch of refinement quite unattainable in their native lands."[1]

An agreeable line of reflection for the ruin-gazer to pursue, as he stands before the solitary massive Tower of St Omer, the sole relic of the Santameri palace which the Catalan adventurers destroyed in 1311. What a life was here lived: this is what we like to reflect on when we see ruined palaces. At Mycenae, what stormy Atridean family scenes; at the emperors' palaces in Naples bay and Capri, what tremendous orgies; in the Palatine palaces what pictures and what statues; in Hadrian's Villa what art and nature imported from abroad, what philosophizing in the halls, what voyaging in revelry down the canal to Canopus; in Knossos what minotaurs and what plumbing; in Nineveh and Babylon what winged bulls. And in Santameri what chivalric jousting and minstrelsy amazed and enlivened the Boeotian plains.

Palaces, châteaux, fortess-castles, whatever category one places them in, these formidable residences were piled up on crags by the Frankish princes about Greece, and in them the princes and their knights kept court. Above the lovely abandoned Byzantine town of Mistrá, whose crumbling streets climb steeply up to the citadel on a rocky spur of Taygetus, William of Villehardouin's thirteenth-century castle looms with broken walls and great towers and keep, seeming part of the mountain range; it is one of the noblest feudal castles of Greece, and here, too, in spite of its discouragingly formidable position with precipices on two sides,

[1]Osbert Lancaster, *Classical Landscape with Figures* (Murray, 1947).

the chivalric life was led; indeed, the Prince had a school of chivalry, to which young nobles flocked from east and west; no expense or luxury was absent in that magnificent court, where "prelates, barons, knights and other gentlemen made their fortunes according to their power, and led the best life that anyone could lead." But William lost Mistrá to the Greeks before the century was out, and his castle passed to the Despots, who built the Byzantine village and the Byzantine churches and convents, and their own huge palace on the lower hill, now a ruined shell, where they kept their Byzantine court and held Byzantine banquets, and it was as different from the vanished Frankish chivalric life as their crowding churches and convents with tiled and clustered domes and exquisite wall paintings are from Gothic architecture, of which nevertheless they have here and there a trace. Above the huddle of roofless churches and houses in the climbing narrow streets, the two great palaces, Frankish and Byzantine, tower against the background of the mountain range.

9

Antiquity is not an essential element in the romantic splendour of mouldering palaces. There is, for instance, King Christophe's huge Haitian palace of Sans Souci, built in 1812 on the precipitous mountains above the village of Milot, twenty miles from the sea, and now a magnificent tropical ruin, five-storeyed, rising above a balustraded terrace on the sweeping double flight of a grand stairway that suggests Versailles. The black king of Haiti determined that his palace should be finer than any in Europe, and more particularly than any in France. It was the palatial glory of the new world, piling up, terrace upon terrace, up the forested mountains above the Plaine du Nord, overlooking the distant sea. It is built of brick and stone and yellow stucco, now peeling and flaking off, and out of the walls and windows and columns and arches trees and creepers push; it is, like all tropical ruins, being drowned in engulfing vegetation. Stupendous in size and beauty, it spreads like a walled town; its courtyards, guest-houses, stables, arsenal, barracks, domed chapel, gardens of fruit and flowers, are on the scale of Knole; the sun-drenched, forest-beleaguered, golden-hued pile, with its arches, grass-grown

that of the new castle at Naples" and fine apartments round it; in the hall was a very beautiful throne; "I fancy that few things or none will be found more beautiful than that throne," and round the hall ran an arcade, beautifully adorned with columns. In the palace the king of Cyprus kept great state, twenty-four leopards, and three hundred hawks. Three hundred years later it still looked well, inhabited by the Turkish Pasha, and with the Lusignan arms over the gate. In the nineteenth century the Pasha still kept state there, sitting on divans, clapping his hands for goblets of sherbet, smoking pipes of jasmine wood with amber heads, drinking coffee out of gold cups studded with diamonds.

II

Standing in Konak square to-day, beside the tall Venetian column of grey granite, among the law courts and government offices, one is haunted by the ghosts of these sherbet-drinking Pashas, those magnificent conquering Venetians, those leopard-keeping Lusignan kings, among the vanished halls, chapels and arcaded galleries that crumbled there until half a century ago, and now are not even dust upon the air.

The ruins of Nicosia and Famagusta have been shamefully treated all down history, by enemy assault, earthquake, the brutal indifference and squalid lethargy of the Turks, the tiresome bustle and officiousness of the British, and the vandalism of the Cypriotes themselves, who until lately used their antiquities to provide stones for new buildings; and here the officiousness and efficiency of the British has been of use; possibly, but for their interference and care, there would be little left to-day of Kyrenia, St Hilarion, or the Latin and Byzantine churches. St Hilarion and Kyrenia, though they were royal residences, rank as castles: really a palace are the ruins of Vouni, on the top of a hill looking over Morphou Bay, three miles west of the Greek city of Soli, famous under the Romans. Vouni palace crowns the hill; near it is the site of a temple of Athena and a vanished township. The palace and temple are both excavated; the palace dated from about the fifth century B.C., it was burnt down in 400. Greek and Persian influences mix in it; its occupants seem to have been Cypriote kings of oriental tastes. Everything, it is said, was of the finest—sculptures, Persian jewellery, living rooms grouped round a colonnaded central court, a magnificent bathing and hot-water system. It is said to represent the typical early Cypriote royal residence. Going round it with a plan, after a steep climb up to it, one may identify rooms, baths and courts; there is no apparent evidence of happy living. It should be one of the pleasures of palace ruins that their luxurious past should drift about them like a cultured and well-fed ghost, whispering of beauty and wealth. Among the great bare masses of stone that lie broken in the sun above the sea at Vouni, the ghosts seem harsh and austere, given to mountain-climbing and bleak, rock-girt situations. I doubt if they lived well at all. About the palace, ruins still unexcavated sprawl down the steep hillside.

Of some palaces, only the whispering ghosts remain; all visible trace is gone. Of these is the immense palace group of the Ptolemies, that stretched along the promontory of Silsileh in Alexandria, and occupied, Strabo said, a third or fourth of the whole city, "for just as each of the kings, from love of splendour, was wont to add some adornment to the public monuments, so also he would invest himself at his own expense with a residence, in addition to those already built, so that now, to quote the words of the poet, 'there is building upon building'". The Mouseion and library were part of the palaces: here flowered the heart of Alexandrian culture. In that colonnaded quarter of the city, between the Canopic Way and the harbour, the Ptolemies reigned in their philadelphian family pride, surrounded by learning, science, astronomers, the noblest library that has ever existed, and a colony of philosophizing Greeks. The Ptolemy palace was taken and occupied by Caesar, to whom arrived, wrapped in carpets, Cleopatra. Later, Anthony reigned in the palace, while Cleopatra bore him children and built to him the temple of the Caesareum, flanked by the two ancient obelisks, later to be towed across oceans to newer worlds. All passion spent, the palace ghosts are to-day scarcely breaths on the air; the promontory where the magnificent arcaded halls and courts stood is now drearily massed with modern buildings; at present no access is possible, for barracks and military men inhabit there. "No one knows how far the buildings stretched inland, or along the shore, or what the architecture was"[1]—all trace has vanished

[1] E. M. Forster, *Alexandria, A History and a Guide* (1922).

for too long. But one may still look over the royal harbour to the sunken island of Antirrhodes where another palace stood; row over it, and you may glimpse below you the drowned island, strewn, they say, with the rocks that were the palace foundations.

As to the palaces, observed Dr Richard Pococke in 1740,

> "when Alexandria was no longer the residence of kings, it is very natural to think that their palace in time fell to ruin, and that the materials of it were removed to the part of the city that was inhabited, and probably also to build the inner walls, though along by the sea there are still great remains and on the shore there are seen several pieces of porphyry and other fine marbles, where the ancient palace stood."[1]

but most of the remains seemed to him rather medieval than Ptolemaic. The island palace of Antirrhodes was as drowned and vanished then as it is to-day, but "there are still seen great ruins in the sea, and they often raise up very fine pillars." Some of the ancient pillars he saw in the porticoes that supported the houses of the new town; "and all over the city are seen fragments of columns of beautiful marble; all so many remains of the grandeur and magnificence of the ancient city."

That much more of the Ptolemy palaces Dr Pococke saw than we can see to-day: but it was little enough. To him, as to us, and as to all travellers for the past many centuries, the palaces that made magnificent the promontory which shut the Royal Harbour on its eastward side were a haunting dream from the past, like the ancient arcaded city itself, built beautifully on its porticoes and vaults round the bay. But it is still the palaces, with the museum and library that were their soul, whose ghosts whisper through this noisy modern business town, whisper of culture and learning, of luxury and beauty, of arrogant and catastrophic family pride. Among the pleasures of ruin these Ptolemaic ghosts have their shadowy prescriptive place.

12

The residence of an ancient royal line: we see it again, very differently, in the walled imperial city on the heights of Gondar,

[1]Dr Richard Pococke, *A Description of the East and Some Other Countries* (1745).

that mountain plateau overlooking the sweep of Ethiopian hill country, gorges, forest, and the great lake of Tana, and, just beneath the plateau, the decayed, half ruinous thatched village that clusters at its foot. Here indeed were palaces: the palaces erected by Ethiopian emperors of the Solomonic line, after they had in the seventeenth century chosen Gondar for their court capital. Each negus erected his residence; the last was in 1736; they stand, ruinous shells of a forgotten grandeur, in their great plateau enclosure, behind broken walls once thirty feet high and over a mile and a half round, battlemented, gated and towered. The first and greatest, the castle of Fasilidas, was built soon after the expulsion of the Portuguese; the architecture, executed by Abyssinian and Indian masons, shows Portuguese influence, and "improbable suggestions of Istanbul and Byzantium."[1] Round about it were built a library, a chancery, wooden and plaster pavilions, later, other palaces.

Ruin took them early; decay, earthquake, sacking, fire; little by little they crumbled, and were never repaired, for Abyssinians find this difficult It was easier for the court to live in the parts still habitable. Abyssinian Bruce observed, when he visited Gondar in 1770, that, though a great part of Fasilidas's palace was now in ruins, there was still ample lodging on the two lowest floors, here the emperor held court, and received visitors in an audience chamber over one hundred and twenty feet long.

The ruin was progressive; by 1830 the Rev Samuel Gobat, a protestant missionary, found the king living "in a little circular house built on the ruins of a part of the palace built by the Portuguese." The clergyman was shown over the palace, "which, although in ruins, is still superior to anything that I should have expected in Abyssinia."

Indeed, it is largely the unexpectedness of the walled city of ruined imperial palaces on a wild Abyssinian hill that gives edge to the pleasure of its odd beauty. That, and the haunting past, where calm Ethiopian neguses sat in state under silken canopies in decorated chambers beneath ceilings formed of Venetian mirrors and ivory painted with stars.

Some visitors have preferred to see the palaces as Portuguese castle fortresses.

[1] David Mathew, *Ethiopia* (Eyre & Spottiswoode (1950)).

"Dominating the region for miles, the principal building stands, magnificent example of a seventeenth-century citadel, a monument to one of the most romantic gestures in the history of the world. Its towers and keeps, its dungeons, its dark, narrow dens, once the quarters of lions kept for the amusement of the garrison, its high surrounding wall, stables, outhouses, guard rooms, sentry boxes, all built of native stone, solid, massive, enduring through the centuries, though in a ruinous state, are still, speaking in terms of ancient ruins, in a fair state of repair."[1]

The Portuguese, said this writer, had laboured on this great castle for thirty years, from 1640 to 1670, and had made Gondar an impregnable highland stronghold. When they were driven out of the country, grass and weeds ran riot in the churchyard, and the castle fell to ruin. "And now hyena and jackal, hyrax and lizard, hold high revel in these silent, crumbling halls."

Thus Mr J. E. Baum. That is a thing about ruins: those who are not too fact-bound can get from them what imaginative pleasure they prefer; Gondar palaces can be Portuguese fortresses or the tabernacles of ancient Amharic sovereignty. Whatever view is taken of their past, you may enjoy those eternally revelling hyenas and lizards in their ruins, and the broken jumble of crumbling towers and walls looking from their rocky height over the spacious wildness of Abyssinian highlands.

13

But ruin and royalty make the best juxtaposition; it is better to remember the emperors. It is the contrast of the high past splendour with present dilapidation that dramatizes the rich and noble decay of the deserted palaces, Hindu and Mogul, of India. Of these, perhaps the most lovely is the marble palace in the deserted Hindu city of Amber in Rajputana. There are several palaces in Amber, that miracle of a ghostly city which has its place elsewhere in this book; the finest is the great ivory-hued marble early seventeenth-century building, standing on a jut of hill above the lake (which once mirrored it, but is now almost dry), an unearthly palace shining in creamy magnolia pallor, with latticed galleries, gilded balconies, alabaster mosaics and

[1] J. E. Baum, *Savage Abyssinia* (1928).

sculptures, pillared Hall of Audience, fountained garden jewelled with smaller palaces and temples, the whole climbing in terraces above the lake, gate beyond gate, court beyond court. Inside, suites of exquisite, inlaid, haunted rooms; "scores of venomous and suggestive little rooms", where was lived "the riotous, sumptuous, murderous life" to which the British government, said Kipling sixty years ago, has put an end. His description of the palace is worth quoting.

"He passed under iron-studded gates whose hinges were eaten out with rust, and by walls plumed and crowned with grass, and under more gateways, till at last he reached the palace, and came suddenly into a great quadrangle where two blinded, arrogant stallions, covered with red and gold trappings, screamed and neighed at each other from opposite ends of the vast space....

"If, as Viollet-le-Duc tells us to believe, a building reflects the character of its inhabitants, it must be impossible for one reared in an Eastern palace to think straightly or speak freely. . . . The cramped and darkened rooms, the narrow smooth-walled passages with recesses where a man might wait for his enemy unseen, the maze of ascending and descending stairs leading nowhither, the ever-present screens of marble tracery . . . all these things breathe of plot and counter-plot, league and intrigue. . . . The Englishman wandered into all parts of the palace, for there was no one to stop him—not even the ghosts of the dead Queens—through ivory-studded doors into the women's quarters. . . . A creeper had set its hands upon the lattice there, and there was the dust of old nests in one of the niches in the wall. . . . There were questions innumerable to be asked in each court and keep and cell; but the only answer was the cooing of the pigeons."[1]

Thirty years before Kipling, Louis Rousselet was given leave by the Rajah to stay in the palace while he explored Amber; he and his companions spent five weeks there; it could not, he felt, have been nicer. He chose for his residence the charming Jess Munder pavilion, all delicate marble trellis work and sparkling mosaics, and a handsome terrace and pomegranate and orange garden outside the windows; it was impossible to picture a more romantic retreat. On the other side of the garden extended a long line of palaces, all exquisite in decoration. He was even given leave to explore the zenana, neglected for a hundred and fifty

[1] Rudyard Kipling, *Letters of Marque* (1896)

years and inhabited by monkeys and a few servants. "The unbroken silence, the glorious view, the fairy-like palace with its Oriental garden, it is impossible to imagine such delightful solitude." The beauty of the linked palaces was enhanced by the silent ruin of the city spreading about it. An incomparable palace, Bishop Heber called it, for its rich decoration, wild beauty of situation, the number and singularity of its apartments, and the strangeness of finding such a building in such a place.

Is the Maharajah who owns Amber as hospitable to-day? He himself prefers to live in his huge palace in Jaipur; to make Amber a comfortable residence would be costly. All these near-perfect palaces—for Amber is not badly ruined—that strew this enigmatic sub-continent in abandoned beauty, raise the question, why does no prince, plutocrat or government official inhabit them? But it appears that Indians like to keep their abandoned cities and palaces lying empty, decaying slowly in the sun, renounced for ever to monkeys, peacocks and pigeons, museum pieces little heeded. Amber has one such palace group; another stands within the gates of the fortress of Gwalior, the Painted Palace, built in the early sixteenth century by the art-loving emperor Man Singh for his queen, and added to by successive dynasties throughout the century. Huge in extent, more masculine and massive than Amber, its battlemented façade has six balconied, pillared and domed towers, delicately arcaded and brilliant with enamelled tiles, most of which are still, after four centuries, in place. The whole effect is of a massive, yet delicate, brilliance. The interior is, compared with Amber, simple and solid. Its situation, on the edge of the steep precipice of the fortress, cliff, standing among ruined Jain temples, with the piled ruins of the ancient town at its base, is magnificent.

The beauty of a palace, as of temples, owes much to incidental factors—a large fortress above it, an ancient city below it, a lake holding its image in green water, valleys and hills and woods as background, submerging jungle drowning it, the sea lapping at its feet, or a shadow-green canal against its walls. Any ruin of a palace posed on a small island, or round a lake, as the tumbling palaces of Sarkhej near Ahmadabad are posed; palaces riven by trees, crowned by creepers and blossom, banyan boughs thrusting through carved windows, wild figs and prickly pears springing

62 Kalendria, coast of Cilicia Engraving by W. H. Bartlett, 1836-8

63 Tortosa from the Island of Ruad Engraving by W. H Bartlett, 1836-8

64 The Château de Tancarville, Normandy, by moonlight. Lithograph, 1820

65 Manorbier Castle, Pembrokeshire. Water-colour by T. H. A Fielding (1781-1851)

up through cracks in marble floors, as in the old Deccan city of Bijapur, with its records of dead glory; palaces where princes have feasted and adventurers have intrigued, as in Motti Jeel of Murshidabad, where Clive and Warren Hastings both inhabited and that now crumble to desolation—these too are good. All over India such palaces crumble and are beautiful. Almost the most immense in extent, and in the number of separate buildings linked by galleries and courtyards (they covered more ground, it seems, than Versailles and the Tuileries), is Akbar's imperial palace at Fatehpur-Sikri, abandoned after fifteen years. The palace has everything that could be desired; a separate palace for each of the wives, a large tank with an island reached by bridges, gardens, pavilions, a columned hall, a folly in the form of a pyramid of terraces (for eunuchs), a little temple for a Guru (for Akbar was entirely broad-minded about religion), a court in which to play purcheesee with human chessmen, a court for the administration of justice, every other kind of court, and innumerable architectural fantasies, all beautiful and mostly now in ruin. Fatehpur must have been such a desirable residence when completed that no one but an Indian Rajah could have deserted it. But Akbar found no difficulty; owing to water troubles he transferred his court to Lahore, and then to Agra, and left his elaborate red stone palace empty but for a few guards. Now it stands deserted; its red buildings, kept bare of encroaching greenery, remind some visitors of a fairy palace, others of barracks.

With many Hindu and Mogul palaces, once of great beauty, the ruin has consisted in vulgar modern destruction and adaptation, such as the British mutilation after the mutiny of Shah Jahan's superb imperial palace in Old Delhi, to make way for barracks. Marble floors and arcaded courts were removed, elegant chambers and courts turned into guardrooms, brick partitions put up, blocking windows and arcades. Louis Rousselet saw it thus in the 1860's; and compared what he saw with the picture of its glories given by travellers in the days of Aurungzeb—the marble-paved courts like fairyland, set with fountains and encircled by marble palaces, their arcaded walls gleaming with gold and silver, ceilings shining like starry skies with bright mosaics, the famous throne-room with its jewelled arabesques

14

Far more ruined are the great Sassanian palaces, which stand in tremendous and lonely majesty about Mesopotamia and Persia. The most magnificent palace ruin in Mesopotamia is probably Ukheidur by the Euphrates. To some travellers the first sight of it has been the most memorable experience of life.

> "It reared its mighty walls out of the sand, almost untouched by time, breaking the long lines of the waste with its huge towers, steadfast and massive, as though it were, as I had first thought, the work of nature, not of man."[1]

Coming nearer, passing through the great bastioned walls of masonry and brick, one enters huge vaulted halls, smaller vaulted chambers, corridors and open courts, walls with blind arcades, stairways climbing up three storeys, windowed bastions, fluted domes, arched doors, tiles of brick and stone. Archaeologists cannot date Ukheidur with certainty. Sassanid in style, was it before or soon after the Arab conquest, or as late as the Abbasid period? It has much in common with the Sassanian Firuzabad and Ctesiphon; but this does not prove it pre-Moslem. There is no Arab account of its conquest, as there is of the taking of Ctesiphon. Probably, therefore, early post-conquest. Whatever its date, it is the most imposing ruin in Mesopotamia; better than Sumarra, better than Ctesiphon, because there is so much more of it. Chosroes I's palace at Ctesiphon, built about 550, of brick, not masonry, on the east bank of the Tigris, opposite the mounds of ancient Seleucia, is a noble fragment, the palace must have been immense, larger than Sarvistan or Firuzabad; all that remains now is the great central vaulted hall and one wall of one wing. The Dieulafoys, seventy years ago, saw the east walls of both wings, and the vault of the hall was still intact. Of all Sassanian buildings except Persepolis, Ctesiphon palace has most renown; less for its present ruin, its huge uncentered vault and carved wall (carving not remarkable, not even good), but for its famous past, the ancient glory of Ctesiphon city, the great Sassanian capital which succeeded Seleucia, the hierarchic grandeur of Chosroes I, the destroyer of Antioch, and the fabulous

[1]Gertrude Bell, *Amurath to Amurath* (Heinemann, 1911).

beauties of the palace as described by its Arab conquerors—the golden throne, the carpet on which Paradise was embroidered in gold and silver and pearls, the great audience hall where the élite society of Persia crowded to pay court. The Chosroes dynasty had that glamour and that fame: the second Chosroes left in Palestine his seventh-century Sassanid palace of M'Shita, an unfinished Persian marvel in the incongruous desert; a domed and vaulted brick building set in a court surrounded by massive limestone walls with rich carving; until early this century this carving was in place, and looked immensely beautiful; it was looted by the Kaiser William for the Berlin Museum, and local Arabs took the rest to build a railway station. But, despoiled as it is, this Persian ruin in a Palestine desert is appealing even to those whom Sassanian architecture leaves cold.

It has been said that only archaeologists see beauty in this architecture, that its interest is historical and architectural, not aesthetic. But the great ruined palaces of Persia impose themselves with a superb strength. These broken domes, great open vestibules, long façades with engaged arcades, great blocks of brick or grey stone, tremendous thick walls, barrel-vaulted rooms, Sassanian carvings—they make their effect rather by mass than detail. Ardeshir's great third-century palace at Firuzabad, with its tremendous ruin-littered courts and domes, chambers, and its approximations to Romanesque, Byzantine and Moslem, would never be called exquisite, it has a kind of elaborate, magnificent clumsiness; but, standing above that sad landscape and the ruined city, towered over by two castles, it is hugely ghostly and impressive. The Dieulafoys were awe-struck by the immense vaulted structure, "*que n'embellit aucun décor*". The vast halls, the enormous arches, the linked chambers of the harem, the domes, the open courts strewn with broken masonry, stood in a plain littered with the remains of a dead city; in front of its great vestibule an artificial lake lay among shards and fragments of stone parapets. It was all, Madame Dieulafoy found, "*triste au possible*", and engendered the melancholy usual in those who survey ruins so long abandoned to the devastations of men and time. James Buckingham, sixty years earlier, was too much engaged in wondering what the building had been to feel this melancholy rhapsody, or anything but curiosity; Robert Byron, fifty years after the learned Dieulafoys, was interested in the place of the palace in the development of architecture; his account of it is the best we have.

Some miles north east of Firuzabad, the ruins of Sarvistan palace lie in a plain, looking, with their great dome, mosque-like and archaically Byzantine.

After these huge Sassanian affairs, the small ruined brick palaces that strew Persia, mud melting back into the soil, seem ephemeral, fragile, charming, set in gardens that will in the end grow over their remains. When they are perished, there will be no digging them up, they will be one with the earth. Not like the Abassid eighth-century palaces now being dug piece by piece, out of Jericho. Nor like the marble palaces fallen broken about Italy, their slabs, sunk deep in vineyards and olive gardens, dug up by contadini and carried in creaking carts by oxen to builders' yards, to find their places in cemeteries, in churches, in new palazzi and villas on the hills, persisting through time and change and mortal chance.

Palaces should be exquisite in death, like the Porphyrogenitus palace in the walls of Byzantium, like the Blachernae palace in the northern corner of the city, like the great chain of imperial palaces disintegrating through the centuries in its western tip. Or like the small ruined palaces that stand in decay in formal grottoed gardens and parks about South Germany and Austria, or the great disintegrating palaces of Russian noblemen, mouldering and discoloured beside artificial lakes, green with weed, used for stables and agricultural implements and lodgings for workers, the windows fallen in. Or the sombrely truculent baronial fortified palaces that range down Italy from north to south and from east to west: castles or palaces, the distinction is nice, they served for both. Or, more delicate, more palatial, the for ever dying, for ever vanishing palaces of China; or the broken-domed Byzantine shells with their dim fading wall paintings where the Despots reigned on Greek hills.

VI

A FANTASY OF CASTLES

THE castle has always been a formidable image, a powerful, intimidating fantasy of the human imagination. The fortress, the citadel, the craggy tower dominating the landscape: it is older than history, as natural to man as the eyrie to the eagle. To defend oneself, to attack others, to live in guarded pride: these are its laudable aims. Until they are ruined, no one but their owners, and those who live under their protection, has liked them; once they are shattered and dismantled, admiration supervenes; they become pets, the most esteemed ruined objects in a landscape, curdling the blood with awe, delighting the soul with majestic beauty.

> Bless'd too is he who, midst his tufted trees,
> Some ruin'd castle's lofty towers sees,
> Imbosom'd high upon the mountain's brow,
> Or nodding o'er the stream that glides below. . . ."

said Payne Knight, voicing the general view of his generation. Looking on these formidable shattered piles, men have been stirred to high moral reflections; they have thought on retribution, on the wickedness and pride natural to those who inhabit castles, and on the ruin into which they have now fallen. "High castles which held many gluttons and thieves stand and teach that fierce gentlemen do not reign long". And,

> Beneath these battlements, within those walls,
> Power dwelt amidst her passions; in proud state
> Each robber chief upheld his armed halls,
> Doing his evil will. . . .

But see what happened to him—

> Though to the clouds his castle seem'd to climb,
> And frown'd defiance to the desperate foe,
> Though deem'd invincible, the conqueror, Time,
> Levell'd the fabric, as the founder, low.

The lizard, and the lazy lurking bat,
Inhabit now, perhaps, the painted room
Where the sage matron and her maidens sat,
Sweet-singing at the silver-working loom.

Though his rich hours in revelry were spent,
With Comus and the laughter-loving crew,
And the sweet brow of Beauty, still unbent,
Brighten'd his fleecy moments as they flew. . . .

Happy baron, one likes to think that he led this amiable and Sybaritish life before he was levelled with his fabric. But, looking on the fortresses that strew all lands, craggy stumps, fierce battlemented towers, mighty walls with loop-hole windows suitable for guns and for boiling oil, huge sprawls of enceintes, massive curtain walls, moats, drawbridges, vaulted halls, winding turret stairs, and all the rest of the castle paraphernalia, one feels that Comus and his crew would have had short shrift, and that the chieftain's moments were probably on the whole less fleecy than bloody. Such appears to have been the opinion of the Portuguese exile poet, Almeida Garrett, who, surveying Dudley castle, saw nothing but the foolish débris of fallen leaves, the fallen walls that choked the moat, and the imagined corpses of those who had perished fighting through the pride or whim of the domineering baron. Garrett took the dark view of castles.

Castles, like temples and churches, have always been reproductive: they generate new castles on their foundations, broken walls, and razed sites. Since all things must have a beginning, one must assume that, where the remains of each castle stand or lie, there was once a first castle: but it was probably pre-historic, a pile of stones and earth without form. It was ruined or taken or merely fell down; on its site and fragments rose a new castle, some cyclopean mass, presently to be ruined in its turn, to make way for massive walls and fortified gates and to move into the recognisable history of two and three thousand years B.C. How many citadels lie, ruin on ruin, on the site of Troy? How many lie below Mycenae and Tiryns and Phaestos? What fortresses preceded all those forts that command and menace the strategic points of Attica, looking across the mountains at Athens as Phyle does? In the massive fort of Phyle with its circular tower,

66 Arches from the demolished Château de Sarcus, re-erected at Pouilly. Lithograph by A. Deroy, 1852

67 The Château de Coucy, Aisne Lithograph by E. B. de Lépinois, 1834

68 Gothic castle in a village near Batroun. Engraving by W. H. Bartlett, 1836

69 The Houses of Parliament on fire, 1834, by William Heath

70 Bombed ruins of the House of Commons, by John Piper

71 Bombed ruins of Coventry Cathedral, by John Piper

Thrasyboulos, expelled from Athens by the thirty Tyrants, settled with seventy-eight martial comrades, looking at Hymettus, Athens, and the Saronic Gulf, and sallied forth to capture the Piraeus and send the Tyrants packing. This is what we think of when we look up at Phyle's walls. For all castles hold their stories. All these kastros, palaeokastros, acropolises guarded by their broken fragments of ancient wall, that stand, battered sentinels, like Eleutherae that guards the pass of Kithaeron, about the mountains and islands of Greece, all the Roman castles of the Campagna, the Volscian and Sabine hills, all the dead Etruscan cities, the castles of southern Italy and of the Trentino, all the Roman-Byzantine-Arab-Frankish castles that ennoble the crags and seaports of Syria, Anatolia, Cyprus and Rhodes, and the desolate mountains of Mesopotamia, all the great Norman and Edwardian castles of Britain, the incomparable medieval castles and Renaissance châteaux of France, the Hohenstaufen palace-castles with which Frederick II decorated and defended Puglia, the dramatic Schlösser above the foaming rivers of Germany, the castle ruins that moulder proudly on the hill-tops of Spain, on the lonely precipices and gorges of the ancient Armenian kingdom of Silicia, Byzantine forts along the orcharded Crimean shores, Anatolian fastnesses, Abruzzi mountain citadels guarding tumbling brown stone villages as ruined as themselves—every one of these has its story and its drama: they are what Anthony Wood would have called "romancey". Here, in those ruined robber-baron keeps that the powerful Roman families and their Gothic invaders threw up in the Colosseum, the Palatine, the tombs, the great baths, any ruin ready to their hand, all about Rome and the Campagna from the fifth century to the fifteenth, the story of feudal Rome was bloodily enacted, the Orsini, the Colonna, the Barberini and the rest waged their wars and fought their feuds, hanged their foes and feasted their friends, broke their pledges and slew their wives. These broken fortresses seem to brood, darkly sinister, looming out of a lurid past. Few are beautiful with the beauty of the medieval castles of Britain and France, the crusaders' castles of the east, the Gothic ruins of Germany; they have the sullen lowering of the defeated bully, and the high provenance of Rome englamours them. All over Italy the feudal castles stand, some almost intact, most shattered or decayed: you may scarcely see a little town of any antiquity which has not its ruined castle gaping blindly down on it. Their histories are only worth examining by those with a great relish for animated slaughter and intrigue; one looks instead at the poise of their broken walls against the back-cloth of olive-grey and pine-green mountain above the pink-washed town and the little stone-jettied port of fishing-boats. The castles, like the towns and ports and mountain villages, are part of the furniture of the mind, they belong to the earliest fairy stories, perhaps to the oldest ancestral memories. In the imaginations of Gothic and Celtic northerners, the most deeply rooted fantasy is the Gothic castle. There they tower on their crags above rivers and lakes, the ruined dwellings of the wicked barons, a few turrets left, or high keeps and battlemented walls, posed ready for the artist, dramatically excessive, satisfying food for the *ruinenhungrige Phantasie* of the nostalgic mind.

In verfallnen Palast und alter Schlosser Ruinen,
Sonst vom Stolze bewohnt, bläht sich die fleckigte Krote.
Auch die Eidechse rauscht vorbei am wusten Gemäuer. . . .

Or, if one prefers dignified landscape to the lizard and the speckled toad, one can say, with Dorothy Wordsworth, "What a dignity does the form of an ancient castle or tower confer upon a precipitous woody or craggy eminence!" But the imagination is stormed by the ruin itself: castle after castle rides crag after crag like battleships riding a high sea: Godesberg, Drachenfels, Falkenberg, Bamburgh, Scarborough, Tintagel, Rhuddlan, Corfe, Gaillard, Coucy, a hundred more such melodramatic visions startle the eyes and haunt the soul. The castled mind is confirmed in its credulous dreams, in its dark aspirations and fears. This is the reality that runs, stealthy and secret, a dark subliminal river, below the threshold of awareness. These are what man, out of some deep need, throws up everywhere that he inhabits; these are what man, in anger and fear, destroys, so that the world is like a fantasy of tumbling towers by Monsù Desiderio. Everywhere *châteaux disparus, verfallene Schlosser, castelli rovinati*, castles in ruin. All about Syria and Palestine they stand, the crusaders' castles we call them, but really also Phoenician, Greek, Roman, Byzantine, and Arab in succession; upon the site the stones were piled and used by each occupier in turn; the crusaders built their great fortresses on ancient towns, taking their columns and stones for foundations; at Byblos the Frankish castle rose out of the Roman theatre. But usually castle grew out of castle, and the Byzantine and Saracen forts that strewed Syria became Latin-French castles, built by the same Greek and Syrian builders. Through each phase the antique Roman columns and stones often sustained the foundations, and still are to be seen. When the crusaders, expelled from their last stronghold in the Holy Land, sailed for Cyprus, the fortresses they left behind were seized and held by Saracens, later to be turned into homes for whole villages. Their *magnum opus*, Crac des Chevaliers on the mountains near Tripoli, that huge fastness of great concentric towered walls, vaulted halls, granaries, store-rooms, stables, chapel, standing high on a spur of rock to be seen across many miles of wild landscape, that jewel in the superb stone chain that the crusaders strung across Syria, had grown from a small Arab castle into a mighty citadel, nearly a city. Almost impregnable, it fell at last to Sultan Beibars in 1271. It was not much ruined; Beibars occupied it, and after him other rulers; later, the Arab population moved in; Crac became a village, full of peasants, cattle, asses, camels, goats and poultry. The Romanesque chapel was turned into a mosque, the great decorated hall and gallery were built over with small houses or used as stables. Better houses were built above, the summits of the walls being knocked down to provide stones. In 1895 its state was horrible—the glory of the Knights Hospitallers was a peasant village, "*croupissant sur son fumier*", freshly mutilated yearly, defiled with the ordure of years; the whole lower story of the second enceinte was covered in dirt, flung down by dwellers on the first floor through holes in the vaulted ceiling. Kala'at el Husn, the Arabs have called it; when Gertrude Bell visited it early this century its topmost tower was inhabited by the Kaimakam, who hospitably entertained her in the guest chamber of the tower: she has recorded the pleasures of a guest in Crac; the coming at sunset on a stormy evening to the Dark Tower, riding through a splendid Arab gateway into a vaulted corridor built over a winding stair, till at last they came into the courtyard in the centre of the keep, where a crowd of village inhabitants surrounded them and the Kaimakam took Miss Bell up the tower to the guest room and an evening of polite hospitality. Next morning,

"I explored the castle from end to end, with immense satisfaction to the eternal child that lives in the soul of all of us and takes more delight in the dungeons and battlements of a fortress than in any other relic of antiquity. Kala'at el Husn is so large that half the population of the village is lodged in the vaulted substructures of the keep, while the garrison occupies the upper towers . . . The keep contained a chapel, now converted into a mosque, and a banquet hall with Gothic windows, the tracery of which was blocked with stones to guard those who dwelt within against the cold".[1]

The internal decoration was Gothically exquisite; and Miss Bell does not mention dirt; perhaps the castle had lately been spring-cleaned. But the real cleaning began with the French, who took over in 1929 and set in hand the gigantic work of clearance, eviction and repair. Now Crac is tidied and restored to a cleaner magnificence than it can have enjoyed since the Hospitallers moved in; it looks what it is, the finest medieval monument in Syria, impressive, beautiful and stupendous, a glorious showpiece; but it no longer looks a ruin. One would have liked to have seen it thirty years ago, with its village of peasants and livestock incongruously swarming in those beautiful halls.

At Tortosa, which has not marched with the times, one may still see this; the castle walls have been chopped and mutilated to accommodate the citizenry, who have built their streets and shops and houses within it; opening out of the great wrecked vaulted hall, carved doorways lead into dirty little houses, stairs climb the walls to terraces and upper storeys, the tenements of the poor; ricketty blue shutters and dingy ragged curtains swing from the narrow casements of keep and massive walls. As a castle, it is hardly recognisable, and the inhabitants of Tortosa do not know it by that name; to them it is just the town within which they live. Its vaulted corridors and arched streets twist down to the sea and the rectangular port; from every cranny swarm mobs of Saracen children to tease the Frankish stranger. "*Quoi de plus original que le formidable donjon de Tortose, plongeant dans la mer . . . la mer d'où l'on attend perpetuellement le secours?*"[2] But no help now arrives from the sea.

[1]Gertrude Bell. *The Desert and the Sown* (Heinemann, 1907).
[2]Réné Dussard, 1934

Acre, too, that once so brilliant, so prosperous, but so often destroyed guardian of its great sweep of bay, with its massive ramparts, is a mazy warren of courts and streets and arches in which it is not easy to identify the form of the Hospitallers' castle. Acre is a jumble of medieval Byzantine and Frankish, sixteenth-century Arab, and the eighteenth and nineteenth century rebuilding and embellishments by Turkish rulers out of the stones of Caesarea and Ascalon. In 1740 Dr Pococke saw no town walls, but he saw the ruin of the "palace" of the Knights of St John, afterwards inhabited by "the great Feckerdine, prince of the Druses". Those splendidly built fortifications, jutting out into the restless sea like a battleship, they have the air of withstanding anything, and did indeed, with the help of Sir Sidney Smith's sailors, withstand Napoleon. Acre frowns on us with an immense prestigious renown; those ramparts against which the green sea breaks as we swim below them are the ramparts of old dream.

There are better crusaders' ruins: there are Saone and Beaufort and Markab, tremendous on their wild mountains, precipitous of approach, shattered giants; there is Chastel Pèlerin, Castellum Peregrinorum, on its seagirt promontory at Athill; built by Greek emperors, says Pococke, but mainly later by the Templars on the ancient foundations. Pococke saw the castle's noble chambers and "fine lofty church built in a light Gothic taste;" he thought it "so magnificent, and so finely built, that it may be reckoned as one of the things that are best worth seeing in these parts". But now, alas, no more to be seen, except by the sailors and soldiers of the State of Israel, who practice round about it those military and marine activities doubtless proper to their kind, but so improperly depriving others of the sight of the great sea castle built by the labour of pilgrims, coveted in vain by Frederick II, the last stronghold of the crusaders in Palestine, quarried ruthlessly in the last century to add to Acre, but still beautifully jutting above the sea in its lovely ruining, and now lost to Frankish pilgrims, they say for good. Sea ruins have a peculiar charm; as the Château de Mer that thrusts out of the pleasant port of Sidon below the balconied restaurants and houses.

In a land of ruined castles, of all periods and types, it is the crusader castles that perhaps most stir our imaginations. That extraordinary, valiant long adventure in conquest, exotic colonization, missionary Christianity spread by the sword in the land that bore it, western chivalry transplanted, more strangely, into the alien east—the whole affair has, it had nine centuries ago, the picturesque quality that excites: its massive ruins, flung about the Levant with such prodigal magnificence, capture us as castles more indigenous less wholly do. The Island of Rhodes, castled and towered all about by the Knights of St John, who held it, with the islands round it and Smyrna on the mainland, for two centuries, planted its feudal pride on the ancient altars and theatres of Greece, and there they stand to-day, the armorial shields and names of knights among the ancient inscriptions and carvings: at Lindus the medieval castle on the high acropolis above a small blue rock-bound bay encloses fragments of Greece—of the temple of Athene which Pindar celebrated; columns and capitals old before the religion of the Knights was born lie jumbled with the proud insignia of the Frankish enterprise; and in the castle ruins villagers of to-day have made their homes. The crusaders' battlemented walls and towers lie, a transient dream, on the island that the Sun God drew up from the depths of the sea and made his bride. But what a dream!

Castles are seldom indigenous. They are apt to be built in apprehensive aggression by conquerors—the Normans in Britain, the Romans and Byzantines all over their far-flung empires. It was the Byzantine emperors, the Franks, and the Venetians who threw up the great defensive mountain and sea castles of Cyprus. Of these the hugest and the most dramatic is St Hilarion, built by the Byzantines on a monastery site in the Kyrenia mountains. Twisting up and up into the sky, terrace above terrace, tower over tower, till it ends in an eyrie that surveys the world, it is a dramatic pile of ruin, rocks, and wild aromatic trees and shrubs springing out of them. Strengthened by the Lusignans, besieged by Frederick II during his assaults on Cyprus, it became a palace of the Lusignan kings; dismantled by the wary Venetians, it is now a vast towered enceinte, a picture-book castle for elf kings, sprawling over two twin crests with its maze of gate-houses, courts, arches, kitchens, cisterns, church, vaulted chambers and halls, terraces, and steep flights of grass-grown steps. Even wilder and more ruinous and haunting the verges of dream is

Kantara, a smaller castle in the mountain range to the north-east, a broken labyrinth of ruin on a dizzying precipice high above the distant green-blue sea that curves into the indented coast. Less a show-place than Hilarion, it is still more utterly a ruined place, given over to desolation. Difficult and fatiguing of access, it is, as the British consul in Aleppo complained, really very much "out of repair". Most of the other Cyprus castles are more tranquil of approach. But Buffavento, the most wildly inaccessible, has always made a strong appeal to ruin-lovers of the Everest breed. A Dutch traveller scaled it in 1683, and did not relish the climb.

"The ascent is difficult and dangerous as ever I made. The greater part of the time we had to climb with our hands as well as our feet, and which ever way we looked we saw only what made our hair stand on end. We took an hour and a half to reach the top. There one only sees the live rock and a number of ruined chambers, and large stone-built reservoirs."[1]

Other travellers, equally fatigued by the ascent, nevertheless greatly admired the luxury and fineness of the fortress-palace when they got there: marble door-jambs, magnificent apartments; the ill-informed decided that it had been the abode of a mighty pre-historic sovereign.

The ramparts of Famagusta citadel stand massive and honey-coloured, against the bastioned and gated walls that enclose the old town of a few Turkish streets and arches, an open square set with palms and ruinous Gothic churches tawny-gold like lions, and the ruins of a Venetian palace. The great fortress, a stupendous maze of walls, vaults, bastions, corridors and towers is largely Venetian: but a hundred years before the Venetians Martoni wrote "the castle of the city is fine, and is nearly all in the sea." The present excavations are uncovering early work. Sixty-five years ago, W. H. Mallock found half the castle walled up and inaccessible, the ramparts were grass-grown, it was a derelict castle guarding a ruinous grass-grown waste of a town. To-day it has been explored and tidied up; tidy it is, but magnificently, startlingly picturesque, a seemingly impregnable rampart guarding sea and land; seemingly impregnable, but now and then, like other impregnable castles, yields. Kyrenia, too, the other Cyprus sea castle, from time to

[1]C. van Bruyn. From *Excerpta Cypria* (C. D. Cobham 1908).

time yields; as a ruin, however, this delightful harbour fortress barely qualifies. We must leave it for the more shattered remains that castle the perhaps over-castled earth. Yes, there are too many. Crusader castles, Byzantine castles, Arab castles in deserts, such as the immense (too immense) Kasr el Heir in the Palmyrene desert, the picturesque decorated Qasr built in the Roman acropolis above Amman, Masada on the Dead Sea, Kerak in Moab, some hundreds more scattered about Syria and Judaea; while to the west of these, Gothic castles frown with noble, glooming menace from the hills on which it has always seemed suitable to erect them, and grand and gay pepper-pot castles such as the fifteenth and sixteenth-century châteaux of France make their defeated gesture. So many French castles have been venally demolished, or reduced to scanty ruins, in the last two centuries; but even now "*mettez la tête à la portière du train et regardez: sur cette colline-là il y aura certainement un château. Sur celle-ci, ou sur une autre*". And most castles are ruined, wholly or in part. You may see fragments of them elsewhere; arcades from destroyed Sarcus ennoble parks and villas by the Oise; at Sarcens there remains only one. A wing remains here, a façade there, the castles like the abbeys, are dispersed. Climb the steep path that winds up some mountain-side in Spain to the medieval castle on its summit; it proves as you approach to be a shell, a façade; a wild fig thrusts through windows, a goat leaps from the broken wall; the satisfied heart receives yet another ruin.

The ruined castles of England, Scotland, Wales and Ireland stand, a chain of stony splendour, linking together the fierce epochs of our Celtic, Roman, Saxon, Danish, Norman and English races. There are Norman keeps built within Roman walls, great clusters of massive round Norman towers, square towers and battlemented walls rearing themselves on steep heights, towered enceintes rising above a lilied moat in sham perfection, as at Bodiam, where all within the walls is ruin; wild and jagged arches and battlements cresting grassy Dorset hills, or climbing Cornish cliffs above a beating green sea, single round towers standing like funnels all over Ireland, tremendous shattered masses, tree-grown, frowning grandly down on the Border country below, guarding the Scottish firths, defending the Welsh ports, dominating the walled cities and cathedrals; small castles on islands, fortified manor houses of timber and stone. There are many hundreds of British ruined castles, and such is British affection for them that in front of each someone or other, and often a whole charabanc, is picnicking, while others climb the walls and towers with cameras. Nothing but the sea-side gives our island race, of high and low degree, a keener pleasure. When we say "a ruin", it is, in childhood, normally a castle that we mean. Henry James thought it was the sense of the past that we like in them; "the sensation of dropping back personally into the past . . . while I lay on the grass beside the well in the little sunny court of this small castle" (Stokesay) "and lazily appreciated the still definite details of medieval life. The place is a capital example of a small *gentilhommière* of the thirteenth century". And so up the corkscrew staircase of the tower "to the most charming part of every old castle . . . the bright dizzy platform at the tower-top".[1]

It may be the past that we seek, or the power, the glory and the romance, or the catastrophe of wreckage, or merely the wonder and the grandeur of a dwelling so unlike our own. Some have had the pleasure of digging out wrecked castles gone to earth, restoring and putting them together, uncovering moats, walls and nutteries from a wilderness of briars and weeds, making there a dwelling and a garden, as at Sissinghurst in Kent. Others have, as the romantic ruin-visitors of the eighteenth and nineteenth centuries found, made their homes among the towers, built their hovels in the walls. Castles, by common consent, should be ruined: Corfe, Loches, Gaillard, San Felice Circeo, all the romantic castles of Italy and its mountainous islands, and of Southern France are more intriguing to most people than Windsor and the châteaux on the Loire, a Salvator Rosa castle on a precipice than the unflawed circle of St Angelo on the Tiber, a Drachenfels than a restored Lutherolatrous Wartburg. A little ruin is best; not so much as wholly to destroy the form: a touch of ruin, such as has romanticized the remarkable chain of the Hohenstaufen castles in Puglia with which Frederick II guarded his south Italian estates and in which he took his pleasures. There, surrounded by *conforts modernes* (or rather, returning, amid Gothic barbarism, to the *conforts anciens* of imperial Rome) the

[1]Henry James. *Castles and Abbeys* (1877).

Stupor Mundi took his Sunday bath, hunted and hawked, and watched the habits of birds. In the largest of them, Lucera, he kept leopards, eunuchs, a harem, and so many Saracens that the city of Lucera was named Lucera Saracenorum; one may still see the remains of the mosque in the castle, as well as of the tall octagonal palace tower. All the castles are damaged, by the assaults of time, man and the heaving earth, looking at Lucera on its hill, one expects leopards, devouring plump eunuchs and urged on by Saracens, to bound out of the broken gateways.

Ruin also adds enormously to the huge Byzantine-Turkish castles that tower on both sides of the Bosphorus, each a climbing pile of round towers and battlemented walls running steeply down to the water's edge, with Turkish houses clustering in their shelter. Built by the Byzantine emperors for defence, they were added to and strengthened by the Turks after the taking of Constantinople; the enormous Roumeli Hissar, standing on a precipitous hill on the Europe shore, with its twelfth-century "Towers of Lethe" and its Turkish wall of 1452; the smaller Anadoli Hissar opposite on the Asia shore, the jaggedly ruined Hieron on the same. The shattered magnificence of these Bosphorus castles conveys the grandeur of Byzantium, and the tenacious Ottoman hold on its conquests; they have the palatial touch, the air of finery, which the crusader and Silician castles lack; they suggest the exotic potentate, as King Christophe's tremendous castle towering on the heights above his Haiti palace suggests it, and the extraordinary impregnable fortress of Dalautabad in Hydrabad, and Kala-i-Dukhtar rearing in terraced splendour its precipice-built walls at Firazabad, and the twisted eye-catcher of Georgian Tiflis.

All these castles in ruin, and a thousand more, climb, a composite fantasy of castelry, about the hills and valleys and winding roads of the mind. They give no security: they are shattered, shot-riddled, they crumble before our eyes. The drawbridges are down, the keep will fall: there is no security, which is what we always knew. Yet still the castles climb the dark crags.

VII

A NOTE ON NEW RUINS

NEW ruins have not yet acquired the weathered patina of age, the true rust of the barons' wars, not yet put on their ivy, nor equipped themselves with the appropriate bestiary of lizards, bats, screech-owls, serpents, speckled toads and little foxes which, as has been so frequently observed by ruin-explorers, hold high revel in the precincts of old ruins (such revelling, though noted with pleasure, is seldom described in detail; possibly the jackal waltzes with the toad, the lizard with the fox, while the screech-owl supplies the music and they all glory and drink deep among the tumbled capitals). But new ruins are for a time stark and bare, vegetationless and creatureless; blackened and torn, they smell of fire and mortality.

It will not be for long. Very soon trees will be thrusting through the empty window sockets, the rose-bay and fennel blossoming within the broken walls, the brambles tangling outside them. Very soon the ruin will be enjungled, engulfed, and the appropriate creatures will revel. Even ruins in city streets will, if they are let alone, come, soon or late, to the same fate. Month by month it grows harder to trace the streets around them; here, we see, is the lane of tangled briars that was a street of warehouses; there, in those jungled caverns, stood the large tailor's shop; where those grassy paths cross, a board swings, bearing the name of a tavern. We stumble among stone foundations and fragments of cellar walls, among the ghosts of the exiled merchants and publicans who there carried on their gainful trades. Shells of churches gape emptily; over broken altars the small yellow dandelions make their pattern. All this will presently be; but at first there is only the ruin; a mass of torn, charred prayer books strew the stone floor; the statues, tumbled from their niches, have broken in pieces; rafters and rubble pile knee-deep. But often the ruin has put on, in its catastrophic tipsy chaos, a bizarre new charm. What was last week a drab little house has become a steep flight of stairs winding up in the open between gaily-coloured walls, tiled lavatories, interiors bright and intimate like a Dutch picture or a stage set; the stairway climbs up and up, undaunted, to the roofless summit where it meets the sky. The house has put on melodrama; people stop to stare; here is a domestic scene wide open for all to enjoy. To-morrow or to-night, the gazers feel, their own dwelling may be even as this. Last night the house was scenic; flames leaping to the sky; to-day it is squalid and *morne*, but out of its dereliction it flaunts the flags of what is left.

The larger ruins are more sad; they have lost more. Nothing can have been more melancholy than the first shattered aspect of the destroyed abbeys before they took on the long patience and endurance of time; they were murdered bodies, their wounds gaped and bled. Their tragedy was like the tragedy of the revolution-destroyed châteaux of France, or the burnt great houses of Ireland, or the cities razed of old by conquerors; the silence brooded heavily round them, as the silence broods over the garden and woods of uprooted Coole. Burnt Hafod crumbled on the mountain like a staunchless grief; Appeldurcombe disintegrated beautifully in all the morbid shades of a fading bruise; Seaton Delaval is sallowed and exquisite in death; Holland House a wrecked Whig dream among gardens. The bombed churches and cathedrals of Europe give us, on the whole, nothing but resentful sadness, like the bombed cities. All the same Monte Cassino put on with wreckage a new dignity, a beauty scarcely in the circumstances bearable; it looked finer than at any time since its last restorations. Caen, Rouen, Coventry, the City churches, the German and Belgian cathedrals, brooded in stark gauntness redeemed only a little by pride: one reflects that with just such pangs of anger and loss people in other centuries looked on those ruins newly made which to-day have mellowed into ruin *plus beau que la beauté*.

But *Ruinenlust* has come full circle: we have had our fill. Ruin pleasure must be at one remove, softened by art, by Piranesi, Salvator Rosa, Poussin, Claude, Monsù Desiderio, Pannini, Guardi, Robert, James Pryde, John Piper, the ruin-poets, or centuries of time. Ruin must be a fantasy, veiled by the mind's dark imaginings: in the objects that we see before us, we get to agree with St Thomas Aquinas, that *quae enim diminutae sunt, hoc ipso turpia sunt*, and to feel that, in beauty, wholeness is all.

But such wholesome hankerings are, it seems likely, merely a phase of our fearful and fragmented age.

Loe here's mine Effigie, *and* Turkish *suite*;
My Staffe, *my* Shasse, *as I did* Asia *foote*:
Plac'd in old Ilium; Priams *Scepter thralles*:
The Grecian *Campe design'd*; *lost* Dardan *falles*
Gird'd with small Simois: Idaes *tops*, *a Gate*;
Two fatall Tombes, *an* Eagle, *sackt* Troyes *State*.

INDEX

Lightning Source UK Ltd.
Milton Keynes UK
UKHW041451070219
336896UK00005B/592/P